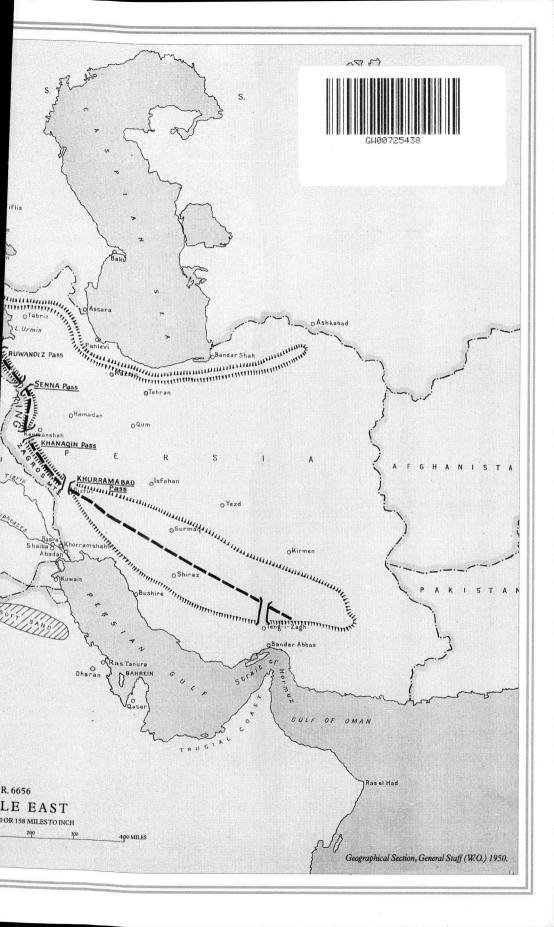

S.

S.

C A S P I A N   S E A

ᵗiflis

Baku

Astara

Tabriz

L. Urmia

Pahlevi

RUWANDIZ Pass

SENNA Pass

Ashkabad

Bandar Shah

Tehran

Hamadan

Qum

Kermanshah

KHANAQIN Pass

P E R S I A

Z A G R O S

Tigris

KHURRAMABAD Pass

Dizful

Isfahan

Yezd

A F G H A N I S T A

Euphrates

Basra

Shaiba

Abadan

Khorramshahr

Surmaq

Kirmen

P A K I S T A N

Kuwait

Shiraz

Bushire

OFT SAND

P E R S I A N   G U L F

Teng-i-Zagh

Bandar Abbas

Ras Tanura

BAHREIN

Dharan

Qatar

Strait of Hormuz

GULF OF OMAN

T R U C I A L   C O A S T

Ras el Had

R. 6656

LE EAST

0 OR 158 MILES TO INCH

200   300   400 MILES

Geographical Section, General Staff (W.O.) 1950.

Egypt and the Defence of the Middle East

The British Documents on
the End of Empire Project
gratefully acknowledges
the generous assistance of
the Leverhulme Trust.

The Project has
been undertaken
under the auspices
of the
British Academy.

BRITISH DOCUMENTS ON THE END OF EMPIRE

General Editor S R Ashton
Project Chairman A N Porter

Series B Volume 4

Egypt and the Defence of the Middle East

Editor
JOHN KENT

Part I
1945–1949

Published for the Institute of Commonwealth Studies
in the University of London

London: The Stationery Office

First published 1998

© The Stationery Office 1998

Introduction © John Kent, 1998

Documents from the Public Record Office © Crown copyright

ISBN 0 11 290560 9

British Library Cataloguing in Publication Data
A CIP catalogue record for this book is available from the British Library

If you wish to receive future volumes from the British Documents on the End of Empire project, please write to The Stationery Office, Standing Order Department, PO Box 276, LONDON SW8 5DT, or telephone on 0171 873 8466, quoting classification reference number 040 30 017

Published by The Stationery Office and available from:

The Publications Centre
(mail, telephone and fax orders only)
PO Box 276, London SW8 5DT
General enquiries 0171 873 0011
Telephone orders 0171 873 9090
Fax orders 0171 873 8200

The Stationery Office Bookshops
123 Kingsway, London WC2B 6PQ
0171 430 1671 Fax 0171 831 1326
68–69 Bull Street, Birmingham B4 6AD
0121 236 9696   Fax 0121 236 9699
33 Wine Street, Bristol BS1 2BQ
0117 9264306 Fax 0117 9294515
9–21 Princess Street, Manchester M60 8AS
0161 834 7201 Fax 0161 833 0634
16 Arthur Street, Belfast BT1 4GD
01232 238451 Fax 01232 235401
The Stationery Office Oriel Bookshop
The Friary, Cardiff CF1 4AA
01222 395548 Fax 01222 384347
71 Lothian Road, Edinburgh EH3 9AZ
(counter service only)

Customers in Scotland may
mail, telephone or fax their orders to:
Scottish Publications Sales
South Gyle Crescent, Edinburgh EH12 9EB
0131 228 4181 Fax 0131 622 7017

The Stationery Office's Accredited Agents
(see Yellow Pages)

and through good booksellers

Printed in the UK for the Stationery Office by
Hobbs the Printers, Southampton

J19961 6/98 C6

Contents

	page
Foreword	vii
Egypt and the Defence of the Middle East: Schedule of contents: parts I–III	xv
Abbreviations: parts I–III	xvii
Principal holders of offices 1945–1949: part I	xxi
Chronological table of principal events: parts I–III	xxvii
Introduction	xxxv
Notes to Introduction	xcv
Summary of documents: part I	ci
Documents: part I	1
Appendix to part I: Extract from the 1936 Anglo–Egyptian treaty	365
Index: parts I–III	371
MAP Middle East defence positions	Front end paper

Foreword

The main purpose of the British Documents on the End of Empire Project (BDEEP) is to publish documents from British official archives on the ending of colonial and associated rule and on the context in which this took place. In 1945, aside from the countries of present-day India, Pakistan, Bangladesh and Burma, Britain had over fifty formal dependencies; by the end of 1965 the total had been almost halved and by 1985 only a handful remained. The ending of Britain's position in these formal dependencies was paralleled by changes in relations with states in an informal empire. The end of empire in the period at least since 1945 involves a change also in the empire as something that was more than the sum of its parts and as such formed an integral part of Britain's domestic affairs and international relations. In publishing official British documents on the end of empire this project is, to a degree, the successor to the two earlier series of published documents concerning the end of British rule in India and Burma which were edited by Professors Mansergh and Tinker respectively.[1] The successful completion of *The transfer of power* and *The struggle for independence*, both of which were based on British records, emphasised the need for similar published collections of documents important to the history of the final stages of Britain's association with other dependencies in Africa, the Middle East, the Caribbean, South-East Asia and the Pacific. In their absence, scholars both from sovereign independent states which emerged from colonial rule, as well as from Britain itself, lack an important tool for understanding and teaching their respective histories. But BDEEP is also set in the much wider context of the efforts made by successive British governments to locate Britain's position in an international order. Here the empire, both in its formal and informal senses, is viewed as an instrument of the domestic, foreign and defence policies of successive British governments. The project is therefore concerned with the ending of colonial rule in individual territories as seen from the British side at one level, and the broader political, economic and strategic considerations involved in that at another.

BDEEP is a sequel, not only to the India and Burma series but also to the still earlier series of published Foreign Office documents which continues as Documents on British Policy Overseas (DBPO). The contemporary volumes in DBPO appear in two parallel series covering the years 1945 to 1955. In certain respects the documents published in the BDEEP volumes will complement those published in DBPO. On issues where there is, or is likely to be, direct overlap, BDEEP will not provide detailed coverage. The most notable examples concern the post-Second World War international settlements in the Far East and the Pacific, and the immediate events of the Suez crisis of 1956.

---

[1] Nicholas Mansergh *et al*, eds, *Constitutional relations between Britain and India: the transfer of power 1942–47*, 12 vols, (London, 1970–1983); Hugh Tinker, ed, *Constitutional relations between Britain and Burma: the struggle for independence 1944–1948*, 2 vols, (London, 1983–1984).

Despite the similarities, however, BDEEP differs in significant ways from its predecessors in terms both of presentation and content. The project is of greater magnitude
than that undertaken by Professor Mansergh for India. Four major differences can be
identified. First, the ending of colonial rule within a dependent empire took place over
a much longer period of time, extending into the final years of the twentieth century,
while having its roots in the Second World War and before. Secondly, the empire consisted of a large number of territories, varying in area, population, wealth and in many
other ways, each with its own individual problems, but often with their futures linked
to those of neighbouring territories and the growing complexity surrounding the
colonial empire. Thirdly, while for India the documentary record for certain matters
of high policy could be encapsulated within a relatively straightforward 'country'
study, in the case of the colonial empire the documentary record is more diffuse
because of the plethora of territories and their scattered location. Finally, the documents relating to the ending of colonial rule are not conveniently located within one
leading department of state but rather are to be found in several of them. As the purpose of the project is to publish documents relating to the end of empire from the
extensive range and quantity of official British records, private collections and other
categories of non-official material are not regarded as principal documentary sources.
In BDEEP, selections from non-official material will be used only in exceptional cases
to fill gaps where they exist in the available official record.

In recognition of these differences, and also of the fact that the end of empire
involves consideration of a range of issues which operated at a much wider level than
that normally associated with the ending of colonial rule in a single country, BDEEP
is structured in two main series along with a third support series. Series A represents
the general volumes in which, for successive British governments, documents
relating to the empire as a whole will be published. Series B represents the country
or territory volumes and provides territorial studies of how, from a British
government perspective, former colonies and dependencies achieved their independence, and countries which were part of an informal empire regained their autonomy.
In addition to the two main documentary series, a third series – series C – will be
published in the form of handbooks to the records of the former colonial empire
which are deposited at the Public Record Office (PRO). The handbooks will be
published in two volumes as an integral part of BDEEP and also as PRO guides to the
records. They will enable scholars and others wishing to follow the record of the
ending of colonial rule and empire to pursue their inquiries beyond the published
record provided by the general studies in series A and the country studies in series B.
Volume One of the handbooks, a revised and updated version of *The records of the
Colonial and Dominions Office* (by R B Pugh) which was first published in 1964, is
entitled *Records of the Colonial Office, Dominions Office, Commonwealth Relations
Office and Commonwealth Office*. It covers over two hundred years of activity down
to 1968 when the Commonwealth Office merged with the Foreign Office to form the
Foreign and Commonwealth Office. Volume Two, entitled *Cabinet, Foreign Office,
Treasury and other records*, focuses more specifically on twentieth-century depart-
mental records and also includes references to the records of inter-departmental
committees, commissions of inquiry and international organisations. These two
volumes have been prepared under the direction and supervision of Dr Anne
Thurston, honorary research fellow at the Institute of Commonwealth Studies in the
University of London.

The criteria which have been used in selecting documents for inclusion in individual volumes will be explained in the introductions written by the specialist editors. These introductions are more substantial and contextual than those in previous series. Each volume will also list the PRO sources which have been searched. However, it may be helpful to outline the more general guiding principles which have been employed. BDEEP editors pursue several lines of inquiry. There is first the end of empire in a broad high policy sense, in which the empire is viewed in terms of Britain's position as a world power, and of the inter-relationship between what derives from this position and developments within the colonial dependencies. Here Britain's relations with the dependencies of the empire are set in the wider context of Britain's relations with the United States, with Europe, and with the Commonwealth and United Nations. The central themes are the political constraints, both domestic and international, to which British governments were subject, the economic requirements of the sterling area, the geopolitical and strategic questions associated with priorities in foreign policy and in defence planning, and the interaction between these various constraints and concerns and the imperatives imposed by developments in colonial territories. Secondly, there is investigation into colonial policy in its strict sense. Here the emphasis is on those areas which were specifically – but not exclusively – the concern of the leading department. In the period before the administrative amalgamations of the 1960s,[2] the leading department of the British government for most of the dependencies was the Colonial Office; for a minority it was either the Dominions Office and its successor, the Commonwealth Relations Office, or the Foreign Office. Colonial policy included questions of economic and social development, questions of governmental institutions and constitutional structures, and administrative questions concerning the future of the civil and public services and of the defence forces in a period of transition from European to indigenous control. Finally there is inquiry into the development of political and social forces within colonies, the response to these and the transfer of governmental authority and of legal sovereignty from Britain to its colonial dependencies as these processes were understood and interpreted by the British government. Here it should be emphasised that the purpose of BDEEP is not to document the history of colony politics or nationalist movements in any particular territory. Given the purpose of the project and the nature of much of the source material, the place of colony politics in BDEEP is conditioned by the extent to which an awareness of local political situations played an overt part in influencing major policy decisions made in Britain.

Although in varying degrees and from different perspectives, elements of these various lines of inquiry appear in both the general and the country series. The aim in both is to concentrate on the British record by selecting documents which illustrate those policy issues which were deemed important by ministers and officials at the time. General volumes do not normally treat in any detail matters which will be fully documented in the country volumes, but some especially significant documents do appear in both series. The process of selection involves an inevitable degree of sifting and subtraction. Issues which in retrospect appear to be of lesser significance or to be

---

[2] The Colonial Office merged with the Commonwealth Relations Office in 1966 to form the Commonwealth Office. The Commonwealth Office merged with the Foreign Office in 1968 to form the Foreign and Commonwealth Office.

ephemeral have been omitted. The main example concerns the extensive quantity of material devoted to appointments and terms of service – salaries, gradings, allowances, pension rights and compensation – within the colonial and related services. It is equally important to stress certain negative aspects of the official documentary record. Officials in London were sometimes not in a position to address potentially significant issues because the information was not available. Much in this respect depended on the extent of the documentation sent to London by the different colonial administrations. Once the stage of internal self-government had been reached, or where there was a dyarchy, the flow of detailed local information to London began to diminish.

Selection policy has been influenced by one further factor, namely access to the records at the PRO. Unlike the India and Burma series and DBPO, BDEEP is not an official project. In practice this means that while editors have privileged access (in the form of research facilities and requisitioning procedures) to the records at the PRO, they do not have unrestricted access. For files which at the time a volume is in preparation are either subject to extended closures beyond the statutory thirty years, or retained in the originating department under section 3(4) of the Public Records Act of 1958, editors are subject to the same restrictions as all other researchers. Where necessary, volume editors will provide details of potentially significant files or individual documents of which they are aware and which they have not been able to consult.

A thematic arrangement of the documents has been adopted for the general volumes in series A. The country volumes in series B follow a chronological arrangement; in this respect they adopt the same approach as was used in the India and Burma series. For each volume in both series A and B a summary list of the documents included is provided. The headings to BDEEP documents, which have been editorially standardised, present the essential information. Together with the sequence number, the file reference (in the form of the PRO call-up number and any internal pagination or numeration) and the date of the document appear on the first line.[3] The second and subsequent lines record the subject of the document, the type of document (letter, memorandum, telegram etc), the originator (person or persons, committee, department) and the recipient (if any). In headings, a subject entry in single quotation marks denotes the title of a document as it appears in the original. An entry in square brackets denotes a subject indicator devised by the editor. This latter device has been employed in cases where no title is given in the original or where the original title is too unwieldly to reproduce in its entirety. Security classifications and, in the case of telegrams, times of despatch and receipt, have generally been omitted as confusing and needlessly complicating, and are retained only where they are necessary to a full understanding. In the headings to documents and the summary lists, ministers are identified by the name of the office-holder, not the title of the office (ie, Mr Lyttelton, not secretary of state for the colonies).[4] In the same contexts, officials are identified by their initials and surname. In general

---

[3] The PRO call-up number precedes the comma in the references cited. In the case of documents from FO 371, the major Foreign Office political class, the internal numeration refers to the jacket number of the file.

[4] This is an editorial convention, following DBPO practice. Very few memoranda issued in their name were actually written by ministers themselves, but normally drafted by officials.

volumes in series A, ambassadors, governors, high commissioners and other embassy or high commission staff are given in the form 'Sir E Baring (Kenya)'. Footnotes to documents appearing below the rule are editorial; those above the rule, or where no rule is printed, are part of the original document. Each part of a volume provides a select list of which principal offices were held by whom, with a separate series of biographical notes (at the end) for major figures who appear in the documents. Minor figures are identified in editorial footnotes on the occasion of first appearance. Link-notes, written by the volume editor and indented in square brackets between the heading and the beginning of a document, are sometimes used to explain the context of a document. Technical detail or extraneous material has been extracted from a number of documents. In such cases omission dots have been inserted in the text and the document is identified in the heading as an extract. Occasional omission dots have also been used to excise purely mechanical chain-of-command executive instructions, and some redundant internal referencing has been removed, though much of it remains in place, for the benefit of researchers. No substantive material relating to policy-making has been excised from the documents. In general the aim has been to reproduce documents in their entirety. The footnote reference 'not printed' has been used only in cases where a specified enclosure or an annex to a document has not been included. Unless a specific cross-reference or note of explanation is provided, however, it can be assumed that other documents referred to in the text of the documents included have not been reproduced. Each part of a volume has a list of abbreviations occurring in it. A consolidated index for the whole volume appears at the end of each part.

One radical innovation, compared with previous Foreign Office or India and Burma series, is that BDEEP will reproduce many more minutes by ministers and officials.

Crown copyright material is used by permission of the Public Record Office under licence from the Controller of Her Majesty's Stationery Office. All references and dates are given in the form recommended in PRO guidelines.

*   *   *   *

BDEEP has received assistance and support from many quarters. The project was first discussed at a one-day workshop attended by over thirty interested scholars which, supported by a small grant from the Smuts Memorial Fund, was held at Churchill College, Cambridge, in May 1985. At that stage the obstacles looked daunting. It seemed unlikely that public money would be made available along the lines provided for the India and Burma projects. The complexities of the task looked substantial, partly because there was more financial and economic data with which to deal, still more because there were so many more territories to cover. It was not at all clear, moreover, who could take institutional responsibility for the project as the India Office Records had for the earlier ones; and in view of the escalating price of the successive India and Burma volumes, it seemed unlikely that publication in book form would be feasible; for some while a choice was being discussed between microfilm, microfiche and facsimile.

A small group nevertheless undertook to explore matters further, and in a quite remarkable way found itself able to make substantial progress. The British Academy adopted BDEEP as one of its major projects, and thus provided critical support. The Institute of Commonwealth Studies served as a crucial institutional anchor in taking responsibility for the project. The Institute also made office space available, and negotiated an administrative nexus within the University of London. Dr Anne Thurston put at the disposal of the project her unique knowledge of the relevant archival sources; while the keeper of the Public Records undertook to provide all the support that he could. It then proved possible to appoint Professor Michael Crowder as project director on a part-time basis, and he approached the Leverhulme Trust, who made a munificent grant which was to make the whole project viable. Almost all those approached to be volume editors accepted and, after consultation with a number of publishers, Her Majesty's Stationery Office undertook to publish the project in book form. There can be few projects that after so faltering a start found itself quite so blessed.

Formally launched in 1987, BDEEP has been based since its inception at the Institute of Commonwealth Studies. The work of the project is supervised by a Project Committee chaired by Professor Andrew Porter, Rhodes professor of imperial history in the University of London. Professor Porter succeeded Professor Anthony Low, formerly Smuts professor of the history of the British Commonwealth in the University of Cambridge, who retired in November 1994. At the outset Professor Michael Crowder became general editor while holding a visiting professorship in the University of London and a part-time position at Amherst College, Massachusetts. Following his untimely death in 1988, Professor Crowder was replaced as general editor by Professor David Murray, pro vice-chancellor and professor of government at the Open University. Mrs Anita Burdett was appointed as project secretary and research assistant. She was succeeded in September 1989 by Dr Ashton who had previously worked with Professors Mansergh and Tinker during the final stages of the India and Burma series. Dr Ashton replaced Professor Murray as project director and general editor in 1993. When BDEEP was launched in 1987, eight volumes in series A and B were approved by the Project Committee and specialist scholars were commissioned to research and select documents for inclusion in each. Collectively, these eight volumes (three general and five country)[5] represent the first stage of the project which begins with an introductory general volume covering the years between 1925 and 1945 but which concentrates on the period from the Second World War to 1957 when Ghana and Malaya became independent.[6]

It is fitting that the present general editor should begin his acknowledgements with an appreciation of the contributions made by his predecessors. The late Professor Crowder supervised the launch of the project and planned the volumes included in stage one. The volumes already published bear lasting testimony to his resolve and dedication during the project's formative phase. Professor Murray played a no less critical role in establishing a secure financial base for the project and in negotiating contracts with the volume editors and HMSO. His invaluable advice and

---

[5] Series A general volumes: vol 1 *Imperial policy and colonial practice 1925–1945* (published 1996); vol 2 *The Labour government and the end of empire 1945–1951* (published 1992); vol 3 *The Conservative government and the end of empire 1951–1957* (published 1994).

Series B country volumes: vol 1 *Ghana* (published 1992); vol 2 *Sri Lanka* (published 1997); vol 3 *Malaya* (published 1995); vol 4 *Egypt and the defence of the Middle East* (published 1998); vol 5 *Sudan*.

[6] Research is currently in progress for a second stage covering the period 1957–1964.

expertise during the early stages of editing are acknowledged with particular gratitude.

The project benefited from an initial pump-priming grant from the British Academy. Thanks are due to the secretary and Board of the Academy for this grant and for the decision of the British Academy to adopt BDEEP as one of its major projects. The Academy made a further award in 1996 which enabled the project to employ a research assistant on a fixed-term contract. The principal funding for the project has been provided by the Leverhulme Trust and the volumes are a tribute to the support provided by the Trustees. A major debt of gratitude is owed to the Trustees. In addition to their generous grant to cover the costs of the first stage, the Trustees agreed to a subsequent request to extend the duration of the grant, and also provided a supplementary grant which enabled the project to secure Dr Ashton's appointment.

Members of the Project Committee, who meet annually at the Institute of Commonwealth Studies, have provided valuable advice and much needed encouragement. Professor Low, the first chairman of the Committee, made a singular contribution, initiating the first exploratory meeting at Cambridge in 1985 and presiding over subsequent developments in his customary constructive but unobtrusive manner. Professor Porter continues in a similar vein and his leadership and experience are much appreciated by the general editor. The director and staff of the Institute of Commonwealth Studies have provided administrative support and the congenial surroundings within which the general editor works. The editors of volumes in stage one have profited considerably from the researches undertaken by Dr Anne Thurston and her assistants during the preparation of the records handbooks. Although BDEEP is not an official project, the general editor wishes to acknowledge the support and co-operation received from the Historical Section of the Cabinet Office and the Records Department of the Foreign and Commonwealth Office. He wishes also to record his appreciation of the spirit of friendly co-operation emanating from the editors of DBPO. Dr Ronald Hyam, editor of the volume in series A on *The Labour government and the end of empire 1945–1951*, played an important role in the compilation of the house-style adopted by BDEEP and his contribution is acknowledged with gratitude. Thanks also are due to The Stationery Office for assuming publishing responsibility and for their expert advice on matters of design and production. Last, but by no means least, the contribution of the keeper of the records and the staff, both curatorial and administrative, at the PRO must be emphasised. Without the facilities and privileges afforded to BDEEP editors at Kew, the project would not be viable.

S R Ashton
Institute of Commonwealth Studies
April 1997

Egypt and the Defence of the Middle East

Schedule of Contents: Parts I–III

PART I   1945–1949

Chapter 1   Collaboration with King Farouk: the Suez base and the definition of
              Britain's post-war requirements in the Middle East, Mar 1945–Dec 1946
              Document numbers 1–89

Chapter 2   The problem of standing on the 1936 treaty and the formation of a plan
              to defend the Middle East, Jan 1947–Oct 1948
              Document numbers 90–125

Chapter 3   New requirements in Egypt and problems in Middle East defence, Nov
              1948–Sept 1949
              Document numbers 126–150

PART II   1949–1953

Chapter 4   The approaching crisis: no Egyptian collaborators, no defence
              agreement and little prospect of defending the Middle East, Oct
              1949–Oct 1951
              Document numbers 151–225

Chapter 5   Violent conflict in Egypt and the demise of King Farouk: defence cuts in
              Britain and a new strategy for global war, Oct 1951–July 1952
              Document numbers 226–315

Chapter 6   Reassessing requirements in the Canal Zone in the light of a new
              approach to Middle East defence, and the involvement of the Americans
              in the attempts to secure a new agreement on the Suez base, Aug
              1952–Feb 1953
              Document numbers 316–368

PART III   1953–1956

Chapter 7   Reluctant to stay but unable to go: Anglo–American conflict over
              Britain's failure to secure a new agreement on the Suez base, Feb–Oct
              1953
              Document numbers 369–446

Chapter 8   The end of Churchill's resistance to the loss of Egypt and the
             Anglo–Egyptian agreement on the evacuation of the Suez base, Nov
             1953–July 1954
             Document numbers 447–541

Chapter 9   The growing importance of the forward Iraqi–Levant strategy for
             Middle East defence and the contradictions of the Baghdad Pact, Aug
             1954–Mar 1955
             Document numbers 542–589

Chapter 10   The collapsing façade of Middle Eastern defence and covert action
             against Egypt, Apr 1955–Dec 1956
             Document numbers 590–648

Abbreviations: Parts I–III

AA	anti-aircraft, air attaché
ACAS	assistant chief of the air staff
Ack-ack	anti-aircraft fire
AEW	airborne early warning
AIOC	Anglo–Iranian Oil Company
AKEL	Reform Party of the Working People (Cyprus)
AM	auxiliary minesweeper
AMC	auxiliary minesweeper coastal
AMCU	auxiliary minesweeper coastal underwater location
AMI	auxiliary minesweeper inshore
ANA	Arab News Agency
ANZAM	Australia, New Zealand, Malaya
ARAMCO	Arabian-American Oil Company
BAD	British Armoured Division
BDCC	British Defence Co-ordination Committee
Bde	brigade
BDEEP	British Documents on the End of Empire Project
BEF	British Expeditionary Force
BJSM	British Joint Services Mission
BMEO	British Middle East Office
BOAC	British Overseas Airways Corporation
Brig	brigadier
BSS	British subjects
BTE	British Troops Egypt
C and R	control and reporting [system]
CB	confined to barracks, coastal battery
CCL	commander-in-chief, Land Forces

Cdo Bde	commando brigade
CIA	Central Intelligence Agency
CIGS	chief of the imperial general staff
C-in-C	commander-in-chief
CINCAFMED	commander-in-chief, Allied Forces, Mediterranean
CINCELM	commander-in-chief, Eastern Atlantic and Mediterranean
CINCNELM	commander-in-chief, Naval Forces, Eastern Atlantic and Mediterranean
COS	Chiefs of Staff
CRC	Council of the Revolutionary Command
DBPO	Documents on British Policy Overseas
DF	day fighter
DMI	director of military intelligence
DNI	director of naval intelligence
ECM	electronic counter measures
EDC	European Defence Community
ESBD	engineer stores base depot
FO	Foreign Office
FRUS	Foreign Relations of the United States
GA	ground attack
GCI	ground controlled interceptor
GOC	general officer commanding
HAFSE	High Authority for Southern Europe
HMC	Higher Military Committee
H of C	head of chancery
ICI	Imperial Chemical Industries
IPC	Iraq Petroleum Company
JAPS	Joint Administrative Planning Section
JCS	Joint Chiefs of Staff
JIC	Joint Intelligence Committee
JPS	Joint Planning Staff
JWPS	Joint War Production Staff, Joint War Planning Staff

KBE	Knight Commander of the Order of the British Empire
KCB	Knight Commander of the Order of the Bath
KCMG	Knight Commander of the Order of St Michael and St George
KCVO	Knight Commander of the Royal Victorian Order
KEK	Cyprus National Party
KG	Knight of the Order of the Garter
Kt	Knight Bachelor
KT	kiloton
LB	light bomber
LOC	lines of communication
LRAF	long range air forces
Lt-Gen	lieutenant-general
MA	military attaché
MAAG	Military Assistance Advisory Group
MDAP	Mutual Defence Assistance Programme (US)
MEAF	Middle East Air Forces
MEC	Middle East Command
MEDO	Middle East Defence Organisation
MFA	minister of foreign affairs
MOD	Ministry of Defence
MT	military transport
MTB	motor torpedo boat
NAAFI	Navy, Army and Air Force Institutes
NATO	North Atlantic Treaty Organisation
NCO	non-commissioned officer
NEACC	Near East Arms Co-ordinating Committee
OF	Overseas Finance (Division, Treasury)
PAO	principal administrative officer
POL	petroleum, oil and lubricants
PT	patrol boat
RAF	Royal Air Force
RCC	Revolutionary Command Council

REAF	Royal Egyptian Air Force
REME	Royal Electrical and Mechanical Engineers
RM	Royal Marines, radio monitoring
SA	South Africa
SAC	Strategic Air Command
SACEUR	supreme allied commander, Europe
SACLANT	supreme allied commander, Atlantic
SACME	supreme allied commander, Middle East
SAS	Special Air Services
SBTA	senior British technical adviser
SBNCME	senior British naval commander, Middle East
SEATO	South-East Asia Treaty Organisation
S of S	secretary of state
SHAPE	Supreme Headquarters Allied Powers, Europe
TA	Territorial Army
TAF	Tactical Air Force
UK	United Kingdom
UNESCO	United Nations Educational, Scientific and Cultural Organisation
UNO	United Nations Organisation
UNRRA	United Nations Relief and Rehabilitation Administration
US(A)	United States of America
USG	United States Government
USSR	Union of Soviet Socialist Republics
VHB	very heavy bomber
WD	War Department
WMD	weapons of mass destruction

Principal Holders of Offices 1945–1949: Part I

UNITED KINGDOM

1. *Ministers* [*]

(a) *Wartime coalition (10 May 1940–23 May 1945) and Conservative caretaker government (23 May–26 July 1945)*

Prime minister	Mr W L S Churchill (10 May 1940)
Lord president of the Council	Mr A N Chamberlain (11 May 1940) Sir John Anderson (Nat) (30 Oct 1940) Mr C R Attlee (Lab) (24 Sept 1943) Lord Woolton (25 May 1945)
Chancellor of the Exchequer	Sir Kingsley Wood (12 May 1940) Sir John Anderson (Nat) (24 Sept 1943)
S of S foreign affairs	Viscount Halifax (11 May 1940) Mr R A Eden (22 Dec 1940)
Minister of defence	Mr W L S Churchill (10 May 1940)
S of S air	Sir Archibald Sinclair (Lib) (14 May 1940)* Mr M H Macmillan (25 May 1945)
S of S war	Mr R A Eden (11 May 1940)* Mr D Margesson (22 Dec 1940)* Lord Beaverbrook (4 Feb 1942) Sir James Grigg (Nat) (22 Feb 1942)**
1st lord of Admiralty	Mr A V Alexander (Lab) (11 May 1940) Mr B Bracken (25 May 1945)
Resident minister, Middle East	Mr R Casey (Ind) (19 Mar 1942) Lord Moyne (28 Jan 1944)* Sir Edward Grigg (21 Nov 1944)

---

* Throughout denotes office not in Cabinet.
** The S of S for war was a member of the Cabinet under the caretaker government.

(b) *Labour government from 26 July 1945 to 8 Sept 1949, the concluding date for part I of this volume*

Prime minister	Mr C R Attlee (26 July 1945)
Lord president of the Council	Mr H S Morrison (27 July 1945)
Chancellor of the Exchequer	Dr H J N Dalton (27 July 1945) Sir Stafford Cripps (13 Nov 1947)
S of S foreign affairs	Mr E Bevin (27 July 1945)
Minister of defence	Mr C R Attlee (27 July 1945) Mr A V Alexander (20 Dec 1946)
S of S air	Viscount Stansgate (3 Aug 1945) Mr P J Noel-Baker (4 Oct 1946)* Mr A Henderson (7 Oct 1947)*
S of S war	Mr J Lawson (3 Aug 1945) Mr F Bellinger (4 Oct 1946)* Mr E Shinwell (7 Oct 1947)*
1st lord of Admiralty	Mr A V Alexander (3 Aug 1945) Viscount Hall (4 Oct 1946)*

2. *Junior Ministers*

(a) *Foreign Office*

(i) Minister of state	Mr R Law (24 Sept 1943) Mr P J Noel-Baker (3 Aug 1945) Mr H McNeil (4 Oct 1946) Mr W Mabane (25 May 1948)
(ii) Parliamentary under-secretary of state	Mr G H Hall (25 Sept 1943) Lord Dunglass (26 May 1945) Lord Lovat (26 May 1945) Mr G Oliver (4 Aug 1945) Mr H McNeil (4 Aug 1945) Mr C Mayhew (4 Oct 1946–2 Mar 1950) Mr K Younger (7 Oct 1947) Lord Henderson (7 June 1948–26 Oct 1951)

3. *Civil servants*

(a) *Secretary to the Cabinet*	Sir Edward Bridges (1938–1946) Sir Norman Brook (1947–1962; additional secretary, 1945–1946)

(b) *Foreign Office*

(i) Permanent under-secretary
     of state

Sir Alexander Cadogan (1 Jan 1938)
Sir Orme Sargent (1 Jan 1946)
Sir William Strang (1 Feb 1949)

(ii) Assistant under-secretary
      of state, responsible
      for Middle East Depts

R G Howe (Aug 1945–Apr 1947)
M R Wright (July 1947–Nov 1950)

(iii) Assistant secretary/counsellor,
      head of Egyptian Dept (African
      Dept from Oct 1948)

P S Scrivener (Mar 1942–Apr 1947)
D W Lascelles (Apr 1947–Apr 1948)
G L Clutton (Apr 1948–Feb 1950)

(iv) Assistant secretary/counsellor,
      head of Eastern Dept

C W Baxter (Sept 1944–Nov 1947)
B A B Burrows (Nov 1947–Dec 1949)

4. *War Office*

(i) Chief of imperial general
     staff (Field Marshal)

Viscount Alanbrooke (25 Dec 1941)
Viscount Montgomery of Alamein
   (26 June 1946)
Sir William Slim (1 Nov 1948)

(ii) Vice-chief of imperial
      general staff (Lt-Gen)

Sir Archibald Nye (5 Dec 1941)
Sir Frank Simpson (1 Feb 1946)
Sir Gerald Templer (1 Feb 1948)

(iii) Director of plans (Brigadier)

C S Sugden (17 Oct 1943)
G S Thompson (13 Feb 1945)
J H N Poett (4 Apr 1946)
G P D Blacker (12 Jan 1948)
W S Cole (14 Mar 1949)

5. *Air Ministry*

(i) Chief of air staff (Marshal of RAF)

Sir Charles Portal (25 Oct 1940)
Sir Arthur Tedder (1 Jan 1946)

(ii) Vice-chief of air staff (Air Marshal)

Sir Douglas Evill (21 Mar 1943)
Sir William Dickson (1 July 1946)
Sir James Robb (1 Jan 1948)
Sir Arthur Sanders (1 Nov 1948)

(iii) Director of plans (Air Commodore)

W L Dawson (19 June 1943)
G H Mills (17 June 1946)
D MacFayden (1 Jan 1949)
Air Vice Marshal H I Cozens (7 July 1949)

6. *Admiralty*

(i) 1st sea lord (Admiral of the Fleet)

Viscount Cunningham of Hyndhope
(1943-1946)
Sir John Cunningham (1946–1948)
Lord Fraser of North Cape (1949–1953)

(ii) Vice-chief of naval staff
(Vice Admiral)

Sir Neville Syfret (1945)
Sir Rhoderick McGrigor (1945–1948)
Sir John Edelsten (1948–1950)

(iii) Director of plans (Captain)

W H D Friedberger (14 Dec 1943)
E W L Longley-Cook (3 Aug 1945)
J F Stevens (10 Jan 1946)
T M Brownrigg (9 Jan 1948)

EGYPT

1. *Government of Egypt*

Prime minister

Ahmad Mahir (9 Oct 1944)
Mahmud Fahmi al-Nuqrashi (Nokrashi)
(25 Feb 1945)
Ismail Sidqi (Sidky) (17 Feb 1946)
Mahmud Fahmi al-Nuqrashi (Nokrashi)
(10 Dec 1946)
Ibrahim Abd al-Hadi (Abdel Hadi)
(28 Dec 1948)
Hussain Sirri (Sirry) (26 July 1949)

Foreign minister

Mahmud Fahmi al Nuqrashi (Nokrashi)
(9 Oct 1944)
Abd al-Hamid Badawi (7 Mar 1945)
Ahmad Lufti al-Saiyid (17 Feb 1946)
Ibrahim Abd al-Hadi (Abdel Hadi)
(12 Sept 1946)
Mahmud Fahmi al-Nuqrashi (Nokrashi)
(10 Dec 1946)
Ahmad Muhammad Khashaba (19 Nov
1947)
Ibrahim Dassuqi Abaza (28 Dec 1948)
Ahmad Muhammad Khashaba (27 Feb
1949)

Minister of war/defence

Saiyyid Salim (9 Oct 1944)
General Ahmad Atiyah (17 Feb 1946)
General Muhammad Haidar (19 Nov 1947)

2. *British Embassy*

Ambassador	Lord Killearn (22 Dec 1936)
	Sir Ronald Campbell (12 Mar 1946)
Minister	R J Bowker (Apr 1946)
	E A Chapman-Andrews (Nov 1947)
Oriental secretary	W A Smart (Apr 1926–Jan 1948)
	T C Ravensdale (Jan 1948–Jan 1949)
Oriental counsellor	T C Ravensdale (Jan 1949)
Counsellor	R J Bowker (Sept 1945)
	R L Speaight (Apr 1946)
	D D Maclean (Nov 1948)

UK COMMANDERS IN THE MIDDLE EAST

High commissioner and commander-in-chief, Palestine (General)	Sir Alan Cunningham (1945–1948)
Commander-in-chief, Middle East Land Forces (General)	Sir Bernard Paget (1944–1946)
	Sir Miles Dempsey (1946–1947)
	Sir John Crocker (27 June 1947)
Commander-in-chief, Middle East Air Forces (Air Marshal)	Sir Charles Medhurst (8 Feb 1945)
	Sir William Dickson (1 Mar 1948)
Naval commander-in-chief, Mediterranean (Admiral)	Sir John Cunningham (15 Oct 1943)
	Sir Algernon Willis (23 Apr 1946)
	Sir Arthur Power (13 May 1948)

Chronological Table of Principal Events: Parts I–III

1945

Apr–June	San Francisco Conference on the new world organisation
June	Soviet demands for bases in the Straits
July	Call for a united front coalition by Nahas to meet Egypt's national demands
July-Aug	Potsdam Conference; Labour government elected in Britain
Sept	Attlee challenges the assumption that Britain should retain exclusive responsibility for the defence of the Middle East
Sept	London Council of Foreign Ministers
Sept	Egyptian notables call for negotiations on British evacuation of the Canal Zone
Dec	Formal Egyptian request to renegotiate 1936 treaty to secure British evacuation of the Canal Zone
Dec	Moscow Council of Foreign Ministers

1946

Feb	Anti-British demonstrations in Egypt
Feb–May	Defence Committee debates inconclusively the importance of defending the Middle East
Apr	Cabinet approves offering the peacetime evacuation of Egypt at the start of Anglo–Egyptian treaty negotiations
May	Anglo–Egyptian treaty negotiations begin in Egypt and fail to produce agreement
May	Chiefs of Staff accept that Middle East oilfields cannot be defended by Britain
July	Resumption of Anglo–Egyptian treaty negotiations
July–Sept	Anglo–Egyptian disgreements over the conditions for reactivating the base
Oct	Anglo–Egyptian treaty negotiations move to London and agreement is reached on a new treaty
Dec	Anglo–Egyptian treaty fails to be ratified owing to different interpretations of the meaning of the Sudan protocol

1947

Jan	Anglo–Egyptian treaty negotiations formally ended
Jan	Attlee accepts that the defence of the Middle East should be one of the three main pillars of British defence strategy

Mar	Bevin decides to stand on the 1936 Anglo–Egyptian treaty
July	Chiefs of Staff protest at the decision to withdraw forces to the levels permitted by the 1936 treaty
Aug–Sept	Egypt goes to the UN over the continued British miltary presence in the Canal Zone
Oct–Nov	Anglo–American Pentagon talks on the Middle East and eastern Mediterranean
Nov	Bevin considers an agreement with Egypt rather than attempting to stand on the 1936 treaty

1948

Jan	British discussions on ways of breaking the deadlock with Egypt
Jan	Anglo–Iraqi treaty revision agreed but disturbances in Iraq prevent ratification
Feb	Montgomery begins to campaign for a commitment to defend western Europe
Mar	Proposals for a Middle East Union drawn up in London
Mar	Staff study 'Intermezzo' on dealing with a Soviet threat to the Middle East in 1957–1958 which leads the Chiefs of Staff to revise their military requirements in Egypt to ensure support facilities for air operations at the outbreak of war
Mar–Apr	Anglo–American–Canadian talks on global war planning
May	Britain withdraws from Palestine
May	First Arab–Israeli War begins
May	First global war emergency plan codenamed 'Doublequick' finalised
June	Passing of the Sudan ordinance
July	Work begins on the first emergency plan for the defence of the Middle East codenamed 'Sandown' and based on the defence of the Tel Aviv–Ramallah line
Aug	Chiefs of Staff require 20,000 troops in Egypt in peacetime
Oct	First long-term plan for the defence of the Middle East finalised
Dec	Second global emergency war plan codenamed 'Speedway' finalised

1949

Jan	First Arab–Israeli war effectively ends with armistice agreements
June	Anglo–Egyptian military staff talks on Middle East defence
July	National government formed in Egypt including representatives of the Wafd
Aug	New American concept for global war which ended the commitment to assist in the defence of the Middle East
Sept	Chiefs of Staff reaffirm their support for a strategy based on defending the Middle East

1950

Jan	Egyptian elections bring the Wafd back to power
Jan	Bevin's talks with King Farouk

Mar	Modification of the defence strategy approved in 1947 in order to give western Europe priority over the Middle East for reinforcements
Mar	Third emergency plan for global war codenamed 'Galloper' finalised
May	Anglo–American–French tripartite declaration on the Middle East conflict
June	New defence policy and global strategy paper taking account of the Soviet atomic explosion and the creation of NATO, which emphasised the importance of the cold war as opposed to hot war but retained the main three pillars of defence strategy geared to defending the Middle East
July	Informal talks on an Anglo–Egyptian base agreement
July	Second emergency war plan for the defence of the Middle East, based on the Tel Aviv–Ramallah line, codenamed 'Celery' finalised
Sept	Review of Middle East defence strategy with consideration of the Lebanon–Jordan and the inner ring defence lines as alternatives to the Tel Aviv–Ramallah line
Sept	Greece and Turkey admitted to NATO as associate members
Oct	US planners criticise the inner ring strategy as constituting the defence of Egypt rather than the defence of the Middle East
Dec	Bevin has a series of meetings with Salah el Din following the end of the informal talks at which he offers the evacuation of combat troops leaving technicians in civilian clothes

1951

Jan	Joint planners accept evacuation of the Canal Zone on condition that an interim peacetime base is established in Israel
Jan	First Malta meeting of British and American commanders to discuss Middle East defence
Feb	General Robertson's visit to Israel
Mar	Bill to nationalise the Anglo–Iranian Oil Company introduced in the Iranian parliament
Mar	Second Malta meeting of British and American commanders to discuss Middle East defence
Apr	Anglo–Egyptian negotiations lead to Egyptian rejection of British proposals for a base agreement
May	Anglo–American discussions on Mediterranean command arrangements lead to US proposals for a separate Middle East Command
May	Nationalisation of the Anglo–Iranian Oil Company implemented
July	Egypt rejects British proposals on the future of the Sudan and the Cabinet assesses the British position if negotiations were to breakdown
Oct	Bills to abrogate the Anglo–Egyptian treaty placed before the Egyptian parliament
Oct	Proposals for a Middle East Command presented to the Egyptians
Oct	Beginning of the Egyptian campaign of violence against the British presence in the Canal Zone
Oct	Conservative government elected in Britain
Oct	Fourth emergency plan for global war, plan 'Cinderella'
Dec	British request to Farouk to replace the Wafd government
Dec	Egyptian measures against British troops in the Canal Zone lead to the near doubling of British forces to 64,000 men

Dec	Revision of British Middle East defence strategy to defend the inner ring line rather than the Tel Aviv–Ramallah or Lebanon–Jordan lines

1952

Jan	British troops kill 43 Egyptians and wound 73 in an attack on a police barracks in Ismailia
Jan	Cairo riots leave 26 dead and 750 buildings burned
Jan	American pressure on the British to resume negotiations
Jan	Dismissal of the Wafd government
Feb	Greece and Turkey admitted to NATO
Feb	Eden proposes the resumption of Anglo–Egyptian negotiations
Mar	British accept that no declaration can be made concerning the resumption of negotiations given the Egyptian insistence on British evacuation and on the unity of Egypt and the Sudan under a common crown
Feb	NATO force goals agreed at Lisbon
Mar	American pressure on the British to make concessions on the Sudan in order to get a base agreement
Apr	Informal talks on the base; the Egyptians insist on the precise evacuation formula agreed in 1946 which is unacceptable to the British
Apr	Outline plan of British intentions in global war, July 1952–December 1952, plan 'Sycamore'
June	Global strategy paper revises the main thrust of British defence strategy laid down in 1947 and looks to reductions in defence expenditure with more emphasis on deterrence and cold war than on hot war
June	Proposal for a Middle East Command replaced by the suggestion of a planning body referred to as a Middle East Defence Organisation
July	Australia sends two air squadrons to the Middle East
July	Examination of a new forward strategy for Middle East defence based on a cover force deployed in the passes of north-east Iraq to delay the Soviet advance towards the inner ring which would require less forces and reduced Middle East deployments
July	Free officers coup in Egypt leads to the abdication of King Farouk
Aug	Chiefs of Staff confirm that British forces in Egypt will be reduced to one division and 160 aircraft in line with the global strategy paper once the situation permits
Sept	General Neguib becomes prime minister
Sept	BDCC(ME) support new forward strategy for Middle East defence
Oct	Neguib wants the resumption of negotiations on the Suez base
Nov	Treasury presses for further reductions in defence expenditure and a radical review of defence policy agreed
Nov	US proposes an Anglo–American formulation of the precise terms of a possible agreement on the future of the base
Nov	COS approve a new forward strategy for Middle East defence and define requirements in Egypt in relation to the new strategy and the agreed force reductions
Nov	Outline plan of British intentions in global war, Jan 1953–June 1953, plan 'Fairfax'

Dec	Joint Planners define three scenarios (Cases A, B and C) under which the base will be evacuated in peacetime and managed in order to make it available in wartime either at the outbreak of hostilities or at three or six months after war begins
Dec	Defence Committee agrees that the evacuation of the Canal Zone will be negotiated on the basis of agreement on the management and reactivation of the base, Egyptian participation in MEDO and Anglo–American economic assistance for Egypt

1953

Jan	Anglo-American discussions on the terms of a base agreement with Egypt
Jan	Military regime in Egypt bans political parties
Feb	Britain and Egypt sign an agreement on the Sudan formally ending the Condominium
Mar	Cabinet approves five-point package for an Anglo–Egyptian agreement involving MEDO, an air defence organisation, maintenance of the base to ensure immediate availability on the outbreak of war (Case A), military aid and a phased British evacuation; Cairo embassy points out that the package will be unacceptable to the Egyptians
Mar	US approve the package with the proviso that Case A is desirable not essential
Apr	Eden enters hospital and Churchill becomes acting foreign secretary
Apr	Anglo–Egyptian negotiations on the base begin
May	Anglo–Egyptian negotiations reach deadlock
May	Dulles's tour of the Middle East leads to a reassessment of US Middle Eastern policy and a decision to take initiatives independently of the British, most notably a defence organisation based on the northern tier
June	Churchill appoints R M A Hankey as chargé d'affaires at the Cairo embassy
June	Churchill suffers a stroke and Salisbury becomes acting foreign secretary
July	US attempts to mediate in the Anglo–Egyptian dispute over the base
Aug	Anglo–Egyptian negotiations on the base resume
Sept	Churchill and Eden return to public life
Sept	New Zealand sends one air squadron to the Middle East
Oct	Anglo–Egyptian negotiations deadlocked over whether British military technicians would have the right to wear uniform, the conditions under which the base would be automatically available, the length of the evacuation period and the numbers of British technicians remaining as the base is evacuated
Nov	Chiefs of Staff express doubts as to whether, in the wake of the agreed reductions in ME forces, it would be possible to reinforce the region with the strategic reserve

1954

Jan	Cabinet considers alternatives if Anglo–Egyptian negotiations fail, including winding up the base
Jan	Churchill expresses a desire to break off the negotiations

Jan	American pressure on Egypt leads to Nasser making a concesssion on the conditions for automatic reactivation of the base
Jan	Muslim Brotherhood outlawed
Jan	US decides to provide military aid to Pakistan
Feb–Apr	Nasser and Neguib battle for political power
Mar	British accept Egyptian concession on the conditions for automatic reactivation of the base and propose the use of civilian contract labour rather than military technicians
Apr	Turco–Pakistani Pact signed
Apr	US–Iraqi military aid agreement
May	Tactical use of nuclear weapons deemed vital to any prospect of successfully implementing the forward strategy
May	Britain expresses a wish to renegotiate Anglo–Iraqi treaty to secure the use of air bases in Iraq
June	Churchill accepts the desirability of evacuating the Canal Zone and reaching an agreement with Egypt
July	Resumption of Anglo–Egyptian negotiations on the base
July	Britain and Egypt sign heads of agreement on the future of the base
July	US requests planning studies on the defence of the Zagros mountains as part of the outer ring
Oct	Britain and Egypt finalise the Suez base agreement
Oct	Australia withdraws its air squadrons from Malta
Oct	Nuri Said visits Turkey to discuss the development of a northern tier defence pact
Nov–Dec	British military planners point to the difficulties of defending the northern tier/outer ring
Nov	Britain and the US agree on the need to make a joint effort to settle the Arab–Israeli dispute
Nov	New Zealand withdraws its air squadron from Cyprus
Dec	Move of Middle East HQ to Cyprus

1955

Jan	Turkey and Iraq announce their intention to sign a defence pact
Jan	Detailed Anglo–American discussions begin on proposals for an Arab–Israeli peace settlement, codenamed Alpha, in which Nasser's role is deemed crucial
Jan–Feb	Arab prime ministers' conference in Cairo
Feb	Large-scale Israeli attack on an Egyptian military camp in Gaza kills 38 Egyptians
Feb	Turco–Iraqi Pact signed
Feb	Eden meets Nasser in Cairo
Mar	Egypt, Syria and Saudi Arabia agree to establish military co-operation
Mar	Cabinet decides to join the Turco–Iraqi Pact
Mar	Combined Anglo–American–Turkish study of defending the Middle East on the northern tier/outer ring
Apr	Britain formally accedes to Turco-Iraqi Pact which becomes known as the Baghdad Pact

Aug	Joint planners deem the retention of Cyprus necessary for the maintenance of British prestige and influence in the Middle East and therefore strategically essential
Sept	Egyptian purchase of Czech arms
Oct	Egyptian–Saudi–Syrian defence pact signed
Oct	Dulles agrees to Iranian accession to the Baghdad Pact
Dec	Templer mission to secure Jordanian accession to the Baghdad Pact fails

1956

Jan	Suez Canal base deemed unnecessary even for cold war purposes
Jan	The Sudan becomes independent
Mar	King Hussein dismisses General Glubb
Mar	Britain abandons the attempts to co-operate with Nasser
Mar	Failure of the Anderson mission brings the collapse of Alpha and leads the US to devise measures, codenamed Omega, to isolate Nasser in the Arab world and undermine his position in Egypt
Mar	Trial of Egyptian military attaché in Baghdad for subversion
July	Nasser nationalises the Suez Canal Company
Oct	Israeli forces attack Egypt
Oct	Britain and France issue an ultimatum requiring the Egyptians to retreat ten miles from the Canal and for the Israelis to do likewise (in effect calling on them to advance to ten miles from the Canal)
Oct	Britain begins bombing Egypt
Nov	Anglo–French forces land in Egypt and seize the northern half of the Suez Canal; Egypt blocks the Canal
Nov	A ceasefire in Egypt is agreed
Dec	Britain agrees to withdraw unconditionally from Egypt

Introduction

In the early days of BDEEP the role of editors of country volumes, as defined in the letters of appointment, was to select key documents related to the nature and timing of the decisions to grant self-government and independence to British dependencies. Yet the end of empire involved historical processes, events and decisions which took place over and above the formal transfer of governmental responsibilities. In the initial conception of BDEEP it was envisaged that a documentary record of such matters could not be left entirely to the editors of the general volumes. Therefore it was proposed that a three-part volume would be devoted to defence and the Middle East covering the years 1945–1956. Those familiar with the documentary record of Britain's relations with the territories of formal and informal empire in the region will be aware of the scale of such an undertaking. Even if Palestine is excluded, it still leaves a series of territories for which there are in excess of 10,000 Foreign Office files. Indeed the British interest and involvement in the region was such that the government had to create an extra Foreign Office department to deal with the volume of work. In addition the fact that the region was a key area in terms of defence strategy, and given priority for reinforcements over Europe until 1950, has resulted in an enormous volume of military records. And then in 1956 there was the Suez crisis which generated a vast quantity of paperwork in its own right.

These problems were addressed at the outset by this editor and a number of people associated with the project. In the course of a lively exchange of views, it became clear that to tackle the whole of the Middle East region would be an impossible task given the constraints on the editor's time and the publishing space. But there was also no consensus on the desirability of making the task manageable by addressing Britain's retreat from Egypt, the most important part of its informal empire, in the form of a standard country volume. While some were keen on this approach others believed that the end of empire involved broader questions of world power, military strategy and economic decline which transcended territorial boundaries. It was not therefore deemed desirable or possible to deal with all such issues in the standard country volume mould. In fact it would be impossible to portray accurately the attitudes, concerns and policies of British decision makers responsible for any Middle Eastern territory without an understanding of the regional approach which dominated their thinking. Consequently while it was decided to change the Middle Eastern volume to one centered on Egypt, there remains a focus on regional problems associated with Middle Eastern defence issues which were often directly related to the British military presence in the Suez Canal Zone. The additional proviso was the exclusion of the details of the Suez crisis from July to December 1956 in the expectation that this will eventually be covered by the Foreign Office volumes in the Documents on British Policy Overseas series.

The purpose of examining defence questions is to examine what determined a British military presence in imperial regions after 1945 and how this presence related to the retreat from empire. The question of whether the cold war was an incentive or a spur to the end of empire is a significant one which needs examination in the context of a proper understanding of how military strategy was geared to the very different requirements of cold and hot war. It is important to be aware of contemporary perceptions of the meaning of the cold war which were very different from the interpretations and analyses found in many standard historical works on the cold war's origins and early development. By the start of the 1950s the British military had quite specifically defined the cold war as all measures short of international armed conflict, which is clearly distinct from understandings of the cold war as the embodiment of Soviet–American relations or as involving the military measures designed to deal with hot war in the form of a global or even a regional conflict.

The subtleties of fighting an essentially political cold war by using, amongst other things, military deployments, have too often been buried beneath an interpretation of all military planning, particularly NATO's, as simply part of the militarisation of the cold war conflict in response to the Soviet military threat. In fact, British defence planners, like their American counterparts, tried to plan for and also to deter a hot war with the Soviet Union (although they never believed the Soviet Union was on the point of starting a hot war) while waging a cold war which required different kinds of forces and deployments. Fighting the cold war sometimes required a combination of political and military measures, but the latter were not the same as those needed to fight or deter a hot war. This distinction between hot and cold war is crucial to understanding that regional defence pacts like NATO, SEATO and the Baghdad Pact were not primarily aimed at defending militarily defensible areas but at fulfilling political functions in terms of the cold war. One of these was to convince the inhabitants of a region that they were facing a military threat from the Soviet Union rather than a political and ideological challenge which military and civilian elites saw as more real and more dangerous.

The special status of the volume inherent in its regional dimension is reinforced by other more obvious differences between informal and formal empire. Egypt in 1945 was technically an independent state whose relations with Britain were influenced by the 1936 treaty.[1] There was thus no power to transfer in the formal sense, no constitutions to make and no interaction between local inhabitants and representatives of the British crown with administrative responsibilities for their welfare. Instead Egypt was dealt with in Cairo and London by members of the Foreign Service. Egyptian affairs were the responsibility of the Egyptian Department and then, after October 1948, the African Department of the Foreign Office. The heads of these departments, most notably George Clutton and Roger Allen who between them held the posts from April 1948 to February 1953, were important drafters of minutes and memoranda on Egyptian policy. At the same time the views of the Chiefs of Staff and the Commanders-in-Chief, Middle East were continually sought, as, often, were those of other Foreign Office departments concerned with Middle East affairs.

In the broad picture of the end of empire, Egypt's role assumes enormous significance. The loss of power in terms of international influence and military and economic strength cannot be buried beneath the transfer of power in the administrative sense. The British empire was perceived by ministers, military leaders and Foreign Office officials as a worldwide system of control and influence whose maintenance in the 1940s and early 1950s was not significantly linked to the retention of administrative responsibilities in the non-self-governing territories. Moreover if there was an area upon which the future of the empire in this broad sense was seen to hinge it would undoubtedly have been the Middle East in which Egypt was regarded as the key territorial player.

The Middle East's significance was linked to Britain's very survival as a world power in military and imperial terms. In the eyes of military leaders it was the only region where Britain had gained success in two world wars. Most British military leaders had served there at some point, and, for all the services, past campaigns in the Middle East and Mediterranean provided key justifications for a future role. These perceptions, along with the location of the Middle East at the heart of imperial air and sea communications, contributed to long held beliefs that Britain's Middle Eastern position had to be preserved at all costs. As Churchill noted in 1941, 'the loss of Egypt would be a disaster of the first magnitude to Great Britain, second only to successful invasion and final conquest. ... It is to be impressed upon all ranks, especially the highest, that the life and honour of Great Britain depends upon the successful defence of Egypt'.[2]

In the post-war years the connection between the life and honour of Britain and the defence of Egypt became the main determinant of defence strategy. Military strategists were to invent a number of other reasons for remaining in Egypt and the Middle East such as the protection of oil, the use of strategic bases and the defence of Black Africa, all of which were generally beyond Britain's capabilities. The use of military strategy to support political goals of prestige and honour was added to Churchill's conviction that for the empire what happened in Egypt would 'set the pace for us all over Africa and the Middle East' (356). Yet as a technically independent state Egypt's relations with Britain fell into the realm of foreign policy in a region where international and regional rivalries were particularly acute.

This situation is reflected in the type of documents reproduced in this volume as compared to the nature of those in other country volumes. Precisely because the loss of informal empire translated directly into a loss of global prestige and influence (whereas the transfer or loss of power in the formal sense was expected to bring compensation in terms of informal influence), government ministers were closely involved in the detailed discussions and decisions about Egypt. These were seen to have enormous implications for Britain's position as a great world power and for the future of the British empire. In much of the colonial empire ministers were not closely involved in the day-to-day contacts with colonial governments and more often than not the Cabinet's role was merely to endorse or occasionally modify key decisions; in the case of Egypt the Cabinet was continually debating and disagreeing about points of detail because of the potential implications for domestic politics and Britain's world standing. Consequently there is an enormous quantity of material covering the papers and deliberations of the full Cabinet and it has not been possible to reproduce it all here. In addition the enormous influence of Conservative back benchers after 1951, given the small government majority, cannot fully be reflected in this volume. However, with an initial majority of only eighteen, ministerial concerns about party opinion were often vital influences on decisions, and worries about opposition from within the party are evident from some of the documents. By contrast, the involvement of many important components of the bureaucracy has made it possible in some instances to illustrate the complex nature of the decision making process right up to prime ministerial and Cabinet levels. One of the volume's main roles has thus been to reveal the nature of, and influences on, the highest levels of the decision making process.

Another key aim of the selection has been to reveal the relationship between military planning and the political requirements of informal empire. Or, put another way, to what extent was foreign policy within the informal empire determined by strategic requirements? In what manner did the apparent need to make provision for Middle Eastern defence in the face of the alleged Soviet threat dictate what facilities Britain needed in Egypt; and to what extent did it provide the basis on which Anglo–Egyptian relations were conducted? Answering such questions has entailed a study of the strategy for defending the Middle East and how this strategy was related to the broader requirements of Commonwealth defence and the global strategy which lay behind it. At the same time it has been necessary to provide a considerable amount of detail on the troublesome negotiations about the future of the British base in the Suez Canal Zone which in 1945 was the largest military base in the world. The aim has been to use an examination of particular problems, like the arrangements pertaining to the Suez base, to illustrate the attitudes of policy makers to larger and more general issues. The arrangements for the British presence in the Canal Zone had obvious links to strategic planning and the overall maintenance of informal empire in the Middle East, which in turn were vital to Britain's standing as a great global power.

Egyptian policy was also closely connected to Sudanese policy, and Britain's future in Egypt was often discussed, at both Cabinet and departmental levels, in the same meetings which dealt with the future of the Sudan. On occasions both Britain and Egypt were keen to use the one issue in order to have an impact on the other, although the Egyptians were more inclined to treat the two issues as inseparable. There has, however, been a deliberate effort to limit reference to the Sudan which is covered in its own right by Douglas Johnson in BDEEP, Series B, Volume 5.

In methodological terms, reference should be made to a number of factors arising out of the key criteria for document selection and the focus of the volume. Firstly, there are the implications associated with the distinction between documents which illustrate attitudes and ideas that may or may not ultimately govern decisions to implement policies, and documents which reveal the actual taking of the decisions. The former may be of enormous interest to historians because of their wide ranging focus or their treatment of particular issues, or because of what they reveal about the writer's assumptions. Yet ultimately they may have had little or no influence on the policies devised to deal with specific problems or the decision making process from which they derived. Indeed, decisions might have been taken to meet party political needs, or for other reasons of domestic policy, or on the basis of retained intelligence assessments which override the memoranda of officials and which might have had a vital influence on the final decision. Such influences are of course difficult if not impossible to document through government records. As far as this volume is concerned the aim is to provide the reader with a knowledge of what the key decisions were while emphasising the difficulties of illustrating all the factors which produced them; it is not expected that the reasons for all the decisions which influenced Britain's relations with Egypt can be determined.

Secondly, there cannot be a fully comprehensive understanding of the decision making process because of the withholding of important material to which editors have not been granted the privileged access normally accorded to editors of official histories. In the case of Egypt, the key omission at the time that the bulk of these documents were being selected concerns the retention of intelligence information. Consequently, although some of the records of the Joint Intelligence Committee have now been released, the activities of the intelligence agencies which were of enormous importance in the Middle East and in the British decision making process are hardly touched upon in this volume. In addition to the role of the Joint Intelligence Committee there are the important activities of MI6 in the Middle East and those of the embassy in Cairo which, before the coup of 1952, had intelligence contacts within the Egyptian government. Available records still tell us nothing about the precise significance of these influences on British policy.

Within the main file series of the Foreign Office and the Ministry of Defence there are significant retentions of files and the removal of papers from within files. In the case of the latter the numbers encountered would probably be measured in thousands rather than hundreds, although many of the withheld military records would not relate to Egyptian or Middle Eastern issues. In the defence series especially, there is also the additional complication that, as a result of the initiative towards more open government, newly released documents have been added to files since they were first examined. To go over hundreds of files again has been too daunting a task, although some interesting material has been unearthed that was previously retained by departments. Moreover there remains the likelihood of new material continually being added as part of an ongoing process.

Another problem concerns the Foreign Office series (FO 141) containing the files of the Cairo embassy which provides a rich historical source. The Cairo embassy was the second largest British diplomatic mission, surpassed only by Washington, partly because the staff of the British Middle East Office came under its establishment. The existence of a minister, an oriental counsellor and other important officials meant that the ambassador often had a series of minutes to read which surpassed in length and variety those available to the secretary of state in London. Thus the views of the men on the spot, other than those contained in telegrams and despatches to the Foreign Office, can be documented and their influence on policy making in London more fully assessed. This is a feature which is unique to the Egyptian volume because records of the colonial governments generally remain in the capitals of the now independent states and are not therefore incorporated into BDEEP volumes. Unfortunately, however, the embassy records come to an end in 1952 with the subsequent files destroyed in 1956 during the Suez crisis.

Thirdly, the emphasis on the particular decisions which were made as part of an ongoing diplomatic drama rooted in defence questions has resulted in a relative lack of attention to economic affairs. Matters associated with Egypt's position in the sterling area and matters arising from Anglo–Egyptian trade and the problems of the sterling balances have not been examined in detail.

Fourthly, an attempt has been made to incorporate a number of reflective minutes and memoranda which illustrate the assumptions and attitudes of officials over and above their writings on the important day-to-day problems of Anglo–Egyptian relations. These, unlike many of their colonial equivalents, do not focus on British responsibilities for the creation of a new political or economic order under the umbrella of nation building, but they do provide insights into the world view of Foreign Service personnel who in some cases had been in the Middle East since the First World War. The responsibility for moulding the Egyptian nation had been slipping from their grasp with the decline of British power, yet dealing with Egypt as an independent state seems not to have rested easily on the shoulders of some British policy makers in Cairo. Documents revealing their attitudes are often fascinating, although they reveal more about the nature of the British than they do about the true character of the Egyptians they encountered. Given the remit of the project, this editor can only express his awareness of the distortions this can produce and hope that one day the Egyptian side of the story will emerge to offset the perspective provided by a record of the British attempts to defend their informal empire in the Middle East.

Fifthly, the complexities of the decision making process pose questions for historians and others interested in such matters which require some initial comments. There can be no doubting the interest shown by government ministers in the detailed questions which are illustrated here. Yet the number of participants in the process of acquiring and presenting information and opinions made it difficult for even the most avid of decision makers to keep track of all aspects of a rapidly changing situation. Advice and information from Cairo, some of it not always welcome to the Foreign Office which might have had different views, had to be considered and acted upon. The military dimension frequently required the opinion of the Chiefs of Staff whose thoughts might conflict with the advice received from the Commanders-in-Chief, Middle East. On occasions the Treasury was also trying to make its voice heard. Yet it is not easy to point to situations when ministers were able to call on the whole range of what was often conflicting opinion. On at least one occasion an important meeting was held to discuss the implications of an assessment that had already been changed (32). Such instances can be significant for an understanding of a decision making process that had to incorporate general requirements while responding to particular events outside British control.

These collective considerations affect any attempt to provide an overall understanding of what exactly constituted British policy and what influenced its determination. To define these two questions is clearly a difficult and often theoretical historical task. It is made somewhat simpler in terms of Egypt and informal empire because there were so many matters, both great and small, which required specific decisions to be taken on a regular basis. Policy in the form of background papers, minutes and letters was time and again in Egypt translated into particular decisions; this makes the task of addressing how policy was made that much easier even if the questions of why it was made remain more elusive.

In terms of the end of empire, or in the case of this volume, the problems stemming from a refusal to end informal empire that led inexorably to the disaster and humiliation of Suez, there are some interpretations of the aims of general policy that should be stated at the outset because they have become part of the editor's thinking and therefore might have influenced his selection of material. In the first place policy was less geared to the ending of informal empire in the Middle East than to preserving it at virtually any cost; this remained so even after Suez, despite the blow to Britain's position the débâcle entailed, because of Britain's close ties to the Gulf states and the regimes in Jordan and Iraq. There was no planned final retreat from the Middle East as a whole, as in areas of formal empire, and the concept of *reculer pour mieux sauter* simply became one of *reculer pour mieux rester*.

Secondly, the reasons for attempting to retain a presence in the Middle East do not essentially relate to the protection of economic interests or the pursuit of realisable strategic goals. Having assumed at the outset that there would be some rational link between the defence of the Middle East and the maintenance of informal empire in general and a military position in Egypt in particular, it soon became clear that this assumption was unsustainable. Many of the documents reveal an emotive or irrational commitment to preserve prestige and status which, as in many areas of human activity, has produced a variety of attempts to employ reason and logic to obscure this fundamental truth.

As regards the particular series of documents from which those making up this volume have been selected, FO 371, Foreign Office original correspondence, is by far the most important. It contains a variety of papers in addition to the letters and telegrams from Cairo and other diplomatic posts in the Middle East. Military records, minutes of inter-departmental meetings, Cabinet committee papers and correspondence with other government departments are all to be found, selectively, in these FO 371 files. The files are conveniently sub-divided into numbered jackets but the order in which these appear is based on their date of registration, not on their date of origin. Thus there is no convenient chronological sequence within files and readers wishing to trace the detailed development of events will also find that the later files in a sequence contain material relating to matters arising several files previously and much earlier in time. This again is a reflection of the volume of paper generated by Britain's relations with Egypt.

The views of Foreign Office officials in London can be related to those held by the men on the spot by using FO 141, the files of the Cairo embassy. It is possible to determine how the ambassador arrived at his conclusions by reading the fascinating and lengthy minutes of his subordinates within the embassy. Particularly important is knowledge of the past Egyptian and Middle Eastern experiences of those serving in the post-war embassy. There was clearly a set of long held traditional views about the nature of Egyptians and the problems and methods of dealing with them.

The key series of military records after December 1946 is DEFE 4, the minutes of the Chiefs of Staff Committee, which until the end of 1946 are contained in CAB 79. The series is not simply a reflection of the Chiefs' discussions as it contains many of the papers submitted by the Joint Planning Staff and the Joint Intelligence Committee. JIC papers are now released up to 1953, with substantial weeding, in CAB 158. DEFE 4 also contains other communications to the Chiefs which eventually form Chiefs of Staff memoranda in DEFE 5 (CAB 80 before 1947). The papers of the Joint Planners are in DEFE 6 (CAB 84 before 1947) but important papers are found in the two main Chiefs of Staff series. Of the other military records DEFE 7 is the Ministry of Defence's general series, DEFE 11 contains the Chiefs Of Staff secretariat files, DEFE 32 the secretary's standard file and DEFE 13 the private office papers of the minister of defence. These series contain important material, including for example the detailed papers outlining the service ministries' requirements that were considered when briefs for British negotiating teams were being assembled. The views of the Air Ministry, the Admiralty and the War Office have not been traced in detail, although series like WO 216, the Chief of the Imperial General Staff's papers, have proved useful. This is partly a reflection of the intention to focus on the regional requirements rather than on the situation in the base itself. In this context the views of the Commanders-in-Chief, Middle East were clearly of more significance than the day-to-day problems of running the base, and in fact key functions like the drawing up of detailed regional defence plans were devolved to the military men on the spot. It should be borne in mind that the British Middle East Office's role was first and foremost to liaise between the civil and military authorities and to make sure the military commanders received advice on political matters. In addition the British Defence Co-ordination Committee, Middle East covered a large area of territory outside the region. The fact that its boundary ran along the northern Mediterranean coast excluding France and Spain but moving inland to include Italy, Greece, Yugoslavia, Bulgaria, Turkey, Iran, Afghanistan and India as well as Black Africa is indicative of British strategic priorities at the end of the Second World War.

Military records are the most difficult and time consuming to work with and there are other problems arising from their use and interpretation. The obvious distinction between operational and planning issues should be self-evident; less clear is the precise nature of the relationship between them. It is not safe to assume, as one might be tempted to do, that strategic planning is an academic exercise designed to produce some theoretical response to any number of possible but unlikely eventualities – a collection of bits of paper which reveal little about real defence issues. In fact these plans do play a role in a number of situations because the advice of the military was frequently sought by the civilian branches of the government in relation to foreign policy issues. On occasion the existence of these plans provided a theoretical frame of reference within which responses were formulated. However, strategic plans often took a long time to percolate through the various committees before they were finally adopted as policy. And it should not be assumed that there was a firm and realistic link between plans and the nature of the forces available to carry them out, except when particular operations were definitely envisaged. In a sense, before the defence cuts of 1952, there was a reasonable chance that the forces necessary to implement the plans to defend the Middle East would become available. However, when cuts and reductions became more and more the order of the day, the nature of the planning did not necessarily change to take account of these new restrictions. When reading planning documents it should always be borne in mind that the resources to implement them were unlikely to have been available, although in some cases the plans themselves do point to the lack of these essential resources. The imperial role of military planners was to decide what needed to be done, often more for political than military reasons, and then to use an ostensibly strategic rationale to promote a particular line of policy within the Whitehall bureacracy.

There are numerous reports of incidents and protests to the Egyptian government after October 1951, when the Suez Canal Zone became a target for terrorist operations, which, like other examples of anti-British actions, are not recorded in detail in the documents reproduced here. Similarly the masses of paper referring to the base installations and military equipment in Egypt and the problems of making adequate provision for them have also largely been ignored. Records of such deliberations on these detailed matters which had major financial implications can be found in several file series including FO 371, DEFE 7 and T 225, the Treasury Defence and Material section. The Treasury became involved in the process of winding up the British peacetime presence after the autumn of 1951 when it attempted to reduce British defence expenditure across the board; and it continued to do so for the remainder of the period covered by this volume. Interestingly, despite the growing importance of the economic aspects, the Treasury became increasingly fearful that these were being ignored by ministers and officials from the foreign and defence ministries. The demands of status and prestige, which were central to the maintenance of informal empire, and which aroused such concern in the rank and file of the Conservative Party, seem to have outweighed any purely financial considerations. T 225 provides the main source of evidence for Treasury concerns which have to be extracted from the mass of correspondence in these files that is duplicated in other series.

Cabinet memoranda are in CAB 129 and the deliberations of the full Cabinet in CAB 128. The most important Cabinet standing committee was the Defence Committee, the minutes and memoranda of which are in CAB 131. It is interesting to compare the type of decision taken by this committee with those taken by the full Cabinet, and to reflect on the amount of information available to both bodies when compared to individual departments and ministers. Under the Labour government the Prime Minister's papers (PREM 8) provide much less material than under the Conservative administrations (PREM 11), particularly that of Churchill. The ageing leader took a keen interest in Egyptian matters despite his advancing years, and without his frequent and decisive interventions in and out of Cabinet the story of Anglo–Egyptian relations would have been a very different one. For several years the prime minister pursued a policy which was clearly at odds with that desired by Eden and the Foreign Office.

There is one final point which again distinguishes this volume from other country volumes. In the Middle East in general and Egypt in particular, the United States played a role in relation to British policy which in nature and extent was different from the influence it exerted in areas of formal empire. The activities of American personnel, in what was an independent state, were on a much larger scale than those undertaken in British dependencies. Often there was a remarkable degree of Anglo–American co-operation between individuals and organisations. On the one hand the British and American military were in frequent contact in and outside the Middle East and the Mediterranean even if they did not always agree on strategy. American supplies and equipment were secretly installed at the Abu Sueir airfield without the official knowledge of the Egyptian government in order to facilitate its future use by the bombers of the US Strategic Air Command. On the other hand, there was also a degree of Anglo–American friction, particularly after May 1953, when the American government made a clear decision to embark on independent initiatives in the Middle East. British Foreign Service officers had a definite view of the American character, just as they did of that of the Egyptian, and it was not generally flattering despite the assumption of a fundamental sharing of common interests. Consequently problems arose on the ground, as between the British and American embassies in Cairo and between the two intelligence services, which are not fully recorded in the official record. At higher levels, Middle Eastern problems in general and Egyptian problems in particular became a cause of concern for President Eisenhower and British Conservative prime ministers. In January 1956 the differences over the Buraimi oasis dispute[3] lay at the centre of Eden's visit to Washington, and under his predecessor Egypt became a subject of extensive correspondence between president and prime minister. In the 1950s the records reproduced here thus have a distinctly Anglo–American flavour, as did all questions of British foreign policy after 1949 if not earlier. In regions of informal empire in particular, the loss of British power and influence was intimately connected to, if not caused by, the corresponding rise of American power.

* * * *

Collaboration with King Farouk and the definition of Britain's post-war requirements in the Middle East, Mar 1945–Dec 1946

When the post-war British position in the region was first discussed by ministers, it was in the context of the defence of the Suez Canal and the role of the proposed international organisation in maintaining peace and security in the region. The deputy prime minister, Clement Attlee, was concerned about the post-war costs of preserving exclusive British responsibility for defending the Suez Canal and the rest of the Middle East and eastern Mediterranean. He was therefore in favour of changing the status quo and making new international arrangements for the security of the Middle East (1). Others, however, saw the maintenance of Britain's exclusive responsibility for the defence of the region as vital because the defence of the Middle East was 'a matter of life and death to the British Empire' (3). The issue was never resolved by the War Cabinet and continued to be a source of debate within the Labour government. By the summer of 1945 Britain's position in the eastern Mediterranean and Middle East was central to the post-war settlement discussions. The future of the Italian colonies, and in particular the arrangements for what was to become Libya, were one source of Anglo–Soviet conflict.[4] The other concerned the future regime in the Straits of the Dardanelles which in 1945 were governed by the Montreux Convention of 1936. The British were prepared to revise the convention to remove the restrictions imposed on the passage of Soviet ships but Stalin saw the Soviet position in the Straits as being directly comparable to the British position in the Suez Canal Zone.

At the Potsdam conference therefore the Russians demanded that they should be given bases in the Straits as Britain had a base in the Suez Canal Zone. Churchill told the Russians that the continuance of international arrangements for the Straits would be preferable and would meet the Soviet Union's needs. This met with queries about Britain's position in Egypt which Eden argued was justified by a bilateral international treaty. Stalin agreed, but pointed out that the British had acknowledged that international arrangements were better. The Turks were opposed to the presence of Soviet forces in the Straits, a fact which the British were keen to emphasise. With the Egyptian demands for evacuation which had appeared after the end of the war in Europe, this distinction between the rival imperialisms no longer applied. On 23 July a message from the Wafd to Lord Killearn, the British ambassador, called for negotiations on Egypt's national demands, and at Potsdam the British were embarrassed by their policies on the control of the Suez Canal and the Straits.[5]

King Farouk was not keen to support Nahas, the leader of the Wafd, but in September an all party group issued a statement calling for a new treaty with Britain to be negotiated on the basis of the evacuation of British forces and the unity of the Nile valley. This demand was particularly embarrassing for the British as with growing calls for evacuation it would be more difficult to argue that the British presence in the Canal Zone, unlike a Soviet presence in the Straits, was justified on the basis of consent.

Mediterranean issues reappeared at the first Council of Foreign Ministers in September 1945 which met under the terms of the Potsdam agreement to draw up peace treaties with Germany's allies. The British could not accept that the Soviets should have bases in the Straits for fear of serious political consequences resulting from an increase in Soviet influence in the eastern Mediterranean.[6] Nor, in the autumn 1945, could they accept an exclusive Soviet sphere of influence in most of eastern Europe in return for Soviet recognition of an exclusive British sphere of influence in the Middle East and eastern Mediterranean. Sir Orme Sargent, a deputy under-secretary of state at the Foreign Office, argued that exclusion from large areas of Europe would be incompatible with Britain's standing as a great world power.[7] The retention of an exclusive sphere of influence in the Middle East in the face of Soviet protests was then justified by the new foreign secretary, Ernest Bevin, on the grounds that post-war Soviet territorial gains made a Soviet sphere of influence unnecessary.[8]

The importance of Britain's position in Egypt in relation to the post-war settlement meant that it was vital to avoid any conflict with the Egyptian government. This was to influence the nature and timing of the talks on treaty revision and the future of the base. On the one hand, because of the alleged importance of Egypt for Middle East defence, the British military sought first to postpone the renegotiation of their presence in order that regional defence needs could be assessed. On the other hand, the Foreign Office was worried that postponing the talks would provide an opportunity for the involvement of the soon to be established UN organisation and the consequent loss of Britain's special position in Egypt.

By the autumn, and in the wake of demonstrations in Egypt, the need for talks was accepted within the broader framework, as yet ill-defined, of Middle Eastern defence. It seemed to officials in London and Cairo that the Egyptian political situation made loyal collaborators in any negotiations hard to find. In the spring of 1945 the lack of a stable, representative government had already produced a conflict between Lord Killearn and the Foreign Office, with the latter keen to work with the prime minister, Mahmud Nokrashi, and especially with King Farouk, both of whom were despised by Killearn (4, 6, 9, 10). Once the need to renegotiate the 1936 treaty was accepted this problem assumed new dimensions.

The resident minister in the Middle East from 1944–1945, Sir E Grigg, later Lord Altrincham, gave the War Cabinet and the new Labour government assessments of the situation in Egypt and the Middle East which combined an element of die hard imperialism with the new spirit of co-operation in which Britain could bring greater economic benefits to the Arab people. His memoranda emphasised the importance of dealing with the Middle East as a region rather than as a number of individual states, particularly in relation to defence issues. Altrincham never doubted that Britain's informal empire in the Middle East could and should be maintained. He defined it in terms of spheres of influence and believed that without it the British way of life could not survive. At the same time he accepted that Britain would have to change the nature of its influence and reduce the scale of its peacetime military presence, especially when close to major population centres (11, 15).

Such ideas were central to the Middle Eastern thinking of Ernest Bevin, whose interest in the empire had developed during his pre-war trade union days. Both Bevin and Altrincham attached more importance to the power and prestige associated with Britain's position in the Middle East than they did to the military and economic realities which threatened its continuation. Although Bevin produced a Cabinet paper arguing that British influence in the Middle East rested on too narrow an economic and social base,[9] lack of resources and the political importance of a military presence meant that the foreign secretary soon adapted policy to the short term needs of British influence and prestige. Attlee, on the other hand, was keen to accept the military and economic realities as determinants of British policy and military strategy in the region whatever the political consequences for British prestige and influence.

As the prime minister began to question the need for the same kind of Middle Eastern deployments in the changed post-war circumstances,[10] the military began to float ideas of a Middle Eastern grouping of states for defence purposes (17) and to emphasise the strategic importance of the region (23). There were, however, a number of problems with regional arrangements in 1945. It was important to avoid further offending the French in the Middle East by plans that appeared to embody exclusive British influence over the region (21). And there was the possibility that regional arrangements would offer the Soviet Union, through the UN, a foothold in what many in London perceived as an exclusive British sphere of influence.

On 20 December the Egyptian government formally requested talks on the revision of the 1936 treaty to secure the evacuation of British forces from the Canal Zone. The delay in getting the negotiations under way was now due to British concerns about the value of any agreement when the political situation in Egypt was deemed so unstable and the ambassador so hostile to the Egyptian prime minister. In the meantime, Egyptian resentment at the continued British presence grew, and on the anniversary of the surrounding of the palace in February 1942, serious disturbances took place in Cairo which contributed to the removal of both Killearn and Nokrashi in the middle of February.

In these circumstances it was unlikely that the British would be able to persuade the Egyptians to accept the continued peacetime presence of British troops. Many in Britain, both in 1946 and subsequently, were slow to grasp the strength of Egyptian feeling on this matter, and in the Foreign Office the head of the Egyptian Department argued that the requirements of the Commanders-in-Chief, Middle East for a peacetime garrison should be insisted on (27).

The Commanders-in-Chief were reluctant to place a figure on British peacetime requirements as there were no plans as to how, and with what forces, the Middle East could be defended. By the time their eventual recommendations for 5,000 combat troops and 300 aircraft were before the COS, they had accepted the view of the embassy in Cairo that complete evacuation would be needed to get an agreement, provided satisfactory regional defence arrangements were in place (32). The issue of Britain's requirements in Egypt was not determined by what specifically would be needed to defend the Middle East; instead it became entangled in the debate between Attlee and Bevin over the general strategic importance of the region in relation to global strategy and the defence of the Commonwealth.

The views of the COS on this were defined by April 1946 on the basis of how they believed the Second World War had been won. This involved the retention of what were termed the main support areas of Britain, the American continent, Africa south of the Sahara, and Australia and New Zealand; these contained sufficient manpower and resources ultimately to achieve victory. It was then a matter of defining in the context of the Second World War what areas were needed to defend the main support areas and the sea communications between them. Given the previous loss of western Europe to the enemy, the Middle East emerged as the key area and as an area from which it would be possible to launch air attacks on the Soviet Union (33). These ideas complemented the arguments of the foreign secretary that the maintenance of

Britain's position in the Mediterranean was vital to its continuance as a great power (35) and that a base in Egypt was essential for such a position.[11]

In 1946 the Defence Committee discussions were not centered on the position in Egypt but on the more general issue of withdrawing from the Middle East as a whole (35). Redeployment in peacetime and retention of the base for use in war meant that evacuation from Egypt could be contemplated by Bevin. The view of the embassy was that evacuation was necessary, and on 11 April the Cabinet agreed to offer the withrawal of British combat troops at the outset of negotiations (37). To the dismay of the ambassdor and of Lord Stansgate, who arrived in Egypt on 15 April to lead the formal negotiating team, the COS initially insisted that combat troops should not include the RAF squadrons and they secured the approval of the Defence Committee for such a line.[12]

The COS remained reluctant to accept complete evacuation of all forces until Major-General Jacob, military assistant to the Cabinet and a member of the British delegation, returned to explain the advantages and disadvantages. The prospect of disorders to accompany those in Palestine, and the delegation's belief that the offer of evacuation would secure Egyptian co-operation and the required peacetime facilities, clearly had an effect (43, 44). Thus the Cabinet approved the Defence Committee's recommendation to offer total evacuation and a phased withdrawal over five years.[13] The subsequent negotiations between 9 and 22 May proved at best a disappointment for the British given that Sidky, the new prime minister, was seen as an improvement on Nokrashi. The Egyptians refused to accept such a lengthy British withdrawal period and argued that the required wartime facilities should not be formally incorporated into the treaty but subject to more informal arrangements of the kind made between friendly and independent sovereign states; this was not acceptable to the Foreign Office[14] or to the military (49). Other bones of contention were the Egyptian reluctance to grant facilities on a threat of war and the areas in which an outbreak of war would automatically produce the reactivation of the base.

The COS were disturbed to learn that the concession on evacuation had not immediately smoothed the way to Britain obtaining what they regarded as its military rights to defend the empire. This key question of what was required in the Middle East to defend the Commonwealth/empire continued to preoccupy policy makers as the negotiations with the Egyptians ran into difficulties in May 1946. The COS produced a paper on strategic requirements in the region which was discussed by the Defence Committee on 27 May. The paper was not detailed enough to satisfy Attlee. Evacuation of the Suez base in peacetime had been agreed but Britain's position in Cyrenaica was uncertain and the possibility of building up a position in East Africa had still to be assessed. It proved impossible for the Defence Committee to endorse the COS's report and Attlee commented that the whole position in the Middle East required re-examination. The prime minister wanted to know what exactly Britain had to defend and what would be Britain's war and peacetime requirements to enable the defence of such areas to be implemented (49).

Attlee was trying hard to inject an element of realism into military thinking about the Middle East, but although the COS produced a revised report the issues were never addressed in precisely the way Attlee required. Rather than define what needed to be defended and what was required to do this, the COS still preferred to concentrate on why the Middle East was so important for British defence strategy. Central to their arguments was the idea that the Middle East was needed to launch air strikes on the Soviet Union. Yet Britain's only long range bomber, the Lincoln, a modified Lancaster, could not fly above 19,000 feet and was capable of hitting only a very small part of the southern Soviet Union. Moreover, with the decision to evacuate Egypt, the need to have strategic bombers immediately available at the start of hostilities meant they would have to be stationed in Cyrenaica, assuming that Britain succeeded in acquiring base rights there. A further problem was that despite the emphasis given to the protection of Middle Eastern oil, Britain's forces were insufficient to do this. As the COS acknowledged, American forces would be required if this goal was to be achieved. In view of subsequent developments, it is also important to note that in 1946 the COS regarded Palestine and Egypt as interconnected and that if Middle East HQ was removed from Egypt it should be located in Palestine (56).

In the wake of the failure to secure agreement on the reactivation of the base and its management in peacetime, Bevin proposed to accept the consultation arrangements desired by the Egyptians through the establishment of a joint defence board (52). Despite COS opposition on the grounds of the security of the Commonwealth (54), the Cabinet decided to pursue the negotiations on the lines of Bevin's proposals. As Attlee stated, there was no more justification for arguing that Britain had to have base facilities in Egypt because they were necessary for the empire's security than for demanding bases from Britain's continental allies (55).

When Stansgate returned to Egypt in July it soon became evident that Britain's agreement to exclude from the treaty the provision of base facilities and the administrative arrangements for them had not solved the problem. The issue of sovereignty over the Sudan had now to be addressed along with the differences over the conditions for reactivation and the timing of the evacuation. The Commanders-in-Chief and the delegation saw no objection to the Egyptian proposals on the latter issues. However, in London there was a determination to ensure the base's availablity if Turkey, Greece or Persia were attacked;[15] by contrast the Egyptians did not want to be involved in a war which did not directly threaten them or other members of the Arab League. This lay behind the dispute over article 2 of the proposed treaty which Stansgate felt was unnecessary (59). Stansgate believed Britain should accept the Egyptian draft of article 2, agree to withdraw all naval forces by 31 March 1947 and to evacuate completely within three years.[16] In the Foreign Office, R G Howe was not inclined to accept the Egyptian article 2, but it was not yet clear whether that, the Sudan or the evacuation period was of greatest significance for the Egyptians (62).

With the disagreement between the Foreign Office and the civilian and military representatives in Egypt, and with Bevin absent in Paris, the matter was discussed by the COS. In contrast to their earlier stance they came out on the side of Stansgate to the extent that they believed an agreement with Egypt was essential. But while Stansgate wanted to end the negotiations because delay would increase suspicions of British reluctance to withdraw, the COS saw no objection to continuing the negotiations despite the opportunity this would give to opposition politicians in Egypt (64, 65).

In the light of these disagreements the prime minister put the issue to the Cabinet which agreed that the negotiators should demand an evacuation period of three years, accept the Egyptian draft of article 2 if necessary, and avoid including in the Sudan protocol anything implying recognition of Egyptian sovereignty (67). Bevin, who was not present at the Cabinet meeting on 1 August, refused to accept his colleagues' decision and wrote to Attlee requesting that the Egyptian version of article 2 be rejected. He argued that it would be necessary in the future to use Egyptian territory if British interests in Iraq or Iran were threatened and that it would be a mistake to surrender the position in Egypt before the forthcoming Arab–Jewish conference on Palestine (69). Instead Bevin proposed yet another draft of article 2 with an additional paragraph that could be used by Stansgate in further negotiations. The issue of whether there should be consultation before reactivation and the areas of conflict which would justify reactivation produced a series of irate telegrams between Bevin and Stansgate in July and August 1946. Stansgate became more convinced that such issues were not sufficiently important to jeopardise the chances of an agreement which he maintained would become more difficult to achieve with the passage of time; if Britain was going to stand firm Stansgate believed it should do so on the Sudan issue, not on article 2 (69–73, 75–77). Bevin, however, believed article 2 was a matter of principle and that the Egyptians, like Arab traders, were setting a high initial price in the expectation of some hard bargaining.

The Egyptians claimed that the British would not be content with the kind of treaty normally concluded between independent states but wanted exceptional clauses 'due to a state of mind which has prevailed for many years' (78). By 21 August the talks were deadlocked and their extension was secured only by the intervention of King Farouk who accepted the three-year evacuation period and made further minor modifications to the draft of the contentious article 2.[17] Farouk also wanted some reference to the unity of the Nile valley under the Egyptian crown which Bevin explicitly ruled out.[18] This, according to Stansgate, was now probably the vital issue. But the British could not fully accept the modifications to article 2, and in early September the Egyptian delegation was still producing redrafts of the latest British draft.[19] Bevin finally decided that to continue in this manner would be undignified.[20] Stansgate was told there was no possibility of a compromise on article 2 and a draft treaty was presented on 17 September as the final British offer.[21] Although the Egyptians rejected it, Sidky was still interested in obtaining a treaty and it was agreed that he should meet Bevin in London in October for talks.

By October Bevin's determination to obtain a satisfactory article 2 was such that he was prepared to abandon his previous insistence on avoiding any reference to Egyptian sovereignty over the Sudan on the assumption that if such a concession were made the Egyptians would accept the British positions on article 2 and the evacuation timing.[22] In the event he was proved wrong to the extent that while the concession on the Sudan might have influenced Egyptian acceptance of the three-year evacuation period, it did not win acceptance of any of the previous British drafts of article 2, despite five meetings with Sidky (85). When agreement was finally secured esentially on the lines of the Egyptian proposals, the Cabinet became aware of the extent of the opposition in the Sudan to the proposed protocol referring to the unity between the Sudan and Egypt under the common crown of Egypt (86). To make matters worse the British discovered from an intelligence source within the Egyptian government that Sidky was claiming that the Sudan agreement ruled out any Sudanese secession from Egyptian sovereignty.[23] As this differed from the British understanding of the London agreement with Sidky, it was imperative to confirm the understandings of the Sudan protocol in writing. Yet before this could be implemented the British learnt that some members of the Egyptian delegation would not accept the text of the treaty or the Sudan protocol (87). Everything now depended on the Egyptian parliament, but success there would be unlikely while the British were insisting on written confirmation of their interpretation of the protocol (88).

The problem of standing on the treaty and the formation of a plan to defend the Middle East, Jan 1947–Oct 1948
On 9 December Sidky fell from power, ostensibly because of his refusal to accept the wording of the British draft letter on the Sudan protocol, and in January 1947 the talks formally ended. King Farouk replaced Sidky with Nokrashi and this immediately opened the question of Britain interfering to produce a government prepared to sign a treaty. As Nokrashi announced his intention to refer the matter to the UN, it was clear that the policy of relying on Farouk had not worked (91). Sir Orme Sargent was one of the advocates within the Foreign Office of abandoning co-operation with Farouk and minority governments in favour of working with the Wafd. The Foreign Office was keener on the idea of co-operation with the Wafd than the embassy and argued that the Wafd would be better placed to win support for any treaty revision. Sargent was also in favour of reverting to a policy of intervention in Egyptian politics to restore the Wafd but Bevin decided to postpone any attempt to remove the existing regime until after the Egyptians had taken their protests about the continued British presence to the UN (101).

Sargent, like the ambassador and the oriental secretary in Cairo, believed that in Egypt and in the post-war world in general there was a feeling that Britain was displaying weakness; this required tough policies designed to show that Britain meant business and to win the respect of Russians, Egyptians and anyone else who believed the British empire could be taken advantage of (96, 97). One way of being tough was to enforce Britain's rights under the 1936 treaty, although Britain was contravening it in a number of ways. The problem was that antagonising the Egyptians was seen as a risky business by the military and the difficulty would increase as Britain reduced its forces in the Canal Zone to the 10,000 troops permitted by the treaty (99). When the Cabinet discussed the question of enforcing treaty rights no conclusions were reached, which effectively left the decisions in the hands of the men on the spot.[24]

The Egyptian intention to go to the UN gave the British yet more problems as there would be international pressure to reduce the 90,000 troops in Egypt at the start of 1947 to the 1936 treaty limit. It was in these circumstances, prior to the Egyptian appeal to the Security Council, that in August 1947 the JPS produced a paper outlining Britain's peacetime requirements in Egypt (103). These requirements were still not linked to any specific strategy and force requirements for defending the region, although (as stated earlier) it was not expected that most of the oilfields could be secured. The military were able to argue that until the future size of the armed forces had been settled it would be impossible to allocate forces to the Middle East (105); they also argued that no regional defence plan could be formulated because of the uncertainty over their position in Egypt and Palestine.[25] However they never suggested that if the forces for defending the Middle East proved to be inadequate then Britain should abandon its position there as Attlee had suggested in 1945 and 1946.

What was becoming clear in 1947, as redeployment (albeit without a defence plan) became more necessary, was that the military were retreating from their 1946 decision to evacuate Egypt. The planners believed that the key to the defence of the Middle East lay in an ability rapidly to establish British forces in Egypt and to operate effectively from the base on the threat of war; this in turn required a nucleus base in peacetime (103).

The desire to remain in Egypt in peacetime was strengthened in September 1947 by the decision to abandon Palestine by May 1948. Palestine had previously been considered essential for the British position in the Middle East but it was now Cyrenaica that assumed this mantle in the eyes of the military (105). The decision to evacuate Palestine meant that the military no longer accepted September 1949 as an evacuation date from Egypt because the movement of stores from Palestine could not be completed before mid-1950. The loss of Palestine and the uncertainty over Cyrenaica only increased the importance of Egypt.

Another reason for the growing importance of Egypt was American interest in the region. In 1947 the British decision to surrender the main responsibility for assistance to Turkey and Greece made the American role in the eastern Mediterranean more important; but it also made it essential for Britain to emphasise its commitment to the rest of the Middle East. More precisely, with the Americans interested in having a base in Egypt available at the outbreak of war, Bevin saw a possibility of receiving US aid for the region if the importance of Britain's role could be demonstrated.[26] At the same time, Bevin was 'opposed to the adoption of a combined Anglo–American policy for the Middle East as this area was primarily of economic and strategic interest to the United Kingdom' (108). The US would be there simply to provide the economic and military resources Britain lacked. This was the rationale behind the Pentagon talks on the Middle East in the autumn of 1947 which covered political and economic aspects as well as military ones and were geared to agreement on general principles; they were not geared to detailed strategic planning for the defence of the Middle East.[27]

American interest in securing facilities in Egypt also made an agreement with Egypt more desirable, especially as one senior State Department official informed the British they would receive only grudging support if they decided to stand on the 1936 treaty.[28] There appeared to be little chance of an agreement, even though Farouk seemed keen to reopen talks, as the military were no longer thinking in terms of the complete evacuation offered in 1946. In an attempt to overcome this problem and to avoid having to renegotiate the 1936 treaty, Bevin proposed a reduction of the British peacetime presence to about one thousand men, leaving the other treaty provisions in force until a regional defence arrangement could supersede the 1936 treaty (109).

By early 1948 the cold war was fully developed and a hot war by accident was more likely. The increased global tension coincided with new Britsh initiatives to create a Third Force in which the Middle East was seen to figure prominently. Inherent in these developments was the conflict between plans to rebuild British power and influence and the need to reduce commitments because of economic weakness. More than anything else, military strategy was affected by such tensions. The Foreign Office was primarily concerned with the political requirements of a global strategy designed until 1949 to regain a position of equality with, and independence from, the Americans and the Russians. Central to this strategy was closer co-operation with western Europe, the political requirements of which began to challenge the primacy given to the Middle East in military strategy. With Montgomery, chief of the imperial general staff, arguing forcefully for a British commitment to fight on the continent, the prime minister was disturbed as his understanding of the agreed 1947 strategy was that it was intended to develop a counter-offensive from the Middle East; western Europe would not be much encouraged by one or two British divisions.[29] The answer provided was that the defence of western Europe was necessary for the defence of the United Kingdom and indirectly to the maintenance of Britain's position in the Middle East.[30] This meant in effect that more resources would eventually have to be provided if Britain was to take on such an important additional commitment.

While moves were made to limit Britain's commitments in the Middle East with the retreat from Palestine and a reduced Egyptian presence, the regional position was not seen as fundamentally threatened because of plans to secure facilities in Cyrenaica, provided a satisfactory decision was reached on the future of the Italian colonies. What was at issue was the evacuation of around 90,000 troops from Egypt in a way which would minimise the cost, secure British rights regarding the use of the base and avoid any damage to Britain's general position. Ideally, as Bevin pointed out, it would have been desirable to have facilities in Egypt and Cyrenaica even though it was still unclear as to precisely what was needed (110). Because there was no specific strategy for defending the Middle East, this could not be used to determine Egyptian requirements which remained primarily linked to general foreign policy goals based on the preservation of Britain's Middle Eastern position.

In early 1948 the Foreign Office decided to sound out the COS on a new approach to the Egyptians.[31] Bevin saw advantages in an agreement which would preserve flexibility in the face of increasing international tensions and the continuing uncertainty over Cyrenaica while gaining American support. More importantly the Commanders-in-Chief, Middle East were of the view that Egyptian co-operation was essential for the effective use of the base;[32] this made standing on the treaty less attractive than a new agreement. Nevertheless the COS wished to reserve their position on a fresh approach because of the impending conclusion of the Iraqi treaty and what they regarded as a general improvement in the atmosphere in the Middle East.[33]

In January Bevin discussed several ways of breaking the deadlock with officials in the Foreign Office and with the ambassador in Cairo; they included leasing the areas in which Britain would retain facilities and the provision of weapons and training to make the Egyptians feel they were being treated as equals (110, 111). Bevin was now also prepared to offer the Egyptian government a date for evacuation in order to meet its condition for any progress on talks. The political requirements of the Egyptians would thereby be met and military experts could discuss Britain's peacetime needs in the Canal Zone.

As earlier, Bevin was convinced that Farouk was likely to be favourably inclined towards accepting British requirements in Egypt (111); this view was reinforced when contacts with the Egyptian government achieved nothing because of disagreements over the Sudan ordinance.[34] Bevin was not prepared to make concessions, believing that the Egyptian government was one of several that 'appeared to think Britain was down and out and could be harassed with impunity' (115). In March it was decided to approach Farouk who had been keen to involve the British in a regional defence arrangement for the Middle East. Such an arrangement could not, in the eyes of the Foreign Office, be a substitute for bilateral agreements which would enable the British to obtain rights and facilities in Egypt (113). However, Bevin was keen on the idea in principle and he proposed a Middle Eastern

Union. Constructed along the lines of Western Union (115), this would form part of the Third Force based on the organisation of the middle of the planet under British auspices. The Middle Eastern Union idea formed part of the proposals which were to be put to Farouk along with the offer of evacuation down to a total of one thousand troops and inter-service talks on the broader question of maintaining the base. There would be no British acceptance of the principle of unconditional evacuation but evacuation would be acceptable as part of an arrangement granting Britain rights to use facilities in Egypt; these suggestions would only be made to Farouk after the ambassador, Sir Ronald Campbell, had made a final attempt to secure acceptance of the Sudan ordinance and to unseat Nokrashi (116, 118). In the short term progress on these proposals was to be undermined by the Sudan issue and the failure to secure Nokrashi's dismissal. In the long term progress was to be hampered by developments in strategic planning that took place in 1948.

Having long asserted that the defence of the Middle East was essential to the defence of the British Commonwealth, the military were also insisting that the use of a base in Egypt before or on the outbreak of war was now essential to the defence of the Middle East (114).[35] Such ideas were reinforced by the study of Middle Eastern defence strategy, codenamed 'Intermezzo', which was based on estimates of British and Soviet force levels in 1957–1958. Its main conclusions were that it would only be possible to prevent a Soviet advance to the Mediterranean and the Persian Gulf by an all out policy of air interdiction on enemy lines of communication; that would require airfields in Egypt and other Mediterranean states and a main base in Egypt on the outbreak of war to provide support facilities for the air forces (120).

The JPS argued that it was no longer possible, because of 'Intermezzo' and the indications from the studies at last being undertaken on an emergency plan for Middle Eastern defence, to rely on measures previously proposed for the maintenance and development of the Egyptian base.[36] The Foreign Office pointed out that if a new treaty was required it would be necessary to reduce the troop numbers in peacetime to below the 10,000 permitted by the 1936 treaty;[37] this was significant because the COS had been arguing that the base could only function with Egyptian co-operation which was unlikely to be secured without a new treaty.

The matter was discussed by Bevin and the minister of defence, A V Alexander, and the consensus was to reduce numbers to the treaty level. This did not prove acceptable to the military who were insisting on the presence of 20,000 troops in peacetime.[38] Further discussions proved inconclusive but the matter was not sent to Cabinet, nor, as far as can be judged, to the Defence Committee; this was almost certainly because Attlee and Cripps were unlikely to support a continued military presence on the scale suggested. While no decisions were taken the continued large scale military presence in Egypt (47,000 troops in October 1948) would serve the needs of the COS.

The emphasis on the defence of the Middle East was continuing to conflict with the requirements of the Brussels Treaty and Western Union. In a brief for the Foreign Office for the Consultative Committee of the Brussels Pact, the military affirmed that Britain's allies should not be told about the extent of the development of the Middle East as a strategic bomber base, nor of the size of the forces Britain intended to deploy there.[39] Yet in the Middle East, plan 'Sandown', the first emergency plan, exposed the limitations of any defence effort even if the COS's requirements in Egypt were met. 'Sandown' was based on the assumptions of plan 'Doublequick' which acknowledged that Britain would be unable to launch an effective strategic air offensive on the Soviet Union and assumed that the Russians would be able to threaten Palestine and Syria with eleven divisions at D+3½ months. Thus 'Doublequick' referred to the need for the demolition of oil installations in Iraq and Persia. The US, it was assumed, would provide support at three and six months and the aim was to hold northern Palestine and southern Syria while forces were built up in Egypt.[40] The Commanders-in-Chief, Middle East who drew up plan 'Sandown' regarded this as somewhat optimistic and noted that because of the need to meet the threat to Egypt, 'The object of the land operations will therefore be to impose the maximum delay on the enemy as far from the Egypt base as administrative resources will allow. The operations will consist of a series of delaying and harassing actions by mobile forces. . . . A prepared defensive position will be constructed on the general line Jericho-Ramallah-North of Tel Aviv' (125). The British had to have peacetime base facilities in Egypt in order to defend the base in Egypt.

New requirements in Egypt and problems in Middle East defence, Nov 1948–Sept 1949

In Cairo it was believed that the 20,000 troops desired by the COS[41] would never be accepted by the Egyptians[42] and it became clear in October that Nokrashi was insisting on the evacuation of British forces before negotiations could even begin. The pro-British Egyptian ambassador in London, Amr, then pressured Farouk to begin talks on the military level (126). The British became increasingly interested in engineering the removal of Nokrashi and using Farouk to ensure that Britain's requirements in Egypt would be met through these military talks. This strategy was seen by the head of the African Department as somewhat risky (127), even though Farouk and Nokrashi had agreed to discussions between Egyptian military experts and the British Commanders-in-Chief at Fayid.[43] However, when progress on the programme of talks was delayed it became increasingly likely that Nokrashi's removal would take place (129). In the event this proved unnecessary as Nokrashi was assassinated by the Muslim Brotherhood.

At the end of 1948 Egypt was in turmoil with the issue of the Sudan ordinance still arousing political tensions that were exacerbated by Arab reversals in the war in Palestine. Nokrashi's assassination and the rise of the Muslim Brotherhood were indications of growing instability. In addition the defeat of the Egyptian army made military rule in alliance with the palace, a solution often favoured by British officials, less feasible (134). Equally, the lack of an Arab–Israeli settlement meant that no significant arms could be supplied to Egypt.

The strong sentiment that a British military presence represented western imperialism and a denial of Egyptian independence was the crux of the British problem in Egypt. It inhibited pro-British, anti-communist Egyptians from endorsing any agreement giving Britain a peacetime military presence in Egypt. Moreover, military strategy made it difficult to justify a presence in terms of Middle Eastern defence given that the British fall back line only defended Egypt and southern Israel. The British would have to hope that an American and Commonwealth contribution or a future increase in military strength would make defending the Middle East a practical proposition.

In the meantime, the Tel Aviv–Ramallah defence line made the base vulnerable to air attack because of its proximity to the Canal Zone and the lack of usable airfields in

Egypt.[44] The first long-term plan for the defence of the Middle East by 1957 expressly ruled it out. Thus, while the specific requirements of Middle East emergency defence plans in 1948 were now influencing what the military required in Egypt, the plans themselves were of dubious practicality and defended only a tiny part of the Middle East. There were also problems justifying the need to defend the Middle East in terms of emergency global war planning in the formulation of plan 'Speedway', the successor to 'Doublequick'. The Western Union powers were increasing their efforts to get Britain to come clean over what forces would be available to defend western Europe; this put pressure on the British to concentrate their resources on the continent. One argument in favour of the Middle East was based on the need to use airfields there for the strategic bombing offensive. Yet by the end of 1948 the COS were stating that the Anglo–American strategic bombing force was not big enough to carry out a strategic attack on Russia and make a significant contribution to the defence of western Europe. Moreover: '... the British bomber force[45] will have too short a range to deliver an effective offensive into Russia. Its primary task will be to assist in the defence of the Middle East and the UK, but it is at present quite inadequate in size to be really effective in preventing the enemy build up in western Europe and at the same time slowing the Russian advance into the Middle East' (128).

There were other weaknesses in plan 'Speedway'. It would not be possible to hold western Europe, and 'the reasonable chance of at least defending Egypt' depended on US reinforcements. It was now expected that one US fighter group would be available soon after D Day and two by D+1 month (more rapid deployment than under 'Doublequick'). Three US divisions, 350 US aircraft and 150 Commonwealth aircraft were expected by D+6 months but these would be available only if the Mediterranean was kept open. The US strategic offensive would require the use of airfields in Britain, Egypt, Aden and Okinawa (128). There were five airfields in Egypt but none of the runways were large enough to take US strategic bombers. In October 1948 the Egyptians had refused to supply the materials for the extension of the runway at Abu Sueir. When they finally agreed to do so in February 1949 the British and the Americans began arguing over who should pay.[46] It took until May 1949 for the Defence Committee to authorise work to begin on Abu Sueir in order that it could take B 29s. In the early summer of 1949 none of this prevented the British military restating the importance of the Middle East in terms of the global strategy defined in 1946 and 1947 (141).

The dependence on an American military contribution did not mean Britain wanted the US involved in any political arrangements associated with plans for Middle Eastern defence. There were concerns about maintaining Britain's dominant position in the region and Bevin was keen to ensure that the Americans were not formally invited to visit Egypt. Bevin was also fearful of the impact of Anglo–American co-operation in the Middle East on the Soviets. In 1949 the foreign secretary remained convinced that Stalin was honouring his December 1945 promise to give Britain a free hand in Egypt and would continue to do so as long as the Americans were not brought into the arrangements for defending the Middle East.[47]

The essential need was to persuade the Americans to provide effective support for the British strategic concept of global war. The planning discussions on this in 1948 had produced an American commitment to the defence of the Middle East once war broke out. Unfortunately this success was negated in 1949 when the Americans produced a new strategic concept for global war (144). Unlike the US navy, which was keen to protect Middle East oil, the US army had never been keen on participating in a Middle East conflict. The journey through the Mediterranean was seen as too hazardous, and with substantial progress in late 1948 towards the creation of NATO, the army could better argue for more commitment to European defence. Unlike the British, the Americans decided in 1949 to choose between European and Middle Eastern defence and to opt for maintaining a bridgehead in southern Spain; this meant abandoning their commitment under plan 'Fleetwood' (the US equivalent of 'Speedway') to send forces to the Middle East in the early stages of a global war. Consequently in the immediate aftermath of this decision the British joint planners concluded that Britain would be unable to attain the three objectives of its defence policy.[48] When the US planners met their British and Canadian counterparts in the autumn of 1949, it was confirmed that no US strategic bombers were to be based in the Middle East (Abu Sueir was now seen only as serving as a staging post for bombers based in Britain, Okinawa and the US) and that there were no suitable targets in the region for the Strategic Air Command. Britain needed the US air force to be employed tactically in the Middle East and the US navy to be used to help keep the Mediterranean open. Without the dropping of atomic bombs by the US SAC in a tactical role, Britain could not defend the Middle East[49] and the Cabinet were informed of that assessment.[50]

Nevertheless British policy makers still claimed they had to retain troops in Egypt in order to defend the Middle East. The talks which began in June 1949 with junior Egyptian officers were designed by the British to gain Egyptian acceptance of their assessment of the threat to the region; this would be followed by discussions on what was needed to deal with the situation. The Egyptians would thus be brought to an examination of what British facilities and Anglo–Egyptian forces were necessary rather than to a discussion of evacuation. Unfortunately the talks made little progress and as a result attention was focused on the supply of military equipment to ensure Egyptian goodwill.

There were differing views as to the wisdom of providing equipment simply to get the required base facilities (147). Moreover the Foreign Office was not entirely convinced of the value of moving towards a settlement with Farouk and a palace government whose position had been weakened by the failures in the war against Israel. In these circumstances doubts about the wisdom of co-operation with Farouk arose and support for the Wafd grew as they were seen as most likely to settle the base question.

During the break in talks in July a change occurred in the Egyptian government which was in line with what the head of the African Department desired (140). Abdel Hadi was replaced by a 'national' government under Hussein Sirry which included the Wafd. However Sirry's assertion that any political settlement would have to be based on evacuation (146) strengthened the belief that it would be best to await the outcome of the elections in Egypt before moving on from the military talks. Yet there were those in the Foreign Office who still advocated an arrangement with King Farouk (148).

The approaching crisis: no Egyptian collaborators, no defence agreement and little prospect of defending the Middle East, Oct 1949–Oct 1951
In January 1950 the long promised elections took place and resulted, to the surprise of the palace, in an overwhelming victory for the Wafd which won 228 out of 319

seats with the next largest group, the Independents, holding a mere 30 seats. The elections also ended the military talks that had been stuttering along under Farouk's auspices. Initially hopes were high in the Foreign Office and in the embassy in Cairo of a new era in Egyptian politics and Anglo–Egyptian relations. All such hopes were eventually to be dashed.

The immediate problem was to reconcile the Egyptian determination to secure evacuation with the Defence Committee's assumption that a peacetime military presence would be retained for the next twenty or thirty years.[51] The departing head of the African Department, G L Clutton, was convinced that the problem of the base was, for the Egyptians, an emotive one in contrast to the practical problems dictating the British approach. He did not believe that compromise was possible unless both sides were prepared to see the problem in practical terms (157). Britain needed an agreement with Egypt to ensure the base's smooth working. But an agreement seemed impossible without evacuation; equally, evacuation would prevent forces being deployed in the early stages of a war which was deemed necessary if there was to be any possibility of defending Egypt.

Moreover, as the Commanders-in-Chief, Middle East pointed out, the defence of a base in Egypt required, not only full Egyptian and Israeli co-operation but also air defence facilities which were not available. Therefore, within the context of existing strategy and resources for the defence of the Middle East, even a base agreement with Egypt would not prevent Russia succeeding 'at one stroke in gaining the majority of her immediate objectives in the Middle East' (159).

When this assessment was received from the Commanders-in-Chief, the military in London were investigating the broader issues of global strategy and the growing conflict between the demands of European and Middle East defence. In June 1950 a review was presented to the Defence Committee which modified the strategy outlined in 1947 in the light of NATO's creation and the Soviet atomic explosion without altering its fundamental assumptions (165). It emphasised the importance of the cold war (a war fought by all means short of international armed conflict), as opposed to hot war, while drawing attention to the links between them. Despite the Soviet atomic bomb the paper argued for a more offensive cold war campaign because of the west's superiority in nuclear weapons. The three pillars of defence remained and therefore the defence of the Middle East continued to be a vital aspect of British defence planning, not least because it was a '*potential*'[52] base for strategic air and other offensive action against the USSR' (165). The defence of western Europe was now seen as an essential part of UK defence and therefore the allocation of resources to the Middle East could not be allowed fatally to undermine the defence of the first pillar. But the planners did not want to earmark existing forces for Europe rather than the Middle East. Given that the military did not believe it likely that even a bridgehead in Europe could be held, it was important not to move bombers from the Middle East to Europe as after the first few weeks the Middle East would be the only theatre where fighting was taking place.[53]

Fortunately, revised assessments were made of the nature and speed of any Soviet advance. These predicted that while the Russians could threaten the Levant with three divisions by D+3 months, the main attack, now with only five divisions, would not take place until D+5 months; this allowed the British more time to deploy to meet the threat (159). Provided Israel was co-operative it also avoided the necessity, in peacetime, of having to deploy large numbers of ground forces in Egypt in the early stages of a conflict. Thus the COS were now prepared to reduce troop numbers below the treaty limit on condition that there was agreement on the arrangements for the air defence of the base (158).[54] The problem of the Tel Aviv line remained, however, in that if the retreat was made to that position, Soviet MIG 15 fighters would be able to operate over the Egyptian base. In addition, the new Ilyushin IL28 (Bison) bomber was now available to the Russians and this could attack Egypt from bases in Iraq once the outer ring was breached.

How best to meet this new situation was examined by the Foreign Office, the COS and the Middle Eastern Commanders-in-Chief in May. It was decided to continue attempting to convince the Egyptians of the danger they faced and offer joint arrangements, particularly with regard to air defence, in order to meet the threat. The nature of any such arrangements had to take account of Egyptian perceptions of equality. Thus the military had to define the extent to which Egyptian personnel could be given the same responsibilities as their British counterparts. In the meantime it was decided to send the CIGS, Field Marshal Sir William Slim, to Egypt to talk to the Egyptians and the Commanders-in-Chief about defence needs and co-operation.

The visit of the CIGS was not seen by the Foreign Office as productive. Despite the positive response of the King, ministers in the Wafd government seemed determined to place political requirements above the so called military realities, due partly, it was believed, to the pernicious influence of the Egyptian foreign minister, Saleh el Din. The Egyptians had made proposals of their own for integrated air defence which would require study and it was therefore deemed inadvisable to make further approaches (166).

Informal talks did nevertheless begin in July 1950 between Sir Ralph Stevenson, the new ambassador, and Saleh el Din. It became increasingly obvious to the British that for the Egyptians obtaining the evacuation of the base outweighed the military issues arising from British assessments of the Soviet threat. Stevenson, however, tried to negotiate on what Slim had defined as necessary for the defence of Egypt: an integrated air defence, a military base, a mobile strike force and a GHQ (169).

In essence the ambassador was attempting to define what could be removed from Egypt in peacetime and whether it would be possible to locate a mobile strike force in Gaza (170). The Egyptians were happy to accept the principle of reactivation and of integrated air defence while the Egyptian air force was built up and trained under British auspices. In return they expected the British to evacuate in peacetime and leave the base in Egyptian hands; they would not accept the principle of joint arrangements in peacetime on a permanent basis (174).

By the end of August the talks appeared deadlocked. To overcome this a senior embassy official suggested the planting of stories alleging a Russian plot to disrupt the flow of the river Nile. He also warned of the deteriorating situation in Egypt if no agreement was reached. The expectation was that with the government unable to deal with domestic economic difficulties, protests and disturbances would take place, and, as in the past, the Egyptian government would have to divert them into anti-British channels (172).

With the British military continuing to claim that they had to have a base in Egypt if they were to defend the Middle East, the difficulties of defending the region were becoming increasingly apparent. The lack of resources and the loss of American help meant that Britain would have to rely on the promise of Commonwealth support.

Even then it was doubtful if more than the area adjacent to the Canal Zone in Egypt and southern Israel could be defended. It was deemed inadvisable to tell the Arab states anything about British military plans as 'the disclosure of the little the United Kingdom can actually do to protect the Middle East would be liable to lower rather than to raise Arab or Turkish morale' (177). In effect the commitment to informal empire had to be maintained, not because of the requirements of Middle Eastern defence, but because of the need to preserve prestige and status. Such was the British approach to the management of decline.

In the wake of 'Galloper' (the successor to 'Speedway', revised as 'Binnacle') and the revision of global strategy in June 1950 (164), a new emergency plan for Middle Eastern defence, plan 'Celery', was drawn up by the Commanders-in-Chief, Middle East. It was criticised by the vice-chief of the imperial general staff, General Brownjohn, because it failed to indicate the extent to which a successful defence depended on Israeli co-operation. Co-operation was vital because the British lines of communication from Egypt would run through the new state. The Israelis would not wish to stand on the Tel Aviv–Ramallah line as that would mean the abandonment of much of Israel. Plans therefore should be based on the defence of the Lebanon–Jordan line, which would not require significantly more troops. Support for the Lebanon–Jordan line was another stage in the process of emergency planning to defend positions that were indefensible with the resources available. Ideally the review wanted Middle East defence based on the inner ring but that would be possible only if the US made up the shortfall in British forces (177).

The review was sent to the US planners who criticised the strategy of defending the inner ring let alone the Lebanon–Jordan line. They argued that the 'Defence of the inner ring does not constitute the defence of the Middle East but the defence of Egypt'. The US and Britain were increasingly at odds over global strategy and Britain was accused of over-emphasising the importance of the Middle East, especially Egypt. The Egyptians too could never understand why Egypt was considered so much more important than Turkey by the British. The Americans also criticised the British for stressing the importance of Middle East oil but failing to plan adequately for its retention. In terms of the threat assessment, the US military believed their British counterparts were under-estimating Soviet logistic difficulties and over-estimating the forces required in a region, which, unlike the British, they did not see as absolutely essential to retain in war (182).

Nevertheless the British military continued to insist that a base in Egypt, manned in peacetime by British troops and pilots, was vital to Middle Eastern defence. An interesting and largely unresolvable question is how many in the Foreign Office and the government appreciated what the commitment to defend the Middle East actually implied when they emphasised its importance. If anything the Middle East's significance received still greater emphasis after the 1950 review and in the wake of the Chinese intervention in the Korean War; the latter could be presented as increasing the importance of remaining in Egypt and defending the Middle East because global war was more likely to break out by accident.[55] Yet if it did, because of the shortage of forces, the COS did not even plan to defend the inner ring but would attempt to hold the Lebanon–Jordan line.[56]

In September 1950 Bevin spoke with the Egyptian foreign minister on the issue of the Egyptians controlling the base in peacetime. The conversation was far from cordial. The lengthy informal discussions conducted by Stevenson in the summer had revealed the irreconcilability of the two sides' positions and produced ill-feeling at a number of levels. The British wanted an agreement and a continued peacetime presence while the Egyptians insisted that the former could be accepted only if the latter was given up. In the face of this deadlock Bevin was prepared to tell Saleh el Din that Britain would look elsewhere in the region for defence facilities and co-operation (179).

Unfortunately this was at odds with the military's insistence on peacetime base facilities in Egypt. While the joint planners were indeed examining the possibility of moving to another base, the military had always been aware of the difficulties involved and especially the cost. The base had to be ready for use immediately in war and would need a British presence in peacetime to make this possible.

Faced with this dilemma, Stevenson attempted to define the available options. Britain could accept the military disadvantages inherent in an agreement acceptable to the Egyptians, or it could leave the base and redefine its Middle East defence strategy by concentrating on strengthening Greece and Turkey; this could be combined with an attempt to defend the Iraqi and Arabian oilfields. The third possibility was to abandon the whole idea of defending the Middle East which, 'from a political point of view', was 'unthinkable'. The ambassador believed that to obtain an agreement Britain would not only have to evacuate but to evacuate within an agreed time period. However, he regarded this as the least objectionable alternative if it was combined with new facilities in the central Mediterranean and the stationing of a mobile strike force in Gaza (180). Whether this would be possible, leaving aside the financial constraints, would depend on the UN agreement on the nature of the new Libyan state.

The Commanders-in-Chief disagreed with the ambassador's conclusions as they did not accept that the Egyptians could take care of the base (180). The battle between military requirements and what was politically possible was to continue, albeit on the bizarre basis that military requirements were to a large extent requirements to do something that was not possible in the short term because of the lack of forces. This became a Cabinet issue after Egypt requested an official statement of HMG's views on the unofficial discussions that had taken place. As anticipated by the embassy, the deteriorating internal situation meant the Egyptian government was keener to focus on external issues to divert the inevitable dissatisfaction. Under pressure to respond, Bevin reconsidered the possibility of a regional arrangement as a means of solving the impasse. One option would be to associate Egypt with NATO now that Turkey and Greece had been admitted as associate members in September 1950. Another would be the creation of a Middle Eastern defence pact, although the ambassador in Cairo had already informed the Foreign Office that a regional defence arrangement would not persuade the Egyptians to accept the presence of foreign troops for an indefinite period.[57]

With the matter soon to be the subject of talks between Bevin and Saleh el Din, the Cabinet examined possible British tactics. Bevin wanted to stand on the treaty if the Egyptians refused to accept a British peacetime presence, but the idea of evacuation, as suggested by Stevenson, was also discussed. In late November, after Nahas had announced that the Anglo–Egyptian treaty of 1936 would be abrogated if no solution was found to the disputes over the Sudan and the base within twelve months, the Cabinet considered an Anglo–Egyptian agreement on the base's use in wartime and a study of the obstacles to an agreement on defence matters in peacetime. If no agreement on the above lines could be achieved, a solution on a multilateral basis would be proposed (186). General Robertson, the commander of Middle East Land Forces, noted the increased urgency of an agreement, but was equally convinced that Britain would have to have peacetime military facilities in Egypt. Robertson regarded the Egyptians as cowards and believed it would be necessary to frighten them in order to get an agreement by making it clear that Britain was prepared 'to meet trouble with trouble' (188). The Cabinet concluded that Bevin should seek agreement on the principle of wartime use with a small strike force of British troops remaining in peacetime. If, however, British requirements could be limited to the wartime use of the base, Bevin suggested that it might be possible to hand the base over to the Egyptians in peacetime, leaving only a number of plain clothes British technicians (189).

Bevin met Saleh el Din four times in December 1950. The foreign secretary assumed a conciliatory stance based on evacuation and the employment of technicians in plain clothes. This could be attributed to the influence of the ambassador but it is more likely that Bevin was affected by the fear that if negotiations did break down it would be better for this to happen over the Sudan issue; concessions were therefore required on the base. After the initial meetings, at which Saleh el Din insisted on British evacuation within a year, the Cabinet had to decide what further proposals, if any, could be discussed (190). In the Middle East, Robertson continued to object to Bevin's proposed concessions, arguing that there was more to running a base than looking after sheds and ammunition dumps. In Robertson's view a base had to be retained by the British in peacetime because it would be necessary for the opening campaign in war.[58]

Meanwhile in London the joint planners accepted evacuation on condition that an interim peacetime base was established in Israel to serve as a substitute main base until the Canal Zone facilities were fully operational again. Upon this basis the COS recommended that all fighting troops should be withdrawn by 1956, after which the base would be leased from Egypt and run by administrative personnel in civilian clothes. In the meantime civilian personnel would be phased in and the guarding of the installations handed over to the Egyptians. Crucially, the internal administration of the base would remain under British control and an integrated air defence system would be established.[59]

The important difference between the COS's proposals and those of Bevin was that the former required the ownership and control of the base installations and equipment to remain in British hands. In Cairo the ambassador was convinced that the maximum Britain could obtain was a more or less effective use of the base for five years in return for an early start on the evacuation of combat troops and a programme to bring Egyptian forces to an agreed strength.[60] In subsequent discussions in the Defence Committee and Cabinet, the opinions of the ambassador were largely ignored, as to accept them would have meant a radical shift in British policy. This was part of a continuing battle between those in favour of meeting the Egyptians' main demands and those determined to modify them to meet British needs other than the generally accepted need for an agreement.

By April 1951 the pressures inherent in the conflicting British desire to appear strong in order to maintain their Middle Eastern dominance while reaching an agreement with Egypt were increasing. As the Cabinet considered what to offer the Egyptians, domestic opinion hardened, particularly in parliament where the Labour majority was small and Conservative concern about Britain's Middle Eastern position was large. Opposition anxieties were shared by Labour supporters following the implementation of the Iranian nationalisation of the Anglo–Iranian oil company in May 1951 and the Egyptian refusal to allow oil tankers to pass through the Suez Canal en route to Haifa. Some believed Britain was being humiliated in the Middle East in ways which were damaging to the Exchequer. In response, the Americans, according to the head of the State Department's Near East Division, George McGhee, were embarking on a new policy because the old discipline of British imperial power had been removed. Essentially this would involve a more active US role with arms shipments and economic aid.[61] In the wake of this decision to woo the Arabs, the Americans did not want the British to take an inflexible stance over negotiations with Egypt (200).

The British attempt to appear reasonable did not satisfy the Egyptians, and when the COS's (as opposed to Bevin's) proposals were put to them on 11 April they were instantly rejected. It was not an unexpected development and the Cabinet had already discussed possible new approaches (198). At a further meeting in May the Cabinet again discussed Bevin's previous suggestion of offering the withdrawal of all combat troops within a reasonable period. Other options which did *not* meet the basic Egyptian demand included a regional defence arrangement. Extraordinarily it was at this meeting that ministers first learned of the additional expenditure involved in the proposal which the Egyptians had just rejected. They decided, however, to raise the issue of the Sudan. If further talks were to break down, Morrison, Bevin's successor, argued that a breach over the Sudan would be preferable to one over the base (202).

The idea of a regional defence arrangement had been given impetus by an American proposal for a Middle East command organisation and defence board (201). This stemmed from the problems produced for NATO by the Anglo–American divergence over global strategy. Different priorities in strategic plans had particular implications for the use of British and American forces in the Mediterranean. During the period of the latest emergency war plan ('Binnacle' was the British revision of 'Galloper' agreed after the Anglo–American–Canadian talks) up to July 1951, there was no prospect of successfully defending the Rhine. The American determination to fight in southern Europe meant that they wanted naval forces in the Mediterranean to support the land campaign there, thus leaving the Middle East to British and Commonwealth forces. These, inadequate though they were, would depend on supplies arriving by sea which suggested a single naval command for the Mediterranean that could preserve Britain's traditional dominance. By March 1951 the Americans had abandoned the idea of a single Mediterranean command under NATO, and wanted the Mediterranean divided, with the British naval command outside NATO. In the light of British opposition to this, the Americans suggested a separate Middle East Command in order to offset the impression that the British naval commander-in-chief would be a subsidiary rather than a supreme commander.

Simultaneously the military were reviewing plan 'Celery', the successor to 'Sandown'. In the discussions more emphasis was placed on the possibility of fighting further north and east on the inner or outer rings during the period up to 1954.[62] This would require support from the Turks who were, however, following the American line and defining their role as supporting NATO's southern flank rather than assisting British and Commonwealth forces in the defence of the Middle East.[63]

In Egypt the situation was worsening as economic problems grew and the Wafd government was perceived as corrupt and incompetent. If, as was likely, the nationalist card was played it would make it impossible for the British to continue to stall in the negotiations. Equally, because of the Iranian nationalisation and the Egyptian interception of Haifa bound British tankers in the Suez Canal, it became even more difficult to contemplate concessions to Egypt. Britain was in a vicious circle: as the situation in Egypt became more difficult an agreement was more necessary but harder to reach (208). A crisis in Anglo–Egyptian relations was rapidly approaching with the Egyptians threatening to abrogate the 1936 treaty.

On 6 July 1951 the Egyptians rejected the British proposals on the Sudan (209). The Cabinet therefore requested an assessment of Britain's position if the negotiations broke down and of the pressures that could be brought to bear on the Egyptians (210). The ambassador believed that an equal partnership in a regional defence treaty was the only basis for agreement, but this would involve accepting the Egyptian right to insist on a British withdrawal from the base (211). Once the Egyptians had made it clear they regarded the talks as over, the situation was deemed so serious that a joint Anglo–American intelligence appreciation of Egyptian views on the Sudan and the base was drawn up by the embassies in Cairo (247).

The American belief that they knew best how to achieve co-operation with Egypt increasingly aroused British resentment. In the case of the base negotiations the US believed the British were too inflexible and that concessions on the Sudan were needed to secure an agreement (213–215). The British, refusing all idea of any compromise over Farouk's title to the Sudan, now sought a way out of the impasse through the establishment of a Middle East Command. If Egypt agreed to participate, Britain would withdraw all its troops from the Canal Zone except those which would be placed under the command of the new organisation. Yet the question remained of how to accord the Egyptians the equality they desired within the regional command structure. As before this eventually came back to the old issue of whether the British would agree to evacuate from Egypt unconditionally (216).

In the short term the MEC idea, which in the view of the embassy would not be acceptable to the Egyptians, failed to prevent a crisis in Anglo–Egyptian relations. Before it was formally presented to the Egyptian government on 13 October, the abrogation bills had been put before the Egyptian parliament on 8 October. The British sought a distraction from their refusal to evacuate Egypt while the Wafd leaders, facing possible corruption charges and continued economic difficulties, needed to cover up internal shortcomings and focus mass discontent on the British.[64] Making a stand against the British by abrogating the treaty was also seen as a means of weakening Farouk's ability to act against the Wafd government.

Violent conflict in Egypt and the demise of King Farouk: defence cuts in Britain and a new strategy for global war, Oct 1951–July 1952

The abrogation of the treaty was followed by a number of measures designed to pressurise the British into withdrawing from the Canal Zone. Buildings were damaged and Egyptian labourers discouraged from working for the British military. Faced by a terrorist campaign, Britain's military commanders in Egypt were eager to take a hard retaliatory line by using sanctions such as stopping the flow of oil to Cairo. The difficulty was that harsh measures were likely to arouse external opposition, notably from the US authorities. As the British considered the prospect of having to impose military government in the Canal Zone, there was also the issue of how far to go in working for the removal of the Wafd (230, 233). The Labour government left office as it had entered it with support for Farouk and the Egyptian military growing within government circles (234).

The decision to cut oil supplies to Cairo aroused considerable criticism and soon had to be abandoned as a permanent measure. In October and November 1951 it symbolised the conflict between the hard line military men on the spot who were prepared to use troops to support Farouk,[65] and Foreign Office officials who were nervous of an all out confrontation with Egypt. Cutting the supplies for a limited period reflected a desire for retaliatory measures which would inconvenience the Egyptians without provoking a crisis.

Proposed solutions to the crisis in Egypt were many and varied. It was widely agreed that the Wafd government would have to be replaced. How this could be done without British concessions or occupation, and more problematically who would take over the reins, nobody seemed to know. The traditional post-1945 panacea of social reform and economic development lacked both the money, which only the Americans had, and the leaders in Egypt prepared to contemplate such ideas (246). As the year drew to a close, fresh incidents continued to occur in the Canal Zone which were met by limited retaliatory measures designed to avoid a complete rupture with Egypt or the collapse of law and order in the Delta.

The Foreign Office and an increasingly harassed ambassador had to consider ways of resuming talks with the Egyptians and also whether and at what point to approach the King with a view to removing the Wafd. In London a working party appointed to examine the implications of economic sanctions against Egypt concluded that sanctions might prove counter-productive by strengthening the existing government. Moreover if Egypt retaliated by denying cotton to Britain, the British economy would be significantly damaged (248).

Stevenson continued to believe that evacuation was essential for an agreement. In response the head of the African Department at the Foreign Office suggested proposing to Farouk British acceptance in principle of the evacuation of combat troops and the turning of the base and the RAF squadrons over to the planned MEC. In Allen's view this did not go very far in meeting the Egyptians but Eden, the new Conservative foreign secretary, thought it went too far and he could not see where the troops would go (251). The military commanders were even less enamoured with any idea of evacuation (254) and Eden decided to offer only negotiations without commitment on the basis of the four-power proposals for the MEC (260).

By the end of December, as a consequence of the abrogation, the number of British troops in Egypt had risen from 35,000 to 64,000 while the number of civilian employees in the Canal Zone had fallen from 58,000 to 2,306.[66] Drastic action in Egypt was one possible way of bringing about a crisis that would force Farouk to act against the Wafd. Another was to rely on Farouk to reach an agreement by recognising his title as King of the Sudan. The latter was the American view as Acheson, the secretary of state, made clear when Eden visited Washington in January 1952. Acheson proposed a package deal whereby Egypt would accept the four-power proposals, agree not to interfere with the existing Sudan regime and allow the Sudanese to exercise self-determination. In return Britain would in some way recognise Farouk's title as King of the Sudan. Eden rejected this approach to an

Anglo–Egyptian settlement as he believed it would lead to serious trouble in the Sudan which Britain would be unable to control.[67]

The continuing trouble in Egypt led officials in London and Cairo to reflect upon the nature and extent of anti-British feeling in Egypt and to question whether any Egyptian government could survive after having made a 'reasonable' settlement with Britain (262). Sir Pierson Dixon, a deputy under-secretary of state in the Foreign Office, concluded that Britain's difficulties stemmed from a lack of power which in turn provoked Egyptian intransigence. Dixon acknowledged that the realistic option was to recognise this and out of necessity to give in to the Egyptian demands. He preferred, however, to distance the Foreign Office from realism, because surrendering to the Egyptians would make it impossible for British power in the world to be rebuilt. Dixon believed that prestige, not just money and troops, was a key measurement of power. Therefore it was vital to avoid a loss of prestige in Egypt while hoping that the US would provide the money and troops Britain lacked (263).

Out of fear of accepting the limitations imposed by a lack of power, the military endorsed the move away from realism with increasing enthusiasm. In part this was prompted by the pressures that were to develop on military expenditure; the new Conservative government was immediately confronted by balance of payments problems and the re-emergence of the dollar gap. It was also prompted by the need, and the opportunity, given the reassessment of the speed of the Soviet advance, to establish a new fall back line of defence further away from Egypt than the Tel Aviv–Ramallah line.

In addition planning a new defence line was influenced by the increasing strength of Turkey's American-supplied armed forces. If the Turks could hold the Soviets it would be more feasible to attempt to defend the inner ring, as opposed to the Lebanon–Jordan line, because no forces would need to be deployed on an east-west axis. However there would be a serious shortage of aircraft and the revision of 'Galloper', plan 'Cinderalla', pointed to a deficiency of 300 planes on D Day rising to 700 at $D+6$ months. In addition there would be a serious deficiency of infantry at $D+180$ days and a grave lack of armour at $D+150$.[68] This did not prevent the adoption of the inner ring as the basis of Middle Eastern defence in a COS memorandum that was designed to cover the period up to December 1954. Despite its perceived political and strategic advantages, the outer ring was ruled out because during the period under review the necessary forces could not be made available in wartime nor deployed in peace. In an attempt to provide some defence of Middle Eastern oil, which required the adoption of the outer ring strategy, the defence of Bahrein was proposed but in the knowledge that British and Commonwealth forces would not be available in 1952 (258).

The role of the Turks in the inner ring was in part connected to the establishment of the proposed Middle East Command. No progress had been made since the idea was first put forward and by the beginning of 1952 military opinions were turning against it.[69] The British had hoped to use the MEC to re-establish the direct US commitment to Middle Eastern defence and so overcome the problem of the base and to involve the Turks more in Middle Eastern as opposed to southern European defence.[70] The latter issue had become entangled in the Anglo–American dispute over command arrangements in the Mediterranean and it was this that preserved the British military's interest in the MEC once Turkey was admitted to NATO in February 1952.

The Americans wanted Greek and Turkish forces in the Mediterranean placed under Admiral Carney's southern command (Atlantic) which would be responsible to SACEUR with no links between the proposed MEC and NATO. They insisted that Turkey and Greece be admitted to NATO before the establishment of a MEC. The British, on the other hand, argued that the MEC should be created immediately.[71] Once Turkey was admitted to NATO there was a perceived need for a MEC to be established in order to divert Turkey from the NATO campaign in southern Europe. The longer the establishment of the MEC was postponed the more Turkey would be drawn into the European orbit.[72]

President Eisenhower was by now arguing for a single naval command in the Mediterranean directly responsible to SACEUR.[73] This would be in line with the new US strategic concept with its emphasis on Europe and would effectively place Britain's Mediterranean fleet under a European command. The British argued that a single Mediterranean commander had to be responsible to the Standing Group rather than to SACLANT or SACEUR, as the conflict of interest between southern Europe and the Middle East could be resolved only by a higher authority; if this was not possible then rather than place the Mediterranean fleet under a US commander there would have to be two Mediterranean commands with a reduction in the naval forces Britain committed to NATO.[74]

By May 1952 it was clear to the British that the Americans were not prepared to compromise over command arrangements. Admiral Fechteler, the US chief of naval operations, did not want to take account of Middle Eastern needs when discussing the Mediterranean theatre, at least until a MEC was set up. Such was the significance of the issue that the Cabinet discussed the matter and the minister of defence, Lord Alexander, submitted a memorandum which argued that Britain should not give way to the Americans (303–304). In an attempt to solve the problem the US ambassador suggested, on his own initiative, that a defence organisation would be better than a MEC. His idea was taken up by the British who passed a memorandum to Washington in June 1952 on a Middle East Defence Organisation.[75]

Early in 1952, however, the MEC idea was still being employed by the Foreign Office as part of its attempts to solve the dispute over the British peacetime presence in the Canal Zone. It was now generally agreed that to obtain a settlement the Wafd would have to be replaced, and following the Ismailia massacre and the Cairo riots on 26 January, Ali Maher formed a new government two days later. In many ways this was a key event because paradoxically the new regime of pashas would now be concerned that by playing the anti-British card it might release uncontrollable forces and thereby threaten the whole society on which its privileges were based.

The new regime at least provided the opening for Eden to go to Cabinet with a proposal to restart negotiations. One initial difficulty was finding an acceptable formula for talks to begin. If this could be overcome and an agenda agreed on, Eden proposed to offer withdrawal of all mobile land forces within twelve months. The base would be turned over to the Egyptians with an air defence organisation controlled by the proposed MEC and the latter would decide what British air defence forces would remain. British military personnel manning the base would essentially be replaced by civilian technicians (267).

Numerous problems attended these proposals. The costs of redeployment would be extremely large, and the shorter the evacuation period the more difficult they would be to bear (268). Moreover, Churchill was not inclined to concede evacuation until British forces had been replaced by allied forces under the proposed MEC (270). Eden was forced to redraft the proposed communiqué on the resumption of negotiations to meet Churchill's objections (272). When this was presented to Cabinet along with a draft despatch instructing the ambassador, the prime minister was still not happy. Two more meetings were necessary before the Cabinet reached an agreement (273–274). Within the Foreign Office, the head of the African Department realised that the minimum British concessions necessary to secure an agreement were not being made. The issue for Allen was whether or not the failure to reach an agreement would bring about a revolution in Egypt (278). There were others in the Foreign Office who still paled at the thought of conceding the principle of evacuation (280). Divisions on this issue existed within the Cabinet, the Conservative Party, the Foreign Office and the embassy, although opinion in the embassy tended to be most inclined to bring British policy on evacuation into line with Egyptian requirements.

On 2 March Ali Maher was replaced by Neguib al-Hilali. This was an improvement from the British point of view as Hilali was deemed to be more likely to take a strong line against the corrupt and anti-British Wafd and more willing to sign an agreement on the base. The Egyptian parliament had been prorogued and if the Wafd could be sufficiently weakened before fresh elections there was the prospect, in Eden's view, of a lasting agreement. He therefore proposed giving the ambassador fresh instructions to permit him greater leeway in establishing a basis for the resumption of talks (281). Before this was discussed by Cabinet, Churchill expressed his objections to running after the Egyptians in search of a settlement. The prime minister instinctively preferred to stand firm; he believed the Egyptians should be bullied into accepting British demands (282). Eden, however, argued that Britain faced either making the best arrangement that was possible or finding itself with a commitment greater than it could bear. If the Canal Zone was to be held by force, disturbances in the Delta would be far too costly in terms of men, money and British commercial interests. Moreover there would be no troops to defend the Middle East as they would all be tied up in Egypt. In claiming that Britain had to negotiate because 'the plain fact is that we are no longer in a position to impose our will upon Egypt regardless of the cost in men, money, and international goodwill' (283), Eden was coming dangerously close to realism.

The Cabinet, however, hauled the foreign secretary back from the brink by opposing the draft of a joint Anglo–Egyptian statement on the resumption of negotiations. Ministers believed that the reference to the evacuation of British forces was not sufficiently tied to the Egyptian government's agreement to participate in the MEC (284–285). It might have been anticipated that although the Wafd had rejected the four-power proposals for an MEC in November 1951, the new regime in the post-Cairo riots situation would be more scared and more pro-British. Churchill took the line that there was no difference between the requirements of the Wafd and the Hilali government except that the former would attempt to use violence to attain their goals (288). In a sense this was true because it would hardly be possible for any opponents of the Wafd to accept what the latter had rejected for fear of the political consequences. But in that case there was no hope of an agreement, and an agreement was increasingly necessary.

Slim re-emphasised to the Defence Committee on 12 March 1952 that a base in Egypt in war was essential. Such a base would only be effective if Egypt were to co-operate, and in order to secure this it might become necessary to withdraw British combat troops in peacetime.[76] Later in the month Slim accepted the withdrawal of combat troops on the understanding that the MEC should be based on British forces in the Middle East with perhaps a move from Egypt to Gaza. The COS endorsed the need to avoid presenting at the outset something the Egyptians would not accept.[77]

The problems of remaining were only to clear to the Foreign Office, if not to Churchill, and an increasingly important difficulty facing the British was US opposition to their stance on the terms for resuming talks. Acheson's arguments were essentially the same as Slim's in that if the base was necessary for the defence of the Middle East, and if Egyptian co-operation was necessary to make the base effective, Britain would have to agree to evacuation in peacetime (292).

Eden therefore presented the Cabinet with the draft of yet another statement to serve as the basis for the resumption of negotiations (291). The draft was not, however, acceptable to the Egyptian prime minister who insisted that the phrase 'the withdrawal of British forces' be replaced by 'the withdrawal of all British naval, military and air forces in line with what had been agreed in 1946'.[78] The proposed statement was also still opposed by Churchill and Alexander because it did not go far enough to link evacuation to the acceptance of a MEC. After two meetings (293–294) the Cabinet decided to omit the offending paragraph referring to the withdrawal of British forces.

Meanwhile, Stevenson had surprisingly persuaded the Egyptian foreign minister to accept the original British draft.[79] Eden therefore proposed reversing the Cabinet decision of 4 April (296) but his colleagues refused, with Churchill arguing against appearing to accept Egyptian responsibility for the defence of the canal at the beginning of negotiations designed to establish a MEC.[80] In the event this was academic as Hilali overruled his foreign minister and insisted on referring to land, sea and air forces.[81] This was unacceptable to the British, including the military, because of the importance attached to air defence measures.[82]

As the prospect of failing to obtain an agreement loomed, the only bright spot from the British point of view was the relative calm in Egypt, helped by Hilali's decision in April to postpone the elections and the government's continued imposition of martial law and censorship. In an attempt to avoid a rupture over the proposed talks there were suggestions in London and Cairo that a more threatening line should be taken with the Egyptians to administer a 'jolt' to the regime (302, 305). But equally there was an awareness of the need to avoid returning to the tensions produced in late 1951 and early 1952, and therefore a concern not to push things too far. The problem was that if an Egyptian government came to an agreement on British terms it would immediately be accused of treachery and would almost certainly be replaced by a more extreme anti-British one (307). And if there was no agreement on Egyptian terms, in any elections Hilali's government would be unlikely to prevail against what was seen as the extremism of the Wafd so Britain would be back in the same difficulty as earlier in the year.

As policy makers grappled with these Egyptian consequences of the decline of British power, reassessments were made of how to fight a global war and whether to maintain Britain's overseas commitments in what were increasingly difficult financial circumstances.[83] In the middle of June 1952 two important and complementary papers were produced by the Foreign Office and the COS on Britain's overseas obligations and on a radically revised global strategy. The first discussed a reduction in Britain's overseas obligations which was seen as desirable on cost grounds (realism) but undesirable because it could bring about a loss of prestige that would be difficult to reverse.[84] The second produced the first fundamental revision of Commonwealth defence strategy since the 1947 paper had confirmed the Middle East as one of the three pillars which would enable Britain and its allies to defend the main support areas in global war (308). The new global strategy paper took account of the development of atomic weapons and Britain's increasingly weak economic position in defining a strategy in which the importance of the main support areas was reduced. In fact preparations for global war were deemed much less significant than deterring war and, more importantly, using the deployment of conventional forces to achieve victory in the cold war. Both papers were keen to emphasise the importance of the US shouldering more of the burdens hitherto born by Britain.

Once it was clear that the idea of a command arrangement was unlikely to produce an American military commitment to the region, this became a key rationale for the proposed MEDO. But differences with the Americans also appeared in the discussions on MEDO which came to be seen primarily as a planning body. The Americans did not accept that only Arab states prepared to make a military contribution should be founder members; nor did they wish to proceed without a significant body of Arab support.[85] Other Arab states, however, would only contemplate a defence arrangement after the Anglo–Egyptian dispute over the base had been resolved. Rather than MEDO bringing about a resolution of the base question, it now appeared that MEDO was feasible only if the base issue was resolved.

With its emphasis on nuclear weapons, the global strategy paper had made a virtue out of a necessity in terms of reduced defence expenditure, but the Treasury was soon to ask for more cuts. Some reductions seemed inevitable in the Middle East although the intelligence assessments, by chance or design, were now playing down the likely Soviet threat to the Levant, and therefore to Egypt, in the early stages of a war. The significance for the base and future planning was that if the Russians were not going to launch a major offensive against the Levant in the early stages of a war, this would again allow the British more time to get forces into position. Not only would this reduce the necessity for the peacetime presence of forces in Egypt (time would allow them to be brought in from further afield); there would also be the possibility of deploying them further north and east even if the plan remained to fall back on the inner ring. In the light of these developments a review process of Middle East defence strategy began which was geared towards adopting what was termed a forward, or Iraqi–Levant strategy with forces initially deployed in northern Iran and the passes of north-east Iraq (311).

Reassessing requirements in the Canal Zone in the light of a new approach to Middle East defence, and the involvement of the Americans in the attempt to secure a new agreement on the Suez base, Aug 1952–Feb 1953
The review of Middle East defence coincided with Treasury demands for more cuts in expenditure. However, the fighting of the cold war and the creation of a nuclear deterrent now assumed priority over fighting global war and thus a strategic reserve, which could intervene in cold war conflicts or a limited hot war, became more necessary. The priority accorded to cold war also meant that the Asian theatre would take precedence over the Middle Eastern one. Consequently, in August 1952 and in line with the global strategy paper, the COS agreed that when the Egyptian situation permitted it, ground forces in Egypt would be reduced to one division;[86] this had important implications for the British position in the Canal Zone. Even more

important was the effect of the proposed cuts on the RAF. There was now no prospect of the air force being able to retain the squadrons originally planned for the air defence organisation; this in turn posed questions about the viability of any plans to provide for the air defence of the base (318).

As the basis of global strategy and Middle East defence was thrown into turmoil in the summer of 1952, events in Egypt were following an even more turbulent course. On 29 June Hilali resigned, ostensibly because of difficulties arising from his anti-corruption campaign. The American embassy, however, believed it was because of his failure to make progress on talks with Britain and that this was the result of Britain's stance on Farouk's title as King of the Sudan. A new government was formed on 2 July with Hussein Sirry as prime minister. The British feared that censorship would be lifted and elections held for a new parliament which would mean the return of the Wafd. The Foreign Office therefore instructed the embassy that the Egyptians should be left to stew in their own juice in the hope that the Americans would talk firmly to Farouk.[87]

However, the Americans, and notably the CIA, were much more interested in talking to the Young Officers movement, led by Anwar Sadat and Gamal Nasser, which was plotting to overthrow Farouk and install General Neguib as president. The British were largely unaware of this, although they did realise that elements in the army were increasingly hostile to the King because of the number of personal appointments he had made to valued posts. Officials in Cairo also believed a military rising was possible, although this came on the night of 22–23 July, just as the embassy was expressing its satisfaction with Hilali's return as prime minister in a much strengthened position.[88] The new regime, with Neguib as a figurehead, reinstalled Ali Maher as prime minister, but then fearful that Farouk would persuade the British to intervene insisted on the abdication of the King on 26 July.[89] British influence in Egypt was never the same thereafter.

The military regime quickly abolished censorship and called for a two-month stocktaking period before considering the future of the base.[90] Churchill was prepared to view Neguib's and Ali Maher's government favourably and urged that it be supported;[91] but he restated his determination not to accept evacuation before satisfactory arrangements for defending the Canal had been made under the auspices of the proposed MEDO (317). The embassy in Cairo was not in the best position to assess the new military leaders, having had little or no contact with them, and this increased the importance of defining a common approach with the Americans. The latter were less concerned than the British about the danger of extremists taking over the government and were more enthusiastic about providing Neguib with military aid of a limited nature (321). On 6 September British concerns increased when Ali Maher was forced to resign because of differences over agrarian reform and Neguib became prime minister, but a joint Anglo–American assessment concluded that the military regime was worth supporting. Eden, however, did not trust the US ambassador, Jefferson Caffery, and differences soon appeared over the nature and timing of such support.

By October 1952, Neguib was showing a keen interest in the resumption of talks to solve the Anglo–Egyptian dispute. The Egyptian leader was eager to get arms, not least the Meteor aircraft that had been on order and partially paid for since 1950.[92] Already the regime was looking for a success that would serve to strengthen its support within Egypt. Unfortunately the keenness of the Egyptian government to negotiate came at a very inconvenient time for the British because of the proposed revision of Middle Eastern strategy on lines of the forward or Iraqi–Levant strategy.

In September the BDCC (ME) came out in support of the new concept in a memorandum for the COS that was extremely critical of the existing inner ring strategy: 'In short the Soviet forces will achieve a large proportion of their Middle East aims while we will achieve none of ours.' It argued that although there were risks in deploying air and ground forces further forward these should be accepted. The military advantage would be to impose further delay on the Soviet advance and allow more time for the strategic offensive to take effect; the Soviets would also be prevented from initially acquiring air bases in Iraq and the Levant which would enable ground attack aircraft to support their advance. The political advantages would lie in the initial commitment to defend more of the Middle East and to bolster confidence in Iraq. The risk would lie in the removal of aircraft from a role of defending the base in the Canal Zone. There would also be the difficulties inherent in basing aircraft in Iraq or Jordan and ensuring that adequate supplies were prestocked there because of the limited transport facilities available (323).

These issues had to be thrashed out against a background of proposed defence cuts which had implications outside the Middle East. The Korean rearmament drive had initially raised the possibility of increasing military strength which was reflected in the February 1952 Lisbon force goals; these had unrealistically committed NATO members to supplying 96 divisions for the defence of western Europe.[93] The British military had circumvented the problem to some extent with the nuclear emphasis in the global strategy paper, but in so doing they effectively abandoned any intention of providing for the conventional defence of western Europe. This reopened the old question of abandoning the continent to its 1940 fate, which the Americans refused to discuss 'however prudent it might be to do so from the military point of view'. When the Treasury produced figures[94] for further cuts, Britain's role in NATO as well as in the Middle East seemed to the military to be under threat (325). The argument went to the Defence Committee on two occasions where the COS argued: 'Our standard of living stems in large measure from our status as a great power and this depends to no small extent on the visible indication of our greatness, which our forces, particularly overseas, provide.' Either resources must be provided to carry out HMG's policy and to support Britain's commitments and status as a great power, or these commitments and Britain's status had to be reduced to a level which the government was prepared to pay for.[95]

Just as the military resources available for the Middle East and the strategy for their use seemed so uncertain, the Foreign Office produced a draft Cabinet paper on defence negotiations with the Egyptians. The reaction of the JPS was yet again to emphasise the need for an agreement to remain in Egypt with Egyptian goodwill unless Britain's whole Middle East strategy was to be revised (328). When the paper was discussed by the COS, there was some disagreement about whether a base in Egypt was essential, given the changed situation that had prompted the recent proposals for a forward strategy. It was agreed that no decision on what precisely was required in Egypt could be taken until studies of the forward strategy had been completed and a final decision on defence cuts had been made. There was, however, still a concern about having an air defence organisation which was shared by the Cabinet when the Foreign Office paper was presented (329, 331, 333).

The British government was now having to stall the Egyptians on an agreement because it was unable to define what form it wanted an agreement to take. For the first time since 1946 there was a possibility that a peacetime military presence in the Canal Zone might not be deemed essential. But as the head of the African Department in the Foreign Office was only too aware, even if there were no military reasons to stay in Egypt, evacuation would have to be on British rather than Egyptian terms for it to be acceptable to the Cabinet and parliament (332).

The British were linking an Egyptian settlement to progress on MEDO and to the review of strategy which in turn was linked to the defence cuts. In November the Americans, keen to break the Middle East logjam, proposed an Anglo–American formulation of the precise lines of a base settlement on which to approach Egypt (335). On 12 November the JPS produced a paper advocating the adoption of a forward strategy as the best means of defending the Middle East whether or not Britain was to remain in Egypt (337). The new strategy was deemed to depend on the development of additional facilities in Iraq and Jordan and the improvement of communicatons through the Levant; the fall back position would be the Lebanon–Jordan line. Not only would this require the co-operation of the Arab states in question; it would also involve considerable expenditure by the British Treasury and this was unlikely to be available except in the long-term future. When the COS discussed the paper it was agreed that the JPS proposal would be the best strategy for defending the Middle East and that a wartime base in Egypt would be necessary to implement it (338). Strategy was not being defined in the light of existing resources.

The next step was to define what peacetime arrangements were needed in the Canal Zone to ensure that the base would be available if the new strategy had to be implemented in wartime. At the end of November the JPS produced a paper outlining three possible scenarios which, to varying extents, would meet Britain's requirements (339). The best and the cheapest was for Britain to retain large numbers of military technicians in the base as this would avoid prestocking except in the most forward areas and enable the base to support the forward strategy from the outbreak of war (Case A). If the Egyptians would not permit British personnel to remain but would allow for the retention of stores and workshops, it would take ninety days for the base to become operable (Case B). If stores had to be evacuated it was estimated that six months would be required to make the base operational (Case C). The prospect of a working base in peacetime might therefore have to be abandoned in order to secure Egyptian co-operation which had always been regarded as essential except when it could be secured only on Egyptian terms.

The COS modified the JPS paper by adding an integrated Anglo–Egyptian air defence organisation to Cases A and B, adding a small number of RAF personnel to Case B and making Case C the same as the JPS's Case B. Finally a new Case D was created embodying the former Case C (340). Before these proposals were finalised by the military, the Egyptians had made it clear that any involvement in MEDO, to which Neguib was not deemed unsympathetic, could be considered only when agreement on the stages and date of the British evacuation had been reached. Moreover the embassy immediately made it clear that the military regime would not accept Case A which did not provide for the complete evacuation of combat personnel in peacetime.[96]

The views of the embassy contrasted with those of the Commanders-in-Chief, Middle East who would not consider anything less than Case A and who argued that if the Egyptians rejected it Britain should sit tight in the Canal Zone (344). The

Commanders-in-Chief also believed that it would not be possible to adopt the forward strategy until MEDO had been established and wished to divorce the Egyptian negotiations from the question of MEDO (345). The COS rejected these ideas, and agreed to accept something between Cases B and C. Their agreement was conditional on Egyptian membership of MEDO (347) and this was endorsed by the Defence Committee.[97] After all this time and after the adoption of a new strategy, the COS were still hedging on complete evacuation in peacetime as only Cases C and D conceded this point. Another problem for those in the Foreign Office and the embassy who saw evacuation as the prerequisite for an agreement was that the Treasury were unhappy because of the costs of redeployment (349).

The arguments on the merits of the various cases were now to involve the Americans whose agreement was to be sought before any proposals were put to the Egyptians. American contacts with the regime were both desired and resented by the British. Resented if the Americans attempted to play a mediatory role; desired if they were prepared to back the British stance. The problem for the Americans was that Case A had long been unacceptable to the Egyptians. The Anglo–American position was straightforward on the general desirability of evacuation, maintenance and reactivation, air defence, participation in MEDO and a programme of economic and military assistance. Less clear cut was the US commitment to an agreement based as closely as possible on Case A, which, minus the aid package, had already been rejected by previous Egyptian governments.

Even though Egypt's economic difficulties had become worse, it was unlikely that the Egyptians would be so desperate for military aid that they would be prepared to give up their demands for complete evacuation. Demand for Egyptian cotton had fallen and although the government intervened, prices were lower than they had been in 1950–1951. Lack of sterling was restricting imports, and as criticism of the regime grew it proved necessary to reimpose censorship.[98] On 16 January 1953 the regime decided to ban all political parties. Once again the British expected the government would be forced to divert attention away from domestic difficulties towards the presence of foreign troops in the Canal Zone.

The more the Egyptians acted in this manner, and the more the government made inflammatory statements, the more difficult it would be for the British to begin negotiations without arousing the fury of right wing opinion within the Conservative Party. Eden, by contrast, was convinced that Britain could no longer use the methods of the last century to preserve its position in Egypt. To do so would be beyond Britain's means and would ensure that no, rather than insufficient, forces would be available to defend the Middle East (364). However, the foreign secretary was also aware that Britain could not agree to withdraw unconditionally if British prestige was to be preserved and Conservative Party opinion appeased. Hence the importance of using the creation of MEDO as a condition for agreeing to evacuate. In addition the establishment of MEDO would satisfy those who wanted a guarantee that freedom of passage through the Suez Canal would be maintained.

Reluctant to stay but unable to go: Anglo–American conflict over Britain's failure to secure a new agreement on the Suez base, Feb 1953–Oct 1953

A package of five points was agreed with the Americans and approved by the Cabinet in March 1953 (374). This involved MEDO, military aid, an air defence organisation, maintenance of the base in peacetime on the lines of Case A and a phased British evacuation. The only US proviso was that the maintenance of the base for use immediately upon the outbreak of war (Case A) was desirable rather than essential.

With Anglo–American agreement secured on a deal which the embassy believed would be unacceptable, the Foreign Office was determined that the Americans should be involved in the actual talks. Without them the head of the African Department accepted that the chances of securing Egyptian agreement to Case A were nil.[99] Case A was much more important to the Commanders-in-Chief than any MEDO, whose motivation was essentially political with regard to domestic opinion within Britain and with regard to opinion in the Arab states and the wider world (381). Indeed the Commander-in-Chief, Middle East Land Forces was opposed to the British insistence on MEDO and on an air defence organisation for which he believed there were insufficient resources (379). Yet Eden insisted that the five points were interdependent and that no agreement could be reached on one without an agreement on all (380), even though the embassy reported Neguib's insistence that evacuation could not be dependent on MEDO.[100]

In the event the Egyptians opposed American participation in the talks which was accepted by the Eisenhower administration.[101] The British now ran into difficulties with the Americans, particularly those in Cairo who clearly realised there was nothing to be gained by presenting the Egyptians with the unacceptable. The American embassy informed the British in Cairo that the military regime was ready to discuss the maintenance of the base and the arrangements for reactivation at the same time as the British withdrawal from the Canal Zone. After the evacuation question had been settled the Egyptians would be prepared to participate in a regional defence organisation.[102]

The British reaction was increasingly one of resentment at what was seen as US reluctance to apply pressure on the Egyptians to comply with what the British wanted. Failing that it was believed that the Americans should support the tactics the British intended to use to secure their demands; these were specifically defined by the Foreign Office and despatched to the ambassador in Washington (380). The Americans found these difficult to accept and began to seek ways of mediating what appeared to be two irreconcilable positions.

Despite concern about the US attitude, Eden was keen to continue the Anglo–Egyptian contacts. Only by getting the Egyptians into detailed negotiations could there be any possibility of securing an agreement. The obstacles were, however, enormous. Both Britain and Egypt had fundamentally irreconcilable requirements based on what was perceived as necessary for national prestige. The nuts and bolts of any agreement mattered little if national honour and international standing could not be satisfied. Each government had to face difficult domestic political situations which made any sacrifice of prestige even more difficult. In Britain the Conservative right was portraying the Egyptian crisis in apocalyptic terms. For Leo Amery it was a chance to rekindle past greatness and he informed Churchill of his 'feeling that the Egyptian business is going to mark a turning point in our affairs. The Middle East and indeed the whole world may realise that we are still alive and have a heart as well as teeth and claws. What is more we may begin to realise it ourselves'.[103]

As Eden contemplated the alleged turning point in imperial history, an air defence organisation was seen as impractical given the planned reductions of British warplanes in the Middle East (387). Moreover, the British commitment to the Middle East was further weakened when the problem of command arrangements in the

Mediterranean was finally resolved essentially in line with American wishes. The Commander-in-Chief, Allied Forces Mediterranean would be responsible to SACEUR for the Mediterranean and Black Sea, although Cyprus, unlike naval forces in the Mediterranean, was to remain under British command. To make matters worse the BDCC (ME) was challenging the concept of defending the Middle East through the new forward strategy with the reduced resources now available. The military men on the spot argued that to succeed it would be necessary to build up local forces as well as retaining a British military presence. Given the global strategy cuts that would reduce British forces in the Middle East to one division and 160 aircraft, the BDCC (ME) believed the initial Russian attacks could not be repulsed. In addition the plans for reinforcing the Middle East were, it was argued, not realistic in that there was no firm commitment to provide the forces to do so either by Britain or its Commonwealth allies. And even if forces were available, it was deemed unlikely that the base in Egypt would be ready to receive them.

The British military were having to confront the fact that the present dearth of resources could not be overcome in the foreseeable future. Prior to and following the Korean war rearmament drive, it might have been expected that the position would improve; now it seemed likely that it would get worse. The BDCC (ME) therefore believed that the 'previous ideas about the defence of the Middle East and of our almost exclusive responsibility for its defence are no longer tenable. . . . So great are the difficulties that some have concluded that a realistic scheme of defence for the Middle East is not possible in our day: yet it is argued, we must maintain a facade of intention to defend it in order to prevent its loss to communism in the cold war' (369).

A difficulty with any such cold war role in Egypt was that the presence of British forces had been producing the very instability and anti-western propaganda that many, especially in the United States, saw as fertile ground for the spread of communism. Moreover, if all Britain's forces in the Middle East were tied up in Egypt, it was difficult to see how they could even play a cold war role elsewhere in the region. As the problems of remaining mounted, increased incidents in the Canal Zone in April 1953 made an agreement seem more unlikely. The Foreign Office began to consider whether it would be better to withdraw in Britain's own time without an agreement. Thus the issue gradually ceased to be one of how Britain could deal with the difficulties of remaining and became one of how Britain could overcome the obstacles to leaving.

Apart from the significant cost of redeployment the problem of leaving was again one of prestige. Given the state of parliamentary opinion it would be necessary to ensure that withdrawal took place in a way that did not appear as if Britain was being forced out by threats. The Egyptians, who had their own problems because of pressure from the Wafd and Muslim extremists, were not unappreciative of British difficulties and saw the advantages that might accrue if they secured British evacuation. As both sides saw benefits in reaching an agreement, informal negotiations were to resume on 20 April without an agreed statement. The professed aim was to make progress by examining issues concerning the base through a number of technical committees and General Robertson was to join the ambassador in the talks. But while agreement was reached on the setting up of the committees, it proved impossible to define their terms of reference. The Egyptians insisted on defining them in advance in order to settle the question of principle involved in the control of the base.

Suspicions were evident on both sides. The British feared that the Egyptians, with German help, were secretly preparing for a more effective guerrilla campaign against British forces in the Canal Zone (389). The Egyptians distrusted the British and suspected that, as in the past, they were dragging their feet in order to remain in Egypt (386). The British wanted Case A in order to retain control of the base installations, whereas the Egyptians were demanding total peacetime control of the base.[104] In effect what the British were being offered was Case C with perhaps some element of Case B and by 30 April the Foreign Office had concluded that this was unacceptable (392). On 6 May 1953 the talks broke up when the Egyptian government was informed that its proposals were unacceptable. For their part the Egyptians could not contemplate the prolonged retention of British technicians or non-Egyptian control of technical facilities in the base. The break-up was followed by Egyptian pronouncements that their rights would have to be won by force.[105]

The failure of the talks coincided with a visit to the Middle East by the American secretary of state, John Foster Dulles, which was to have dramatic consequences for the British position in the region. Dulles visited the Middle East and North Africa between 9 and 23 May 1953 and came away shocked by the extent of anti-British feeling he encountered. In the short term the visit persuaded the United States to make greater efforts to resolve the Anglo–Egyptian dispute. The Americans attempted to impress on the British that the package as a whole, like Case A, would not be acceptable to the Egyptians and this was endorsed in a personal message from Eisenhower to Churchill (399). It was not welcomed by the prime minister who tried to convince the Americans to back the British position (400). Churchill was seeking a confrontation with Egypt and was not inclined to give way to Egyptian demands whether on Case A or anything else.

In the long-term Dulles decided that US policy would have to be developed more independently of the British, which led him to attach much less importance to Egypt and to devise a new basis for Middle Eastern defence.[106] The changes in American policy were to some extent part of the process which had begun in the wake of the nationalisation of the Anglo–Iranian Oil Company. The pro-British, ex-Rhodes scholar, George McGhee, had advocated greater US involvement in Middle Eastern affairs in order to assist the British achieve common cold war goals. Dulles acted on the assumption that while co-operation with Britain was desirable for the unity of the western alliance, it should not involve the US supporting what were deemed unpopular and outdated British policies. In Dulles's eyes the British were no longer best suited to play the leading role in countries like Egypt where the opposition they had engendered was not compensated for by adequate military or economic power. If the countries of the Middle East were to unite against the spread of communism Britain would have to adapt its stance and the United States would have to play a more significant role.

In defence terms this would mean more US military and economic aid to encourage pro-western states to build up their own armed forces in opposition to the Soviet Union. In such a scenario Britain's role would be much reduced, and if the aim was actually to defend the Middle East, Egypt would also assume less significance. The idea that Dulles began to develop in the wake of his May 1953 visit was the construction of an alliance system based on the northern tier states of Turkey, Iraq, Iran and Pakistan. His efforts to realise this goal were to exacerbate regional conflicts and to lead to Britain's involvement in what became known as the

Baghdad Pact. The creation of the pact was subsequently to modify Britain's approach to the façade of Middle East defence and to contribute to the collapse of Britain's predominant position in the region.

In the wake of the break-off of discussions, the Americans began to play a firmer role as mediators in the dispute. At the same time, with Churchill as acting foreign secretary and Robert Hankey installed as chargé d'affaires in the Cairo embassy, there was a considerable hardening of British attitudes. No longer would the embassy repeatedly inform London that their proposals would not be acceptable to the Egyptians. The hardening of British policy continued in July when, in the wake of Churchill's stroke, Lord Salisbury acted as foreign secretary. The desire to avoid giving in to the Egyptians and a willingness to soldier on without an agreement rather than accept an unsatisfactory one became stronger, as did the determination to insist on Case A. All the disadvantages inherent in this strategy remained. The base was costly and ineffective, and the conflict in the Canal Zone reduced the credibililty of what was now acknowledged as the façade of Middle East defence.

As before the Foreign Office considered the pros and cons of a number of possible solutions to the Egyptian imbroglio and continued to evaluate the difficulties if no agreement was reached. Now, however, the role of the US was more crucial, and in early July the acting foreign secretary went to Washington to discuss the question with the Americans. It was suspected that the US embasssy in Cairo had leaked the three British cases to the Egyptians and this contributed to an outpouring of bitter criticism of the mediatory American approach to Middle Eastern problems (405, 410). The Americans, while broadly sympathetic, disagreed with the British over the particular stance they were taking towards the negotiations. However, the Egyptian decision to break off the talks in May was reversed once it became clear to them that the Americans were not going to provide full backing against the British; this led to the resumption of discussions in August and Salisbury's visit to Washington was an attempt to get US support for the British position. Salisbury was determined that Britain should stand firm on Case A and resist any US pressure to move towards Case C. He also wanted an agreement which would remain in force for an initial period of five years. In addition the Cabinet insisted that the conditions under which the base would be made available should include, not only aggression or the threat of aggression against Turkey, Iran or any Arab state but the existence of general war (411, 415).

When Salisbury arrived in Washington he received the Egyptian proposals for the future management and reactivation of the base which were to be embodied in an agreement of three years duration (417). These were essentially American proposals put to the Egyptians as something that might be acceptable to the British and only slightly modified by Cairo.[107] But they were unacceptable to the British and the Cabinet agreed that they could not be used as a basis for resuming negotiations (418). An open breach with the Americans was avoided when Dulles agreed that while there were Anglo–American differences over the detailed proposals, the United States was prepared to support Britain in principle (419).

The British justification for the need to obtain a 'satisfactory' agreement was specifically defined in terms of preserving a base in peacetime in working order and ensuring its availability in war. The COS opposed any suggestion that defence efforts should be concentrated solely on ensuring the survival of the UK; to abandon significant cold war commitments overseas, as in Egypt, would make hot war more likely and cause grave damage to Britain's position, influence, security and commerce.[108] For the right wing of the Conservative Party and others with a commitment to British greatness whatever the reality of military and economic power, the Egyptian question linked the particular military arrangements made for the Canal Zone with the general requirements of British imperialism at a crucial moment in the empire-Commonwealth's history. Egypt, where the challenge to British prestige and status could not be diverted into Commonwealth co-operation or adapted to new forms of control or influence, was still perceived as the cornerstone of the imperial edifice. Julian Amery saw evacuation of the Canal Zone as the end of the Commonwealth as an independent force in the world. He believed the Asian states would leave, while in eastern, central and southern Africa the evacuation would be seen as a betrayal that would open the continent to communism (377).

One consideration in the minds of those who became known as the Suez group, was the symbolism of the Canal itself and they exerted pressure to ensure that in any agreement with Egypt guarantees should be provided regarding freedom of navigation. A large amount of shipping carrying goods which were of importance to Britain passed through the Canal, but it was the appearance rather than the substance of the situation that mattered most to those worried about the future of the Commonwealth and Britain's continued recognition as a great world power. In reality the Suez Canal Convention of 1888 already provided for the right of passage through what was a vital international waterway. What mattered to many in London was whether Britain appeared to have responsibilities in the region which would symbolise the nation's importance. There was no more potent symbol than the Suez Canal.

Some reference to the Canal in any new agreement was important to the Conservative imperialists and provided another hurdle to be overcome in the talks which resumed in August 1953. Initially the talks stalled on whether British technicians should receive instructions direct from London or through the Egyptian authorities. The difficulties which then emerged concerned the duration of the agreement, the numbers of technicians and the length of their stay, and the conditions under which the base would be reactivated. The period of withdrawal of combatant troops was also an issue; an air defence agreement which had assumed such significance in the past had been dropped. For the Egyptians, if fewer technicians were left behind, it would be easier to accept longer time periods for the eventual withdrawal of both combatant troops and technicians. They believed the agreement should not be for more than five years whereas the British, having abandoned the idea of not fixing a time period, demanded a ten-year agreement. On availability the Egyptians would accept reactivation only if an Arab state was attacked but the British wanted automatic availability if an Arab state or Turkey were attacked, and immediate consultation if Iran was attacked or if any of the above mentioned countries were threatened with attack (424, 426).[109]

These issues were discussed in August and September between the British and Egyptian delegations with Robert Hankey in charge of the civilian team. On 8 September General Robertson reported to the Cabinet that the Egyptians could be induced to accept a seven-year agreement made up of eighteen months for the withdrawal of combatant troops, three further years with 4,000 technicians and a final two and a half years with a reduced number of technicians. The Egyptians, he believed, would not accept automatic reactivation in the event of attacks on Turkey or Iran. There were further obstacles in that the Egyptians did not accept that the technicians should have the right to wear uniform. They were not prepared to include a reference in the treaty to freedom of navigation in the Canal, nor to grant Britain air staging post rights (432).

Robertson's proposals were endorsed by the Cabinet, which also agreed that the delegation should seek to insert a clause on freedom of navigation in the Canal in the preamble to the treaty and to obtain automatic availability in the case of an attack on an Arab state or in the event of UN action to resist aggression (434). The Egyptians had insisted on no more than five years for the duration of an agreement but in the event they proved ready to compromise on six, albeit without approval from the Council of the Revolutionary Command (CRC). They accepted the reference to the Canal provided it took note of Egyptian sovereignty but would not agree to a staging post (442).[110] The idea of a six-year agreement was unacceptable to the British (437).

At the beginning of October the Egyptians spelt out their position on the specific issues of the withdrawal of combatant troops, automatic availability and uniform, all of which for them constituted a breaking point. Withdrawal had to take place within eighteen months from the conclusion of an agreement in principle, as opposed to the signing of the final detailed agreement; technicians in uniform were not acceptable; and automatic availability could apply only in the event of an attack on an Arab state (440). By then the Cabinet had decided to inform the Egyptians that Britain had made its final offer and that no further attempts would be made to reach a compromise (439).

As Britain contemplated the breakdown of negotiations, the War Office estimated that the base was costing between £40 and £50 million per year when Britain was faced with a reduction in American aid and, with German rearmament, paying the occupation costs in Germany. But having decided to make no further concessions, the British could not simply break off the negotiations. The Americans were unhappy at the prospect of technicians' uniforms determining whether or not facilities would be obtained in Egypt.[111] And there were broader considerations associated with what the breaking point should be. From the British point of view it was preferable to have the talks fail on the issues associated with the effective running of the base which had yet to be properly addressed. The Egyptians, however, were reluctant to talk about such matters as the duties of the base commander until questions of principle had been settled (441).

There was therefore a reason for continuing talks and the delegation believed that, other than on availability, the differences were small enough to be overcome. The delegation's view was that it would be possible for both sides to accept withdrawal within fifteen months of the agreement in principle, a new draft pertaining to uniform and a seven-year agreement with a reduced number of technicians after four and a half years (442). The Cabinet decided to follow the recommendations of the delegation with minor drafting changes on the uniform issue, but the Egyptians rejected the British proposals. There was thus no agreement on uniform, the numbers of technicians who would remain for the final one and half years of the seven-year agreement now accepted by the Egyptians, or the conditions under which the base would be automatically available. There was also no agreement on staging rights and the consultation process for renewing or terminating the agreement (445). While Robertson continued to believe that an agreement in line with British requirements was both possible and desirable, others like Churchill and Hankey saw little or no advantage in the kind of agreement now being sought (450, 452).

The end of Churchill's resistance to the loss of Egypt and Anglo–Egyptian agreement over the evacuation of the Suez base, Nov 1953–July 1954
Militarily the defence of the Middle East was becoming increasingly impractical as the implications of defence cutbacks sank in. It was now a question of maintaining forces to convince friends and enemies alike of the seriousness of British intentions, rather than catering for the region's actual defence needs. As Sir John Harding, the chief of the imperial general staff, put it, the issue was whether to maintain 'the effective semblance of military power in the Middle East' (451). Rather than plan to provide the necessary forces to defend the Middle East as a whole, Britain would have to think more about protecting its increasingly important economic interests in the Persian Gulf and ensuring that British prestige was not damaged by any arrangements for the Canal Zone.[112]

Military cuts were forcing the British to look more to indigenous forces and to a strategic reserve which could be deployed in the Middle East to bolster the inadequate remaining troops. In conditions of global war this featured a key element of unreality as it was assumed that a Soviet nuclear strike would make conditions at British ports so terrible that the despatch of any Middle East reinforcements would be unlikely.[113] There was also the problem of how and where to redeploy the forces that would be left in the region when the base in Egypt had been evacuated.

This latter issue lay at the heart of the problem for officials grappling with the need to make reductions in British Middle Eastern forces. The Foreign Office believed an agreement would enable the cuts to be implemented, whereas staying put in the face of Egyptian opposition would make them impossible. Moreover, if a key rationale for a defence presence in the Middle East was to demonstrate the seriousness of Britain's intentions, this was unlikely to be achieved if a reduction in forces was accompanied by a failure to reach an agreement with Egypt and the abandonment of the base (457, 465).

Churchill, unlike his foreign secretary, opposed any agreement which might be interpreted as 'scuttle' and suggested the despatch of air and land forces to Khartoum to intimidate the Egyptians (456). The prime minister continued to regard forcing the Egyptians into submission as a better option than negotiations (466). For Churchill, the breaking off of negotiations would enable Britain to regain the freedom to redeploy its Middle Eastern forces at a time and in a manner of its choosing and thus avoid the approbrium of a scuttle. For Eden and the Foreign Office, failure to reach an agreement would appear much more of a scuttle as all rights in the base would be abandoned and Britain would be faced with the dangerous and costly task of evacuating civilian and military personnel in the face of Egyptian hostility (465). There was general agreement on the need for a solution to the Egyptian problem that would maintain and strengthen British influence in the Middle East through preserving the semblance of power. How best this could be achieved continued to be a matter of debate in 1954 (468–469, 472).

On 12 January Eden presented the Cabinet with three alternatives if negotiations failed. He proposed to state that in the event of failure Britain intended to alter its arrangements in the Middle East and to wind up the base. This would not deprive Britain of its existing treaty rights and when the treaty expired in 1956 Britain would accept arbitration on the terms of its revision and on the arrangements for the future defence of the Canal (472, 478).

Before the Cabinet discussed these proposals, ministers received another memorandum from the COS and a further note by Eden on the legal position (475, 479). The COS were prepared to make concessions on uniform and to accept serious military disadvantages in order to obtain an agreement. Eden was nervous about the political implications of the former, but had always been prepared to contemplate the latter. Churchill remained opposed to making concessions and preferred to break off the negotiations.(477).

The Cabinet agreed to urge the Americans to pressurise the Egyptians into supporting the British proposals which had been put forward in October (480). The Americans duly informed Nasser that no aid would be forthcoming until the heads of agreement had been signed. Nasser's response was that it might be possible for the Egyptians to concede on availability if Turkey was attacked but not Iran. The Egyptians were definitely not prepared to concede on uniforms (483).

American pressure on the Egyptians was important in helping Nasser win over the more hard line members of the Revolutionary Command Council for the concession on Turkey. When this was studied and discussed in London, it emerged that Nasser's concession on availability would be militarily more advantageous than the British proposal of October 1953. Unfortunately this was not entirely welcome to the Cabinet because it would also be *perceived* as a British concession which deviated from the final October offer (489). The Cabinet was now inclined to modify the evacuation plan recommended by Eden by reducing the troops to the level permitted under the 1936 treaty rather than by evacuating completely (484–485). This was likely to arouse Egyptian resentment, and as the British would have difficulty evacuating without Egyptian co-operation it was therefore self-defeating (493). On this the supervising under-secretary of the African Department agreed with the COS that a declaration of standing on the treaty rights would produce guerrilla activity which would make the detailed evacuation plan out of the question.[114]

The debate in early 1954 on the Egyptian base took place in yet another period of uncertainty regarding the British approach to Middle Eastern defence and the broader requirements of global strategy. Not all of the problems stemmed from the growing pressures on British defence expenditure. In January 1954 the Americans finally decided that their new approach to the cold war in the Middle East, and the provision of forces for hot war, would involve military aid to Pakistan and the creation of a Turco–Pakistani Pact which was duly signed in April 1954. The next step would be the provision of aid to Iraq in order to strengthen further the northern tier of states which was to replace Egypt as the main pillar of American cold war and military strategy in the region. This threatened to undermine Britain's predominant position in Iraq as American resources would produce much greater quantities of aid than Britain. The chief of the air staff also complained that the Americans failed to realise that the supply of arms could be used by Britain as a bargaining counter to obtain base rights.[115] It therefore became much more important for Britain to revise the Anglo–Iraqi treaty which was to expire in 1957 and which enabled the RAF to use facilities at Habbanyia and Shaiba. In order to persuade the Iraqis to agree to provide facilities for Britain it would be necessary to convince them of the value of a British military role in the defence of their country. But the British plans for defending the Middle East were based on the inner ring and, despite the commitment to deploy forces in forward positions in north-east Iraq, it was not the intention to defend those positions against a Soviet attack (494). The British thus had to consider alternative defence plans which would require extra forces if Iraq were to be defended, or find some other way of retaining their military position in Iraq.

The option of extra forces had been out of the question for some time. Both in the Middle East and Europe the position was that force goals were regarded as ideals rather than as targets.[116] The Iraqis therefore had to be convinced that Britain could defend them when it was most unlikely that this would be possible. This required much greater emphasis on the forward strategy and visible signs, such as pre-stocking in Turkey, that the British intended to fulfil the commitments they were unable to meet. Ironically, in February 1954, the chief of the air staff deemed its success to be dependent on Iraqi confidence in British support.[117] The irony of Britain's position was made clear in a JPS paper which pointed out that unlike 1952, when the forward strategy was first discussed, Britain could no longer rely on a fully developed base in Egypt. Once the forces in Egypt were redeployed, Britain's position would be much weaker and therefore it would be more difficult to persuade the Middle Eastern countries that Britain intended to defend them.[118]

Meanwhile ministers were considering withdrawing from the Canal Zone without an agreement and in a manner linked to the 1936 treaty which was certain to produce Egyptian hostility and make it unlikely that the withdrawal could be accomplished successfully. Officials in the Foreign Office and Treasury were aware of the problem (498–499) and it was the politicians, led by Churchill, who were refusing to face up to the difficulties of an increasingly absurd situation. With no resolution as yet in sight, an internal political crisis in Egypt effectively ruled out any further talks. Nasser and Neguib were battling over the future constitution and the exercise of personal power. With the outlawing of the Muslim Brotherhood in January 1954 the regime became totally dependent on the army for support and was likely to remain so unless there was a return to a parliamentary system. On 25 February Neguib resigned and Nasser became prime minister. Disturbances followed, including a number of serious anti-British incidents in the Canal Zone. Neguib, who appeared to favour a presidential system of civilian government, was reinstated as president two days later and as prime minister on 8 March following an announcement by the Revolutionary Command Council that a constituent assembly would be created in July. Any successful negotiation of a British withdrawal would have been beneficial to the regime and therefore in mid-March the Egyptians made clear their wish to resume negotiations. However by 14 April Nasser was back as prime minister and a further purge of old guard politicians took place. The Command Council seemed back in control although the commitment to permit the re-establishment of political parties remained.[119]

In March Eden was even more convinced that an agreement was necessary and he produced a series of new proposals, even though Harding had changed his mind and now saw no value in an agreement.[120] The Egyptian concession on Turkey was accepted and to solve the uniform problem Eden proposed to use civilian contractors rather than military technicians in the base. In return the Egyptians would be asked to extend the duration of the agreement from seven to twenty years (503). On 22 March, after two discussions, the Cabinet agreed that Eden should explore with the Americans detailed proposals for the maintenance of the base by civilians (505).[121]

The Foreign Office was concerned that further delay on an Anglo–Egyptian agreement would prejudice Britain's position in Iraq. With the Americans pressing ahead with aid to Pakistan, the Foreign Office began to attach greater importance to defence arrangements with Iraq as part of the American-inspired northern tier. Yet Churchill was still hoping to use American participation in, or support for, Middle East security arrangements as a way out of Britain's difficulties in Egypt.[122] The prime minister had failed to grasp the change in American policy which attached much less significance to Egypt and to which the British would have to adapt if they were to preserve their position in the Middle East and Iraq.

The new emphasis on Iraq and the northern tier was in part intended to prevent the Americans undermining British influence in the Middle East. As Selwyn Lloyd, minister of state at the Foreign Office put it, Britain should retain the initiative in obtaining a desirable settlement with Iraq and hold off US influence.[123] Hence the commitment to treaty negotiations with the Iraqis and to a revised forward strategy. British influence in the Middle East had long been linked to defence arrangements and, as the COS argued, in order to maintain Britain's position as a world power it was necessary to retain the existing overseas forces and bases except those in Korea, Trieste and Egypt.[124] The use of nuclear weapons was to be the key element in the new forward strategy façade in the Middle East and they were also seen as a more general means of maintaining global influence.[125] If Britain used atomic weapons in the Middle East, which, however, were not yet operational, this would reduce the scale of the Soviet advance, allow for the possibility of holding the passes of north-east Iraq and convince the Iraqis of the effectiveness of Britain's commitment to their defence and of the British need for air bases (514).

As discussions continued on this modification of Middle East defence strategy, the Commanders-in-Chief were expressing some unease about Eden's idea of civilian contractors for the Egyptian base. Their preference was to accept the Egyptian position on uniform in exchange for Nasser's concession on Turkey as this would be more likely to produce an agreement (511). For domestic political reasons, Conservative ministers were reluctant to make concessions to the Egyptians on uniform whatever the views of the military, or indeed the Treasury who were concerned that the costs of civilian contract labour were higher than those of military technicians. As a result the Foreign Office suggested a smaller or nucleus base in Egypt in order to keep down the costs of contract labour (515).

This was compatible with the new forward strategy based on the use of nuclear weapons because it was not expected that forces would be sent to the Middle East in the early stages of a war. Thus there would be no need for a large base to maintain them until much later. By 22 June 1954 the service departments had accepted the contract labour scheme and the Cabinet formally endorsed it as the basis of a new approach to the Egyptians (523, 525).

The timing of negotiations would depend on the scale of the anti-British incidents in the Canal Zone. Towards the end of June there was a marked improvement and negotiations formally resumed on 10 July when the Egyptians were presented with a British draft heads of agreement (531). The British hoped to extend the withdrawal period from fifteen months to two years and to extend the duration of the agreement from seven to twenty years. They justified this on the grounds that the *Egyptians had conceded* that an attack on Turkey would produce automatic availability and that Britain had agreed to employ civilian contractors for maintaining a nucleus base rather than use military technicians for dealing with more extensive facilities.

Stevenson pointed out that the Egyptians were deeply committed to the fifteen-month withdrawal period and irrevocably committed to the seven-year duration period (534). But for political reasons the government preferred to extend the seven-year duration period. This difficulty was compounded by the fact that both the Treasury and the COS preferred to extend the withdrawal period because it would allow for the removal of a greater volume of stores and leave fewer items to be abandoned to the Egyptians.

After a memorandum on the outstanding issues had been prepared on 23 July[126] it was agreed to send the secretary of state for war, Anthony Head, to Egypt. He joined the negotiating team on 25 July and his proposals for a seven-year agreement with an evacuation time of twenty months were discussed in Cabinet on 26 July.[127] The heads of agreement were signed on this basis (541), leaving the detailed arrangements to be worked out in accordance with the agreement.

The growing importance of the Iraqi–Levant strategy for Middle East defence and the contradictions of the Baghdad Pact, Aug 1954–Mar 1955

As the nine years of difficulties in Anglo–Egyptian relations appeared to be ending, new and disturbing questions arose in relation to Britain's contribution to the defence of the Middle East. Britain faced even more problems in producing a rational policy for Middle East defence designed to do anything other than defend British pretensions to be a great world power with important responsibilities. In 1954, British military planners were focusing more on Iraq, given its position in the northern tier. It was a shift essentially produced by American initiatives and economic power rather than by technological developments or the changing nature of the Soviet threat. As constraints on defence expenditure grew, the goal of Middle East defence became increasingly geared to defending prestige and status from Arab and American challenges as opposed to meeting a military threat from the Soviet Union. In the words of Sir Neville Brownjohn, as British strength in the Middle East declined it became more important to show that Britain meant business there.[128] As the difficulties of providing military forces increased, the political need to defend a greater area also grew. Defence cuts and the idea of a strategic reserve, the proposed use of nuclear weapons to reduce the speed and effectiveness of the Soviet advance (both of which made a large, readily available base in Egypt less necessary), and the American interest in the northern tier all contributed to a reassessment of the forward strategy in order to attempt to hold the passes in north-east Iraq. Yet in the summer of 1954, when the Americans initially requested planning studies for the defence of the Middle East based on the Zagros mountains, the CIGS stated it would not be possible in the face of a heavy enemy attack.[130] By contrast, the BDCC (ME) did not want to rule out the possibility in view of the effect of the strategic nuclear offensive.[131]

This debate on what was militarily possible paled into insignificance in relation to what had to be done to preserve British prestige and credibility in the Middle East. Maintaining Britain's position in Iraq, which was dependent on a military presence under a new guise, was clearly vital. Also important was a presence in a Cyprus under British sovereignty where the new Middle East GHQ would be located. The military argued for the retention of British sovereignty in Cyprus for political reasons and acknowledged that the strategic argument was subordinate. However as Sir William Dickson, the chief of the air staff, remarked, 'the need to demonstrate our presence in the Middle East is not a good argument to use'.[132] The JPS were equally convinced of the supreme importance of political factors in relation to Britain's overseas military presence, and with regard to Cyprus they noted: 'Above all we must strengthen our position as a major power and thus maintain our influence in the councils of the world.'[133] In broader terms the JPS still believed that the military means to exert British influence as a world power and to meet Britain's cold war requirements had to take preference over preparations for a global conflict with the Soviets.[134]

In Iraq, prime minister Nuri Said had informed the British in August 1954 that after elections in September he wanted to hold secret talks on defence within the framework of a regional defence pact.[135] Once the elections were over, the Iraqi leader visited Turkey to discuss the idea of developing a northern tier. Nasser had already ruled out the extension of the Arab League security pact. This produced a dilemma for the British. A northern tier defence treaty would provide the perfect cover for the retention of the facilities they needed in Iraq to symbolise their power and influence in the Middle East. Yet there would also be disadvantages as Egypt was opposed to any immediate western involvement in Middle Eastern defence arrangements.[136] In addition Nasser was determined to build up the strength of the Arab League rather than become involved in defence arrangements with Iraq, Turkey and Pakistan (556). Arousing Egyptian hostility was seen in the Foreign Office as to some extent discounting the benefits that had been gained through the Anglo–Egyptian agreement (549).

The problem of preserving good relations with the main Arab states was compounded by the difficulty of convincing them of the effectiveness of Britain's contribution to Middle East defence. The withdrawal from the Canal Zone and the significant reduction made in Britain's peacetime presence could in theory be compensated for by the use of nuclear weapons and the reinforcement of the region by a strategic reserve in Britain. But Britain did not have nuclear weapons for operational use, and in the unlikely event of the reserve being ready and available for the Middle East, the military still doubted if overseas theatres could be supplied from the UK in the face of the Soviet nuclear assault on seaports (551). Moreover, after 1956 automatic overflying rights in Egypt would lapse and Britain would no longer be able to guarantee rapid airborne reinforcements of the Middle East.[137] Finally, it was deemed necessary to supply forces deployed in Iraq through Basra yet according to JIC estimates Basra would be liable to attack between D+38 and D+40.[138] Not surprisingly the Foreign Office wanted to conceal the nakedness of British reinforcement plans (559).

A further difficulty was the Arab–Israeli dispute which prevented the effective courting of the Arab states through large scale arms supplies designed to help them defend the Middle East. More generally it was difficult to see how the Middle East could be united against an external threat when many of the states in the region felt themselves more threatened by their neighbours. In November 1954 the British and the Americans agreed on the need to produce a settlement to the Arab–Israeli dispute, and detailed discussions began at the official level in January 1955. This futile effort became embodied in a peace plan codenamed Alpha which in turn became hopelessly entangled in the Anglo–American attempts to create a regional defence organisation.

In January 1955 the dilemma facing the British was whether to proceed with a northern tier arrangement advocated by Nuri and the Americans, or to wait for the possible involvement of the Egyptians in an organisation based on the Arab League. The latter would have more chance of uniting the Arab world in a defence agreement, but it would not be acceptable to the Egyptians before the final evacuation of British forces from the Canal Zone. Under the terms of the 1954 agreement this would not take place until 1956. By that time the opportunity to retain military facilities in Iraq under the umbrella of a regional defence agreement would have been lost. Within the Foreign Office, C A E Shuckburgh, the supervising under-secretary of the Middle East Departments, maintained that the Arab–Israeli conflict should be addressed before attempting to set up a regional defence organisation. In early 1955, the British, to the annoyance of the State Department, were keener to postpone the creation of a regional defence agreement than the Americans (568).

However, following an announcement on the 13 January that the Iraqis and the Turks intended to sign a defence pact, pressure on the British to join increased, and not just from the Americans. The ambassador in Baghdad, Sir Michael Wright, was enthusiastic and told Nuri not to be deflected by the Egyptians.[139] Eden minuted his approval and a senior official, J G Ward, argued that although Shuckburgh had warned of a price to be paid for damaging relations with Egypt, the 'bird in the hand' of the Turco–Iraqi pact was worth more than the risks of waiting to formalise any defence relations with the Arab world. This was said to be justified in relation to the latest defence strategy (573), which had been defined to satisfy the political requirements of maintaining British prestige and influence in the Middle East. Shuckburgh's suggestion of waiting until the settlement of the Arab–Israeli issue did not find favour. However damaging Shuckburgh's policy might have been in relation to facilities in Iraq, the long-term consequences of rejecting it were equally damaging because Egyptian co-operation was essential for any attempt to achieve an Arab–Israeli settlement.

Nasser's absolute refusal to support a northern tier defence scheme was based on a number of aspirations and fears. They included a desire to maintain Egyptian leadership of the Arab world and a concern that close association with the west would destroy what credit had been gained from the 1954 base agreement; this would further weaken Nasser's domestic position already under threat from a number of sides. There was also a danger that American aid would be directed more firmly towards the Iraqi-sponsored organisation. The Egyptian government was not alone in opposing the northern tier defence scheme. The French, suspected by Eden of attempting to wreck the Turco–Iraqi Pact,[140] were concerned that their influence in the Levant would be undermined, especially if Iraq used the defence treaty to absorb Syria; they were also fearful of what action Nasser might take in Africa if he was isolated from the Arab world (575–576). The Israelis were also disturbed by the prospect of a regional defence organisation containing Arab states. As the British ambassador, Sir John Nicholls pointed out, the pact would strengthen the hands of those Israelis who argued that Israel would always be ignored unless it exploited its nuisance value by adopting an aggressive foreign policy.[141]

The negotiations over the Turco–Iraqi Pact continued until the end of February, partly because Nuri was suspicious of Turkish designs on Mosul and was determined to avoid providing an opportunity for Turkish troops to enter Iraqi territory (583). When finally signed on 24 February 1955, the pact was limited to an agreement to exchange military information, to provide mutual assistance regarding arms production, and to engage in joint studies of co-operation in the event of an attack on either party.

The British were left with the formal decision of whether to join this seemingly innocuous association and the Cabinet gave its approval on 15 March. The Baghdad Pact, as it was subsequently known, was so hated and feared by many of the important Middle East players that it proved to be the catalyst for the developing crisis which ultimately engulfed the Middle East in 1956 with the second Arab–Israeli war. This conflict, which began with a French and British approved Israeli invasion of Egypt, led to the destruction of most of the remaining British influence in the Middle East with the humiliating débâcle at Suez.

The Egyptian opposition to the pact became increasingly clear in March 1955 with the announcement that an alternative defence grouping was to be formed by Egypt, Syria and Saudi Arabia (581). With alarming speed the desperate British attempt to cling on to defence facilities in order to maintain a position in the Middle East escalated into a competition with Egypt over which defence grouping should carry out military tasks that were beyond both of them. Politically, it was important for the British to persuade the as yet uncommitted Arab states to join their defence grouping, even though the Egyptians had not made their agreement with the Syrians and the Saudis into a formal treaty.

Eight days after the Cabinet agreed to join the Turco–Iraqi Pact based on the American idea of the northern tier, the COS produced a paper geared to this concept. The Middle East was now to be defended on the outer ring and the forward strategy based on the inner ring was to be replaced. Throughout the closing months of 1954, the military planners had pointed to the obvious difficulties of holding the Soviets on the line of the Zagros mountains (the outer ring) even with the use of tactical nuclear weapons. Given that Britain would have only one armoured division and eight RAF squadrons in the region the lack of resources was evident. The planners not only emphasised the need for the strategic nuclear offensive and the tactical use of nuclear weapons (nuclear interdiction) to reduce the weight of the Soviet attack, but pointed to a number of other criteria which would have to be met. These included the availability of Commonwealth forces and stockpiling in peacetime (563). Although the use of nuclear weapons had boosted hopes of providing more than a facade of defence, the failure to meet these criteria and the remote prospect of being able to reinforce the Middle East theatre in global war soon restored the pre-nuclear status quo of the façade.

The outer ring defence concept was examined with the Turks and the Americans in March 1955 and a detailed report produced. The greatest shortfall of available forces was in aircraft where the predicted deficit ranged from 275 to 487; the higher estimate was actually greater than the total aircraft available in the theatre (580).[142] To make matters worse, the Americans were refusing to store nuclear weapons in bases not under US control and they would therefore have to be flown in, by which time the Soviets would have had time to launch two nuclear strikes. A further factor was that in the estimated shortfall of ground forces of between two and four divisions, the British armoured division was included in the total of available forces, even though it would in fact be in Libya and other parts of the region and there would be no means of getting it to the Zagros mountains before D+42. More generally the COS stated that British forces would be 'so widely dispersed in Cyprus, Jordan and Libya and reinforcements from the United Kingdom and the

Commonwealth so doubtful of arrival, that short of a drastic reorganisation and reappraisal of the logistic factors involved, our contribution was certain to be ineffective'. The COS believed that without redeployment to more forward areas, Britain's military contribution could not fulfil Britain's commitments under the pact or maintain Britain's influence and position in the Middle East against the growing interests of the US (587).

The collapsing façade of Middle East defence and covert action against Egypt, Apr 1955–Dec 1956

In these inauspicious circumstances, Britain formally acceded to the Turco–Iraqi Pact on 2 April 1955. The pact was to be the basis, allegedly, for uniting the Middle Eastern states against the Soviet menace. In reality it was an attempt to fix another layer of prestige and credibilty to Britain's declining economic and military power. The Baghdad Pact had to succeed if the informal British empire was to be maintained. Yet it was detested by the Egyptians who were vital to the Anglo–American efforts to set-tle the Arab–Israeli dispute. Moreover, not only did the pact sour relations with the Egyptians, it also brought to the surface every latent conflict and rivalry existing within the Middle East. If the Soviets had wanted to stir up trouble in the region they could have produced nothing better than the Baghdad Pact.

As Nasser attempted to woo Arab states away from the Baghdad Pact, his position was threatened by another problem. On 28 February 1955 Israeli defence forces launched a large scale attack on an Egyptian military camp in Gaza. In part the raid was seen by Ben Gurion, the new Israeli defence minister, and Moshe Dayan, the chief of staff, as revenge for the Egyptian executions of Israeli intelligence saboteurs who had been responsible for blowing up British and American buildings in Cairo in an attempt to poison relations between Egypt and the west.[143] The assault on Gaza killed thirty-eight Egyptians and effectively postponed progress with Alpha for several months. Nasser responded by organising raids into Israel and by increasing the strength of the Egyptian armed forces. Already insecure, Nasser's domestic position was further threatened if nothing was done to offset Israeli attacks. Nasser had therefore to secure arms as well as undermine the Baghdad Pact. The west, for its part, could not afford to erode Israeli military superiority until the conflict with the Arabs was brought to an end. But this could not be achieved unless Egypt was prepared to lead the Arab states down the road to peace, and this in turn would not happen while the Baghdad Pact was producing such divisions in the Arab world.

In the US there was now a realisation that the Baghdad Pact was going to be singularly unhelpful in making Alpha succeed. The Americans, like the British, were divided over how best to deal with the problem. How far should Nasser be appeased by turning away from the northern tier? Should the pact be left to wither or should efforts be made to reconcile the two rival defence groupings? Should Nasser be isolated by persuading more Arab states to join the pact and forcing him to come into line? Or should the pact be developed only by including non-Arab states? These issues were debated throughout 1955 and caused considerable conflict between London and Washington. In May it seemed to be accepted in Britain that no encouragement should be given to any Arab state bordering Israel to join the pact even though the Turks were working for Lebanese accession.[144] However by the autumn the British were making renewed efforts to bring Arab states into the pact.

In August the JPS were adamant that British influence and prestige in the Middle

East could not be maintained without the retention of Cyprus. The essentiality of the Egyptian base had been replaced by the essentiality of the threatened facilities in Iraq. These had now been secured, but British facilities in Cyprus, deemed to depend on British sovereignty, were under threat so they too became for a while essential for the British military. The reason was now not to defend the Middle East, which was allegedly being done through the Iraqi passes, but because 'British influence and prestige in the Middle East as a whole could not be maintained without the retention of our present military position in Cyprus, which is therefore strategically essential' (597).

A further factor relevant to British influence and prestige, and therefore of strategic importance for the military, was the successful American testing of the hydrogen bomb in 1952 which increased the significance of nuclear weapons. The need for these weapons to convince the Middle Eastern states of Britain's importance to their defence was matched by a determination to acquire the right number of them to convince the world, and particularly the Americans, of Britain's importance as a great world power. This was part of a shift towards defining military requirements more in political terms, as Britain became less capable of providing adequate military resources. More particularly, as part of the ultimately unsuccessful attempt in 1955 to agree on a long-term defence strategy,[145] it was noted that the pattern of British forces would no longer depend on what was militarily necessary but on the minimum required to achieve Britain's political aims. Unless Britain could continue to play a full part in the cold war, including limited war, it would lose its position as a great world power.[146] Thus the size of Britain's nuclear force could not be defined in military terms, not least because the Americans were refusing to provide details of the Srategic Air Command's targeting plans. What mattered was that the nuclear deterrent should be large enough to give Britain a say in allied strategic plans.[147] Equally no defence cuts could be accepted which threatened Britain's position as a world power, her position in NATO or her leadership of the Commonwealth.[148]

Defining a defence strategy that would maintain great power status was clearly related to the maintenance of Britain's position in the Middle East. In September 1955 new problems appeared, which, like the Baghdad Pact, made it impossible for all of Britain's Middle Eastern aims to be achieved. These stemmed from Nasser's decision to purchase arms from the Soviets. Israeli military superiority in the region would be undermined within a year, the time needed for the arms to be absorbed. The British feared that if nothing was done the Israelis would attack the Egyptians to prevent the loss of military superiority, and thereby enable the Soviets to interfere in the Middle East on the side of the Arabs. But taking action could be equally disastrous. To outbid the Soviets over Egyptian arms supplies would, even if Britain could afford it, be seen as rewarding those states which had turned to Moscow; to provide more arms to pro-western states like Iraq would increase Israeli insecurity and would have to involve the Americans who would be seen as supplanting Britain as the dominant regional power. Supplying the Israelis to compensate for the Arab arms would weaken Jordan's military position and make it impossible for Britain to meet her treaty obligations to King Hussein. The invidious British position produced a number of extreme suggestions as to how to escape from it, including the abandonment of Israel and the overthrow of Nasser (599).

After consultation with the Americans (602), no drastic action was decided upon and no dramatic counter-measures were taken. The American ambassador in Cairo, Henry Byroade, was in favour of abandoning the Baghdad Pact in order to assist plan Alpha, but the British came to see the extension of the pact as a way of showing displeasure with Nasser while strengthening their own position. The dilemma of the arms deal was that to be too tough with Nasser would drive him further into the arms of the Soviets, while to do nothing would involve a loss of British face in the Arab world.[149] Eden, now prime minister, found this increasingly hard to take as Egyptian propaganda against the Baghdad Pact, against the British position in their dispute with the Saudis over Buraimi and against British colonialism in general became more strident.

The importance of expanding the Baghdad Pact increased by the end of October 1955. It was needed to offset the carrot of Aswan dam aid required by Alpha and also in response to Egyptian support for the Saudis as the Buraimi crisis deepened. At the beginning of October the British believed that Dulles had agreed to the inclusion of Iran, a non-Arab state, in the Baghdad Pact (602),[150] but the head of the Foreign Office was keen to persuade other Arab states to join (610). Sir Ivone Kirkpatrick's stance ignored the more cautious elements in the Foreign Office who doubted the wisdom of Jordanian accession. Eden, despite doubts over the timing, was in agreement with the permanent under-secretary's hard line when Byroade urged the British to allow a few more months for Alpha to succeed before extending the pact, noting: 'The stronger the Northern tier the better Nasser will behave'.[151]

The Americans were as divided as the British over the expansion of the pact, but in London the issue was part of a broader discussion within the Foreign Office over whether Arab states could be persuaded to take a line independent of Egypt (611). It was a question of whether co-operation with Egypt was essential to Britain's Middle Eastern position or whether working with other Arab states, in opposition to Egypt, would eventually force an end to Egyptian hostility. On the one hand the British were infuriated by what they regarded as incessant anti-British propaganda (630), while on the other Nasser gave repeated assurances of his desire to co-operate with the west in meeting the communist challenge (617, 623). To isolate Nasser not only meant abandoning plan Alpha but risking further Soviet–Egyptian co-operation.

By the beginning of 1956 strategic planning, in line with the Baghdad Pact, was focused on the outer ring. Yet as the military acknowledged: '. . . we have neither the men nor the money in current circumstances to make the Baghdad Pact effective militarily' (628). The idea was to fall back on the Zagros mountain passes from an initial position in the Elburz mountains south and west of the Caspian Sea in Iran. To implement the strategy successfully was said to be dependent on the US strategic offensive and the tactical use of nuclear weapons (622). But as the JPS made clear, with no nuclear weapons likely to be available before 1959, 'it was the primary concern of existing deception plans for the Middle East to cover up this nuclear deficiency by portraying a nuclear capability for our forces in the theatre now'. Since Britain was 'deceiving both the Soviets and our allies with regard to our nuclear capability' the lack of such a capability was on no account to be revealed (621). It was, however, acknowledged that defending the Middle East in global war was much less important than the cold war need to prevent the peacetime destabilisation of the region (620).

In January the Egyptian base was deemed no longer necessary even for cold war purposes and the base would be more of a liability in any global war involving the use of hydrogen bombs (618). There was also the difficulty of supplying forces in the northern tier from Egypt which prompted discussion of an alternative approach to Middle East defence with more attention being paid to the oil producing regions of the Persian Gulf and less to the eastern Mediterranean and the northern tier (624, 627). Politically this would have a damaging impact on the Baghdad Pact which was still perceived as the best way of preventing Nasser gaining influence in the region.

Growing tensions between Britain and Egypt produced concerns that the Egyptians might abrogate the 1954 agreement or take measures against the few remaining forces in the Canal Zone which Britain would be powerless to prevent. Such would be the perceived damage to British prestige that the military began to argue for total abandonment of the base and redeployment elsewhere to avoid possible humiliation; this would be accompanied by an announcement that Britain would not want to renew the 1954 agreement when it expired in 1961 (625). Having struggled to obtain an agreement to safeguard British prestige, the same considerations now seemed to require its abandonment.

In global war Jordan was now more important than Egypt as an air base for the launching of tactical nuclear strikes and for maintaining British lines of communication. While this might have been a reason for concern over the troubles in Jordan and the dismissal on 1 March 1956 of the Arab Legion commander, General Glubb, the overriding consideration for the British military was the political necessity of supporting Iraq and the countries of the Baghdad Pact by maintaining a Jordan friendly to the west:[152] 'Existing facilities and the stationing of forces in Jordan are not essential to UK strategy, but overriding political considerations demand the retention of UK influence and interests in Jordan. This involves the retention of British forces in Jordan for the present'.[153]

As Iraq's relations with Egypt deteriorated from January to March 1956 with the trial of the Egyptian military attaché in Baghdad for subversion, the battle for influence between Britain and Egypt and their supporters centred on Jordan. The nature of this battle was now increasingly defined by MI6 whose operative in Cairo was allegedly managing a source named Lucky Break. The source claimed to have access to the highest levels of the Egyptian government.[154] The intelligence received, whether genuine or not, had a significant impact on the small circle of policy makers in London who were privy to it. It portrayed Nasser as an ambitious, anti-western leader aiming to take over the Middle East and it strengthened the hard liners in London, especially the prime minister. The hard liners were increasingly frustrated by plan Alpha's requirement for co-operation with Nasser, when to them it appeared necessary to wage a diplomatic war against Egypt through the expansion of the Baghdad Pact.

A further consideration aroused British concerns about Egypt in early 1956. Up until February the British had always believed that the danger of war in the Middle East came from Israeli action. However undesirable in a military sense, politically this at least offered the prospect of joining with the Arabs, particularly Jordan to whom Britain had treaty obligations, against Israel. From February the British began to change their assessment[155] which raised the prospect of intervention, under the tripartite declaration,[156] on the side of the Israelis; this would mean the end of British influence in Jordan and the rest of the Arab world, with all the perceived consequences for British oil supplies.

Those who still looked to an Arab–Israeli settlement as the key to the cold war battle and the maintenance of British influence in the Middle East were now reliant on a link between the Baghdad Pact and an Arab League security pact which Nasser seemed willing to consider (632). This would be the only way to reconcile the conflicting requirements of Alpha and the Baghdad Pact. However, by the end of the first week in March, Alpha had finally collapsed. Eisenhower had sent a personal emissary, Robert Anderson, to the Middle East in January 1956 in an attempt to achieve a settlement. The mission travelled back and forth between Cairo and Tel Aviv until on 6 March Nasser informed Anderson that he could not attempt to win Arab acceptance of any peace plan agreed with the British and the Americans by putting it forward as an Egyptian proposal. This removed at a stroke the main reason for concentrating the peace efforts on Egypt as the country able to sell a settlement to the rest of the Arab world. It also sounded the death knell of a British policy which aimed at ending the Arab–Israeli dispute and uniting the Middle East against the Soviet threat in order to maintain Britain's position in the Arab world (634).

As the Americans considered how best to respond to the collapse of Alpha, the British opted for a policy of outright hostility to Nasser (635). Based on 'absolutely reliable information', Eden informed Eisenhower that Nasser aimed to unseat Nuri Said and the King of Iraq, overthrow King Hussein and King Idris of Libya and establish Arab republics in French north Africa before finally removing King Saud.[157] For MI6 this would be the prelude to the Middle East falling under complete Soviet domination. However influential British views might have been, the Americans drew up another secret plan, codenamed Omega, designed, in co-operation with Britain, to destabilise Nasser's regime in order to convince him that he should work with the west rather than collaborate with the Soviet Union. The Americans hoped that by the use of economic weapons, black radio broadcasts and the isolation of Nasser in the Arab world, the Egyptian leader would return to the western fold; the British were more inclined to see Omega as a way of bringing down Nasser and enabling Iraq and the Baghdad Pact to serve as the focus of Arab unity.

Anglo–American discussions on the details of Omega began at the end of March and although some extreme British ideas were rejected, plans went ahead for the overthrow of the Syrian government as a means of isolating Nasser. Initially the British were also quite open in their criticism of the Egyptian leader and the British press revealed that Britain planned to hit back at him. This contrasted with the Americans who were attempting to conceal their change of policy. The idea of a 'cover policy' was eventually adopted by the Foreign Office,[158] but by then it was too late to leave any doubts about British intentions in Nasser's mind (637, 638). With Nasser aware of the British change of policy the battle for Middle Eastern influence entered a new phase. On 26 July in retaliation against the hostile policy adopted by the British and the Americans, which culminated in the decision to withdraw the Aswan dam finance, Nasser nationalised the Suez Canal Company.

The humiliation this entailed for Britain led ultimately to the invasion of Egypt in a vain attempt to remove Nasser and make good the damage he had inflicted on British prestige and status in the Middle East. The result was that all Britain's justifications for maintaining a presence in the Middle East were temporarily or permanently destroyed. The Suez invasion saw Britain attacking an Arab state when it was in the Middle East to protect the Arabs from a Soviet invasion. The Suez invasion closed the Suez Canal which Britain had to protect to ensure the passage of Middle Eastern oil. The Suez invasion witnessed an Arab–Israeli conflict which

Britain had been attempting to prevent in order to deny the Soviets greater influence in the region. The Suez invasion reinforced the air barrier in the eastern Mediterranean which Britain needed to cross to support its forces that were committed to the Baghdad Pact. The Suez invasion elevated Nasser's status in the Arab world. And the Suez invasion alienated the US with whom Britain needed to co-operate in the region and strengthened American influence which had to be avoided if Britain was not to be overshadowed.

The invasion occurred in the middle of a government review of Britain's position in world affairs which conceded that Britain had attempted to do too much since 1945. In the Middle East the maintenance of vital oil supplies was deemed to depend more on the friendly co-operation of the producing and transit countries rather than on the actual strength of British forces in the region (641); and it was suggested that these forces should be kept to a bare minimum (645). But Britain still attempted to invade and occupy part of a country in a manner which the instigator of the enterprise had ruled out in 1951 when Britain's military capabilities in Egypt were much greater.

The emotive nature of the Suez invasion stemmed from the loss of prestige resulting from Britain's failure to achieve a *modus vivendi* with Egypt despite the ultimate success of the base negotiations in 1954. Britain did not want to make political or military concessions for fear of being perceived as weak. Yet the very weakness of Britain's position combined with regional conflicts to ensure that no financial or military offerings could be made to win over the Egyptians. This was bound to be troublesome because Britain was competing, not just for power and influence over Egypt with Egyptians but with Egypt over power and influence in the Middle East.

The initial claim of Bevin and the Labour government that they sought an equal partnership in defence matters with Egypt was fraudulent because of the emotive need to appear the dominant force in the Middle East. Thus the initial negotiations over evacuating the base were conducted by Bevin, the Foreign Office and the military, if not by Stansgate, on the basis that they had the right to make demands on the Egyptians. It was claimed from the start in 1945–1946 that this right, based on the importance of empire-Commonwealth defence, was linked to the importance of defending the Middle East. Strategy passed through a number of different phases and plans, all of which after the abandonment of the Tel Aviv–Ramallah line were at best regarded as implausible. Until 1953 the British claimed that they needed facilities in Egypt to carry out a defensive strategy which from 1951 they were never likely to achieve with their increasingly limited resources. Even when the base became unnecessary for the implementation of what existing military forces could not hope to achieve, Britain could not afford to accept the Egyptian demand for evacuation.

The British clung more to prestige as their power declined. As time went on the military themselves privately acknowledged the importance of using British forces for political rather than military purposes. With the exception of Attlee, the image of power became more important than its exercise to virtually all policy makers who were reluctant to accept the reality of economic and military decline. Goals deemed to require Egyptian co-operation were in effect justifications for policies to preserve status and prestige.

By 1953 the base had become militarily worthless and by the end of the year most policy makers were desperate to get out. They could not afford to go without an agreement with Egypt and they could not afford to stay without an agreement with

Egypt. Yet the negotiations dragged on as the Egyptians were determined to establish independence and the British determined to preserve the prestige necessary for the appearance of regional dominance. In the end, as the right to wear the Queen's uniform became more important than the cost of the base, it was perhaps only the fact that Churchill became convinced that the damage to prestige from not signing an agreement would be greater than it would from signing one that enabled the British to withdraw from Egypt in 1956.

Their return a few weeks later marked the ultimate humiliation for Britain. It effectively ended the military commitment that they had fought so hard to retain as a symbol of power and influence. But Suez did not initially change their efforts to retain influence in the Middle East or to abandon the Baghdad Pact (647–648). Only gradually did the British come to revise their strategy for defending the Middle East which, as the Gulf states became more important in political and economic terms, came to focus more on the Persian Gulf than the northern tier. The axis was a line of defence from the west coast of Africa to the Persian Gulf and on to the Indian Ocean islands, Singapore and the antipodean dominions. It was a line which Attlee had suggested in 1946 in order to save money and avoid conflict. With an eye to Anglo–Egyptians relations, readers will judge the value of postponing that retreat in terms of the cold war, informal empire and the management of decline.

*   *   *   *

The transliteration of Arabic names in the main body of the documents and introduction has been adopted to represent the contemporary general usage of the 1940s and 1950s. Document headings do not therefore reflect the most accurate transliteration often used by modern day Arab historians. Readers should be aware of the lack of uniformity in the transliteration of Arabic which partly reflects different historical influences. In Syria and Lebanon the use of 'ou' rather than 'u' reflects French influences with its emphasis on the phonetic importance of the sound of Arabic letters which have no equivalent in English. This was generally used by Egyptian officials in their correspondence with the British which was in French. British officials were not however entirely consistent (hence Nasser, Nasr and Nasir), and to avoid confusion the list of office holders provides the more accurate transliteration as well as the form generally used in the documents.

*   *   *   *

In the preparation of these volumes I have benefited from help and advice from a number of people, notably Amr al-Baho, Ronald Hyam, Douglas Johnson, Brenda and Nicola Kent, Kate Morris, Kirsten Schulze and my Suez students at the LSE. I am also grateful to Michael Thornhill for sending me a copy of his Oxford D Phil thesis 'Britain and the Egyptian question 1950–1954'. The fact that these volumes appear in the meaningful and coherent form identifiable with BDEEP is entirely due to the efforts of Steve Ashton, the general editor. Steve has made an enormous contribution to the project as a whole and his patience, and rigour regarding style, organisation and attention to detail, have been invaluable as an antidote to my more slapdash methods.

Notes to Introduction

1   The 1936 Anglo–Egyptian treaty is reproduced in appendix I.

2   BDEEP Series A, vol 1, S R Ashton and S E Stockwell, eds, *Imperial policy and colonial practice 1925–1945*, part I, 25.

3   The Buraimi oasis crisis stemmed from the territorial disputes in south eastern Arabia following the attempts of the British and Ottoman empires to define spheres of influence there. The new state of Saudi Arabia rejected the Anglo–Turkish boundary line in 1934, although the dispute did not become serious until 1952 when Saudi Arabia seized one of the villages in the oasis. Lying on the boundary of the shaikdom of Abu Dhabi and the Sultanate of Muscat, the Buraimi oasis became more significant in relation to the oil exploration activities of ARAMCO. The British, keen to maintain their role as protector of the Trucial States, wanted to take the dispute to arbitration. Despite initial US reluctance to put pressure on the Saudis to agree to arbitration, the Americans helped secure Saudi acceptance of arbitration in 1953. However it was then abandoned by the British amidst accusations of Saudi violations of the arbitration agreement. Eden's decision, approved by the Cabinet in October 1955, to use the Trucial Levies to retake the oasis, provoked a significant if temporary crisis in Anglo–American relations. As well as economic rivalry, the dispute illustrated the importance the US attached to preserving good relations with the Saudis for broad, cold war reasons and the fact that the British did not support this when their prestige and influence in the Gulf were at stake.

4   For the Italian colonies issue in 1945, see BDEEP series A, vol 2, R Hyam, ed, *The Labour governmment and the end of empire 1945–1951*, part 3, 273 and 274.

5   Foreign Relations of the United States (FRUS), *The Conference of Berlin (Potsdam)*, vol II, *1945*, pp 365–367, 372–373. The Americans made two separate records of this conversation which disagree only in that Cohen's record attributes the Soviet remarks to Stalin while Thompson's notes attribute them to Molotov. This exchange is not fully recorded in the British records of the meeting.

6   John Kent, *British imperial strategy and the origins of the cold war 1944–49* (London, 1993) p 61.

7   FO 371/47881, memorandum by Sargent, 2 Apr 1945, reproduced in G Ross, ed, *The Foreign Office and the Kremlin: British documents on Anglo–Soviet relations, 1941–45* (Cambridge, 1984) no 35.

8   FO 371/50795, no 8222, note by Bevin on Heaton-Nicholls (South African high commissioner) to FO, 6 Oct 1945.

9   CAB 129/2, CP(45)174, 17 Sept 1945.

10   CAB 129/1, CP(45)144, 1 Sept 1945; reproduced in Hyam, *op cit*, part 3, 273.

11   CAB 131/2, DO(46)48, 2 Apr 1946.

12   CAB 131/1, DO 12(46)2, 15 Apr 1946.

13   CAB 128/5, CM 37(46)1, 24 Apr 1946.

14   FO 371/53296, no 2172, FO tel no 960, 16 May 1946.

15   FO 371/53306, no 3140, FO tels 3 and 4, 18 July 1946.

16   FO 371/53308, no 3299, Alexandria tel 33, 25 July 1946.

17   FO 371/53310, no 3638, Alexandria tel 86, 25 Aug 1946.

18   FO 371/53310, no 3639, FO tel 68, 26 Aug 1946.

19   FO 371/53311, no 3752, Alexandria tel 113, 3 Sept 1946.

20   FO 371/53311, no 3807, FO tel 103, 9 Sept 1946.

21   FO 371/53311, no 3772, FO tel no 106, 12 Sept 1946.

22   FO 371/53314, no 4213, conclusions of FO meeting in Paris with embassy officials to discuss the Anglo–Egyptian treaty, 4–5 Oct 1946.

23   FO 371/53318, no 4834, Cairo tel no 1711, 18 Nov 1946. Anglo–Egyptian differences over the Sudan

protocol are extensively documented in BDEEP series B, vol 5, Douglas H Johnson, ed, *Sudan*, part I, chapter 2.

24   CAB 128/9, CM 38(47)1, 22 Apr 1947.

25   DEFE 4/7, COS 128(47)5, 15 Oct 1947, JP(47)133, 9 Oct 1947.

26   T 236/1274, minute by E W Playfair, 19 May 1947.

27   For details of the talks, see FRUS, *The Near East and Africa*, vol V, *1947*, pp 485–627.

28   FO 371/62984, no 4279, minute by D Scott-Fox, 10 Sept 1947.

29   DEFE 4/10, COS 18(48), 4 Feb 1948.

30   DEFE 5/10, COS(48)30, 7 Feb 1948.

31   DEFE 5/10, COS(48)6, Sargent to Hollis, 3 Jan 1948.

32   FO 371/69192, no 308, note by Campbell on Egyptian alliances, 6 Jan 1948.

33   DEFE 4/10, COS 3(48)4, 7 Jan 1948, annex II, Hollis to Sargent, nd.

34   The Sudan ordinance, which was passed in June 1948, originated in proposals made by the Sudan Administration Conference of Mar 1947. The conference recommended the establishment of a Legislative Assembly and an Executive Council to replace the Advisory Council for the Northern Sudan and the Governor-General's Council. The Egyptians contested the recommendations on the grounds that they had not been consulted. They claimed that they had the right to put forward proposals of their own and submitted detailed criticisms of the recommendations, describing them as inadequate in that they did not fulfil their avowed purpose of associating the Sudanese more closely with the central government. From a British viewpoint, given that the reforms were also intended to restrict Egypt's influence in the Sudan, the Egyptian response was said by the FO to be 'potentially very embarrassing' (FO 371/62949, no 6364, minute by D W Lascelles to Bevin, 9 Dec 1947, reproduced in Johnson, *op cit*, part I, 144. Chapter 3 of Johnson's *Sudan* volume provides extensive coverage).

35   PREM 8/1231, minute by Shinwell, 20 Apr 1948.

36   DEFE 4/14, COS 102(48)3, 19 July 1948, JP(48)72, 1 July 1948.

37   FO 371/69176, no 4734, G L Clutton to Group Captain D C Stapleton, 24 July 1948.

38   DEFE 5/12, COS(48)191, 23 Aug 1948.

39   For the reasons for this relating to inadequate runways, see p lv.

40   DEFE 5/11, COS(48)110, 18 May 1948. The strategic bombing would have to be left to the Americans but in 1948 there were no runways in Egypt large enough to take B 29s.

41   The COS were also insisting on the use of depots and workshops in the Tel el Kebir area which was outside the area allocated to the British under the 1936 Treaty.

42   FO 371/69176, no 6558, minute by Campbell, 16 Oct 1948.

43   FO 371/69195, no 7772, FO tel 248, 1 Dec 1948.

44   DEFE 4/20, COS 50(49)1, 1 Apr 1949, JP(49)29, 30 Mar 1949.

45   The force was 160 aircraft.

46   FO 371/73552, no 1050, M N F Stewart to R H Melville (Air Ministry), 16 Feb 1949. Work on the runways, with shared Anglo–American costs, was not completed until Nov 1952.

47   FO 371/69176, no 5067, record of meeting between Alexander and Bevin, 24 July 1948; FO 371/73570, no 574, minute by Bevin, 19 Jan 1949; FO 141/1400, no 1, minutes by E A Chapman Andrews, 31 Dec 1949 and Campbell, 3 Jan 1950.

48   The three main objectives were the defence of Britain, the defence of the sea communications between the main support areas and the defence of the Middle East.

49   DEFE 6/10, JP(49)126, 3 Nov 1949; DEFE 4/24, COS 131(49)8, 8 Sept 1949, JP(49)85, 5 Sept 1949.

50   CAB 129/37/1, CP(49)209, 19 Oct 1949.

51   DEFE 4/30, COS 57(50)9, 5 Apr 1950, JP(49)168, 24 Mar 1950.

52   Editor's emphasis.

53   DEFE 4/30, COS 63(50)2, 24 Apr 1950, JP(50)40, annex, 20 Apr 1950.

54   *Ibid.*

55   DEFE 4/38, COS 188(50)3, 29 Nov 1950.

56   DEFE 4/39, COS 13(51)2, 17 Jan 1951, JP(51)1412, annex, 17 Jan 1951.

57   FO 141/1396, no 181, minute by Sir R Stevenson, 13 Nov 1950.

58   DEFE 4/38, COS 210(50)4, 19 Dec 1950.

59   FO 141/1436, no 16, FO telegram 75, 25 Jan 1951.

60   FO 141/1436, no 16, Cairo tel 63, 26 Jan 1951.

61   FO 371/90127, no 1, record of meeting with G C McGhee, 3 Apr 1951.

62   DEFE 5/31, COS(51)282, 7 May 1951, appendix, DCC(51)35, 21 Apr 1951.

63   DEFE 5/30, COS(51)210, 10 Apr 1951.

64   FO 371/90137, no 206, minute by D V Bendall, 14 Sept 1951.

65   FO 371/90144, no 368, C's-in-C tel 32602, Robertson to Slim, 23 Oct 1951.

66   FO 371/96859, no 25, Fayid tel no 3, 31 Dec 1951, (received 10 Jan 1952).

67   FO 371/96918, no 26, Washington tel 108, 10 Jan 1952.

68   DEFE 5/35, COS(51)686, 28 Nov 1951.

69   DEFE 4/51, COS 8(52)5, 15 Jan 1952.

70   DEFE 4/53, COS 57(52)2, 25 Apr 1952.

71   DEFE 4/51, COS 9(52)4, 18 Jan 1952.

72   DEFE 4/53, COS 47(52)3, 1 Apr 1952.

73   DEFE 4/51, COS 14(52)6, 25 Jan 1952, JP(52)10, annex, 23 Jan 1952.

74   DEFE 4/53, COS 60(52), 5 May 1952; DEFE 4/53, COS 63(52)4, 8 May 1952, JP(52)59, annex, 7 May 1952.

75   DEFE 4/54, COS 71(52)2, 23 May 1952; DEFE 4/54, COS 87(52)8, 16 June 1952.

76   CAB 131/12, D 1(52)5, 12 Mar 1952.

77   FO 371/96972, no 13, note by Slim, 20 Mar 1952; DEFE 4/53, COS 47(52)2, 1 Apr 1952.

78   FO 141/1457, no 84, Cairo embassy memorandum, 22 Mar 1952; FO 141/1467, no 21, BDCC tel 651, 26 Mar 1952.

79   FO 371/96928, no 251, Cairo tel 676, 7 Apr 1952.

80   CAB 128/24, CC 40(52)1, 9 Apr 1952.

81   FO 371/96928, no 262, Cairo tel 690, 9 Apr 1952.

82   DEFE 4/53, COS 50(52)5, 8 Apr 1952.

83   The dollar gap for the second half of 1952 was projected to reach £175 million (CAB 130/77, Gen 411/1, 18 June 1952).

84   CAB 129/53, C(52)202, 18 June 1952. Reproduced in BDEEP series A, vol 3, D Goldsworthy, ed, *The Conservative government and the end of empire 1951–1957*, part 1, 3.

85   DEFE 4/54, COS 89(52)6, 23 June 1952.

86   DEFE 4/55, COS 98(52)3, 8 July 1952, JP(52)69, 7 July 1952.

87   FO 141/1453, no 53, draft Cairo tel 32, 2 July 1952; FO 141/1453, no 54, draft Cairo tel 33, 2 July 1952; FO 141/1453, no 66, FO tel 1099, 13 July 1952; FO 371/96876, no 184, Cairo tel 997, 4 July 1952.

88   FO 371/96877, no 197, Cairo tel 1045, 20 July 1952; FO 141/1453, no 72, Cairo tel 1059, 22 July 1952.

89   M T Thornhill, *Britain and the Egyptian question, 1950–1954* (unpublished Oxford D Phil, 1995) pp 88–89.

90   FO 371/96932, no 394, Cairo tel 1168, 4 Aug 1952.

91   FO 371/96880, no 347, minute by Churchill, 26 Aug 1952.

92   FO 371/96933, no 425, Cairo tel 1504, 9 Oct 1952.

93   M Dockrill, *British defence since 1945* (London, 1989) p 50.

94   The figures were presented to the Cabinet as part of the 1953–1954 defence programme in CAB 129/55, C(52)316, 10 Oct 1952.

95   CAB 131/12, D(52)41, 29 Sept 1952; CAB 131/12, D(52)45, 31 Oct 1952.

96   FO 141/1462, no 56, minute by M J Creswell, 4 Dec 1952.

97   CAB 131/12, COS 12(52)4, 11 Dec 1952.

98   FO 371/96883, no 463, Cairo despatch 265, 17 Dec 1952.

99   FO 371/102798, no 53, minute by R Allen, 9 Mar 1953.

100   FO 371/102798, no 65, Cairo tel 477, 14 Mar 1953.

101   CAB 128/26/1, CC 20(53)5, 17 Mar 1953.

102   FO 371/102798, no 65, Cairo tel no 494, 16 Mar 1953.

103   FO 371/102764, no 100, Amery to Churchill, 21 Mar 1953.

104   FO 371/102701, no 21, Cairo tel no 112, 13 May 1953.

105   PREM 11/485, Cairo tel 758, 6 May 1953; FO 371/102701, no 21, Cairo tel 112, 7 May 1953.

106   FRUS, *The Near and Middle East,* vol IX part I, *1952–1954,* p 384. Dulles's visit is covered in vol IX part I, pp 1–167 and his conclusions, which were discussed at the 147th meeting of the National Security Council on 1 June, in vol IX part I, pp 379–386.

107   FRUS, *The Near and Middle East,* vol IX, part II, *1952–1954,* pp 2108–2114.

108   DEFE 5/47, COS(53)332, 9 July 1953; DEFE 5/47, COS(53)336, 11 July 1953.

109   FO 371/102859, no 46, Cairo tel no 1180, 11 Aug 1953; FO 371/102859, no 56, Cairo tel no 1222, 24 Aug 1953.

110   PREM 11/485, Cairo tel 1342, 23 Sept 1953.

111   FO 371/102816, no 488, Washington tel 2027, 25 Sept 1953.

112   DEFE 4/66, COS 130(53)3, 17 Nov 1953.

113   DEFE 4/66, COS 125(53)2, 3 Nov 1953.

114   FO 371/108473, no 10, minute by R Allen, 15 Feb 1954.

115   DEFE 4/67, COS 140(53)4, 8 Dec 1953.

116   DEFE 4/67, COS 139(53)1, 4 Dec 1953.

117   DEFE 4/68, COS 19(54)2, 19 Feb 1954.

118   DEFE 4/69, COS 22(54)2, 3 Mar 1954, JP(54)24, 26 Feb 1954.

119   FO 371/108327, no 3, Cairo tel 261, 25 Feb 1954; FO 371/108327, no 12, Cairo tel 292, 27 Feb 1954; FO 371/108327, no 26, Cairo tel 325, 6 Mar 1954; FO 371/108327, no 30, Cairo tel 338, 9 Mar 1954.

120   DEFE 4/69, COS 32(54), 22 Mar 1954.

121   CAB 128/27/1, CC 21(54)2, 22 Mar 1954.

122   CAB 128/27/1, CC 29(54)2, 15 Apr 1954.

123   CAB 128/27/1, CC 37(54)3, 2 June 1954.

124   DEFE 4/70, COS 53(54)1, 10 May 1954.

125   *Ibid*, COS 54(54), 12 May 1954.

126   CAB 129/70, C(54)251, 23 July 1954.

127   CAB 128/27/2, CC 53(54)4, 26 July 1954.

128   DEFE 4/72, COS 92(54)5, 27 Aug 1954.

129   DEFE 5/53, COS(54)212, 25 June 1954.

130   DEFE 4/71, COS 82(54)1, 14 July 1954.

131   DEFE 11/115, C's-in-C, Middle East tel 956, 11 Aug 1954.

132   DEFE 4/72, COS 94(54)2, 6 Sept 1954.

133   DEFE 4/72, COS 96(54)1, 8 Sept 1954, JP(54)81, 6 Sept 1954.

134   DEFE 4/73, COS 111(54)2, 27 Oct 1954, JP(54) note 22, 21 Oct 1954.

135   DEFE 5/54, COS(54)278, 26 Aug 1954.

136   FO 371/110788, no 84, Cairo tel 1777, 7 Dec 1954.

137   DEFE 5/54, COS(54)318, 1 Oct 1954.

138   DEFE 11/115, JP(54)11 OR, annex, 18 Aug 1954.

139   FO 371/115487, no 126, Baghdad tel 73, 29 Jan 1955.

140   FO 371/115490, no 226, minute by Eden, nd, on Baghdad tel 117, 12 Feb 1955.

141   FO 371/115494, no 351, Tel Aviv tel 48, 28 Feb 1955.

142   The discrepancy in the estimated shortfall was partly explained by whether or not it was assumed that nuclear weapons were available at H-hour.

143   W S Lucas, *Divided we stand: Britain, the US and the Suez crisis* (London 1991) p 43.

144   FO 371/115510, no 779, minute by C A E Shuckburgh, 3 May 1955; FO 371/115507, no 708, Ankara despatch 74, 12 Apr 1955.

145   If it continued to have to meet the expenditure targets of the Treasury, it was believed in 1955 that any long term defence strategy would not be acceptable to all three services until strategic policy had been reappraised in the light of knowledge of the effects of the hydrogen bomb. The reason was that if choices had to be made between supplying conventional forces to NATO for hot war in Europe, fighting the cold war on a global basis or maintaining a deterrent, the role of one or more of the services would be seriously diminished. Thus Britain would have to continue to maintain all three, however impossible it became. More particularly Britain would have to ensure that Commonwealth priorities were not discarded for NATO priorities if they conflicted (DEFE 4/78, COS 56(55)1, 12 July 1955, JP(55)61, 8 July 1955).

146   DEFE 4/78, COS 56(55)1, 12 July 1955.

147   DEFE 4/78, COS 60(55)2, 22 July 1955, JP(55)67, 20 July 1955.

148   DEFE 4/79, COS 80(55), 6 Oct 1955, JP(55) note 19, 4 Oct 1955.

149   DEFE 5/61, COS(55)253, annex, 5 Oct 1955.

150   Dulles in fact opposed Iranian membership at a National Security Council meeting on 7 Oct 1955 and appeared to have been converted only after the signing of the Egyptian–Saudi–Syrian defence pact on 27 Oct (N J Ashton, *Eisenhower, Macmillan and the problem of Nasser: Anglo–American relations and Arab nationalism, 1955–1959* (London, 1996) p 56).

151   PREM 11/859, note by Eden on Cairo tel 1609, 2 Nov 1955.

152   DEFE 4/85, COS 33(56)2, 20 Mar 1956, JP(56)64, annex, 16 Mar 1956.

153   CAB 131/17, DO(56)7, 22 Mar 1956.

154   W S Lucas, *op cit*, p 109.

155   DEFE 4/84, COS 23(56)4, 24 Feb 1956.

156   The tripartite declaration required the US, France and Britain to consult over possible action to deal with violations of the 1949 Arab–Israeli armistice agreements.

157   US National Archives, RG 59, State Department Central Files, 641.74/3–2256, memorandum by E Wilson, 21 Mar 1956. Cited in W S Lucas, *op cit*, p 109.

158   On Omega see W S Lucas, *op cit*, pp 108–141 and US Declassified Documents, 1988, 000866.

Summary of Documents: Part I

Chapter 1
Collaboration with King Farouk: the Suez base and the definition of Britain's post war requirements in the Middle East, Mar 1945–Dec 1946

NUMBER			SUBJECT	PAGE
		1945		
1	War Cabinet Suez Canal Committee meeting	13 Mar	Minutes on the Canal's future administration	1
2	Mr Attlee	20 Mar	War Cabinet memo, 'Future defence policy in the Suez Canal area: report of the Suez Canal Committee'	4
3	Mr Eden	13 Apr	War Cabinet memo, 'Defence of the Middle East'	6
4	Lord Killearn to Sir R Campbell	14 Apr	Letter about political situation in Egypt, + *Minute* by P S Scrivener [Extract]	9
5	PHPS Committee paper, annex for COS	18 Apr	Draft aide mémoire on future defence policy in the Canal area	12
6	Sir R Campbell to Lord Killearn	5 May	Letter (reply to 4) on importance of King Farouk's position [Extract]	14
7	Lord Killearn to FO	16 May	Tel on need to retain a predominant position in Egypt	15
8	Sir E Grigg	23 May	Memo on farewell talk with King Farouk [Extract]	16
9	FO to Lord Killearn	28 May	Tel giving instructions on discussions with Egyptian government	17
10	Lord Killearn to FO	23 June	Tel advocating firmness in talks with Egyptian government, + *Minutes* by A V Coverley-Price & P S Scrivener	18
11	Sir E Grigg	2 July	War Cabinet memo, 'Imperial security in the Middle East'	20
12	P S Scrivener to Mr Bevin	3 Aug	Minute on Anglo–Egyptian treaty and internal development of Egypt	34

NUMBER		SUBJECT		PAGE
		1945		
13	Sir W Smart	29 Aug	Internal embassy minute on timing of treaty negotiations	37
14	Lord Killearn to FO	1 Sept	Tel on discussion with Nokrashi about Egyptian aspirations [Extract]	38
15	Lord Altrincham	2 Sept	Memo, 'British policy and organisation in the Middle East' [Extract]	39
16	FO internal paper	17 Oct	Memo on need to work with King Farouk	50
17	JPS paper for COS Committee	9 Nov	Report, 'Middle East policy' [Extract]	52
18	COS Committee meeting	9 Nov	Minutes on formation of Middle East confederacy	52
19	JPS paper for COS Committee	9 Nov	Report, 'Revision of the Anglo–Egyptian treaty' [Extract]	53
20	COS Committee meeting	9 Nov	Minutes on revision of Anglo–Egyptian treaty	54
21	COS Committee paper, annex	2 Dec	FO memo on Middle East confederacy	55
22	Lord Killearn to FO	6 Dec	Tel on terms and conditions of treaty revision	57
23	JPS paper for COS Committee	27 Dec	Report, 'Anglo–Egyptian treaty – comments of Commanders-in-Chief, Middle East and Admiralty', + *Annexes*	59
24	COS Committee meeting	27 Dec	Minutes on Anglo–Egyptian treaty revision	67
		1946		
25	Lord Killearn to FO	9 Jan	Tel on treaty relations with Egypt and Middle East	68
26	Mr Bevin	18 Jan	Cabinet memo, 'Revision of the Anglo–Egyptian treaty of 1936', + *Annexes* [Extract]	69
27	P S Scrivener	2 Mar	Minute on Anglo–Egyptian treaty revision	75
28	R J Bowker to FO	6 Mar	Despatch constituting Lord Killearn's resumé of his time in Egypt	77
29	R J Bowker to FO	10 Mar	Despatch on the military requirements in Egypt of the C's-in-C, Middle East	80
30	FO	12 Mar	Note of FO departmental meeting on Anglo–Egyptian treaty revision	82

NUMBER			SUBJECT	PAGE
		1946		
31	Sir R Campbell	25 Mar	Internal embassy memo on talk with Sidky about Egyptian desires to be treated as equals [Extract]	83
32	COS Committee paper, annex	27 Mar	Memo by C's-in-C, Middle East, 'Military requirements in the revision of the Anglo–Egyptian treaty'	85
33	COS paper for Cabinet Defence Committee	2 Apr	Report, 'Strategic position of the British Commonwealth'	94
34	R G Howe to Mr Bevin	4 Apr	Minute on peacetime requirements in Egypt	101
35	COS Committee meeting	5 Apr	Minutes on strategic position of the British Commonwealth	102
36	Sir R Campbell to FO	9 Apr	Tel on base evacuation question	105
37	Cabinet meeting CM 33(46)4	11 Apr	Conclusions on offer to evacuate base at start of treaty negotiations	106
38	Lord Stansgate (Cairo) to Mr Bevin	17 Apr	Tel on Britain's initial negotiating position	106
39	COS Committee meeting	18 Apr	Minutes on views of British delegation in Egypt	108
40	Lord Stansgate (Cairo) to Mr Bevin	22 Apr	Tel on preliminary talks with Egyptians	109
41	C's-in-C, Middle East to COS	22 Apr	Tel on Britain's initial negotiating position	111
42	Sir W Smart	23 Apr	Internal embassy memo on the problem of negotiating with existing Egyptian government	113
43	COS Committee meeting	24 Apr	Minutes on offer of complete evacuation	113
44	Cabinet Defence Committee meeting	24 Apr	Minutes on offer of complete evacuation [Extract]	116
45	Mr Bevin	24 Apr	Cabinet note, circulating a note to British delegation by Sidky	118
46	Cabinet meeting CM 42(46)1	6 May	Conclusions on public announcement of Britain's withdrawal from Egypt	120
47	Sir W Smart	24 May	Internal embassy memo on King Farouk's role in the negotiations	122
48	Lt-Gen C Allfrey (Cairo) to Field Marshal Lord Alanbrooke	25 May	Letter on future treaty negotiations	123

NUMBER   SUBJECT   PAGE

1946

49   Cabinet Defence   27 May   Minutes on problems in Egypt, Palestine   125
        Committee meeting   and Cyrenaica

50   Cabinet meeting   27 May   Conclusions on suspension of treaty   130
        CM 52(46)1   negotiations

51   Sir R Campbell   5 June   Letter on likely Egyptian reaction to   130
        to R G Howe   British aid

52   Mr Bevin   5 June   Cabinet memo, 'Revision of Anglo–   131
                                             Egyptian treaty', + *Annexes*

53   Cabinet meeting   6 June   Conclusions on new draft treaty   137
        CM 57(46)1

54   COS paper   7 June   Report, 'Revision of Anglo–Egyptian   141
        for Cabinet   treaty'   [Extract]

55   Cabinet meeting   7 June   Conclusions on continuance of treaty   143
        CM 58(46)   negotiations

56   COS paper   18 June   Report, 'British strategic requirements   146
        for Cabinet Defence   in the Middle East'
        Committee

57   JPS paper, annex   17 July   Report, 'Egypt – revision of treaty'   166
        for COS Committee

58   Mr Bevin   18 July   Tel on timing of proposed British troop   168
        to Lord Stansgate   withdrawal
        (Cairo)

59   Lord Stansgate (Cairo)   21 July   Tel on article 2 of proposed treaty   168
        to Mr Bevin

60   Mr Bevin   22 July   Tel on article 2 of proposed treaty   170
        to Lord Stansgate
        (Cairo)

61   P A Dove   25 July   Internal embassy note of meeting with   171
                                             Hassan Youssef on obstacles to an
                                             Anglo–Egyptian agreement

62   R G Howe   29 July   Minute on the apparent impasse in   174
                                             negotiations

63   Sir W Smart   29 July   Internal embassy memo, 'Review of the   174
                                             Anglo–Egyptian treaty situation'

64   Lord Stansgate (Cairo)   29 July   Tel on attitude of Egyptian government   176
        to Mr Attlee

65   COS Committee   30 July   Minutes   on   details   of   proposed   177
        meeting   evacuation

66   Sir O Sargent   30 July   Tel on Anglo–Egyptian treaty negotia-   179
        to Mr Attlee (Paris)   tions

NUMBER			SUBJECT	PAGE

1946

67	Cabinet meeting CM 76(46)7	1 Aug	Conclusions on instructions to British delegation	180
68	Egyptian delegation to British delegation	1 Aug	Note on Egyptian position in treaty negotiations	181
69	Mr Bevin to Mr Attlee	4 Aug	Minute opposing Cabinet's decision on article 2 of proposed treaty [Extract]	185
70	Mr Bevin to Lord Stansgate (Cairo)	5 Aug	Tel giving instructions to British delegation	186
71	Lord Stansgate (Cairo) to Mr Bevin	6 Aug	Tel on article 2 of proposed treaty	187
72	Mr Bevin to Lord Stansgate (Cairo)	7 Aug	Tel giving instructions to delegation	189
73	Lord Stansgate (Cairo) to Mr Bevin	8 Aug	Tel complaining of mishandling of negotiations	190
74	Mr Bevin to Lord Stansgate (Cairo)	8 Aug	Tel on article 2 of proposed treaty	191
75	Mr Bevin to Lord Stansgate (Cairo)	8 Aug	Tel reporting conversation with Amr on treaty negotiations	192
76	Lord Stansgate (Cairo) to Mr Bevin	10 Aug	Tel on article 2 of proposed treaty	193
77	Lord Stansgate (Cairo) to Mr Bevin	12 Aug	Tel on dangers of falling back on 1936 treaty	195
78	Mr Bevin (Paris) to Lord Stansgate	13 Aug	Tel on article 2 of proposed treaty	196
79	Lord Stansgate (Cairo) to Mr Bevin	21 Aug	Tel reporting meetings with Sidky, Amr and Hassan Youssef	197
80	Sir W Smart	30 Aug	Internal embassy memo on political intrigues in Egypt	199
81	Sir R Campbell to FO	11 Sept	Tel on political conflicts affecting Egyptian delegation	200
82	DO to dominion governments	30 Sept	Circular despatch summarising Egyptian reply to latest British treaty proposals	203
83	Mr Bevin for Cabinet Defence Committee	23 Oct	Memo, 'Anglo–Egyptian treaty negotiations'	205

NUMBER		SUBJECT	PAGE

1946

84	Cabinet Defence Committee meeting	24 Oct	Minutes on Anglo–Egyptian treaty negotiations [Extract]	206
85	FO	25 Oct	Draft of Anglo-Egyptian treaty	208
86	Cabinet meeting CM 96(46)3	14 Nov	Conclusions on Sudan protocol and proposed Anglo–Egyptian treaty	211
87	R J Bowker to FO	26 Nov	Tel summarising Egyptian delegation's stated opposition to proposed treaty	213
88	R J Bowker to FO	29 Nov	Tel on problem of exchanging letters on Sudan protocol	214
89	Mr Bevin (New York) to FO	6 Dec	Tel suggesting text of letter to Sidky	215

Chapter 2

The problem of standing on the 1936 treaty and the formation of a plan to defend the Middle East, Jan 1947–Oct 1948

1947

90	Sir O Sargent to Mr Bevin	1 Jan	Minute on likely situation in Egypt if talks break down	216
91	Sir O Sargent to Sir R Campbell	27 Jan	Letter on bringing the Wafd back to power	218
92	Lord Stansgate for Mr Bevin	8 Feb	Memo on why the treaty negotiations failed [Extract]	219
93	COS paper for Cabinet Defence Committee	7 Mar	Memo, 'The defence of the Commonwealth'	220
94	Sir R Campbell to FO	12 Mar	Tel suggesting a tougher policy towards Egypt	223
95	Sir O Sargent to Mr Bevin (Moscow)	15 Mar	Tel on possibility of replacing existing Egyptian government	224
96	Sir O Sargent to Mr Bevin (Moscow)	28 Mar	Tel on inadvisability of concessions to Egypt [Extract]	225
97	Sir W Smart	2 Apr	Internal embassy memo on the need to frighten Egyptians	226
98	Sir O Sargent to Mr Attlee	3 Apr	Minute on issue of concessions to Egypt	227

NUMBER			SUBJECT	PAGE

1947

99	J P E C Henniker to Mr Bevin	24 Apr	Minute on difficulties of enforcing British rights under 1936 treaty	229
100	Sir O Sargent to Mr Bevin	5 May	Minute on possibility and desirability of removing Nokrashi	230
101	FO	6 May	Record of inter-departmental meeting with Treasury on unseating Nokrashi and Egyptian sterling balances	235
102	Sir O Sargent to Lt-Gen Sir L Hollis	29 May	Letter on reduction of troops in Egypt to treaty levels	237
103	JPS paper for COS Committee	6 Aug	Report, 'Middle East defence – military requirements in Egypt', + *Annex* 1 [Extract]	238
104	FO internal paper	11 Oct	Memo opposing attempts to break Anglo–Egyptian deadlock	241
105	JPS paper for COS Committee	4 Nov	Report, 'Redeployment of Middle East forces' [Extract]	243
106	COS Committee paper	18 Nov	Letter from FO to Lt-Gen Sir L Hollis on military requirements in Egypt, + *Annex* [Extract]	246
107	M R Wright	20 Nov	Minute on new factors affecting possible Anglo–Egyptian agreement	249
108	COS Committee meeting	21 Nov	Minutes on Washington talks on Middle East policy	251
109	Mr Bevin to Mr Attlee	15 Dec	Draft minute on how best to approach Egyptians	254

1948

110	FO	10 Jan	Note of departmental meeting on Egypt and Sudan [Extract]	257
111	FO	20 Jan	Note of departmental meeting on future talks with Egyptians [Extract]	261
112	E A Chapman Andrews	7 Feb	Internal embassy note of conversation with Azzam on Arab regional defence arrangements	263
113	Mr Bevin to Sir R Campbell	14 Feb	Tel giving instructions on responding to King Farouk	264
114	Lt-Gen Sir L Hollis to Sir O Sargent	11 Mar	Letter on military requirements in countries adjacent to Egypt	266
115	FO	12 Mar	Note of departmental meeting on Sudan ordinance and military questions in Egypt	268

NUMBER   SUBJECT   PAGE

1948

116   D W Lascelles   23 Mar   Minute on defence proposals and   270
                                           Egyptian government attitudes

117   E A Chapman Andrews   Mar   Internal embassy draft memo, 'Egypt   271
                                           and defence: suggested manner of
                                           approach to King Farouk'

118   E A Chapman Andrews   25 Mar   Internal embassy minutes on evacuation 273
       & Sir R Campbell   –1 Apr   from Egypt

119   J M Troutbeck (BMEO)   21 Apr   Despatch on Middle East nationalist   274
       to Mr Bevin   agitation, + *Enclosure*: note from
                                           British subject resident in Middle East

120   C's-in-C, Middle East   13 May   Report, 'Staff study "Intermezzo"'   277
       paper   [Extract]
       for COS Committee

121   JIC Committee paper   12 July   Report, 'Middle East defence policy – 280
       for COS Committee   potentialities and scale and direction of
                                           attack – 1950', + *Annexes*

122   COS Committee   25 Aug   Minutes on postponing rundown of   286
       meeting   forces in Egypt

123   M R Wright   10 Sept   Letter on finance for military require- 288
       to E A Chapman   ments in Egypt   [Extract]
       Andrews

124   Mr Bevin   13 Sept   Letter on views of COS on military   289
       to Mr Alexander   requirements in Egypt

125   JPS paper   11 Oct   Report on emergency planning for   290
       for COS Committee   Middle East defence

Chapter 3

New requirements in Egypt and problems in Middle East defence, Nov 1948–Sept 1949

1948

126   E A Chapman Andrews   19 Nov   Internal embassy minute on attitude of   296
       to Sir R Campbell   King Farouk to military talks and new
                                           Egyptian government

127   G L Clutton   7 Dec   Memo on the instigation of military   297
                                           technical talks with Egypt

128   COS Committee paper,   16 Dec   Report on global war emergency plan   299
       annex   ('Speedway') for period to July 1950

129   Sir R Campbell   21 Dec   Internal embassy minute on technical   305
                                           talks and timing of Nokrashi's removal

NUMBER			SUBJECT	PAGE

1949

130	E A Chapman Andrews to G L Clutton	7 Jan	Letter on effect of Palestine issue on possibility of an agreement with Egypt	307
131	Mr Shinwell for Cabinet Defence Committee	Jan	Note on long-term policy in Egypt	307
132	Mr Bevin for Cabinet Defence Committee	21 Mar	Memo on Anglo–Egyptian technical defence talks	310
133	Cabinet Defence Committee meeting	22 Mar	Minutes on Anglo–Egyptian defence talks, + *Annex* 1: tel on talks between Field Marshal Sir W Slim and King Farouk	312
134	Brig C Price for COS Committee	23 Mar	Note circulating a minute by Mr Bevin & an FO paper on Middle East defence agreements	316
135	D J D Maitland	26 Mar	Minute on future nature of Egyptian regime	319
136	Sir R Campbell to FO	30 Mar	Tel reporting talk with Gen H Pyman and Abdel Hadi on Middle East defence	319
137	Air Marshal Sir W Dickson	1 Apr	Internal embassy record of talk with Sir R Campbell and Abdel Hadi	320
138	Sir R Campbell to FO	15 Apr	Tel on timing of Anglo–Egyptian discussions	325
139	COS Committee meeting	17 June	Minutes on Egyptian equipment requirements [Extract]	327
140	G L Clutton	24 June	Minute on value of bringing Wafd into Egyptian government	329
141	JPS paper, annex for COS Committee	6 July	Report, 'Overall strategic concept for war in 1957' [Extract]	331
142	JPS paper, annex for COS Committee	15 July	Report, 'Middle East strategy and defence policy', + *Appendix* "A" [Extract]	334
143	War Office paper, annex for COS Committee	21 July	Note on military talks and Egyptian requirements	346
144	COS Committee meeting	3 Aug	Minutes on Anglo–American military talks on new American strategic concept	349
145	COS Committee meeting	5 Aug	Minutes on supply of equipment to Egypt and nature of future discussions [Extract]	354
146	E A Chapman Andrews to M R Wright	5 Aug	Letter reporting talks with Hussein Sirry and Hassan Youssef	356

NUMBER		SUBJECT	PAGE

1949

147	COS Committee meeting	12 Aug	Minutes on supply of equipment to Egypt	357
148	D J D Maitland	17–24 Aug	Minutes on obtaining desired Egyptian agreement	359
149	D J D Maitland & G L Clutton	5–7 Sept	Minutes on response to Egyptian request for talks [Extract]	361
150	JPS paper for COS Committee	8 Sept	Report, 'Examination of US strategic concept for war 1950/51'	362

Appendix to Part I

Extract from the 1936 Anglo–Egyptian treaty   365

1   CAB 95/18, SC(M) 1(45)1   13 Mar 1945
'The future administration of the Suez Canal': War Cabinet Suez Canal Committee[1] minutes

[The Suez Canal Committee met for the first time on 11 Oct 1944 when it considered a paper by Eden stating responsibility for the defence of the Canal should be Britain's in perpetuity. Attlee, who had doubts about such a proposal, wanted the question to be considered by the COS. Ralph Assheton, financial secretary to the Treasury, proposed that Britain acquire the Canal Zone with territorial compensation for Egypt in Cyrenaica. In the light of these differences and of discussions on the creation of a Public Utility Service to administer the Canal, a series of papers were produced as a basis for the further discussion reproduced below.]

The Committee had before them:—

(a) A Memorandum by the Minister of State, to which was annexed a Paper giving an outline of the detailed arrangements suggested for the carrying out of the proposal for the administration of the Suez Canal by an organisation on the lines of a Public Utility Service. The Memorandum asked the Committee to decide whether to recommend to the War Cabinet that our future policy should be based on the annexed Paper, or on some variant of it, or whether it would be better to concentrate now on securing our objective in the matter of defence, and to defer the question of the administration of the Canal until a later date. (S.C.(M)(44)7).

(b) A Memorandum by the Financial Secretary to the Treasury outlining the practical and financial objections to the scheme for the administration of the Canal on the lines of a Public Utility Service, and supporting the alternative proposal, namely, that we should now concentrate on securing our objective in the matter of defence. (S.C.(M)(45)2).

(c) A Report by the Chiefs of Staff Committee covering a Report by the Middle East Defence Committee on the future requirements for the defence of the Suez Canal. (S.C.(M)(45)3).

(d) A Note by the Minister of State covering a despatch from the Minister Resident in the Middle East commenting on the Report by the Middle East Defence Committee on future requirements for the defence of the Suez Canal. (S.C.(M)(45)4).

Mr. Law said that after giving the matter further consideration, he was convinced by the arguments in the Memorandum by the Financial Secretary to the Treasury, and therefore favoured the second alternative.

Mr. Peake said that the financial objections to the scheme for establishing the Public Utility Service were very great, particularly as we should be expropriating the Suez Canal shareholders and the Egyptian Government at a time when profits from the Canal were at their zenith. He felt that if matters were left until the concession began to run out, pressure could be exerted which would result in smaller Canal dues. The political objections to the scheme were also serious. The Foreign Office suggested that the management might be placed by the Public Utility Service in the hands of a Board of ten—three of whom would be British, three French, three Egyptian, and one from some other nationality, such as the Dutch. He felt that the

---

[1] The meeting was attended by Mr Attlee (chairman), Lord Cranborne (DO), Mr Alexander (Admiralty), Mr Law (minister of state, FO), Mr Stanley (CO), Lord Leathers (minister of war transport), Mr Peake (financial secretary to the Treasury) and N Young (Treasury).

United States and the Russians would undoubtedly require a share in the control if the Canal were vested in an international organisation. The Treasury therefore strongly favoured the alternative proposal to try and secure our defence objective, either by a new Convention or by bilateral negotiation with the Egyptians.

Our present position under the Anglo–Egyptian Treaty was reasonably satisfactory until 1957, and the Treaty provided for an extension. If we got a mandate from the United Nations, we could proceed to negotiate with the Egyptian Government, and we should be more likely to be successful in our negotiations if we did not arouse their hostility by trying at the same time to introduce drastic changes in the administration.

Lord Leathers thought that there were many arguments against the Public Utility Service proposal, though he did not share the view that traffic in the Canal would decline. There was likely to be a very large traffic of oil tankers, and even if air transport reduced the passenger traffic the cargo going through the Canal would still be heavy. Our defence objective was of the first importance. He hoped, however, that in concentrating on that an opportunity of strengthening our share in the control would not be lost.

Mr. Alexander said that he was impressed by the financial calculations of the Treasury, but he thought that the political dangers were over-emphasised. He thought that if we could go for something on the lines of the arrangement for the Panama Canal, which was almost an international affair, we could resist any Russian pressure to share in the control. The Russians were anxious to revise the Montreux Convention, and in return for concessions there they might be ready to concede something to us in Egypt. He was in favour of international control for an undertaking which, though vital to our own interests, was also of great importance to the whole world.

Mr. Attlee said that he too favoured international control. He would like to see the Americans taking part, not only in the control but in the defence. He thought that it was high time that the Americans took their share in policing the waterways of the world. Up to the present we had borne the whole burden of this task, while others had profited from it. It was quite wrong that an international waterway of this importance should be left in the exclusive possession of the Egyptians. The whole cost of defence fell on the British taxpayer, and he felt that it was time that someone else took a share.

Lord Cranborne agreed with the viewpoint of the Treasury. He very much doubted whether we should be able to exclude the Americans and the Russians from control of an international Utility Service, and the Americans might well wish to have a share in the control without bearing any of the burden of defence. In principle there was a good deal to be said for international control, but in practice the system did not seem to work out advantageously. The international control of Tangier was a case in point. There was certainly no international control of the Panama Canal.

Colonel Stanley said that it was not his understanding of the position which would arise under a World Organisation that every nation should participate in the policing of every part of the world. Surely there would be spheres of responsibility allotted to different nations. He felt that the Canal was one which should be allotted to us.

Lord Leathers said that the issue before the Committee was fundamental. Were they, or were they not, to examine the problem of the Canal on the basis of the necessity for British control of the defence? The Middle East Defence Committee and the Chiefs of Staff were quite definite on this point, and were not prepared to see even the French taking a hand in the defence authority. He thought that the United States would certainly demand a share in any international control, and might bear their part in the defence.

Colonel Stanley said that the interest of our Colonial Empire was to see the Canal run economically. To buy out the present owners would place a financial burden on the Canal administration which would prevent any economy for many years to come. There was no power under which we could dispossess the French shareholders except by agreement. The French could not be forced to abandon their rights. Finally, the Company was an Egyptian one.

Mr. Attlee thought that the necessary pressure could be brought to bear on the French if the United Nations declared that the great waterways of the world were to be placed on an international basis.

Mr. Alexander thought that the Committee should go back to their original viewpoint, which was first that the present position was unsatisfactory in that we had an insufficient share in the control, and secondly that the time was now ripe for a bold change in the status of the Canal.

Lord Cranborne pointed out that the Canal was in some respects only part of the Middle East, and he doubted whether it would be to our advantage to have the Russians taking part in the control of the Canal, or stationing troops there. It might be desirable to have the Americans in, but he felt that each of the nations should shoulder the burden for a certain area, and that we should certainly desire to shoulder the burden in the Middle East.

Discussion then turned upon the wider defence questions presented by the Mediterranean and the Middle East, and the possible dangers to which the Canal might be exposed. It was pointed out that the Chiefs of Staff in their Report had not considered what possible enemies might exist, but had drawn up the requirements which ought to be fulfilled in any agreement reached on the defence of the Canal. They gave a list of the powers which it would be necessary for the defence authority to wield in peace and war.

After further discussion, the view was generally expressed that it would be desirable to settle the general lines of our policy in relation to the defence of the Canal before dealing with the wider question of its future administration. The Committee felt, however, that before proceeding further with their task they would have to ask the War Cabinet for guidance on the general nature of the defence arrangements in the Mediterranean and Middle East under a World
X Organisation, and on the attitude of His Majesty's Government to the idea of bringing other powers into the control, and into the defence arrangements, not only of the Suez Canal, but of the Middle East as a whole. Was it the policy of His Majesty's Government that the responsibility for the defence of the Suez Canal should be vested in ourselves in perpetuity? Or should we seek to associate the Americans, and perhaps other Powers, under the aegis of the World Organisation? Would it be contrary to the policy of His Majesty's Government for the Russians to be associated with us and other nations in the Middle East and on the Canal?

The Committee then turned to the comments by the Minister Resident in the Middle East (S.C.(M)(45)4).

Mr. Peake drew attention to paragraph 11 of the Paper, in which Sir Edward Grigg stated that we had closed the Canal to enemy shipping in the course of the present war. This statement was not correct. We had not closed the Canal. We had merely taken steps to prevent any shipping approaching it, and thus being in a position to defend free passage.

The Committee:—

(a) Instructed the Secretary to draft for their consideration a Report to the War Cabinet on the lines of the discussion which had taken place, and seeking guidance on the questions affecting defence policy outlined in X above.

(b) Invited the Minister of State to consult H.M. Ambassador in Egypt as suggested in paragraph 11 of his Memorandum (S.C.(M)(44)7). Consultation should be on the basis of the various hypotheses which had been put forward for the control and the defence of the Suez Canal.

2 CAB 66/63, WP(45)197 20 Mar 1945
'Future defence policy in the Suez Canal area: report of the Suez Canal Committee': War Cabinet memorandum by Mr Attlee (chairman)

In accordance with the terms of reference remitted to us by the War Cabinet, we have been investigating the various factors bearing upon the long-term policy to be adopted by His Majesty's Government on the future of the Suez Canal. We find it necessary to ask for a measure of political guidance from the War Cabinet on certain points before we can proceed to finish our task.

2. It is unnecessary in this Report to set out the full background to our study. This was contained in a Memorandum submitted to the War Cabinet by the Secretary of State for Foreign Affairs on the 7th September, 1944 (W.P. (44) 507). Broadly speaking, there are two sides to the problem of the future of the Suez Canal. The first is the general method of administration which we should seek to secure. The second is defence. The two sides are related in that arrangements for the administration must be such as to secure to the defence authority for the Canal the powers which it requires.

3. The Committee first considered the future administration of the Canal. Various alternative suggestions were put forward in the Foreign Secretary's Memorandum. The issue was finally narrowed down before the Committee to two alternative courses of action, namely—

(a) That we should now work towards the conversion of the present Canal Company into a Public Utility Service under the control of the United Nations, on the general ground that an undertaking of this magnitude and international importance ought no longer to continue to be in the hands of a profit-making concern. It would be necessary to secure French and Egyptian agreement to this policy, and this might involve financial compensation both to the shareholders of the Canal Company and to the Egyptian Government, which under existing arrangements is due to receive complete possession of the Canal in 1968. The scheme for international administration of the Canal would provide for United Nations supervision, and for the carrying out of the actual administration by a small efficient and expert body representative of the maritime users of the Canal.

(b)   That we should not seek to change the existing arrangements for the administration of the Canal, at any rate until much nearer the date when the concession lapses, but that we should concentrate as our immediate aim on securing satisfactory arrangements for the defence of the Canal. The arguments in favour of this course of action, which is supported by the Chancellor of the Exchequer, are partly political and partly financial. It is suggested that international management would be bad management; that the United States and Russia, and possibly others, would desire to have a voice in the control; that the suggestion for a change would cause offence to French prestige; and that the United States would fear that some similar proposal would be put forward for the control of the Panama Canal. The financial argument is that compensation would be fixed at what may prove to have been the crest of the wave of the Company's prosperity, and that the financial burden resulting from this compensation would mean that all hope of any reduction in the level of dues would have to be abandoned for 60 years. A bargain made now would therefore be likely to be a desperately bad bargain.

4.   Before making any recommendation on the above courses of action, the Committee felt it necessary to examine the other side of the problem, namely, defence. We were immediately brought up against the validity or otherwise of the British objectives as stated by the Foreign Secretary in his Memorandum, as follows:—

"(a) that responsibility for the defence of the Canal should be vested in His Majesty's Government in perpetuity;
"(b) that the Canal dues should be fixed at the lowest rate compatible with efficient administration with a reasonable return to the shareholders, including the Treasury;
"(c) that the Canal should be so administered as to facilitate the exercise of His Majesty's Government's defence responsibilities."

5.   The crux of the matter is the validity of the first objective. This has so far been stated by the Foreign Office as an axiom. It is strongly supported by the defence authorities in the Middle East and by the Chiefs of Staff and is fully accepted by some members of the Committee. Others, however, feel considerable doubts about this objective.[1] They feel that there is much to be said, not only for international control of the Canal, but also for international responsibility for its defence, as being more in harmony with the aims which His Majesty's Government are trying to realise in the new World Organisation. The considerations advanced in favour of this view can be summarised as follows:—

(a) It is desirable on general grounds that an undertaking of such importance to the world at large should be under international control, and not under the control of a single country, such as Egypt, or of a profit-making company.

(b) If this is admitted, then the burden of defence should also be shared among the nations. The time has gone when Great Britain could afford to police the seas of the world for the benefit of others. The United States and Russia are composed of large compact land masses, and this geographical fact tends to cause them to limit their commitments to the immediate vicinity of their territory. We, on the other hand, have an Empire which straggles across the world, and which involves us in heavy commitments in many directions. There is a tendency on all sides to leave us

---

[1] Mr Attlee and Mr Alexander.

to carry the burden of security over large areas of the world, which burden falls very largely on British taxpayers and on British man-power. This is a state of affairs which should not be allowed to persist, as otherwise our resources will be strained beyond the breaking-point.

(c) The defence of the Suez Canal cannot be viewed separately from the general defence problem of the Eastern Mediterranean and Middle East. Are we alone to be responsible for keeping the peace throughout this area? Would it not be to our advantage that other nations, and particularly the United States, should share in the problems of security and defence in this part of the world? (It may be argued that it would not be in our interests to associate Russia in the control of the Suez Canal, and in the maintenance of its security. It is not certain, however, that the Russians would necessarily wish at any rate in present circumstances to take an active share in these matters, especially if Russia gets satisfaction over the revision of the Montreux Convention.

(d) The advantages of international assistance in the burden of maintaining security in the Middle East could be combined with a larger British share in the administration of the Canal. As the principal user of the Canal, and as the senior partner in the security of the area as a whole, we should be entitled to such a share.

(e) It would be much easier to get the French and the Egyptians to acquiesce in new arrangements for the administration of the Canal if its control and security were declared to be the concern of the United Nations, than if we attempted to establish the predominance of Great Britain alone.

6.   In view of the above considerations the Committee felt it necessary to ask the War Cabinet to instruct them whether or not in their further examination of this matter they should proceed on the assumptions:—

(1) that responsibility for the defence of the Canal should be vested in His Majesty's Government in perpetuity; and
(2) that His Majesty's Government for political and strategic reasons regard it as desirable that Great Britain should play the predominant part in the defence and political control of the Middle East.

3   CAB 66/65, WP(45)256   13 Apr 1945
'Defence of the Middle East': War Cabinet memorandum by Mr Eden

[On 27 Mar the PHP[1] produced a paper 'Security in the Eastern Mediterranean and the Middle East' examining Britain's requirements in Egypt in the light of broader power political assessments of the Middle Eastern situation. It argued that if Britain failed to maintain its prestige in the region the Arab states might throw in their lot with the USSR, and that it was essential for Britain to secure general recognition of its predominant interest in the Middle East and its right to play the leading role in the area. On the other hand the acquisition of rights and facilities to defend the region might conflict with Britain's policy of avoiding Soviet hostility (CAB 79/31, PHP(45)10, 27 Mar 1945).]

---

[1] In 1943 the Post Hostilities Planning Committee was established as the successor to the Military Sub-Committee of the COS. It reported to the FO as well as to the COS and the Armistice and Post-War Planning Committee. The head of the FO Economic and Reconstruction Department sat on the committee whose remit was to put forward solutions to problems arising from the occupation of enemy territory in so far as such problems were connected with the instruments of surrender or with questions of general strategic importance. In 1944 the PHP Committee became the Post Hostilities Planning Staff.

In their report on future defence policy in the Suez Canal area (W.P. (45) 197 of the 20th March)[2] the Suez Canal Committee formulate two questions, *viz.*; should they proceed on the assumptions:—

(1) that responsibility for the defence of the Canal should be vested in His Majesty's Government in perpetuity;

(2) that His Majesty's Government, for political and strategic reasons, regard it as desirable that Great Britain should play the predominant part in the defence and political control of the Middle East.

2.   In leading up to these questions, the Committee remarked that the Foreign Office had hitherto regarded assumption (1), viewed as an objective, as axiomatic; but that certain members felt there was much to be said in favour of international responsibility for the defence of the Canal as being more in harmony with the aims which His Majesty's Government are trying to realise in the new World Organisation. The arguments in support of this view are contained in paragraph 5 of the report, sub-paragraphs (a) to (e). In particular, it is pointed out that, in the case of the United States and Russia, geographical facts tend to cause them to limit their defence commitments to the immediate vicinity of their territory, whereas the British Empire, being dispersed over the globe, involves us in commitments in many directions of a nature to strain our resources to breaking-point. It is suggested that it would be to our advantage that other nations, notably the United States, should share in the problems of security and defence in the Middle East generally, and that it might be easier to induce the French and Egyptians to acquiesce in new arrangements for the administration of the Canal if both its control and its security were declared to be the concern of the United Nations rather than of Great Britain alone.

3.   I understand that any satisfactory reply to the two questions put by the Committee must take into account not only our future available resources, but also world (and in particular United States) opinions and tendencies, and must conform to them if we are not to be faced, later on, with pressure to reverse our policy. My submission, however, is that both questions must be answered in the affirmative, and in endeavouring to justify that submission I shall examine the questions first of all from the point of view of the Middle East itself and secondly from the broader standpoint of world security into which our Middle Eastern arrangements must be fitted.

4.   The Middle Eastern area (*viz.*: Egypt, Palestine, Transjordan, the Levant States, Iraq, Saudi Arabia and the Persian Gulf), with Egypt and the Suez Canal as its core, is the meeting place of two continents and, if Turkey be added, of three. It is thus one of the most important strategic areas in the world, and it is an area the defence of which is a matter of life and death to the British Empire since, as the present war and the war of 1914–18 have both proved, it is there that the Empire can be cut in half. Consequently, we are bound to give the Middle East an extremely high priority when allotting our available resources to the areas where we have responsibilities. For this reason alone, we cannot afford to resign our special position in the area (even though in an emergency we may be able to accept the help of others

---

[2] See 2.

in defending it) and allow our position to be dependent on arrangements of an international character.

5.   Secondly, the Middle East is the sole really large source of oil outside America which is available to us. Recent studies indicate that in ten years' time neither the British Empire nor even the United States will be able to exert their full war effort in case of need without the oil supplies of the Iraq–Persian Gulf area.

6.   There is a further consideration. The quality which the Middle Eastern peoples recognise above all others is strength. If we retained our position there during the early part of the present war, it is because the Middle East never lost confidence in our resolution and in our ultimate ability to win through. If once we go to the lengths of inviting other Powers permanently to share the burden which we have hitherto carried in the Middle East, the countries concerned will construe our action not as statesmanship but as abdication: at best they would become confused and revert to the game of playing off the Powers against each other: at worst they would identify themselves with the interests of the newcomer whom they conceived to be the strongest. Our present position would thereby be forfeited: it is questionable whether it could ever be retrieved.

7.   To turn to the more general considerations outlined earlier in this memorandum, it is true that His Majesty's Government are pledged to support the organisation of security by international co-operation. But the World Organisation, when it comes to devise practical means of ensuring peace, can scarcely proceed otherwise than by giving one Great Power special defence responsibilities in its particular area or areas: and the effectiveness of the World Organisation in the last resort in carrying out its decisions will depend on the efficiency of the defence facilities available there to the Great Power concerned. Whether, in a more or less distant future, this principle will give way to a more general sharing of responsibility it is difficult to say. Our hope and intention would be that any provision we made on our own account for the security of the United Kingdom and the Commonwealth would receive the eventual sanction of the World Organisation, by which it would be regarded as a contribution to the general security, and therefore as an arrangement to be adopted and fitted into the World Organisation's security arrangements. But at the present moment each of the Great Powers is, in fact, in the same position in the areas it considers vital to it as is this country in the Middle East. The position of the United States in relation to the Panama Canal is identical with our own in relation to the Suez Canal, as is the position of Russia with regard to certain areas of Eastern Europe. It is a practical certainty that, at present at any rate, those Powers would decline to share their special responsibilities with us (and it would be a grievous drain on our resources to seek to claim a share) and we are equally entitled to exclusive facilities (so far as we consider them expedient) in our own vital area. I recommend, then, to my colleagues that, pending the establishment of the World Organisation and its Military Staff Committee, His Majesty's Government should secure the vital interests of the British Empire and Commonwealth in the Middle East by their own means. In so far as this involves treaty arrangements with the nations of the Middle East, I might add that the conclusion of freely negotiated treaties can hardly be challenged as an undemocratic method and that such treaties have brought undeniable benefits to the countries concerned.

8.   I do not consider, therefore, that our claim to a predominant rôle in the defence and political control of the Middle East is out of harmony with the general

international background. But I have one final point to make, namely, that the earliest possible consultation should take place on this subject with the Dominions, two of which (Australia and New Zealand) have always shown an acute—and highly justifiable—interest in the defence of Egypt and the Suez Canal. Solidarity with the Dominions on this issue would strengthen our position *vis-à-vis* the United States, and their practical assistance—were they disposed to afford it—would lessen the strain on our resources, to which the Committee drew attention, which would be imposed by our assuming sole responsibility for security in the Middle Eastern area.

4   FO 371/45920, no 1406   14 Apr 1945
[Political situation in Egypt]: letter from Lord Killearn to Sir R Campbell on the gloomy outlook. *Minute* by P S Scrivener   [Extract]

[Ahmed Maher, Egyptian prime minister since Oct 1944, was murdered by a member of the Muslim Brotherhood (Ikhwan) following his bringing of Egypt into the war in Feb 1945. The idea that the Wafd were in decline stemmed from their loss of 'nationalist' credibility following their installation in power by the British in Feb 1942 and their refusal to take part in the elections of Jan 1945.]

I feel, though you already know it, that it is worth while recapitulating the unpromising state of affairs at the moment out here.

The Wafd fell last autumn largely through their own folly. I was not here at the time which was fortunate, for it has thus been easier to avoid any open breach between us and the Wafd. And incidentally, (as you have doubtless read between the lines of my official reports), it is owing very largely if not entirely to that, that the Wafd have kept so quiet and behaved with (for them) unusual discretion during the months since they were ejected from office. Their one lapse—and it was a very bad one—was their manifesto against Egypt's entry into the war, which was the stupidest of stupid blunders.

They were succeeded by Ahmed Maher who was the one and only man who had a hope of making a reasonable success. He had in fact been put in by the Palace: he knew in advance that he could count on full Embassy support. And so it worked out—and things seemed to be set fair for some little time to come. But naturally I had not failed to impress upon King F. in the friendliest way that in installing Ahmed Maher and his coalition H.M. had come well down into the direct political arena which had its dangers and its great responsabilities [sic]: that we all of us hoped it was going to be a success and that certainly the Embassy, from the background, would always be ready to lend a helping hand to the new P.M.

Matters seemed set reasonably well: and my relations with Ahmed Maher were progressing admirably. We understood one another and could meet and exchange ideas in the best possible of moods and an atmosphere of mutual understanding and collaboration.

Then came the murder, and poor little Ahmed Maher to whom for many years past I had been genuinely attached was "liquidated". He was succeeded, as he had to be, by a very different kettle of fish, Nokrashi.

Ahmed Maher's death was a real tragedy. He was, in my view, the only man capable of carrying the country over what, at the best, was only an interim period.

And so we found ourselves faced with Nokrashi in his stead—a narrow, pig-headed, hair-splitting obstinate schoolmaster! With no vision, no real statesmanship. Not unsound as regards basic attachment to the Anglo–Egyptian connection: but totally without qualification for the job of P.M. to which he had been so suddenly and accidentally elevated. Not only that, but with no following in the country where he had always been regarded as—what he indeed was—the party C.G.S. [chief general secretary] of Ahmed Maher, and nothing more.

Add to this a Finance Minister (Makram)[1] hardly on speaking terms with the new P.M.: and as a matter of common knowledge out for his own hand and inspired especially with the spirit of vengeance against Nahas and the Wafd whom he was determined at whatever cost, to see put behind the bars.

And if that were not enough, the above "mixture" has more recently been capped by the addition of Bedawi as Foreign Minister! You, from your early days here, will almost certainly remember Bedawi? An exceedingly able and agile lawyer, but an extreme nationalist. Who by nature and by training looks at every comma and every dot with the suspicion that it veils a trap of some sort. In short the last possible person to put in charge of foreign affairs.

To mitigate this pretty hopeless lay-out, I had of late been fortunate in having little Amr P. Very luckily for us, Hassanein[2] (who has for long been both weak and undependable) went out of action last November (he all but pipped, and in my opinion is quite liable to do so still at any minute) and suggested to me that whilst he was laid up I should use Amr as a discreet channel with King F., with whom (owing to his racquet prowess) Amr stood particularly well. As you know, this arrangement proved a gift from the Gods: and by the regular use of it, we have been able to surmount many difficulties which by direct approach to the Government would have been quite hopeless. For the plain fact always remains that this outfit is a Palace outfit—and will always do the Palace bidding.

Then, unfortunately, the endemic Egyptian suspiciousness triumphed once more. And even Hassanein, who had sponsored him, became jealous of Amr whom, by the usual poison in his ear, Hassanein ending by suspecting as out to supplant him in his job of permanent adviser to King F.!

And so, after various delays, Amr finally had to leave for his post in London, despite the fact that Hassanein is still ill in bed and out of action more or less indefinitely.

The net result of all this is that I am now left without my Amr to act as emissary—and even advocate—with King F. And equally that I am left face to face with Nokrashi and the even more impossible and unresilient Bedawi.

We had a good example of Nokrashi—and I was glad that a British Cabinet Minister should see it for himself—when Swinton[3] was here and I took him down to discuss aviation matters with him. Swinton dealt with him in a masterly way which I hope may prove to have worked in that particular issue. But my point is that that is the man, and that is the combination with whom we *may* have to deal over really big questions—such as defence of Egypt, Treaty Revision, Suez Canal and I know not what.

A pretty gloomy outlook—indeed an outlook that could hardly be more discouraging.

---

[1] Makram Ebeid leader of the Independent Wafdist bloc or Wafd Kotla party which he founded in 1942 when expelled from the Wafd for publishing a 'Black Book' detailing corruption within the party.
[2] Hassanein Pasha, chief of the Royal Cabinet.
[3] Lord Swinton, minister for civil aviation, 1944–1945.

Naturally we must carry on as best we may: and I think the records will show that such is my usual habit. But you cannot make a silk purse out of a sow's ear: and the particular ear we have to deal with is even less silky[4] than usual!

One has naturally pondered what the alternatives are? I don't know *any* answer—and would prefer not to attempt one at present. The Wafd are gaining ground in my opinion (I have never wavered from the belief that they have always had at least a 60% majority in the country), and will continue to do so proportionately as the stock of the present team falls. They have (luckily for them) been left out of the San Francisco Delegation which gives them full freedom to criticise whatever is done there. Cloth, food and supplies are shorter in the country than ever. In fact, the Wafd seem to me to be "sitting pretty". Nonetheless my own feeling is that it will do them good to stay out in the wilderness yet awhile. It should sober them up and give them time to reflect on their stupidities and fatuities whilst in office. So that—in my estimation—it will be better that they should not return just yet awhile.

Where, in all this, does King Farouk get off? That is another and a big question. I think myself that his is a very much dickier situation then either he or anyone else yet realises. The majority party is out of office and he has made them his sworn enemies; the country is quite capable of serious social unrest at any time; he has gone out of his way to insult and make an enemy of a vindictive and dangerous intriguer like Nashaat; he is not on speaking terms with his uncle Hussein Sirri;—*and* his relations with his Queen are the subject of public gossip and scandal! Not a particularly rosy picture. At the same time there *is* another side to it. Since the strong medicine of Alamein he has greatly changed his tune and is now affability itself—especially to our rather naive soldiers and (especially) airmen. This incidentally has carried with it the great advantage of his being willing, at Amr's prompting, to put the present Government in their places when required and to compel them to play the game by us. But with the departure of Amr that channel, I repeat, has dried up. And nothing save a moribund Hassanein, still in bed, to take his place!

On top of all this, an American drive which small men such as Nokrashi and Bedawi are not at all above using in the hope of undermining our predominant political position.

So there you are! A very jolly outlook. Just at the moment perhaps it doesn't vitally matter. And my role remains that of friendly observer, waiting on events. But when, as I anticipate, Egypt once more becomes a vital strategic centre or base; when in fact our war effort turns and increases in the Far East, this attitude of detached and friendly indifference to internal politics, may no longer be the right one.

There again it seems to me we can only "wait and see".

I apologise for this long rambling effusion. But it's a Saturday afternoon and I felt there was no harm in letting you know my trend of thought.

Minute on 4

This letter generally recapitulates the criticisms of Nokrashi Pasha which Lord Killearn has voiced ever since Nokrashi came into office. Hitherto HE has reported any word of unfavourable comment and has left Nokrashi's virtues, if any, to be inferred. But people who have known Nokrashi for years are insistent that he *does*

---

[4] An FO official wrote 'sowish' under 'silky'.

possess considerable virtues beneath his rather forbidding exterior, and I think the embassy should use such people to build a bridge between them and Nokrashi. The answer to Lord Killearn is really to remind him of the saying of ?Talleyrand 'Il faut tirer parti de tout, même de ce qui déplaît'.

The big question mark in Egyptian politics at the moment is whether the (Nahas) Wafd is a spent force or not. Lord Killearn evidently thinks it is not: but there are competent observers who hold the opposite view. . . .

P.S.S.
28.4.45

5   CAB 81/46, PHP(45)13, annex   18 Apr 1945
'Future defence policy in the Suez Canal area': draft aide mémoire by the Post Hostilities Planning Staff for the COS

[In the summer and autumn of 1944 an argument had developed over the political actions recommended by the PHP in terms of taking measures to incorporate as much of Germany as possible into a Western bloc. The FO objected to what it regarded as unwarranted interference in the political aspects of foreign policy making and it was agreed that henceforth the PHPS would concern itself only with military questions and would not therefore require a FO representative. The PHPS continued to provide papers for consideration by the COS until the end of the war, covering such questions as security in the Eastern Mediterranean and Middle East, military aspects of the Yalta conference and advice to British representatives on the European Advisory Commission. By the time this paper was prepared the COS had already agreed with Eden that the defence of the Suez Canal should remain a British responsibility in perpetuity (CAB 79/31, COS 90(45)14, 6 Apr 1945).]

Introduction

1.   The Suez Canal Committee has asked the War Cabinet whether or not they should proceed on the following assumptions:—

Assumption   I—That responsibility for the defence of the Canal should be vested in His Majesty's Government in perpetuity.

Assumption II—That His Majesty's Government, for political and strategic reasons, regard it as desirable that Great Britain should play the predominant part in the defence and political control of the Middle East.

2.   Certain members of the Suez Canal Committee maintain that "international responsibility" for the defence of the canal would be more in harmony with His Majesty's Government's general policy.

3.   The Chiefs of Staff may wish to enter a caveat to the effect that decisions on this subject, particularly in connection with our relations with the U.S.S.R., should not be regarded as final, pending consideration of British strategic requirements throughout the world, a review of which is now in preparation.[1]

---

[1] This was to be the final task of the PHP and resulted in PHP (45)29, 29 June 1945, 'The security of the British empire'. See BDEEP series A, vol 1, S R Ashton & S E Stockwell, eds, *Imperial policy and colonial practice 1925–1945*, part I, 43. This document attached greater importance to the Indian Ocean than the Middle East but was soon overtaken by the debate on the Middle East's importance that arose out of Anglo–Soviet disagreements at the post-war peace conferences between July and Sept 1945.

4.   Since the defence of the Suez Canal cannot be viewed separately from the general defence problem of the Middle East, we deal first with Assumption II.

Assumption II

British interests in the Middle East

5.   British strategic interests in the Middle East are:—

(a) Oil.

(b) Sea and air communications. Because the British Empire "straggles across the world", the British Empire will be the chief sufferer from their disruption.

(c) A main administrative base and location for an Imperial Strategic Reserve.

(d) British territories and States to whose defence we are committed.

(e) Internal Security. Unrest in the Middle East would have repercussions throughout the Moslem world, including India.

6.   In order to secure these important interests it is essential that His Majesty's Government should continue to play the predominant part in the direction and control of Middle East defence policy.

Transfer of responsibility to the United Nations

7.   Assumption by the United Nations of direct and joint responsibility for the security of the Middle East would deprive us of our predominant role in the defence of the Middle East, and would therefore be militarily unacceptable. Moreover, any such arrangement would be inefficient.

8.   It would, however, be acceptable for the security of the Middle East to be declared the concern of the United Nations, provided that the effective control of defence policy was assured to His Majesty's Government. This might be achieved under some regional security scheme.

Participation of other powers

9.   In view of the manpower stringency and the weakness of our strategic position, it is (apart from political considerations) to our advantage that other nations should share in the burden of the defence of the Middle East. We should welcome assistance from the U.S.A., the Middle East States themselves, and France.

10.   *U.S.A.* The help of the U.S.A. could be of great value—greater than that of any other country. In a major war, her early and active assistance would be essential. It would, therefore, be greatly to our advantage that she should accept definite military commitments in the Middle East in peace time, so as to ensure her early intervention in war. Her interest in Middle East oil resources might make her willing to accept such commitments.

11.   *Middle East States.* Our Middle East defence policy will, in any event, require the full co-operation of the Middle East States themselves, particularly Egypt.

12.   *France.* French help in the defence of the Middle East would be desirable, but not at the price of seriously antagonising the Arabs. Though other powers have not done so, His Majesty's Government have recognised that France has a special position in the Levant. She has large financial interests in the Canal and in Iraq oil.

13.   *U.S.S.R.* Although some Soviet participation in defence arrangements in the area may be unavoidable, such participation should for strategic reasons be limited as far as possible.

14.   Any participation by other powers must be subject to the proviso that our authority in all matters affecting the security, internal and external, of the Middle East as a whole remains effective.

Assumption I

Defence measures in the Suez Canal area

15.   Both in peace and war, it will be essential to secure compliance by the Egyptian Government and by the Canal Company (or its successor) with defence requirements in the neighbourhood of the Canal. The Chiefs of Staff have already reported on this subject, and have indicated the type of requirements involved, e.g., security measures. Some assistance from other countries in the provision of military resources will be welcome even in this area but, for reasons of administrative efficiency, and to avoid giving the Egyptians and the Canal officials the opportunity to play off one power against another, it is essential that one power should be in a position of effective authority with regard to these local measures.

16.   British strategic interests are intimately affected. The mobility of any imperial strategic reserves in the Middle East will greatly depend on our having freedom of movement, both through the Suez Canal and across it. It would not be acceptable that any power other than Great Britain should be responsible for the control of defence measures in the neighbourhood of the Canal.

Conclusions

17.   We conclude that, subject to a review of British strategic requirements throughout the world, the assumptions propounded by the Suez Canal Committee should be revised to read as follows:—

(a) The defence of the Canal cannot be separated from the defence of the Middle East as a whole.

(b) His Majesty's Government regard it as essential that Great Britain should play the predominant role and retain a position of effective authority in all matters affecting the security, internal and external, of the Middle East as a whole. Subject to this it is important to obtain the assistance of the Middle East States themselves, France, and particularly the U.S.A.

(c) Responsibility for control of defence measures in the neighbourhood of the Canal should be vested in His Majesty's Government.

6 FO 371/45920, no 1406   5 May 1945
[Political situation in Egypt]: letter (reply) from Sir R Campbell to Lord Killearn on the importance of King Farouk's position   [Extract]

Thank you very much for the review of the Egyptian political situation contained in your personal letter of April 14th.[1]

It was certainly an unpleasant trick of fate which eliminated Ahmed Maher and confronted you with the Nokrashi–Bedawi combination. You have all my sympathies

---

[1] See 4.

in your task of shepherding it along the road we want it to follow; I only hope that non-official Britons in relations with Nokrashi, e.g. C. Delaney, may so use their personal contact with him as, so to speak, to soften him up at any rate to some extent for the official exchanges, and be useful to you in this way. From your descriptions of him, these exchanges must, I fear, at best be irksome and wearisome. As regards Amr, I do not think that the present arrangement can be prolonged indefinitely, or even for a long time. We can defend it for a while on the ground that it is excessively difficult for the Egyptian Government to choose among the personalities available, a suitable nominee for the key post of Ambassador here, but a lot of people will sooner or later begin asking awkward questions about the absence of an Ambassador, and it seems to me that you would be perfectly justified in pressing fairly soon—say in a few months—for Amr to be recalled to his former sphere of usefulness and succeeded by an Ambassador who really need only be a respectable figurehead. In fact if anything happens to Hassanein I should anticipate your being anxious to do this at once.

The King's position, as you say, is certainly interesting. We feel, and I believe that you agree, that we want neither an uncontrolled Wafd nor an uncontrolled King. Clearly no man can say how the Egyptian internal political scene is going to develop, but it almost looks as though *none* of the existing parties can be relied on to guide Egypt along the road of political realism in external, and social reform in internal, politics. It might for example be held that the Wafd is too corrupt, the Saadists too doctrinaire, the Liberals too paralytic, the independents too independent, the Watanists too unrealistic and the Moslem groups too obscurantist. If this is accepted, the importance of the King's position becomes enhanced, and the case for a satisfactory succession to Hassanein is strengthened. . . .

7   FO 141/1043, no 1   16 May 1945
[Anglo–Egyptian treaty revision at San Francisco]: inward telegram no 1092 from Lord Killearn to FO on the need to retain a predominant position in Egypt

[The end of the war in Europe brought calls for the evacuation of British troops from Egypt and the union of Egypt with the Sudan. The lifting of press censorship in June 1945 increased the demands for an early review of the 1936 treaty which gave Britain the right to station troops in the Suez Canal Zone in peacetime.]

My telegram No. 992 [2nd May: attitude of Egyptian Delegation at San Francisco].[1]

2.   Subject to fundamental difficulty of commenting without knowing fully what line United Kingdom Delegation are taking in relevant discussions at San Francisco, my view on the principle involved is that it will be the height of absurdity if one of the fruits of our victory is to be the abandonment of our predominant position in Egypt. As already recorded I should deplore any such decision.

3.   If, as is possible, the retention of our predominance entails being a little rough with Egypt, I should be fully prepared to be as rough as required. Bedawi's paper is a clear attempt to sabotage the Treaty on juridical grounds.

---

[1] The San Francisco conference to finalise the establishment of the new United Nations Organisation met from 25 Apr 1945 to 26 June 1945.

4.   The most urgent practical point in Bedawi's paper is the indication that Treaty revision will be forced on to the Agenda of the San Francisco Conference by the argument of the Egyptian Delegation that they cannot sign any instrument on the lines of the Dumbarton Oaks proposals,[2] unless they are promised an early release from such of their obligations under the Treaty as are inconsistent with the undertakings to which they would be subscribing. But this objection could be met no less effectively by a promise that Egypt and His Majesty's Government would be called upon to enter into a new agreement under VIII(B)(5), than by a promise that Egypt should be allowed to tear up the Treaty. I assume that there must be many other nations represented at San Francisco who will have to make some sort of reserve with regard to their existing bilateral treaties and that a general reserve of this nature may prove to be necessary.

5.   In any case I hold that we should not admit that the Treaty can be revised before 22nd December, 1946, when it falls due for revision by mutual consent. If legal adjustments of its terms are required consequent on San Francisco, then will be the time to consider a redraft. I take it that our Delegation will ensure that (if necessary) the point is sufficiently covered under whatever may be agreed to at San Francisco.

6.   As to regional arrangements, my view remains that it would be sheer madness to admit the French and the Russians to any degree of control over Egypt, under any form. I should also be opposed to American participation, though that would, at a pinch, be less repugnant than participation by the other two. But to agree to any weakening of our predominance here would in my view be to admit to "losing the peace" with a vengeance. By winning the war we have proved not only that we are prepared to stand up for our rights, but that we can effectively do so. I should be fully prepared, on your instructions, to make that point completely clear to Egypt.

---

[2] The Dumbarton Oaks conference met in two sessions to conduct exploratory discussions on a world security organisation to replace the League of Nations with a new UN organisation. The first, in which the US, the USSR and Britain participated, met from 21 Aug 1944 to 28 Sept 1944. The second, in which China replaced the USSR, met from 29 Sept 1944 to 7 Oct 1944. The meetings helped prepare the ground for the San Francisco conference.

8   PREM 8/23   23 May 1945
[Anglo–Egyptian relations]: memorandum by Sir E Grigg on his farewell talk with King Farouk   [Extract]

[In the summer of 1945 Grigg had a room in the Cabinet Office while winding up the affairs of the resident minister in the Middle East. As a result of the conversations he had there with Sir Edward Bridges, the Cabinet secretary, the latter received copies of the two memoranda written by Grigg earlier in the year (see 11, 15) and circulated to the caretaker government. Grigg wanted the new prime minister to see them along with the last two pages of his record of the farewell meeting with King Farouk printed below. The meeting covered a large number of issues including Farouk's views on the disaster which Churchill's election defeat would bring, the Russian threat, Zionism and the Hashimites. Grigg regarded the record as so confidential that he could not officially send a copy to the FO and the only other copy had gone to Churchill (PREM 8/23, minute by Sir E Bridges, 29 Aug 1945). Attlee read the record of Farouk's remarks and made no comment.]

... Then, almost pleadingly, he said in words which I can (two hours later) closely reproduce:—

> "I will say to you what I cannot say to my own countrymen and have never yet said to anyone else. If I said anything of the kind in public here, I would only defeat myself. I know that my father was right. England is Egypt's best friend and I know that I can never make progress for my people here without England's guidance and help. We shall need it for years and years—certainly for my life. I don't exaggerate my own importance; but here I am, and I want to do my best for Egypt. I know, too, that Egypt is important to you, and that I can do more for Anglo–Egyptian friendship than any one else. Please believe me, I don't want to make much of my own influence and place. Other Arab rulers are in much the same position as I, but Egypt is perhaps the most critical country in your relations with the Middle East. If you will understand my difficulties and come halfway to meet me, I will meet you halfway at once. If you will go a third of the way, I will go two-thirds—with your help. But you must understand how sensitive we are. There is little you can't do with us, if you do not hurt our dignity and will treat us as partners in a common task. My Ministers are not much use. I cannot yet find any younger or better men to put in their place. Our Parliament is unrepresentative—a totally undemocratic farce. I know our future depends in all things on English help. But it must be unobtrusive help, if it is to be real help. I have given you my confidence as I have never given it to any one else. I feel you understand this country and its place in the Middle East. I know I can rely upon you not to give me away and only to report this conversation where you think it may be of use. I have kept you very long, but I have long wanted to speak to you like this."

I said, very sincerely, that I deeply appreciated his confidence and the frankness with which he had spoken his mind on his fears and hopes of us. I felt sure that both his country and mine had much to gain by such mutual frankness of speech. He could count on me to utter no word of what he had said to me except in quarters where I was sure it would be of use.

He said "Bon voyage, and please come back".

9   FO 371/45921, no 1657   28 May 1945

[Anglo–Egyptian treaty revision]: outward telegram no 812 from FO to Lord Killearn on the attitude of the Egyptian government and the line to be taken in discussions with King Farouk

[The instructions contained in this telegram intensified the dispute between the FO and Killearn over which groups in Egypt were the most desirable collaborators for the British. The ambassador, rejecting the FO views, believed that King Farouk and his team of ministers under Nokrashi were not only hopeless but dangerous (FO 141/1043, no 19, Cairo tel 1180, 30 May 1945).]

Your telegram No. 1092.[1]

See my telegram No. 955 to San Francisco.

There is unfortunately no escape from the fact that legally speaking, Egyptian Government will be justified in claiming that entry into force of Charter of World Organisation and disappearance of League of Nations will necessitate revision of Anglo–Egyptian treaty.[2] But this is not to say that we do not fully share your dislike of their tactics.

2.   Prospects of the rough approach to Nokrashi do not appear to us very promising; and we suggest that in this matter the person to work on is the King with his intense nervousness of Russian interference (and over-all responsibility for the present Coalition). It could be represented to His Majesty that the practical outcome of the success of his Government's policy (not that we propose to allow it to succeed) would be to undermine British influence in Egypt and throw open the country to international, and particularly Russian, influence, with results which have already been troubling His Majesty's imagination. His Majesty would, in consequence, be well-advised to ensure that his Government abandon their policy of legalistic sabotage of Anglo–Egyptian collaboration, and concentrate instead on working with His Majesty's Government in the framework of the new organisation with a view to the creation of conditions which would allow Egypt to tackle, undisturbed by external influence, the economic and social problems which call so urgently for treatment and in which His Majesty has so often expressed his interest.

3.   You may if you think it useful approach His Majesty on the foregoing line. Such action would not, we think, compromise the source of your telegram No. 992 since by tabling the amendments in San Francisco telegram No. 205 (particularly references to "reconsideration of treaties" and military alliance) the Egyptian Government seem to have sufficiently disclosed their hand.

---

[1] See 7.

[2] The Egyptians were also likely to argue that the treaty obligations imposed on Egypt were incompatible with the new world security organisation (FO 371/45921, no 1883, minute by P S Scrivener, 3 June 1945).

10   FO 371/45921, no 2054   23 June 1945

[Anglo–Egyptian relations]: inward telegram no 1401 from Lord Killearn to FO advocating a show of firmness in discussions with the Egyptian government. *Minutes* by A V Coverley-Price and P S Scrivener

[The minutes reproduced with this telegram, which were approved by the permanent under-secretary, Sir A Cadogan, formed the basis of a telegram to Cairo. Later on the day that the telegram was despatched, Churchill minuted on telegram 1401: 'Should we not support?' Cadogan justified the FO's actions on the grounds that the time was not right for the return of the Wafd and that action which might precipitate a crisis should be avoided until the political situation in Egypt was clearer. The FO doubted if a more reasonable successor to Nokrashi could then be found and Cadogan believed that there was no reliable candidate who would co-operate with Britain (FO 371/45291, no 2054, minute by Cadogan, 30 June 1945).]

The time has come when it may be salutary to speak [grp.undec.] openly to the Egyptian Prime Minister.

2.   There is a clear disposition to depart from that spirit of loyal collaboration to which we have been accustomed in the past, and for which we have the right to look from any government of this Allied country.

3.   As instances I quote the following: 1) civil aviation 2) Assuandam 3) tenders for railway material 4) anti treaty manoeuvres at San Francisco.

4.   I am disposed to indicate to the Egyptian Prime Minister that if this goes on we on our side shall be driven to put the screw on; and that we have as levers not only supplies (such as fertilisers, kerosine, cloth, phosphates) but purchase of Egyptian cotton.

5.   As in the last case I should first prepare the ground through Hassanein Pasha. Thereafter I would once more see King Farouk. I would then see Nokrashi Pasha and tell him the position.

6.   I submit it is time we should show firmness and determination with these folk. I believe it to be the only language that in their present inflated mood they will understand. It will incidentally do no harm if it is known that we have once more asserted ourselves which is what the public here expect us to do. I should of course make it clear throughout that we were not interfering with internal politics and that we have no intention or desire whatever of doing so that we were simply recording hard incontrovertible facts and that if they expect the customary goodwill from us, they must prove their goodwill to us by deed.

Minutes on 10

My feeling is that, from the widest point of view, Lord Killearn is in a dangerous mood. He is justifiably irritated by Egyptian procrastination and obstruction, but the application of the screw at this moment would be damaging to our prestige and influence elsewhere: all the more so if it were successful in eliminating Nokrashi, for we should quite clearly have achieved the result by pressure.

Departure from loyal collaboration (paragraph 2) is not a purely Egyptian misdemeanour: we see the same thing in France, Yugoslavia, etc. Threats to cut off the very supplies which Lord Killearn has himself declared to be essential for the populace in order to prevent disorders which give Nokrashi an excellent weapon with which to prove that we do not have the interests of the people at heart and that Lord Killearn's talk about preventing disturbances is so much "blarney".

The red jacket attached suggests that Nokrashi may soon be thrown out owing to his incompetence and the dissatisfaction which he is engendering in his own party, and it would be folly on our part to strengthen his hand by the threats proposed, which might also lose us much of the present feeling in the provinces that British rule brings the greatest benefits. It is all very well to say that Lord Killearn would make it clear that we were not interfering, etc. But the mere assertion of this doubtful argument would not necessarily lead to its acceptance by anyone. We have made our attitude about Syria clear, but it is not universally accepted.

I am sure that for the time being we must bear and forbear and that, in the end, we should achieve more by the cultivation of the friendship of the King and, if possible, by the removal of the resentment and uneasiness inherent in the continuation of the Lampson régime of unpleasant memory (in the King's mind).

Meanwhile we can be quite firm about the Aswan priorities and the need for improved internal distribution, etc. But already increased shipping and other relaxations are depriving us of some of our levers, e.g., in regard to fertilisers.

A.V.C-P.
24.6.45

I agree generally. Lord Killearn is at the moment in a state of exasperation with almost everyone in Egypt. We have parried one attempt to get Nokrashi sacked; and I do not think that *at the moment* it would in any case be right to confront H.M.G. with a row with Egypt for which there is not some *very* good reason based on the conduct of the war (which there isn't). Lord Killearn finds it very difficult to allow this Egyptian Government the rope to hang themselves, but they seem to be engaged in tying the knot for him!

? Reply to the general effect that, while we have every sympathy with Lord Killearn's views, we are not anxious to take drastic action of a nature to precipitate a possible crisis until both the political situation at home is clearer and the situation created by the San Francisco Conference has been more fully studied and appreciated.

P.S.S.
24.6.45

11   CAB 66/67, CP(45)55   2 July 1945
'Imperial security in the Middle East': War Cabinet memorandum by Sir E Grigg

This is a political memorandum. Its purpose is to discuss the following subjects from the standpoint of Imperial security in the Middle East:—

(a) the nature of British interests and aims in the Middle East;
(b) the most promising political method of dealing with the Middle Eastern States;
(c) the varying importance to us of those States;
(d) the attitude to be adopted by His Majesty's Government towards other Powers in the Middle East.

2.   The memorandum also contains some tentative ideas upon the Naval, Military and Air dispositions which seem best fitted to maintain security within the political and financial conditions which are likely to govern us. These ideas, I need hardly say, are purely for discussion; I count upon my Service colleagues in the Defence Committee to criticise them with the utmost freedom from their several points of view. But one principle of action I am concerned to emphasise, namely, that our defence arrangements must be closely allied both to our political aims and to the political situation in the Middle East if they are to be effective in protecting our vital interests, because we are now entering an era in which political considerations will infallibly predominate. I do not mean by this that policy in the form of guarantees of security should not be closely governed by our military capacity to honour the obligations which we undertake. Nor do I mean that the effectiveness of our policy will not very greatly depend upon the strength which we

are able to deploy in case of need, as also upon the knowledge among the peoples concerned that the strength and the organisation for deploying it will be ready at call when the need arises. Security cannot be ensured by statesmanship and diplomacy alone; it must also be based on strength. What I mean is that we shall not be able in peace to ride roughshod over political considerations as we have done at necessity in war, and that, accordingly, no system of security will prove adequate which is not wisely fitted to the political conditions and character of the Middle Eastern States.

Our vital interests in the Middle East

3.   The British Empire, in contrast to the self-contained land-masses of the American and Soviet Unions, is a *co-operative commonwealth of widely separated peoples*; and the resources necessary to its existence are as widely scattered as the peoples themselves. Its life and strength therefore depend upon the freedom of its communications; it could not survive as a co-operative system, nor could most of its individual peoples escape subservience to some foreign rule, if its communications were effectively dominated and liable to severance by some foreign Power. In the nineteenth century Britain's naval predominance was sufficient to guarantee the safety of the whole. In the second half of the twentieth century Britain, though still immensely powerful, would not be the equal of the American or Soviet Unions if she ever stood alone. Even the British Empire as a whole must have powerful Allies; but its coherence must be Britain's first concern because her status and influence depend upon the fact that she is the parent State, and still the strongest State, in a family of peoples who broadly support her policies and believe that the Empire is as essential to their freedom and welfare as to hers. Egypt and the Levant have long been of great strategic importance to the British Empire, as witness Napoleon's attempt to seize them early in his career; but the cutting of the Suez Canal, the development of the air arm and of air communications, and the vital necessity of controlling adequate supplies of mineral oil for lubrication and motive power have made all the communications which run through the Middle East, together with the oilfields in Iraq and Southern Persia, absolutely indispensable to its cohesion and security. It results that the whole region of the Middle East is now an essential link in the Imperial system, a centre in which are gathered essential arteries of communication and an essential source of power.

4.   The Middle East is therefore a region of life-and-death consequence for Britain and the British Empire in four ways:—

(a) as an indispensable channel of communications between the Empire's Western, Eastern and Southern territories;

(b) as a strategic centre, control of which would enable an enemy to disrupt and destroy a considerable part of the British Imperial system and to deprive Britain herself of many supports and resources essential to her status and influence as a major Power;

(c) as the Empire's main reservoir of mineral oil;

(d) as a region in which British political method must make good, if the British way of life is to survive.

The vital importance of those four considerations has been established by hard experience in both world wars.

Our aims in the Middle East

5.   The island of Cyprus, lying just West of the Fertile Crescent, is the only territory in this region over which we hold full sovereignty. Palestine is a mandated territory, and its future is subject in some considerable measure to international agreement. All the other Middle Eastern countries are independent States except Transjordan, whose independence will very soon be equally complete, and the two Levant States, whose position *vis-à-vis* France is still precarious. We have, therefore, to face the fact that protection of our vital interests in the Middle East will depend upon the collaboration which we can obtain in several independent States and one Mandated State. Neither the American [sic] nor the Soviet Union can be said to depend in this manner upon its relations with a group of independent States far from its own boundaries; and neither certainly has an interest comparable to ours in close relations with the group which constitutes the Middle East. Neither, therefore, will sacrifice anything essential to its standing as a Great Power by entrusting the main responsibility for peace and security in the Middle East to Britain, whereas Britain would be seen and known to have sacrificed a position vital to her strength if she surrendered that responsibility to any other Power. I assume accordingly that Britain's claims to be recognised as the major Power most deeply concerned in the regional security of the Middle East will be acknowledged by the World Security Council and the United Nations when the organisation of world security against war is being worked out.

6.   Even so, the task before us in the Middle East is unusual and most difficult. We cannot expect the sensitive young nationalist movements of the Middle East to accept direction and control from us merely because it is necessary to us. We must persuade them that their major interests and ours coincide, and we must seek to give them the guidance and co-operation they need in the form which will be most acceptable to them. The difficulty of all this has been very largely overlaid during the last five years. Non-co-operation has on occasion lifted an ugly head, but in the main ready co-operation has been the rule. During the war we have enjoyed an unlimited range of facilities under our treaties with Egypt and Iraq. We have used our mandatory position in Palestine and our semi-mandatory position in Transjordan for war purposes without sting or check. We have entered the two Levant States and secured from them a practically unlimited complaisance towards our military convenience as well as our military necessities. We are established in various enemy territories whose future international status is still to be defined. British officers and other ranks are admirable ambassadors. They have eased our relations with the local peoples in many important ways and created an atmosphere of friendliness towards us throughout the Middle East. This friendliness is a very important element; it spreads an absolutely invaluable aura about the immense prestige which the record of the Empire in the war has restored to us. But it cannot be taken for granted. Arab and Egyptian sentiment is notoriously changeable; unwise action, inconsiderate policy, can transform it (as Sir Kinahan Cornwallis[1] has often observed) almost overnight.

7.   War has now passed completely from the Middle East, though this region is still an essential base; and we have to deal with States which have forgotten the

---

[1] Sir Kinahan Cornwallis, director of Arab Bureau, Cairo, 1916–1920; Egyptian Civil Service 1919–1924; adviser to minister of the interior, Iraq, 1921–1935; ambassador to Baghdad, 1941–1945.

necessities of war and are wholly concentrated upon their national rights as earnest of all they hope to achieve in peace. To finish the Far Eastern war with despatch, we must prolong in almost all essentials our military occupation of the Middle East. But it is imperative to realise that the manner in which we acquit ourselves during this last stage of war and the transition from war to peace will profoundly affect our future relations with the Arab States. We must ride them with the loosest possible rein asking rather for co-operation than insisting upon rights, unless compelled to do so, humouring their national sensitiveness in every possible way, caring for their essential interests, and remembering that Imperial security in the future will depend in no small degree upon the skill and tact with which we now discharge a very exacting and complex task.

8.   Our governing aim in the Middle East should therefore be, not to dominate its peoples or dictate how they shall live, but to preserve them against any other domination, to help them to help themselves towards political stability and social advance, to make them feel that their interests coincide with ours, and thus to secure the fullest possible measure of co-operation from them in matters of policy and in arrangements for defence. The most important factors in achieving that aim will be:—

(a) Friendship with Middle Eastern Rulers and Governments.
(b) Security against sedition and widespread popular discontent.
(c) Security against external propaganda designed to cause unrest.

The Middle Eastern States are socially unbalanced and primitive; they all exhibit, in varying degrees, a dangerous contrast between poverty and wealth. The greatest risk to security in the nearer future will be political and social discontent. This will indubitably be exploited by Soviet propaganda (and with some reason) if it is not providently guarded against by a policy of steady reform and betterment.

9.   The main essentials will be close attention to the trappings of national independence (the outer form will always matter more than the inner method of this part of the East), and the use of all the influence we can exert to secure progressive policies in questions of land tenure, employment, justice, education, poverty and health. Sedition in this region, though it spring from poverty and misrule, is certain, like Arabi's rebellion, to take an anti-foreign and therefore anti-British bent when once it breaks out. There is already in existence much fanaticism which attributes the evils of Middle Eastern society solely to foreign exploitation and self-interest. We shall therefore not be able to exert the necessary influence unless we handle the problems of transition from universal to Far Eastern war and from that to final peace with great consideration, and unless we keep the friendship and secure the co-operation of Rulers and Governments. We completely misunderstood the situation after the last war, and have suffered much in consequence. If we fail again, the Soviet Union will assuredly inherit the influence which we shall have lost. That, for the next twenty years at least, will be the main danger from the side of Russia in the Middle East. She will always be ready (her evangel demands it) to exploit the wickedness of "Western Imperialism," if we do not see that genuine progress is made towards a better state of society than at present exists.

10.   Policy is not enough of course by itself. It must be based on strength. But we could never afford to maintain the strength which would be necessary to protect our vital interests, if our political aim and method failed to secure the goodwill and co-

operation of the Middle Eastern States. The character of the Empire is, moreover, its greatest asset by comparison with the elemental power of the only major State which may seriously challenge its position in the Middle East. We must prove and justify that character to the full in the Middle East, if the Empire is to continue to exist.

Importance of the various states

11.   Certain other political observations fall to be made before any attempt to assess the importance, from the standpoint of Imperial security of the individual Middle Eastern States.

12.   Though we shall, I should like to insist, be acknowledged as the major Power responsible for peace and security in this region, we shall not be able to afford any vagueness or imprecision in the measures of co-operation which we shall require of the various States. Naval and air bases, cantonments and training areas, the protection of oilfields, pipe-lines, terminal ports and essential communications by water and land are not matters which can be left to chance or dealt with solely on the line of least political resistance without regard to the claims of effective defence. We shall have to obtain the lease of essential bases and the grant of other facilities by treaty or perhaps better still by a pact of mutual defence negotiated as part of the new world order with individual States. We shall be entitled to obtain all this and strengthened in the process of obtaining it, by the fact that we shall be the major Power chiefly responsible to the World Security organisation for the peace of the Middle East; but we should also aim at the establishment of a genuinely co-operative scheme of defence, the local States contributing all they can in such a way as to complement our own forces and agreeing to the regular arrangement of joint exercises between our forces and theirs. It is also to be hoped that equipment will be broadly the same throughout the area, so that joint training may be facilitated and supply problems simplified in time of need.

13.   While, moreover, the general scheme of defence, particularly as regards the air, must be organised in the greatest possible depth so that we command so far as practicable the coast lines flanking our sea routes and the areas outside the region itself whence air attack upon it may most effectively be launched, there are certain areas of exceptional importance and also certain vulnerable points within the region which necessitate especially clear and solid understanding with certain Middle Eastern States. These are—

(a) the area of the Suez Canal and the terminal ports;
(b) the main naval base in the Eastern Mediterranean at Alexandria;
(c) the pipe-line from Northern Iraq to Haifa and the port and installations at Haifa itself;
(d) the oilfields in Iraq and Southern Persia;
(e) the port and installations at Abadan;
(f) the whole line of communication by land and air running from the Mediterranean sea-board through Palestine, Transjordan and Iraq to the Persian Gulf.

It will be manifest from this short list that Egypt, Palestine, Transjordan and Iraq must be the central factors in our scheme of defence. The security of the Austrian Empire in Italy used to be based upon a scheme of defence embracing four mutually supporting cities, and this central strategic area was known as the Quadrilateral.

Egypt, Palestine, Transjordan and Iraq do not form a Quadrilateral but rather a strategic spine in which all four are essential vertebrae. We cannot afford to lose our position in any one of them or even to see it seriously weakened. They support and depend on each other.

14.   One other consideration requires emphasis. There is no doubt that after the war the Arab States will be extremely averse to the presence of foreign garrisons in their territory, more especially in or near great centres of population where their presence is necessarily prominent. The only exception is Transjordan, where the Amir Abdullah and his people are unlikely, I am told, to object in any way to the grant of cantonments and training areas, provided the co-operation of Transjordan troops is welcomed in joint exercises and the present great friendliness of our relations is not disturbed. In other Arab States, not least Egypt and Iraq, we shall, I believe, be wise to reduce our demands for permanently located troops to a minimum. The great measure of co-operation and the bases which we shall need in those States will be much easier to obtain if we use our command of the air to keep our main forces out of sight. Provided we have the *essential bases*, adequately protected and duly equipped, we shall be able to count upon regular exercises with air squadrons, air-borne troops and (where convenient) truck-borne troops from outside to show that the strength which is necessary to security exists. The more such exercises can be organised as joint exercises with local troops and air forces, the more popular will they be and the stronger will be our scheme of combined regional defence. It follows from this method, if adopted, that Palestine will be of exceptional importance as the only territory (apart from Cyprus) where the administration is in our hands and where our facilities will be unlimited in time of peace.

15.   To these general observations I would add a few notes, as concisely as possible, upon the individual States.

Cyprus
16.   I begin with Cyprus because (apart from Aden, which is not well situated to serve the main purpose here in view) it is the only territory completely under British sovereignty in the Middle East. Our hold upon the people of Cyprus is not as sure as it should be in view of the important part which the island must play in our Middle Eastern system of security. The sentimental desire of the great majority of the Greek population (four-fifths of the whole) for union with Greece, which has always been strong, is gathering new strength from two factors—the wind of national and racial self-consciousness which is fanning such movements everywhere and the dislike of being governed by foreigners, which is blowing equally hard in most parts of the world. We can only answer that Greece is not strong enough to guarantee the independence of Cyprus and that, if we ceased to guarantee it, the island would soon be dominated by another great Power. It always has been and always will be so dominated until the lion lies down with the lamb. But this is not a convincing answer to a delightful people with an immense capacity for political argument but no experience of self-government. Cyprus will not be a reliable member of our Middle Eastern security system unless we can persuade her that she is more likely to find safety and attain self-government within that system than in any other that is open to her. The material development of the island is making considerable strides with generous help from the Colonial Development Fund, but we shall not retain the loyalty of the island by material benefactions of that character alone. Two other

things are essential—to show that we can give it security, and to associate its people as fully as possible not only with our plans of development but also, I am convinced, with our scheme of defence. There are no better examples of British character nor interpreters of the British point of view than British Service men. It is, moreover, by genuine co-operation in defence and by serving with British officers and men that the inferiority complex in our smaller partners (which largely inspires their nationalism) can best be cured. It is of great importance that a declaration of our intentions in Cyprus should be made without delay, since the Union-with-Greece movement is very strong and is being exploited by the local Communists for their own ends. Silence of a negative character will not stem the movement or prevent it from causing disturbances which, like those in Greece, will probably find sympathy in America, even though the only gainer by weakness or surrender on our part would be a third great Power.

17. I had hoped that Cyprus might be developed as the main Fleet base in the Eastern Mediterranean, where such a base is assuredly required. The harbour at Famagusta will have in any case to be greatly improved for civil purposes, if the projects in prospect under the Colonial Development Fund are to mature. I understand now that Alexandria is to be preferred to Cyprus as the main Fleet base in this region, because the island, though valuable as an advanced air base, is so sited as to make adequate defence against air attack from the north impossible. The establishment of a small naval base, which is, I believe, considered desirable, and of an advanced air-base would, however, do much for the island and strengthen our hold upon its people, especially if British troops were also located there. In the case of internal unrest in the Middle East it would be a valuable small base on British territory for all forces.

Egypt

18. We have a hard and searching task before us in Egypt. The pashas and land-owners have accumulated prodigious fortunes in this war. Few have any genuine public spirit, and they are practically untaxed because they control all possible elected governments. The student intelligentsia is always in a state of suppressed ferment; it is growing rapidly and somehow or other will have to be employed. The rank and file of the Army and Police are badly paid. The fellahin (apart from those who are working for wages under us) are far worse off than before the war. Nationalist sentiment is intense. Xenophobia is always seething below the surface. Trouble is bound to take a violently anti-British turn if living conditions deteriorate and grievances multiply in the process of demobilisation, as they may only too easily do. But for the admirable conduct and habitual good temper of British troops, it would have broken out ere now—for Cairo still looks like an occupied city with camps all round it and in some of its parks.

19. It will be extremely hard to negotiate a satisfactory new treaty in the conditions which are likely to prevail; for there is no part of the Middle East in which our influence will depend so much upon our success in helping the local ruler to make progress in such vital matters as employment, land-tenure, education and health, and in tackling the people's awful poverty. For a long time we shall be the potential butt of nationalism and xenophobia because of our long and close association with the country, and a very little unwisdom on our part would make our standing extremely precarious. In these conditions the following seems to me the best we can do from the defence point of view:—

(a) to offer to evacuate Cairo at the earliest possible date, provided facilities (b), (c), (d) and (e) are conceded to us;

(b) all the facilities necessary to establish and keep in readiness a main Fleet base at Alexandria;

(c) cantonments and training facilities on the Great Bitter Lake in addition to the forces and facilities necessary (see despatch on Suez Canal) for the defence of the Canal Zone;

(d) a leased area and an agreed co-operative scheme of air defence and training to be worked out between the Air Forces of the two countries;

(e) continuance of the undertaking to afford us all the facilities we may require in time of emergency or of actual war.

The Ambassador emphasises (and I fully concur) that it may be particularly difficult to secure the necessary facilities for a main naval base at Alexandria in time of peace. The arguments for it are strong, since there is no alternative equally removed from possible air attack from the north and most of the necessary expenditure has already been incurred. It is to be remembered, moreover, that Alexandria is in full working order, whereas a new main base would not be available for some years owing to the work requiring to be done and the probable shortage of skilled engineering staff. It may be necessary, therefore, to press our need of Alexandria despite any political difficulties which the proposal may create. But the difficulties are likely to be grave, and they should not be overlooked.

Palestine

20.   The conception of a security system with the Canal, Palestine, Transjordan and Iraq for its central vertebrae is incompatible with the partition of Palestine. I cannot indeed see how any conceivable system of British security in the Middle East can be reconciled with the partition of Palestine. The worst political feature of partition, namely its alienation of the whole Arab world, is almost equalled by its military defects, which are the alienation of the Palestine coast, the dependance [sic] upon treaty rights for the defence of Haifa and the pipe-line, and the reduction of British tenure to a land-bound Jerusalem State possessed of highly controversial frontiers and surrounded on all sides by uncertain friends if not by positive enemies. It is indispensable to Imperial security in the Middle East, as also for the discharge of our responsibilities in this region to the new World Order, that Palestine should be administered by Britain as an undivided whole. It is equally indispensable that there should be no armed forces in it but those which the British administration controls. It is only so that communications can be controlled, troops dispersed as may be necessary, airfields maintained, Haifa and the pipe-line adequately secured, and inter-racial friction reduced to a minimum. Palestine and Transjordan must constitute the core of our Middle Eastern system of security. To disrupt that core by creating an independent State upon the Palestine sea-board and alienating Transjordan would be to undermine our whole Middle Eastern position. Egypt and Iraq will certainly be difficult from time to time in the future as in the past, but Palestine and Transjordan will be reliable buttresses in all weathers, provided we administer the former and cement the loyal friendship shown us by Ruler and people alike in the latter when no other free and uninvaded State in the world was making war in common with us and our fortunes were at their lowest. The Middle Eastern

Defence Committee is unanimous in the opinion that the partition of Palestine would, from the military standpoint, spell irremediable disaster.

Transjordan

21.   Transjordan has been throughout the war the most friendly and helpful of the Arab States. The Arab Legion fought for us in our darkest hours against other Arab forces and is a model, with its admixture of British and local officers serving above or under each other without distinction of race, of what may be done with Arab man-power, provided only the best British officers are posted to it and the right method pursued. Her loyalty is vital to us, for her territory lies on the central spine between Palestine and Iraq and also marches with Syria. But for the loyalty of Transjordan we should, for instance, have had to face a steady infiltration into Palestine of Arab bands from Syria, Saudi Arabia and Iraq coming to support the rebellion which broke out in 1936. In the future the friendship of Transjordan will be even more valuable, if we are to complete our trust in Palestine with success and keep the peace of the Middle East. It is noteworthy that the present Prime Minister of Transjordan was born and raised in Palestine, as also was his predecessor in that post—both loyal friends of Britain and competent for their work. It may well be that some of the Arab leaders which Palestine requires may be drawn from Transjordan in the years immediately ahead; and it will depend upon our relations with Transjordan whether or not they help us in the task of building up in Palestine a peaceable bi-racial State. I am convinced that the development of even closer military co-operation with that territory and careful attention to the military model of the Transjordan Arab Legion, which has proved its worth, may do much to strengthen our political ties with the Amir and his people and thereby to reinforce our central bastion in the Middle East.

Iraq

22.   The friendship of Iraq cannot be guaranteed, but if we pursue the line of policy established by Sir Kinahan Cornwallis in the last four years, avoid the mortal offence of subordinating Syria to French ambition or Palestine to Zionism, maintain our cordial relations with the Hashimite family, and send her really good men, her friendship ought not to be difficult to retain. (Second-raters are instantly detected in every part of the Middle East and reduce our standing immeasurably.) It should not, however, be necessary to station large forces in Iraq if a scheme of combined defence with regular joint exercises is organised, and the movement of forces from Transjordan and Palestine in case of emergency is carefully provided for. The three vital areas in Iraq are the oilfields in the North and the area of Habbaniya towards the South and Shiba [?Shaiba] from which the South Persian oilfields and Abadan would have to be defended. In these areas leased bases should be obtained, if possible.

The Levant States

23.   In view of the certainty that neither of the Levant States will grant France bases or other military facilities and of the fact that we have imposed upon ourselves a self-denying ordinance in France's favour, it is necessary to recognise that Syria and the Lebanon will constitute something in the nature of [a] military vacuum. The future of the republican institutions which both have adopted is problematic, since monarchy is the traditional centre of stability in these still primitive and semi-settled

parts; and it is also doubtful whether the Lebanon will be able to make good as a separate State. It may be desirable at a later date to bring them more closely into the defence scheme of the Middle East, particularly if (as seems possible) the Americans put new oil installations at Tripoli, bring a new pipe-line to it, and develop it as a terminal port. But the States are anxious to play their part as members of the world security order and also of the Arab League, and they may be counted upon to grant the necessary facilities for Middle Eastern defence in that guise, whether or not their present configuration as separate States and their present systems of Government survive. Russian propaganda is making itself felt in the towns, and the French have encouraged it blindly as an offset to British influence. Turkey is determined not to relinquish the Hatay, and might take steps to increase her holding if the opportunity seemed inviting. It is even possible that she might be encouraged to do so by Russia as compensation for losses elsewhere, if Russia had made sure of her general subservience to Russian policy. Internal instability and the conflict of rival Arab ambitions in the States themselves might well create the opportunity. It is therefore of serious importance that the States should not remain a debatable land exposed to strife between competing neighbours and systems of Government, but should come into the co-operative system of Middle Eastern security set up by us as reasonably stable partners. The Hashimite family seems at present rather lacking in potential rulers of solid quality; but it is more deeply rooted in Arab tradition than any other. Its growing fear of Russia will always keep it pro-British, and I think we should unobtrusively foster the traditional regard which is felt for it.

Saudi Arabia

24.   The power and influence which Saudi Arabia can exert in Middle Eastern affairs depends on a single factor, the prestige and masterful personality of King Ibn Saud. This is now waning because of his great age, and it will vanish altogether when he dies. Saudi Arabia will then become another military vacuum. She seems likely to be rent by internal conflict, and a revival of Wahabi fanaticism may cause some trouble on her frontiers. But these are domestic tribulations against which her neighbours can protect themselves and are not likely to endanger in any way the broad security arrangements which we should base upon Egypt and the central spine of Middle Eastern defence—Palestine, Transjordan, Iraq. American oil interests are deply [sic] concerned in the province of Nefd, which may well become a separate and affluent State. I shall be commenting later upon our relations with America in the Middle East. It will suffice to say here that, so far as I can see, the greater the American interest in any part of the Middle East, the better for us.

Concluding points

25.   There are three concluding observations which I should like to add to this very summary study of our relations with the Middle Eastern States.

26.   It will be seen, in the first place, that no attempt has been made in this Paper to discuss the strength which we should maintain in the Middle East or the location of our forces. So far as the army is concerned, the latter is being studied by a Re-Deployment Committee, which will deal with purely military considerations. In Cyrenaica the Royal Air Force are understood to attach importance to the Hump east of Benghazi, and Tobruk may be equipped to serve as a small naval base and port. Air bases in Kenya and Rhodesia will also be desirable.

27.   Secondly, I must make it clear that I have not attempted in this rough study to deal with one over-riding consideration, namely, finance. The question of what we can legitimately afford for defence in the Middle East is greatly complicated by such problems as the risk of local inflation and the size of the sterling debt, and lies entirely beyond my competence. I can only say, with deep conviction, that we cannot afford to be weak, and would therefore call attention to one measure which may assist to reduce considerably the high cost of defence.

28.   Military expenditure is most economically incurred where, so far as possible, it will serve a double purpose and pay two separate dividends. The use of Kenya and Rhodesia as rear bases and of Cyprus as an advanced base would conform to this principle. Other cases would be Palestine and Transjordan where grants-in-aid must, in any event, be made for development. Yet another is Cyrenaica. I cannot see what British purpose a grant to Ethiopia would serve comparable with any of these or others which I could enumerate.

29.   Thirdly and lastly, I would emphasise the importance of reducing to a minimum the visible permanent troops in Egypt and Iraq. The less we insist in these countries the more they will want us to stay. We should make the utmost of our command of the air and of all modern facilities for the rapid transport of troops, concentrating the latter in areas where they are a political asset rather than a liability and making their presence felt elsewhere by regular joint exercises with local forces of all sorts. I submit, moreover, that the adequacy of road and rail communications should be carefully studied with special attention to our liabilities in the Iraqi and Persian oilfields and at the head of the Persian Gulf. What we should aim at is a well-planned skeleton with bases and communications adapted each to each, which can be rapidly clothed with muscular flesh should the emergency arise. And we must never forget, in the defence arrangements which we make, how vital the friendship or otherwise of the brave but ignorant and volatile Arab peoples will always be to Imperial security in the Middle East.

Relations with other powers in the Middle East

30.   There are three Powers of great consequence to us outside this area which can also make themselves felt to our advantage or disadvantage in the Middle East. They are France, Russia and the United States.

France

31.   France has a great tradition and a powerful cultural influence in the Middle East, and she attaches deep importance, mainly from the standpoint of prestige, to her position in the Levant States. First as the protector of Christians, later as the apostle of her own rich culture, and finally as the Mandatory Power, she has struck deep roots in both countries, and she feels that a loosening of her hold will be of serious disadvantage to her as well as bitterly painful to French sentiment. But her record since the last war tells profoundly against her, and she has, despite our support, to reckon with determined opposition on the part of the United States and Russia to her claim of privilege and pre-eminence. She also has the Arab League against her, since the only two subjects on which that new creation is solidly united are fear of Zionist [sic] and opposition to French pretensions in the Levant.

32.   It has been argued that the natural xenophobia of the Arab world might turn exclusively against Britain, if it lost its fear of the Jews and also its fear of the French.

There is no question that the peoples of these countries are apt to blame the foreigner who is closest to them when they have cause for discontent, and that British standing here will be seriously imperilled if we are not consistently wise and understanding in our political technique; but, given that essential proviso, I do not believe that the elimination of France as a Middle Eastern Power would be embarrassing to us, because the fear of Russia is so great. In other ways, moreover, we stand to lose much more than we stand to gain by backing France, because to identify ourselves with her pretensions is to identify ourselves with a colonising aim and method which are anathema to all the Arab States. The Arab League would not be interesting itself in Morocco, if it were not determined to make an end by all means of France's Frenchifying cult. France seems unable to produce men capable of understanding the mind and winning the heart of the virile, inconstant and warm-blooded Arab peoples. We have all we need of such men and we ought not to compromise their value to us by refusing to recognise that they and the French type which prevails in the Levant are oil and vinegar respectively to the Arab peoples.

33.   It is therefore of serious importance to us that France should be dissuaded from the purpose on which she seems at present set, of attempting to re-establish a special position in the Levant by reinforcing her troops. But even if she desists from that, her considerable interests in the Levant will have to be regulated by an agreement of some sort, and we shall have to face the certainty that neither in military matters nor in diplomatic status nor in education or commerce or finance will the Levantine peoples concede anything to her which they do not concede on equal terms to other nations, more especially ourselves and the United States. The American Government is, I understand, determined on that principle, and we shall only throw away the friendship and trust which we at present command in the Levant if we attempt to engineer its peoples into any other course. It is, moreover, of the first importance that we should work in the closest possible accord with America throughout the Middle East. To persist in backing French ambitions against American and Russian declarations and also against the fixed resolve of the Levantine peoples themselves would be to compromise our own vital interests without gaining anything for France. The only gainers would be third parties.

34.   Is there any other way in which we may, with due regard for our own vital interest, preserve some special status for France in the Middle East? There is no doubt that, if we could de so, we would thereby prove the single-mindedness of our desire to heal the wounds of spirit which are torturing the new régime in France. The only conceivable way would be to take France into partnership in our general responsibility for the peace of the Middle East. I wish with all my heart that we could do this, for no one more truly or strongly believes in the importance of rebuilding the prestige of France. But for all the truth and strength of that wish, I would regard any such attempt at partnership in the Middle East as calamitous. Amongst many reasons for this opinion drawn from my recent experience of French standing and French policy in this region, I select one as being conclusive in itself. If there had been any hope of loyal co-operation in such a partnership, France would already have given us such co-operation in the single-minded efforts which we have made on her behalf in the Levant. In place of co-operation she has given us suspicion and contempt of our advice; and the jealousy which she has shown in the Levant would be still more pronounced and still more unfortunate if it were allowed to spread its contagion over the whole range of our security system in the Middle East.

35.   Since I was then a Private Secretary to the Prime Minister and responsible for close liaison between No. 10 and the Foreign Office, I have a vivid recollection of the range and pertinacity of French intrigue against us in Turkey and the Levant during the years 1921–22, when France was nominally working in close and loyal accord with us on a mutually agreed policy. The result, my colleagues will remember, was a grave humiliation—the first of a long series to shake the prestige of Britain as victor over Turkey, liberator of the Arab peoples, and reconqueror of Jerusalem. The complex of mind in France which sapped against us then persists ineradicably. It is in truth only blindness to the facts of history and of national character to believe that France can ever be made a loyal co-operator in this region. Elsewhere, yes, if we can eliminate this purely local sore; but in the Middle East, never—it is for France, as I believe, a psychological impossibility. She cannot forgive either us or herself for much past history. Us, for instance, she cannot forgive for the fact that while French culture is much more deeply implanted than ours in Egypt and the Levant, British arms have all the glory and British influence has become predominant. Herself she can never forgive for the fact that she refused to enter Egypt with us in 1882 and that our primacy there has even [?ever] since been unchallengeable. It is true that she acknowledged that primacy when the *Entente* was established in 1904 in return for our acknowledgement of her primacy in Tunis and Morocco; but that has not changed her inner feelings on the subject. Finally, she seems incapable of realising that her dependence on colonial troops is fatal to her standing with the Levantine peoples. There have been many Indian and British colonial troops in the Middle East, but they have never been[2] used for imposing our domination on the Arab peoples; and troops from the United Kingdom have a splendid record and reputation throughout the region.

36.   I hope I shall not seem to have strayed beyond the sphere of my Middle Eastern responsibilities in dealing thus frankly and at length with the problem of France in the Levant. I have done so only because I have satisfied myself by five months' study of the Middle East that we cannot continue much longer to support French claims to predominance in the Levant without paying very heavily for it. There is no room in the Middle East for a French and a British sphere of influence. It is useless to say that France is to have a special position, since, whatever we may say, events and her own record have made it impossible. We therefore only damage ourselves without helping her by saying it. The Arab League is solid in two things only—opposition to French pretensions in the Levant and to the creation of a Jewish State in Palestine. I have tried in another paper to show that in Palestine we can dispel the fears of the Arab League while doing full justice to the Balfour Declaration. For France in the Levant we simply cannot secure more than a settlement of her affairs in conformity with Levantine, American and Russian declarations that no nation is to have a privileged position in Syria and the Lebanon; and we cannot afford the running sore which is caused by her present attitude on the question, since it will poison our own relations with the whole Arab League and gravely compromise a friendship which is vital to imperial security.

---

[2] An FO official had underlined the words 'they have never been' and noted in the margin: 'What of 1920 in Iraq?'

The Soviet Union

37.   There is no doubt that Russia is spreading wide tentacles throughout the Middle East. I do not believe, however, that her purpose is aggressive or deliberately unfriendly to us. She is merely suspicious, opportunist, and ready to spread the leaven of her political and economic evangel in any quarter of the Middle East which shows signs of social maladjustment or unrest. The whole region is full of such signs, and I do not for my part believe that parliamentary institutions, very imperfectly adapted from ours, will be found capable of dealing with the awful problems of poverty, disease and ignorance, since to these problems the governing oligarchies of pashas and landowners which control all action in the legislatures are for the most part blindly indifferent. If the Middle East is to be healed of these disorders, it can only be through enlightened, personal rulers who are willing, whatever the outward form, to take strong action on disinterested advice. We may find such action practicable through the King of Egypt, who is, I believe, conscious of the danger and amenable to unobtrusive advice, and the Hashimite family in Transjordan and Iraq. If we fail to secure action through these rulers, who are masters of traditional obedience and personally popular with their respective subjects, there will be widespread ferment which Russia will exploit. Russian propaganda, so far as it can be traced, is at present moderate enough, but it is being sown in fertile ground, and the fear of it amongst the rulers and the wealthy oligarchies is intense. There will be no security for us in the Middle East, whatever forces we maintain in it, if we fail to guide its Governments into some reasonable measure of our own regard for social justice, education, and the elementary claims of health.

The United States

38.   America is the only true partner which we shall find in building up a solid structure of social and military security in the Middle East. Her work in education and health has already been of great value to these countries, which all, for instance, send students to the American University and training hospital in Beyrouth. We shall not need her military backing in the form of engagements other than those which she may accept in the new World Order for the maintenance of peace, provided that we have her moral backing in our Middle Eastern policy and her co-operation in solving the economic problems which the era of transition will present. But she is our natural ally, because her leaders at home and her representatives on the spot for the greater part think and feel as we do upon the welfare of the Middle Eastern States, and because her major interests coincide with ours in that she needs security for the exploitation of mineral oil, aviation bases, and social contentment rather than unrest. The only serious grounds of trouble with her lie in differences over Palestine, in the widespread feeling amongst her eager traders that we are pursuing a dog-in-the-manger policy for our own selfish interest, and in the ignorant ideas of British Imperialism which hold the American mind with unrelenting force. I have urged elsewhere that we should secure American co-operation in developing Palestine as an undivided bi-racial State under a new mandate or trust. On the other two grounds of difference, which have struck deeper roots, we shall need much skill and patience for the presentation of our case. But the facts are on our side, if only we can get them across. For the rest, it seems to me that we should welcome and foster in every way open to us the rapidly growing interest of America in the peace and progress of the Middle East.

39.   America's sudden presentation of demands for a military mission and air bases in Saudi Arabia demand some special reference, though they may prove to have been made without the full knowledge or support of the American Government. It is to the interest of the British Empire that America should have commitments in the Middle East. We cannot compete with her in financial largesse to Saudi Arabia, and there is no reason why we should object to her having a military mission and air bases in that Kingdom so long as she consults beforehand frankly with us, does nothing which conflicts with our general defence scheme, acknowledges our primacy as representatives of the world security order in the Middle East, and gives us (on the ground of common interest in the peace and welfare of this region) her moral backing in the whole of that task. American goodwill and understanding will be important when we come to new settlements in Egypt, Palestine and Iraq, and we must try to eliminate the danger of rivalry with her in any field out here. Her representatives on the spot have often been most difficult, and Americans in general on the lower level are loud in their complaints against us. We must therefore make room for American partnership wherever we can do so without sacrificing something vital to our own interests and try to establish an atmosphere of give-and-take. What matters most, in the field of security, is an official acknowledgement by the American Government of our primary interest and responsibility in the Middle East. It is understood that President Roosevelt acknowledged it more than once, but there is no record here of any formal declaration or understanding on the point. It is greatly to be hoped that our special position in the Middle East has been satisfactorily established at the San Francisco Conference.

12   FO 371/45923, no 2630   3 Aug 1945
'Egypt': minute by P S Scrivener to Mr Bevin on the Anglo–Egyptian treaty and the internal development of Egypt

[The FO was in no hurry to begin re-negotiating the 1936 treaty because of the need to assess the outcome of the San Francisco conference. In July the leader of the Wafd, Nahas, publicly called for the formation of a 'united front' coalition to begin negotiations to meet Egypt's national demands; this led Farouk to back away from any immediate revision of the treaty out of fear that the British would want Nahas, whom the king detested, returned to power. By August Bevin had decided to tackle the Levant problem before dealing with Egypt (FO 371/45924, no 2716, minute by P Dixon, 8 Aug 1945). However on 22 September an advisory group of Egyptian notables issued a statement saying that the time had come to negotiate a new alliance with Britain based on evacuation of the Canal Zone and the unity of the Nile valley.]

The present phase of Anglo–Egyptian relations dates from the Anglo–Egyptian Treaty of 26th August, 1936, which finally established Egypt as an independent country, terminated the British military occupation, provided for mutual support in the event of war, and authorised His Majesty's Government to maintain military and air forces in the Suez Canal area in peacetime for the defence of the Suez Canal. The revision of the treaty was foreseen after twenty years at the request of one party, or after ten years with the consent of both. Any revision must provide for the continuation of the alliance, and for mutual aid in war including the grant of all the facilities (ports, railways, etc.) which it is in Egypt's power to provide. The continued presence of

British forces in Egypt is subordinated to the question when, and whether, Egyptian forces will be able, unaided, to secure the defence of the Canal. If, after twenty years, no agreement can be reached on this question, international arbitration is foreseen.

2.   The Treaty had only been ratified a short time before its implementation became a matter of immediate practical politics. During the war it worked exceedingly well—indeed it is doubtful whether its negotiators ever expected it to work as it has worked with Egypt a non-belligerent, which was the position up to February, 1945. Pending the conclusion of the Japanese war, the treaty is still in full operation, but the question of its revision has for some time been canvassed in Egypt, and now, in consequence of the signature of the San Francisco Charter, has become an issue for early consideration by His Majesty's Government. This issue is, however, necessarily subordinate to the more fundamental question of the system under which His Majesty's Government contemplate that the security of our imperial communications in the Middle East shall be safeguarded.

3.   It has hitherto been regarded by His Majesty's Government as axiomatic that the defence of the Suez Canal should be ensured by Great Britain and Egypt in partnership, and that this country should, in relation at any rate to defence measures, maintain a form of British Monroe doctrine so far as Egypt is concerned. During the recent discussions of the Ministerial Committee which has been examining all aspects of future policy towards the Suez Canal, the question was, however, propounded whether, in fact, this state of affairs should be taken for granted, or whether it was not desirable, on various grounds, to share our responsibilities with the other great Powers, notably the United States and the Soviet Union. The view of this Office, as endorsed by Mr. Eden, was that we should continue (for the reasons given in WP(45)256)[1] to play the decisive rôle in defending the Canal jointly with Egypt. But the question still awaits decision.

4.   As the Egyptians have been swift to appreciate, the new Charter of the World Organisation, by the very fact of substituting itself for the Covenant of the League of Nations, has rendered certain sections of the Anglo–Egyptian Treaty out of date. Apart from the purely juridical aspect, the position is affected in various ways which are examined in an Office memorandum now under consideration by the Chiefs of Staff. Suffice it to say here that there is a strong suggestion that we should be well advised to proceed with the revision of the treaty, in the light of the lessons learned during the war, in order that we may have ready for embodiment in the new world security system an agreed system of defence of the Suez Canal.

5.   It is now necessary to mention the internal development of Egypt, and the situation which would confront our negotiators assuming, for the sake of argument, that we wished to renew negotiations for an up-to-date military alliance with Egypt as a cog in the machine of world security.

6.   Broadly speaking, the internal history of Egypt since 1918 has, in the nature of things, been shaped by three forces, viz. Egyptian nationalism, whose embodiment was Saad Zaglbul [sic] Pasha[2] and his party, the Wafd: the Egyptian monarchy, whose outlook is *primarily* selfish and dynastic: and His Majesty's Government who are

---

[1] See 3.

[2] Saad Zaghlul, Egyptian nationalist who took part in the revolt of 1882 to eradicate foreign rule. Founder of the Wafd he led the delegation to London to demand freedom from British rule at the end of World War I and became prime minister of Egypt's first parliamentary government in 1924 before his death in 1927.

faced by the necessity of safeguarding their strategic interests (leaving aside for the moment their commercial and other interests) against the manoeuvres of both the other parties. The operation of this triangle of forces has led to many interesting results, and, having regard to Egypt's position in relation to the German and Japanese wars, is still continuing, though in a lesser degree so far as His Majesty's Government are concerned.

7.   Egyptian policy since 1918 has been expressed by the slogan "Complete independence for Egypt and the Sudan". The Sudan will be dealt with in another paper, but so far as Egypt is concerned this is still the declared policy of every party, and, in theory, will continue to be the policy until all British troops have been withdrawn and until Egypt can govern (or mis-govern) herself *in vacuo*. Individual Egyptians see quite clearly that such a policy, particularly in the light of the lessons of the last six years, is unreal and totally unconstructive in that it has led to the essential problem facing Egypt—viz. social reform—being thrust into the background. But no Egyptian statesman has yet had the courage to declare that Egypt cannot (and never will be able to) stand alone militarily; that her correct policy is to collaborate internationally with His Majesty's Government as being the Great Power which has an interest in defending Egypt and from which Egypt has nothing to fear; and that behind the shield of British influence she should apply her energies and her immense wealth to introducing a tolerable social system. But it must be repeated that the Egyptian maximum demands in any negotiation must be expected to be the evacuation of Egypt by all foreign troops.

8.   The nearer Egyptian "independence" approached, the more did the Wafd party tend to disintegrate. At present it is in three pieces. The main body, led by Nahas Pasha, is in opposition: one secessionist group is the leading party in the present Coalition;[3] and another, formed and led by the Egyptian Minister of Finance, is a minor member (if a fractious one) of the same Coalition, which is kept together (with some difficulty) by the influence of the King who put the combination in office. Our own relations with the present administration may be described as politically fairly good but personally difficult. It is regarded by His Majesty's Ambassador as insufficiently representative and collectively inadequate to speak for Egypt in a first-class negotiation such as the revision of the present treaty.

9.   A word should be said in conclusion about the attitude of His Majesty's Government to Egyptian internal affairs. Since the treaty was signed, we have intervened in those affairs only on grounds justified by the treaty, and specifically by those articles that bind Egypt to accord us the fullest military facilities and not to carry out a policy inimical to the alliance. Thus we removed a pro-Axis Prime Minister in 1940 and installed (to fill a dangerous vacuum) in 1942 the only Prime Minister (Nahas Pasha) who was at that moment willing *and able* to implement the treaty. Similarly, we dissuaded King Farouk on two occasions from summarily dismissing the said Prime Minister (who is personally detested by His Majesty) on the ground that such action would have led to internal disquiet and jeopardised the efficiency of Egypt as a base for the Allied armies. When Nahas was finally dismissed as a result of actions admitting of no reasonable defence (and long after active hostilities had ceased) we stood aside. If we decide to negotiate a fresh treaty with

---

[3] The Saadists under Nokrashi.

Egypt, we shall probably have to take steps (see above) to secure the presence of an administration qualified to commit the whole Egyptian people. This task will be an exceptionally difficult one owing to the personal factors involved, but it is unnecessary to examine it in this very general survey.

13 FO 141/1043, no 51   29 Aug 1945

'Anglo–Egyptian treaty': minute by Sir W Smart on the timing of the proposed treaty negotiations

With reference to a recent suggestion that we should take the first step and ask the Egyptians to negotiate a revision of the Treaty, I have, since my return from leave, been thinking over this question very carefully, and I have come to the conclusion that it would be to our advantage to do nothing to raise the question prematurely.

The present position is that the Egyptian Government has announced its intention of opening negotiations with us for Treaty revision but is showing no hurry to commence. Our information is that the Palace and the Government are not at all anxious to start the ball rolling because they fear that it may result in a demand for a United Front to negotiate with us, a development which would open the door to a return of the Wafd to power. The Wafd, on the other hand, is vociferously urging immediate opening of the negotiations and taunting the Government with reluctance to do so because of its unrepresentative character. It is possible that the Government may be forced by this outcry to make an approach to us, but it is not certain whether this will be forced on them in the immediate future or not. If they are forced to approach us, we could then suggest the advisability of a United Front without provoking the suspicion (as would be the case if we took the first step) of a deliberate attempt to bring the Wafd back to power: in other words, of interfering in internal politics as on the occasion of past returns of the Wafd to power.

In any case, as it is at present exceedingly difficult to create any unity among Egyptian parties, we would be able to sit back for some time on the Anglo–Egyptian Treaty of 1936 and say that we were ready to talk when Egyptians were agreed among themselves.

Incidentally, one possibility should not be lost sight of. Supposing we take the first step and demand a United Front with the result that the present Government's position is so weakened that the Wafd returns to power, it is quite possible that the Opposition will then boycott the elections and refuse to take part in the Treaty negotiations under the direction of the Wafd. The Wafd probably represents slightly over half the country but we could not safely negotiate such a Treaty without the participation of so strong an Opposition. We should then be in almost the same position as we are now with the present Government, particularly as Nahas is not a good life [sic] and, if he were to disappear, the Wafd would certainly be unable to implement any Treaty without the co-operation of the non-Wafd elements.

Our whole strategic requirements in the Middle East are likely to be profoundly modified by the development of the atomic bomb and other new implements of warfare. It is quite possible that we shall no longer require the large strategic reserves, the enlarged Air Force set-up, the Naval arrangements at Alexandria, at any rate on the scale at present advanced by their protagonists. For all we know, the future may require only police forces to assist by their propinquity in the maintenance of security in the whole of the Middle East region. Until, therefore, we see more clearly into the future, we would seem to have every interest to hold our hand as long as we can. Meanwhile what is of the utmost importance to us is to maintain the goodwill of all this Egypto–Arab world in order to prevent Russian infiltration in one form or another. It is thus supremely important that we should not take any unnecessary action which would arouse the hostility of these countries against us. Any effort to impose on Egypt an Anglo–Egyptian Treaty giving us more than we got in 1936 is bound to create a hostile Egypt and cannot be successful except by the use of force. Any attempt to use force would involve appeals by Egypt to the United Nations organisation and would therefore be impracticable. I think, therefore, that any such requirements by us can only be obtained through the Security Council, and to get this through the Security Council we must come to an understanding with at least the United States. Trouble is brewing in other countries in the Middle East, particularly in Palestine. It is surely imprudent for us to take any hasty action which would provoke trouble in Egypt at the same time.

In short, as I see the situation, we should wait and see as long as possible.

14   FO 371/45924, no 2901   1 Sept 1945
[Anglo–Egyptian relations]: inward telegram no 1991 from Lord Killearn to FO reporting a discussion with Nokrashi on Egyptian aspirations   [Extract]

Egyptian Prime Minister for the first time revealed his hand last night in regard to Egyptian "aspirations". Talk was informal and friendly but at times outspoken and I left with renewed conviction that His Excellency, though personally agreeable and suave, was a real tough customer [grp. omitted] most extreme Nationalistic sentiments amount almost to an obsession.

2.   Regarding treaty revision, His Excellency kept harping on Egyptian national pride and injured feelings: nothing would satisfy him but removal of every British soldier from the country. Now was the psychological moment for us to take the initiative. Why were we so "afraid" of Egypt? She had proved her good faith and loyalty during the war. But she now expected that the last trammels upon her sovereignty should be eliminated: it would be really dangerous for us to dally or delay in doing so. He of course (as is his habit) placed the blame for all Egyptian ills upon us: to which I gave the usual answer that that was not commonsense and might be taken as read. I had no knowledge yet of what the views of His Excellency were about revised defence arrangements, but could imagine they might be far reaching. It was surely a matter of hard fact what was required and if Egyptian side could only realise specific dangers which had to be provided against, and agreed with us as to the best method of meeting them [grp. undec.] problem would become much easier and less of political issue. The British tax-payer would not foot the bill for one British soldier not genuinely regarded as necessary to secure our essential and legitimate needs. ...

15 CO 732/88, no 5a   2 Sept 1945

'British policy and organisation in the Middle East': memorandum by Lord Altrincham

1. As a funnel of communication between the western, eastern and southern peoples of the British Commonwealth, as their richest reservoir of lubricant and motive oil, and furthermore as an area in which, without desiring to dominate ourselves, we cannot allow any other Power to dominate and must preserve for ourselves the maximum of friendship and goodwill, the Middle East is no less vital to Britain than Central and South America to the United States, or than the eastern and western glacis of the Russian landmass to the Soviet Union. It was not for nothing that we sent to Egypt in 1940, when this island was in imminent jeopardy of invasion, the only armoured division of which we stood possessed. It was no mere accident that the whole face of the war began to change after our victory, two years later, at Alamein.

2. Having now reaped the military fruits of that decisive event, we must not allow ourselves to forget that the moral of the strategy which brought it about applies to peace no less than war, though peace demands that we shall pursue our aims by policy instead of force. It is a fact that the circle of friendship upon which Britain's welfare and influence will now depend has its centre in the Middle East, because the loss of primacy in that region would deprive the Commonwealth of its coherence and much of its power. But the harvest of our immense war effort in that region is still to be repeated; and we can make our primacy there secure, like the United States and Russia in the regions which are vital to them, only by the wisdom and firmness of our policy, combined with the maintenance of trust in our constancy and goodwill. We must, moreover, recognise (as the United States and Russia have without question already done) that the Middle East is a region with a unity of its own, and ensure that our organisation is adapted to that all-important fact both in the region itself and in Whitehall.

3. There is no time to lose. Since the intense co-ordinated effort which first took decisive effect at Alamein, we have lost in the Middle East something of our clarity of purpose and singleness of aim. We cannot afford the unco-ordinated departmental activities or the many-sided and in some ways shortsighted expenditure which have marked our proceedings there for some little time; nor must we allow ourselves the persistence of a war mentality and heaviness of touch inconsistent with the disappearance of military exigency in its former compelling forms. The tragedy of the moment is that important parts of our immense war establishment in the Middle East, such as the Middle East Supply Centre and the Administration of Occupied Enemy Territories which are indispensable for the transition period and may become permanent, have been rapidly depleted of experienced and irreplaceable men, while other parts, which have no use except for war, seem to be proof against retrenchment and reform.

4. Both features in the situation—the decay of institutions which are indispensable and the persistence of some which are not—are bad for our standing in the Middle East. We are dealing with rulers and peoples whose goodwill towards us has been formed in a hard school, but whose sensitiveness, mutability and proneness to xenophobia are certainly not exceeded in any part of the world. They will turn

from goodwill to hatred against us, as they have against France, if we forfeit their trust or offend their pride or fail to help them in their manifold needs to the full measure of our power. It is not an easy task in the complex of problems bequeathed to us by past commitments or created by the war. Our power is circumscribed in many ways and we shall succeed only by the most careful adjustment of ends to means and means to ends. I am convinced that in peace as in war this will need planning on a regional scale, directed of course from Whitehall but applied upon the spot by the best regional organisation to [sic] which we can devise and afford.

5.   Some of the mechanism which has served us in war is, as I have said, still indispensable, and it will need for its operation all that are now left to us of the experts who have worked it through the war's emergencies and strains; but the war system and method are now completely out of date and must be radically changed. We have a new world to deal with in the Middle East, profoundly different from that which existed before the war, and we cannot afford to blunder with it as we blundered in Egypt after 1918. I will try to analyse very briefly the outstanding elements in this new world in order to suggest the main lines of policy and the kind of organisation by which, as it seems to me, its problems may best be solved.

I. Problems of policy

Nationalism and the Arab League

6.   The Middle East is a complex of peoples newly awakened to the sense of nationhood and instinct with the virtues and vices of nationalism in its most sensitive form. The war has greatly intensified the passion for sovereign independence which nationalism nurtures everywhere; but in the Middle East it has done something more. It has given a sense of unity to the whole group of peoples which they have never possessed hitherto; they mean to stand together in defence of their national rights and common Islamic culture against the outer world, and they have already created an instrument for joint action in the Arab League. If the Middle East were to be isolated in a vacuum, they would soon return to their internal feuds; but the sense of external pressure is (with good reason) extremely strong, and it operates in two ways by making them conscious of a common danger as well as determined to govern themselves. The Arab League is therefore a reality which will gather to itself increasing trust and power. But while it expresses the demand of its members for independence from foreign domination of any kind, it also feels the need of a big brother amongst the Great Powers who will help the Arab people to security and progress without threatening their independence or hurting their pride. The bitter reaction of the Arab League against French pretensions in Syria and its gratitude towards Britain for her disinterested aid are eloquent examples of the trend of Arab sentiment, which we ourselves must not fail to recognise in our own dealings with the Arab world.

7.   It is in this setting that we have to study the means of maintaining our primacy in the Middle East during the formative and in some ways revolutionary period which we are now entering. The problems are political, military and economic, and I will deal with them in that order, while observing that the economic are the most difficult and also the most certain to determine the future of our relations with the Middle Eastern States. Success in our economic policy, which touches the life of the peoples at a thousand points, will greatly ease our path in other respects; but neither military prestige nor political and diplomatic skill will

atone for bad handling of economic questions. The fundamental issue is how best to unravel the economic tangle left by the war and how much of the help needed by the Middle Eastern States we can afford to give. The consideration must, moreover, be mutual, if the help is to be adequate and the progress real.

The political aspect

8. The most urgent political problem is at present the future of Palestine. That question is no longer one to be settled by the Mandatory Power under the general supervision of the League of Nations. There can be no lasting prosperity for the Jews in Palestine, and certainly no considerable expansion of the present settlement of Jews, without the goodwill and co-operation of the members of the Arab League. It is astonishing that people here and in America should speak so glibly of creating a sovereign Jewish State in Palestine and of merging it in a federated Greater Syria without regard to the plain declarations on the subject which have issued from the Arab States and the Arab League. I do not suppose that the Middle Eastern representatives at the present Foreign Office Conference will be prepared to modify the advice which they gave at the Fayoum Conference five months ago, nor have I anything to add myself to the views which I have already expressed. But it is important to emphasise here that the Palestine question is a regional question, not a question merely between the Arabs of Palestine and the Jews to be settled autocratically by distant Powers, and that no solution will ensure stability and progress in Palestine which is not acceptable to the Arab and Moslem world. The moral is that in working out their responsibilities in Palestine His Majesty's Government will have to co-ordinate the methods and instruments through which their policy is formed and carried out. They will need, I submit, to treat Palestine as a Foreign Office rather than a Colonial Office affair, and also to have a representative entitled to deal in their name, on regional questions such as this, with the Arab regional organisation, namely, the Arab League. I will come later to the method by which this may be arranged.

9. There are two other political subjects which I should like to underline. The first is the importance of recognising the independence of Transjordan without further parley. Transjordan is the only Arab State which fought on our side in the crisis of the war, despite the minatory and anti-Zionist propaganda which poured at a decisive period from the German-controlled radio at Bagdad. It was therefore most unfortunate that she should have been the only Arab State not invited to San Francisco; our conduct towards her tallies most imperfectly with the line we have taken in Syria and the Lebanon. It is to be presumed that when recognised as independent she would come into the Foreign Office sphere. This is largely a question of prestige; but, like all such questions in the Middle East, it strongly affects the Amir and his people, who have proved themselves faithful friends.

The military aspect

10. Another question of prestige may soon become acute. Our military organisation in the Middle East is still all-pervasive; and though it is well within our Treaty rights, it is of great political importance that all signs of military occupation should now be rapidly withdrawn. Cairo in particular is an occupied city. It was the natural centre for military headquarters, and a host of auxiliary organisations also inhabit many of the city's chief buildings and a surrounding network of camps. The

statue of Saad Zaglul, Egypt's nationalist hero, stands at the island end of the Kasr-el-Nil bridge, looking towards the Citadel. On its right is one of Cairo's most charming parks, still a military camp. On its left is the Alamein Club, a token of Egyptian gratitude to our fighting services and the scene not only of much invaluable recreation but of formidable parades. Across the Nile the statue faces the Kasr-el-Nil barracks and the Semiramis Hotel, the largest in Cairo and still a military headquarters despite the acute lack of accommodation of which the innumerable travellers through Cairo complain. This investment of a nationalist monument is symbolic, and I mention it on that account, since I came to feel with increasing discomfort that our criticism of French display in Damascus and Beyrut did not tally with our own conduct elsewhere. The explanations are, of course, weighty. Egypt has been the centre of an essential war-base, even since the war passed out of Africa. But Egyptians may be forgiven for feeling that the magnitude of our military occupation three years after Alamein has not been entirely justified by the needs of the latter phases of the war against Germany or the war with Japan.

11.   We shall now no doubt be drawing in our military horns throughout the Middle East, and it is of great political moment that we should do so rapidly and of our own volition before nationalist feeling on the subject takes an aggressive or explosive turn. But the process will affect profoundly the economy of most of the Middle East, more especially of Egypt, and I would therefore plead for the prompt establishment of civil control over all those forms of it which will affect labour, industry and employment, house property and civil interests of other kinds. The conduct of demobilisation, derequisitioning, disposal, &c., will form an important part of that process, to which I have already referred, of unravelling the economic tangle left by the war. It is a regional problem in many essentials, and it must be guided by the advice of financial and economic experts who understand local as well as world conditions at this difficult time. Such advice cannot be made available in every territory. In peace, as in war, it must be centralised.

12.   The other main military problem is that of future security against war. We have relied in this war upon our mandatory rights in Palestine and Transjordan and our treaties with Egypt and Iraq. These have served us well. But there can be no question of renewing the treaties in their existing form. They are already being denounced as incompatible with national independence and the Charter of the United Nations, and we are bound by our obligations under that Charter to make our essential contribution to the security of the Middle East in conformity with its terms. Here again the problem is regional. What is needed is a co-operative regional scheme of security to which we contribute what the Middle Eastern States cannot afford and dovetail our arrangements into theirs. It is only so that the use of bases and other rights indispensable to defence against aggression can be properly secured and that the scale of our own contribution can be brought within our means. India, the East African Colonies, Southern Rhodesia and the South African Union will all have a substantial interest in the plan and may conceivably desire to participate in it, since peace and security in the Middle East will always be of great importance to them. The articulation of the plan may involve separate treaties with individual States; but, if so, such treaties must be worked out as part of the general plan. Here, once again, it seems essential that His Majesty's Government should have on the spot, in addition to its missions in the individual States, a representative empowered to deal on lines prescribed by its military advisers with the Arab League and the Middle East as a whole.

13.   One other point which will differentiate the new security arrangements from the old should be clearly borne in mind. National susceptibilities will never be agreeable to the presence of foreign garrisons or occupying forces, particularly in or near great towns. It is therefore essential that the arrangements should be in no way offensive to national pride. Though rights conferred under the Charter of the United Nations as part of a co-operative plan will certainly be more acceptable than rights implying the protection of a single great Power, the location of British forces in the Middle East should conform to political good sense, efficiency being assured by joint exercises with the forces of the co-operating States. The rapid development of air defence and transport makes this possible to an extent which could not have been thought of before the war.

The economic aspect

14.   Our economic problems are as searching in the Middle East as elsewhere, and their importance is supreme, since our manner of dealing with them will intimately affect all classes and deeply influence their attitude towards us. They fall broadly into four divisions.

15.   First and foremost comes finance. Our expenditure in the Middle East has been, and still is, immense; it must be greatly reduced. Arising out of it we have the problem of the sterling balances and of providing a sufficiency of hard currencies to pay for imports which we cannot at present supply ourselves. I presume that Treasury control over the many Departments which are spending in the Middle East will now be greatly reinforced, and that something like a Middle Eastern budget within our means will be carefully worked out. The broad lines of policy and the limits of expenditure must obviously be laid down in Whitehall; but the policy should be framed in close collaboration with experts who know the conditions of the Middle East, and its application should be entrusted to experts on the spot, since without intimate local knowledge immense political harm may be quite unwittingly wrought.

16.   Secondly, there is the question of food supplies and of the various controls established in the war which cannot be summarily and completely relaxed. The Middle East Supply Centre will cease to function at the end of the year, but some central Middle Eastern organisation will be indispensable, in my opinion, to take its place. There is no one available, to my knowledge, with the necessary experience except the present Director. I mention the fact in order to show how seriously essential staff has been reduced. Men of the necessary capacity can easily find employment elsewhere, and they are naturally leaving posts in which their prospects are uncertain and their status much below their deserts.

17.   Thirdly, there are the problems created by our vast expenditure and our manifold war activities, which have in some respects transformed the primitive economies of the Middle Eastern States. ... The poverty-stricken masses, particularly in Egypt, are suffering gravely from shortage of supplies and from the inflated cost of most of the necessities of life. Unemployment is already in evidence, and demobilisation of war industries is bound to swell its ranks. Here yet again the unravelling of the war tangle with least damage to the peoples and our standing in their eyes must depend upon the advice of local British experts in close touch with local needs and conditions of life.

18.   Fourthly come the grants-in-aid which we make in Palestine, Transjordan and the Occupied Enemy Territories. I do not know that any of these can be fairly

reduced; some will certainly have to be increased. I can only suggest that the location of our troops should be planned in such a way as to pay, where possible, a double dividend, the expenditure which they entail enriching the local population, and to some extent reducing the need for grants.

Social justice and betterment

19.   I am convinced that, apart from liquidation of the liabilities contracted in the war, which should not be done without the most careful attention to its social and economic effects, Britain will stand or fall in the Middle East by her influence upon the promotion of social justice and betterment, claiming no arbitrary power over or even open influence upon its national Governments, but helping and advising unobtrusively at request, so that all parts of the population can feel the benefit of progress in opportunity, education, living conditions and health. This will call for much quiet wisdom, backed by true creative enthusiasm, amongst our representatives on the spot. The narrower political, diplomatic and military modes of thought would leave us in the lurch, and it is high time that we reverted to a greater tradition, high time that we rekindled throughout the Middle East the ideal which inspired Lord Cromer's[1] historic régime in Egypt when Britain first supplanted the Turkish Empire there. Arabi's rebellion, which caused our intervention, was in its origins a rising of the poor against intolerable oppression, the Kourbash, the Corvée, the whole mechanism of local and foreign exploitation which ground them in the dust; and Cromer, despite the capitulations, transformed their lot in life.

20.   The Cromer technique is indeed no longer suitable, for nationalism will not abide the control which he exercised over the whole machine of Government, nor will it any longer tolerate the open constraint of rulers and the arbitrary making and unmaking of Governments which we have thought desirable at some moments since Cromer's time. But this change of the conditions under which our influence must be used does not affect by one iota the truth that we shall enjoy no primacy in the Middle East, nor ultimately any standing in the eyes of its peoples, if we fail, with the immense material power and moral influence which we possess, to secure a steady improvement in opportunity and standards of life for both the fellahin and the partly-educated but struggling poor just above the peasant class. In some territories this leaven is already working. I felt its presence in Transjordan and Irak; and we have certainly done something (apart from the effects of Jewish development) for the people of Palestine. But in Egypt, the richest and yet the poorest of the Middle Eastern States, which is the gate and key in many ways of the whole Middle East, we have done less than nothing for the helpless poor for many years past. Worse—in the preoccupation of fighting for our life (which is, indeed, strong but to my mind insufficient excuse) we have, though we controlled so much and helped in many ways, allowed the contrast between wealth and poverty to reach a dangerous state. Another Arabi will arise (with much hidden foreign support) if this long deterioration is not effectively reversed.

21.   It is then essential to recognise that social conditions in the Middle East, especially in Egypt, present us with a categorical imperative, if we are to be true to

---

[1] Lord Cromer, 1st Earl of; minister plenipotentiary in the Diplomatic Service; controller general Egypt, 1879; agent and consul general, Egypt, 1883–1907. Cromer retired in 1907 and was granted £50,000 by parliament in recognition of eminent service in Egypt.

the civilising mission with which we first entered its life. But we cannot shoulder this great responsibility without good men and some new expenditure, particularly on general education and also on education for health. The United States and France have done much in the educational field, and we have many struggling institutions, such as schools and Lady Cromer's dispensaries; but they are much in need of help. Another Great Power, Russia, will infallibly exploit a failure on our part to make our influence in these directions more felt, and she will not be niggardly of expenditure or of agents, unobtrusively organised for infiltration till the tumours burst. The danger to security will not, in fact, be a danger of open armed aggression, but a danger rather from within, of widespread social discontent and unrest, which Russia (having a genuine evangel, whatever the method by which it is pressed) will not refrain from stimulating and turning to her own use.

22.   Our help and advice must go to the rulers, since the selfishness and corruption of the propertied classes cannot be mitigated without strong action on the rulers' part. They are all desperately afraid of communism, but most of them are unwilling to understand that the only method by which communism may be defeated is reform and betterment. Here lies our opportunity and our task. The King of Egypt, who is (like his country) the gate and key to much that is necessary for our standing in the Middle East, has, I am convinced, good qualities of head and heart. He is able, popular and young—so young that in the course of nature he is likely to reign for the thirty or forty critical years which will decide the fate of the Empire in the Middle East.

23.   But if help and advice from us are to meet with success, they must be quietly and self-effacingly given, asked for and not imposed. The task before us therefore calls for two things—good men and security behind those men, so that they may be independent enough of the Asiatic Governments which employ and pay them to retire with firmness if they meet with too much obstruction to be surmounted by goodwill and tact. It is also desirable that many of the political officers who have done such excellent work in Arab service during the war, such as those introduced by Sir Kinahan Cornwallis in Irak, should be maintained at our charge as consuls, in which capacity they can render much of the same service and will more than repay their cost. Without a Middle Eastern Service for training, harbouring at need and giving independence to picked political advisers and specialists, we shall find it hard—I believe, impossible—to hold our own or discharge our all-important task.

II. Organisation

Departmental responsibility

24.   The present division of responsibility for the territories of the Middle East between the Foreign Office and the Colonial Office is largely due to the personality of the Ministers who held those two portfolios in Mr. Lloyd George's post-war Coalition Cabinet. Whatever the reasons existing then, the division is now out of date, since the region has attained a unity of its own with a range of problems belonging rather to the international than the colonial sphere. Transjordan will presumably pass to the Foreign Office when its independence is recognised. It would be well if Palestine and Cyprus, in both of which our local policy must depend in large measures upon our policy towards and relations with foreign Powers, were also transferred. I would suggest the same for the Occupied Enemy Territories. Their future also depends upon international agreement; and though the War Office has administered them admirably under war conditions, the method has its

drawbacks and those for which we remain responsible should come under civil administration when their future is no longer in doubt. I will deal later with the administrative rearrangement which would be required. The urgent need of a Middle Eastern Service of some kind seems to me to reinforce the case for fixing responsibility upon a single Secretary of State.

Inter-departmental committee in Whitehall

25.   Not that British interests in the Middle East can even be regarded as the exclusive concern of a single Department in Whitehall. While the responsibility for policy should, in my opinion, rest upon the Foreign Office, because our policy throughout the Middle East belongs mainly to the sphere of foreign affairs, the Treasury, the Service Departments, the Board of Trade and the Ministries of War Transport, Information and Food are all of necessity implicated in that policy in different degrees, the rôle of the Treasury being especially critical and delicate. I understand that the need for close inter-departmental liaison in Middle Eastern affairs is to be met by the creation of an inter-departmental Middle Eastern Committee in Whitehall. I would have warmly welcomed such a Committee while I was Minister Resident, if it had been a Cabinet Committee which met with reasonable frequency and gave decisions at the Ministerial level without undue delay. But it is also important to secure that questions of real local moment are put up to Ministers in a digestible form, and this is not likely to be done unless another committee is formed at the official level to which all questions involving more than one department are promptly referred and tackled in a systematic way. An established and accepted machinery for inter-departmental consultation at the official level can do much to prevent that sense of frustration because answers are either inadequate or entirely lacking which so often overwhelms our representatives oversea.

26.   To summarise, I think I shall be speaking for all my former colleagues in the Middle East if I say that the three following provisions in Whitehall would help them considerably:—

(a) Close liaison between all the Departments concerned, with special regard for those officials who have an intimate knowledge of Middle Eastern affairs.

(b) Special attention to economic questions, which are now the main crux.

(c) Prompt submission of such questions as need it for Ministerial decision, so that irritation may be precluded so far as possible among local Governments and decisions neither unduly delayed nor given (in default of higher guidance) by junior clerks. (There is a file upon the Middle Eastern Agricultural Committee which illustrates the possibilities of delay and what it sometimes costs.)

Organisation in the Middle East

27.   No organisation in Whitehall will, however, atone for lack of organisation in the Middle East. The Fayoum Conference agreed unanimously upon the need of a "nucleus" without specifying at all clearly to whom it should be responsible locally or of what it should consist. The papers are no longer at my disposal, but I think it will be found that, under Sir Wilfred Eady's[2] invaluable inspiration, they made an unanswerable case. For my part, I submit that the office of the Minister Resident should be reorganised in four main branches with the following allocation of subjects:—

---

[2] Joint 2nd Secretary, Treasury, 1942–1952.

(a) *Political*. Arab League business—collation of political information from all Middle Eastern territories—civil administration of Occupied Enemy Territories—education—publicity.

(b) *Economic*. Finance—food supplies and economic controls—action affecting industry and employment—trade and commerce—demobilisation and disposals—collation of information regarding economic needs, cost of living, health and conditions of life throughout the Middle East.

(c) *Security*. Defence plan—co-operation with local forces—location and movement of British forces—intelligence (including security arrangements against criminal groups).

(d) *Establishments*. Advice on pay and local allowances—local administration of Middle Eastern Services—transport.

I do not pretend that these suggestions are either fool-proof or complete. They are submitted as a basis of discussion roughly indicating the main duties which the office should discharge.

28. As to location, the office must, I think, remain in Cairo, where it already is. Cairo is a natural centre of communications in the Middle East, capital of its richest and most populous State, and headquarters of the Arab League.

29. Until lately the office was responsible to the Minister Resident, a member of the British Government divorced from his Cabinet colleagues and stationed without diplomatic status in the capital of an independent foreign State. Since the portfolio has now been abolished, I need not enter into its difficulties and inconveniences except to say that it could not in my opinion have been properly retained unless the office of Minister Resident had been combined with that of Ambassador, at any rate for the transition period. There were inconveniences about that course also, but they appeared to me less than those of any other proposed. I discussed the matter more than once with the two Ambassadors who were my colleagues during the greater part of my time, Lord Killearn in Cairo and Sir Kinahan Cornwallis in Bagdad. I am not entitled to quote their opinions, which were privately expressed; but I presume they will both be available to the Secretary of State during the conference and I hope they will both be consulted on the point, since it has a definite bearing on the question as to who should be head of the Middle Eastern Office in Cairo now that the post of Minister Resident has gone.

30. I have insisted again and again in the course of this paper that the Middle East has a regional unity which should be recognised in our organisation for dealing with a variety of subjects which are by their nature regional affairs, and also that all our representatives there should be responsible to the Foreign Secretary. It is clear that the Foreign Office must be able to deal when necessary with the Arab League, which itself deals with all Middle Eastern affairs and seems certain to grow in power. Clearly, too, the British representative who deals with the Arab League should have behind him an office on [? or] a chancery fully seised [sic] of all the Middle Eastern questions in which the League is concerned; and he can hardly be of a rank below that of Ambassador. I would add that the most difficult questions of which the Ambassador in Cairo will have to dispose are in their essence Middle Eastern questions such as the treaty question and most of the economic questions which I have briefly reviewed. The Ambassador in Cairo is the senior diplomatic representative of His Majesty in the Middle East, and no other representative of His Majesty's Government in Cairo should vie with him in authority or prestige. For all

these reasons and also to confer upon it the status which it needs, I submit that the Ambassador in Cairo should be head of the Middle Eastern Office, which would serve him as a second chancery covering Middle Eastern as distinct from purely Egyptian affairs, and that he should be empowered to act as the representative of His Majesty's Government *vis-à-vis* the Arab League.

31.   There is good precedent for this proposal in so far as prestige and authority in Egypt is concerned. Lord Cromer as British Agent controlled all British activities in Egypt; and Lord Salisbury, who was not only Foreign Secretary but Prime Minister during the better part of Lord Cromer's long tenure, was concerned in many Egyptian affairs. The Middle East is now a complex to the creative and co-ordinating spirit which informed the Cromer régime, and it is from His Majesty's principal representative that such inspiration and co-ordination should properly come. But there is an important difference between Lord Cromer's and the present time. The Middle East apart from Egypt belonged then to the Turkish Empire, and it was with Turkey that Lord Cromer was concerned in many Egyptian affairs. The Middle East is now a complex of sovereign States; and while the Ambassador in Cairo should in my opinion be empowered, like the Minister Resident, to deal with the Arab League and with questions common to all the Middle Eastern States, it is imperative that his authority should in no way derogate from the prestige and authority of the Heads of His Majesty's Missions in other Middle Eastern territories.

32.   The importance of this consideration cannot be over emphasised. The success of our policy in the Middle East will depend in very large measure upon the establishment of relations of intimacy and trust between His Majesty's representatives and the Governments to which they are individually accredited. Their relations with the Rulers in particular are of critical importance, since it is mainly to the Rulers that we must look for progressive policies and measures helpful to the poor. I can only say that, but for Cairo where he lived, the Minister Resident was not to my knowledge an embarrassment to His Majesty's representatives, and that the activities of his office were as a general rule most welcome to them. The Cairo embarrassment, which was difficult for both parties whatever their mutual confidence, would be removed by the arrangement I propose, and I do not see why the Ambassador in Cairo should be more of an embarrassment to our other representatives as head of the Middle Eastern Office than the Minister Resident was.

33.   Every system has its drawbacks and difficulties; every official relation can be prejudiced by lack of consideration and tact. But the system I propose has been tested by experience, and I am convinced that, with due consideration and tact, it can be satisfactorily worked. It is not, however, the Cairo view that really matters most; the opinion of His Majesty's representatives in other territories affords the better test. There have been considerable changes in our diplomatic representation in recent months; but Sir Kinahan Cornwallis saw the system at work for almost five years as Ambassador in Bagdad from 1941 to 1945 and can therefore comment on it from a wealth of experience. I would add that with a Minister on his staff the Ambassador in Cairo should be able to visit his colleagues in other capitals from time to time as opportunity serves. He would also, I presume, invite them to Cairo for any important business in the Middle Eastern Committee (see next paragraph) which particularly concerned their respective States. I suggest, moreover, that a Middle Eastern Conference such as was held in April last in the Fayoum should be held annually. The value of the Fayoum Conference was, I think, recognised by all who attended it.

34.   The Middle Eastern Defence Committee has, I understand, been abolished. It was perhaps an anachronism as such; but something of the kind seems to me desirable, and its place might usefully be taken by a Middle Eastern Committee of wider scope. If constituted, its chairman should be the Ambassador, with power to give decisions within limits laid down by the Cabinet. Its other members should be the Commanders-in-Chief of the three Services, the heads of the four branches of the Middle Eastern Office, and any other Middle Eastern authority whom the Ambassador wished to invite.

35.   All important telegrams to and from the Middle Eastern Missions would presumably be repeated to the Middle Eastern Office, as in the past. It would also undoubtedly facilitate business for other Departments in Whitehall if on departmental matters communications passed between them and the Middle Eastern Office direct.

A Middle Eastern Service

36.   Proposals for the creation of a Middle Eastern Service have been current for some time. They originated, I think, with Sir Kinahan Cornwallis in a despatch from Bagdad and were supported by my predecessor as Minister Resident as well as by myself. These would need to be extended if, as I hope, the Foreign Office becomes responsible for the whole of the Middle East. It is true that the Foreign Office is not an administrative office in the Colonial Office sense; but it has made a signal success of the Sudan Service because it has known how to attract the right type of young man and given considerable freedom to its administrators on the spot. Would it not be possible now, when our mission in the Middle East is calling for a Service imbued with the spirit which has transfigured the Sudan, to create a Middle Eastern branch of the Foreign Service? If so, it should have two branches—an administrative branch which would comprise the administrative services in Palestine, Cyprus and the Occupied Enemy Territories as well as the Sudan; and a specialist branch which would include the Middle Eastern Office, the technical advisers who will be needed, and perhaps also the political officers with Middle Eastern experience who will be required for special Consular and intelligence work. The officers in the administrative branch would be organised on Sudan lines; those in the specialist branch would, I hope, be given appropriate Foreign Service rank. The creation of some such Service with a high status and prestige is greatly needed in order to retain officers who will otherwise be lost, attract new ones of the right type, and build up the *esprit de corps* which will be necessary to command success in our great Middle Eastern opportunity and task.

37.   I am sure I need not apologise for ending this hastily written and most inadequate paper with a word on British Imperialism in the new world emerging from the war, since everyone who understands the importance to Britain of the Middle East knows that our ancient quality has to prove itself equal to novel and highly exacting conditions amongst the lovable but sensitive and mutable peoples of that critical part of the earth. Britain is no longer the equal of the United States or Russia in material resources and capacity for war; but she can still be the greatest of all countries in her power for helping the smaller and more backward peoples towards greater abundance and freedom under law in a world at peace. With her long liberal tradition, her natural human-kindness and her wide knowledge both of diplomacy and government, she has to show, and she can under a good Government show, that she is not an exhausted and declining but still, as of old, a creative and pioneering influence, stronger by her character than dollars can ever be, stronger

also by her appeal to normal human aspirations than those who serve the Communist ideal. Britain still has a powerful attraction for the weak of which her great Allies are not as yet possessed.

38.   I would like to quote in this context a short extract from a writer of lifelong Socialist faith. More than thirty years ago, in 1912, Mr. H. G. Wells wrote this:—

> "The Empire must live by the forces that begot it. ... There was never anything like it before. Essentially it is an adventure of the spirit, sanguine, discursive, and beyond comparison insubordinate, adaptable, and originating. ... It has a common medium of expression in the English tongue, a unity of liberal and tolerant purpose amidst its enormous variety of localised life and colour. And it is in the development and strengthening, the enrichment, the rendering more conscious and more purposeful, of that broad creative spirit of the British that the true cement and continuance of our Empire is to be found."

That was written in a different age, before the two world-wars. But it is truer than ever to-day, except that the Empire must serve and bind to itself even more peoples than its own, if it is to spread its tolerant and human way of life in these hard and cruel times. It will be our fault, ours who inherit its opportunities after the mighty war effort which it has made, if it fails, in Bacon's phrase, to continue "growing upon the world." And amongst foreign peoples, it is above most for those of the Middle East that the broad creative spirit of the British, more adaptable and originating, more conscious and more purposeful than in the slothful years between the wars, should now recover and display to the full its ancient, quickening power.

16   FO 371/45927, no 3526   17 Oct 1945
'Egypt': FO memorandum on the need to work with King Farouk

[The memorandum was forwarded to Sir O Sargent by R G Howe who proposed that if the secretary of state approved it Lord Killearn's opinion on approaching King Farouk should be sought. Howe pointed out that the difficulty was that Lord Killearn was so identified by every Egyptian mind with the policy of support for Nahas that Farouk would regard any approach by Killearn as not sincere (FO 371/45927, no 3526, minute by Howe, 18 Oct 1945).]

Political forces in Egypt consist broadly of the King and the coalition Government which he has brought into existence and maintains; the Wafd, led by Nahas Pasha; and His Majesty's Government.

2.   The King would like to eliminate his rival Nahas from the political scene and to establish the Throne as the dominant continuing political force in the country. He is deterred from the realisation of this desire by fear of the possible reaction of H.M.G. who have more than once *during the war* intervened in Nahas Pasha's favour. He has, therefore, let it be known that, if H.M.G. will "quit the arena" and give him a free hand, he in return will see that H.M.G.'s strategic interests in Egypt are fully provided for and will do all in his power to lead Egypt along the road to social reform and to the creation of a real democracy in the country in place of the present rather insincere imitation. In the immediate future he will curb the embarrassing enthusiasm of his Government and other politicians for Treaty revision and will see that there are no disorders.

3.   Nahas Pasha, who when in power angled for promises of active support from H.M.G. in the anticipated showdown with the King, is at the moment down but by no means out.

He wears the mantle of the legendary Saad Zaghloul and commands the allegiance of a majority of Egyptians; and this despite the corruption and inefficiency of his late administration, his dictatorial tendencies and his known antagonism to the King. Nahas is now both in opposition to the King and suspicious of H.M.G. and is exploiting his nuisance-value by outdoing the Government in demands for Treaty revision.

4. At present H.M.G. are getting the worst of both worlds; the King and his Government are unamenable and the Wafd suspicious. To enable us to break out from this position there appear to be two alternative courses: one is by direct intervention to secure a more complaisant Government: the other is to collaborate with the King. The first course involves further direct intervention in Egyptian affairs, and seems for that reason inopportune at least until the second has been tried and proved a failure.

5. It is therefore proposed that H.M.G. should let the King know that H.M.G. are prepared to resume the rôle of interested spectators but on the condition that they receive satisfactory assurances that their imperial strategic interests are fully safeguarded, that His Majesty will lead a genuine movement for social and political reform, and that there is no political victimisation of the leaders of the Wafd Party. In adopting this attitude we should be acting consistently with our response to Nahas' approaches (see paragraph 3) when he was in office viz. that the relations between people and monarchy were a matter for the Egyptians alone.

6. In taking this step we should, however, be clear about its implications. It must not be supposed that the King, at heart, likes us, and still less democratic progress, more than anyone else in Egypt. And, even if he were initially sincere we might, by acquiescing in the elimination of Nahas, place His Majesty in a position of such power that even a more honest man than he would soon forget about his assurances to us. For one side of the triangle of forces in Egypt might well disappear overnight. Despite the pretensions of the Saadists and the Makramites there is no dispute in reality as to Nahas' position as the successor to Saad. But with his removal the succession would really be in dispute. It is more than likely that the present Wafd would disintegrate. Numbers of its adherents would be attracted to the Saadists and possibly also to the Makramites. The rump might never again be able to present itself seriously as an alternative Government, and the only Governments possible in Egypt would be coalitions (of varying composition) holding office at the King's pleasure. In such circumstances the King might well be tempted to flout our wishes.

7. Nevertheless if there is to be serious social reform in Egypt the King seems the only available instrument for its realisation. For reforms mean money which in turn can only come from taxation of the rich. And such taxation can probably only be imposed by the will of the King. If His Majesty is in a sufficiently strong position he should be able to impose it either by decree or even by obliging a Government dependent on him to force legislation through a Parliament of landowners and capitalists rent by party differences. This, then, is one good reason for backing the King. For the rest, existing Egyptian politicians and parliamentary institutions have proved themselves bankrupt of ideas and all seem equally incapable of breaking away from parrot phrases. The Monarchy has prestige and it has continuity. Let us give it a run. It is—and, let us hope, will remain—susceptible to pressure; and if it proves in fact hopelessly reactionary we can think again.[1]

---

[1] Bevin commented: 'I am very doubtful about this. I would prefer the CIGS to have his talks first and then consider the whole matter.' The CIGS visited Egypt in Nov 1945.

17   CAB 79/41, COS 269(45)2   9 Nov 1945
'Middle East policy': report by the JPS to the COS, 6 Nov 1945
(JP(45)276)   [Extract]

In anticipation of instructions, we have examined a paper by General Paget, Commander-in-Chief, Middle East, in which he proposes the formation of a Middle East Confederacy.

General Paget's proposals for a confederacy
   2. General Paget considers that nationalism, amounting to xenophobia, is now becoming so strong throughout the Middle East that we cannot hope to satisfy our strategic requirements in that area by normal negotiation and treaties. He, therefore, proposes that we should associate the Middle East with ourselves in a Confederacy, co-ordinated by a council of all member states.

   General Paget visualises the Confederacy embracing all the states (less Persia) now included in the term Middle East, and all those territories for which Great Britain is responsible including East Africa.

   The object of the Confederacy would be mutual defence. Each member state would subscribe to the mutual defence system in proportion to its resources, the British contribution being to supply deficiencies, where for technical, financial or other reasons a member state was unable to fulfil its obligation to the Confederacy.

   In this way, General Paget considers that the Middle East states would feel that their sovereign rights were being respected and that they would have a common interest with us, as we have with them, in the security of the Middle East as a whole, or of any member state therein. They would thus be more likely to grant us the military facilities which we require in the Middle East than if they considered that we were interested only in the retention of our special position in that area, for our own benefit. ...

18   CAB 79/41, COS 269(45)2   9 Nov 1945
'Middle East policy—formation of a confederacy': COS Committee
minutes

The Committee had before them a report by the Joint Planning Staff[1] commenting on a paper by General Paget in which he proposed the formation of a Middle East confederacy.

Lord Cunningham said that he liked the J.P. paper but wondered whether this proposal for a multi-sided confederacy might not produce more difficult practical problems than a series of bilateral agreements. The following were among the political difficulties which the establishment of a general confederacy might raise:—

   (i) Russia would consider the Confederacy a Middle Eastern Bloc aimed against the Soviet Union.

---

[1] See 17.

(ii) A purely Military Confederacy would be impossible; it would be a political confederacy as well and from the nature of things would begin to look like the Arab States plus the U.K. and Palestine; in other words the Arab League with the U.K. as an associated member.

(iii) Palestine would occupy a very uneasy place in such a Confederacy.

(iv) The General Confederacy would presumably be presented to the World Organisation as "A Regional Arrangement". It would probably take us at least as long to promote the Confederacy as it would for the World Organisation to become established. The Security Council instigated by Russia and France would probably intervene before the bonds of the Confederacy were sealed.

(v) If the Levant States were to be included how could France be left out whose dominant position in Syria and the Lebanon we have recognised?

(vi) What about the United States who had for a long time been trying to establish a U.S. Military Mission in Saudi Arabia? More important than all the Arab States thrown together was co-operation with the United States whose economic stake in the area was already considerable.

For the above reasons, it seemed to him that the Foreign Office might prefer to pursue the partnership conception with individual States, working up gradually, perhaps, to a more ambitious scheme.

Lord Portal and *Sir Archibald Nye* suggested that the paper as drafted might be sent to the Foreign Office for their views. To this the First Sea Lord agreed.

Sir Archibald Nye then referred to a personal telegram which he had received from the C.I.G.S. suggesting that the Joint Planning Staff should be instructed to put forward proposals for a key plan of defence for the whole of the Middle East on the basis of a Confederacy.

Air Commodore Dawson[2] asked whether the Joint Planning Staff could await the views of the Foreign Office on the paper now before the Chiefs of Staff before beginning work on the defence plan.

The Committee:—

(a) Instructed the Secretary to send the J.P. report to the Foreign Office with a request for their views;

(b) Instructed the Joint Planning Staff to prepare proposals, in the light of the Foreign Office comments on the above report, for a key plan of defence for the whole of the Middle East on the basis of a Confederacy.

---

[2] Air Commodore W L Dawson, director of plans, Dept of Chief of Air Staff.

19 CAB 79/41, COS 269(45)3 9 Nov 1945
'Revision of the Anglo–Egyptian treaty': report by the JPS to the COS, 6 Nov 1945 (JP(45)189) [Extract]

[The FO had become worried that the new UN Security Council, once established, would become the arbiter of any disputes about the treaty. Therefore there was a case for tackling treaty revision as soon as possible and a need to produce a government in Egypt which would be disposed to conclude a revised treaty on the basis of the continuance of Britain's special position as protector of Egypt and the Suez Canal (CAB 80/96, COS(45)506, annex, 2 Aug 1945).]

In anticipation of instructions, we have examined a letter from the Foreign Office, covering a memorandum as to the effect of the United Nations' Charter on the Anglo–Egyptian Treaty and the British position in Egypt. The Foreign Office enquire whether the Chiefs of Staff concur in the conclusion of the memorandum that the revision of the Treaty should be undertaken as soon as possible. In that event the Foreign Office request the Chiefs of Staff to recommend what military clauses should be included in a revised Treaty.

Timing
2.   From a purely military point of view, there is much to be said for delaying treaty revision until the political situation is clearer regarding Russian claims to a position in the Mediterranean area, and until more is known of the effect of atomic energy on our future strategy.

On the other hand, Egyptian pressure for immediate revision of the Treaty has increased and it has been proposed that the Prime Minister should make a statement which concedes the principle of revision. Moreover, it would be preferable that negotiations should be conducted between ourselves and Egypt alone rather than through the World Organisation which might give other Powers an opportunity of interfering in the defence arrangements which we wish to make in the Middle East.

We agree, therefore, that early revision of the Treaty should be undertaken if the Foreign Office consider such action is advantageous. . . .

20   CAB 79/41, COS 269(45)3   9 Nov 1945
'Revision of the Anglo–Egyptian treaty': COS Committee minutes

The Committee had before them a report by the Joint Planning Staff[1] on a letter from the Foreign Office covering a memorandum concerning the effect of the United Nations charter on the Anglo–Egyptian treaty and the British position in Egypt.

Lord Cunningham said that he would like to have the report further examined in the Admiralty from the point of view of strengthening the naval considerations governing the military requirements of a revised treaty.

In the course of discussion, the following points were raised:—

(i) It was pointed out that the military considerations governing the revised treaty had been based on the assumption that there would, in future, be no obstacle to our stationing military forces in Palestine. If there was any prospect of our ceasing to enjoy military facilities in that country, at least comparable to those we had at present, this would seriously affect our military requirements in Egypt. This should be emphasised when sending the paper to the Foreign Office.

(ii) *Brigadier Thompson*[2] pointed out that a much stronger case could be made for basing air forces in Egypt than land forces, since the land defence of the country ought to be conducted well in advance of its frontiers. A strong case could, however, be made out for basing a part at least of the air forces in the country to be defended.

---

[1] See 19.

[2] Brigadier G S Thompson, director of plans, Dept of the CIGS.

(iii) *Lord Portal* said that the present treaty stipulated that up to 400 pilots might be stationed in Egypt. He noticed that under the new proposals we would be requiring the right to station up to 300 operational first line aircraft in Egypt.

Air Commodore Dawson said that this figure left a margin of some 2 squadrons over the forces estimated to be necessary.

(iv) *Lord Portal* suggested that the word "airfields" ought to be included within the bracket in paragraph 13 of Annex II.

(v) *Sir Archibald Nye* suggested the following amendments to paragraph 4 of Annex I and to paragraph 7 of Annex II. He said that paragraphs 8 and 9 of Annex II would more properly come under Section IV (General Clauses).

Para. 4, Annex I. Last sentence to read—

"We consider that we should make it clear to the Egyptians in the course of negotiations that we would make every endeavour to avoid stationing any of these forces in the Nile Valley."

Para. 7, Annex II. Penultimate sentence to read—

"The proportion of these forces including Headquarters personnel to be located in the Nile Valley to be reduced to the minimum number compatible with the requirements of military efficiency."

In discussion, it was suggested that before sending the paper to the Foreign Office, the comments on it of the Commanders-in-Chief, Middle East, ought to be obtained. This could be done while the paper was under further examination in the Admiralty.

The Committee:—

(a) Took note that the First Sea Lord would have the report further examined in the Admiralty;

(b) Instructed the Secretary to send copies of the report, incorporating the above amendments, to the Commanders-in-Chief in the Middle East for their comments;

(c) Agreed to give further consideration to the report in the light of the comments from the Middle East, and from the Admiralty, when received.

21   CAB 80/98, COS(45)678, annex   2 Dec 1945
[Middle East confederacy]: FO memorandum on General Sir B Paget's proposal for a Middle East confederacy

As requested in paper J.P.(45) 276 of 6th November,[1] the Foreign Office have considered from the political standpoint General Paget's proposal for a Middle East Confederacy (C.O.S.(45) 616 (0)).

2. In principle, we see considerable advantage in treating the problem of security in the Middle East on a regional basis. In the first place, as the Joint Planning Staff have pointed out, the problem of the defence of the area is in fact a regional problem. Secondly, a multilateral system would offer the Arab States a kind of psychological

---

[1] See 17 and 18.

set-off to the dominant partnership represented by His Majesty's Government. Thirdly, it would complement the regional economic and social policy on which His Majesty's Government have embarked. Fourthly, since the Arab Governments themselves are thinking in terms of Arab unity, as witness the development of the Arab League, they would tend to favour a regional approach to the question of defence. Fifthly, such an approach would be calculated to harmonise with the eventual World Organisation of the United Nations. Sixthly, a regional approach might calm popular agitation in Egypt for treaty revision, as indicating that the problem was being dealt with on a new and up-to-date basis instead of on the basis of out-of-date treaties.

3.   At the same time, the scheme has the following weaknesses from the political point of view. The Confederacy ought preferably to include Egypt, Iraq, Palestine, Transjordan, Syria, the Lebanon, Saudi Arabia and the Yemen. In other words, it would be desirable that it should include Palestine together with all the members of the Arab League. But it would not be possible to include all the territories of the Arab League. Syria and the Lebanon cannot be included without bringing in the French, which would be politically impracticable. The inclusion of Saudi Arabia might lead to complications with the Americans. It seems in any case doubtful whether we need any military facilities in Saudi Arabia or indeed in the Yemen. So far as Iraq is concerned, our present arrangements with that country give us everything we require, and if we were to scrap the present Anglo–Iraqi Treaty we might not get anything so satisfactory in its place. In the case of Palestine and Transjordan, we are at present in the position of enjoying in these territories all the military facilities which we require. By this process of elimination it seems that it is only in the case of Egypt that we must embark on fresh negotiations with the object of securing our military requirements; and we do not consider that the solution of the problems arising there would be in anyway facilitated by arranging for the participation in the negotiations of, say, representatives of Iraq, Saudi Arabia and Transjordan.

4.   Moreover, in the case of Egypt, the time factor must be taken into account. Public opinion in Egypt is becoming increasingly restive on the subject of treaty revision, and it may be imperative to open at any rate preliminary discussions at an early date. Actually, this suits our book for it is in any case desirable that fresh arrangements should if possible be concluded with Egypt before the opening of the negotiations for military arrangements between the Security Council of the United Nations Organization and individual states. Otherwise we fear the Egyptians might well take the line that any bilateral arrangements with us were superfluous.

5.   We consider therefore that, for practical reasons, negotiations with Egypt must necessarily be undertaken on a bilateral basis. But, having regard to paragraph 2 above, we recommend that it should be explained to the Egyptian Government that His Majesty's Government no longer regard the defence measures to be adopted in Egypt by the Egyptian and United Kingdom Governments in partnership as a matter purely of concern to their two countries, but rather as an essential element in the security of the whole Middle Eastern area and one which they would hope in due course to see merged into a regional scheme, in which certain of the countries comprising the Arab League would be active participants, and to which the others would signify their agreement. Such a regional scheme would moreover ultimately take its place in the scheme of world security to be worked out by the United Nations Organization. We are at present considering in what form this idea could best be

embodied in any new treaty. In any case we consider that there would be advantage in restricting the main articles of the treaty to the broad principles of the alliance, and dealing with the details of the military arrangements in an annex (c.f. the present Immunities Convention) or even in a separate military Convention.

6.   We have further considered the position in Palestine from the point of view of the freedom of the United Kingdom to station troops and enjoy all necessary military facilities in that country, and in particular the advisability of designating Palestine as a "strategic area" in the trusteeship agreement into which His Majesty's Government propose ultimately to enter in respect of Palestine. We have come to the conclusion that on the whole it would be preferable not to designate Palestine as a strategic area, since (a) this would expose His Majesty's Government to possible obstruction (however partisan) on the Security Council and (b) that designation of the Holy Land as a strategic area might arouse the opposition of public opinion in the United States and elsewhere. At the same time nothing in the Charter affects the right of the administering authority to take such measures for the defence of the territory as it sees fit, and should such defence arrangements in Palestine as His Majesty's Government deem essential be seriously questioned when it is sought to place Palestine under trusteeship, it would be open to His Majesty's Government to decline to agree to any terms of trusteeship which prejudiced this right. In that event and pending agreement the territory would continue to be administered on the basis of the status quo.

22   FO 141/1043, no 10   6 Dec 1945
[Anglo–Egyptian treaty revision]: inward telegram no 2552 from Lord Killearn to FO on the terms and conditions of securing an agreement

Scrivener's secret letter J/G to Bowker of 12th November.

I have now received from Commander-in-Chief a copy of Joint Planner's paper J.P. (45)189(Final)[1] of 6th November, together with Middle East telegram No.CCL/61 to Cabinet Offices of 26th November giving the comments of the three Commanders-in-Chief on the Joint Planner's proposals. Incidentally this telegram was sent without prior consultation with me. The following are my comments on these two papers.

2.   The Commanders-in-Chief agree with the Joint Planners on the desirability of an early approach to the Egyptian Government on the question of Treaty revision. If this is to be done—and I am not prepared to differ from the view that an early approach may be desirable—the fundamental question arises, can we negotiate with the present Egyptian Government? My own view remains that even if there were any prospect of their agreeing to our terms (and I cannot conceive a more unpropitious combination than Nokrashy and Bedawi) it would be most unwise to do so: and that we should need something (on the lines of 1936) representative of all Egyptian parties, including the Wafd which is the big opposition party at present. Despite the King's detestation of Nahas Pasha, I doubt if Wafd participation in a Treaty revision delegation would be possible without him. My views on possible method of dealing

---

[1] See 19 and 20.

with the internal political situation are given in my telegram No.2498, though I am well aware of the difficulties in the way.

3.   The next point to be settled is where the negotiations are to take place—here in Egypt as in 1936, or in London? If in Egypt, then we should need Service members. Are they to be delegates? or (as in 1936) advisers to His Majesty's Ambassador who, in theory if not in fact, did the negotiating?

4.   If negotiations are to be in Cairo, it would be important that we should have competent assistance on the United Nations Charter in order to meet the hair-splitting arguments on the subject which will certainly come from the Egyptians (especially from Bedawi if he is still in office).

5.   To summarise my views on these points. We need a receptive and comprehending Egyptian Government to deal with. At present we have nothing approaching that standard (c.f. their attitude over the aviation agreement). A Hussein Sirri would increase the chances of successful negotiations 100%. Wafd inclusion in the Egyptian Delegation will be essential. But we must be prepared to face the fact that our refusal to negotiate with the present Government without all party participation will raise a storm among all non-Wafdist elements and will indispose King Farouk.

6.   As regards the specific recommendations of the Joint Planners about our future military requirements in Egypt, my comment is as follows. While most sensible Egyptians will really be only too glad to see adequate British forces available to defend them at short notice, nevertheless with the growing popular clamour, encouraged by all parties, for complete withdrawal, it will be extremely difficult to get any Egyptian Government to accept a Treaty which specifically provides for retention of British armed forces in Egypt in any form in peacetime. This will be our great, and, as some (including Oriental Minister) think, insurmountable difficulty. For this reason I have little doubt that the best chance of getting our military requirements accepted is to present them as part of the defence requirements of the whole Middle East area on a partnership basis. This was the main theme of the Chief of the Imperial General Staff's talks here and met with a warm response from King Farouk. I therefore agree with the Commanders-in-Chief that the approach to the Egyptian Government should be represented as being an attempt to carry out the idea of collective security (accepted by both Governments at San Francisco) as the Anglo–Egyptian contribution to the whole scheme. Thus, in the words of the Commanders-in-Chief, the "regional aspect should be stressed" and the defence requirements which will have to be specified should be related to the defence of the Middle East generally, to which Egypt herself is bound, and would like to be bound, to make a contribution. The Foreign Office memorandum on the effects of San Francisco on the Anglo–Egyptian Treaty (paragraphs 15 and 16) points out the grave difficulties in negotiating a revision of the Treaty as a "regional arrangement" under Chapter VIII, but goes on to suggest that it might be argued after it has been negotiated that it constitutes such an arrangement. This will be hard to get the Egyptians to agree to in terms, but we might be able to persuade them that close collaboration with us in Middle East defences would be their best contribution to collective security. In this connection I would suggest that the military authorities should consider how it might be possible to make the mutuality of the defence arrangements that they want more apparent, even if not more real, than under the old Treaty.

7.   The Commanders-in-Chief are clearly thinking on these lines when they suggest that it should be pointed out that the troops which they require to be stationed in Egypt are not repeat not to be there for purposes of internal security (even in collaboration) and not repeat not for the security of the Suez Canal, but are to be stationed here as part of our mutual contribution to the security of the Middle East, stressing the regional aspect but only as a part of the general world scheme of collective security under the United Nations plan. On similar lines is the suggestion of the Joint Planners that troops should not be maintained in the Nile Valley i.e. presumably that they should be stationed near the Canal or at the Ports. I understand that General Paget is in favour of a start being made with this as soon as possible and I have already entered a caveat about such action in advance of Treaty revision (my letter to Mr. Howe of the 16th November).

8.   I agree also with the Commanders-in-Chief that it is desirable that there should be no limitation of numbers in the revised Treaty, and their observation that such limitation would relate the presence of the troops to the defence of Egypt, whereas the relation it is desired to set up is to the defence of the Middle East, although I doubt if any Egyptian Government would swallow this argument. Another helpful point for negotiation is the suggestion of Commanders-in-Chief that military personnel at the administrative base should be limited as far as possible, and supplemented by civilians in charge of installations of a technical nature which it will be necessary to maintain in peace time. If, however, these civilians are, as is suggested, to be serving under the Egyptian Government, then the installations will have to be coloured as Egyptian. They would have to be nominally for the joint use of the two allies, although no doubt in practice the British troops would mainly work them.

9.   You will appreciate, of course, that any approach about Treaty revision will at once raise the question of the Sudan, about which it will likewise be extremely difficult to find a formula which any Egyptian Government will feel able to accept, though I might just remind you of what Amin Osman[2] said to me last summer about Nahas' probable attitude—see my telegram No.1799 of 8th August.

---

[2] Amin Osman, pro-British figure not formally a member of the Wafd but who played a key liaison role between Nahas and Killearn in Feb 1942 and who became minister of finance in the wartime Wafd government. He was assassinated by the Ikhwan after the war.

23   CAB 79/42, COS 289(45)5   27 Dec 1945
'Anglo–Egyptian treaty—comments of Commanders-in-Chief Middle East and Admiralty': report by the JPS to the COS, 21 Dec 1945 (JP(45)300). Annexes

As instructed we have re-examined our report[1] dealing with the revision of the Anglo–Egyptian Treaty, in the light of the comments of Commanders-in-Chief, Middle East and the Admiralty.[2] We have taken into account a telegram from Lord Killearn.[3]

---

[1] See 19.   [2] See 20.   [3] See 22.

Middle East comments

2. The Commanders-in-Chief, Middle East, raise three main points, with which Lord Killearn is in general agreement:—

(a) The defence of Egypt cannot be divorced from that of the Middle East as a whole.
(b) As a corollary of (a) no limit should be placed on the size of our garrisons in Egypt.
(c) Every effort should be made to avoid any appearance of infringing Egyptian sovereign rights.

As regards (a) and (c) above we entirely agree with the importance of both these points. We have, however, already taken account of (a) in our examination, in which we expressed the view that, on the assumption that we continued to enjoy Military facilities in Palestine at least comparable to those we have at present, our requirements in Egypt would be likely to be the same whether or not she became a member of a Middle East Confederacy.

(c) is of importance particularly in regard to the method of approach and presentation of our requirements to the Egyptians, and these are matters for the Foreign Office to decide. We have prepared our paper, in consultation with them, with a view to giving the Foreign Office clear information as to our needs in any revision of the Anglo–Egyptian Treaty; we accept that the Foreign Office in presenting our requirements will not always use the background reasoning that we have given to them. We have, however, made certain amendments to our report in order to avoid any possible misunderstanding on this subject.

With regard to (b) we agree that it would be greatly to our advantage not to specify a limit in numbers to our garrison forces, and we have already said in our report that we should prefer not to be limited to any specific figure. It would, however, in our view, be unrealistic at this time to expect the Egyptian Government to give us a blank cheque in respect of the numbers of British forces to be stationed in their country in peace-time. We consider therefore that a limit should be decided now, so that if during discussion it becomes necessary to state a figure, His Majesty's Government's representative may be fully briefed.

Admiralty comments

3. The Admiralty point out that for the next two or three years there is a requirement to retain existing ammunition depots, while global redistribution of ammunition and explosives is being carried out, and that subsequently there will be a need to maintain a quantity of ammunition as a strategic reserve in Egypt.

Recommendation

4. In the light of the above comments we have revised our original report[4] as amended by Chiefs of Staff[5] in the form of a letter, which we recommend should be sent to the Foreign Office. New or amended paragraphs are underlined or side-lined.

---

[4] See 19.   [5] See 20.

Annex to 23: draft reply to Foreign Office letter C.O.S.(45)506(0)

We have considered your letter forwarding a memorandum on the effect of the United Nations Charter on the Anglo–Egyptian Treaty and the British position in Egypt.

Timing
2.   From a purely military point of view, there is much to be said for delaying treaty revision until the political situation is clearer regarding Russian claims to a position in the Mediterranean area, and until more is known of the effect of atomic energy on our future strategy.

On the other hand, it would be preferable that negotiations should be conducted between ourselves and Egypt alone rather than through the World Organisation which might give other Powers an opportunity of interfering in the defence arrangements which we wish to make in the Middle East.

We agree, therefore, that early revision of the Treaty should be undertaken if the Foreign Office consider such action is advantageous.

Considerations governing the military requirements of a revised treaty[6]

British strategic requirements in the Middle East
3.   The general strategic background to our position in the Middle East was considered in two Staff Studies[7] which were provisionally approved by the Chiefs of Staff. We consider that there is at present no reason to change our view that the retention of our special position in that area is an essential feature of our imperial strategy.

Our military requirements in the Middle East may be stated broadly as follows:—

(a) In war, or threat of war, similar facilities to those which we have enjoyed in Egypt under the present Anglo–Egyptian Treaty.
(b) In peace:—
    (i) The security and use of the Suez Canal and such other facilities as we may require for our Imperial communications to India, Australasia and the Far East.
    (ii) The preparation and maintenance of base installations for use by our forces in war.
    (iii) The right to station forces in strategic areas, and to move forces in and through the Middle East.

Political considerations
4.   *Arab nationalism.* There is a rising tide of Arab nationalism throughout the Middle East, which in Egypt expresses itself in an agitation for the withdrawal of British forces from the country. It is, however, difficult to assess to what extent this represents the real wishes of responsible Egyptians. H.M. Ambassador to Egypt recently expressed the opinion that the Egyptians did not know what they really wanted, and the present agitation was mainly political and nationalist.

It seems likely, therefore, that we shall in any revision of the Treaty, have to make

---

[6] This is the revised version of that part of JP (45)189 not printed in 19.
[7] cf BDEEP series A, vol 1, S R Ashton & S E Stockwell, eds, *Imperial policy and colonial practice 1925–1945*, part I, 43; also CAB 81/46, PHP(45) 10, 21 Mar 1945.

concessions to Egyptian nationalism which will enable the Egyptian Government to save face with its own people *and avoid our appearing to infringe Egyptian sovereignty*. Such concessions might take the form of a complete withdrawal from large centres of population. *Our negotiations might well be assisted if we present our demands to Egypt as their contribution at the present time to an overall defence scheme for the Middle East.*

5. *Russian aspirations.* We must take account of Russian aspirations to the trusteeship of Tripolitania. If Russia were to get the sole trusteeship of Tripolitania, she would be in a position to build up forces which could constitute a threat to Egypt and the Suez Canal. Against such a threat we would have to have forces west of the Suez Canal, in either Egypt or Cyrenaica. We understand, however, that should the Russians be granted the sole trusteeship of Tripolitania by the World Organisation, it is safe to assume that His Majesty's Government will insist on our obtaining a similar trusteeship of Cyrenaica. If, therefore, the Russians were enabled to instal forces in Tripolitania, it would not necessarily follow that we should require to locate large forces in Egypt since forces could, in that case, be kept in Cyrenaica, or moved there when a state of emergency was impending.

6. *Palestine and the Middle East Confederacy.* In assessing our military requirements in Egypt, we have assumed that the political status in Palestine will remain such that we continue to enjoy military facilities at least comparable to those we have at present. From this we consider our requirements in Egypt are likely to be the same whether or not she becomes a member of an Arab Confederation as suggested by General Paget.

Military considerations

7. *War.* In war we are likely to have to conduct operations based on Egypt. We shall, therefore, require in war the full facilities in that country which we have enjoyed in this war.

8. *Peace.* Our communications through Egypt together with the necessary facilities must be assured to us in peace.

In addition, it will be necessary in peace to maintain or develop base installations in Egypt, for the use of our forces in war. The Egyptians will clearly be unable to undertake this work without British assistance and we shall, therefore, need a certain number of technical and specialist personnel permanently in Egypt to ensure the preparedness and efficiency of our base. *It may be possible for a considerable proportion of these personnel to have civilian status.*

It will not be necessary to maintain large forces in Egypt in peace. We do, however, require a small land force which would be available, if required, to ensure the protection of our administrative personnel and establishments of all three Services and of our vital communications in the event of internal disorder; we do not consider that we can rely entirely on the Egyptians for the safety of these interests. Some air force units will be necessary to provide a stiffening to the Egyptian air defences and a nucleus from which we can expand in an emergency.

It is not necessary that our forces should be in the Nile Valley except in so far as is necessary to supervise the preparation and maintenance of base installations. Moreover, they could be represented to the Egyptians as being required not for any internal security commitment, but as our immediate contribution to the defence of the Middle East as a whole.

Military requirements

9.   At Appendix I we discuss in the light of the above factors, the broad individual requirements of the three Services in peace.

At Appendix II we have set out the draft heads of the military, naval and air clauses which we consider should be included in a revised Anglo–Egyptian Treaty.

APPENDIX I[8]

Military requirements in peace

Naval requirements

1.   *Availability of Alexandria as a naval base.* With the exception of normal berthing facilities and the periodical use of two airfields in the vicinity of the port for training purposes, we shall have no operational requirements in peace at Alexandria.

We shall, however, need to arrange with the Egyptians that the port facilities, installations and local defence arrangements which will be required in the event of war, when the port would again become a naval operational base, are adequately developed and maintained.

2.   *Defence, salvage and storage facilities in the Canal area.* So long as we give the Egyptians the necessary equipment, and adequate technical advice and assistance as regard its working, there would be no objection to such facilities being under Egyptian control in peacetime.

We shall however require to hold the existing ammunition depots for two or three years and subsequently it will be desirable to maintain a strategic reserve of ammunition in the Canal area.

Army requirements

3.   *Main administrative base.* In order that our installations may be in a fit state to support immediate operations in war, they will have to be maintained at a high standard during peace. It will also be necessary to replace obsolete equipment and stock up depots as the occasion arises.

To a great extent these installations could be maintained in peace by civilian labour recruited in Egypt. It would be necessary to employ a certain number of Service personnel for control and supervision. These might be included on the strength of a Military Mission.

4.   *Garrison troops.* It will be necessary to station some garrison troops in Egypt, *not only as part of our share in the overall defence of the Middle East at the present time, but also* to insure against Egyptian failure adequately to safeguard our communications, military installations and administrative personnel.

In our negotiations with the Egyptians however, we should disclaim any intention of interfering in Egypt's sovereign right to be responsible for her own internal security, and we must concentrate upon the requirement of forces for the defence of the Middle East as a whole. We should prefer as a result not to be limited to any specific figure for the number of troops in Egypt. If, however, it becomes necessary to agree upon a figure, we consider that this should not be less than 5,000 men in combatant units. This figure would allow us to station in Egypt one brigade group which is the smallest formation which can operate as such.

---

[8] This is the revised version of annex I (not printed) to JP(45)189.

We consider that we should make it clear to the Egyptians in the course of negotiations that we would make every endeavour to avoid stationing any of these forces in the Nile Valley.

Air requirements

5.   In order to ensure in war the air defence of Egypt and the Middle East as a whole, we shall require to maintain an air garrison in Egypt in peace. In war, attack from the air is likely to come quickly and in greater strength than the Egyptians by themselves can possibly hope to deal with. In order to satisfy the Egyptians, the garrison may have to be confined to the Canal Zone or other designated area. Under conditions of modern air warfare, it is, however, impossible to ensure the air defence of Egypt from any one area of the country. Moreover, we shall wish to prepare installations for the reception of a greatly increased number of squadrons of all types in war. Our object is, therefore, to obtain the right to base our squadrons in a designated area, and, in conjunction with the Egyptians, to construct and develop in other areas, such additional airfields, signals network, radar installations and repair and maintenance depots as we may consider necessary to enable us to expand our air forces appreciably in war or on a threat of war.

6.   If it is necessary to state a size limit to our air forces, we are anxious to adopt a nomenclature which will not be unduly restrictive and will allow for future changes and development in formations, air crew compositions, etc. We consider that we shall require the right to station in Egypt up to 300 operational first line aircraft together with the necessary ancillary units, although it may not be necessary for all these squadrons to be permanently stationed in Egyptian territory. Squadrons concerned in air trooping should not be included in this total.

Transit rights

7.   We require the right and facilities to stage through Egypt such Imperial forces as His Majesty's Government may require.

Emergency requirements

8.   If in the opinion of His Majesty's Government a period of apprehended International Emergency arises, an Anglo–Egyptian force of sufficient size to meet the threat, shall be built up on Egyptian soil.

APPENDIX II[9]

Draft heads of the naval, military and air clauses
in a revised Anglo–Egyptian treaty

Continuation of alliance

1.   The Alliance with Egypt to continue, without prejudice to the obligations of Great Britain and Egypt under the Charter of the United Nations.

---

[9] This is the revised version of annex II (not printed) to JP(45)189.

In time of war or threat of war

2.   When, in the opinion of His Majesty's Government, a state of emergency exists, or when enforcement action is contemplated by the Security Council of the United Nations involving use of Egyptian territory, Imperial forces of all descriptions shall have complete freedom of movement into and within Egypt by road, rail, air, sea and inland waterway and the full use of telecommunications, ports, airfields and maintenance facilities.

In time of peace

Section I—naval clauses

3.   With a view to ensuring in co-operation with the Egyptian armed forces, the defence of Egypt, the Egyptian Government to earmark *and where necessary maintain* in time of peace ready for use on the outbreak of war, or the threat of war, the following facilities:—

At Alexandria, Port Said, Suez and the Canal Area

(a) *Accommodation*. Establishments and training schools on a scale similar to those required for Fleet purposes in 1942.

(b) *Facilities for Administration*. Such repair facilities, storage and base installations as may be considered necessary to effect a rapid expansion to a scale adequate to maintain a fleet (of the approximate size of that of 1942) in war. [This provision must permit of the retention for two or three years of the existing ammunition depots and subsequently of a strategic reserve in the Canal Area.]

(c) *Local Defence Arrangements*. Such nucleus local defences as may be adequate to ensure when expanded to war scale, the defence of the ports, the Suez Canal, and the enforcement of the Examination Service.

(d) *Aircraft repair*. Aircraft repair facilities as a nucleus ready for expansion in time of war, to an extent comparable to 1942.

4.   Apart from reserving facilities mentioned above, His Majesty's Government also wish for freedom for naval aircraft, disembarked from H.M. ships visiting Egyptian ports, to visit local airfields in Egypt.

5.   *Planning*. His Majesty's Government will assist with technical advice in the planning of harbour works, positioning of moorings; and alterations or improvements in fixed defences.

Section II—army clauses

6.   *Facilities for administration*. The right for His Majesty's Government to maintain such existing base installations throughout Egypt as it may consider necessary for the efficient maintenance of the garrison (including such requirements as may be necessary for a garrison in Cyrenaica) in peace and war, and such as will enable a rapid expansion to full war scale, when the necessity as covered by paragraph 2 arises.

7.   *Garrison troops*. In view of the mutual interest of the Egyptian Government and His Majesty's Government in the overall defence of the Middle East, and of the security of the Suez Canal, His Majesty's Government and the Egyptian Government to collaborate for this purpose. His Majesty's Government to have the right to maintain in Egypt the necessary forces.

The proportion of these forces, including Headquarters personnel, to be located in the Nile Valley, to be reduced to the minimum number compatible with the requirements of military efficiency.

Access to suitable training areas to be provided for these forces.

Section III—air clauses

8. *Air passage.* The Egyptian Government to allow full rights of air passage through Egyptian territory to all H.M. aircraft whether training, ferrying or in transit.

9. *Emergency landings.* The Egyptian Government to afford all necessary aid and facilities to H.M. aircraft forced landing in Egyptian territory or territorial waters.

10. *Airfields and anchorages.* His Majesty's Government to have exclusive rights to the airfields and flying boat and seaplane anchorages constructed in the Canal Zone [as defined in Annex to Article 8 of the 1936 Treaty] including the right to develop them as may be necessary in the light of:—

(a) Increasing size and speed of modern aircraft.

(b) Adequate dispersal of aircraft and administrative installations.

(c) Increasing size and complication of air force ground organisation.

11. *Air defence of Egypt.* His Majesty's Government to have the right in agreement with the Egyptian Government to construct air defence installations inside or outside the Canal Zone. Such installations (e.g. airfields, radar, signals network, etc.) to be integrated with such air defence system as the Egyptian Government may set up through the medium of the British Military Mission.

12. *Depots and installations.* His Majesty's Government to have the right to build and maintain such stores, repair and maintenance facilities as may be necessary in the opinion of His Majesty's Government to maintain, in the event of war, a joint Anglo–Egyptian air force adequate for the defence of Egyptian territory.

13. *Training.* H.M. air forces to have the use of adequate bombing, gunnery and R.P. [radar protection] ranges and low flying areas.

H.M. air forces to take a full part in all exercises of the Egyptian air defence system in conjunction with the Egyptian air forces.

14. *Air sea/desert rescue.* The Egyptian Government to assist His Majesty's Government in the provision of such air sea/desert rescue arrangements as may be considered necessary.

15. *Size of force.* The total number of British operational first line aircraft stationed in Egypt shall not exceed 300 together with the necessary ancillary personnel for administrative and technical duties. Insofar as it is compatible with the adequate air defence of Egypt these will normally be stationed in the Canal Zone [as defined in Article 8 of the 1936 Treaty].

Section IV—general clauses

16. *Fuel.* The Egyptian Government to agree that adequate facilities shall be earmarked in peace for the bulk storage and distribution of fuel oils, petrol and lubricants for use by H.M. forces in the defence of Egypt in time of war.

17. *Staging of imperial troops through Egypt*

(a) The right for His Majesty's Government to stage through Egypt such Imperial forces as His Majesty's Government shall require.

(b) The right to construct in the Canal Zone or in such other areas as may be agreed sufficient accommodation and facilities for such personnel and for aircraft in transit under the trooping by air and air mobility programme. Aircraft and ancillary personnel engaged in trooping by air and air mobility shall not be included in the air force ceiling laid down in paragraph 15 above.

18. *Right of movement.* The Egyptian Government to provide means of communication to and from the localities where Imperial forces are situated, and landing and storage facilities for supplies at Port Said and Suez. British administrative detachments to be located at the latter ports to handle stores.

19. *Roads.* The Egyptian Government to undertake to construct and/or maintain the roads specified in Annex to Article 3 of 1936 Treaty and such roads as are agreed to be necessary for the maintenance and movement of Anglo/Egyptian Forces.

20. *Scientific development.* In view of the new methods of warfare constantly being devised, His Majesty's Government and the Egyptian Government to consult together from time to time with a view to building such special installations and generally equipping the defences of Egypt, as may be expedient for the full protection of their mutual interests in wars.

21. *Military mission.* The Egyptian Government to accept a Mission representative of all three Services to whose advice they shall pay due regard on defence matters of interest to both Governments.

22. *Time of move.* The movement of British forces to the new areas shall be timed with due regard to the construction by the Egyptian Government of adequate accommodation, administrative facilities, and means of communication and to the disposal of surplus stocks.

24 CAB 79/42, COS 289(45)5 27 Dec 1945
'Revision of Anglo–Egyptian treaty': COS Committee minutes

The Committee considered a report by the Joint Planning Staff[1] concerning the revision of the Anglo–Egyptian Treaty in the light of the comments that had been received from the Commanders-in-Chief, Middle East, and the Admiralty and of *the views of Lord Killearn.*

Vice Admiral McGrigor, referring to the last sub-paragraph of paragraph 8 of the Annex, suggested that the presence of British Forces in the Nile Valley was so important that the phrase in the second sentence "Moreover, they could be represented to the Egyptians. ..." should be re-drafted to read "Moreover, they should be represented to the Egyptians. ..."

Major General Simpson, referring to the penultimate line of paragraph 4 of the Annex, suggested that our demands were only a part of the contribution by the Egyptians to the overall defence of the Middle East. This sentence should be re-drafted accordingly. He suggested that a new paragraph should be added as paragraph 9 to Appendix I that "in carrying out these negotiations, efforts should be made to persuade the Egyptians to look to the future and realize that the ever-changing methods of modern warfare make it necessary to keep defence

---

[1] See 23.

requirements flexible and subject to alteration as necessary by agreement between the two Governments. His Majesty's Government's representatives should endeavour to discourage a state of mind which regards defence arrangements made now as immutable".

He agreed that the word "garrison" should be omitted throughout the Report.

Air Vice Marshal Dickson suggested that it was undesirable to state the exact limits of the R.A.F. Force to be stationed in Egypt in paragraph 15 of Appendix II, and that this paragraph should be re-drafted in accordance with the wording of paragraph 7 referring to the Army, which was drafted in much more general terms.

In this connection, he felt that the Annex did not explain clearly enough the reason for not wishing the exact number of troops to be mentioned in the draft Heads of Agreement, and suggested that this point should be further emphasised in paragraph 6 of the Annex. He further suggested that paragraph 6 should be split into two, the first part to deal with Palestine and the second part to deal with Middle East Confederacy.

The Committee:—

Instructed the Secretary to despatch the report as amended in discussion, as a memorandum by the Chiefs of Staff Committee to the Foreign Office.

25   FO 371/53282, no 132   9 Jan 1946

[Anglo–Egyptian treaty revision]: inward telegram no 36 from Lord Killearn to FO on the necessity of considering treaty relations with Egypt and the Middle East

Mr. Bowker's telegram No. 2376

Feeling in Egypt towards us is deteriorating owing to:

(1) Absence of reply to Egyptian request for treaty provisions negotiations;

(2) Reuter reports on comments of British newspapers suggesting that Egypt will get neither evacuation nor her Sudanese requirements;

(3) Anglo–French agreement about Middle East interpreted as sacrifice of the smaller nations even Great Britain's allies to power politics;

(4) Our hereditary failure to prevent Russia from devouring Persia;

(5) Moscow Conference which apart from excluding Egypt from the peace conference, is interpreted as a sacrifice by Great Britain and the United States of the small nations to Russian exhortation without any counter-balancing guarantees against Russian aggressions in the Middle East.

2.   As indicated in the telegram referred to above, further delay in handling question of treaty relations between Great Britain and Egypt as well as other Middle East countries is working against our interests here in that it leaves the field free to extremist agitators and to Russian promotion of such agitation—compare with recent Russian press. It is obvious also that Egypt, which is now becoming a centre to which representatives of all the Arab countries are continually coming for conferences etc. is infecting the rest of the Middle East with her feeling. The longer we delay in handling this treaty problem, the greater the danger of extremist [gp. undec.] ity and agitation possibly leading to disorder.

3.   In considering what policy we are to adopt regarding treaty relations with Egypt and the Middle East, I would urge that we bear strongly in mind one essential factor, namely that although possibly Egypt may be prepared to temporise about the Sudan it is certain that with her present Government (or possibly any other—though of that I am not so sure) she will not, except under duress, sign any new treaty giving us the right to maintain troops in Egypt and except, just possibly, as part of a defence scheme the Middle East on a partner-ship basis (see my telegram No. 2552 of 1945).[1] Failing acceptance of such a scheme, we must then be prepared either for force or for other military arrangements e.g. stationing of troops in Cyrenaica and Palestine with military, naval and air bases maintained in Egypt by Egyptians in liaison with our military naval and air authorities and ready for immediate occupation by us in the event of apprehended international emergency. That would be the most we could get out of Egyptians by consent. It will no doubt be realised that in view of Russia's progress and of growing propaganda regarding the Middle East, the Egyptians, and no doubt other Middle East states are no longer so likely to acquiesce in treaties or agreements after pre-war model. I venture to submit that it is necessary for us now to take bold and new view of our requirements in these parts. Unless we can obtain satisfactory assurances from Russia and the United States that they will not interfere, it would be disastrous to antagonise the whole of the Middle East by trying to force on it agreements which it will reject with consequent deterioration of feeling of its peoples towards Great Britain and a consequent tendency on their part to play with the idea of Russian support against us.

---

[1] See 22.

26   CAB 129/6, CP(46)17   18 Jan 1946
'Revision of the Anglo–Egyptian treaty of 1936': Cabinet memorandum by Mr Bevin. *Annexes*   [Extract]

[The Foreign Office had prepared a note for the Cabinet on treaty revision which was sent to the Chiefs of Staff for approval and became the annex to COS(46)8, 12 Jan 1946. The FO and the COS agreed that there would be advantages in bilateral talks, rather than talks under the auspices of the World Organisation, and the FO also argued that an Anglo–Egyptian treaty should 'form the security agreement which Egypt may be required to conclude with the Security Council under Article 43[1] of the Charter of the United Nations, or shall at any rate form the basis of such an agreement'. Therefore it was desirable for the treaty to be ready before Egypt could undertake negotiations on security arrangements with the United Nations. The difficulties the Foreign Office foresaw were

---

[1] Article 43 states:
'1. All members of the United Nations, in order to contribute to the maintenance of international peace and security, undertake to make available to the Security Council, on its call and in accordance with a special agreement or agreements, armed forces, assistance, and facilities, including rights of passage, necessary for the purpose of maintaining international peace and security.
2. Such agreement or agreements shall govern the numbers and types of forces, their degree of readiness and general location, and the nature of the facilities and assistance to be provided.
3. The agreement or agreements shall be negotiated as soon as possible on the initiative of the Security Council. They shall be concluded between the Security Council and members or between the Security Council and groups of members and shall be subject to ratification by the signatory states in accordance with their respective constitutional processes.'

[(1) the Egyptian government contained no representatives of the largest political party – the Wafd; (2) the emnity between the King and the Wafd; (3) that the PM and minister of foreign affairs were temperamentally unfitted to undertake such important negotiations; (4) that while HMG were anxious to avoid interference in Egypt's internal affairs the issues were so important that it would be necessary to voice British anxieties about the existing government to the King whose influence was deemed to be keeping it in power (CAB 80/99, COS(46)8, 12 Jan 1946). None of these points were put to the Cabinet which considered Bevin's paper produced below on 22 Jan and approved discussions with the Egyptians on the lines of the instructions set out in annex (CAB 128/5, CM 7(46)5).]

I circulate herewith, for the information of my colleagues (Annex A), a translation of a Note, received from the Egyptian Government on the 20th December, which contains the anticipated demand for the revision of the Anglo–Egyptian Treaty of 1936, and more particularly for the withdrawal of British forces from Egypt in time of peace. I recommend that a reply agreeing in general terms to a review of our present arrangements should be sent, and attach a draft (Annex B) for concurrence.

I should explain that the principles of those articles of the present treaty which are of the greatest importance from our point of view, viz, those establishing the alliance and providing for the extended facilities to our forces in time of war, are automatically renewable *in any revision of the Treaty* (Article 16 of the Treaty). We should, of course, insist on this renewal as a point of departure. The remaining articles deal with the military facilities afforded us by Egypt in time of peace, the Sudan, and various political questions of a general nature. A number of these articles (notably those relating to the League of Nations) are in any event out of date and since the whole Treaty of 1936 is based on the League of Nations and the Covenant, it cannot be contested that some revision is necessary and is called for now.

In addition, I am satisfied that it would be unwise, if not impossible, in the light of the state of public opinion in Egypt and of the international situation in general to take our stand on the letter of the present Treaty which excludes the possibility of revision before the end of this year. I contemplate that the new Treaty (reproducing, as I have said, the essential features of the old) should be bilateral in character, but should be drafted so as to fit into a regional defence system for the Middle East as a whole (such as I hope to bring about in due course). The Treaty would be related to the United Nations Organisation in some suitable form, possibly as an arrangement for "collective defence" such as authorised by Article 51 of the Charter. I also agree with the advice of the Chiefs of Staff that is essential to press for facilities for the maintenance of British land and air forces in Egypt in time of peace in order that the aid to be given in emergency may be effective and sufficiently speedy.

As regards the Sudan which, like the question of peacetime facilities for our troops, constitutes a major difficulty (and offers little scope for compromise), His Majesty's Governments have repeatedly refused to abandon their responsibilities towards the Sudanese peoples, amongst whom the idea of nationhood has already taken shape. It is out of the question for His Majesty's Government to accede to the request which will probably be made of them, viz, to recognise *sole* Egyptian sovereignty over the Sudanese. They must, I submit, maintain firmly the standpoint that the future of the Sudan belongs neither to this country nor to Egypt, but to the Sudanese themselves, whose own wishes must be taken into account in any new arrangements which may be devised. Our further tactics must depend on Egyptian reactions to this standpoint.

As regards procedure, I am satisfied that we should follow the precedent of 1936 and clear the ground by preliminary conversations in Cairo conducted by His Majesty's Ambassador and by the Service Commanders acting as His Excellency's technical advisers. Apart from the practical inconvenience of receiving an Egyptian delegation in London during the coming weeks, the discussions would be conducted in the glare of publicity, which in my view would greatly increase the likelihood of a breakdown.

The general lines of the instructions which I would propose to issue to Lord Killearn are annexed as Annex C.

Annex A to 26: note of 20th December, 1945, from the Egyptian government

The Egyptian Government, certain that they are interpreting a unanimous national sentiment, consider that the manifest interests of Anglo–Egyptian friendship and alliance demand that the two parties should revise, in the light of recent events and of their experience, the arrangements which govern their mutual relations at the present time.

2.   It is certain that the Treaty of 1936 was concluded in the midst of an international crisis at a moment when the spectre of war was already appearing, and it is to these circumstances that it clearly owes its present form.

3.   Further, Egypt only accepted it under the pressure of necessity and as a testimony to the loyalty and sincere desire for collaboration which inspire her towards her Ally.

4.   The Treaty thus appeared as a link in the chain of measures taken and of agreements concluded to prevent the war which was menacing the world, or to repel aggression if war could not be avoided.

5.   If Egypt accepted the Treaty with all that it implied in the way of restrictions on her independence, it was because she knew that they were of a transitory character and were destined to disappear at the same time as the circumstances and events by reason of which they had been agreed to.

6.   In fact, the war has exhausted the principal objectives of the Treaty and opened the way for the adoption of a new system which would take the place of arrangements established as much under the influence of a mistrust which had not yet entirely disappeared in 1936 as under the inspiration of military conditions which recent events have essentially modified.

7.   The international events which have upset the world, the Allied victory which has brought the last war to an end, the agreements destined to maintain the peace and security of the world, render several of the provisions of the Treaty superfluous and without justification.

8.   Moreover, it is not the letter of the text of agreements which decides their efficacity, but rather the goodwill of the peoples in consenting to them and the spirit governing their application.

9.   Nothing proves better the loyalty with which Egypt honours her obligations than her assistance to her Ally during the whole of the war, in the course of which she gave the most concrete evidence of her fidelity to her alliances and of her sincerity in her friendships.

10.   The British Government, at the time of trial, obtained from their agreement with Egypt more than the text stipulated and much more than the most optimistic British negotiators had certainly been able to contemplate.

11.   Therefore, now that the circumstances which determined the particular character of the Treaty of 1936 have changed, it has become necessary to revise it in order to bring it into harmony with the new international situation; its clauses which detract from the independence and the dignity of Egypt no longer correspond to present conditions.

12.   The presence of foreign forces on our soil in peace-time, even if stationed in distant areas, is still wounding to national dignity, and can only be interpreted by Egyptian public opinion as the tangible sign of a mistrust which the British Government themselves, we believe, must regard as unjustified.

13.   It would be better for the two countries that their relations should be founded on mutual understanding and confidence.

14.   Egypt, conscious of the needs imposed on her by the defence of her territory and of the responsibilities which her participation in the organisation of the United Nations entails for her, will, moreover, shrink from no sacrifice in order, in the immediate future, to place her military potential in a state enabling her to repel aggression pending the arrival of the reinforcements of her Allies and of the United Nations.

15.   For this reason, and in view of the unanimous urge of the Egyptian people and their ardent desire to see their relations with Great Britain established on the basis of an alliance and a friendship which will no longer be inspired by past prejudices or out-of-date doctrines, the Egyptian Government express their confidence that these views will be shared by their Ally, and that the British Government will take steps to fix an early date for an Egyptian delegation to proceed to London to negotiate with them the revision of the Treaty of 1936.

16.   It goes without saying that the negotiations will include the question of the Sudan and will be inspired by the interests and aspirations of the Sudanese.

Annex B to 26: draft reply to Egyptian government

Your Excellency,

I have the honour to acknowledge receipt of the note of the 20th December, 1945, by which the Egyptian Government request His Majesty's Government in the United Kingdom to fix an early date for negotiations for the revision of the Anglo–Egyptian Treaty of Alliance of the 26th August, 1936.

His Majesty's Government have been well aware of the desire which has been manifested in Egypt for discussions with them on this subject, and if they have not hitherto responded formally to these expressions of opinion by their Allies, the reason has lain first in the continuous pressure of events arising out of the termination of hostilities, and, secondly, in the necessity of examining the provisions of the Anglo–Egyptian Treaty in the light of the Charter of the United Nations and also of the lessons taught by those hostilities. And in this connexion His Majesty's Government, without wishing at the present stage to examine in detail the contentions in the Egyptian Government's note, take leave to observe that one of these lessons was the essential soundness of the fundamental principles on which the Anglo–Egyptian Treaty of 1936 was based.

It is the policy of His Majesty's Government to consolidate in a spirit of frankness and cordiality the close co-operation, achieved by Egypt and the British Commonwealth and Empire during the war, to which Your Excellency's note bears testimony, and to place it on a footing of full and free partnership, as between equals in the defence of their mutual interests, and with full respect for the independence and sovereignty of Egypt. Therefore, notwithstanding the provisions of Article 16 of the Treaty of 1936, His Majesty's Government in the United Kingdom declare themselves willing to undertake, with the Government of Egypt, a review of the treaty arrangements between them in the light of their mutual experience and with due regard to the provisions of the Charter of the United Nations for ensuring international peace and security. Instructions will shortly be sent to His Majesty's Ambassador in Cairo to hold preliminary conversations with the Egyptian Government to that end. His Majesty's Government in the United Kingdom take note that the Egyptian Government desire that the forthcoming discussions should include the question of the Sudan.

Annex C to 26: memorandum

I suggest below the lines on which the preliminary conversations with the Egyptian Government might be conducted. But first of all it is necessary to describe the relationship between the revised Treaty and the Charter of the United Nations.

From the point of view of pure advantage, it would suit us best to represent the Treaty as an arrangement of collective security within the meaning of Article 51 of the Charter rather than as a "regional" agreement within the meaning of Articles 52 to 54 because—

(a) It is not certain whether such a Treaty can qualify as a regional arrangement since, according to Article 52, one of the purposes of a regional arrangement is the development of the pacific settlement of local disputes through local agreements.
(b) The Egyptian Government are known to be opposed to the idea that the Treaty constitutes a regional agreement.
(c) Furthermore, there is an awkward provision in Article 53, viz, that no enforcement action is to be taken under a regional agreement without the authorisation of the Security Council, whereas there is no limitation on the exercise of collective defence in Article 51.

On the other hand, from the broad standpoint of United Nations policy, it would be difficult for His Majesty's Government *openly and in terms* to relate the revised Anglo–Egyptian Treaty to Article 51 of the Charter which, however reasonable in itself, is in effect in the nature of an "escape clause" and an admission that the international security system may not prove effective in practice.

In general, therefore, and certainly at the outset of the preliminary conversations, it will be well to avoid reference to any specific security articles in the Charter, though it is realised that in discussion at any rate we may be forced to do so before long. The object of the treaty can in fact be generally defined as strengthening by mutual co-operation the contributions which each party will be able to make to the maintenance of international peace and security in accordance with the provisions of the United Nations Charter.

1. *Defence*

It should be explained to the Egyptian Government that His Majesty's Government are anxious to raise the question of the defence of Egypt from the level of a purely bilateral understanding by which Egypt, to judge from the Egyptian note, feels herself placed in an inferior position, to the level of a general partnership between the Middle East States and His Majesty's Government for the safeguarding on the one hand of the integrity and independence of those States, and on the other of the security of the British Commonwealth which, as conclusively demonstrated in the course of two world wars, can be vitally threatened by an attack on the Middle Eastern area. In this matter the Middle Eastern States and the Commonwealth stand or fall together. The suppression by an aggressor of the independence of the Middle Eastern States or of the independence of any one of them threatens to divide the Commonwealth. Similarly, any undermining by an aggressor of the British position in the Middle East threatens the stability of the individual Arab countries. All the experience of the last war, moreover, goes to show that smaller countries, however tenaciously they may defend themselves, must inevitably be overrun by an aggressor unless they can receive full and immediate support from a Power possessing a military *and economic* potential comparable to that of the aggressor. If Egypt in the last war was spared the rigours of enemy occupation it is due to the fact that under the Anglo–Egyptian Treaty there was in Egypt the nucleus of a force capable of defending Egyptian territory and counter-attacking in its turn. And it must be remembered that every aggressor from the dawn of history has extended his ambitions to the Middle Eastern area. No more fatal error could be made by the Arab States than to suppose that their deliverance in 1941–43 has of itself averted the danger of attack for all time. The United Kingdom and their Allies of the United Nations have pledged themselves to construct and to operate an international system for safeguarding world security, but until this edifice is completed regional partnership will be required, and the military advice at the disposal of His Majesty's Government has convinced them that the defence of the Middle East can and should be organised on a collective basis.

In the light of the foregoing considerations His Majesty's Government regard it as essential that—as is in fact provided by Article 16 of the treaty of 1936—the Alliance shall continue in accordance with the principles contained in Articles 4–7: and that in particular the aid promised by Egypt under Article 7 in case of war or emergency should be confirmed and redefined in the light of experience. Once this point is conceded, it should be explained that, in order that this aid shall be fully effective, His Majesty's Government consider it necessary to have certain facilities in the Middle East countries in time of peace; and in particular they must be able to station in the area, and particularly in Egypt as one of the countries indicated by geography no less than by *industrial* development as regional bases, the minimum forces necessary to provide the nucleus of a war-time establishment for the defence of the area as a whole, and to ensure continuous collaboration in training and the use of technical devices and armaments. Moreover, in the present state of development of military aviation the burden on a small State, or States, of maintaining the necessary defensive forces to ensure against long-range bombing attack (with all its consequences) would be intolerable however great the national spirit of sacrifice.

His Majesty's Government will therefore ask the Egyptian Government first of all to reaffirm Articles 4–7 of the existing treaty and then to agree in principle to provide the Imperial forces with the necessary administrative, base and communications facilities, and to allow for a term of years the presence on her soil of those British forces considered necessary, as part of the contribution which Egypt is ready to make to the security of the Middle East.

His Majesty's Government will also ask the Egyptian Government for permission to construct certain defences and to stage through Egypt such Imperial forces as may be required. His Majesty's Government will, in addition, raise with the Egyptian Government the question of the retention of the British Military Mission.

The details of these arrangements which must cover the three fighting services and are necessarily of considerable complexity will require to be elaborated in a military convention either to be annexed to, or to be concluded separately from, the main treaty of alliance, and it would, in the view of His Majesty's Government, be right that the States of the Arab League should be appraised of these arrangements (and of those which His Majesty's Government will set on foot in Palestine and may seek elsewhere in the area) with a view to their endorsement by the League and to the ultimate formation of a military confederacy between His Majesty's Government and the countries of the Middle East embracing as wide an area as is required. The proposals which His Majesty's Government will lay before the Egyptian Government for this purpose have been so drawn up as to fit into an overall defence scheme for the Middle East area.

2. *Political articles*

His Majesty's Government are ready to discuss with the Egyptian Government the modification or, as the case may be, suppression of those Articles of the 1936 Treaty which the passage of time and developments in the international field have rendered out of date, viz., Articles 1, 2, 3, 6, 10, 13, 15, 16 and 17. . . .

27 FO 371/53286, no 942   2 Mar 1946

[Revision of Anglo–Egyptian treaty]: minute by P S Scrivener on British requirements in Egypt

[The problems associated with the unrepresentative Egyptian government and the emnity between King Farouk and the Wafd faced the British with increasingly difficult problems in February. On 4 February, the anniversary of the surrounding of King Farouk's palace by British tanks in 1942 in order to install a Wafd government under Nahas, there were a number of anti-British demonstrations. One Egyptian newspaper published a cartoon of Egyptian tanks bombarding the British embassy, and the Chamber of Deputies suspended its session for five minutes as a sign of mourning. In this anti-British atmosphere where Farouk stood to benefit from hurt Egyptian national pride, the Wafd could only attack the King and Nokrashi's unrepresentative government by condemning the proposed treaty negotiations as incompatible with Egyptian sovereignty. On 11 Feb the British ambassador, Lord Killearn, a supporter of Nahas not the King, reported that the situation was not conducive to successful treaty negotiations. He was then replaced and a new Egyptian PM, Sidky Pasha appointed following Nokrashi's resignation on 15 Feb. Killearn's replacement, Sir R Campbell, was told before leaving for Egypt in March that it had been decided to work with King Farouk as the chief element of continuing stability and not to attempt to force Nahas into power (FO 371/53304, no 2955, Cairo tel 1183, 2 July 1946). On 21 Feb an anti-British demonstration produced attacks on British establishments in Cairo which, according to the British, led to troops firing in self-defence. The Egyptians claimed that the incident was sparked by a British army lorry driving into a crowd with fatal consequences and that subsequently fifty people were killed or wounded by the British.]

It might be advisable before Sir R. Campbell's departure to consider very carefully, and if necessary put to the Cabinet, the question whether we should acquiesce in the removal of British forces of all arms from everywhere in Egypt in peace if Sir R. Campbell's powers of persuasion fail to ensure the acceptance of a peace-time garrison.

2.   I am personally convinced that the insistence of the Chiefs of Staff on retaining a peace-time garrison in Egypt is justified, on political as well as military grounds, *unless* the over-all defence of the British Empire can be assured by substituting for the Egypt-Palestine-Transjordan-Irak bastion the East African bastion *plus* through communications with West Africa. (I have assumed that when the Secretary of State contemplates withdrawal from Egypt he has this alternative in mind. The Chiefs of Staff are now considering it). My reason is that the Egyptians cannot be trusted to maintain unaided (or, let us say it frankly, unprompted) the military framework which must exist in peace-time if the area is to be properly defended in war. In fact confidence in Egyptian capacity to organise their resources and to maintain public order is lacking—and rightly lacking. Egyptian administrative inefficiency and mob violence persist in 1946 just as they did in 1882: and the argument that if there are no British troops in Egypt there will be no demonstrations is totally fallacious: Egyptians will riot about anything.

3.   The reasons in favour of giving way on this issue are broadly (1) that the Egyptians are unanimous in their insistence on evacuation and (2) that proceedings in U.N.O. have shown virtually unanimous support for the proposition that foreign troops shall only remain in a sovereign state with the approval of the Government of that state; and that as no Egyptian Government would approve the presence of foreign troops in Egypt, we should be defeated if the matter came before the Security Council.

4.   I am not convinced of the validity of (1) but assuming its truth we find ourselves under (2) in the interesting position that the body responsible for preserving world peace would be invited to take action which could not fail to jeopardise world peace, viz. weakening the British Commonwealth at one of its vital points. It will be agreed that history has proved that a weakened British Commonwealth is the most potent *negative* cause of war.

5.   The argument in this form is hardly suitable for use in the Security Council, but it does seem to me that the Council would be incurring a terrible responsibility before history if it *did* order us out of Egypt. And we have had indications from secret sources that the Egyptians do not view with unmixed glee the prospect of hauling us before the Council. Doubtless the recent proceedings of the Council will have confirmed them in these doubts.

6.   There is the further consideration that this country is very much on trial at the moment. We can, without an undue appearance of weakness, withdraw from many places; but there would be something unpleasantly symbolic about our departure from Egypt. As a gesture of acceptance of a new international conception it might look very well; but unfortunately no other great Power is prepared to make such gestures, and our own would therefore be calculated to discourage our friends and encourage our enemies. Setting an example seems akin to suicide, internationally speaking.

7.   If, on the other hand, the East African bastion *is* a military possibility (or even an improvement on the present edifice, whose foundation is the shifting sand of Arab

—and Jewish—politics) we can start off as at present planned, and if we can ensure the continuation of the peace-time garrison, so much the better for financial reasons and reasons of general convenience. If we cannot, we can give way gracefully and demand whatever delay may be necessary to develop the East African base—say five years (and I suppose we should have to develop an enormous air base in the Sudan). But failing this possibility I believe we ought to stand fast in Egypt, and face riots and the Security Council if necessary. In such an eventuality the assurances given to the Secretary of State by Stalin would assume capital importance.[1] Can they be relied upon?

---

[1] At the Moscow Council of Foreign Ministers in Dec 1945 Stalin suggested to Bevin, presumably in the hope of reciprocal concessions in the Straits or parts of Eastern Europe, that he would welcome a continued British presence in certain areas of the world, ie Egypt.

28 FO 371/53288, no 1135 6 Mar 1946[1]
'Swan-song': inward despatch no 101 from R J Bowker to FO constituting Lord Killearn's resumé of his time in Egypt

In 1934 I left China after seven years as head of the British Legation there. It was a wrench to leave. In 1946 I quit Egypt after twelve years with an even greater wrench.

2. I reached China (for my second period of service there) in October 1926. There was an intensive nationalist drive in full flow against us as the principal foreign Power. When I left China in January 1934 common sense had prevailed, the drive had been diverted, and once more Great Britain occupied pride of place with practically every Chinese War Lord and political party. We were on terms of marked amity with the Kuomintang, the Nationalist party, which by that time ruled the land and which had been specially violent against us. It was an invaluable lesson—how to get on terms with a strong nationalist movement.

3. In January 1934 I landed in Egypt with no previous local knowledge and no local prejudice. The problem had much similarity to that in China in 1926. A strong nationalist drive—which in Egypt, as in China, took the form of an essentially anti-British movement: but with the fundamental difference that in Egypt British interests were of a more compelling nature owing to the geographical situation of Egypt lying as she does right athwart the communications of the British Commonwealth. The complex was otherwise much the same: but the technique was necessarily different to suit the different need. In China one had been a spectator, interested, but in a sense passive. In Egypt Fate had decreed that such passivity was not feasible. Egypt was an essential link in British world security.

4. What was the position? On the throne King Fuad, an astute and unscrupulous Monarch, but a Monarch who in the last resort knew full well on which side his bread was buttered. He might gird at the British and frequently did: but he was fully conscious that the security of his throne depended in the last resort upon British support. Against him—and against us—was the Wafd, the popular nationalist party

---

[1] The despatch was not received until 11 Mar 1946.

pledged to secure the independence of the country. It was a three-legged stool—King Fuad, the British and the Wafd. When things became difficult we could always rely on King Fuad to beard—and if necessary scotch—the Wafd in their more violent anti-British, *i.e.,* pro-independence, attitude.

5.   When I reached Cairo there had been no personal contacts between the British High Commissioner and Acting High Commissioner and the Wafd for several years. Yet the Wafd even then were the majority political party in the country.

6.   It was evident that this was not a wholesome lay-out. But when as one of my first probing efforts I invited *all* political leaders to a garden party at the Embassy, I well remember King Fuad's scorn at what he termed a futile attempt to copy British methods and to bring all Parties together. This political *impasse* continued, with the one exception of a better contact between the Embassy and all political parties, until Mussolini took a hand and by his adventure in Abyssinia so impressed the Egyptian political leaders that, under the Government of Ali Maher, they agreed to coalesce and for the first time a United Front was created which rendered the negotiation of a Treaty with us not only desirable but imperative. It is to the credit of King Fuad that not only did he realise this, but that, as the last act of his reign, he encouraged and created it. The result was the Treaty of Alliance of 1936, in which the Wafd, our enemies of earlier days, played the dominant and most whole-hearted part under Nahas Pasha.

7.   Then King Fuad died: and his son King Farouk, an immature boy reigned in his stead.

8.   As observed earlier, his father King Fuad, with all his many faults, had always realised which side his bread was buttered; unfortunately his son was not only ignorant of that, but did not even know where the butter came from. He was young, immature and badly led by Ali Maher. And it was a tragedy—none of his doing—that owing to the death of his father he had been recalled from his studies in England before he had had any real chance to benefit by them. Upon return he was easily misled by Ali Maher; and it was not long before the latter persuaded his young Sovereign into dismissing the Wafd Government at the end of 1937. There followed the Government of Mohamed Mahmoud Pasha,[2] who vainly tried to govern decently and constitutionally against incessant Palace interference and arbitrariness until finally he was forced out of office by the Palace and replaced by Ali Maher Pasha,[2] with whom came almost immediately after the cataclysm of the late war. The Government of Ali Maher developed cold feet and adopted an attitude of neutrality which had certainly never been anticipated by any signatory of the Treaty of Alliance. It is true that this attitude of benevolent neutrality on balance suited our book. But it showed an attitude of mind on the part of Egypt which was unfortunate—an attitude of moral cowardice which, as the war turned against us, developed into a deliberate policy of reinsurance with the enemy. This had to be checked, and first of all Ali Maher, the arch insurer, had to be got rid of. But he had done much harm and fifth-columnism and defeatism were rampant with the more than tolerant encouragement of the Palace. Finally, with Rommel at the gates and rampant defeatism abroad, stern measures had to be adopted and a Government called to office which not only had the support of the people but a will to support Great Britain loyally, as prescribed by the Treaty.

9.   The crisis was shortly afterwards met and successfully passed with the victory of Alamein, which was strong and convincing medicine. But the rancour of the

---

[2] Former leader of the Liberals and prime minister, 1937–1939.

events of the 4th February 1942, lingered, and after two years of admittedly inefficient and corrupt Government, the Wafd handed their heads to King Farouk on a charger and were dismissed from office.

10. Ahmed Maher took the helm: and was generally admitted as the only politician capable of keeping the ship of State reasonably stable. But fate intervened, and he was murdered by a half-baked fanatic for declaring war against the Central Powers in order to qualify for membership of the United Nations.

11. With Ahmed Maher gone, matters rapidly deteriorated. His successor, Nokrashi, was quite nakedly the nominee of the Palace and the vendetta between the Palace and the Wafd yawned ever wider. The Palace *coup*, in ejecting the Wafd and installing their nominee Ahmed Maher, had foundered. And it could only be a question of time till the failure of the Palace *coup* forced a further change. This occurred last month when, on the issue of Treaty Revision, things got really out of hand, and Sidky Pasha, the most corrupt if also the most able of Egyptian statesmen, found himself called to office.

12. Such briefly is the sequence of events.

13. Meantime, with the war successfully over, British technique had altered— what had been regarded as both legitimate and indeed essential to repel the enemy, was no longer the order of the day. Non-intervention in Egyptian politics was convincingly proclaimed; and the rôle of the British representative was henceforth to remain aloof and let internal bickerings and political squabbles take their course as being no direct concern of ours.

14. A convincing and pleasant theory—yet in the long run is it possible? For Egypt continues to occupy the same geographical position as she always has done: she continues to be right athwart the Suez Canal and our imperial communications. Furthermore the Middle East has gained greater political and strategical importance than ever before; *and* the Arab League has been born and shows unexpected signs of growth and vigour. To sit back and remain splendidly aloof from Egyptian internal politics sounds extremely attractive in theory: and in normal conditions would be unchallengeable as politically sound. But with Egypt situated as she is, how long will that be possible? Can we allow Egypt to disintegrate and deteriorate at her own sweet will? Can we even stand by and, in the extremest case, allow any other Power to replace us here? Can we in short admit any substantial diminution of our predominance? With all deference I gravely doubt it.

15. I am leaving Egypt in a few days' time. I regret to record that in my judgment the internal situation was never worse. It will not be for me to handle the situation further nor to deal with the task of adapting to Egyptian national aspirations and the post-war international outlook the Anglo–Egyptian treaty of 1936, which, all in all, stood us in good stead through the war. This I admit carries a tinge of regret. For with powder in the gun I maintain that in the East it is usually unnecessary to discharge it. The knowledge we mean business is enough.

16. Certain facts stand out:—

(1) Great Britain cannot in the long run disinterest herself completely in Egyptian domestic affairs. Partnership is splendid but nature has ordered there must be a senior partner.

(2) The Egyptians are essentially a docile and friendly people, but they are like children in many respects. They need a strong but essentially a fair and helpful

hand to guide them: "firmness and justice" is the motto for Egypt, just as it used to be for the Chinese.

(3) The present cleavage between the Palace and the Majority Party (the Wafd) is fraught with the gravest danger.

(4) The present Sovereign is in many respects old beyond his years. But he is vindictive, like his father, badly advised and politically short-sighted. Hitherto the Throne has been regarded as the most permanent element of stability in the country. The position of the Throne, however, has been shaken by King Farouk's policy of interfering too openly in Party politics and, what is more serious, trying to compete with the Wafd in demagogic appeals to elements of disorder, which have been greatly strengthened by this two-fold appeal to them. These elements are also being played upon by Communist agents with the result that many of them are now indulging in violent attacks on King Farouk himself. The deplorable social conditions in Egypt, which the King's Government, in spite of many platonic expressions of desire for social reform by the Monarch, have done nothing substantial to alleviate, are naturally being exploited by Communist agents and confused in the popular mind with nationalist objectives. The Throne is thus in the midst of social and nationalist conflict, of which no one can see the end, but in which it is clearly exposed to grave danger. His Majesty should therefore be urged on every possible occasion to make his peace with the Opposition, be on terms with all political Parties alike, and encourage popular opinion to have its way instead of the present system of faked elections and Palace-imposed Governments. Otherwise there will be an explosion, almost certainly involving the Throne itself, and equally certainly involving considerations of British policy and interest that may well impel British intervention, possible on a large scale.

17. So much for my swan song. Should these disjointed thoughts, jotted down in the intervals of packing up, be held to have any value either at home or to my successor in office here they will have served their purpose.

---

29   FO 141/1081, no 7   10 Mar 1946
[Anglo–Egyptian treaty revision]: despatch no 350 from R J Bowker to Mr Bevin on the military requirements in Egypt of the Commanders-in-Chief, Middle East

With reference to my despatch No. 312 of 1st March, I have the honour to transmit herewith copy of a letter[1] from the Secretary of the Commanders-in-Chief Committee to the Secretary of the Chiefs of Staffs Committee in London covering a memorandum by the Commanders-in-Chief, Middle East, setting out what, in their view, are the military requirements which will need to be safeguarded in any revised Anglo–Egyptian Treaty. As you will see, this memorandum takes as its point of departure the general principles laid down in your telegram No. 25 Saving of January 25th last.

---

[1] The letter and covering memo are not printed.

2. The Commanders-in-Chief prepared their memorandum without prior consultation with this Embassy, and in my opinion, they have placed their requirements too high. The only advantage that they appear to offer Egypt is the removal of troops (other than the two General Headquarters) from Cairo when accommodation is ready elsewhere. More than this has already been conceded under the present Treaty under which the General Headquarters would not remain in Cairo: this proposal, therefore, provides no sort of basis for agreement to-day; and indeed, I see no possibility of persuading any Egyptian Government, except under threat of force, to accept the continued presence in Egypt of British troops to the extent envisaged in the enclosed memorandum. If it became known—as it inevitably would—that we were insisting on such terms, we should have to expect an immediate aggravation of the present already tense internal situation and a recurrence of anti-British riots, possibly on a scale with which the Egyptian authorities would be unable—or unwilling—to cope. We could also expect that the Egyptian Government would refer the whole question of Treaty revision and the British occupation to the Security Council of the United Nations.

3. In paragraph (6) of my telegram No. 2552[2] of December 6th last, I emphasised the importance of bringing out the regional aspect of our defence requirements in Egypt and the point that defence in this country was a joint Anglo–Egyptian responsibility. The Commanders-in-Chief have taken this point into consideration, but I feel that it will need more than the use of the phrase "joint defence" to induce the Egyptians to accept their requirements. The Egyptians are suspicious of joint action with us, just as they are suspicious of the word "partnership." They will need to see present and real needs in any proposals if they are to be induced to accept them: the doubtful honour and glory of token participation in the British defence arrangements for Egypt, which is really all that it is proposed to offer them, will not be enough.

4. Apart from these general considerations, I feel bound to comment on the fact that the Commanders-in-Chief still look on Egypt as the only possible main centre for British forces in the Middle East. Thus, in paragraph (5) of their memorandum, they say that "the limitations of the port facilities and the internal communications in Cyrenaica and Palestine require that the forces in the Middle East are based on Egypt." In paragraph (13) they maintain that in addition to Headquarters, British Troops in Egypt, there must still be a General Headquarters, Middle East Forces, that "for it to exercise its functions effectively there is no satisfactory alternative to a location in Egypt" and that "a location in Cairo would facilitate liaison with the Governments and staffs of countries included in the Middle East confederacy." Naturally, it is more convenient to have General Headquarters, and the main body of British troops, in Egypt. But the Egyptians are bound to oppose any such plan to the bitter end, and I think it would be most advisable to examine urgently what measures will be necessary, (for example, development of port facilities) in order to provide suitable accommodation elsewhere.

---

[2] See 22.

30 FO 371/53288, no 1151   12 Mar 1946
[Anglo–Egyptian treaty negotiations]: FO note of a meeting in Mr Bevin's room on 11 Mar 1946

A meeting took place in the Secretary of State's room at 6 p.m. on March 11th at which Sir Orme Sargent, Sir Ronald Campbell, Mr. Howe, Mr. Dixon and Mr. Lambert were present.

The object of the meeting was to discuss the question raised in Cairo telegram No. 438 of March 8th, namely whether His Majesty's Government should negotiate with the Egyptian delegation appointed by the present Egyptian Government or whether they should insist upon the Wafd participating in the negotiations.

The Secretary of State thought that we must accept the delegation which had been appointed by the Egyptian Government. It was for the King of Egypt and his Government to say who were to negotiate on their behalf. Any agreement reached must not, however, be repudiated. If the question was raised in the House of Commons as to whether the Egyptian delegation now appointed were entitled to speak for Egypt, he proposed to reply that the delegation had been appointed and duly authorised to negotiate the revision of the Anglo–Egyptian Treaty and that His Majesty's Government were entitled to suppose that they were authorised to speak for Egypt.

The Secretary of State then described how he envisaged the general defence scheme for the Middle East area. He was in favour of our defending this area so far as possible from British or British-controlled territories and not from foreign territories the governments of which were reluctant to have British forces quartered on their soil. Thus, a large and perhaps the main British base would be at Mombasa and other bases would be in Iraq and Transjordan if, as was probable, the Governments of those territories agreed. There might also be a base at Cyprus, but the *Secretary of State* was averse to transferring Cyprus to Greece and then renting a base from her there, lest this should form a precedent for the Dodecanese being returned to Greece and the Russians renting a base in those islands. Certain bases, including air bases, would require to be rented and maintained in a state of full preparation in Egypt in the Suez Canal zone, but they would not be occupied in peace-time unless the Egyptian Government agreed. The general conception of "partnership" in these matters with Egypt and other Middle East countries would in fact be one operating *inwards* from surrounding British territories and not *outwards* from the foreign territories themselves.

The Secretary of State restated his view that it was most desirable that British troops should be removed as soon as possible from Cairo and Alexandria, in order to prepare a better atmosphere for the Anglo–Egyptian Treaty revision talks. He understood that the Chiefs of Staff were now arranging to remove two divisions from Egypt to Tripolitania, and he hoped to receive their firm answer on this subject at a meeting of the Defence Committee on March 15th.

31   FO 141/1081, no 20   25 Mar 1946
'Record of personal conversation with Ismail Sidky Pasha':
memorandum by Sir R Campbell on Egyptian desires to be treated as
equals   [Extract]

I met Sidky Pasha last night at Sir A. Keown-Boyd's[1] house, as arranged.

Sidky began by saying that he was not going to talk politics or military matters but had wanted as soon as possible to make contact on a personal basis in order to give me a psychological picture of the Egyptian scene in relation to the Treaty question. Having said that he was a warm friend of Great Britain and that he keenly desired, and was convinced of the necessity of, close friendship between his country and mine, he plunged into his theme.

There had, he said, been a very marked evolution in Egypt in the last 12 years. Education had spread much more widely and intellectually progress had been considerable. A far larger number read and thought and studied foreign affairs—this had naturally stimulated national consciousness and a feeling of intellectual equality. The tempo of this evolution had been increased by the war and the general spirit it had created and by the accompanying political developments such as the allied statements of their objectives, the Atlantic Charter, San Francisco. The war was over and people asked themselves why the spirit of the allied statements should not be applied to and in Egypt. They could see no reason now for the continuance of restrictions on full Egyptian independence and equality.

For several decades now Egyptians had received education on British lines. They talked English, their mental processes were English, thousands went to the United Kingdom for their education, where many proved themselves at least the intellectual equals of their British fellows.

It was fully realised that a small power needed a more powerful friend. For Egyptians this friend could only be Great Britain not only because of obvious practical reasons but also because of sentiment engendered by English education etc. But the results of Egyptian experience and often prowess in this field of English education also created a keen aspiration to treatment as equals. Egyptians were a sentimental people and if we really gave them equal treatment, nationally and individually, they would follow their inclinations and respond in full measure and give us their unstinted and warm friendship. Egyptians knew they needed an alliance with Great Britain; they wanted an alliance and friendship with us, but above all real friendship. Their friendship, once gained, would secure for us all that an alliance without friendship would secure, and more. They wanted both alliance and friendship, but friendship, without which the alliance would have little value, could only be gained if they were treated on a footing of real equality.

The presence of British troops in Egypt was not compatible with a sense of being treated as equals. In Egyptian eyes it both implied a wish on our part for domination (how did this square with our general professions?) and meant domination. Whatever might be our intentions it put us in a position to interfere in Egyptian affairs and in

---

[1] Sir A Keown-Boyd, oriental secretary to the high commissioner for Egypt, 1922; director general of foreign affairs of the Egyptian government, 1922; director general of the European Department of the Egyptian Ministry of the Interior, 1922–1937.

practice this meant that we would not always be able to resist the temptation to interfere. Even if our Government did not, a soldier could not forget he had a sword and this, in general intercourse, must tend against treatment of Egyptians as equals. This and the general relative position of the two countries gave Egyptians a feeling of being under foreign domination and of humiliation. Sidky instanced the incident of February 4th.[2] He had been present and as an Egyptian patriot, even a great patriot, he could not but feel indignation.

Egyptians then wanted an alliance, but on a footing of real equality. The basis should be that of two friends, a big and a small one, but equals in status. There could not be friendship unless it was of a kind in which the smaller friend could say to the larger not "I want to do such and such: may I?" but "I am going to do such and such". Sidky was certain that as friends, we could together contribute all that was necessary to the defence of our common interests, without it being necessary for British troops to be in Egyptian territory. He was no military expert and anyhow did not that evening mean to discuss military matters, but his common sense forbad him to believe in the need for British forces in Egypt. What were ten thousand troops one way or another? Egyptians had seen millions in their country during the war. (I thought it well to interpose here that the B.T.E. had furnished a nucleus round which the reinforcements could rally). In his view there was at the present time no real or imminent external danger. At most it was infinitesimal. But should danger arise Egyptian friendship would produce all we should need. The Egyptian Army had greatly improved and could be really good. There was a body of 400 officers of really superior quality. Egypt could, and intended to, have an army of 1½ million. It was with such sentiments and such convictions that he had assumed office when summoned by his sovereign.

Sidky urged therefore that we should convert the present feeling abroad in Egypt into real friendship, and avoid the risk of causing it to deteriorate into dislike and even hostility.

During the course of his remarks Sidky referred to the comparison Egyptians made between our actions in withdrawing troops from Syria and the Lebanon and Indonesia, and our failure to withdraw them from here. I said that the cases were not on the same footing. The presence of British troops in Egypt was provided for by a freely negotiated Treaty in which Egypt had given her agreement to their presence. Sidky agreed but said that the comparison was nevertheless made and the contrast felt. This was not unnatural with the passage of years and the events that had taken place. He said, in this connection, that Egypt had not much relished the statement in the note from His Majesty's Government of January 26th[3] that one of the lessons of the recent hostilities was the essential soundness of the fundamental principles on which the Treaty of 1936 was based. The surprise I expressed elicited from Sidky the explanation that the Treaty had always been regarded as a first step towards further changes in Egypt's favour: that it had been accepted without enthusiasm but as this first step and because of the prevailing international situation: that the agreement to the presence of British troops was not regarded as a recognition of the material difference between the capacity of each party to contribute to mutual defence, but as a humiliating symbol of continuing British domination to which Egypt must for the moment submit. He endorsed the principle of alliance and friendship, but with

---

[2] cf 27, note.   [3] See 26, annex B.

emphasis on friendship greater than on alliance. But he deprecated the provision (as he put it) to submit Egyptian foreign policy to Britain (Article 5). (I said this was surely common form in Treaties of this kind and bound both parties: while Sidky admitted this, he said the presence of British troops gave the provision an unequal character). He also remarked that Article 7 was humiliating in its restrictions on the aid which Egypt might bring to Great Britain. (I asked whether this was not, then, regarded as moderation in British demands on Egypt rather than a humilitating restriction. Sidky said it was not and that its purpose had been clearly and woundingly shown in the war). I gathered that it was both these points that were behind the statement, in the Egyptian note requesting revision of the Treaty, that the Treaty implied mistrust of Egypt. Sidky at one moment said that Egypt wanted an association, "a partnership" with Great Britain, i.e. equal treatment. I said that I understood the use of this word, which had the meaning he had given it, had given offence. Sidky said it had been misunderstood: that a big boy had to expect suspicion from a small one: the small one had suspected that the word hid something. I told Sidky that the Secretary of State certainly intended the word to express a wish to treat on a basis of equality. Sidky said he believed this and welcomed it and that Amr Pasha had reported a conversation in which Mr. Bevin had said this. Sidky went on to say that treatment and discussion on a basis of equality however had no value unless it had the consequence of creating a state of equality. He urged that this should be the object of our negotiations.

Sidky emphasised his contention that there should be no "zones of influence". They were anachronistic as an idea and there was, with the establishment of U.N.O., no need for them. I said he could be sure that the Secretary of State did not think in terms of anachronisms, and that he did not approach the question of Treaty revision with a prejudiced mind. (Further than this, in our present state of uncertainty, I did not dare go).

Sidky at one moment made remarks tending to the argument that U.N.O. provided all that was necessary in the way of security for our mutual interests. I suggested that there was a period to provide for before U.N.O. defence arrangements got going. He did not entirely dismiss this, though he saw no immediate danger, and seemed finally to suggest that he did want an Anglo–Egyptian arrangement for defence. I said that surely what was required was that we should prepare an Anglo–Egyptian brick which could fit into a broader edifice. He expressed agreement.

Sidky seemed to accept the proposition that the two countries had an obligation so to arrange their affairs that by their friendship and provisions for mutual defence they contributed to the peace and security of the world. . . .

32   CAB 80/100, COS(46)95, annex   26 Mar 1946
'Military requirements in the revision of the Anglo–Egyptian treaty':
memorandum by the Commanders-in-Chief Committee, Middle East,
for the COS Committee

[The difficulties in deciding how to deal with the Egyptians over the treaty negotiations were compounded by the uncertainty as to what facilities Britain needed in Egypt in peacetime. Central to this question was the kind of responsibilities Britain intended to maintain in the Middle East and the overall approach to be adopted for the defence of the region. Attlee's desire to transfer some responsibilities to other UNO members, opposed by Eden (see 2), remained undiminished and the issue re-emerged in September 1945, when, in response to a memorandum by Bevin and Hall (FO 371/50792, no 6540, 25 Aug 1945) on the future of the Italian colonies, Attlee again challenged the conventional assumption that Britain should retain exclusive responsibilities for the defence of the region. (CAB 129/1, CP(45)144, 1 Sept 1945, see BDEEP series A, vol 2, R Hyam, ed, *The Labour government and the end of empire 1945–1951*, part 3, 273). This opened a detailed debate on the necessity of defending the Middle East for the future defence of the Commonwealth and on the strategy to do so successfully. However the COS had no global or Middle Eastern emergency plan[1] and claimed that the consideration of global strategy should await assessments of the impact of nuclear weapons. Nevertheless the military response to Attlee's memorandum was given careful consideration in the service ministries and the conclusions summarised in a paper produced for the COS on 13 Feb (CAB 131/2, COS(46)43). In response on 2 Mar Attlee produced a paper for the Defence Committee (CAB 131/2, DO(46)27 to which the COS summary was attached, see Hyam *op cit*, 276) challenging the desirability and the practicality of maintaining Britain's military position in the Middle East to which Bevin responded (CAB 131/2, DO(46)40, see Hyam *op cit*, 277). Discussion by the Defence Committee on the importance of defending the Middle East was postponed until the COS had produced an overall assessment of the strategic position of the British Commonwealth (CAB 131/2, DO(46)47, 2 Apr 1946, see 33 and 35 for the discussions). The Middle East C's-in-Cs' paper on the military requirements in Egypt needed to implement a Middle Eastern defence strategy not yet decided upon did not reach the COS until 23 Mar and did not become a paper for consideration until 27 Mar. By then, the C's-in-C having seen the embassy's criticism (see 29), had changed their views on the need for a permanent peacetime presence in the Suez base. In order to facilitate the beginning of treaty negotiations the C's-in-C were prepared to accept a phased withdrawal of British forces, but evacuation was deemed to be dependent on a satisfactory settlement of the regional security problem (FO 371/53289, no 1309, Cairo tel 548, 25 Mar 1946). The head of the Egyptian Department opposed such a concession on the principle of a phased withdrawal until the Defence Committee and the COS had pronounced on DO(46)40 and the idea of a main base in E Africa (FO 371/53289, no 1309, minute by P S Scrivener, 26 Mar 1946). As a further complication, at the Defence Committee on 27 Mar, Bevin, who had been considering the possibility of leasing the base, rejected Sir R Campbell's view that the Egyptians would want Britain to evacuate Egypt completely. The foreign secretary argued that the question of evacuation turned on the ultimate location of Britain's Middle Eastern forces and that discussions with the Egyptians should be delayed until the COS reported on his and the PM's memos (DO (46) 40 and 27) on Mediterranean strategy (CAB 131/1, DO 9(46)3, 27 Mar 1946). Therefore the covering letter sent by the secretary of the C's-in-C Committee to which this document forms the annex referred to military requirements which the Middle East commanders no longer saw as necessary and had been overtaken by events.]

Method of negotiation

1. His Majesty's Ambassador has submitted for Foreign Office approval a paper based on the Section headed "DEFENCE" in telegram No. 25 SAVING of 25th January, 1946. If this paper with which we agree receives the approval of the Foreign Office, it is intended that it should form the basis of the British case in the preliminary conversations with the Egyptian Government.

It contains the following relevant extracts:—

(a) "The military problem of Egypt should be raised from the level of a purely bi-lateral under-standing to the level of a co-operative arrangement between the Middle East States and His Majesty's Government for the safe-guarding on the one hand of the integrity and independence of those States and on the other of the

---

[1] Emergency plans are plans to deal with an enemy (ie Soviet) attack with the forces available at the time and cover periods of approximately 12 months into the future.

security of the British Commonwealth which, as conclusively demonstrated in the course of two world wars, can be vitally threatened by an attack on the Middle Eastern Area."

(b) "All the experience of the last war, moreover, goes to prove that smaller countries, however tenaciously they may defend themselves, must inevitably be over-run in a modern war unless they can have full and immediate support from a Power possessing the military and economic potential, essential for the maintenance of large naval, military and air forces."

(c) "The United Kingdom and their Allies of the United Nations have pledged themselves to construct and to operate an international system for safeguarding world security, but until this edifice is completed regional co-operation will be required, and the military advice at the disposal of His Majesty's Government has convinced them that the defence of the Middle East can and should be organised on a collective basis."

(d) "His Majesty's Government consider it necessary to have certain facilities in the Middle East countries in time of peace. They wish to be able to station in the area, and particularly in Egypt as one of the countries indicated by geography no less than by industrial development as a regional base, the minimum forces necessary to provide the nucleus of a war-time establishment and a general reserve for the defence of the area as a whole and to ensure continuous collaboration in training and the use of technical devices and armaments. Moreover in the present state of development of military aviation the burden on a small state or states of maintaining the necessary defensive forces to ensure against long-range bombing attack (with all its consequences) would be intolerable, however great the national spirit of sacrifice, and equally vulnerable are those small states without adequate Naval power to defend themselves from attack by sea."

(e) "His Majesty's Government therefore trust that the Egyptian Government will not hesitate to reaffirm the principles set out in Articles 4–7 of the existing Treaty, to provide the Imperial forces with the necessary administrative base and communications facilities, and to allow for a term of years the presence on Egyptian soil of those British forces considered necessary as part of the contribution which Egypt is ready to make to the security of the Middle East. His Majesty's Government will also ask the Egyptian Government for permission to construct certain installations and to stage through Egypt such Imperial forces as may be required."

Future developments

2. In carrying out these negotiations, an effort should be made to persuade the Egyptians to look to the future and realise that the ever changing methods of modern warfare make it necessary to keep defence requirements flexible and subject to alteration, as necessary, by agreement, between the two Governments. His Majesty's Government's representatives should endeavour to discourage a state of mind, which regards defence arrangements made now as immutable.

Political assumptions

Middle East confederacy

3. Since the principle in Article 8 of the existing Treaty is incompatible with an approach to the Egyptians on the basis of an overall defence scheme for the Middle

East it is assumed that this principle will be completely superseded, unless we fail to obtain acceptance of the idea of collective defence of the wider area of the Middle East, in that case we shall have to fall back on our original position as defined in Article 8 of the 1936 Treaty.

Libya

4.   Account must be taken of Russian aspirations in Tripolitania.[2] If she were in a position to build up forces in that territory they would constitute a threat to Egypt. Against such a threat we should require forces West of the River Nile. It is assumed that we should be entitled to station them in Cyrenaica insofar as it is practicable to do so.

Palestine

5.   In assessing our military requirements in Egypt we have assumed that the political status in Palestine will remain such that we continue to enjoy military facilities at least comparable to those we have at present.

Essentials of British strategy in relation to Egypt

6.   Whilst the retention of our special position in the Middle East remains an essential feature of Imperial strategy, we must disclaim any intention of interfering with Egypt's Sovereign right to be responsible for her own internal security. Our position in Egypt must in future be justified by our ability to contribute to the defence of the Middle East as a whole. The limitations of the port facilities and the internal communications in Cyrenaica and Palestine require that the forces in the Middle East are based on Egypt.

7.   The British strategic interests in Egypt which must thus be covered are broadly as follows:—

(a) *In war.* There is no alternative to Egypt as the vital part of the Middle East base in any future major operations. We shall therefore require in war full facilities such as we are entitled to under Article 7 of the present Treaty.

(b) *In impending threat of war.* In the war of 1939/45 we were fortunate in that Italy did not declare war until June 1940. In future we are likely to get less time. Modern weapons are likely to make necessary more extensive and widely dispersed preparation when we are under "threat of war" than heretofore. It may therefore be necessary to increase our army and air forces in Egypt and introduce our Naval Forces before a state of emergency exists and it is essential that all the necessary facilities should be available when an emergency impends.

---

[2] The Russian claim for designation as a trustee power was made at the San Francisco conference. At the Potsdam conference in July 1945, a Soviet paper called for the foreign ministers to prepare proposals for the future of the Italian colonies having in view the possibility of establishing a trusteeship system exercised by individual states or by the USSR, the US and Britain jointly. On 23 July 1945 at Potsdam, Molotov, the Soviet foreign minister called for some form of joint trusteeship for the Italian colonies. As this idea was not acceptable it was agreed that the future of the Italian colonies should be considered at the first Council of Foreign Ministers (*FRUS, The Conference of Berlin (Potsdam) 1945*, record of sixth meeting of foreign ministers, pp 281–283, 288). When it met in Sept 1945, it was agreed that the issue should be dealt with by the foreign ministers' deputies (*FRUS*, vol II, *General: Political and Economic Matters*, record of fifth plenary meeting, 15 Sept 1945, pp 192–193).

(c) *In peace*

(i) *Communications*. The use and security of our communications through Egypt, together with all facilities on which their efficient working depends. These communications include the Suez Canal, and such other land, sea and air facilities as are required for our Imperial communications to India, South and East Africa, Australasia and the Far East.

(ii) *Stationing and movement of armed forces*. The right to station adequate army and air forces with all necessary material, in strategically satisfactory areas. The administrative effort and financial expense of maintaining more than a very small garrison in Cyrenaica would be prohibitive. The need to station forces in Egypt therefore remains. These forces must, incidentally, be in sufficient strength and contain the necessary elements to protect essential British interests.

We shall also require the right to move forces and material in and through Egypt.

(iii) *Base facilities*. The development and maintenance of up-to-date base installations, including the necessary defence and movement facilities, for our use in war, and adequate arrangements sufficient to ensure that Naval facilities are kept in a state of high efficiency so that they are ready immediately to sustain a fleet at short notice in an emergency.

Requirements in Egypt in peace

8.   The broad requirements specified above need some elaboration in respect of the facilities which we require in peace. The following paragraphs amplify the general requirements for all three Services and the particular requirements for each individual Service.

General requirements

Staging of imperial forces through Egypt

9.   In order to stage through Egypt such Imperial Forces and material as His Majesty's Government shall require we must have the right to construct (in areas to be agreed) accommodation and facilities for forces in transit. Those facilities will include those required for personnel, aircraft, and other material moving under the "trooping by air" and "air mobility" programmes.

Stationing of British forces in Egypt

10.   No firm estimate is yet available of the strategic reserves to be stationed in the Middle East and the forces which we can, or want to, station in Egypt are likely to vary from time to time. Thus it is impossible to forecast our requirements with any degree of certainty. In a treaty which is likely to endure for a long time it is highly undesirable to accept any numerical limitation.

11.   It is our intention, subject to paragraphs 14, 30 and 41 below, that such forces should be stationed in areas to be agreed outside the Nile Valley and away from the main centres of population.

12.   The movement of British forces to their new locations must however be timed with due regard to the construction of adequate accommodation, amenities, administrative services, and means of communication, and to the disposal of surplus material.

Headquarters

13. In addition to the local Headquarters of the British Forces in Egypt, a General Headquarters, Middle East, will be essential. This includes Army and Air components together with a Naval element for liaison purposes. For it to exercise its functions effectively there is no satisfactory alternative to a location in Egypt. Any move within Egypt should only be to a permanent location the preparation of which would involve considerable expense and time. A location in Cairo would facilitate liaison with the Governments and Staffs of countries included in the Middle East Confederacy and it might even be possible to create the beginnings of a joint Headquarters representing all members of the Confederacy.

Right of movement

14. We shall require the means of communication to and from the localities where Imperial forces are situated and landing and storage facilities at Port Said and Suez, and also the necessary arrangements to cover the movement of military cargo on commercial account through the port of Alexandria. The right to move hazardous cargoes must be included.

It will also be necessary to construct and/or maintain and develop such roads and railways as are agreed to be necessary for the maintenance and movement of Anglo–Egyptian forces.

Fuel

15. We shall require the Egyptian Government to agree that adequate facilities shall be earmarked in peace for the bulk storage and distribution of fuels, oils, petrols and lubricants for use by our forces in time of war.

Technical advice

16. In order to assist the Egyptian Government in peace in the maintenance and development of the facilities which will be required by both the British and Egyptian Forces in war, or the threat of war, it will be necessary for His Majesty's Government to supply technical advisers to the Egyptian Government. The duties of these advisers, both military and civil, in co-operation with the Egyptians, will be to review, and as necessary revise, the existing arrangements and to supervise the maintenance and development of all facilities in Egypt which will be necessary for both the British and Egyptian Forces in war.

Allied forces

17. In war, or threat of war, British, Dominion and Colonial Forces would require facilities in Egypt as would those of other Allied countries. It may however be sound tactics not to mention this requirement to the Egyptians in the Treaty but to rely on them to allow it when the occasion arises.

Costs

18. The costs arising out of the foregoing proposals will be a matter for subsequent discussion and should be appropriately apportioned amongst the members of the Confederacy with due regard to the overall burden borne by the several members.

Military requirements in peace

Naval requirements

Size of fleet

19.   For planning purposes it may be assumed that the size of the Fleet, which will be based in Egypt in war, or threat of war, will approximate to that of 1942.

Naval facilities in Egypt

20.   In peace it will be necessary to ensure that Alexandria is effectively developed and maintained for use as a Naval operational base in war, or the threat of war, and that all the other facilities in Egypt which will be required by the Egyptian and British Navies, including Naval aircraft, on the outbreak of war, or the threat of war, are also immediately available to sustain a Fleet at short notice in an emergency.

21.   The Naval requirements at Alexandria, Port Said and Suez, the airfields required for naval aircraft and naval requirements in the Suez Canal and its vicinity must, therefore, be kept in peace in a modern and up-to-date condition.

22.   The facilities which will be required to achieve this object are specified below:—

(a) *Those installations which will be required in peace to hold naval reserve stocks*

   (i) Reserve stocks of ammunition, torpedoes, mines, air stores and aircraft must be held permanently in the vicinity of the Canal.

   (ii) For two or three years the existing ammunition depots elsewhere in Egypt must also be retained until disposal of their stocks of ammunition has taken place.

(b) *Those defences and facilities which must be maintained and developed in peace*

   (i) *Local defence arrangements*: These will include fixed harbour defences, boom and asdic defences, Port War Signals Station, examination service, harbour defence craft, local minesweeping and mine watching services and Radar installations.

   (ii) *Communications*: These will include all the necessary W/T facilities, including the Delta W/T Station.

   (iii) *Repair facilities*: Such facilities, including a berth for a floating dock, as may be necessary to effect a rapid expansion to a scale adequate to maintain a fleet in war.

   (iv) *Harbour works*: Harbour Works and moorings sufficient for immediate use of a fleet in war, or threat of war.

   (v) *Aircraft repairs*: Aircraft repair facilities as a nucleus ready for expansion in time of war. This will entail keeping H.M.S. "PHOEHIX" on a care and maintenance basis in peace.

(c) *Facilities which require to be earmarked for use in time of war, or threat of war.*

   (i) *Accommodation*: This will include:—

      A. An Eastern Mediterranean Operational Headquarters.

      B. Local Naval Headquarters at Alexandria, Port Said and Suez.

      C. Headquarters for organisation of sea transport.

      D. Accommodation for Royal Naval and Allied personnel.

(ii) *Training establishments*: These will include:—
Sites for training in Gunnery, including an anti-aircraft range, Radar, combined training, torpedoes, mining and mine sweeping.
(iii) *Storage*: This will include installations for stocks of fuel, naval and victualling stores and for ready use armament and air stores in the vicinity of Alexandria.
(iv) *Base installations*: These will include a coastal forces base, a minesweeping base, Naval Air Stations, Boom Defence Depots and Administrative Depots such as Supply Offices, Armament, Victualling and Naval Stores Offices, etc.
(d) *Facilities which may be required in the future*
It cannot be foreseen with any certainty to what extent the methods of warfare will change and it will be necessary to keep defence requirements flexible and subject to alteration. As an example, it is probable that passive defence measures to accord with the latest developments of warfare will be an early requirement.

Co-operation with the Egyptian navy

23.   In war the Egyptian and British Navies will be required to work together in defence of the coasts of Egypt and in the maintenance of sea communications. It will, therefore, be desirable that both Navies collaborate in peace in order to prepare for their joint functions in war.

24.   It would be to the mutual advantage of both Nations if the Naval technical advisers included in their duties advice to the Egyptian Government on the administration, maintenance and operation of the Royal Egyptian Navy and if the coastal and anti-aircraft defences in the vicinity of the Egyptian ports and the Egyptian Naval forces were exercised in co-operation with the British Naval forces during the periodical visits of the latter to Egyptian waters.

Naval forces

25. There will be no necessity for British warships or Naval personnel (with the exception of the technical advisers and Naval representatives at General Headquarters) to be stationed permanently in Egypt in peace after the disposal of Naval stores and material has been completed, provided that adequate arrangements can be made for the guarding of the Naval reserve stocks.

26.   Finally, in peace it will be necessary for the Royal Navy to be permitted free and unrestricted entry into Egyptian ports and for Naval aircraft to have the right to visit airfields in Egypt on prior notification alone.

Army requirements

Strength of army in Egypt (see also para. 10)

27.   If in the last resort it becomes unavoidable to mention a figure, the Chiefs of Staff consider that it should be *NOT LESS THAN* "5,000 men in Combatant Units". Since all personnel not protected by the Geneva Convention might be held to be "combatant" any such clause will require careful drafting. Headquarters, technical advisers, Administrative units and personnel in transit should be excluded from any stated total.

Training areas

28.   Suitable training areas and access to them will be required.

Administrative base

29.   We shall require the right to construct, maintain and develop jointly with the Egyptian Government such base installations, industrial and agricultural resources throughout Egypt as we may consider necessary for the efficient maintenance of our joint forces in the Middle East in peace and to hold our reserve stocks for war, including such new installations as the future needs of modern war may dictate.

30.   The scale and preparedness of the base must permit of a rapid expansion to full war scale. This will require the earmarking and maintenance of certain installations in time of peace which can be taken over for military purposes at short notice when the threat of an emergency impends. These facilities must by their nature be located in the industrial and populated areas of Egypt to make use of the accommodation, labour and public utility services where these are available and may in peace time be operated or maintained, as mutually agreed upon. These may be under the direction of the Egyptian Government, or operated by civilian firms, or by Egyptian labour with a British cadre. Subject to the numbers not being unduly swollen these British cadres might be included in the total of advisers.

31.   In our negotiations we should point out the positive assets which Egypt will gain by these proposals, such as an increased industrial potential, modernised factories, increased port and rail facilities and trained labour which the Government can make full use of during peace. These developments will be leading Egypt along the path towards a modern industrialised nation.

Air requirements

Size of air forces

32.   In order to ensure in war the air defence of Egypt and the Middle East as a whole we shall require to maintain air forces in Egypt in peace.

33.   It is not desirable to give definite figures but, should we be pressed so to do we should stipulate 300 operational first line aircraft exclusive of air transport squadrons, air training and ancillary units and Air C. P. squadrons.

34.   We shall require to base our squadrons in designated areas. Air Headquarters and administrative personnel in the Nile Valley should be reduced to a minimum compatible with the requirements for a joint air defence.

35.   We shall require to provide these air forces with the necessary administrative facilities and amenities on the lines indicated in paragraphs 29 and 30.

Air defence of Egypt

36.   It will be necessary for us to have the right, in agreement with the Egyptian Government, to construct joint Anglo–Egyptian air defence installations. Such installations (e.g. airfields, radar, signals network, etc.) to be integrated with such air defence system as the Egyptian Government may set up.

Training

37.   It will be necessary for our air forces to have the use of adequate bombing, gunnery and R. R. [radar reconnaissence] ranges and low flying areas and areas in which to co-operate with both British and Egyptian armies.

38.   British air forces to take a full part in all exercises of the Egyptian air defence system in conjunction with the Egyptian air forces.

Airfields and anchorages

39.   We require to have exclusive rights to the airfields and flying boat and seaplane anchorages constructed as defined in Annex to Article 8 of the 1936 Treaty including the right to develop them as may be necessary in the light of:-

(a) Increasing size and speed of modern aircraft.
(b) Adequate dispersal of aircraft and administrative installations.
(c) Increasing size and complication of air force ground organisation.

We require to construct and develop, in conjunction with the Egyptians, such additional airfields and signals network as we may consider necessary to enable us to expand our air force appreciably in war or on threat of war.

Depots and installations

40.   It will be necessary to build and maintain such stores, repair and maintenance facilities as may be required in the opinion of His Majesty's Government to maintain our joint forces in peace.

41.   It will be necessary to maintain on a cadre basis, jointly with the Egyptian Government, such depots and installations to enable us to expand our joint forces in war or on threat of war. These depots and installations must necessarily be near the centres of population to take full advantage of skilled civilian labour and the industrial potential available.

Emergency landings

42.   We shall require the Egyptian Government to afford all necessary aid and facilities to our aircraft forced landing in Egyptian territory and territorial waters and it must be ensured that this provision will allow as to deal with the salvage, repair and safety of aircraft on crash sites.

33   CAB 131/2, DO(46)47   2 Apr 1946
'Strategic position of the British Commonwealth': memorandum by the COS for the Cabinet Defence Committee

The Prime Minister has asked for an appreciation of the strategic position of the British Commonwealth in the light of our resources and of modern conditions of warfare.

We have accordingly reviewed our strategical requirements throughout the world, confining ourselves to the fundamental issues involved, so as to present a broad picture of what, from the defence point of view, our vital interests are.

We have related this examination primarily to a possible policy discussed by the Prime Minister. This policy we understand to be that we should concentrate our preparations in peace and our defence in war upon those areas and communications which are vital to us. The implication is that these are the United Kingdom, the American continent and the White Dominions. As a corollary to this we should cut our commitments in other parts of the world which are nearer to the areas of potential conflict.

2.   A conflict with Russia is the only situation in which it at present seems that the British Commonwealth might again become involved in a major war. In such a conflict it would be vital to obtain the early and wholehearted participation of the United States on our side. We have, therefore, in the following review, considered our strategical position, having particular regard to the possibility of a war in which the British Commonwealth and the United States, with such allies as they could obtain, were confronted by Russia and her satellites.

3.   If Russia be taken as the potential aggressor we must consider:—

(a) Main support areas on which our war effort must be based, and which it is therefore essential for us to hold, and the communications between them.

(b) Other areas of strategical importance in which we wish to retain our influence in order to protect our main support areas, and ensure that we do not start a future war in an unfavourable strategical position.

In considering the above, we must bear in mind the relative position of ourselves and Russia as regards man-power and war potential which will result from the maintenance or loss of our position in any particular area.

Main support areas and communications between them

4.   By the term "main support areas" we mean those areas which contain concentrations of man-power, industrial potential or sources of food or raw material, such that they are essential to our war effort.

5.   It is clear that the following will be our main support areas:—

(a) The United Kingdom.
(b) The American continent, including South America.
(c) Africa south of the Sahara, including East Africa.
(d) Australia and New Zealand.

The position of the United Kingdom is peculiar in that it contains 63 per cent. of the white man-power of the British Commonwealth and an even greater proportion of its industrial potential, but is at the same time in a highly vulnerable position geographically. Eventually it may be possible to build up the war potential of the Dominions to such an extent that the relative importance of the United Kingdom will be diminished, but short of mass emigration and the wholesale transfer of industry, which at present appears impracticable, the contribution of the United Kingdom in war-making potential will remain so high that, in spite of its vulnerability, it must continue to be classified as a main support area.

6.   The position of India also requires consideration. Uncertainty as to her political future makes it unwise, at the present time, to regard her as a main support area. The airfields in North-West India are of great importance, as the attached map shows,[1] and have great offensive possibilities. India is, however, with the exception of the United Kingdom, more exposed to air attack than the other main support areas.

On the other hand, her geographical position, together with the proportion of the man-power of the Commonwealth which India is in a position to provide is so high

---

[1] Maps not printed.

and her industrial and supply capacity, which is already increasing, is potentially so great that we consider that it will undoubtedly be of the greatest importance that India should remain in or closely allied to the Commonwealth and take her place as a main support area in the future.

We have not included India as a main support area in our present review, but we consider it essential that the country should be so developed and the political situation stabilised so as to allow her to take her place as a main support area at the earliest possible moment.

7.   Communications between the main support areas will mainly be by sea through the Atlantic, Pacific and Indian Oceans. These are of vital importance. In particular, if the war potential of the United Kingdom is to remain available it is essential that her Atlantic sea communications are kept open.

The use of the sea and air communications through the Mediterranean may be of very great importance owing to the saving both of shipping and of time thereby achieved. Although, from the point of view of our broad strategy, we cannot classify this route as vital in the same way as are our Atlantic communications, the extent to which our freedom of action is and must remain dependent upon limitations of shipping makes it of very great value.

We must also point out that the security of the alternative shipping route via the Cape, which serves either the Mediterranean or the Far East theatre, depends almost entirely on South African co-operation.

Effect of withdrawal to main support areas

8.   It may be argued that we should concentrate our preparations in peace upon the preservation of our main support areas only and of the communications between them, and that outside these areas we should cut our commitments to the minimum. Such a policy might claim the double advantage, not only of reducing our commitments, but also of placing between ourselves and the potential aggressor very considerable areas, thereby lessening the chance of conflict.

9.   We suggest, however, that it would be a fallacy to suppose that, where territories of strategic importance are concerned, hiatus areas would exist for long between zones of Russian interest and those of our interest. If we cut our commitments and thereby lose our predominant position in such areas, these areas with the war-making potential they contain will, sooner or later, be dominated by Russia. If we move out in peacetime, Russia will move in, pursuing her policy of extending her influence by all means short of major war to further strategic areas.

10.   A policy of concentrating upon the defence of our main support areas would result in adding to the Russian-controlled area and therefore to the war-making potential at her disposal, the following:—

(a) All Europe less the United Kingdom.
(b) North-West Africa.
(c) The Middle East and North-East Africa.

11.   These additions to Russian-controlled territories would have a far-reaching effect on the security of our sea communications. The communications between the main support areas of the American continent and Southern Africa and Australia could still be maintained, though those in the Atlantic would be threatened from

bases in North-West Africa. Communications to the United Kingdom, however, would be gravely threatened through the possession by the enemy of the entire Atlantic coast line from the North Cape to French Morocco. Our Mediterranean communications would, of course, be cut.

Because of the great distances involved, our air communications would be severely restricted in war and we would lose the ability to reinforce by air with the shorter range types.

Under the circumstances, it is doubtful whether the industrial potential of the United Kingdom could be sustained. The threat to its sea communications, coupled with the direct threat by air attack and long-range bombardment from the mainland of Europe, would introduce a grave risk that the United Kingdom would be reduced to a Malta-type existence, contributing little to the main war potential.

12.   Should the U.S.S.R. dominate all the areas given in paragraph 10, she would gain immense additional resources in man-power. As well, she would approximately double her steel-making capacity and acquire substantial additional oil production.

13.   It is therefore clear that a policy of withdrawal into our main support areas would produce the following results:—

(a) It would render the position of the United Kingdom, if not untenable, at least one of the utmost gravity in which the industrial potential of this country would, to all intents and purposes, be lost. Both India and Southern Africa would be threatened.

(b) It would add considerably, perhaps even decisively, to the man-power and war potential at the disposal of Russia.

In addition, it would greatly reduce the possibility of carrying out offensive operations against areas of importance to the enemy, would add greatly to the depth of his defences and would correspondingly reduce the depth of our own, thereby depriving us of the time necessary to organise our defence.

14.   If a war with Russia should occur, we are certainly likely to have to give ground in some of these areas, but we should on no account weaken ourselves in peacetime by surrendering our influence in areas of major strategic importance in advance of a war.

Areas of strategic importance other than the main support areas

15.   From the preceding section it is clear that, if we concentrate our preparations in peace upon our main support areas only, we should be at a very grave disadvantage from the start of a conflict. We must, therefore, consider the extent to which we should maintain our influence in additional areas which will enable us to:—

(a) Ensure the security of our main support areas.

(b) Ensure that at the start of a conflict we have sufficient depth in front of our vital areas to allow the necessary time both for us to mobilise our own forces and for the resources of the United States to be brought into play.

(c) Deny to the probable enemy the opportunity of developing in peace important additional resources and war potential.

(d) Attack areas of importance to the enemy at the outbreak of a war.

16.   In considering our strategic requirements forward of our main support areas, the main factor to be taken into account is the very great numerical superiority in land forces which the Russians would be likely to enjoy in the event of war.

In face of this we shall have to rely upon two main factors:—

(a) The maintenance of our lead in the scientific and technical fields.
(b) Our sea and air power.

These factors coupled with Russia's geographical position and economic self-sufficiency lead to the consideration that threat of attack by air or long-range weapons will be our one effective military deterrent to Russian aggression. It is therefore of the greatest importance that we should retain control of the necessary bases to render such attacks possible. Of the main support areas at present assured to us only the United Kingdom is so placed that it could constitute a base for this purpose, and the attached map shows that the United Kingdom alone is clearly insufficient.

17.   In the light of the above, we consider that there are the following areas, the value of which must be examined:—

(a) Western Europe, including Scandinavia.
(b) The Iberian Peninsula and North-West Africa.
(c) The Middle East and North-East Africa.
(d) India.
(e) South-East Asia.

We examine below the strategic importance of each of these areas.

Western Europe
18.   In view of the direct threat to the United Kingdom which would result from the loss of France and the Low Countries, and of the threat to our sea communications which would result from the loss of Scandinavia, it is clearly of the greatest importance to us that Western Europe should not fall under Russian domination. Moreover, the man-power and industrial resources of this area would represent a major increase in the war potential at the disposal of Russia. Although in the event of war it may not be possible entirely to prevent this in view of the very great preponderance of Russian land forces, we should at least be prepared to give the countries of Western Europe the support necessary to ensure that in peace they do not fall under Russian influence.

Iberian Peninsula and North-West Africa
19.   We have already indicated the importance of this area for the security of our Atlantic communications, both westwards and southwards, and therefore for the defence of the United Kingdom. If this area were under Russian control, we should, in addition, be denied access to the Western and Central Mediterranean immediately war broke out. In peace our position in Western Europe as a whole would be adversely affected.

Middle East
20.   It may be argued that we can afford to abandon this area, that we should thereby place between ourselves and a potential enemy large tracts of difficult

country, and thus compel him, in order to extend his influence further, to fight at the end of long and difficult lines of communication, and that we are unlikely in any case to be able to hold the area in war.

21.   The strategic importance of the Middle East lies in the following facts:—

(a) It forms the land-bridge between the continents of Europe, Asia and Africa and controls the Eastern Mediterranean and one of the main gateways into the Indian Ocean. It offers therefore the easiest route for a European-Asiatic Power into the African continent.

(b) Control of the area Egypt-Palestine would provide the Russians with a ready-made base area which could be built up by short sea route from Russia itself and which then would enable them to extend their influence both westward and southward into Africa. Such an extension would prejudice our position both in North-West Africa, the importance of which we have already shown, and in the Indian Ocean. It would be the first step in a direct threat to our main support area of Southern Africa.

(c) Control of the Middle East will give us the essential depth in front of our main support area in Southern Africa and the highly important area of India to give us the time necessary to organise the defence of these areas.

(d) Of those areas in which we can reasonably expect to maintain our influence in peace, the Middle East is the nearest to the important Russian industrial and oil-producing areas of Southern Russia and the Caucasus. It is also an area from which many other important industrial centres of Russia could be subjected to long-range attack. Our Middle East air bases are therefore a valuable deterrent to Russian aggression.

(e) The immense importance to us of the oil supplies of this area has been stressed in a recent paper by the Minister of Fuel and Power. We should clearly do our utmost to maintain our position in the area as long as we can in war and should certainly do so in peace.

India

22.   The value of the war potential of India has already been stressed. If India were to fall under Russian domination, it is unlikely that we could maintain our position in South-East Asia and Russian influence would then extend up to the outer defences of Australia. Airfields in North-West India are, apart from those in Iraq, the nearest of those at present under our control to certain important Russian industrial areas in the Urals and Western Siberia.

Provided that the Russians do not gain control of one of the main entrances to the Indian Ocean, India should be relatively easily defensible and should pay a good dividend in man-power and supply potential for the effort which we should have to expend. If, however, the Russians did gain such control, India would be all the more important as a striking base.

South-East Asia

23.   The strategic importance of this area is considerable in relation to the defence both of India and Australia. We should therefore do our utmost to preserve our position there.

Summary

24.   Our strategic requirements in addition to the security of our main support areas and the communications between them may therefore be summarised as the establishment and maintenance of our position in:—

Western Europe, including Scandinavia.
The Iberian Peninsula and North-West Africa.
The Middle East, particularly Egypt and Palestine.
India and South-East Asia.

25.   We do not suggest that in all the above areas a display of military force in peacetime is essential in order to prevent the spread of Russian influence. Our influence can be established and maintained in varying ways, by political action, and by our economic policy as well as by the presence of armed forces. In some cases political action may be all that is possible or required, in others the actual presence of armed forces may be necessary.

It does not, therefore, follow that our strategical requirements as set out above result in the maintenance of large-scale forces which it is quite clear the country cannot afford to maintain in peacetime.

26.   The requirements set out above are based solely upon strategical considerations. We note, however, that in his memorandum[2] to the Defence Committee the Foreign Secretary sets out the political and economic considerations of our position, particularly in the Mediterranean and the Middle East. He points out that—

(a) From a political point of view our presence in the Mediterranean is vital to our position as a great Power. On it depends our influence on Spain, France, Italy, Yugoslavia, Greece and Turkey, and with that goes all that we stand for as the last bastion of social democracy.

(b) We have strong interests in Egypt and in Iraq, where the oil is now one of our greatest economic assets.

(c) It is essential to maintain the Mediterranean as a trade route and as a trade area, to utilise both and to maintain the principles of Western civilisation in that area.

(d) We may require to develop within the United Nations Organisation a 'Western Zone' including Scandinavia, the Low Countries and France. Our ability to bring such an organisation into existence will depend upon our retaining our position in the Mediterranean.

These arguments, with which we are in full agreement, show that as regards Western Europe, the Mediterranean and the Middle East, our political, economic and strategic requirements coincide.

Conclusions

27.   We conclude that—

(*a*) The main support areas upon which our war effort must be based will be the United Kingdom, the American Continent, Southern Africa and Australia. The security of these areas is essential.

---

[2] See reference in note to 32.

Every effort should be made to develop and stabilise India as an additional main support area.

(b) The sea and air communications between our main support areas in the Atlantic, Pacific and Indian Oceans are of vital importance. Communications through the Mediterranean, though not vital, are of great importance particularly in relation to economy of shipping.

(c) By concentrating in peace upon our main support areas only, we should place ourselves in an unfavourable strategic situation at the start of any future conflict. We must, therefore, establish and maintain our influence in other areas of strategic importance since we must assume that, if we do not, our influence will be supplanted by that of Russia, whom we must at present consider as our most probable potential enemy.

(d) These additional areas are Western Europe including Scandinavia; the Iberian Peninsula and North-West Africa; the Middle East, particularly Egypt and Palestine; India and South-East Asia.

If these areas were to fall under Russian domination:—

(i) The security of the United Kingdom would be directly threatened.

(ii) Our vital sea communications, particularly those in the Atlantic would not be secure.

(iii) We should lack the essential depth in front of our vital areas to allow the necessary time both for us to mobilise our own forces and for the resources of the United States to be brought into play.

(iv) We should have relinquished to Russia important sources of man-power and war potential.

(v) We should be deprived of bases outside the United Kingdom from which the threat of air action would be a deterrent to Russian aggression and from which we could, at the outset of a war, conduct offensive operations, which might indeed be the only effective means of defence open to us.

28. Our main strategic requirements are based principally upon facts of geography and the distribution of man-power and natural resources which do not change. We consider therefore that the basic principles of our strategy set out above will not be radically altered by new developments in methods or weapons of warfare.

34   FO 371/53218, no 3476   4 Apr 1946
[Evacuation of Egypt]: minute by R G Howe to Mr Bevin on peacetime requirements in Egypt

The Chiefs of Staff have now reported (D.O. (46)48 of April 2nd) that "our strategic requirements make it necessary that we should maintain certain forces in Iraq, Palestine, Egypt and certain other areas of the Middle East" and that "if the defence of the Middle East on a regional basis is to become a reality" the main headquarters cannot be in East Africa but could most suitably be located in the Suez Canal Zone. The report also makes it clear that while a subsidiary base could be developed in East Africa, "it would not be possible to develop the area into a major base comparable to Egypt in the recent war" the essentials of which are "a major industrial potential, first-class communications, and a plentiful supply of both skilled and unskilled labour".

Translated into the terms of the present Anglo–Egyptian discussions, this means that the original decision of the Chiefs of Staff and the Cabinet—that we must secure base facilities in Egypt in peace *and* the right to station one brigade group there—is confirmed,[1] with the addition that we must also secure facilities for G.H.Q., Middle East, in the Canal Zone.

H.M. Embassy in Cairo have warned us that failure to concede the Egyptian demand for the total evacuation of Egypt by British forces may lead to serious tension and disorder. It has been the Department's view (see note in J 1306/G) that unless the Chiefs of Staff be assured *notwithstanding* the withdrawal of British forces from Egypt, His Majesty's Government should stand firm on the Cabinet's original proposals. Indeed they have doubts whether the Egyptians can be trusted to maintain, unaided and unguided, the necessary military installations in peace-time; and graver doubts whether they can maintain the state of public security which is essential in a main base area in peace-time. Finally, they have drawn attention to the political disadvantages of withdrawal (particularly immediately following outbreaks of violence) from an area historically under British influence; and to the possibility that withdrawal would stimulate demands in Iraq for a British withdrawal from the country. The Department recommend therefore that the conclusions of the Chiefs of Staff should be accepted, that H.M. Ambassador in Cairo should be informed accordingly and that the Commanders-in-Chief should be warned to prepare (unobtrusively) for possible widespread disorder if negotiations break down on the question of evacuation, though it is by no means certain that they will do so. Moreover it has yet to be seen what reception will be accorded to the proposal that we should offer a lease of a base in the Canal Zone.

---

[1] The peacetime requirements of roughly a brigade group were endorsed by the COS in 1945, see 23 and 24. The Cabinet merely referred to 'the minimum forces necessary for the nucleus of a wartime establishment', see 26, as the C's-in-C, Middle East were to provide an update of requirements to the British negotiators, see 32.

35   CAB 131/1, DO 10(46)2   5 Apr 1946
'Strategic position of the British Commonwealth': Cabinet Defence Committee minutes

The Committee had before them:—

   (i)   a memorandum by the Prime Minister and Minister of Defence (D.O. (46) 27);
   (ii) a memorandum by the Secretary of State for Foreign Affairs (D.O. (46) 40);
   (iii) a report by the Chiefs of Staff (D.O. (46) 47).[1]

Lord Alanbrooke said that the Chiefs of Staff had based their report on the contingency of a war with Russia, the U.S.A. being our ally. From this premise they had reviewed the vital support areas and communications which we ought to maintain for the conduct of such a war. Between the support areas there existed

---

[1] See 33.

zones in Western Europe, the Iberian Peninsula, North West Africa and the Middle East, from which if we withdrew our influence, it must be assumed that it would be supplanted by that of Russia. It was unsound to concentrate in peace upon our main support areas only, for by so doing, we should place ourselves in an unfavourable strategic situation at the start of any future conflict. If we withdrew our influence from the Mediterranean, we should lack the essential depth in front of our vital areas to allow the necessary time both for us to mobilise our own forces and for the resources of the United States to be brought into play. Moreover, we should be deprived of bases outside the United Kingdom, from which the threat of air action would be a deterrent to Russian aggression, and from which we could at the outset of a war conduct offensive operations.

The Prime Minister said the zones outside the main support areas could be termed "protective" zones, but they included in Europe the Western Mediterranean, and in the Middle East groups of comparatively weak nations. If the security of these groups was to be assured, they were in need of a strong defensive organisation to support their resources. Would the British Empire be able to provide sufficient forces to guarantee this support? He considered that Russian policy in the Middle East might take the form of gradual infiltration of political influence and ideologies. We might be faced with a gradual series of political intrigues, whereby in the event of war, the Russians would have manoeuvred into a position to enable them to move at once, by previous agreement into bases in that area. In his (the Prime Minister's) view it was very doubtful if we could provide the forces on such a scale as would be necessary to support a "forward" policy in the Mediterranean and Middle East.

Lord Tedder said it was essential that in any future war with Russia we should gain time at the outset to enable us to mobilise our resources. The necessary delays could best be imposed by air action, and for this, it was essential that we possessed bases in the protective zones from which we could operate. If a conflict broke out in the Middle East, where the terrain to a certain extent limited operations to definite seasons, the use of air action might well delay an enemy advance sufficiently for us and the Americans to mobilise our resources. The first reinforcement we should receive from the Americans would be their heavy bomber force, but their use would be severely curtailed if we lacked the bases from which they could make their power felt immediately.

Lord Alanbrooke agreed and said that although it was too early to estimate precisely the effect of the tactical use of atomic bombs, our attacks on the depots and bases from which any enemy advance was maintained, might well cripple such an advance for a long period. The small garrisoning force which the Chiefs of Staff had proposed should remain in the Middle East area, was militarily a small premium to pay for ensuring that we obtained the time necessary to mobilise our resources at the start of a major war. If there was no opposition to an enemy advance into the Middle East, we should be faced at the outset with an immediate threat to the security of our support areas and communications, and the prospect of losing the whole of the Middle East oil supply.

The Foreign Secretary said he agreed with the Chiefs of Staff that we must maintain our influence in the Mediterranean. It was impossible to retain the necessary diplomatic strength if military support was withdrawn, and in his view, Russia only respected nations which had the power to command respect. At the same time, our presence in the Mediterranean served a purpose other than military, which was very important to our position as a great Power. Through this area we brought influence on Southern Europe, Italy, Yugoslavia, Greece and Turkey. Undoubtedly, if we left the Mediterranean, Russia would move in, and the Mediterranean countries together with their commerce and trade, and their importance to our economy would be lost to us. Thus without the necessary facilities and bases for defence in the Mediterranean, it would be impossible to maintain the influence of our foreign policy in Southern Europe. From the political point of view therefore, it was essential to maintain the Mediterranean as a trade route and trade area, and to utilise both to the best of our advantage. The plan put forward by the Chiefs of Staff whereby only a small garrison remained in the canal area as the nucleus of a Regional Defence Organisation designed to support the Middle East States, seemed sound. It could, he thought, be defended before the United Nations Organisation as being compatible with the Charter. It was important to remember that if we did sacrifice the Mediterranean and concentrated our forces elsewhere, it was still necessary for us to obtain supplies; abandoning this area would mean a great loss to both our peace and war-time economy, trade and manpower. In his opinion, a thorough development of the Middle East trade areas, particularly in the belt stretching from West Africa to East Africa could offset the cost of retaining the small defence commitment in the Mediterranean. Moreover, we must seriously endeavour to ensure that the regional defence scheme would function efficiently and do all in our power to train the armed forces of countries such as Egypt, Iraq, and Saudi Arabia to a standard capable of meeting the needs of modern warfare.

The Secretary of State for the Dominions said he was agreeably surprised at the small force which the Chiefs of Staff thought necessary to retain in the Middle East. In view of the manifest military and political advantages both in the event of a war with Russia, and to our peace and war-time economy, he could see no reason for withdrawing our influence from the Mediterranean area.

The Prime Minister said that the issues involved were of such far reaching consequences that the problem would require further consideration before a definite decision could be taken. In particular he was very concerned at the vulnerability of the United Kingdom, and he considered that this should be the subject of a special examination. It would be necessary also to await the outcome of the special commission which was to study the potentialities of East Africa as a strategic base and as a trade development area.

The Committee: —

Gave general approval to the plan governing the recommendations of the Chiefs of Staff as set out in DO (46) 47 as a provisional basis for discussion at the forthcoming Conference with Dominion Prime Ministers and

(a) subject to further consideration being given to the security of the United Kingdom: and

(b) pending the findings of the Commission which is to look into the Foreign Secretary's suggestion for opening up the route across Africa.

36 FO 141/1081, no 95   9 Apr 1946

'Treaty revision: question of evacuation': inward telegram no 636 from Sir R Campbell to FO on the question of evacuation

[The difficulties in the way of an Anglo–Egyptian agreement appeared to increase on 5 Apr when the FO learned that Sidky had rejected the idea of Britain leasing the base and wanted a bilateral agreement rather than a treaty that would form part of a regional defence agreement (FO 371/53290, no 1507, Cairo tel no 610, 5 Apr 1946).]

It seems to me that the question which His Majesty's Government have to decide is whether (1) they can at the outset agree to evacuation pure and simple and construct a Treaty of friendship and alliance on that basis, relying upon the relief and goodwill which this course of action might create, in order to secure in a separate instrument the base, facilities etc. in Egypt which they consider essential for the security of the Middle East; or (2) whether they must insist on including in the new Treaty of friendship and alliance provision for the security requirements of the Middle East whether it is agreed to willingly by the Egyptians or not.

2.   (1) is clearly a gamble and I would hesitate to assert that it would come off. At the same time, unless His Majesty's Government declare their readiness to negotiate on a basis of evacuation without qualification, I very much doubt whether a free and amicable agreement can be reached. It is just conceivable that a "base" and "facilities" could be so disguised and camouflaged that the delegation and the Government would be willing to accept it and that the Wafd and the public would implement it, but this is certainly doubtful and for it to be at all possible the base and facilities would have to take an extremely moderate form.

3.   (2) could no doubt be put through by pressure and force. Quite apart from the difficult position in which we should in that event find ourselves because of declared opposition to the negotiation of Treaties under duress, there is in this course of action also an element of gamble. We could no doubt put down and keep down (at some cost in men, material, money and of the peaceable conditions we desire) any resultant popular outburst. But even supposing there was no such out-burst we should quite probably meet in peacetime with non-co-operation and perhaps even sabotage and a general expression of ill-will which would hamper the operation and utility of our base in peace-time and create serious difficulties and diversion of effort from the real enemy in war-time. No doubt also the Egyptians, in spite of their aversion from bringing in the Russians, would feel obliged to refer to the United Nations Organisation.

4.   It is obviously extremely difficult to decide which course of action to take. My own feeling is that if we declare our readiness to evacuate we might be able to secure beforehand, in some form or other, an undertaking to conclude a military convention giving us what we require in the way of a base and facilities if these were in an extremely moderate form and if they did not involve the presence, in peace-time, of combatant troops. The difficulty of course is that having undertaken to evacuate and having concluded a Treaty of friendship and alliance on that basis, we might find ourselves unable to secure subsequent and separate Egyptian agreement to a base and facilities to satisfy even the minimum security requirements. We would then be in a weakened position from the point of view of meeting these requirements and of forcing our views on Egypt. On the other hand it will take some months for our troops to withdraw (and I believe the Egyptians understand and accept this fact) so that for a considerable period we would still be in a position to enforce our views.

5. It seems just on the cards that the support of King Farouk might be secured for a solution on these lines and that he might be willing and able to make Sidky Pasha agree. His Majesty sent for General Paget on April 6th to secure an explanation of what was involved by a "base". General Paget tells me that His Majesty was most friendly, considerably more so than at previous audiences the General has had. He thinks that His Majesty took the points he made but he did not express agreement and the General cannot be sure that he did in fact agree. He is reporting direct to C.I.G.S.

The foregoing is drafted purely from the point of view of calculating the best political action for the achievement of our strategic ends.

37 CAB 128/5, CM 33(46)4   11 Apr 1946
'Egypt': Cabinet conclusions on the offer to evacuate British troops at the start of negotiations

The Foreign Secretary said that he had been considering whether the Delegation which was to negotiate the revision of the Anglo–Egyptian Treaty should indicate at the outset of the negotiations that His Majesty's Government were willing to withdraw British troops from Egypt. He had come to the conclusion that it would be expedient, as a matter of tactics, to make this offer at the outset. He had asked the Chiefs of Staff to consider the military implications, and he would not settle the final form of the instructions to the Delegation until he had received their comments. Meanwhile, he would be glad to have the views of his colleagues in the Cabinet.

After a short discussion the Cabinet:—

(1) Agreed that, subject to the views of the Chiefs of Staff, it would be expedient, as a matter of tactics, if any offer by His Majesty's Government to withdraw British troops from Egypt were made at the outset of the negotiations for the revision of the Anglo–Egyptian Treaty,

(2) Invited the Secretary of State for Dominion Affairs to inform the Governments of the Dominions in due course of the instructions given to the British Delegation on this point.

38 FO 371/53291, no 1699   17 Apr 1946
[Anglo–Egyptian treaty negotiations]: inward telegram no 679 from Lord Stansgate[1] (Cairo) to Mr Bevin on Britain's initial negotiating position[2]

[Following the Cabinet's decision to approve the principle of offering troop withdrawals at the outset, Bevin's detailed ideas, not revealed to the Cabinet, were put to the COS who discussed them on 12 Apr (CAB 79/47, COS 59(46)4). Bevin's suggestion was that the

---

[1] Stansgate arrived in Egypt on 15 Apr 1946 as head of the formal British delegation and held a series of informal talks with King Farouk and prime minister Sidky which the ambassador had already begun. Discussions between the two delegations began on 9 May after an exchange of notes and ended on 22 May. Stansgate returned to London for consultations at the beginning of June and talks resumed on 3 July and continued without agreement until 26 Sept.

[2] All telegrams from Lord Stansgate referred to in 1946 were sent through Sir R Campbell and although the delegation and the ambassador were sometimes resident in Alexandria no distinction will be made between communications between the latter and London or other destination as opposed to those going in or out of Cairo.

[delegation be authorised to state British policy at the outset as (a) the complete evacuation from Egypt of all British combatant troops (as opposed to those troops maintaining the base) (b) the maintenance by Egypt, with British collaboration, of naval, land and air administrative and air defence organisations (c) permission for the transit of troops and aircraft, and for the maintenance requirements of the transit organisation (d) the creation of a regional headquarters to be located in the Canal Zone (e) the provision of equipment for the Egyptian forces. As a result of their discussions of these five points the COS drafted a paper (DO(46)56) which was considered by the Defence Committee on 15 Apr (CAB 131/1, DO12(46)2). In the light of the COS views instructions were sent to the British delegation the following day (FO 371/53291, no 1659, FO tel 718, 16 Apr 1946). The telegram contained instructions to negotiate on the basis of Bevin's five points with the qualification that if possible combatant troops should not include the fighter squadrons, but as a last resort the delegation might agree to their withdrawal as soon as the Egyptian air force had reached sufficient strength to provide a peacetime garrison, and provided British control over long range bomber bases would be retained for many years to come.]

We have received your telegrams Nos. 718 and 719 and have discussed them at a full meeting of the delegation. As a result we have prepared an aide-mémoire in which we have sought to interpret your instructions. Text of aide-mémoire is in my immediately following telegram.

2. Your instructions differ in several important respects from the line which has been suggested in a number of telegrams by the Ambassador and Commanders, and go further than the five points in your telegram No. 688. Their estimation of the situation in Egypt is that the best chance of getting our military requirements is to start by offering complete evacuation of all British troops and not only of combatant troops. They [?grp. omit.] it is only by making a gesture of this kind that the requisite atmosphere of good-will will be created in which the Egyptian Government will be prepared to co-operate in general defence arrangements of the kind desired in the Canal zone. Unless a promise of complete evacuation without conditions is made, they think it possible that the Egyptian delegation may refuse to open negotiations, that the Government may fall, and that there may be grave disorders.

3. Since my arrival I have had an opportunity of appreciating the situation, and fully share these views. In any case we all think it would be a mistake to start by tabling formal proposals based on your instructions before the full Egyptian delegation. It is unwieldy in size and disunited: discordant elements (especially Makram Ebeid) are bound to try to exploit and publicise proceedings for their own political ends and so the fewer the contentious issues of principle that are brought before them the better. We therefore intend to take the opportunity of calls which I shall pay tomorrow or next day on Sidki Pasha and the King to sound them out on the basis of the aide-mémoire.

4. It may be that the proposals in the aide-mémoire will be sufficiently moderate to come as a relief to King Farouk and Sidki Pasha, and that we shall find it possible to proceed to formal negotiations on this basis. On the other hand it may well be that the reaction we get will be such as to make it clear that nothing less than an opening promise of complete evacuation can form the basis for successful negotiation. If this happens I shall of course refer to you before taking any further step. It is unlikely that any serious business will take place between Friday and Monday 22nd April, but first formal meeting between the two delegations is almost certain to be on Tuesday, when I shall have to take a positive line. If therefore I have to refer to you after seeing Sidki Pasha and the King it will be essential for me to have a reply with further instructions by Monday at the latest. I am sending this telegram in the hope that it will facilitate arrangements in London.

39   CAB 79/47, COS 62(46)6   18 Apr 1946

'Revision of Anglo–Egyptian treaty': COS Committee minutes on the views of the British delegation in Egypt

[Tel 679 was considered by the JPS who drafted a letter to the FO for the COS to approve agreeing to Stansgate's proposal only if the negotiations could not be started on any other terms (CAB 84/81, JP(46)84 (F) annex, 18 Apr 1946.]

The Committee had before them a telegram[1] from the British Delegation in Egypt to the Foreign Office setting out their views as a result of a discussion held after receiving from the Foreign Office the instructions approved by the Defence Committee.

Sir Rhoderick McGrigor said he had discussed the instructions sent by the Defence Committee to the British Delegation in Cairo with the First Sea Lord before the receipt of this telegram. He was very concerned with the somewhat pusillanimous attitude we were adopted towards the Egyptians. In his opinion, it was incorrect tactics to disclose all our concessions at the opening of discussions, and he would have preferred that we should have conducted the discussions on hard bargaining, and reserved our concessions until the appropriate moment.

Lord Alanbrooke referring to the telegram said the Delegation appeared to hold the view that there should be no provisos to accepting the evacuation of our troops from Egypt. When the Chiefs of Staff had agreed to the principles set forward by the Foreign Secretary at the Defence Committee, they had stipulated two provisos. In the first place the necessity of maintaining the base installations which supplied our forces deployed in Palestine, and secondly, the need to retain fighter squadrons until such time as the Egyptian Air Forces were efficient enough to carry out the role of modern air forces. In the immediate future, there could be no question of evacuating the base supply depots in the Canal Zone, otherwise the whole of our position in Palestine would be jeopardised.

Lord Tedder said our desire to retain air forces in Egypt did not conflict with our concession to evacuate our force. It was purely a question of timing in that the air force squadrons must be retained until we were satisfied that the Egyptians could replace the squadrons efficiently.

In discussion, it was agreed that the provisos mentioned by the Chiefs of Staff did not conflict with the principle of evacuation. The problem of the maintenance of our base personnel and facilities for supplying Palestine could be a matter of negotiation and applied similarly to the evacuation of air force squadrons. It was not thought that the headquarters which was to be retained in the Canal zone as the Control Centre for the Middle East Regional Defence Scheme, could be argued as conflicting with the decision to evacuate our troops.

The Committee:—

(a) Instructed the Joint Planning Staff to examine the telegram from the British Delegation, and to prepare a draft reply to the Foreign Office.

(b) Agreed to meet at 4 p.m. 18th April, to discuss the draft reply by the Joint Planning Staff.

---

[1] See 38.

40   FO 371/53292, no 1735   22 Apr 1946
[Anglo–Egyptian negotiations]: inward telegram no 713 from Lord
Stansgate to Mr Bevin on preliminary talks

[The views of the COS on 18 Apr were immediately made known to the FO on the basis
that anything less than they had previously agreed prior to Stansgate's tel 679 of 17 Apr
was unacceptable unless negotiations could be started only on the basis of his proposals.
This was reflected in the instructions sent to Cairo on the same day (FO 371/53291, no
1699, Cairo tel no 744, 18 Apr 1946).]

We have now reached the position foreshadowed in paragraph 4 of my telegram No.
679.[1] That is to say we have exhausted the possibilities of progress in preliminary
talks with the King and with Sidki Pasha and can no longer avoid coming into the
open at official meetings with Egyptian Delegation. We have now got to commit
ourselves to formal proposals. In order that you may come to a decision in the full
knowledge of the facts as seen here, I am attempting in this telegram to lay them
once more before you. Certain phrases in your telegram No. 744 seem to us here to
show that you do not understand the situation in Egypt and the kind of impasse into
which the King and the Egyptian Delegation have got in view of public feeling which
they are partly responsible for having created.

2.   The choice before us seems to me to be as follows. The first alternative is to go
forward to formal negotiations on the basis of the proposals in your telegram No. 718
and your telegram No. 719. After a number of interviews and conversations with His
Majesty and Sidki Pasha it is quite clear that the Egyptian Delegation would reject
these proposals and demand complete evacuation. There are no arguments which we
can employ in support of our proposals which carry any weight with the Egyptian
Delegation in comparison with the fears which press upon them on every side. We
have tried our utmost to convince His Majesty and Sidki Pasha that our proposals are
themselves extremely moderate, that they represent the minimum required both for
the future safety of their country and that without an organised base here our help
would come too late to save them. They are totally unable to view our proposals in
this light partly out of ignorance of military affairs which prevents them
understanding the necessity for large administrative installations in Egypt itself, but
much more because they know that they have no chance whatever of representing
our proposals to their delegation, to [?grp. omtd.] militarists and to their people, as
compatible with Egyptian independence and sovereignty. Complete evacuation of
Cairo and Alexandria means little to them as we are already committed to that under
the 1936 Treaty which they consider we have so far shown no sign whatever of
fulfilling. Removal from Egypt of combatant troops means little because it simply
involves substitution of a considerable number of British administrative troops and
some fighter squadrons for 10,000 men and 400 pilots permitted in 1936 Treaty. The
whole of our proposal appears to them to be an elaborate attempt in a new guise to
perpetuate our hold on the country. We are convinced that though naturally they are
out to get all they can essentially there is no bluff in their attitude.

3.   The attitude of the rest of the Egyptian delegation is bound to be much more
intransigent than that of His Majesty or Sidki Pasha because they are afraid of
popular feeling, if they do not succeed in securing complete evacuation. We have

---

[1] See 38.

heard the opinions of all those, officially and unofficially who are in a position to form a judgement upon Egyptian matters. They are unanimously expressing the view that the Wafd and Muslim brethren will seize on anything short of complete evacuation as a pretext for arousing the passions of the people. The whole articulate portion of the nation has asserted a demand for our evacuation not once but time after time.

It is certain that the Government would not be able to hold the position and that there would be disorders. Even if the Government had the will to use the police and the army to the full, the latter are doubtful quantities. Former are not numerous enough to cope with prolonged disorder, and the army, and especially the junior officers, would be in sympathy with popular agitation. The British force would have to be employed to safeguard the Europeans and possibly to keep essential services going. The situation might get completely out of hand and no Egyptian Government in these circumstances could avoid an appeal to U.N.O. We could, in theory, oppose such an appeal on grounds that there is in existence the 1936 treaty but it is hard to see how we could do this in the face of the Persian and Syrian precedents and at a time when large scale anti-British demonstrations would be in progress in this country.

4.   Our considered opinion therefore is that if you decide to adopt this alternative you must do so in the certainty that you will either have to give way in negotiation or be prepared to carry our proposals through by force and face an appeal to U.N.O. In either case you will sacrifice the friendship of Egypt and lose all chance of willing cooperation.

5.   If our negotiations with the Egyptians fail and we proceed to impose our wishes on Egypt by force if necessary, we shall not only destroy the liberty of our influence in this country but we shall find ourselves on bad terms with some or all of Arab neighbours. This would play right into the hands of Russia, who, without stirring a finger would see our friendship with the Arab world gravely impaired and would have the pleasure of helping to force us out of Egypt altogether by public opinion expressed through U.N.O. Meanwhile Russia herself will no doubt have done the right thing by Persia ostensibly enough to figure as a good boy by contrast with us. In such circumstances Egypt and the Arab world would begin to look away from us. Whether they would look towards Russia is a matter for speculation but we should not lose sight of the possibility. Certainly Communism here would receive a stimulus.

6.   Second alternative is to "come clean" ourselves and to offer complete evacuation of all British troops from Egypt and to settle a date by which it will be complete. This would mean that assistance which we should be able to give to Egypt in peacetime would be limited to collaboration between Staffs and to maintenance by the Egyptians of administrative installations with the assistance of British technical personnel in mufti. There is little doubt that the Egyptians would meet us half way in facilitating operation of any scheme worked out on these lines and of course they would give us complete freedom of action in Egypt at a time of apprehended emergency and in war.[2] But it would be wrong to imagine that this plan would get us everything we want in peacetime. Strategical implications are likely to be serious.

---

[2] An FO official sidelined this sentence and commented in the margin: 'ha! ha!'

Nevertheless we should secure Egyptian friendship and co-operation in full measure and this is surely something that is worth more than a position gained at the point of the bayonet.

7.   Choice before us is not easy and neither alternative will give us everything we want. On political grounds Ambassador and I and our political advisers recommend that we should adopt the second alternative. It is essential however that we should retain the initiative in negotiations. It would, in our opinion, be fatal to be forced in negotiation to recede from our position once we had decided to go forward on first alternative. To do so would merely be to make sure of worst of both worlds. If the second alternative is chosen we consider that we should be empowered to make public announcement at the opening of negotiations on the following lines. We should say that it was the settled policy of His Majesty's Government to consolidate Anglo–Egyptian Treaty of Alliance as a [2 grps, undec. ? free association of] equal nations who have interest in common. In pursuance of this policy His Majesty's Government were proposing to withdraw all British armed forces from Egyptian soil and to conduct negotiations with the Egyptian delegation with the object of arranging details of this withdrawal and for the purpose of making satisfactory arrangements for mutual assistance in emergency in accordance with the spirit of the alliance.

8.   Commanders-in-Chief are telegraphing separately to Chiefs of Staff on the military aspect of the alternatives.

9.   If we are to retain initiative it will be necessary to table our proposals or to make an announcement on Thursday or Friday of this week at the latest. I am sending General Jacob[3] home tonight so that he will be available to give any further explanations of the local situation which you may require to help you in coming to a decision.[4]

---

[3] Maj-Gen E I C Jacob, Brigadier Major of the Canal Brigade, 1936–1938; military assistant to the Cabinet, 1938–1946, and member of the British treaty delegation. Left the army to become controller of Foreign Services of the BBC 1946.
[4] Stansgate re-enforced his belief in the desirability of immediately offering complete withdrawal and negotiating on the timing in a personal letter to Bevin (FO 371/53292, no 1796, 22 Apr 1946).

41   FO 371/53292, no 1723   22 Apr 1946
[Anglo–Egyptian negotiations]: inward telegram no 81 from Commanders-in-Chief, Middle East to COS on Britain's initial negotiating position

1.   Following are our views on Military implications of alternatives put forward in Cairo Telegram No. 713[1] to Foreign Office.

2.   Alternative (1). Forcing proposals on Egypt will cause major internal security problem. Forces available sufficient to secure essential Service installations, airfields and lines of communication, but will involve commitment present reserve of one division for Palestine. Reinforcements of one division one armoured brigade together

---

[1] See 40.

armoured troops necessary to restore and maintain order. Necessary also to concentrate all isolated detachments and isolated civilians and in case of latter evacuation of those not essential to British interests must be considered. Some cruisers and destroyers would be desirable at Port Said and Alexandria and sea transport lift would be necessary in the event of breakdown of railway to Palestine or evacuation of civilians.

3. Alternative (2). Complete evacuation both combatant and administrative. Evacuation will be a long and costly process entailing provision of extra accommodation first in Canal Zone for reception of personnel and stores from Delta and second in final location personnel less technicians and supervisors in mufti working under Egyptian Government. Minimum military requirements for Middle East base are as stated in aide memoire text of which signalled in Cairo telegram No. 680 to Foreign Office. Egyptian proposals no substitute for these since control of stores and material constituting war reserves and representing millions of British taxpayers' money would be vested in a foreign government and not with responsible commanders. Nor would it be possible to rely on drawing on these reserves for operations elsewhere in the Middle East. Whilst Palestine can in time be made administratively self contained as regards garrison some administrative backing will be required and if not available from Egypt reserves must be held elsewhere. Turnover modification and security of stores on secret list also requires army war reserves of certain stores should not be under control of a foreign government. The maintenance and development by the Egyptians of administrative storage and defence facilities including airfields and maintenance units with the assistance of British advisors [sic] and technical personnel would be acceptable to R.N. and R.A.F. provided due regard is paid to British advice.

4. Implications of adopting alternative two are therefore that certain essential base installations now in Egypt must be provided elsewhere. In view of inadequate ports and communications in Palestine and Cyrenaica and possible closure of Mediterranean in war consider vicinity of Mombasa and Aden as only alternatives to Canal Zone though given time arrangements could be made to hold equipment for one or two divisions in Palestine. This would entail large construction and stores movement programme.

5. Only alternative to Egypt is Palestine. Provided Egyptians would maintain communications and accommodation for shadow GHQ in peace which would be immediately available for us in war.

6. Conclusions from above are:

(a) Alternative one likely cause major internal security problem involving reinforcements one division, one armoured brigade, Adm. troops together with additional warships and sea transport with also loss good will of Egyptians.

(b) Alternative two necessitates complete evacuation and provision of certain army base installations and movement out of Egypt and of great tonnage of army stores.

(c) If alternative two adopted GHQ must move out of Egypt.

(d) But a friendly Egypt should ensure free use of railways, docks, labour, etc., in war together with maintenance of certain storage and workshop accommodation and provision shadow GHQ in peace.

(e) Complete.

42   FO 141/1081, no 146   23 Apr 1946
[Anglo–Egyptian treaty revision]: memorandum by Sir W Smart on the problems of negotiating with the existing Egyptian government

If we succeed in negotiating a new Anglo–Egyptian Treaty with the present régime, the Treaty will have to be ratified by an Egyptian Parliament. Quite apart from the fact that the present Parliament was elected on a boycott by the Wafd of the elections, it was not elected on a Treaty revision issue. The right thing, therefore, would seem to be for the Government to go to the country on the new Treaty.

We have asked King Farouk and Sidky for guarantees that the Treaty will not be repudiated and they have given us assurances to that effect, which are, of course, only binding on the present régime. Presumably the present régime will either refer the new Treaty to the present Parliament for ratification or go to the country and cook the new elections. If the present régime got away with ratification by the present or another inadequately representative Parliament, there would not be a cessation of anti-British agitation, with consequent disorders on occasion, because the Wafd, which is the majority Party, would agitate even more fiercely after than before the Treaty. It is out to get back to power and will not be deterred from agitating against the Treaty even if it happens to be a good one for Egypt.

In 1929, after Mohamed Mahmoud brought back the draft Treaty from London, we insisted that the Treaty should be submitted to the country under a régime of free elections. The Wafd, during the elections, refused to express an opinion on the Treaty and maintained the slogan that their views must be expressed under the cupola of the Parliament. As a matter of fact when they got back into power they did not express their views in Parliament before going to London for negotiations. They tried to get from us more than the Mohamed Mahmoud Treaty and the negotiations failed.

Presumably, under our present policy of complete non-interference in the internal affairs of Egypt, we have to leave it to the present régime to decide how the Treaty is to be ratified and to refrain from any interference in securing free elections with a view to ratification of the Treaty by the country. However, we must bear in mind, as indicated above, that ratification by the present régime would not produce tranquillity in Egypt, though a Treaty favourable to Egypt would strengthen the present régime and facilitate its task of squashing attempts of the Wafd to make disorder.

43   CAB 79/47, COS 64(46)9   24 Apr 1946
'Revision of the Anglo–Egyptian treaty': COS Committee minutes on the offer of complete evacuation

The Committee had a general discussion with Major-General Jacob[1] on the progress made by the British Delegation in Cairo on the revision of the Anglo–Egyptian Treaty.

---

[1] See 40, note 3.

Major-General Jacob then gave the background which led to the culmination of the Delegation's advice on the two alternative courses of action.

The British Delegation had drawn up an Aide Memoire, based on their instructions from H.M. Government. In consultation with the Political Advisers and Commanders-in-Chief, they then considered the tactics whereby our requirements should be put across. They had reached the unanimous conclusion that the correct action was first to sound the King and the Egyptian Prime Minister, in order to reach some basis on which a reasonable chance of a successful outcome of the negotiations could be guaranteed, and to avoid an impasse from which later it might be difficult to withdraw.

Every member of the Egyptian Delegation was publically committed to accepting nothing less than the total evacuation of all British troops from Egyptian soil. In the past, anti-British demonstrations had been confined to students and extremists, but today, the Egyptian Delegation's attitude was supported by all articulate levels of Egyptian opinion. Moreover, the Wafd Party, who were not included in the Egyptian Delegation, were awaiting the opportunity of any signs of concession on the part of their Delegation from this principle, in order to stir up trouble. The result was that the Egyptian Delegation were supported in their convictions by the political atmosphere of the country, and even by fear of attacks on their lives, if they wavered.

The attitude of the King was such that whilst he was more receptive to our requirements for certain defensive facilities, he would be unlikely to override or modify the Egyptians' claims in the face of public opinion.

The Egyptian Police Force could be used to deal with disorders on the assumption that the will to prevent disorders was present in the Egyptian Government, but their size limited them from being effective if disorders were sustained longer than 48 hours. Similarly, the Army who were resentful of long relegation to the position of inferiority without equipment, were permeated with the nationalist feeling, and would be an unreliable factor in any major outbreak.

The causes of Egyptian resentment towards our presence were apparent in the obvious physical signs of our military activities in Egypt. In Cairo, main buildings such as the G.H.Q. Kasr el Nil, the Citadel and the Semiramis Hotel were the centre points from which large numbers of British forces moved to and fro. Moreover, our forces enjoyed exemption from Egyptian jurisdiction, and large areas were set aside for our exclusive use.

The Egyptians pointed to the precedents of withdrawal from Persia, Syria and the Lebanon, and were resentful of our continued presence in Egypt.[2] Their attitude towards their own defence was that the danger from the West had disappeared, and

---

[2] The Egyptians were referring to the events in 1945 and 1946 in which the British played a key role in ensuring the withdrawal of foreign troops from the Levant and Iran in accordance with the wishes of the indigenous leaders. In the summer of 1945 British troops prevented the Free French from going back on a wartime promise to grant the Syrians independence and aroused enormous hostility from de Gaulle. In early 1946 when the Soviets refused to withdraw troops from Iran in accordance with Iranian wishes and their agreed obligations, the British supported the US in taking action at the UN and in confronting the Soviet Union which led to the withdrawal of Soviet troops in May 1946. There were obvious similarities with the Iranian situation in that the British, by keeping more than 10,000 troops in Egypt, were, like the Soviets, in breach of an international agreement and arousing the hostility of the local government, even though the Anglo–Egyptian treaty, unlike the Soviet agreement with Iran, did permit some troops to remain in the Canal Zone.

that the danger from the East was remote. They had no real appreciation of the cost of providing modern defensive installations and armed forces. They looked to U.N.O. to guarantee to them freedom from aggression, and whilst they recognised that British support was necessary in time of emergency, they thought that British forces could be located near to the territories of Egypt, in either Libya or Palestine but not in Egypt. Their whole attitude was thus a combination of ignorance and pride, through which it was most difficult to introduce and obtain their acceptance of the conception of a regional defence organisation.

The method which could be used by our Delegation to secure our requirements was either to persuade the Egyptians of the realities of the situation, or to fight our demands through. The latter action would invove [sic] us in a situation, the outcome of which it would be almost impossible to foresee, particularly if there was simultaneous trouble in Palestine. On the other hand, if we conceded unequivocally that we would withdraw our troops completely, there were definite chances of obtaining certain concessions in the resultant negotiations.

On this basis the Treaty would be founded on goodwill and friendship. It was likely that full facilities would be granted in Egypt in time of war or in time of apprehended national emergency. In peace, the Egyptians would probably maintain, though in a reduced state of efficiency, the port facilities, railways, roads, oil installations and airfields. We would probably retain a certain measure of influence on the maintenance of workshops and signal networks, but would probably not obtain adequate facilities for the supervision of the storage of warlike stores that we had contemplated putting into the Middle East base.

We might gain facilities for the transit of troops in peacetime, and the right to take part in occasional joint air exercises. It was probable that we could maintain close touch between military staffs, perhaps through a Mission. The Egyptians might agree to maintain a Headquarters and Signals Organisation earmarked for operation in war, and to be available in time of apprehended emergency, but not for use in peace.

Finally, the Delegation considered that the Egyptians would allow a reasonable time for the withdrawal of our forces and installations, say three years, provided there was constant physical evidence that our withdrawal promises were being fulfilled. The Delegation had ample grounds both from the King and the Egyptian Prime Minister for believing that the Egyptians would agree to the majority of the concessions he had outlined, provided we categorically stated that we would evacuate Egypt.

In a full discussion of the alternative courses of action put forward by the Delegation, it was apparent that the political effect of pressing for our full requirements would almost certainly lead to disorders which would call for the despatch of the large reinforcements specified by the Commanders-in-Chief.[3] There was also the risk of ruining our relations with Egypt, and the possibility of being pilloried in the Security Council. If Egypt resorted to the Security Council, it would provide useful propaganda ammunition for Russia and might result in the Russians obtaining some footing in the area under the guise of U.N.O. supervision.

Complete evacuation would not obtain the minimum military requirements which were considered essential and would thus confront us with the serious problem of finding these requirements outside Egypt. The likely serious situation in Palestine

---

[3] See 41.

emphasised the importance of retaining in the immediate future some base facilities in Egypt from which our troops in Palestine could be maintained. On the other hand, the Delegation advised that by following this course, we should obtain the friendly co-operation of Egypt which would enable negotiations to proceed for full facilities in war, and in peace time for the maintenance by Egypt of communications, workshop accommodation, port facilities, etc., in a reasonable state of efficiency. But there was no guarantee that after we had stated that we intended to evacuate Egypt, the Egyptians would grant these facilities if an emergency did arise; and the extent to which the military requirements would be met could only be assessed as negotiations proceeded.

However from the military point of view, there was no doubt that the first alternative involved the greater disadvantages, and there was thus no alternative but to recommend the second alternative as the lesser of two evils.

It was agreed that a minute containing their views should be submitted to the Prime Minister.

General Ismay[4] suggested that the minute to the Prime Minister should set out fully the disadvantages of the two courses of action recommended by the Delegation and the repercussions on the chances of obtaining our minimum essential military requirements. The position of the Chiefs of Staff should be made quite clear that their recommendation was the only action they could take in the light of political advice from the British Delegation in Cairo.

The Committee:—

(a) Took note of the telegram from the Commanders-in-Chief, Middle East, setting out their views on the military implications of the alternative courses of action recommended by the British Delegation in Cairo;

(b) Instructed the Secretary to prepare a draft minute for submission to the Prime Minister in the light of the above discussion;

(c) Agreed to consider (b) above at 2.45 p.m., and providing agreement was reached to submit the minute to the Prime Minister in time for consideration by the Defence Committee that afternoon.

---

[4] General H L Ismay, military secretary to the Cabinet.

---

44 CAB 131/1, DO 14(46)2   **24 Apr 1946**
'Revision of the Anglo–Egyptian treaty': Cabinet Defence Committee
minutes on the offer of complete evacuation   **[Extract]**

The Committee had before them a minute by the Chiefs of Staff containing their views after consultation with General Jacob and after consideration of the contents of the recent telegrams[1] from the British Delegation in Cairo.

Lord Alanbrooke said the Chiefs of Staff had examined the alternative courses of action put forward by the Delegation in Cairo. Course 'A' if successful, was the only one which would give us all we required in Egypt for the general defence of the Middle East. The Delegation advised, however, that the political effect of pressing for

---

[1] See 40, 41.

our full requirements involved the risk which they regarded as a practical certainty, of disorders necessitating the despatch of considerable reinforcements to Egypt to restore and maintain order; permanently ruining our relations with Egypt; and opening the way for Egypt to refer the case to the Security Council.

On the other hand, Course 'B' would not get us the minimum military requirements which they considered necessary, and would confront us with a serious problem in meeting these requirements outside Egypt. The Delegation advised that we stand to secure the friendly co-operation of Egypt, but it was by a definite sacrifice to our military position. The Chiefs of Staff had therefore decided in the face of these two inescapable alternatives, that to follow Course 'B' would be the lesser of the two evils.

Major-General Jacob then gave the background which led to the culmination of the Delegation's advice on the two alternative courses of action. . . .[2]

In answer to questions from *Mr. Bevin, Major-General Jacob* said that the Delegation had ample grounds both from the King and the Egyptian Prime Minister for believing that the Egyptians would agree to the majority of the concessions he had outlined, provided we categorically stated that we would evacuate Egypt.

The question of establishing a Joint Military Board or similar body with the Egyptians, at the same time leaving ourselves free to conduct conversations with other countries concerned in a regional defence agreement, would probably be agreed to by the Egyptians, as this would fall within the cover of general staff conversations for the security of the area.

There were already indications of the type of concession the Egyptians would be prepared to agree to in the example of Alexandria. The Royal Navy were evacuating Alexandria very quickly, and their two main requirements, that of the Naval Wireless Station and the stores dump in Alexandria, had successfully been turned over to British civilian manning. On the general question of base facilities, there was the possibility that we should be able to introduce a limited number of civilians to run certain of our organisations, but nominally they would remain under Egyptian control.

Mr. Bevin said that he would prefer the evacuation programme to take place over a period of five years instead of the anticipated three. We could, if necessary, agree that all our troops and installations would be evacuated by 1951. He stipulated the five year period as by then we should be in a better position to assess from the international situation the trends of world events. Moreover, the extra two years would enable a better assessment of the strength of the United Nations Organisation in upholding the peace of the world.

The first requirement was for us to evacuate Cairo as quickly as possible. There was a possibility that in the period before complete evacuation, the Egyptians would realize the necessity of our presence in the Canal Zone to ensure the efficient working of the regional defence scheme.

Major-General Jacob said there was a likelihood that the Egyptians would agree to a five year evacuation period. The important point from their point of view was not so much the time taken for evacuation, as the principle that we had agreed to a timed evacuation programme with a firmly agreed date for final and complete evacuation. The Treaty concluded at the end of the negotiations would ensure that there was no

---

[2] Major-Gen Jacob then repeated his statement made earlier at the COS Committee, see 43.

question of the Egyptians disowning their promised facilities in time of war or apprehended emergency.

The Prime Minister, summing up the discussion, said there was inevitably a general measure of agreement on allowing the Delegation to pursue Course 'B'. He would recommend this to the Cabinet with the proviso that in negotiations on the details of evacuation, we should press strongly for allowing the evacuation period over five years, namely, 1951 as the date by which time all British troops and installations would be withdrawn from Egypt.

The Committee:—

Agreed to recommend to the Cabinet:—

(a) that the Delegation should be authorised to open the negotiations on the basis of the second alternative proposed by them, i.e. on the principle of the complete evacuation of all British forces from Egypt; and

(b) that the delegation should be instructed to try and obtain in negotiation a period of five years in which to complete the evacuation.

45   CAB 129/9, CP(46)170   24 Apr 1946
'Revision of Anglo–Egyptian treaty': note for the Cabinet by Mr Bevin circulating a note presented to the British delegation by Sidky

[On Apr 24 the Cabinet considered CP(46)170 and the recommendation of the Defence Committee that Britain should offer at the outset of negotiations complete evacuation of all British troops from Egypt by a specified date. The Cabinet authorised the delegation to proceed on that basis with all troops evacuated from Egypt within five years. In discussion emphasis was laid on the importance of securing full Egyptian agreement with the estimate that it would be physically impossible to complete the process in less than five years. It was deemed most important to avoid any impression that withdrawal had been offered merely to gain time. The Cabinet agreed that from this point of view it would be helpful if a public announcement could be made, with the concurrence of the Egyptian government, making it clear that they accepted the British estimate of the time required to complete the withdrawal (CAB 128/5, CM 37(46)1, 24 Apr 1946).]

I circulate for the information of my colleagues a translation of a note presented to the British Delegation by the Egyptian Prime Minister.

Note with 45

On Saturday the 20th April Sedky [sic] Pasha summoned the officers forming the military bureau attached to the Egyptian Delegation for the Negotiations and communicated to them the aide memoire which had been handed to him on the previous day by His Excellency the British Ambassador and Lord Stansgate.

Their first reaction was wholly unfavourable.

Sedky [sic] Pasha explained to them that he was only asking their technical opinion on the matter.

He begged them to study the British suggestions objectively putting all considerations of sentiment to one side.

"The suggestions should", he told them, "be regarded from the following angle".

"We are two allies of unequal strength who may have to face a powerful and rapid act of aggression launched by an enemy of not less strength than Great Britain. Whatever Egyptian preparations may be, the defence cannot be immediately in a state capable of repulsing the invader; our British allies must therefore intervene at once and they consider that the defence may prove to be ineffective without the presence in our country of a nucleus forming in advance an "allied administrative base" whose composition is set out in detail in the note and whose purpose will be to prepare in time of peace for the reception of troops and re-inforcement formations.

"Consider this without being influenced by the political aspect of the suggestion; I only ask you for a military opinion".

The members of the bureau have handed their opinion, in the form of the attached note, to Sedky [sic] Pasha this evening.

The Prime Minister, after a personal examination of the British aide memoire which was handed to him on the 19th April[1] and of the above note from his military bureau, can only give his entire support to the latter's conclusions. He adds the following considerations which will be the last after the series of considerations which he has developed orally or in writing in recent days.

1.   There is no longer any doubt that, in the form set forth in the Aide Memoire communicated on the 19th April, the base asked for in Egyptian territory constitutes a veritable military occupation of this territory.

2.   This base, to which is added a British air force contingent, presents such a variety of aspects—including notably a veritable headquarters belonging to a foreign army—that the fiction consisting in saying that it simply involves an allied base cannot take away its true character from it.

3.   By the arrangement suggested by the Aide Memoire the alliance between the two countries is reduced to a military tutelage exercised by a big country over a smaller country which will rapidly degenerate—as in fact has happened—into political supremacy. An alliance based on equality cannot involve more than consultations and conversations between Staffs to arrive at a rational use of forces and preparation in common of defence plans.

4.   Egypt would go as far as possible in this way since she envisages a development of the cultural help to be furnished by British schools for military instruction and a harmonious choice of the arms to be employed.

5.   The development of the power and effectiveness of the new Egyptian army, planned as a sign of the true and final liberation of the country, could not but suffer from the position of inferiority which would be created by the presence of a British base, of which the undoubted influence would halt or discourage many initiatives. The facts of a recent past are there to prove it.

6.   The same influence will continue to be exercised in the political field notwithstanding the assurances, often dictated by incontestable good faith, which are offered. This is ground on to which the present note does not wish to venture, since it would involve needlessly the examination of a past which gave little reason for confidence.

7.   After the final disappearance of the reasons which determined the measures contemplated by the treaty of 1936, a country like Egypt could not agree that its independence should remain at the mercy of new and various reasons which the political repertory is never at a loss to discover. An independent country should provide for its own security from its own resources, and this should be so in Egypt's

---

[1] This was based on FO tel 718 that produced Stansgate's protests in Cairo tel 713, see 40.

case; she does not want to fail in this task, but her dignity as a free country cannot but refuse to alienate her independence as a result of exaggerated and almost imaginary anxieties as to probable dangers. And if this could be explained to some extent before the last war, it would no longer be understood, since the creation of the mechanism of world security inaugurated at San Francisco, how an independent country could cheerfully allow its liberty to be fettered by benevolent agreements of doubtful efficacy.

8.   It is now apparently a question of a danger from the East, just as later on, and even after the end of the alliance, it may be a question of quite a different danger resulting from the difficulties of the moment, or from any other product of the always fertile imagination of Chancelleries.

9.   It is not the aim of the present note to expatiate on the extent of the dangers to which world peace is exposed. But may we remark that these perils are often presented in a light in which a sometimes deliberate pessimism plays a leading part. Russian policy is certainly disturbing; but it is more suspicious than dangerous, and if the danger which it presents can arise from its immediate and neighbouring interests, Egypt cannot in any case be the country against which its first act of aggression would take place, an act which distance and the presence of other intermediate countries, placed under British rule or influence, would render as inexplicable as it was inoperative.

10.   In brief, and whatever may be the goodwill of the Egyptian negotiator or his influence on his compatriots, he would find it, if not impossible, at least very difficult to convince them that their hopes for the independence of their country and the integrity of its territory will have been substantially realised by the application of the last suggestions contained in the British note.

In regard to Sedky [sic] Pasha personally, he regrets that he cannot support such suggestions, which, moreover, are far from being in accordance with the terms of his mandate.

11.   And since in regard to Great Britain, the friend and ally of his country, he has obligations dictated by loyalty and sincerity, he owes it to himself to issue a warning that, as he has many times pointed out, a movement of public opinion (stimulated to an equal degree by different causes and currents) may at any moment transform itself into an action which it was possible to repress or contain at the beginning of the present political campaign, but which may subsequently elude all control.

46   CAB 128/5, CM 42(46)1   6 May 1946

'Egypt': Cabinet conclusions on the public announcement of Britain's withdrawal from Egypt

The Prime Minister said that the discussions at the meeting of Foreign Ministers in Paris were narrowing down to the strategic position in the Mediterranean, and the Foreign Secretary had reported that it would be helpful to him in these discussions if it could now be publicly declared that it was the policy of His Majesty's Government to withdraw all British troops from Egypt. At their meeting on the 24th April the Cabinet had agreed that, at the outset of the formal negotiations for the revision of the Anglo–Egyptian Treaty, the British Delegation should make the offer of complete evacuation, but they were to make it clear that it would take five years to complete the withdrawal of all troops. This offer had been communicated to the Egyptian Delegation, and it was known that they would seek in negotiation to secure agreement to complete the evacuation in a shorter time. The British Delegation had, therefore, reported to the Foreign Secretary that, while there would be no objection to announcing that it was our policy to withdraw from Egypt, the Egyptian Government would be strongly opposed to our stating publicly at this stage that the evacuation would not be completed for five years. The British Delegation themselves deprecated any public reference to the five-year period, since this would cause such consternation in Egypt as to prejudice the chances of negotiating a satisfactory agreement. They therefore suggested that an announcement should be made in the following terms:—

> "It is the considered policy of His Majesty's Government in the United Kingdom to consolidate their alliance with Egypt as one between two equal nations having interests in common. In pursuance of this policy negotiations have begun in an atmosphere of cordiality and goodwill. The Government of the United Kingdom have proposed to withdraw all British naval, military and air forces from Egyptian territory, and to settle in negotiation the stages and date of completion of this withdrawal and the arrangements to be made by the Egyptian Government to make possible mutual assistance in time of war or imminent threat of war in accordance with the alliance."

Sidki Pasha had agreed that an announcement in these terms might be made by the British Delegation as having his full concurrence. The Foreign Secretary had said that, from the point of view of his discussions in Paris, it would be convenient if authority could be given for this announcement to be made that day.

In discussion the view was expressed that we should not be hurried into making a declaration of our intention to evacuate from Egypt, before we had any assurance that the Egyptian Government would agree upon a reasonable period for the completion of the evacuation or would accord the facilities which we desired for bringing British troops back into Egypt on a threat or actual outbreak of war. Dominion Ministers had been anxious that in the course of the negotiations we should secure satisfactory facilities for military bases in time of war. Was it not likely that our negotiating position would be impaired if at the outset we made a public declaration containing an unqualified offer of complete evacuation?

The point was also made that the recent agreement between the Soviet and Persian Governments regarding the exploitation of the oilfields in Northern Persia might be found to threaten the security of our oil concessions in Central Persia which were of vital importance to us. This increased the importance of maintaining our position in the Middle East; and it seemed hazardous to make an unqualified offer of withdrawal from Egypt until we had secured an alternative location for military bases in the Middle East which would safeguard our oil supplies.

On the other side, it was pointed out that the Cabinet had already agreed that it would be impracticable for us to seek to maintain our existing position in Egypt by the use of force. In present circumstances we could only secure military facilities there by agreement with the Egyptian Government. The issue, therefore, resolved into one of tactics—should we secure a more favourable atmosphere in which to negotiate a satisfactory agreement if at the outset we made a public offer of complete evacuation? The British Delegation in Egypt had always advised that such a declaration would create an atmosphere in which it would be easier for them to negotiate a satisfactory agreement, both on the period within which the evacuation should be completed, and also on the defence obligations to be accepted by Egypt; and they had only abandoned the idea of a public declaration because of the Cabinet's earlier insistence that the period of five years should also be mentioned. The concluding phrases of the announcement now proposed would make it clear that we had still to settle in negotiation the stages and the date of completion of the withdrawal and the arrangements to be made by the Egyptian Government to facilitate mutual assistance on a threat or actual outbreak of war.

It was the view of the Cabinet that the balance of advantage lay on the side of making a public announcement in the terms proposed by the British Delegation in Cairo.

The Cabinet:—

(1) Invited the Minister of State to arrange for the British Delegation in Cairo to be authorised to make an immediate public announcement, in the terms set out above, declaring that the United Kingdom Government had offered to withdraw all British troops from Egypt and to settle in negotiation the stages and date of completion of this withdrawal and the arrangements to be made by the Egyptian Government to facilitate mutual assistance on a threat, or actual outbreak, of war.

(2) Took note that the Prime Minister would inform Dominion Ministers at their meeting later that day of the circumstances in which His Majesty's Government had authorised this announcement.

47   FO 141/1082, no 235   24 May 1946

[Anglo–Egyptian negotiations]: minute by Sir W Smart on the role of King Farouk

[On 8 May the British delegation received the Egyptian reply to their memorandum agreeing to withdraw in five years. The Egyptians considered that withdrawal could be completed in twelve months. They believed the treaty should not contain references to the employment of British military experts or technicians by the Egyptian government (although they would employ them where necessary) because the maintenance of the base must not comprise any obligations for the Egyptians other than those foreseen in parallel circumstances between two sovereign and independent states. In these inauspicious circumstances the two delegations began their official talks. Article 5 in the British draft was soon to be a further bone of contention. It read: 'The High Contracting Parties agree that in the event of a war involving either of them, or of imminent menace of war, or of apprehended international emergency, their respective armed forces will take the necessary measures in close co-operation with each other, and that British forces of all arms shall receive all facilities and assistance, including the use of Egyptian ports, roads, railways, airfields and telecommunications, in accordance with the Egyptian system of administration and legislation. The Egyptian government will take all the administrative and legislative measures, including the establishment of martial law and effective censorship, necessary to render these facilities and assistance effective' (FO 371/53295, no 2158, 15 May 1946). By 16 May the FO was aware that the Wafd would not be bound by the results of any negotiations based on the non-realisation of the unity of the Nile valley (the separation of Sudan from Egypt) nor by any military alliance deemed to nullify the effect of British evacuation by compromising Egyptian independence (FO 371/53296, no 2173, Cairo tel 872, 15 May 1946). The FO had also expressed concern about the Egyptian reluctance to include in the treaty any assurances with regard to the maintenance of facilities and installations in the Canal Zone (FO 371/53296, no 2172, FO tel 960, 16 May 1946). On 19 May the British and Egyptians exchanged draft treaties with the British draft containing the substance of the original article 5 split into two articles. Article 5 now stated that the measures taken in close co-operation would be for the purposes of mutual assistance with article 6 listing the facilities and assistance to be granted to the British (FO 371/53297, no 2305). Sir R Campbell described the Egyptian draft as a childish effort (FO 371/53296, no 2204, Cairo tel 904, 19 May 1946). On 22 May Cairo confirmed the Egyptian refusal to make provisions in the treaty for military arrangements and base installations (FO 371/53298, no 2286, Cairo tel 920, 22 May 1946). The COS concluded on 24 May that the talks seemed unlikely to lead to all Britain's military requirements being met (CAB 79/48, COS 82(46)2).]

I cannot help feeling sceptical about King Farouk's attempts to get the Egyptian Delegation to accept the views which he previously expressed to Lord Stansgate and the Ambassador in the sense of the granting of military facilities to us in some form or other. After all we have to remember that this is the régime which His Majesty has himself installed and maintained by force against a majority Party. The present régime is entirely dependent on the goodwill of the King. It is difficult to believe that, if His Majesty really took up a courageous, statesmanlike attitude, he could not induce the Delegation to be more forthcoming. I think that the truth of the matter is that he is trying to make us think that he is a good boy struggling with difficult people, while in reality he is careful not to compromise himself at all in the eyes of the nationalist extremists, whom he has fostered, and is therefore leaving the whole burden on his puppet Government in the strong hope that the latter will be able to get out of us enough to satisfy these extremists. He would then emerge as a one hundred percent nationalist Monarch, for the success would be attributed to him rather than to his puppets.

If the Wafd régime were negotiating with us, we should hold Nahas responsible for the conduct of the negotiations and expect him to manipulate his Delegation and public suitably. That is what he did in 1936. That is the rôle which King Farouk should play when his own régime is in charge. However, I do not imagine that there is much chance that His Majesty will play this rôle.

48   WO 216/658   25 May 1946

[Anglo–Egyptian negotiations]: letter from Lieutenant-General Sir C Allfrey[1] to Field Marshal Lord Alanbrooke on the future course of the negotiations

I thought it might be helpful if I wrote and told you some of the things we are thinking about in connection with the Treaty negotiations.

There is a strong feeling on the Army side here that we are being very skilfully jockeyed from position to position, and that eventually someone or our side must firmly call a halt, and say that we will accede no more. At the very beginning, when discussions took place as to whether we should offer complete evacuation before the negotiations started, we were always led to believe that if we offered complete

---

[1] GOC British troops Egypt and army member of the British delegation representing the C-in-C Middle East Land Forces.

evacuation, then the Egyptians on their side would make everything much easier in the negotiating period, and we thus should get practically everything we wanted by free offer by the Egyptians. The goodwill which was supposed to be produced by our very considerable gesture does not seem to be manifest, and the Egyptian Delegation on their side seem to be very loth to commit themselves to paper in the form of any guarantee to us. We are now told that if we accept a somewhat indefinite Treaty, we shall in fact get all we want by subsequent arrangements between the military staffs of the two countries; but there seems to be no machinery by which we can subsequently put the pressure on if we do not get what we want.

The present situation is that Sidky has produced an avant-projet-conjoint, and has said that he *thinks* that he can get his Delegation to agree to it, but of this we have no guarantee; and it is this avant-projet which Stansgate has sent home to the Foreign Office with Mr. Beckett[2] by air. Article IV in this avant-projet refers to the high contracting parties being involved in an unprovoked war, but does not specifically mention an "apprehended emergency", or some similar phrase. If this is omitted, it is not necessarily implicit that we can make plans for, or not before agression [sic] has actually taken place, and this we think is completely unacceptable. If, on the other hand, an "apprehended emergency" is included, and the Egyptians are sincere in their wish to help us by mutual staff talks subsequent to the Treaty, then it would seem that the subsequent Article V would give us pretty well all we want to ensure that we could carry out our commitments in the event of a threat of war or war out here. My own view is that there is a very reasonable chance of the Egyptians being co-operative after the signing of the Treaty, and I also think that once the Treaty is signed the political temperature will drop, and that as the Egyptians get more frightened with the possibility of Russian agression [sic], so their willingness to co-operate will increase.

It would seem, therefore, that there are three courses open to us:—

Course A
To say that the present conditions are unsatisfactory as they do not give us sufficient guarantee, and that we will drop negotiations and revert to the 1936 Treaty. (Presuming this is legally possible).

If we do this there would undoubtedly be disorders, and probably serious ones. But the possibility of the loss of a few lives may have to be accepted sometime or other, and I personally think that the bogey of disorders is being used to the full by the Egyptians in order to blackmail us. As to what happens after we have taken up this stand it is difficult to forecast, but we must not do it now or later unless our Government is prepared to stand by their decision if arraigned in front of UNO, with all its consequences. We should certainly forfeit good-will by adopting this course.

Course B
To insist that the "apprehended emergency" is added to Article IV of Sidky's avant-projet, and to sign a thin Treaty on this basis.

If we do this, we shall retain good-will, and no doubt great pressure will be brought to bear on us to give a time-limit by which our total evacuation will be

---

[2] W E Beckett, legal adviser, FO; member of the treaty delegation.

complete. We are anxious to clear out of the big cities, Treaty or no Treaty, and are perfectly prepared to have this period defined; and I think it would be reasonable also to define a subsequent period in which we should evacuate combatant troops not required for the parts of the base still in Egypt. But we *must* not be jockeyed into giving a final date of shorter duration than five years hence, by which evacuation will be complete.

If we adopt this course, we can then get down to it with the military staffs, and in the course of the next year we can watch the political temperature and the international situation, and can be certain whether or not the Egyptians are going to co-operate sincerely. If at the end we find that the military agreement means little or nothing, then we must be prepared to say that they have broken the Treaty, that we therefore propose to tear it up, and that we are not going to move any of our installations from Egypt at all. It will be seen that by adopting this course, which is a gamble, we do in fact leave ourselves some form of cover should things go wrong, but this is only so provided that it is agreed that if necessary the Government are prepared to be firm a year hence. When this situation arises, it would be for decision at that time whether we hold ourselves here by force, or whether we then go to Course C below.

Course C
To come right into the open now with the Egyptians, and tell them that without guarantees the scheme is unacceptable, and that we propose to evacuate totally, in our own time, and to establish a base elsewhere which we are certain will function in war.

If we did this we should have a Treaty of friendship with the Egyptians, but definitely no Treaty of mutual assistance, as we should point out that this would be impossible. It would be extremely expensive, I presume, but it would at least mean that for the defence of a vital part of the Empire we were not depending on promises without guarantees. It might be that if we faced the Egyptians with this proposition they would then lose their nerve, and give us the guarantees that we require. In their present frame of mind and inconceivable conceit, my own view is that they would not give us these guarantees.

Conclusion
Having discussed the matter locally, you will see that we have recommended to the Chiefs of Staff the adoption of Course B.

P.S. Under present agreement there will be no guarantee that the Egyptians will carry out their side of the contract *after* we go – nor do I think there can be.

49   CAB 131/1, DO 17(46)1   27 May 1946
'Strategic requirements in the Middle East': Cabinet Defence Committee minutes on the problems in Egypt, Palestine and Cyrenaica

The Committee had before them a memorandum by the Chiefs of Staff on our strategic requirements in the Middle East.

The Chiefs of Staff introducing the paper stated that the report was an attempt to show the relationship between the problems at present under separate negotiations, namely, those in Egypt, Palestine, and Cyrenaica, and brought out the position not previously examined of the relationship of Cyrenaica to our Middle East Strategy. Whilst this area was chiefly important for air and naval bases the Army would only locate there certain administrative and internal security units.

The *Prime Minister* said present conditions made it difficult to assess the degree of certainty of obtaining the minimum military requirements. Egypt was a foreign state and we would have to respect her sovereignty in any negotiations for military rights. The future of Cyrenaica was doubtful and the uncertainty [sic] internal problem of Palestine emphasised the insecurity of developing that country as a main base. There were several points which he would wish to clear later in discussion, in particular the necessity for locating the main military Headquarters as far forward as Palestine, but before discussing the Chiefs of Staff report in detail he requested the Secretary of State for Foreign Affairs to inform the Committee of recent discussions with the American Ambassador in this country on the Middle East situation.

Mr. Bevin then gave the Committee the gist of his discussions with the United States Ambassador, the record of which is contained in the Secretary's Standard File.

Mr. Bevin then gave his views on the three Middle East States under discussion.

Egypt

Since the 1936 Anglo–Egyptian Treaty we had neglected to fulfil our obligations under the terms of this Treaty. There appeared to have been no intention in the past to move Service Headquarters Installations and forces from the Cairo Area into the Canal Zone. Moreover, some administrative functions (such as the Records Office) had been added to the Headquarters Organisation for which from his information, there appeared to be no necessity, as such administration could have been effected from the United Kingdom. This decentralization had increased the size of our occupation forces and emphasised our presence in the Capital of Egypt. Our failure to fulfil our obligations under the Terms of the 1936 Treaty would lose a measure of sympathy in the United States and would provide an awkward case to defend if the matter was referred to the Security Council. For this reason it was essential that our forces should begin evacuation of Cairo to the Canal Zone at once irrespective of the trend of our negotiations in Egypt.

On the subject of the necessity for a Headquarters to be located in peace in either Egypt or Palestine, he was not convinced that such a Headquarters could not be situated at some distance from the Middle East, e.g. in Kenya, or the Sudan, and our present communications redesigned to serve a new Reserve Area, south of Egypt. If this could be done the Canal Zone could then be regarded as a forward base and the negotiations pressed to obtain the necessary facilities in the Middle East Area. He felt confident that if this policy was adopted we should be able to carry both the United States and Dominions opinion in support of our requirements. For the present it was not his intention to take further action regarding the negotiations for the revision of the Treaty until he was aware of the outcome of the Arab rulers Conference. The results of this meeting should be available about 28th May by which time our policy towards the negotiations should be crystallised. In the meantime he proposed that Lord Stansgate as Head of the British Delegation should be recalled to London for consultation.

Cyrenaica

It was not at present possible to assess the outcome of the Foreign Minister's discussions on 15th June, concerning the future status of Cyrenaica. Originally the United States had proposed that Libya should be placed under the United Nations Trusteeship. At the recent Foreign Ministers' Conference the United Kingdom had claimed trusteeship for Cyrenaica, only after the proposal had been tabled for the Italian Colonies to be returned to Italy under United Nations Organisation supervision. The Americans were apprehensive lest our claim should be pressed as Russia might use this claim as a bargaining point to obtain similar facilities in the Dodecanese. Nevertheless it would be valuable if the Chiefs of Staff could prepare an assessment of our military requirements in Cyrenaica on the assumptions that we either totally evacuated Egypt and retained no military rights of entry, or that we obtained the military facilities for which we were now negotiating.

Palestine

The future of Palestine was uncertain. Before proceeding with the intended negotiations with the Americans on the next step regarding the fulfillment [sic] of the Anglo–American Commission's report on Palestine, he wished to ascertain the legal position, on the assumption that Palestine, Cyrenaica and the Sudan were allotted to our trusteeship under the United Nations Organisation of our stationing armed forces in those countries without designating them as strategic areas. At present he was under the impression that if any area was designated a Strategic Area the supervision under the aegis of the Security Council would introduce foreign influences.

The *Prime Minister* asked on what grounds the Chiefs of Staff considered it necessary to locate the main Service Headquarters as far forward as the Canal Zone or Palestine. If the Middle East Area was to be the vital point in any future war he would have thought that the Headquarters should have properly been placed further away from the main centre of conflict. Moreover to locate a large Service Headquarters in this area was to advertise our intentions and to promote suspicions of our reasons for maintaining military facilites [sic] and forces in the Middle East.

The *Chiefs of Staff* said that a central Headquarters had been found essential in the last war and it would be essential in any future war in order to control a major conflict. Such a Headquarters must in peace be located as near as possible to the centre of communications. The Middle East Communication Centre was the focus, not only for the Middle East but for the whole Empire Communication System. The necessity for a Headquarters in peacetime was based both on this and for providing a centre in which there could be a rapid change from peace to wartime control. Naturally the peacetime Headquarters would be a fraction of the size of a War Control Centre but the development in modern methods of war necessitate our peacetime facilities being available for an immediate switch to a wartime basis.

Egypt was the Middle East focus for all communications and political activities. Thus in war the regional Headquarters should be located in Egypt, but if this proved impossible in peacetime another location as near as possible to Egypt would have to be selected. In this connection a Headquarters located far to the South of Egypt would find it impossible to conduct naval operations in the Mediterranean.

Orders had already been despatched to the Middle East Commanders-in-Chief to prepare plans for the transfer of the Service Headquarters from Cairo to the Canal Zone.

In connection with the reduction of our forces, in Egypt considerable progress had been made since June 1945. On this latter date there had been in Cairo 3 Brigades together with 71,000 administrative troops, this had been reduced to 1 battalion, plus 38,000 administrative troops. The strength of G.H.Q. Middle East had been reduced by November 1945 to 2,400, was now 1,900 and pressure was still being exerted to reduce this complement even further. Administrative installations had been reduced in Cairo by 25% of the original figures for June, 1945 and in Alexandria by 75%.

Mr. Dalton said he was again impressed with the possibilities of using Kenya and East Africa as the main base for our reserves in the Middle East. He was greatly concerned at the adverse sterling balance existing in Egypt and the implications that administrative forces were still being maintained in Egypt when they could be located elsewhere. Unless expenditure was greatly reduced in the future we should be in the impossible position of borrowing money from the Egyptians in order to maintain our forces in Egypt. He hoped partially to offset the present adverse sterling balance by negotiating financial adjustments by the sale of military stores and equipment to the Egyptians which we should leave in that country after our evacuation. The Treasury would wish to be closely associated with the Service Ministries with any negotiations to this end.

Lieutenant-General Simpson said although military negotiations had not yet reached the stage of the disposal of stores and equipment he would certainly ensure that the Treasury were informed and consulted on all matters affecting such disposal.

Mr. Strachey[1] suggested that the possibility of Russia over-running the Middle East, would turn largely on the degree of interest evinced by the United States in the Middle East which in turn would depend on our attitude towards Egypt and Palestine. The deterrent to any pre-conceived Russian aggression in this area, would be the considerations of meeting United States and United Kingdom solidarity and not the numbers of troops or facilities which we maintained in the Middle East.

Mr. Bevin said the security of our Middle East oil resources had not been considered in detail in the report. This was one of our most important strategic interests and would be vital to us in time of war. Moreover the security of the United States oil interests would also largely determine the assistance that we might expect to obtain from the United States.

Lieutenant-General Simpson said that plans for the defence of our oil resources had been prepared in war but we did not possess in peace sufficient troops or facilities in the areas concerned to guarantee the security of the oil fields in Persia and Iraq in the event of a large scale attack. Present plans dealt only with the security of the oil fields against sabotage attempts.

Lieutenant-General Roberts[2] in reply to a question from the Prime Minister said that the Record Office in the Middle East had been established to deal with the rapid

---

[1] John Strachey, parliamentary under-secretary of state for air.
[2] Lieutenant-General O L Roberts, War Office.

and changing status of units due to the fluid conditions in war. With the advent of peace these conditions had become even more fluid because of changes caused by demobilisation, disbandment and the rundown of units. The organisation dealt with the reinforcement, release, statistics and information connected with each individual in the Middle East Area. The strength of the Record Office was a little over 1,000 officers and men and was calculated on a scale of one clerk for every 450 officers, one clerk for 600 other ranks and one clerk for every 1,000 Prisoners of War in the Middle East Command. If this organisation was transferred to any great distance away from the Middle East Headquarters the efficiency of the demobilisation and reinforcement organisation would be greatly jeopardised. The Record Office could move away from Cairo to the Canal Zone, but this would depend on accommodation. The experience of war had shown that the nearer it was to the main Service Headquarters the more efficiently would the administration of 400,000 personnel in the Middle East function. The Record Office was not duplicated in the United Kingdom. If it was transferred to the United Kingdom it would entail establishing smaller advance units wherever the Services were located throughout the Middle East and would, taken as a whole, require greater manpower to operate. As the strength of the Services ran down the strength of the Record Office would proportionately decrease.

Mr. Hall[3] said he had made preliminary investigations into the implications that would arise on the stationing of armed forces in Palestine should we not wish to designate the country as a strategic area. The difference between Trusteeship and Strategic Trusteeship lay in the type of supervision effected by the United Nations Organisation. Under the latter contingency supervision was exercised by the Security Council and might introduce those States who could claim to be directly concerned and who could thus claim a part responsibility in the Trusteeship. He agreed that the whole matter needed careful examination and suggested that the Colonial Office should undertake this examination in consultation with the Foreign Office obtaining such military guidance as necessary from the Chiefs of Staff Committee.

Mr. Bevin suggested that the Dominions should be consulted before decisions were taken on our strategic requirements in the Middle East. Their agreement to whatever policy was adopted would be of material benefit to defending, if the need arose, our Middle East policy before the United Nations Organisation.

The Prime Minister, summing up the discussion, said it was apparent that it would not be possible for the Defence Committee to endorse the Chiefs of Staff report under discussion. It was clear that our whole position in the Middle East required re-examination to determine our exact strategic requirements in the Middle East with particular reference to what in the Middle East would it be essential for us to defend in a possible future war, to determine what would be our wartime requirements to defend these essentials and what would be our peacetime minimum military requirements on which we could expand in war and from which we could have access to those facilities required in war.

There was general agreement with this view.

---

[3] George Hall, secretary of state for the colonies.

50   CAB 128/5, CM 52(46)1   27 May 1946
'Egypt': Cabinet conclusions on the suspension of negotiations

The Cabinet were informed that the Defence Committee had now directed the Chiefs of Staff to expedite the completion of plans for the removal of British Headquarters staff from Cairo.

The Foreign Secretary said that a difficult stage had been reached in the negotiations for the revision of the Anglo–Egyptian Treaty. He had thought it expedient to ask the United States Government to impress upon the Egyptians the importance of an early and satisfactory settlement of these issues; and he hoped that the United States representative in Cairo would shortly be instructed to make representations in this sense both to the King of Egypt and to Sidki Pasha. Meanwhile, the situation was to be debated in the Egyptian Parliament; and he also understood that at their forthcoming meeting the representatives of the Arab States intended to discuss, not only the report of the Anglo–American Committee on Palestine, but also the general strategic position in the Middle East. In these circumstances, it seemed expedient that the negotiations in Cairo should be suspended for a time; and the Prime Minister therefore proposed to recall the Secretary of State for Air for consultations in London later in the week.

51   FO 141/1216, no 1   31 May 1946
[Economic and social reform in Egypt]: letter from Sir R Campbell to R G Howe on likely Egyptian reaction to British aid

Please refer to Secretary of State's remarks in his speech on Egypt on May 24th on British assistance for Egypt in the economic and social sphere.

2.   I do not think we should bank too much on this wish on the part of H.M.G. being particularly pleasing to the Egyptians. I have for some time been doubtful on the point, in particular in connection with the Middle East Office and have been coming to the conclusion that if we wish for success in the policy of which that office is the instrument we should be very careful about the way we use it and present it. I may have further ideas to put forward on this later on. In general what I have been thinking is roughly as follows:—

3.   Social betterment in Egypt is likely to appear to the over-sensitive Egyptians as being none of our business. There is likely to be a feeling that if they want our assistance (and I am sure they do) they will ask for it, but that a unilateral statement and practical demonstration on our part that we wish and intend to help in this field and that it is an act of policy arising from our political and strategic interest in Egypt and the Middle East, are a proof of condescension and of a propensity for looking on Egypt and other Middle Eastern countries as pawns in our imperial policy. There have already been silly statements connected with the Treaty negotiations that Egypt will find evacuation of our troops has only meant the substitution for military domination of domination in other fields e.g. the economic field.

4.   These being the lines on which my thoughts had been moving I at once felt a doubt about the reception here of the passage in Mr. Bevin's speech that I have referred to. Sidky Pasha's remarks in his speech in the Senate on May 27th therefore

did not particularly surprise me. I read them as intended to show that this matter is one for the Egyptian Government to deal with itself and as a gentle reminder that Mr. Bevin's declared intentions have for Egyptians a slight flavour of interference. (Sidky's remarks may also of course have been influenced by the desire to refute any suggestion that the present Egyptian Government are not fully alive to the necessity for social and economic reforms and are not taking them in hand—internally Sidky is making rather a point of this—but the other motive springing from feelings of national dignity and independence was, I am sure, present also). Since writing the foregoing I hear that Kamel Selim[1] has in fact admitted to Lord Stansgate that Sidky's remarks were intended as a retort courteous to Mr. Bevin, though possibly based on an unskillful Arabic translation of the Secretary of State's remarks.

5.   I think the thing is largely a question of presentation and of setting about our work very quietly; and this letter is only intended to suggest that care in presentation and method is desirable. Things of course look differently from different ends of the line.

6.   While on this question it might be worth mentioning another point. In general the people who profess the Mohamedan religion set less store by questions of material well-being than we are inclined to do and they tend to prefer to be content with a mere subsistence level, if anything better can only be got at the price of something they do not relish. If this is so, we must not expect to reap much gratitude for any insistence on improving the material lot of Mohamedan populations. This perhaps applies more to the tillers of the soil than to the industrial workers. But the former are in the great majority here. The case might of course be different in this respect if we could again have a Cromer to carry out reforms and put our assistance into practice. Then a new Cromerian legend might be created amongst the fellaheen and gratitude redound to us. But for this to be possible our position vis-à-vis of Egypt would have to be very different from what it has become, and the new Cromer would have to occupy in Egypt a position of no less preeminent authority than that of his proptype [sic]. As it is, even if we were to have success in insisting on the Egyptians improving the lot of the fellah, with our help, any results of our insistence would be too remote for the fellah to attribute these to us.

7.   I think the Secretary of State should be aware of the foregoing.

8.   I am sending a copy of this letter to Cornwallis.

---

[1] Kamel Selim, secretary general of the Egyptian Council of Ministers and secretary general to the Egyptian treaty delegation.

52   CAB 129/10, CP(46)219   5 June 1946
'Revision of Anglo–Egyptian treaty': Cabinet memorandum by Mr Bevin. *Annexes*

Since my last report to the Cabinet on the 27th May[1] I have had the opportunity of personal consultation with Lord Stansgate in regard to the position which has been

---

[1] See 50.

reached in the Anglo–Egyptian negotiations. This position is, briefly, that the Egyptian Delegation have refused (and I am assured that the refusal is final) to embody in a new treaty, or in any published treaty instrument, (a) clauses similar to those of the 1936 treaty which promised this country, in the case of war or international emergency, all facilities which Egypt could offer, "including the use of ports, aerodromes and means of communication" and the right, after consultation, to send in troops, (b) certain new provisions which we desired about the maintenance of installations and facilities in peace-time. The attitude of the Egyptian Delegation is, however, that we shall obtain the substance of what we require through the medium of staff conversations and agreements between the military authorities of the two countries. Such agreements would not, however, be published and they would not be binding on the Egyptian State, *i.e.*, a future Government could refuse to implement them.

2.   At first it appears that we have reached a complete deadlock, and that the Egyptians are offering us no real possibility of filling the vacuum which I have pledged His Majesty's Government not to allow after the withdrawal of our troops. It has, however, been represented to me that in actual practice the implementation of any defence scheme maintained in peace-time on Egyptian territory and by Egyptian personnel depends on the goodwill of the Egyptian Government and the Egyptian people, and that this holds good *whatever* provisions may, or may not, figure in our treaty arrangements, published or unpublished. Thus, even if the provisions of the 1936 treaty were textually reproduced in the new treaty, an unfriendly Egyptian Government could, in an emergency, sabotage them without great difficulty. For instance, even under the 1936 treaty, His Majesty's Government were not the sole judges of the existence of an emergency. There was to be consultation as provided for in the agreed minute which forms part of the treaty. It would be open, therefore, to a hostile Egyptian Government to refuse to admit that an emergency had come into existence. Contrariwise, a friendly Government might give us (as in 1940–44) far more extensive facilities than were ever defined in writing. In any event it is useless to have facilities for the re-entry of troops if there are no adequate installations available for them, and there was nothing in the 1936 treaty to provide for this. From a practical point of view the maintenance of installations, &c., is more important than a treaty right of re-entry after consultation. The only method by which we can secure the maintenance of these installations is through arrangements between the two military staffs carried out by a friendly Egyptian Government.

3.   This being so, I have endeavoured so to readapt certain provisions of a new draft treaty, to which Sidky Pasha *personally* (though so far not the Egyptian Delegation) has given his assent, as to replace, in a manner acceptable to Egyptian opinion, the (in Egyptian eyes) inadmissible provisions of the 1936 treaty. The result is contained in articles 4, 5 and 6 of the annexed draft treaty (Annex I)[2] which are intended to provide, through the mechanism of arrangements between the two staffs, for the necessary action in time of emergency including the maintenance of the installations and facilities required for use in an emergency. My colleagues will observe that I have adopted the device of a Joint Defence Board (on the analogy of the United States–Canada Defence Board formed in 1940), the function of which will be

---

[2] Annex I is not printed. For the earlier British drafts of article 5, see 47; for a summary of the revised British draft and the Egyptian proposals for article 5, see 57.

"to keep under review the international situation and to consult with a view to advising and recommending appropriate action to the two Governments upon all events which may threaten the security" of the Middle East or the vital interests of the two countries, and thus, in fact if not in name, plan the facilities, &c., granted to us in war or emergency by the old treaty. I would refer my colleagues in this connexion to Sir R. Campbell's telegram No. 1009, a copy of which is annexed (Annex III) which indicates that support for the idea of a Joint Board will be forthcoming from the King of Egypt. The evacuation protocol (Annex II—see Articles III and IV) provides for the co-ordination of the evacuation with the plans for the future drawn up by the British and Egyptian military staffs. This is my proposal for filling the vacuum.

4.   In my view, it is unnecessary to insist that the military staff arrangements which are foreseen by these three articles (notably Article 6) should be complete before the treaty is signed. The treaty only becomes operative on ratification, and inevitably an interval of at least three months must elapse between signature and ratification. The discussions between the two military staffs can continue in this interval, and progress can be assessed. Consequently we shall, if necessary, have in connexion with the ratification of the treaty, a further opportunity of using influence with the Egyptian Government to carry out the scheme by saying that we are unable to ratify unless the Egyptians show that they are in fact ready to do so.

5.   After ratification, we should, as I have already said, still be dependent on the loyal fulfilment by Egypt of her obligations under the proposed treaty. This would have been just as much the case if the treaty had contained an elaborate military convention. In both cases it would be open to us, if Egypt is not carrying out her obligations, either (a) to change our military plans and arrange for our bases to be elsewhere, *e.g.*, Cyrenaica, or (b) if we thought fit, express our disquietude to the Security Council about the unsatisfactory position of the Middle East as regards defence and try and arrange for the Security Council to make alternative demands on Egypt by way of a security agreement under Article 43 of the Charter. In any case, we should be on far better ground in going to the Security Council as suggested after Egypt had failed to fulfil her obligations under a new treaty which she has freely accepted after the Charter had come into force than we would be if we went to the Security Council *now* on the ground that Egypt had failed to conclude a new Treaty of Alliance, on terms which we considered suitable, namely a treaty containing elaborate written terms because we could not believe in Egypt's good faith.

6.   For the rest I would point out that the proposed treaty only abrogates the corresponding articles of the 1936 treaty, which are appended in Annex I, and leaves the Sudan article untouched, as the Egyptians have stated that they wish to deal with the Sudan in a separate protocol, a course which is desirable from our point of view also. It is of course understood that the financial implications of the proposed treaty arrangements (which are under examination in Cairo) will require further consideration. Some idea of the problems arising in this connexion is given in the note which appears in the draft evacuation protocol as Article IV. But I would make it clear that we have never had to incur expenditure in regard to the provision of accommodation for our forces which, but for the war, we should have incurred under the 1936 treaty. If we regard Egypt as a vital Imperial connexion, we must be prepared now to pay for installations, communications and other facilities. Our negotiators must be empowered to negotiate in the last resort a

generous financial settlement, though naturally they would secure the best financial terms they can.

7.   If the Cabinet approve. I would authorise His Majesty's Ambassador in Cairo to explain to Sidky Pasha our proposals on the lines of paragraph 3 above and enquire whether it is worth while for Lord Stansgate to return to Cairo to continue the negotiations on that basis, which represents a very great concession to the point of view expressed by the Egyptian Delegation.

Annex II to 52: draft protocol relating to the withdrawal of the British forces from Egypt

The Government of the United Kingdom of Great Britain and Northern Ireland and the Egyptian Government:

Having regard to abrogation by the Treaty of Mutual Assistance signed this day of the Treaty signed in London on the 26th August, 1936, which provided for the stationing in Egyptian territory of certain British forces: and

Desiring to settle by agreement the arrangements for the withdrawal from Egypt of the British forces which are at present there and for the removal, or disposal, of the large installations, stores of material and equipment, and communications facilities, which those forces have made or accumulated in Egypt as a result of the war 1939–45: and

Further considering that these arrangements should be such as to provide that the withdrawal of the forces should take place as soon as possible, and to secure that both this withdrawal and the removal and disposal of the material, equipment and facilities should be co-ordinated with the arrangements agreed between the competent military authorities of the two Governments in accordance with Article 6 of the Treaty of Mutual Assistance signed this day having in view the continued security of the Middle East, including all territories adjacent to Egypt:

Have agreed as follows:—

Article I

(i) Not later than .... from the date of the entry into force of the Treaty of Mutual Assistance signed this day:—

(a) All British forces shall be withdrawn from the cities of Cairo and Alexandria, and from the Nile Delta;
(b) the total number of British forces in Egypt shall be reduced and certain field formations of the Army and certain operational and training units of the R.A.F. shall be withdrawn from Egypt;
(c) all Naval forces shall be withdrawn from Egypt except a small number of personnel, directly concerned with the withdrawal of the military and air forces referred to in Article I of the Protocol.

Article II

Not later than .... from the date of entry into force of the Treaty of Mutual Assistance signed this day, all combatant troops of the Army and all operational and training units of the R.A.F. shall be withdrawn from Egypt and no British military, air force or naval personnel will be retained in Egypt other than those required during the period covered by Article III for the operation and removal of the installations, stores of material and equipment and communication facilities made or accumulated in Egypt by the British forces during their presence in Egypt.

Article III

The installations, stores of material and equipment and the communication facilities made or accumulated by the British forces in Egypt shall be removed or disposed of, or be placed at the disposal of the Egyptian forces, in accordance with plans which shall be drawn up and agreed by the Staffs of the British and Egyptian forces. These plans shall be such as to co-ordinate, in the interest of the continued security of the Middle East including all territories adjacent to Egypt, the removal and disposal of the installations, stores of material and equipment and communication facilities with the arrangements agreed between the competent military authorities of the two Governments in accordance with Article 6 of the Treaty of Mutual Assistance signed this day. The British naval, military or air force personnel retained under Article II of this Protocol, in connexion with the installations, stores and facilities to be removed or disposed of, or placed at the disposal of the Egyptian forces, shall be withdrawn from Egypt as each installation, store and facility is removed or disposed of in accordance with this plan.

Article IV

Note

[Article III above provides for the removal or disposal of installations, stores and material and of communication facilities in accordance with plans to be drawn up and agreed between the British and Egyptian military staffs. The idea is that these plans should provide:—

(1) for certain installations to be maintained in Egypt by the Egyptians for joint use in time of emergency. Some of the installations to be so maintained exist now and others have to be constructed. We should be willing to construct these and to pay a generous share of the cost.

(2) that certain stores of material and equipment shall be guarded in Egypt by the Egyptians for use by the British forces if, in time of emergency, they return to Egypt. These stores of material and equipment to remain the property of His Majesty's Government and the Egyptians to employ some British technical personnel as their servants for the purpose of helping the Egyptians to look after them and also of teaching the Egyptians.

(3) that the Egyptians should purchase some material and equipment and possibly some installations of ours for the exclusive use of their own forces.

It will consequently be necessary to have a financial provision either here or in some annexed letter dealing with the payment by the Egyptians for the stores and equipment and installations which they purchase for their own use. Another question is what the Egyptians should pay for installations left in Egypt for joint use.

Everything which the British forces leave in Egypt will be handed over to the Egyptian Government either for their sole use or for maintenance for joint use or for guarding for British use according to the category in which they fall.

It will be seen that nearly all these detailed arrangements must be left to be settled by the plans of the two military staffs and they cannot appear either in the Treaty or in the Evacuation Protocol. It may be possible, however, to insert something here about handing over to the Egyptian Government installations, &c., which are left.]

Article V

The provisions of the convention relating to Immunities and Privileges signed on the 26th August, 1936, will continue to apply to the British forces until their withdrawal is complete in accordance with the provisions of the present Protocol.

Article VI

This Protocol shall be ratified and the instruments of ratification exchanged at the same time as those relating to the Treaty of Mutual Assistance signed this day.

This Protocol shall be regarded as an integral part of the Treaty of Mutual Assistance. In witness whereof:

Annex III to 52: inward telegram no 1007 from Sir R Campbell to Mr Bevin, 2 June 1946

Your telegram No. 782 instructed us to try to secure some benefits of the Joint Defence Board on the lines of the United States–Canadian arrangement. Egyptian negotiators rejected this out of a ludicrous fear engendered by the misapprehension of the words "on a Ministerial level" fear which prevented them from reading the next words saying the Board would "meet from time to time." This ridiculous incident is a revealing example of the depth of morbidness to which the Egyptians have been plunged by their state of raw-nerved sensibility—a state of which we have perforce to take account as a genuine factor in the situation.

Misapprehension has, however, been removed by our explanation and when we mentioned it recently to King Farouk he seemed to like the idea of a Joint Board. At our last audience His Majesty spontaneously referred to it as something which might meet the difficulty over action in an emergency (and facilities) and recommended that we should study its possibilities. He did not think that the Egyptian delegation ought to feel unable to accept something on these lines. He suggested a mention of it in the treaty provisions themselves.

Since then Hassan Youssef Bey, in private conversation with a member of the Embassy staff, has twice referred to the United States–Canadian Board. The Minister for Foreign Affairs showed considerable interest in the arrangement between Canada and the United States concerning Alaska highway when Lord Stansgate mentioned it to him on the 1st June.

2. Though doubtless His Majesty's Government suggested a Joint Board chiefly as a piece of mechanism to give staff contacts proposed by Egyptians an elementary concreteness and permanency, I wonder whether we could not now extend scope of suggestion and use it in conjunction with Article 5 of *avant-projet* to get round present impasse and at the same time actually to secure our requirements.

3. It seems possible that a Joint Board system if mentioned in Article 5 as a means of filling out provision of that article might both ensure for us the necessary facilities and even render possible requisite action in emergency period. This might be more possible if it were combined with understanding about disposition of Egyptian and British forces in case of Egyptian military action in limitrophe countries (Foreign Office telegram No. 1077).

4.   Joint Board would then constitute a method both of consultation and of action.

5.   Question of what happens in case of disagreement on the Board remains.

Presumably, disagreements would go to heads of the two Governments. (King Farouk toyed with the idea that heads of the Board might be the two heads of State as being Commanders-in-Chief of forces so that the matter might be dealt with on military as distinct from political basis. But this is doubtless impossible constitutionally.)

If there was [? dispute] at this level could His Majesty's Government contemplate reference to an umpire satisfactory to both parties?

If so, would the President of the United States, King Ibn Saud or Arab League be expedient?

6.   Sidki Pasha has said he thinks he could get the Egyptian Delegation to accept Article 5 of *avant-projet*.

King Farouk has said the same and acting head of Royal Cabinet has said that His Majesty would be able and ready to force acceptance of Article 5 in conjunction with a Joint Board system to which reference would be made on that account. Joint Board would be in substitution for a military convention.

7.   His Majesty would, of course, be encouraged and helped in such action if we gave definite *and really early* dates for withdrawal of H.Q. and all troops from the cities and of combatant troops from the delta and the rest of Egypt. I am sure that we should in any case determine to overcome all practical and financial difficulties in the way of rapid withdrawal from the cities, &c., and early communication of dates to the Egyptian Government.

8.   I believe we must face the fact that the Egyptians will not accept as part of treaty or close tie up with it a military convention or similar document of detailed and comprehensive character we put forward.

9.   I do not know how far ideas put forward above are acceptable as I am still without text of United States-Canadian Joint Defence Board arrangement or any comments upon it. I hope we may be sent early information since in case there is anything in the idea it seems a pity not to be able to utilise interest shown on Egyptian side.

10.   Above is subject to concurrence of Lord Stansgate, to whom it may be useful as bringing together the ideas we have discussed.

53   CAB 128/5, CM 57(46)1   6 June 1946
'Anglo–Egyptian negotiations': Cabinet conclusions on the new draft treaty

The Cabinet considered a memorandum by the Foreign Secretary (C.P. (46) 219)[1] on the negotiations for a revision of the Anglo–Egyptian Treaty.

The Foreign Secretary said that this memorandum had been prepared after discussion with the Secretary of State for Air and his advisers who had returned from Cairo. It was clear that the Egyptian Delegation would not agree to embody in a new

---

[1] See 52.

Treaty clauses giving us the right on a threat, or actual outbreak, of war to send troops into the country or to have military facilities of the type given by the 1936 Treaty. Nor would they be ready to include the alternative provisions which we desired regarding the maintenance of installations and facilities in time of peace. Their attitude was that we could obtain the substance of our requirements through the medium of staff conversations and agreements between the military authorities. It was now for the Cabinet to consider whether or not we should be prepared to accept something on these lines. He realised the dangers of acceptance. At the same time, he felt that in practice the implementation of any defence scheme short of the peacetime occupation of the country by our forces (which we had agreed must come to an end) was dependent on Egyptian goodwill. He had therefore attempted, in Articles 4, 5 and 6 of the draft Treaty annexed to his memorandum, to provide for consultation on defence matters through the medium of a Joint Defence Board on the analogy of the United States-Canada Defence Board. A protocol would be attached to the Treaty providing for the terms of the evacuation and Articles III and IV of the draft of this protocol, which was also attached to his memorandum, provided for the evacuation to be co-ordinated with the plans for the future to be drawn up by the military Staffs.

The *Foreign Secretary* said that his draft Treaty was an adaptation of an earlier draft to which Sidky Pasha had personally agreed, and he thought that the proposal now introduced for a Joint Defence Board might also appeal to the Egyptians. While the first reaction of the delegation had been unfavourable, the King had been attracted by it. On the one hand it would carry with it no implication of inferiority and, on the other hand, it would give Egypt an assurance regarding her own defence.

In drafting these Articles he had had it in mind that Egypt might herself be associated under the Covenant of the Arab League with other Arab States in a regional security organisation and that our association with her in a Joint Defence Board might open the way to association with that regional organisation. He had also had it in mind that agreement on these lines might form a useful precedent in the negotiation of a Treaty with India.

The *Secretary of State for Air* said that, having discussed matters fully with every member of the Egyptian delegation, with the King and with many prominent Egyptians, he had no doubt whatsoever that the Egyptians were unanimously of the opinion that the new Treaty could not include provisions which would appear to place Egypt in a position of inferiority. They were, however, perfectly ready to consider any proposal for a Treaty between equals.

The *Secretary of State* pointed out that the 1936 Treaty only entitled us to keep forces in Egypt for the defence of the Canal. During the war we had enjoyed facilities far in excess of these and we still maintained in the country a large headquarters organisation and air bases for long-range attack. He understood that we now had some 200,000 troops[2] in the country, in addition to 100,000 prisoners of war. We could not pretend that the existing Treaty entitled us to all the facilities we now enjoyed and we could not expect to obtain recognition of them in the present negotiations. The only argument we could use to persuade the Egyptians to cede them to us in the Treaty was that we enjoyed them at the moment and would not willingly give them up. The Cabinet must realise that the alternative to a Treaty on

---

[2] See 55.

the lines now proposed would be an Egypt united in hostility to us and supported by the Arab world.

The very large number of British troops at present stationed in the centre of Cairo and Alexandria was, understandably, a constant irritant to the Egyptian public; and it was of the greatest importance that, without waiting for the result of the negotiations, as many as possible of these troops should be moved as soon as possible either out of the country or to some place where they would be less conspicuous. It should be possible in a matter of a few weeks to hand back to the Egyptians buildings in the centre of Cairo at present occupied by us, for instance, the Citadel, and the more than [sic] could be made of any such gesture the better.

The Chief of the Imperial General Staff said that the Chiefs of Staff had not yet had time to consider the Foreign Secretary's draft as fully as they would wish. When the proposal had been made that we should agree to evacuate Egypt, the Chiefs of Staff had understood that we had hoped to obtain complete freedom to return in an apprehended emergency. It now appeared, however, that we were not to obtain even this. He felt that we had embarked on a slippery slope of concessions. Our first concession, designed to secure the goodwill of the Egyptian negotiators, had not been successful. It was now suggested that we should make a second. Was there any assurance that it would be successful either? He could not but remember the analogy of the Irish ports.

In his view, the proposals for a Joint Defence Board gave us no firm assurance. The Board could only "advise and recommend" action to the two Governments. It might well be that the advice of the Egyptian members of the Board would carry little weight with their Government. Moreover, any agreements made would not be published, and there would be nothing to prevent a future Government from refusing to implement them.

Finally, he emphasised that in the conditions of modern war it was more than ever important for defence purposes to be ready with our defence preparations before the outbreak of war. Article 5 of the draft Treaty gave us no guarantee that those essential preparations could be made.

The discussion which followed turned mainly on the question whether it would be practicable to persuade the Egyptian Government to accept Treaty provisions which laid on them specific obligations to give us military facilities on a threat, or actual outbreak, of war. There was general agreement that it would be advantageous if specific provisions on these lines could be included in the Treaty. Ministers felt, however, that the question now at issue was, not what we should like to see included in the Treaty, but what we could persuade the Egyptian Government to accept. And all concerned in the negotiations at Cairo were satisfied that there was no practical possibility of persuading the Egyptian Government to accept a Treaty containing provisions on the lines of Article 7 of the Treaty of 1936. There was indeed good reason why the Egyptian Government, from their point of view, should be unwilling to accept such a provision. Their acceptance of these obligations would mean that, by our own action, we could at any time involve them in war. Our self-governing Dominions would not accept such a position: they insisted on reserving an independent right to decide whether they would join in any war in which the United Kingdom became involved. Yet they had all the common ties implied by membership of the British Commonwealth. Why should Egypt, which was an independent State accept obligations which were not undertaken by the Governments of the British Dominions?

As against this it was suggested that, though Egypt was an independent State, her defence interests were the same as ours and it was her geographical position rather than any Treaty obligation which would implicate her in any war in which we were involved. It was pointed out, however, that these arguments could be applied to Holland and Belgium; but it was not contended that on this account the Governments of those countries should accept Treaty obligations giving us military facilities in their territory for the defence of British interests.

It was further argued that, if we stood out for specific Treaty provisions authorising the maintenance in Egypt of the military facilities which the Chiefs of Staff now had in mind, we should be asking for more than had been guaranteed to us by the terms of the 1936 Treaty. We had in fact established larger installations, and maintained more troops, in Egypt than was justified by the letter of that Treaty. The facilities which we had secured in Egypt had been gained by the goodwill of the Egyptian Government and went far beyond the specific obligations assumed by them under the Treaty of 1936. To this extent past experience suggested that it was preferable to rely on good relations with Egypt rather than the precise words of a Treaty provision.

It was also to be remembered that the Treaty of 1936 had been negotiated when Egypt lay under the threat of Mussolini's imperialism. That threat had now passed; and, as the Treaty itself contemplated revision after ten years, it was natural that the Egyptians should expect us to be willing to negotiate a new Treaty which involved them in lighter obligations. The fact was that we could not expect now to negotiate a new Treaty which laid upon the Egyptian Government the same obligations as those which they had been willing to assume in 1936. If we decided to take our stand on the terms of the 1936 Treaty, we could not expect to secure, without the goodwill of the Egyptian Government, the same military facilities which we had been able to secure in the past. And if we attempted to maintain our position in Egypt by force, it was to be assumed that the resulting situation would be brought to the notice of the Security Council. It was in these circumstances that our advisers in Cairo suggested that we should refrain from pressing our demand for specific Treaty provisions about military facilities and should rely on the goodwill which we should thus win to secure by informal arrangements the assurance we needed that military facilities would be accorded to us in Egypt on a threat, or actual outbreak, of war.

At the same time, it was recognised that it would be desirable, if possible, to strengthen the provisions of Articles 4, 5 and 6 of the new draft Treaty. Thus, it might be possible to strengthen the drafting of Article 4 so as to secure a greater measure of assurance that the recommendations and advice of the Joint Defence Board would be accepted and implemented by the two Governments.

The Foreign Secretary said that he was not committed to the wording of the present draft and would be glad to consider any amendments which could be devised for this purpose.

The Secretary of State for Dominion Affairs suggested that it might be useful to study the precise terms of the agreement between the United States and Canada for the setting up of their Defence Board.

The Lord Chancellor suggested that the Egyptian Government might perhaps be willing to accept a provision to the effect that in the event of a threat, or actual outbreak, of war the Egyptian Government should notify His Majesty's Government and the latter should be under an obligation to come to their assistance.

Points in further discussion were:—

(a) *The Foreign Secretary* recommended that we should be ready to bear the cost of building the temporary accommodation we should need in the Canal zone. Under the 1936 Treaty the Egyptian Government should already have built this accommodation, but this had not been done and he did not think it would serve any useful purpose to endeavour to persuade them to pay for it now.

The Chancellor of the Exchequer agreed with this view. At the same time, he reminded the Cabinet that Egypt was the second largest holder of sterling balances, about which there would have to be negotiations later on. We should not, therefore, be unduly generous in these negotiations, but should endeavour to ensure that the Egyptians paid a fair price for installations and equipment which were to be handed over to them.

(b) Articles I and II of the draft protocol contemplated that specific dates would be prescribed for the various stages of the withdrawal of British troops from Egypt. What were the dates which were to be inserted in these two articles?

The Chief of the Imperial General Staff said that it would probably be possible to complete the first stage of the evacuation within about a year, particularly if an early decision could be taken as to the future site of the Middle East headquarters.

The Foreign Secretary said that the Egyptian Government were not likely to be content with so long a delay. We should, in his view, aim to have completed this stage at the latest by March 1947.

The Cabinet:—

(1) Invited the Foreign Secretary and the Chiefs of Staff to consider what amendments could be made in the new draft Treaty and protocol annexed to C.P. (46) 219 with a view to meeting the points which had been raised in the discussion.

(2) Agreed to resume their consideration of the Foreign Secretary's memorandum at a further meeting on the following day.

54   CAB 129/10, CP(46)224   7 June 1946
'Revision of Anglo–Egyptian treaty': report by the COS to the Cabinet
on the implications of developments since Dec 1945   [Extract][1]

. . .

9.   The latest position as disclosed by CP (46) 219[2] is that the Egyptian Delegation have refused to embody in a new Treaty any clause which would give us the facilities which we require in the event of war or the imminent threat of war. They argue that we should get what we require through "staff conversations and agreements between the military authorities of the two countries." In our view such agreements would not be worth the paper on which they were written. Apart from the fact that the function of military authorities is inherently advisory, the Egyptian military authorities are not only completely incompetent but also devoid of influence or prestige with their Government or their countrymen. In other words, this latest

---

[1] The first section of the COS paper reproduces the military's detailed requirements in Egypt as defined at the end of 1945, see 23.

[2] See 52.

proposal involves yet another retreat from a position which was admittedly at very best a gamble. We have no hesitation in saying that from the point of view of the security of our vital interests in the whole Middle East area, it is completely unacceptable.

10.   It remains therefore to find an alternative. In attempting to do so we recognise that we are encroaching into the political field, but in a problem of this kind it is impossible to draw a hard and fast line between what is political and what is military.

11.   It seems to us that there is a tendency on the part not only of the Egyptian Government but also of others to underrate British rights and British interests in this matter. The following are some of the facts, boldly stated: —

(i) We have twice saved Egypt, but we have only been able to do so because we have had the necessary facilities.

(ii) At the end of a world war there is bound to be a lot of clearing up to be done. It cannot be expected that all the vast installations and arrangements which are involved in waging total war can be cleared away immediately the fighting stops. After all the period of emergency is still in force.

(iii) It is true that foreign troops, enemy prisoners and military dumps are still on Egyptian soil, but is this a hardship comparable to what we, their Allies, have to bear, with conscription still in force and vast occupational forces all over the world? And is it in any way comparable to what they would have had to bear had we not saved them?

(iv) We are doing our very best to clear out the Delta with all speed. We should have thought that there would be no harm in telling the Egyptians that the Chiefs of Staff instructed the Commanders-in-Chief, Middle East as far back as the 30th April, 1946 that it was imperative to get out of Cairo at the earliest possible moment, and that they followed this up on the 30th May with a peremptory order (C.O.S. (M.E.) 87).

(v) We cannot get away from geography. It so happens that Egypt occupies a unique position in relation to the group of states known as the British Commonwealth of Nations. In the long run, therefore, the security of this area is as vital to the British as it is to the Egyptians themselves, and we surely cannot be expected to forego our minimum security requirements there. When one thinks of the steps that Russia has taken in the Baltic and the Balkan States to secure her frontiers, surely what we are asking in Egypt is a very little thing?

(vi) We went to the limit of our military concessions in our opening offer in the hope of securing the goodwill of the Egyptians. The only response we have obtained is to receive further pressure to withdraw our requests for our minimum military facilities.

12.   In our opinion, the above points should be emphasised as strongly as possible to the Egyptian Government.

13.   We consider that the facts set out in paragraph 11 give us the right to demand that satisfactory arrangements for mutual assistance in emergency or in time of apprehended international emergency should be publicly recognised by the Egyptian Government, in such a way as to form an integral part of any revised Agreement which may be negotiated.

14.   From the foregoing, it will be seen that the revised Draft Treaty proposed by

the Foreign Secretary in C.P. (46) 219 does not meet our minimum military requirements unless it is fundamentally altered in the following respects.

(a) *Article 5.* There is no mention of the "menace of war" or of "an apprehended international emergency'. It *must* cover the pre-war period: otherwise our measures will be too late. The phrase "apprehended international emergency" should therefore be inserted after "the event of war".

(b) Article 4 of the draft Protocol should no longer be in the form of a note but become a definite part of the Protocol. Furthermore, it would have to set out in full detail the minimum military facilities which we require.

(c) If Article 5 and Article 4 of the draft Protocol are revised as above, Article 4 of the Treaty would become redundant and could be omitted.

15.   If, on the other hand, H.M.G. should, despite our representations, decide to proceed with the idea of a Joint Defence Board, as set out in Article 4 of the new Draft Treaty, we consider that for the reasons given in paragraph 9 it could be improved by establishing a Joint Anglo–Egyptian *Council* on a Ministerial level. This Council could, of course, be advised by a Joint Defence Board on the lines proposed by the Foreign Secretary.

16.   We must, however, categorically state that this alternative would still fall short of our minimum military requirements, and does not provide the necessary safeguards for achieving these requirements.

55   CAB 128/5, CM 58(46)   7 June 1946
'Anglo–Egyptian negotiations': Cabinet conclusions on the continuance of negotiations

The Cabinet resumed their discussion of the memorandum by the Secretary of State for Foreign Affairs (C.P. (46) 219)[1] regarding the negotiations for a revision of the Anglo–Egyptian Treaty. They also had before them a report by the Chiefs of Staff (C.P. (46) 224)[2] commenting on the proposals in C.P. (46) 219.

The Chief of the Imperial General Staff said that the Chiefs of Staff could not regard the proposed Joint Defence Board as an adequate safeguard for our minimum military requirements. There was no reason to believe that the Egyptian military representatives on the Board would be competent or would carry any weight with their own Government; and, under these new proposals, even more than under the proposals already put to the Egyptian delegation, it would be a gamble whether the Egyptians would, in fact, give us the facilities that we required. From the military point of view the Chiefs of Staff must therefore advise that the new proposals were unacceptable. The Chiefs of Staff could see no alternative to their previous recommendations and felt that to secure the facilities which we needed and which, in view of the considerations set out in paragraph 11 of C.P. (46) 224, we were entitled to demand, certain fundamental amendments in the draft Treaty attached to C.P. (46) 219 would have to be made. In particular the provision for the Joint Defence Board should be omitted, we should be given the right to enter Egypt in an

---

[1] See 52.   [2] See 54.

"apprehended international emergency," as well as in the event of war, and the Treaty should set out the minimum military facilities that we required.

The Chiefs of Staff realised that the Cabinet might feel unable to accept these proposals. In that case, they considered that the proposal for a Joint Defence Board could be improved by establishing a Joint Anglo–Egyptian Council on a Ministerial level, advised, if need be, by a Joint Defence Board on the lines proposed by the Foreign Secretary.

The Chief of the Imperial General Staff added that there had been a misunderstanding at the previous meeting as to the number of troops at present in Egypt. The number was, in fact, only about 106,000, of which 68,000 were British, including one division in reserve for Palestine. The British troops in the Cairo district had been reduced from 71,000 in August 1945 to 38,000, and a further 4,000 were leaving shortly. Considerable reductions in our installations had been made over the last twelve months. He had earlier in the day seen General Paget and impressed on him the urgency of removing our troops from Cairo and Alexandria. General Paget appreciated the position and had said that it should be possible to move his headquarters to the Canal zone within nine months, though they would probably have to live in tents for a while.

The Foreign Secretary said that it must be remembered that the alternative to a new Treaty acceptable to the Egyptians was not the retention of our present position in Egypt. The facilities we enjoyed at present were far greater than those given by the 1936 Treaty; and it was very doubtful how far we could actually rely on that Treaty to give us our minimum military requirements in the face of a hostile Egyptian Government. Article 7 of the Treaty must be read in conjunction with the Agreed Minute attached to it which provided that there should be mutual consultation before an emergency arose; and the Law Officers had advised that, though the Treaty might be kept on foot by a refusal on the part of His Majesty's Government to agree to a revised Treaty, the provisions of Article 7 would be of little value if, when an emergency arose, the Egyptians were unwilling to implement the spirit of the Treaty. It must also be remembered that in such crcumstances [sic] any facilities enjoyed under this Treaty would come to an end in ten years' time. For all these reasons he did not feel that the 1936 Treaty provided firm ground on which to stand. Thus, the real choice before the Cabinet lay between a new Treaty freely negotiated with the Egyptian Government, and the maintenance of our position in Egypt by force. He did not think that the British people or Parliament would regard the latter alternative as an acceptable course. On the other hand, he was convinced that the Egyptian Government would not agree to a new Treaty which specified the minimum military facilities that we required; nor, for historical reasons, would they accept the proposal that the Joint Defence Board should be supplemented by a Joint Council on a Ministerial level.

In accordance with the Cabinet's decision at their meeting on the previous day, he had considered what amendments might be made in the draft Treaty annexed to C.P. (46) 219 and he now proposed that in Article 6 the phrase "the steps which should be taken to enable the armed forces of the two High Contracting Parties effectively to resist aggression" should be amended to read "the steps which should be taken to enable the armed forces of the two High Contracting Parties *to be in a position* effectively to resist aggression." The words added implied that preliminary arrangements would be made before an emergency arose. He also proposed that Article 4 should be redrafted on the lines shown in the Annex to this Minute. The revised draft emphasised that both countries shared in the obligation to discharge the common task, and, by providing that the competent military authorities on the Joint Defence Board might be assisted by such other representatives as the two Governments might appoint, would enable Egyptian Ministers to be associated with the Board. The fact that the redraft was based on the agreement setting up the United States-Canada Defence Board should commend it to the Egyptian Government. If we could obtain a Treaty on the lines of that attached to C.P. (46) 219, with the modifications he now suggested, we should, in his view, be in a more satisfactory position than we had ever been under the 1936 Treaty.

The Lord Chancellor[3] said that, short of using force, the only alternative to the Foreign Secretary's proposal was to rely on the terms of the 1936 Treaty. Unless we had the goodwill of the Egyptian Government, this Treaty would in effect expire after ten years and even in the period during which it remained in force would not give us what we wanted, since a hostile Egyptian Government could easily render its provisions nugatory by denying on any particular occasion that the situation was such as to justify our intervention. Moreover, though he believed that the point was a bad one, it was arguable that the 1936 Treaty had lapsed with the end of the League of Nations.

In discussion there was very full realisation of the weight of the arguments advanced by the Chiefs of Staff. In particular, it was appreciated that reliance on the terms of the revised Article 4 meant taking a considerable risk at a time when there was no firm assurance of any other base from which our Middle Eastern interests could be protected.

The Minister of Fuel and Power[4] emphasised that the oil resources in the Middle East were vital to our security. We could not afford to leave them unprotected.[5]

The following points were also made:—

(a) If negotiations were resumed on the basis of the revised Article 4, our negotiators should insist that the functions of the Joint Defence Board should include the co-ordination of measures for mutual defence in the region of the Middle East and not merely in the territories adjacent to Egypt; and if a firm attitude were adopted in the negotiations, it should be possible to secure this. It was most important that we should not give the Egyptians an impression of weakness, since they would be only too ready to exploit it.

(b) Confidence was expressed in the ability of the British Staff representatives who would serve on the proposed Joint Defence Board to ensure that provisions on the lines proposed by the Foreign Secretary would work satisfactorily.

(c) Nothing in politics was stable and we should remember that the situation in Egypt would not necessarily always be so unfavourable to us as at the moment. Would it not be possible during the period over which the withdrawal of our troops from Egypt would be spread to foster by unofficial means a more friendly attitude towards us?

(d) The withdrawal of troops from the Cairo district would mean a considerable loss to the Egyptian business community. Might it not be advisable to spin out the negotiations in the hope that the Egyptians would realise what they stood to lose economically by the withdrawal of our troops and so be brought into a more reasonable frame of mind?

---

[3] Lord Jowitt.   [4] Mr E Shinwell.

[5] The military had already acknowledged that their strategic requirements in Egypt would not enable them to defend the oilfields of the Middle East, see 49.

In reply it was pointed out that it was now eight months since the original request for a revision of the 1936 Treaty had been made and that there was every indication that further delay would only serve to make the Egyptian Government more irreconcilable. Further, it was only too likely that any economic distress due to the withdrawal of our troops from the Cairo district would be attributed to our continuing presence elsewhere in Egypt.

(e) *The Secretary of State for Air* pointed out that Article 5 of the *avant-projet*, which Sidky Pasha hoped the Egyptian Delegation would accept, gave good grounds for the belief that a satisfactory basis of agreement could be achieved by the approach recommended by the Foreign Secretary.

(f) It was suggested that if, as the Foreign Secretary had indicated, it was proposed to bring Ministerial representatives into the Joint Defence Board discussions it would be desirable to substitute the words "together with" for the words "assisted by" in the second sentence of the revised draft of Article 4.

Summing up the discussion, *The Prime Minister* said that the Chiefs of Staff had very properly drawn attention to the fact that the Foreign Secretary's proposals did not give us an assurance of the facilities which we should require in the event of war or the imminent threat of war. The Cabinet must, however, consider what would be the alternative to proceeding with these proposals. It seemed clear that to stand on the 1936 Treaty would not give us what we wanted and we should therefore be driven to remain in Egypt forcibly on the ground that only by doing so could we safeguard our military security. There was no more justification for this than for our claiming that our neighbours on the Continent of Europe should grant us bases for our defence. Our oil interests in the Middle East were indeed important, but our ability to defend them would only be impaired if we insisted on remaining in Egypt against the will of the Egyptian people and so worsened our relations with the remainder of the Arab world. For these reasons he was convinced that the proposals made by the Foreign Secretary should be accepted, and it was clear that this was the general view of the Cabinet.

The Cabinet:—

(1) Agreed in principle that the negotiations for the revision of the Anglo–Egyptian Treaty should be continued on the general lines proposed by the Foreign Secretary in C.P. (46) 219.

(2) Agreed that Articles 4 and 6 of the draft Treaty annexed to C.P. (46) 219 should be revised on the lines which had been suggested by the Foreign Secretary.

(3) Took note that the Foreign Secretary would obtain the views of His Majesty's Ambassador in Cairo on the draft Treaty and Protocol as so revised.

56   CAB 131/3, DO(46)80   18 June 1946
'British strategic requirements in the Middle East': report by the COS to the Cabinet Defence Committee

We have reconconsidered [sic] our Report on Strategic Requirements in the Middle East in the light of the discussion at the Defence Committee on the 27th May, 1946.[2] Our revised conclusions are summarised below. The full report is annexed.

---

[1] See 49.

We have considered the problem against the background of war with Russia, not because we assume that such a war is inevitable, but because it represents the greatest, and indeed the only, menace which is apparent at the present time, and is by far the most difficult situation with which we may have to deal.

Summary

Expanded in annex
Paragraph reference

I   Strategic Background

(a) The fundamental basis of Commonwealth Defence is the security of the United Kingdom, of the Dominions and of the communications between them.

(b) The security of the United Kingdom itself is vital. But to limit our strategy to the local defence of this country would permit an enemy to concentrate unimpeded his entire effort against us, and would expose us to gradual reduction by the proportion of long-range weapons and aircraft that would penetrate our defences.   3

(c) If Russia were the enemy, her great superiority of man-power would necessitate our making the maximum use of our technical and scientific superiority and particularly of our air power to strike back at the enemy's vital centres, war potential and communications. In war with Russia, bases in the United Kingdom alone would not be sufficient for this task. The Middle East provides the only air base from which effective offensive action can be undertaken against the important Russian industrial and oil-producing areas of Southern Russia and the Caucasus.   3

(d) Without at least some of the Middle East oil supplies we would be incapable of developing our full war effort.   4

Appendix I.

(e) By holding the Middle East we shall obtain defence in depth for East and Southern Africa, and may also secure the through route of sea communications via the Mediterranean, Suez Canal and Red Sea.   5

(f) In the Middle East geographical factors enable us to redress the balance of man-power. In Palestine, and north of it, the Russians would be fighting at the end of long and difficult lines of communications.   6

(g) Thus from the Middle East we can attack Russian vital interests and so impede her effort against the United Kingdom and its communications, and can conduct this offensive from bases secure against land attack except by forces with which we can compete.   6

(h) Russian intentions are considered to include a resumption of her traditional policy of southern expansion. If we abandon the Middle East in peace, or fail to defend it in war, Russia will replace us.   7

(i) The forces necessary to guard against threats from an enemy based in the Middle East would not be less, and might well be more, than would be required for the defence of the Middle East itself.   7

To sum up. It is, therefore, of great strategic importance to hold the Middle East in order:—

Expanded in annex
Paragraph reference

(i) not to prejudice the security of the United Kingdom, the other main support areas of the Commonwealth and the communications between them, 8

(ii) to retain the necessary air bases from which to assume the offensive and attack areas vital to the enemy, 8

(iii) to secure our essential oil supplies, 8

(iv) to deny to Russia the means of, firstly, securing her most vulnerable flank and, secondly, of establishing a formidable base from which to extend aggression towards our main support areas and their communications. 8

II. *In war: areas essential to the defence of the Middle East and the forces and facilities required*

(a) *Egypt and Palestine*. The security of Egypt and Palestine is vital to the defence of the Middle East. 10

(b) *Cyrenaica*. Although Cyrenaica cannot be classified as equally vital it is of the greatest importance to be free to operate from there. 11
Appendix III.

(c) *Oil supplies*. At the very least some of the oil from the Middle East will be essential to the maintenance of our full war effort. At present the oil producing areas essential to us include Koweit,[2] Southern Iraq and Persia. 12

(d) *Administrative requirements*: Although our main support areas and intermediate supply bases will be outside the Middle East, it will be necessary to locate in Middle East certain minimum stocks and administrative facilities, of which the bulk will have to be in Egypt. 15–18

(e) *Headquarters*. It will be essential in war to have a joint headquarters, and Egypt alone fulfils all the requirements. 19
Appendix II.

(f) *Provision of forces*. It is practicable, with the active assistance of the Dominions, to provide the necessary forces for the defence of Egypt and Palestine without prejudicing the security of the United Kingdom. But to have any hope of maintaining the necessary oil supplies from the Middle East we would require the assistance of the Americans. 14

III. *Our minimum military requirements in peace to enable us to fulfil our tasks in war*

(a) *Egypt*: In the event of the previous evacuation of our forces from Egypt we shall require an effective guarantee that the Egyptians will develop and maintain the necessary naval, military and air bases, facilities and stocks, and make these available to us as soon as His Majesty's Government consider that a state of emergency has arisen. 10, 20,
21, 28.

---

[2] Both spellings—Koweit and Kuwait—appear in this document.

Expanded in annex
Paragraph reference

(b) *Palestine*. We must retain the right to locate in Palestine any forces we consider necessary, and we must have complete control of the organisation of defence of this area.   10, 21,
                                                                         24, 25.

(c) *Cyrenaica*. The proposed withdrawal of our forces from Egypt increases the importance of Cyrenaica in peace. We shall require to locate there nucleus forces for the defence of our sea and air communications in the Eastern Mediterranean, certain equipment and stocks, a part of our strategic bomber force, and possibly part of our strategic reserve.   11, 15,
                                                                            25.
                                                                  Appendix III.

(d) *East Africa*. When it is possible to form a true strategic reserve this could well be located in East Africa, but it would be desirable to have the right to station it temporarily in Cyrenaica. Dependent on the results of the present examination of East Africa, much of our administrative and base facilities could be located there.   22, 28.

(e) *Headquarters*. A joint headquarters will be required. If it cannot be located in Egypt, Palestine is the best alternative in the Middle East.   27
                                                                   Appendix II.

(f) *Oil supplies*. In view of our present dependence on existing Middle East oil supplies and our inability fully to provide for their defence, it is of the first importance:—
                                                                    Appendix I.

  (i) to associate the United States in the defence of oil producing areas;
  (ii) to press forward with investigating the possibility of obtaining oil
  and establishing adequate refineries in less vulnerable parts of the
  Middle East.

(g) *Arab states*. All our defence requirements in the Middle East, including the maintenance of our oil supplies, demand that an essential feature of our policy should be to retain the co-operation of the Arab States.

IV. *Conclusions*

Our conclusions emerge, step by step, throughout the above summary.

   Our overall conclusion is that it is essential to the security of the British Commonwealth to maintain our position in the Middle East in peace and to defend it in war.

Annex to 56

In the light of the discussion in the Defence Committee we have revised our report on Strategic Requirements in the Middle East.

   Our report below sets out:—

(I) The strategic background against which we assess the importance of the Middle East.

(II) Areas essential for the defence of the Middle East in war and the forces and facilities required.

(III) Our minimum military requirements in peace to enable us to fulfil our tasks in war.

I. *Strategic background*

Commonwealth defence

2.   The fundamental basis of Commonwealth Defence is the security of the United Kingdom, of the Dominions and of the communications between them.

Security of the United Kingdom

3.   Of these, the security of the United Kingdom itself, with its high proportion of the Commonwealth man-power and industrial potential is vital.

Great Britain, on account of her size and geographical position, is extremely vulnerable to attack from the air and from modern long range weapons.

If, however, we attempt to limit our strategy to the local defence of this country, we should permit the enemy to concentrate unimpeded his entire effort against us. Although our land, sea and air power should be capable of protecting us from invasion, modern weapons and air forces, operated from the Continent, would still prove a serious menace.

The Joint Technical Warfare Committee have given us their opinion that a proportion of the enemy aircraft and projectiles, which could be launched against us, would penetrate any defence methods which are likely to be developed in the foreseeable future. The cumulative effects of such enemy attacks would, in the end, prove decisive if we rested purely upon the defensive. If Russia were the enemy, to counter-balance her great superiority in man-power it would be essential for us to maintain and exploit to the utmost our technical and scientific superiority especially in respect of air power. Given secure and suitably located bases, air power would give us the means of striking quickly and hard at the vital centres of the enemy war potential, action which would be immediately essential in order to relieve the pressure of attacks on the United Kingdom. Some of this counter-offensive could be undertaken from the United Kingdom, but if we regard Russia as the potential enemy many of her vital centres are out of range from United Kingdom; her most vulnerable flank is in the South-East, where most of her oil industry is located. It is only from the Middle East area that effective air action can be taken against this flank. Thus, an offensive strategy conducted from bases both inside the United Kingdom and in the Middle East area is an essential complement to the defence of the United Kingdom itself.

Oil supplies

4.   The importance to us of the Middle East oilfields is examined in detail at Appendix I. From this it will be seen that on the maintenance of our position in the Middle East depends the security of great oil resources, some at least of which will be essential to the development of our full war effort. Furthermore, maximum peace production is essential to our economy and to the building-up of reserves.

In a recent appreciation, the J.I.C. have brought out the fact that the Abadan oil production constitutes 40 per cent of British controlled production. If this were cut off an acute oil famine would develop throughout the Empire. Abadan is therefore of the highest importance to the economy of this country and the Empire. If we were to pull out of the Middle Eastern Area we would make it a very simple matter for Russia to acquire control of this source of oil, and to cripple our strength both in peace or in war. Moreover, the importance of Middle Eastern oil to America is becoming more and more apparent and widely realised. We can, therefore, reasonably hope that a time is coming when America will be more willing to take an interest and perhaps a share in the responsibility for maintaining our position in the Middle East generally.

We are forced to the inescapable conclusion that if there were no other reasons for maintaining our position in the Middle East the problem of our oil supplies would demand that we should do so. A further conclusion is that it should be an essential part of our policy to retain the co-operation of the Arab States.

Security of the dominions and communications to them

5.   To ensure the security of the Dominions we need defence in depth, and, just as for the United Kingdom, we need to maintain the communications to them.

If we hold the Middle East, in addition to the advantages we have already stated, we shall also obtain the defence in depth of East and Southern Africa.

We may also secure the through route of sea communications via the Mediterranean, Suez Canal and Red Sea. We do not maintain that the loss of this line of communications would be immediately fatal. But the effects of its loss might well prove so. Shortage of shipping has been a crux of two world wars and the alternative route round the Cape entailed, at the height of the Libyan campaign, a 33 per cent. increase of effort in general shipping and 50 per cent. increase in tanker tonnage.

Ability to hold the Middle East

6.   The approaches to the heart of the Middle East from the north are canalised through Palestine which is protected on the west by the sea and on the east by large desert areas. In Palestine the Russians would be fighting at the end of long and extremely difficult lines of communication from Eastern Europe through Turkey or from the Caucasus through Eastern Turkey, Northern Iran and Northern Iraq. Taking into account the pressure on these communications which we should be able to exert from the air, we do not consider that the size of the forces required to defend the vital areas of the Middle East would be beyond our resources. In fact, in the Middle East, geographical factors enable us to redress the balance of man-power.

Thus from the Middle East we can attack Russian vital interests and so impede the effort which she could otherwise direct against the United Kingdom and its communications, and our base there would be secure against a land atack except by forces comparable to those which we could put in the field against them.

India, however, offers facilities for offensive air action against certain areas in Russia.

Russian intentions

7.   Russian intentions in the Middle East have been examined in a recent J.I.C. paper, and it is evident that she is reassuming her traditional policy of southern expansion. If we abandon our position in the Middle East in peace we must assume that Russia will replace us. If we do not defend the area in war there can be no doubt that Russia will occupy it.

If the Russians occupy Egypt they will secure their vulnerable flank against air assault. They will also obtain a forward base so that, instead of being at the end of long, difficult, and vulnerable lines of communication, they will be free to build up their strength, gain fresh impetus and thus be able to support large forces further afield. By these means they can either develop a serious threat to our main support areas of Southern Africa and India, or by steady extension westward eliminate us from the Mediterranean, gain the ports of North Africa and eventually the domination of the African Atlantic seaboard.

The forces necessary to guard against the threats from an enemy based in the Middle East would not be less, and might well be more, than would be required for the defence of the Middle East itself.

Finally, Russia would secure valuable additional resources of oil.

Summary

8.   The salient facts which emerge are that if we abandon the Middle East:—

(a) We shall prejudice the security of the United Kingdom and the communications to it.

(b) We should lose possession of the air bases which are most important to our assumption of the offensive and from which we could attack areas vital to the enemy. We consider that these bases are within our power to hold.

(c) We should lose an area which is the world's greatest potential source of oil and on which at the present time we rely for some, at least, of our essential requirements in peace and war.

(d) Russia would be permitted effectively to secure her most vulnerable flank.

(e) Russia would be able to establish a formidable base from which to extend aggression towards our main support areas and their communications.

The forces necessary to guard against a threat from this region would not be less than would be required for the defence of the Middle East itself.

II.   *Requirements in war*

Essential areas

9.   In order to obtain our strategic requirements it is clearly not necessary to defend the whole area normally included in the term Middle East. It is therefore necessary to decide what are the essential areas.

10.   *Egypt and Palestine*. Egypt is the political and geographical centre of the Middle East and the hub of communications. It controls the land route from Asia to Africa, the entry into the Indian Ocean and, owing to its port facilities and industrial capabilities, forms the natural base for forces operating in other areas of the Middle East. Through it runs the Suez Canal, which is essential if we are to use the through Mediterranean sea route and which is in any case of very great importance in order to enable the main ports of Egypt and Palestine to be reached from the south. In fact, if we can retain Egypt we achieve all our main strategic aims with the exception of the safeguarding of the oil supplies. Egypt is therefore clearly an essential area.

The defence of Egypt cannot be conducted effectively from Egyptian territory alone. The land approaches to Egypt from the north are canalised through Palestine, and it is in Palestine and in the difficult country north of it that the main land defence of Egypt will have to be conducted. The air defence of Egypt will also require the location of certain forces and installations in Palestine. Forces operating in Palestine will have to use Egypt as their forward supply base.

Egypt and Palestine are therefore interdependent.

11.   *Cyrenaica*. We have already shown the importance of the Mediterranean to

us in war. In order to retain control of the Eastern Mediterranean it will be necessary to station certain forces in Cyrenaica. Although we cannot classify Cyrenaica as vital in the same way as Egypt and Palestine, it is clearly of the greatest importance to us that we should be free to operate from there in war.

12.   *Oil producing areas.* It has been shown in Appendix I that at the very least some of the oil from the Middle East will be essential to the maintenance of our full effort in peace and in a future war.

Strategically the most easily defensible areas from which to draw oil would be from South-Eastern Arabia and the Arabian Red Sea littoral. The Ministry of Fuel and Power have advised us, however, that there is no prospect in the near future (ten to fifteen years) of satisfying our essential requirements from these areas alone. At the present time the oil production from the areas at the head of the Persian Gulf, *i.e.,* Koweit, Southern Iraq and Persia, would also be required, but that from Northern Iraq would not be essential. It is possible that if development is pressed forward in Arabia and is successful, we should progressively be dependent less and less on the supplies of oil from the areas at the head of the Persian Gulf, and might be able eventually to meet our requirements from Bahrein and the fields south of it which might be found. Whether this could be carried further and our dependence reduced to areas outside the Persian Gulf, it is impossible to estimate. At the present time development in this region is not being pressed forward at the same scale as in the areas Koweit and to the North.

Thus the oil-producing areas essential to us for the maintenance of our war effort at present include Koweit, Southern Iraq and Persia. It is of strategical importance that development should be pressed forward in South-Eastern Arabia and in other parts of the Middle East less vulnerable than the head of the Persian Gulf, though on economic grounds and in order to build up reserve stocks this should not be at the expense of continued full production in peace from the existing fields in more vulnerable areas. It is also of strategic importance that refineries should be developed in other areas less vulnerable than Abadan.

Forces required for the defence of the Middle East in war

13.   *Scale of Russian effort against the essential areas.* Taking into account the difficult nature of the terrain and the lack of communications, it has been estimated that the Russian forces which could be maintained in the Middle East would be as follows:—

(a) *As far south as Southern Syria:* 8 Divisions (numerically equivalent to 5–6 British Divisions).
(b) *In Northern Iraq:* 8 Divisions (numerically equivalent to 5–6 British Divisions).
(c) *In the Persian Gulf area:* 15 Divisions.

For simultaneous operations in (b) and (c) above the total in these two areas would be limited to 17 Divisions.

These calculations are based solely on the existing capacity of the road, rail and sea communications to maintain Russian ground forces. The figures may, in fact, be an over-estimate since they make no allowance for the maintenance of accompanying air forces and take no account of the disruption of the communications by our own air action; on the other hand, they do not allow for the possibility of Russian Supply by air.

Practicability of providing the forces required for the Middle East while still ensuring the defence of the United Kingdom

14.   In considering the provision of forces we must assume, firstly, that there will be some warning of impending war and a corresponding period of expansion of the Defence Services, and, secondly, that with the outbreak of war the whole man-power of the country would be mobilised and due allocations made to the Services:—

(a) *Naval forces.* The object of the Royal Navy, assisted by the Dominion Navies, is the security of the sea communications of the Commonwealth. We must provide forces adequate for this task. If this is done, it will undoubtedly be possible to provide the naval forces required for the Middle East, as well as those necessary for the defence of the United Kingdom and its immediate communications.

(b) *Land forces.* In our opinion the defence of the United Kingdom against invasion must rest primarily on the superiority of our sea and air power. The army will, however, remain responsible for protecting the country against such forces as penetrate these defences. In addition, there will be heavy commitments for anti-aircraft defence and assistance to the Civil Defence services. On the assumptions detailed above, however, some formations would be available for service in the Middle East.

With these forces and those which we consider the Dominions should provide, we are satisfied that we could meet our commitments in Egypt and Palestine.

Even with the maximum assistance of the Dominions, it seems unlikely that sufficient forces would be available to hold Iraq and Persia as well as Egypt and Palestine. With the aid of air power, however, we should be able to cause delay to a Russian advance to the Persian Gulf.

If, therefore, we are to retain the essential oil-producing areas, we shall need the assistance of the Americans, who also have highly important oil interests there, and who, as is shown in Appendix 1 are likely to themselves become more dependent on Middle East oil.

Even allowing for the timely arrival of the Americans, it might still not be possible to hold the oil-fields at the head of the Persian Gulf; in any case oil production in this area is likely to become difficult owing to enemy air action.

We consider, therefore, that it should be a definite part of our policy to aim to associate the United States in the defence of the Middle East oil-fields, and, as we have already said, to develop oil production and refineries in less vulnerable areas of the Middle East.

(c) *Air forces.* The security of the United Kingdom will depend, among other factors, on our ability to hit out and to take offensive action in the early stages of war. Our strategic bomber force is a weapon which can be used quickly. In order to use it effectively it is essential that it should be so based that it can reach the enemy's vital areas. The only effective way of using strategic bombers quickly against Russia is to have an adequate proportion of that force stationed in the Middle East, from which the enemy's vulnerable and comparatively exposed flank can be reached.

With regard to other air forces required for defensive and tactical purposes, we consider that, assuming a proper use of our technical and scientific superiority and given a due allocation of man-power, we should, with the aid of the Dominions, be able to supply the forces required both for the defence of the United Kingdom, and for the Middle East area.

Facilities required in war

15. *Operational requirements*. To enable the forces of all three services to operate effectively in war it will be necessary to make provision for the following:—

(a) *Navy*. Operational bases at Alexandria and Aden. Advanced Naval bases at Tobruk, Haifa, Port Sudan, Bahrein and Mazirah Island. In addition it would be of considerable value if Benghazi and Massawa were available.

(b) *Army*. Location of the main land forces in Palestine. Reserve formations in Egypt, where they will be centrally placed to move as required.

(c) *Air Force*

(i)   Location in Egypt (with certain units in Palestine and Cyrenaica) of Air Forces for the defence of Egypt and the communications to it.

(ii)   Location, mainly in Palestine, of air forces to support the land forces.

(iii)   Bases in Egypt for the strategic bomber force.

16. *Administrative base requirements*. Owing to the increasing range and power of modern weapons it will be necessary to locate our main base installations as far as possible in areas remote from the scene of actual conflict. We have already shown that our main bases in a future war will be in our main support areas – the United Kingdom, the Dominions and possibly India.

17.   It will be necessary, however, to have certain installations and stocks nearer to the Middle East than the main support areas. These should, we suggest, be located in the area Port Sudan, Aden, East Africa. The last named appears to provide the only area capable of any considerable development, and this question is now under consideration.

18.   Certain minimum stocks and administrative facilities will have to be located in the actual theatre of operations. In war the bulk of these will have to be located in Egypt which alone possesses the necessary communications, man-power and industrial capacity with ports giving access to the Mediterranean and Indian Ocean.

19. *Headquarters*. It will be essential in war to have a joint headquarters to deal with operations, administration and politico-military problems in the Middle East as a whole.

This headquarters should:—

(a) be located at the political and geographical centre of the area and be at the hub of communications;

(b) contain both the operational and administrative staff for all three services;

(c) be reasonably near to the tactical commanders in order that Commanders-in-Chief may keep in close touch with them. It should not, however, be so far forward that its security will be affected by fluctuations of the battle front.

Egypt is the only location which satisfactorily fulfils all these conditions in war. See Appendix II.

III.   *Requirements in peace*

20.   If we are to fulfil our tasks in war it will be necessary:—

(a) To locate in the Middle East in peace the necessary minimum nucleus required for expansion in war.

(b) To maintain our predominant position in the area so as to ensure that the

Arab World does not gravitate into the Russian orbit, and so as to strengthen Turkish resistance to Russian pressure.

21.   We have shown that in war Egypt will form the keystone of the defence of the Middle East and that we shall require to locate there reserve army formations, a considerable proportion of our Middle East air forces, the major part of our forward administrative facilities for all three services and our regional headquarters.

If our offer of evacuation made to Egypt during the recent negotiations is fully implemented we shall, at best, only be able to keep there in peace certain stocks and administrative facilities which the Egyptians themselves will maintain. The effects of this are that:—

(a) We must have an effective guarantee from the Egyptians that they will develop and maintain the necessary naval, military and air bases together with their defences and make these available to us as soon as His Majesty's Government consider that an emergency has arisen.

(b) We must allow for the likelihood that, whatever guarantee we may receive, the Egyptians may not maintain the bases we require at full efficiency and will be unwilling to compromise their neutrality by allowing us to occupy them long in advance of a war. We may, therefore, well not be able to operate from Egypt at full efficiency from the outset.

(c) We must, therefore, locate elsewhere in the Middle East those parts of essential nucleus which would hitherto have been situated in Egypt.

Requirement for forces

22.   Apart from the fact that considerable British forces are likely to be required in Palestine for some time to come, we consider that in any case we could not dispense with the presence of some British forces in the Middle East.

The defence of the area in war could not be assured if we were dependent soley [sic] upon moving in forces at the last moment. This does not imply that we must maintain there in peace the full forces which we consider would be required in war. In order, however, to ensure that our defence is ready in time, a "foot in the door" will be necessary and certain preparations will have to be made on the spot in peace.

The extent to which the presence of armed forces is necessary in peace in order to maintain our influence is primarily a political question. It would seem to us, however, that we are unlikely to be able to persuade Turkey of the reality of our continued support or obtain that co-operation in defence matters which we require from the Arabs without tangible proof of our determination to stand by them which the presence of armed forces provides. We do not think that the small force which we might station in Cyprus, the only British possession in the central Middle East area, would be sufficient to achieve this object or that forces stationed in East Africa would have the required effect.

Location of forces

23.   *Naval*. Naval forces operating in the Middle East area in peace will be based on Malta, Aden and Ceylon.

24.   *Land forces*. Palestine will form the core of the land defences of the Middle East in war and it is politically one of the most important areas of the Middle East. Both in order to maintain our influence and to ensure its security we should,

therefore, wish in any case to keep certain land forces in Palestine, and have complete control of the organisation of the defence of this area.

Once the internal situation allows, however, it will be possible to reduce our permanent peacetime garrison in Palestine to comparatively small proportions and to form a true strategic reserve. This could well be located in East Africa in peace and moved forward to Egypt in war. But to guard against the possibility that an early move into Egypt might not be possible, it would be desirable to have the right to station it temporarily in Cyrenaica.

If we are allotted the trusteeship of the latter area we shall not normally require to locate there more than the small land forces necessary to ensure internal security.

It does not appear possible to station in the oil-producing areas more than the small land forces which we at present have there. As we have already said, it is of great importance to associate the Americans in the defence of the area. If they could be brought to take the necessary protective measures it would be of considerable assistance towards meeting the defensive commitment in this area.

25.   *Air forces*. The nucleus of the fighter defence of Egypt must be stationed in peace in an area from which it can conveniently and quickly be moved to its war stations. Certain of the units required can be located in Palestine, but the limited airfield accommodation there will make it highly desirable that some should be located in Cyrenaica, where in any case fighter facilities will be necessary in war for defence and to cover communications.

The location of the strategic bomber force is a matter of greater difficulty. Ultimately this will operate from Egypt in war, but there is no certainty that this would be possible in the early stages and we regard it as of the greatest importance that we should have, from the outset, fully operational bomber bases within striking distance of the important targets in South-West Russia and southern Europe. East Africa is too far distant to fulfil this requirement although rear bases might be maintained there. Airfield accommodation will not be available in Palestine which will in any case be too vulnerable in war. We, therefore, consider it essential that we should be able in peace to locate our Middle East strategic bomber force in Cyrenaica.

Administrative and base requirements

26.   An examination is now in progress of the extent to which it will be possible to develop East Africa as a base. Depending on the result of this examination it should be possible to locate there much of our administrative and base facilities and to reduce those required in the forward area to comparatively small proportions.

Of the installations and stocks held forward it should be possible to locate a proportion in Egypt in peace, to be maintained by the Egyptians under the terms of the Treaty. The remainder of those in the forward area must be located in Palestine or Cyrenaica. The capacity of Palestine is limited and in present conditions the internal security commitment will be large. It seems certain that we shall require to locate in Cyrenaica in peace certain units, equipment and stocks.

Regional headquarters

27.   We consider that in peace a joint regional headquarters will be required which can consider the defence problems of the Middle East as a whole and carry out the necessary co-ordination throughout the theatre. This headquarters need not in peace be large and need not include many of the administrative sections and units which

have grown up round the present Headquarters owing to its being located alongside the main administrative base. The Naval Commander-in-Chief, Mediterranean, will in any case have his permanent Headquarters at Malta in peace and will be represented at the joint Headquarters by a Senior Naval Officer, Middle East.

The Headquarters will be located in Egypt in war. We have considered at Appendix II possible alternative peacetime locations. Our conclusion is that if the Headquarters cannot be located in Egypt in peace, Palestine is the best alternative.

General effect of withdrawal of forces from Egypt in peace

28.   Our strategic requirements in the Middle East in peace are to a great extent governed by our undertaking to withdraw from Egypt and by the uncertainty of the safeguards which we may be able to obtain in our treaty with Egypt. The broad effects of these are:—

(a) The strategic importance of Palestine has increased. Unless we are free to take there what military measures we consider necessary in peace our whole position in the Middle East will be jeopardised in war. We must, therefore, retain the right to locate in Palestine any forces we consider necessary, and we must have complete control of the organisation of defence of the area. This will also enable us to provide a visible sign of our influence in an important area of the Middle East.

(b) The strategic importance of Cyrenaica has greatly increased. It is of the greatest importance that we should have the right to locate there certain units, equipment and stocks. A more detailed analysis of our requirements is at Appendix III.

(c) The importance of the development of East Africa as an administrative base has increased.

APPENDIX I

The importance of British oil interests in the Middle East

Commercial

During the past decade the Middle East has emerged as potentially the world's greatest oil reservoir. Vast new deposits have been discovered in the area as a result of which Middle East oil reserves are now estimated to represent 30 per cent. of the total known oil reserves in the world.

North America has 40 per cent. at present, but the picture may well be changed in a few years, due to increased production in the Middle East and increased consumption in America.

A summary of an official oil commission report to the United States Congress in 1945 shows this—

World oil production and reserves

Area	Production (Millions of Tons)		Estimated Reserves (Proven Fields only.)
	1945	(1950 Est.)	
North America	236	211	2,905
South America	63	60	1,240
U.S.S.R.	25	35	1,000
Europe (excluding U.S.S.R.)	8	8	75
Asia	2	10	175
Middle East	26	60	3,045
	360	384	8,440

2.   It is extremely unlikely that new discoveries in North America, already very fully prospected, will allow the U.S.A. to maintain her position and it is possible that before long she will cease to be an exporting country; in fact, it is probable that, during the next decade, the Middle East will supplant North America as the World's principal oil-exporting area. This is largely due, of course, to the low *consumption* in the Middle East.

3.   Long-term insufficiency of U.S.A. natural oil resources is now widely assumed both in official and commercial circles.

The following may be deduced:—

(a) There will be a gradual decline, and an eventual cessation, of exports from the U.S.A. and an absorption of South American oil in the U.S.A. markets.

(b) In consequence, *all* countries not possessing large indigenous reserves and hitherto largely dependent on America, will have to turn to the Middle East—*i.e.*, to the very great natural but as yet largely unexplored reserves of Persia, Iraq and Arabia. The only other (at present) known reserves of great magnitude are in U.S.S.R. territory. Oil-fields so far discovered in Europe are relatively inconsiderable, and even those of the East Indies are believed to be of secondary importance.

4.   The fact is that, in a world requiring more and more oil, the British Empire contains only a negligible quantity.

But, at a rough estimate, Britain controls 70–75 per cent. of present Middle East production and about 60 per cent. of Middle East estimated reserves.

The Abadan, Haifa and Suez refineries are British controlled.

The Middle East provides a source from which Empire requirements can be met with "Sterling oil" as opposed to "Dollar oil."

Strategical

5.   During the last war, as in World War I, oil played a decisive part, and on the operational fronts accounted for half the tonnage which had to be shipped.

Within a year of the outbreak of World War II our stock levels in spite of all our preparations were a cause for concern—our strategic reserves were to a large extent absorbed by the sharp rise in Service consumption.

6.   In the final stages of the war all Allied production and refining facilities were at full stretch, but there was virtually no margin of reserve in the Allied oil supply programme. Requirements of the United Nations (excluding Russia) were at the rate of 320 million tons per year; production at 1 million tons per day kept pace with these requirements, but only because production in America was stepped up, above the economical working limit, to an extent unlikely to be repeated.

7.   It is inconceivable that during the next decade ships, tanks and aircraft will use a fuel other than a petroleum derivative.

It is most unlikely that in a major war the oil requirements will be at a lower rate than in the late war—(aircraft jet engines use 30 per cent. more fuel than piston engines).

The British Commonwealth would thus require oil at the rate of at least 50 million tons a year.

8.   The Post Hostility [sic] Planning Staff in a recent paper assumed a war in the period 1955–60; and concluded that without Middle East oil production supplies

would fall short of requirements by 40 million tons a year if the British Commonwealth were engaged in a war and *the U.S.A. were neutral*. If the U.S.A. were also at war, as our allies, the deficit would be increased to 53 million tons a year. A deficit of this size was considered by the Ministry of Fuel and Power to be so big that they felt there was no possibility of taking effective measures to bridge the gap, and they therefore considered that the Middle East oil resources could be truthfully classified as "vital" to the full development of the war effort of the British Commonwealth and the U.S.A.

9.   If (hypothetically) the most pessimistic estimate of our strategic position resulting in the most conservative estimate of our consumption is attempted, we might assume the following:—

(a) We have retired from the Mediterranean and the Middle East.
(b) We have no European Allies but the Dutch are friendly.
(c) The U.S.A. are neutral.
(d) India is not in the British Commonwealth.
(e) There has been no increase in civilian consumption (rationed).
(f) Services consumption at the average rate of World War II.
(g) Merchant ship bunkers at the average rate of World War II.

We then have for the British Empire at war:—

Civilian requirements	15 million tons per year.
Service requirements	13 million tons per year.
Merchant Navy bunkers	10 million tons per year.
Total	38 million tons per year.

10.   To meet these requirements we might have from "Sterling" resources:—

	(Optimistic estimate)
From East Indies	8 million tons per annum (50 per cent. from Sumatra, where the future position is uncertain).
From U.K. (including substitutes)	1 million tons per annum.
From Trinidad	2½ million tons per annum.
From Venezuela	14 million tons per annum.
Total	25½ million tons per annum.

Thus leaving a deficit of at least 12 million tons per annum even under the circumstances most favourable to low consumption.

11.   It is thus quite clear that in the event of a major war during the next 10 to 20 years the British Commonwealth, without the Middle East, would have annual deficit of something between 12 and 53 million tons of oil, depending on the circumstances. The deficit could only be made up from:—

A. America, *if* the U.S.A. were neutral *and* adopted rationing. (But if the Middle East oil resources were overrun by a third Power it cannot be assumed that the U.S.A. would be neutral in view of her interests there. If the U.S.A. were also fighting the deficit would be larger by some 13 million tons per annum–vide paragraph 6 above.)
B. The Middle East.

12.   It is important not to be short of oil.

Germany (in both wars), Italy and Japan in the moment of defeat had not run out of men, weapons, explosives or food but they were desperately short of oil.

Analysis of Middle East oil reserves

13.   In considering the Middle East as a source of supply to make up our deficit in a major war, it must be remembered that a very large area is involved. From the deposits in Northern Iraq to those in Southern Arabia is some 1,500 miles.

The estimated reserves of proved oilfields are:—

Country	Reserve (Million Tons)	Interest
Persia	900	British
Iraq	700	Anglo–American
Kuwait	700	Anglo–American
Bahrein	35	} American
Saudi Arabia	600	
Qatar Peninsular	100	Anglo–American
Egypt	10	Anglo–American
	3,045	

At the present time production of crude petroleum from Middle East areas is at the rate of some 32,000,000 tons per annum. Of this just under 20,000,000 tons is being produced in Persia. During the next five years it is estimated that production in the Middle East may increase to 50/60,000,000 tons, of which from 10 to 20 million tons per year will flow by pipe line to the Mediterrancan.

14.   There are very large-scale developments planned for the immediate future in the Kuwait oilfields which, when completed, would together with the production from the oilfields further South go a long way to compensate for the loss of the Persian and Iraq fields if these are considered indefensible.

Every effort should be made to hold Kuwait, but if this area also is indefensible then even greater efforts must be made to develop as quickly as possible the maximum production from the oilfields to the South of Bahrein. This could only be done by the full co-operation of the American commercial interests.

It is estimated that, given sufficient urgency, a high rate of production from the Southern Persian Gulf area might be achieved within 5 to 15 years.

Importance of Middle East oil to the U.S.A

15.   During recent years American oil companies, faced with the prospect of decreasing supplies at home, have turned with increasing urgency to the Middle East and after the British have the most important interests, especially in Arabia.

The following is the position as at present known:—

	U.S. interest. per cent.
Iraq Petroleum Coy.	23¾
Covering practically the whole of oil producing areas in Iraq.	
Kuwait Petroleum Coy.	50
Bahrein Petroleum Coy.	100
Californian Arabian Standard Oil Coy.	100

Very large concessions in Saudi Arabia of which proved areas are in Haza. Plans are now being developed for a 24-inch pipe line from Arabia to the Mediterranean.

Persia. It is understood that American interests are preparing to negotiate for a concession in Persia.

Refineries (100 per cent. American).

(1) *Bahrein,* working.

(2) *Raz Tanura,* working at present on small scale but large expansion in progress.

(3) *Tripoli* (Syria), large refinery proposed, and concession to build recently obtained.

Haifa. Refinery owned by Anglo–Iranian Oil Coy. and Royal Dutch Shell Coy., but the Americans have the right to refine part of their output of Iraq crude oil there.

Conclusions

16.   (i) Middle East Oil is essential to us in peace and war.

(ii) There is no considerable quantity of oil in the British Empire.

(iii) Apart from North America most of the World's oil lies in the Middle East.

(iv) Without Middle East oil the British Commonwealth and the U.S.A. could not fight a war on the same scale as in 1945 unless unforeseen developments occur.

APPENDIX II

Joint regional headquarters

Need for a headquarters in war

The speed of modern warfare, the increasing interdependence of the three Services with the consequent necessity for joint decisions on a high level, and the impossibility of divorcing military factors from political considerations, have all emphasised in the past war the need for locating a central or regional headquarters within each theatre of operations, and at the nerve centre of communications. We consider that the possible conditions of future war, when time may become even more important, will further emphasise this need.

2.   Such a headquarters will be concerned primarily with the planning and conduct of operations. Although there will be an administrative element, the headquarters should not be confused with an administrative base, which controls the smooth forward flow of men and materials from base installations, requires a considerably larger establishment, and is generally located well to the rear of the scene of operations.

Location in war

3.   In war the headquarters should be located at the political and geographical centre of the area and be at the hub of communications. In addition it should be reasonably near to the tactical commanders in order that Commanders-in-Chief may keep in close touch with them and exert a personal influence on their forces. This at the same time avoids the adverse morale effect on forward troops which comes from siting the headquarters in rear areas out of touch with the fighting and living conditions of the front line. It should not, however, be so far forward that its security will be affected by fluctuations of the battle front.

These general considerations make Egypt the unquestionable location for a Middle East headquarters in war.

Need for a headquarters in peace

4. The outcome of any future war may well depend on the result of our initial actions, and we must therefore have in peace a nucleus headquarters, which could rapidly be expanded in war. This peace-time headquarters would be much smaller than that visualised in war, since it need not include many of the administrative sections and units which have grown up round the present headquarters. The duties of this headquarters in peace would be to co-ordinate all inter-service matters, including intelligence, and to prepare defensive plans to be put into effect on the outbreak of war. There would also be inter-service problems of a political nature in the Middle East area which will require joint consideration on the spot.

Location in peace

5. It would be preferable to locate in peace the headquarters for the Middle East in Egypt where it will have to be in war. Since, however, we have agreed to withdraw our forces from Egypt in peace we examine below possible alternative locations. We shall, however, require the Egyptians to prepare the necessary accommodation and communications for the war headquarters so that the move to Egypt can be made immediately on the outbreak of war.

6. We consider that East Africa and Malta are too far away from the political and geographical centre of the area and a headquarters located in either of these places would be out of touch with subordinate commands. In addition, since the headquarters of the naval C-in-C. must be in the Mediterranean a headquarters in East Africa would divorce him from the other two Cs-in-C.

We are, therefore, restricted to Cyprus, Cyrenaica or Palestine, whose relative merits we discuss below:—

(a) *Move to Egypt on the outbreak of war.* All these countries are equally well placed for a quick move of the headquarters to Egypt on the outbreak of war, with some balance in favour of Cyrenaica and Palestine, since land communications would be available.

(b) *Position in the area.* A regional headquarters in Palestine would be in close touch with the most active part of the zone, and would also be well placed for political and intelligence co-ordination. Both Cyprus and Cyrenaica, on the other hand, would be somewhat remote from the political scene and out of touch with our main forces.

(c) *Internal security.* The internal security problem in Palestine would result in a heavy guarding commitment. In both Cyprus and Cyrenaica the commitment would be considerably lighter.

(d) *Tenure.* Cyprus has the great advantage of being British territory. Although the future status of Palestine has not yet been decided, our tenure there is more certain than that in Cyrenaica.

(e) *Accommodation.* In view of the fact that Palestine is a developed and built-up area, we consider it reasonable to suppose that accommodation could be made available there and a move from Egypt could be carried out with less delay than to any other area.

The provision of accommodation in both Cyprus and Cyrenaiea on the scale required would present considerable problems.

7. On balance, we consider that Palestine should be selected as the peace-time location for the joint regional headquarters.

APPENDIX III

Military requirements in Cyrenaica

Strategic requirements

We have shown that Cyrenaica will be required in war to provide:—

(a) A base from which the strategic bomber forces could operate in the early stages of the war before re-deployment to Egypt has taken place.
(b) Bases for fighter defence with the necessary ground organisation.
(c) Port facilities for naval forces and bases for air forces required to protect sea communications in the Eastern Mediterranean.
(d) Staging facilities for our East–West air transport route.

We should also require to locate in Cyrenaica sufficient ground forces to defend the facilities detailed above.

2. We now examine our minimum military requirements in Cyrenaica in peace on two assumptions, namely:—

A. We were able to obtain the rights and facilities in Egypt for which we are now negotiating.
B. We agreed complete evacuation of all forces, installations and stores from Egypt.

A. *Requirements assuming facilities in Egypt*

3. In peace we shall require to maintain a nucleus for the base installations and facilities outlined in paragraph 1 above, together with forces to man them. We discuss these requirements fully below.

4. *Navy.* In War, Alexandria will be the operational base for naval forces in the Eastern Mediterranean. In Cyrenaica, Tobruk and Benghazi will be required as advanced bases from which convoy escorts, coastal forces, mine-sweepers and light forces can operate both for the protection of our sea communications and for attack on enemy forces.

5. In peace, we shall require the clearance and reconstruction of Benghazi and Tobruk, and limited storage space for ammunition, fuel and naval stores for use in war. All other facilities will be provided on a mobile basis on the outbreak of war.

6. *Army.* We do not visualise stationing in Cyrenaica more than a peace-time garrison of about one brigade for the guarding of airfields and other facilities and for the maintenance of internal security. Although we may eventually locate a strategic reserve in East Africa and plan to move it forward to Egypt in war, we must guard against the possibility that an early move into Egypt might not be possible. Therefore, it is desirable to have the right to station it temporarily in Cyrenaica.

7. *Air.* Although we have based our requirements in Cyrenaica on having in Egypt on the outbreak of war airfields and facilities for operating our air forces, we must assume that there will be a period after the outbreak of war during which, while the Egyptian bases are being brought into full operation, we shall have to depend for our strategic air offensive primarily on Cyrenaica. We must therefore make provision

for that part of our strategic bomber force which we shall expect to be in the Middle East in the early stages of a war to operate from Cyrenaica. We think it reasonable to assume that this would be of the order of twelve long-range bomber squadrons.

It is not possible to assess the period during which the whole of this bomber force will have to operate from Cyrenaica, but it is logical to assume that it will be limited. To reduce to a minimum our commitments in peace we consider that for such a period this number of squadrons could operate from four airfields.

We should wish to develop these bases and to maintain them at an efficient standard in peace either by basing there our Middle East bomber force, or by arranging frequent visits of the force to the area.

8.   In addition we should require in Cyrenaica facilities for:—

(a) A fighter force for the defence of the country and of sea communications and a small maritime air force to carry out anti-submarine operations and offensive operations against enemy shipping in the Eastern Mediterranean.

It is essential that these forces should operate effectively immediately on the outbreak of war. Airfields adequately equipped and with good dispersal facilities, together with a ground control organisation for fighter defence manned by a skeleton staff, will therefore be required.

Our airfield requirement can be met in peace by the maintenance and improvement of certain of the existing airfields.

(b) A proportion of the force allotted for the fighter defence of Egypt.

The limited airfield accommodation in Palestine will necessitate stationing in Cyrenaica, in peace, part of the nucleus force for the fighter defence of Egypt. This force will move into Egypt on the outbreak of war and could be accommodated in peace on those airfields prepared for the defence of Cyrenaica.

(c) Air staging facilities for our air communications and for the reinforcement route.

Through air staging requirements are at present being met by the airfields at El Adem and Benina. These are well placed for our East–West air traffic and should fulfil our requirements in war.

9. Though in peace we shall not need to station in Cyrenaica forces of the size required at the outbreak of war, we must ensure that our organisation there remains effective.

This can be achieved by basing nucleus forces in the area combined with visits by aircraft based elsewhere.

10.   To summarise, our requirements in Cyrenaica in peace to support air forces required in that country on the outbreak of war will be:—

(a) The development of four existing airfields to long-range bomber standards.

(b) The maintenance and improvement of certain airfields for fighter defence and small maritime air forces.

(c) The provisions of a fighter defence ground organisation manned by a skeleton staff.

(d) The maintenance and development of existing air staging facilities at El Adem and Benina.

(e) The right to operate such forces in the country as are required to keep these facilities effective.

11. *General*—We may require storage facilities for equipment, which for reasons of security or maintenance cannot be left in Egypt, but which may be required in that country on the outbreak of war.

B. *Requirements assuming no facilities in Egypt*

12. Egypt is the only country on which operations in the Middle East can be based in war. We must therefore continue to plan on the assumption that we shall return to Egypt on or immediately after the outbreak of war and there can be no question of developing Cyrenaica as a substitute.

The general effect in peace, however, of failing to obtain the rights and facilities in Egypt for which we are now negotiating, would be to make it all the more important to have facilities elsewhere from which to fill the operational gap before we can commence operating from Egypt. This would greatly increase the importance, although not correspondingly the size, of those requirements in Cyrenaica detailed above.

57 CAB 79/50, COS 112(46)2, annex   17 July 1946
'Egypt-revision of treaty': report by the JPS to the COS, 16 July 1946 (JP(46)140)

[In the wake of the Cabinet's decision of 7 June (see 55) Stansgate was authorised to resume negotiations in Egypt. Meanwhile attempts were made in London, at the highest level, to re-draft the British version of the treaty, essentially to incorporate new proposals on the joint defence board and on article 5, although the issues of the evacuation's timing and the nature of its stages also remained to be settled. On 10 July a new Egyptian draft was received (FO 371/53305, no 3050) and sent to the JPS for comments. The JPS report (CAB 84/83, JP(46)140, 16 July 1946) in the form of a draft reply to Attlee was considered by the COS the following day along with several Alexandria tels. Tel 9 of 14 July (FO 371/53305, no 3076) and tel 10 of 17 July (FO 371/53306, no 3138) dealt with the withdrawal of combat troops. Tel 9 also focused on the differences between article 2 in the Egyptian draft treaty and the equivalent article 5 in the British draft. The Egyptian article 2 stated: 'In the event of Egypt becoming the object of armed aggression or in the event of armed aggression against Great Britain in the countries adjacent to Egypt, the High Contracting Parties shall consult together immediately in order to undertake such common action as may be recognised as necessary, until such time as the Security Council has taken the necessary measures for the re-establishment of peace'. The revised British draft of article 5 stated: 'The High Contracting Parties agree that, subject always to the provisions of the Charter of the United Nations, their respective armed forces shall, in the event of war involving either of them and endangering their security in Egypt and neighbouring territories, take the necessary measures, in close co-operation with each other, for the purposes of mutual defence'. The British wanted consultation in the event of threats to their security short of war. The Egyptians argued that this was provided for through the medium of the proposed joint defence board and the second paragraph of article 3 of their draft stated: 'The Board shall meet as often as may be necessary . . . . and in order to examine, if need arises, the military repercussions of the international situation and, in particular, of all events which may threaten the security of the Middle East, and to make in this respect suitable recommendations to the two governments, the appropriateness of which it will be for the latter to decide'. The C's-in-C, having learnt of Sidky's rejection of the British article 5, were prepared to accept the Egyptian draft which, unlike the British draft referred to the Middle East without the qualification of territories neighbouring Egypt. Moreover, tel 9 also reported the C's-in-C's willingness to withdraw all combat troops from Egypt by 31 Mar 1947. This was qualified in tel 10 (not seen by the COS before their meeting) by the intention of the new C-in-C MELF, Gen Dempsey, to camouflage some combatant forces within the remaining administrative troops. The COS incorporated the points in JP(46)140 into a minute to the PM from Gen Ismay, printed below, which formed an amended draft of the annex to the JPS paper.]

The Chiefs of Staff have examined the text of the Draft Treaty proposed by the Egyptians as amended by Lord Stansgate's Telegram No. 9.

2.   It seems to them that the proposed Draft does not specifically cover the following essential military requirements:—

(a) It does not guarantee legal immunities for British troops pending their withdrawal.

(b) It does not commit the Egyptians to give us all the necessary facilities on threat of war.

(c) It does not even commit the Egyptians to consultation with a view to action unless countries "adjacent to Egypt" are involved.

(d) It does not provide for air transit rights in peacetime, about which the Chiefs of Staff are writing separately.

(e) No mention is made in the Terms of Reference of the Joint Defence Board of:—

   (i) Communications
   (ii) Facilities to be placed at our disposal.

3.   The Chiefs of Staff do not feel themselves competent to judge the extent to which the wording proposed by the Egyptians may be held to meet these requirements, since this is a matter which can only be decided by legal experts. They wish merely to record that, from the military point of view, it is essential that all the points given in paragraph 2 above should be safeguarded.

4.   There is a further point. Paragraph 9 of Lord Stansgate's telegram suggests that there is some misunderstanding in Egypt about our programme of evacuation from the Delta, as recommended by the Chiefs of Staff and approved by the Defence Committee. (D.O. (46) 21st Meeting, Item 2, Conclusion (i)). This may be summarised as follows:—

"(a) The evacuation of Service Headquarters to be carried out as soon as possible;

(b) The evacuation of the remaining British forces from Cairo and Alexandria to the Canal zone to be completed by 31st March, 1947;

(c) The total evacuation of Egypt to be completed within five years; provided that within three years:—

   (i) Decisions on our long-term future position in the Middle East are taken in sufficient time to enable us to make alternative arrangements elsewhere in the Middle East; and

   (ii) We receive assurances that the Egyptians will efficiently maintain the facilities we subsequently require."

5.   The Chiefs of Staff have been informed that the Foreign Office have already brought the misunderstanding to the notice of Lord Stansgate, but they think that it would be advisable to telegraph the approved programme, as set out above, to Lord Stansgate again, in order to obviate the possibility of any further misconception.

6.   I am sending a copy of this minute to the Foreign Secretary.

58   FO 371/53306, no 3138   18 July 1946

[Anglo–Egyptian treaty negotiations]: outward telegram no 5 from Mr Bevin to Lord Stansgate on the timing of the proposed withdrawal of British troops

> [Attlee delayed replying to Gen Ismay (see 57) until he had consulted Bevin. The FO view on article 2 was dictated by the perceived need to use the base if aggression occurred outside the Middle East and in particular if Turkey, Greece or Persia were attacked. Stansgate was therefore instructed to insist on the British draft of article 2[1] (FO 371/53306, no 3140, FO tels 3 and 4, 18 July 1946).]

Your No. 10 of July 17th about evacuation of combatant forces from Egypt.

The evacuation of all combatant troops from the Canal Zone by 31st March, 1947 would create just such a vacuum in Egypt as I promised Parliament I would avoid.

The Prime Minister is most insistent that we should not go back on this.

The intention is that no distinction shall be made between combatant and administrative troops so far as evacuation from the Canal Zone is concerned and that they should be "run down" together. The plan approved by the Defence Committee is as follows:—

(a) The evacuation of Service Headquarters to be carried out as soon as possible;

(b) The evacuation of the remaining British forces from Cairo and Alexandria to the Canal Zone to be completed by 31st March, 1947;

(c) The total evacuation of Egypt to be completed within five years; provided that within three years–

   (i) decisions on our long-term future position in the Middle East are taken in sufficient time to enable us to make alternative arrangements elsewhere in the Middle East; and

   (ii) We receive assurances that the Egyptians will efficiently maintain the facilities we subsequently require.

Please work to the above plan in your negotiations over the evacuation protocol.

---

[1] Henceforth references to treaty articles correspond to their numbers as they appear in the Egyptian draft.

59   FO 371/53306, no 3183   21 July 1946

[Anglo–Egyptian treaty negotiations]: inward telegram no 17 from Lord Stansgate to Mr Bevin on article 2 of the proposed treaty

Your telegrams to Alexandria 3, 4, 5, 6, 7 and 8.

You will remember that when I returned to London in June we went carefully into the question of just how far we could insist on inclusion in a new treaty of what we considered to be all our essential military requirements. You then agreed and your view was later endorsed by the Cabinet that we could only enforce our full military requirements by a military occupation, and that this was a step which we were certainly not prepared to take.

2. It was agreed therefore that:—

A. We must obtain most satisfactory kind of goodwill treaty we could by mutual agreement.

B. It would be impossible to tie down Egyptian Government in advance to take what we might consider to be necessary action in the event of threat of war i.e. that Egyptian Government must formally retain the right to make their own decision as to what they considered to be appropriate action in any given set of circumstances.

C. Too much reliance could not be placed upon form words included in a treaty, since future action by Egyptian Government both as regards maintenance of an efficient base and co-operation in war or threat of war, would depend largely on their goodwill.

D. Although a treaty on these lines would not be entirely satisfactory from military point of view it would be better than nothing, and that there was no better alternative.

E. Decisions to be taken by Chiefs of Staff were not therefore upon what they must insist (since ex-hypothesi we have no means to insist) but what alternative measures in view of unsatisfactory position inside Egypt, they must take outside Egypt.

3.   Policy outlined above specified, we understood our brief for resumption of negotiations. On this basis we were to get what we could and we were to bear in mind the need to obtain Egyptian agreement to a form of words which would make the treaty defensible at home.

4.   It appears to us however that instructions and comments contained in your telegrams under reference are not quite in line with this policy. If we must insist that Egyptian Article 2 is amended as you now propose, if it is *vital* to have Egyptian *agreement* that we can if necessary use Egypt as a base for our operations in the event of for instance a Bulgarian attack against Greece, if the requirements of Chiefs of Staff are *essential*, it appears to us to be certain that negotiations must break down and that we will be faced by alternatives of either being content with no treaty at all or undertaking a military occupation. Both these alternatives were considered in London and rejected, and if a deterioration in international situation or some other reasons has led to a reversal of this Cabinet decision, and of our brief as a delegation, an entirely new situation will have arisen here.

5.   As we see it at present we are within reach of obtaining agreement of treaty articles which as we have explained in my telegram No. 9 we believe covers substance of our own draft treaty which only recently was put forward to the Egyptians as the settlement of our requirements. There remains:

(a) Evacuation Protocol.

I am drafting separately the text of a draft which we have prepared and which covers both immunities and transit rights until completion of evacuation. I must emphasise that it is becoming increasingly clear with the lapse of time, it is the actual evacuation from Egypt of British uniformed personnel that has become the vital issue. I hope to see Sidki Pasha tomorrow and will press for an evacuation protocol on the plan of your telegram No. 5. I must warn you however that we consider that there is little chance of success, since all indications are that Egyptians will insist on specific completion date.

(b) Sudan Protocol.

It was agreed before I left London that it would be wise policy to leave discussion on the Sudan Protocol until agreement had been reached on treaty articles and the evacuation protocol. When discussions take place I will of course bear in mind the point you make. Egyptians have already made it clear that they will not leave this question in the air.

6. You expressed the hope in your telegram No. 3 that a final settlement will be arrived at which will enable you to come out about August 5th. If we are to continue on the present lines and negotiate a treaty of goodwill, doing the best we can to include our requirements, I am hopeful that we may be able to welcome you here early August. I do urge however that how much we can get and how much goodwill will be at the disposal of Joint Defence Board depends a great deal upon our being able to conclude these negotiations quickly and without raising further suspicions and animosity. You appreciate I am sure that even intelligent and cosmopolitan members of the Egyptian Delegation often cannot be persuaded that our points are reasonable. They cannot understand the requirements of modern war; they are afraid of being involved in defence of purely British interests; they are unreasonably suspicious of our intentions as a result of 60 years occupation; they are assumingly handicapped by an ignorant dislike and an unscrupulous, hostile opposition. If we must insist on the points raised in your telegrams, in particular in your revised draft of Article 2 and if we can make no compromise in our evacuation programme, we are all convinced that there is no chance whatever of obtaining a treaty of goodwill at all. I would moreover stress that there is no possibility of ensuring our requirements by verbal jugglery of the texts. We will get Egypt to fulfil her obligations as an ally either (a) by Egyptian goodwill or (b) by the use of force. The day for the sword will only come when it is clear that there is no Egyptian goodwill. It has not come yet. My detailed comments on certain points in your telegrams under reference are contained in my immediately following telegram.

8. Commanders-in-Chief agree entirely from a military point of view with your assessment in your telegrams under discussion of our requirements for the defence of the Middle East, but they nevertheless endorse our estimate of the possibilities and course we recommend.

60　FO 141/1082, no 422　　　　　　　　　　　22 July 1946

[Anglo-Egyptian treaty negotiations]: outward telegram no 43[1] from Mr Bevin to Lord Stansgate on article 2 of the proposed treaty

Your telegrams Nos. 17[2] and 18.

I accept your definition of the policy laid down by the Cabinet more particularly the statement in paragraph 3 of your telegram No, 17 that "we were to get what we

---

[1] This telegram was numbered incorrectly and therefore out of sequence. This was pointed out by the embassy in Cairo who asked the FO for a correction. It should have been tel 18 but no correction seems to have been made. The next FO tel to Alexandria was duly numbered 19.
[2] See 59.

could, and we were to bear in mind the need to obtain Egyptian agreement to a form of words which would make the Treaty defensible wisdom." I have no intention of creating a situation which would necessitate our undertaking a military occupation, and I do not really think that my telegrams under reply can bear such a construction. In redrafting Article 2 I was alive to the necessity of finding words which the Egyptians could reasonably be asked to accept, and I see no reason why Sidky should not be asked to accept my version when it can be pointed out to him that it is futile to argue and consult when you are being attacked. You have got to act, and action should already have been determined by the Board. I cannot understand your hesitancy in representing these very sensible propositions to Sidky, and I beg you to do so. If he rejects our proposals it will be a pity; but we shall be no worse off than we are now. There is no need to define "neighbouring countries" (nor yet to specify Greece and Turkey, which I mentioned by way of background only), and surely we need not assume in advance that everything we put forward will be rejected? All I am trying to do is to get quite clear what our respective standpoints and obligations are. I have been over the ground with Amr, and explained all this to him. He said he thought that our proposals in regard to Article 2 were reasonable and promised to inform the King and his Government (but please do not quote him). It is therefore important that you should press these points also on Sidky.

Finally in dealing with these people it is very necessary to display the utmost firmness. I have done so in talking to the Ambassador, and with your support of my attitude I have every hope that we shall obtain improvement in the Egyptian text which we hope for.

61 FO 141/1082, no 432   25 July 1946

[Anglo-Egyptian treaty negotiations]: note by P A Dove[1] of a meeting with Hassan Youssef on the obstacles to agreement

[By 21 July the FO were aware in reference to article 2 that Sidky believed his colleagues would never accept treaty obligations in the event of a threat of war and that Stansgate found it difficult to believe the negotiations could be allowed to break down on such a point (FO 371/53307, no 3216, Alexandria tel 22, 21 July 1946). On 25 July, Stansgate reported Sidky's conviction that it would be impossible not to announce an evacuation date or to announce a date of five years. He also stated his view that Britain should accept the Egyptian draft of article 2, agree, in the light of Bevin's tel 5 (see 58), to the evacuation of all naval forces by 31 Mar 1947 and that a period of three years should be proposed for the complete evacuation of the base (FO 371/53308, no 3299, Alexandria tel 33, 25 July 1946).]

In the course of a conversation with Hassan Bey Youssef today, I began by remarking that he must have been hearing a good deal from Amr Pasha recently. How was he: was he still optimistic about the negotiations.

Hassan Bey replied that Amr was in fact telephoning once a day and that this morning for the first time he had struck a depressing note. Following his last

---

[1] 2nd secretary at the Cairo embassy.

meeting with Mr. Bevin, Amr had been very optimistic because the conversation had largely centred on Mr. Bevin's plans to visit Egypt early in August for the signing of the Treaty. Hassan Bey said that Sidky had also telephoned him this morning and appeared not only to be pessimistic about the results of yesterday's meeting with the British Delegation, but also to be nervous about the reactions of his own Delegation when he met them on Saturday. Sidky felt and Hassan Youssef agreed with him that the Delegation might well charge him with the failure of his mission and bring about the fall of his cabinet.

I asked what were the obstacles which were regarded as so insuperable. Hassan Bey said 'evacuation and the Sudan'. Our insistence on five years as a period for total evacuation was obviously unacceptable and Sidky could not be expected to have the slightest chance of getting this across his delegation or the country. Egyptians as a whole would simply lose all confidence in the sincerity of our offer to evacuate and would feel that on the contrary we had every intention of remaining. These fears were further substantiated by no early date being given for the evacuation of combatant troops, which we had previously led them to expect. He had also heard that the telephone system for G.H.Q. on the Canal was going to take six months to install: this surely gave a very solid impression of permanency.

I asked whether this was really a fair estimate of the position. We had really no idea how long total evacuation would take and our wish was that it should be left to the Joint Board to supervise the running down of troops, stores and installations in such a way that no vacuum would be left between the termination of that process and the effective birth of a nucleus base under Egyptian control. Two factors therefore controlled the date of final British evacuation: (1) the physical considerations of winding up and disposals, and (2) the safe merging of that process into the new system of Egyptian control; and no one on the British side felt able to predict even approximately when that process would be complete. But since the Egyptians had insisted on being given a date, the best we could do was to give a figure inside which we could be reasonably sure of completing the evacuation, though this figure might bear little relation to reality. Was it not therefore better to leave the time limit out of the Treaty and to build up Egyptian confidence in the competence of the Joint Board to see that evacuation was completed at the earliest possible moment. Hassan Youssef was sure that this would not be sufficient, but why could it not be left to the Security Council or some such disinterested third party to determine the rate of evacuation. If such a provision were made in the Treaty he could assure me that it would not be necessary to include a time limit. I said that that was an interesting suggestion.

At this juncture Hassan Bey was called away to speak to Montaza on the telephone.

On his return Hassan Bey turned to the question of the Sudan. He said it was his turn to ask me what was our difficulty in accepting the very simple and reasonable protocol which the Egyptian Government had put forward. I replied that our only anxiety was that we should not in any way prejudge the ultimate wishes of the Sudanese. We felt very strongly that they were in the middle of a continuing process of development which in their own best interests should not be disturbed and our hope was therefore that the Sudan question should be left open with provisions for joint study and discussion after the Treaty was signed. Surely the Egyptian proposal to establish in the Treaty Egyptian sovereignty over the Sudan was in fact pre-judging the issue. Hassan Bey replied that this was far from being the Egyptian intention. He said I would surely acknowledge without going into legalistic arguments the existence of "some Egyptian sovereignty" and all the Egyptians wanted *pour sauver l'apparence* was some reference to this in the Treaty. Without it, what standing would they have in future discussions on the Sudan, since they had virtually no share in the administration. The Egyptians were only really concerned in the Nile waters and in maintaining their rightful interest in the Sudan until such time as the Sudanese were in a position to determine their own future; and when that time came he agreed that the Sudanese should be perfectly free to renounce Egyptian sovereignty if they so desired.

Hassan Bey finally turned to the question of Article 2 of the Egyptian draft treaty. He informed me that Mr. Bevin had asked Amr to consider the example of a Russian attack on Iraq and the desirability of instant preparedness of the Egyptian base in that event. Hassan Bey said that the answer to that question was that if the first bomb fell on Iraq, the second would fall on the Suez Canal and Egypt would be automatically at war. I asked what happened if the second bomb did not fall on the Suez Canal which might just as easily be the case. Our anxiety was over the time factor in the swift movement of modern war. If Egypt were to wait for attack to reach the limitrophe countries, which in the older conceptions of war was quite reasonable, we felt sure it would be too late. Hassan Bey frankly agreed with this view and assured me that if we could satisfy the Egyptian Government on the evacuation and Sudan issues the Egyptians would not stand on area limitation in Article 2.

I finally came to the real purpose of my mission and informed Hassan Youssef that Lord Stansgate and the Ambassador felt it was time they had another talk with His Majesty and hoped that H.M. might feel able to receive them sometime soon. They did not, however, wish to give rise to undesirable speculation, which might be the case if they were to be received officially with the usual attendant publicity. Would it perhaps be possible for them to be granted an audience informally and without publicity. Hassan Bey hesitated a little and then explained that his telephone talk, which had interrupted our conversation, had been with H.M. who had just studied Sidky's report of yesterday's meeting with the British Delegation. H.M. had appeared to be "very upset". Hassan Bey therefore advised against an audience if Lord Stansgate and the Ambassador could show no advancement on yesterday's position. If, on the other hand, they felt able to offer something such as the introduction of a third party into the evacuation protocol or a concession to Egyptian feelings over the Sudan, would I let him know at once and an audience would be arranged. He knew that H.M. would take particular pleasure in acting as an intermediary in the attempt to solve either of the two outstanding crucial problems.

Throughout our conversation I was impressed by the frankness and openness of Hassan Youssef's argument which appeared to be free from the bargaining motive. As ever the obsession was with face-saving which in both the major issues seemed genuinely to be the crux of the Egyptian difficulties, although there was in the case of evacuation the added complication of suspicion about our intention to leave.

62 FO 371/53308, no 3299   29 July 1946
'Alexandria telegram no 33': minute by R G Howe on the response to the appparent impasse in the treaty negotiations

A partial answer has already been sent to this telegram in the shape of our telegram No. 22 to Alexandria summarising the Secretary of State's conversation with Amr on July 25th. It is to be noted that Amr did *not* mention the Sudan.

The position now seems to be that we have reached an impasse. To begin with, we cannot compromise, or give way, on the question of Egyptian sovereignty over the Sudan. Secondly, the Secretary of State has always insisted that he *must* have five years to "run down" in Egypt to enable the international situation to clear. Thirdly, the Article 2 as drafted by the Egyptians represents (on the Egyptians own showing) a "Polish guarantee". It is in fact perfectly obvious, now that the Egyptians have been brought up against essentials that they do not intend to collaborate in adequate measure for Middle East defence. This being so, we seem faced with the necessity of telling them that we are not prepared to commit ourselves to an alliance with them on the terms offered, and that we should prefer to have our hands entirely free. As regards the Sudan we shall continue to be bound by the agreements of 1899; and we shall continue our policy of evacuating (1) the cities and the Delta to the Canal Zone, and (2) subsequently from Egypt in accordance with (1) the programme already laid down and (2) the practical limitations which govern the rate of evacuation from the Canal Zone. A point for consideration, however, is whether we should not, before recommending this course to the Cabinet, suggest that Sidky should pay a visit to London (as he has expressed readiness to do) and make a last attempt, away from the poisonous atmosphere of Cairo, to convince him of the soundness of our case.

See now Alexander [sic] telegram No. 35[1] which rather suggests that we have not yet quite reached the impasse. If Hassan Youssef can be relied on, Article 2 is not the chief stumbling block as Sidky represents it to be and that there may be room for a compromise solution on the time limit for evacuation and the Sudan protocol. Whilst standing on Article 2 it might be possible, if the Egyptians insist on a time limit for evacuation from the Canal, to meet them here. After all Sidky's offer of two years on the Canal would bring us to March 1949. The Secretary of State has asked for 1951. It looks as if there is a possibility here of a compromise on 1950. As far as the Sudan is concerned, I see very little possibility of compromising on the question of the sovereignty over the Sudan.

---

[1] Reporting the conversation between P A Dove and Hassan Youssef, see 61.

63 FO 141/1082, no 435   29 July 1946
'Review of the Anglo–Egyptian treaty situation': memorandum by Sir W Smart

The following observations are not intended to influence the negotiations but to be an objective examination of the situation.

None of us could be expected to see last year how the Treaty problem would develop. At that time none of us had in mind a limitation of the operation of an

Anglo–Egyptian Treaty to Egypt and limitrophe countries though we were aware of the ideas of Egyptian extremists, such as Fikri Abaza,[1] about turning Egypt into a sort of Switzerland. My personal opinion was that, in view of the internal situation in Egypt, we should agree to evacuation of Egypt and content ourselves with advanced bases in Cyrenaica and Palestine, a main base further south and military facilities in Egypt for the timely return of our troops in the event of war. If we had been able to get down to negotiations with the Egyptians before the end of last year, we might have got a satisfactory Treaty with Egypt on these lines. Owing to the delay in opening negotiations, the extremists, as we had warned the Foreign Office at the end of October, got possession of the field and negotiations finally opened with the Egyptians in an extremist mood. Owing to our U.N.O. policy, we were unable to do the necessary for securing the Cyrenaica forward base. We finally agreed to the evacuation of Egypt and proceeded to negotiate with Egypt for the necessary military facilities in Egypt., etc. In these negotiations hitherto the Egyptians have refused to give us adequate guarantees for military facilities in Egypt and to ensure our return to Egypt in the circumstances which would require our return if we were to be enabled to defend our positions in the Eastern Mediterranean and the Middle East. The Egyptian attitude indicates a desire to keep Egypt out of any war between Great Britain and Russia unless Egypt herself is attacked. The provision regarding limitrophe countries cannot be regarded as a serious contribution, since Russian aggression would obviously be directed against non-limitrophe countries, which would only be involved later in the proceedings. We would, therefore, have no contractual right to use Egypt as a military base when it became necessary for us to repel Russian aggression in the rest of the Near and Middle East.

It can be taken for granted that the terms of the Anglo–Egyptian Treaty will powerfully influence the course of Treaty revision in Iraq, where we may also find ourselves militarily evicted on similar lines. Transjordan may quite well follow suit. The Hashimites and their supporters may quite well not like these developments but will probably have their hands forced.

Our oil supplies in Iraq and Southern Persa would thus be undefendable. I believe that it is thought that we might defend the Southern Persian oil wells from India, but, with an independent India, this seems a dubious proposition.

The Egyptians at the same time are obviously aiming at getting rid of the obstacles which prevent their substituting Egyptian for British domination in the Sudan. If they succeed in this, they will cut our trans-African communications and weaken our Colonial positions in East Africa.

We are thus faced with the possibility of our military eviction from the Middle East, with the possible exception of Palestine, which in present circumstances will be an uneasy foothold, and a weakening of our Central African positions. If we cannot persuade the Egyptians to abandon their present attitude, our U.N.O. policy forces us to yield to their demands, with the wider consequences indicated above. The result would seem to be a danger of a liquidation of the British Empire, as apart from the Dominions, if the latter would still stick to a Great Britain thus weakened [sic]. Our only hope would be that once we have gone from the Middle East and the Sudan, all

---

[1] Egyptian journalist and the editor of *Al-Musawwar* favoured by the Revolutionary Command Council in 1952.

these countries would, on the analogy of the old Turkish Empire, develop friendly relations with us similar to those which existed between Turkey and Great Britain during the 19th century, seek our support to stem the Russian tide, and eventually drift into military agreements with us which would enable us to give them some effective support against a Russian aggression. It is possible that this is the only course open to us.

In the past the British Empire, in view of its military weakness, has been reluctant to undertake land military commitments on a large scale, except in India. In 1882 and 1919 we deviated from that policy; the maintenance of these recent land commitments is perhaps beyond our power. The trouble is that now our oil supplies, without which, in the absence of the development of atomic or other power to replace oil we cannot wage war or even live industrially, lie in this region, which we are apparently unable to defend.

64 FO 371/53308, no 3332   29 July 1946
[Anglo–Egyptian treaty negotiations]: inward telegram no 39 from Lord Stansgate to Mr Attlee on the attitude of the Egyptian government

Egyptian Delegation met together all day on Saturday to consider views of His Majesty's Government explained to Sidky Pasha at our last interview as reported in my telegram No.33. As a result of this meeting Sidky Pasha called alone on the Ambassador and me this morning.

2.   Sidky Pasha made to us an oral and personal communication of which a translation is contained in my immediately following telegram.

3.   We then discussed at length on an unofficial basis the attitude of the Egyptian Government as set out in this communication. Sidky Pasha emphasised as regards Article 2 that if a threat developed in the Middle East, the Joint Board would make its recommendation and the Egyptian Government would of course agree to take the necessary action in time. He remained adamant however that they could not accept in advance a commitment to action in the event of war or of a dangerous situation arising outside limitrophe countries without the right to make final decision. This would be an infringement of sovereignty. We could not move him from this position.

4.   As regards evacuation, Sidky Pasha repeated that he appreciated and had emphasised to his delegation the necessity for agreeing to a reasonable time for the evacuation and hand over for which he had suggested two years. He said he understood also our anxiety regarding the present international situation. This threat however could not last for ever and in 2½ years time (you notice slight advance in time) we should know where we were both as regards the international situation and the state of Egypt's preparedness. It was not possible to plan on the basis of an international threat of indefinite duration. He assumed that in discussion of our evacuation that we would keep to our original expressed intention to withdraw columns of troops at an early stage of the programme.

5.   In the discussion on the Sudan, Sidky Pasha agreed that a joint commission should be set up but maintained the Egyptian view that investigations must be on basis of unity of the Nile Valley i.e. Egyptian sovereignty. Only faint note of concession was that in the course of conversation he appeared to consider the

possibility that the Egyptians might be ready to reserve by a purely unilateral statement their position on Egyptian sovereignty. He seemed ready to accept [? gp. omitted ? as] mandatory principle of preparing the Sudan for eventual right to secede from Egyptian sovereignty.

6.   Both Sidky Pasha and we advanced the familiar arguments on points on which differences exist and solution is as you see exactly as reported in my telegram No. 33. It is clear both from reports which have reached us and from his attitude during this interview that the Egyptian delegation is unanimous and that Sidky Pasha speaks with confidence of their full support. He was very friendly and much calmer than when we last met him.

7.   Sidky Pasha finally told us that a note had been prepared setting forth the Egyptian position which would be handed to us after Wednesday's meeting of his delegation. He would beg us to bring it to the official attention of His Majesty's Government. It seems to us probable intention is that this note should be eventually used if need be as a manifestation in vindication of Egypt's position to the world – whether or not an actual appeal to United Nations Organisation is made. It may be significant that Hafez Afify Pasha had an hour's conversation with the Prime Minister yesterday.

8.   Our views remain as set forward in my telegram under reference. We would add that if no solution can be found regarding the Sudan protocol it appears to us that we would be in a stronger position if it can be shown that the negotiations have broken down on that issue.

9.   Sidky Pasha expressed his readiness to go to London to continue there the negotiations with our delegation including Mr. Bevin. We confined ourselves to noting this suggestion. I do not imagine Mr. Bevin will wish to be involved in the negotiations and a further objection is that it is difficult for an Egyptian delegation or part of one away from Egypt and out of touch with their public opinion to make any serious concession. I would be very glad of your views on this suggestion. I must emphasise that the situation here remains critical. A breakdown is widely announced in most sections of the Arab press though Sidky Pasha has officially denied that this is true. We do *not* consider that time is on our side but believe beside that every week reduces both what we may hope to get and the goodwill necessary to make our military projects work. I would therefore be greatful for earliest possible reply.

65   CAB 79/50, COS 119(46)1   30 July 1946

'Anglo–Egyptian treaty – evacuation': COS Committee minutes on detailed proposals in Alexandria tel 33

The Committee had before them a minute by the Secretary annexing a copy of a telegram prepared by the Foreign Office in reply to telegrams Nos. 33 and 35 from Lord Stansgate, which they wished to despatch to the Prime Minister for approval before instructing Lord Stansgate.

The Committee then discussed two main points contained in the draft telegram, namely—

(i) The proposal to compromise on the date, i.e. 1950 for the total evacuation of all our forces from Egypt including the Canal Zone;

(ii) If this compromise is shown to be impossible, that "we are not prepared to commit ourselves to an alliance . . . . . and that we should prefer to have our hands entirely free".

In discussion of the point at (i) above, it was recalled that the period of five years in which all British forces were to be evacuated from Egypt was proposed originally by the Foreign Secretary, who considered that by then we should be in a better position to assess the international situation. Although the stated period was therefore principally a political matter, from the military point of view there was a period under which material considerations, such as the physical problems inherent in evacuating certain base installations and the necessity to locate and construct a new reserve base outside Egypt, made it impossible totally to evacuate Egypt in less than three years. This point had also been covered by the decisions of the Defence Committee, when they had agreed that the evacuation of Egypt should be completed within five years subject to two provisos. The Chiefs of Staff opinion therefore, was that total evacuation could not be effected in less than three years, and that this programme should preferably be either four or five years.

With regard to (ii) above, the prospect of no Treaty with the Egyptian Government if they did not accept a compromise about the dates for total evacuation, was unacceptable from the military point of view. A complete breakdown in negotiations resulting in no guarantees whatsoever from the Egyptians, opened the whole question of our future military position in the Middle East. It would mean that the military concessions which we hoped to gain under the present agreements from the Egyptians to maintain facilities for our use in Egypt and of the establishment of the Defence Board, would be discarded. Moreover, a breakdown in the negotiations would at this stage almost certainly precipitate serious disturbances in Egypt, which would jeopardise our position in the whole of Egypt, including the Canal Zone.

The forces at our disposal in Egypt precluded the imposition of our wishes in regard to the Treaty with the Egyptians. It was therefore a question of obtaining the greatest concessions from the Egyptians by negotiations, without pressing the issue to a complete breakdown. There was no question that from the military point of view it would be better to accept the conditions so far agreed to by the Egyptians, than to risk the prospect of no Treaty and no military facilities, guarantees or rights remaining to us in Egypt.

Even though this position had been reached, it would not obviate further negotiations with the Egyptian Government explaining our requirements that there should be an adequate guarantee of assistance in time of war, and that it was not so much a question of the form of the present wording, but of obtaining guarantees (if necessary by discussing proposals put forward by the Egyptian Government) to this end.

The Committee:

Instructed the Secretary to draft for their consideration, a reply to the Foreign Office, commenting on the proposed telegram in reply to Nos. 33 and 35 from Lord Stansgate, in the light of the above discussion.

66   FO 371/53308, no 3313   30 July 1946

[Anglo–Egyptian treaty negotiations]: outward telegram no 726 from Sir O Sargent to Mr Attlee (Paris)[1]

[Attlee informed Sargent that he believed breaking off the talks and falling back on the treaty would be unsatisfactory. Meanwhile he would await the COS's detailed views (see 67) and then the matter would be discussed by the Cabinet (FO 371/53308, no 3366, Paris tel 420, 31 July 1946). The views of the COS were duly sent to the FO on 31 July (FO 371/53309, no 3419, letter from Hollis to Sargent.)

Alexandria telegrams Nos. 33 and 35.

Read together, and assuming that Hassan Youssef is to be relied on, these two telegrams indicate that the Egyptians have had a shock on being confronted squarely with the fundamentals of the position, but that we have not yet *quite* reached an impasse. We cannot compromise, or give way, on the issue of Egyptian sovereignty over the Sudan. (This possibility has been reviewed since the Cabinet originally approved the Foreign Secretary's recommendation that we should stand fast, but the review has only confirmed his opinion). Nor can we give way on Article 2 since the Egyptian draft commits us, on the Egyptians' own showing, to a "Polish guarantee", and shows that the Egyptians are determined to shirk if possible collaboration in adequate and timely defence measures for the Middle East. On the other hand, while standing fast on our own draft of this article, it might be possible to meet the Egyptians on the time-limit for evacuation from the Canal. Sidky's offer of two years would bring us to March 1949. The Foreign Secretary has always thought in terms of 1951. We might, subject to the views of the Chiefs of Staff, be able to compromise on 1950. We might also be able to meet the Egyptians over the Sudan in some way *other* than the question of sovereignty. But if a compromise as above is definitely shown to be impossible, we are satisfied that we should tell the Egyptians that we are not prepared to commit ourselves to an alliance with them on the terms which they offer, and that we should prefer to have our hands entirely free. As regards the Sudan we should consider ourselves bound by the agreements of 1899 and the Nile Waters Agreement of 1929; and we should continue our policy of evacuating the cities and the delta to the Canal Zone in accordance with the present programme and subsequently of evacuating the Canal Zone itself within the limitations laid down by practical considerations. It might even be possible to salvage, by an exchange of notes, the idea of the Defence Board.

We also agree with your suggestion that the moral of the two telegrams under reference maybe [sic] that we should not take Sidky's "last word" pronouncements as necessarily final as regards Article 2, for example, it would appear that although Sidky says "no" the King means "perhaps", so that if we stand firm we may yet get "yes". Telegrams Nos. 39[2] and 40 from Alexandria also show that Sidky is not entirely immovable (see his remarks about the evacuation date) that he does not want to break, and that he is prepared to come here himself. (In telegram No. 40 "Article 4 of the" should read "Sudan".)

---

[1] Attlee was in Paris for the Peace Conference which began in public on 29 July and which was convened to finalise the treaties with Germany's allies that had been discussed at the two Paris Councils of Foreign Ministers earlier in 1946. He flew back specially for the Cabinet on 1 Aug.
[2] See 64.

The above are the views of the Department which, as you will have heard, were considered by the Chiefs of Staff today. We understand that their views, which have not yet reached us in detail, are that it is essential that a treaty should be signed, and that for this reason they must differ from the conclusions recorded above. We shall telegraph again when we have been able to study Chiefs of Staff's views in detail.

67   CAB 128/6, CM 76(46)7   1 Aug 1946
'Anglo–Egyptian treaty negotiations': Cabinet conclusions[1] on instructions for the British delegation

The Cabinet discussed the latest developments in the Anglo–Egyptian Treaty negotiations, as reported in telegrams Nos. 33, 35, 39[2] and 40 from the Secretary of State for Air. These telegrams indicated that difficulties had arisen over three points:—

(i)   the timing of the programme of evacuation;
(ii)   the proposal in Article 2 of the draft Treaty that British Forces should have the right to re-enter Egypt if hostilities broke out in neighbouring countries other than those adjacent to Egypt; and
(iii)   the claim that the Egyptian Crown had sovereignty over the Sudan.

Though no reply had yet been received to the latest communication addressed to the Egyptian Delegation, it was desirable that the British Delegation should be given guidance as to the line which they should take on the points at issue.

The Cabinet were informed that, so far as concerned the programme of evacuation, the Chiefs of Staff would see no objection to a compromise on a period of three to five years, but that they regarded a period of three years as the absolute minimum. With regard to Article 2 of the draft Treaty, while the Chiefs of Staff would prefer to see a provision in the Treaty guaranteeing that British troops would be able to enter Egypt in the event of a dangerous situation arising in countries such as Iraq or Syria, they felt that the primary consideration was that we should secure a Treaty with Egypt and they would therefore be prepared to agree to the limitation proposed by the Egyptian Delegation rather than face a complete breakdown in the negotiations. The Chiefs of Staff thought it essential that a firm stand should be made on the question of the Sudan.

The Prime Minister said that he doubted whether anything material would be obtained by insisting on the acceptance of the British version of Article 2 of the draft Treaty. Since Egypt was vital to our position in the Middle East, we were bound to go to her assistance in any case in which she was threatened; and it would not help us to have a provision in the Treaty authorising the entry of British troops into Egypt in certain circumstances if the Egyptian Government were determined to evade their obligations under that provision. He agreed that a firm stand should be made with regard to the Sudan. It would, of course, be open to the Egyptian Government to make a unilateral declaration on this matter, but we should resist the inclusion in the protocol of any words admitting the sovereignty of the Egyptian Crown over the Sudan.

---

[1] Bevin was absent from the meeting due to illness but Sargent attended along with the three service chiefs.
[2] See 64.

As regards the proposal that Sidky Pasha should come to London, while it might in the end be necessary to agree to this, he would prefer that the negotiations should continue in Cairo.

The Cabinet:—

Agreed that the British Delegation should negotiate for a compromise on a period of not less than three years for the completion of evacuation; should accept the Egyptian draft of Article 2 of the Treaty, if it appeared impossible to obtain the willing agreement of the Egyptian Delegation to the British version; and should resist the inclusion in the Sudan protocol of any provision implying recognition of Egyptian sovereignty over the Sudan.

68   FO 371/53308, no 3399   1 Aug 1946

[Egyptian position on the treaty negotiations]: note[1] from the Egyptian delegation to the British delegation

Well before the opening of the present negotiations, the Political Committee, set up by the Egyptian Government to define the main lines of Egyptian post-war foreign policy, had reached the conclusion that it was in Egypt's interest to maintain her traditional friendship with Great Britain and to conclude with her, within the framework of United Nations Organisation, a treaty of alliance on the model of those concluded between equally sovereign and independent States.

In fact, in her attachment to the democratic principles which Great Britain defends, Egypt preferred after the war to follow a policy of friendship with Great Britain in the same way as, during the war, she had resolutely ranged herself in the camp of the Democracies.

On the other hand, Egypt decided to develop her armed forces and to modernise her armaments, in order herself to ensure the effective defence of her territory until U.N.O. would be able to intervene to re-establish peace. In modern war, such a defence places a heavy burden on the States undertaking it.

Egypt is disposed to face up to this task.

To be sure, the alliance with Great Britain strengthens the defensive position of Egypt, until such time as the Security Council can effectively intervene; but, for her part, Egypt renders a great service to Great Britain in freeing her from certain responsibilities and from certain very heavy burdens which she had formerly assumed.

But a country which agrees to enter into such an alliance has the right to demand that its independence should be fully respected. If, in the name of this independence and in order to defend it, the country takes on heavy military burdens, it does not do so in order to give away its independence to an Ally in exchange for the latter's support.

It is accordingly with a strong desire to reach an agreement quickly that the Egyptian Delegation entered into negotiations with the British Delegation for the conclusion of a Treaty of Alliance which she had herself proposed. For its part, before the opening of the negotiations the British Government has declared and has confirmed that Great Britain was disposed to conclude a treaty on new foundations

---

[1] The note was enclosed with despatch no 910 of 1 Aug.

respecting the independence and sovereignty of Egypt and in accordance with the aims and principles of the United Nations Charter.

Nevertheless, from the beginning, the Egyptian Delegation has been forced to take notice of a tendency, on the part of the British, not to be content with a Treaty of the type of those concluded between independent States, but on the contrary to wish to maintain, in one form or another, exceptional clauses taken from the 1936 Treaty and inspired by a state of mind which has prevailed for many years.

The British side has successively proposed the lease for a long period of a part of Egyptian territory, the maintenance of aerial formations in the Canal Zone on a permanent footing, the establishment in Egypt of administrative military bases under British control, the installation at the Canal of an "allied" headquarters for the execution of security measures concerning the whole of the Middle East, the employment for an unspecified period of time of British Military technicians and, finally the creation, for the execution of the clauses of the Treaty, of two non-consultative Mixed Boards, one of the General Staff and the other at Ministerial level.

The British Delegation has, furthermore, asked that British troops should be able freely to enter Egypt and to enjoy all facilities in the case of a simple threat of war or of urgent international necessity. Finally, it has submitted a draft of a Military convention which is only a re-edition of the 1936 Treaty.

The Egyptian Delegation has, in the course of the discussions, never ceased to make it clear that these proposals, inspired by the spirit prevailing in 1936, were in formal contradiction with the principles which ought to have been the foundations of the Treaty and which the British Government had itself accepted; they were equally incompatible with the principles of the United Nations Charter.

The Egyptian Delegation has opposed these proposals, which were finally abandoned by the British.

It was even more careful to adopt this watchful attitude because, in the course of the negotiations, it did not perceive, on the part of the British, an unreserved desire to respect Egyptian independence. For example, in the conversations between the Military experts of the two Delegations, the British officers have clearly revealed their tendency to consider Egypt as the only base possible for defence of the Middle East, and our officers have had indications that important British General-Staffs were to remain in contact with the Suez Canal Zone.

This state of mind has awakened a certain scepticism towards the declarations of principle of the British Government [;] a section of public opinion has thus been led to find in the Joint Defence Board, although it was a purely consultative instrument, a danger of interference in Egyptian internal affairs.

The Egyptian Delegation has, however, given proof, in the course of these long discussions, of a great spirit of conciliation with a view to arriving at a satisfactory agreement.

After numerous exchanges of views, it has finally sent to the British Delegation a draft Treaty which, within the strict limits of Egyptian independence, takes largely into account the last British amendments.

Nevertheless, in the essential article of the draft Treaty, Article 2, the Egyptian Delegation aimed to make clear that the Treaty should only apply in the case of a war "not provoked" by one or other of the Contracting Parties. It retained the expression "limitrophe countries" instead of the much wider expression "neighbouring countries" which included countries more or less distant and outside the possibilities of Military intervention by Egypt. Finally, the delegation aimed to specify that a consultation between the two Allies ought to precede the common action which they would have to undertake. This consultation, elsewhere normal, is not of a kind to complicate or even to delay common action, of which the methods of execution would already have been drawn up by the Joint Defence Board and approved by the two Governments. Egypt, if her territory is threatened, has an interest greater than that of Great Britain in the speed of common action and in an immediate intervention.

After waiting more than two weeks, the Egyptian Delegation has been informed that its amendments have been rejected by the British Government.

In fact the terms that have been offered by the British Government marked their desire to take exaggerated precautions in the Treaty which do not conform to hard realities and are the manifestation of a lack of confidence in their future Ally, and it is this mutual confidence which the Egyptian Delegation considers to be the fundamental element in the Treaty.

Consequently, as a result of the meeting of the Egyptian Delegation, which examined the last British position, new versions of Article 2 have been proposed by the British Delegation. The expression "neighbouring countries" has been replaced by "neighbouring territories" and the formula "endangering their security" has been replaced by the more precise and more adequate expression "leading to hostilities". In fact allusion has been made to the consultations envisaged in Article 3. These new British amendments do not satisfy the Egyptian Delegation insofar as their demands relate to unprovoked war and to limitrophe territories. And furthermore, the consultations which they envisage are the preliminary consultations of the Joint Board, while the Egyptian side demands that the two Governments should consult at the moment when it would be necessary to take a decision on the common action to be undertaken. On the other hand, before the opening of the negotiations the Egyptian people unanimously made known their two essential aspirations: evacuation of the country and unity of the Nile Valley by uniting Egypt and the Sudan under the Egyptian Crown, aspirations which the Egyptian Delegation have put forward and justified in their note of introduction to the negotiations.

The presence of foreign troops on its territory cannot be tolerated by a free country in the new world born of the war. The United Nations Organisation has affirmed this principle without possible doubt in its debates on the maintenance of foreign forces in Syria, the Lebanon, and Iran. But even if the outworn conceptions of the Treaty of 1936 are maintained, the evacuation of the towns of Cairo and Alexandria by British troops ought today to be a *fait accompli*. As it is, there is still in actual fact in Egypt, and notably in these two towns, a British army on a war footing. Yet in all other countries where it was necessary for foreign troops to penetrate by reason of the war, the withdrawal of these troops was begun on the cessation of hostilities, and the evacuation of these countries is almost everywhere complete.

It is true that the British Government announced that it would evacuate Egypt, but when it is a matter of putting it into execution, the British Delegation claims for this operation a maximum delay of five years. Even if one admits that the terms of the Treaty of 1936 are still in operation, only small contingents of British troops could remain in the Suez Canal Zone and these only for ten years.

Thus all that Egypt would obtain on this essential question would be a delay of five years on the limit envisaged in the 1936 Treaty. The Egyptian Delegation cannot obviously accept the prolonged presence of British troops in Egypt whilst all other countries are free of the presence of foreign troops, above all at the moment when Egypt and Great Britain are endeavouring to put their relations on a new footing and conclude a new alliance in conformity with the principles of the Charter of the United Nations.

Furthermore, the Egyptian Delegation would recall here that during the war Egypt has gone beyond the obligations which the Treaty of 1936 imposed on her, and her co-operation during this period difficult for the British Empire and for the cause of democracy certainly deserves quite a different return.

But the defenders of the prolonged delays and those who would wish to see the re-establishment of a Military occupation seem to wish to make use of Egypt in their own interests under British supremacy, and not to treat her like an equal country and one of the same standing.

As regards the Sudan also, the British Government have not yet agreed that the negotiations to be undertaken to determine its future status should be based on the principle of the recognition of the Unity of the Valley of the Nile under the Crown of Egypt.

Now this recognition is a question preliminary to the negotiations. In fact, the Egyptian Delegation cannot agree that the sovereignty of Egypt over the Sudan should be a matter for negotiation, for this would be to admit that it can be contested and would make open to question an inalienable right which all Egyptian governments have never ceased to affirm and to maintain, sometimes despite difficult circumstances, and which for its part Great Britain has also recognised through the statements of its responsible statesmen, before and after 1899.

In fact Egypt has all rights over the Sudan without any exception whatsoever, and thousands of Egyptians have died to assure the Unity of the Valley of the Nile.

Although Egypt has been deprived of the full extent of her administrative rights in the Sudan, it is to her that the Sudan owes her present economic situation. The great public works which have been executed, the railways, the ports, the chief installations, as well as the economic apparatus, have been created with Egyptian money and effort, and it is Egypt which has always met the successive deficits in the Sudan budget.

Egyptian sovereignty over the Sudan has always shown care for the wellbeing of the Sudanese and even now Egypt has only in view their interests and their development on a basis of democratic principles.

In these circumstances it cannot be admitted that Great Britain should invoke the interests of the Sudanese to contest the principle of the Unity of the Valley of the Nile under the Crown of Egypt.

The Sudan does not at present form a political entity, and it is in the interests of the Sudanese to form part of an organised state instead of to live under an abnormal régime.

Egypt, to which the Sudan is united by historical bonds, is more than any country the State to which the Sudanese should attach themselves, since she can at one and the same time offer the advantages of a State endowed with a modern administrative organisation and on the other hand assure them of a complete understanding of their interests because of their geographical situation and the similarity of race, religion and language.

After four months of laborious negotiations, the Egyptian Delegation can only show its disappointment in face of the results of these conversations, since it entered into these negotiations with the desire to conclude a treaty with Great Britain rapidly.

The Delegation is compelled to observe that the text of one of the essential articles of the draft Treaty which it proposed in reply to the latest British amendments has been rejected, and that on the two national demands of evacuation and the Unity of the Valley of the Nile it has received no satisfaction, either in the British proposals or in the conversations on these subjects.

The Egyptian Delegation, in these circumstances, can only express its regret that the negotiations, which it entered into with hope, have reached a point at which it can only stand on the proposals contained in the last texts handed to the British Delegation.

69 FO 371/53309, no 3519   4 Aug 1946
[Anglo–Egyptian treaty negotiations] : minute by Mr Bevin to Mr Attlee opposing the Cabinet's decision on article 2   [Extract]

Prime Minister

I have been considering the Cabinet conclusions of last Thursday, August 1st, about the Egyptian negotiations.[1] I have, on the basis of them, drafted the attached instructions to Stansgate and would like your concurrence to them.

2.   As you will see, I am suggesting that Stansgate, rather than give in to the Egyptians and accept their Article 2, should submit a further alternative which meets the Egyptian objections to our present draft while securing our strategic interests. There are a number of reasons which convince me that it would be wise to try for this:—

(1) We must try and secure, even after we have evacuated Egypt, that we are able to use Egyptian territory should our interests be threatened, say in Irak or South Persia. I am thinking five or ten years hence.

(2) With the discussions on Palestine about to start I am anxious to avoid the appearance of having given in to and curried favour with the Arabs. Moreover I believe that our position in the forthcoming negotiations will be stronger vis-à-vis both Arabs and Jews if we have reserved our strategic position in Egypt. If we have forfeited our position in Egypt it will be difficult to appear disinterested over Palestine.

(3) I believe that it would be wrong tactically to give way over Article 2 at this stage. The Egyptians have already secured great concessions from us. I think Stansgate is too ready to give in when bargaining, with Arabs who invariably pitch their demands too high and expect, as in the market-place, that they will meet considerable resistance from the other side. . . .[2]

---

[1] See 67.

[2] The rest of the minute referred to the evacuation protocol and proposed a time period of three years from the ratification of the proposed treaty rather than from the signing of the agreement.

70   FO 371/53308, no 3333   5 Aug 1946[1]

[Anglo–Egyptian treaty negotiations] : outward telegram no 30 from Mr Bevin to Lord Stansgate on the line to be taken in the treaty negotiations

[Bevin's refusal to accept the Cabinet decision led the FO to redraft instructions to Stansgate taking account of the foreign secretary's views in a way which did not simply modify the Cabinet decision but effectively overturned it. The initial draft telegram instructed Stansgate to stand firm on the Sudan while also noting the importance attached by HMG to obtaining a more favourable version of article 2. In line with the Cabinet decision (see 67), it did however make clear that the Egyptian version of article 2 would have to be accepted as a last resort. The draft, which Bevin wanted sent to Attlee for approval (see 67), was then radically altered by Sargent and became the telegram produced below. It is impossible to be certain which draft Attlee saw. A note by the resident clerk states that tel 30 and tel 31 (which contained the redraft of article 2) were approved by Attlee and despatched at 11.10pm on 4 Aug. Oddly, tel 31 was sent at 12.20am before tel 30 at 1.15am on 5 Aug.]

Cabinet have discussed your telegrams Nos. 33, 35, 39[2] and 40.

We seem to be placed in the position, that, unless we give way on all points to the Egyptians, we get no Treaty. His Majesty's Government cannot conscientiously give way all round. They consider that Sidky should be faced bluntly with the outstanding feature of these negotiations, namely, the fact that since they started we have met the Egyptians on practically every issue they have raised, whereas their own response to our requests has been both slight and grudging.

3.   As regards Article 2 we have carefully studied the reasons as given in paragraph 6 of your No. 33 why the Egyptian negotiators object to our draft. They apparently read into it an obligation upon Egypt to go to war herself in the event of hostilities outside the limitrophe countries, e.g. in Iraq. We do not intend the Egyptians to be committed to such an obligation; but what we must secure is that in the event of war involving Great Britain in some part of the Middle East or the Eastern Mediterranean both inside and outside the limitrophe countries we will ourselves be able to enter Egypt. Such entry would not automatically oblige the Egyptians to declare war. Indeed the last war is sufficient evidence of the possibility of our using, and incidentally, defending, Egyptian territory without this involving the Egyptians in war. There would be no harm in pointing this out.

4.   I have tried my hand at a further version of Article 2 which is given in my immediately following telegram.[3] As you will see this redraft commits us both to joint action in the event of war in Egypt or the adjacent countries. From a study of paragraph 5 of your telegram No. 33 I gather that the Egyptians would probably be prepared to accept this. In the event of war in the neighbouring countries, i.e. in the

---

[1] The telegram was drafted on 4 Aug but sent on 5 Aug.

[2] See 64.

[3] The draft of article 2 in tel 31 stated: 'In the event of Egypt or countries adjacent to Egypt becoming the object of armed aggression the High Contracting Parties agree to take in close co-operation such action as may be necessary until the Security Council has taken the necessary measures for the re-establishment of peace.

In the event of a threat to the security of any of the neighbouring countries of Egypt the High Contracting Parties agree to consult together in order that such action should be taken as may be recognised as necessary until the Security Council has taken the necessary measures for the re-establishment of peace'.

Eastern Mediterranean or the Middle East, we will be obliged to consult together in order to undertake necessary action. What I have in mind is that this part of Article 2 should cover a situation in which we alone would be taking action after both parties have consulted.

5. I do not believe that this re-draft is inconsistent with the expressed intentions of the Egyptians and I would be glad if you would propose it to them in place of their draft.

6. On the question of the Sudan the Cabinet stands absolutely firm. His Majesty's Government cannot compromise on this. Nor can I see anything in your No. 44 received since the Cabinet met which adduces any new argument in support of the Egyptian demand. The Egyptian Government can of course make a unilateral declaration on this matter; but we can accept no form of words in the protocol which admits the sovereignty of the Egyptian Crown.

7. On the question of evacuation I understood that originally the Egyptians did not wish to mention a date. I agreed to this and had it in mind that it would be one of the matters for the Defence Board to settle. Once a date is mentioned we will be pressed to evacuate whether a Treaty is secured or not; but we are determined to hold to the 1936 Treaty rights in the Canal Zone if no revised Treaty is obtained. Would you therefore work to a compromise on the lines that evacuation should be completed within three years of the date of ratification of the Treaty unless it is otherwise agreed by the High Contracting Parties on the recommendation of the Defence Board. Three years from the date of ratification is our minimum. This leaves you nothing to play with. You should, therefore, make a claim for four years. If the Egyptians themselves propose three years you should keep bargaining for a longer period realising that as a last resort you can fall back on three years.

8. The Cabinet considered Sidky's proposed visit to London and decided that in the end we may have to agree to this. But we should prefer you to continue to negotiate in Egypt on the lines of the above for the time being.

9. My attitude is best expressed by what I said in the House of Commons on May 24th that there must be no vacuum in Egypt. The Egyptian proposals would amount to something very like it. All they seem willing for is a goodwill Treaty involving heavy obligations for the defence of the vital interests of Egypt and ourselves without providing the wherewithal to honour them. I must say Sidky's attitude is not as responsive as I had been led to expect at the time when Jacob and Beckett returned.

71 FO 371/53309, no 3412   6 Aug 1946
[Anglo–Egyptian treaty negotiations]: inward telegram no 46 from Lord Stansgate to Mr Bevin on article 2 of the proposed treaty

Your telegrams 30[1] and 31

I am not quite clear what your intentions are regarding your new draft Article 2.

2. I agree that this redraft is not inconsistent with the expressed intentions of the Egyptians i.e. that they are prepared to go to war in the event of an attack on Egypt or the limitrophe country (this is [? gp. omitted ? they] say covered by their Article 2)

---

[1] See 70.

and to consult with a view to taking joint action in the event of war further afield (this they say is covered by their Article 3).

3.   Juridically speaking it appears to us that the Egyptian draft and our old as well as our new draft all involve the same commitments i.e. to concert such action as may be *agreed* to be necessary in any ideal set of circumstances. Omission however of the wards [sic] "consultation together" in the first part of your new re-draft and the inclusion of your second part makes this war clause firmer, and more comprehensive. It increases perhaps the moral obligation. We appreciate that it will make the treaty on the face of it more readily defensible at home.

4.   You say however in paragraph 3 of your telegram No. 30 that although you did not in your previous draft article 2 intend that there should be an obligation upon Egypt to go to war herself in the event of hostilities outside the limitrophe countries, what we must secure is that in the event of war involving Great Britain in some part of the Middle East, both inside and outside limitrophe counties, we will ourselves be able to enter Egypt. You suggest that we can relieve their fears that they need be involved in war (or should it be "committed to a declaration of war") and that there would be no harm in pointing out to Egyptians that the last war was sufficient evidence of the possibility of our using Egypt as a military base without necessarily involving the Egyptians in war.

5.   The Egyptians are, it is true, flatly opposed to any commitment to war outside the limitrophe countries. (This is the underlying reason for their insistence that a war situated inside and outside the limitrophe countries should be dealt with in separate articles). But the Egyptians are also suspicious that we intend to re-occupy Egypt according to our own judgment and in the case of a war which [grp. omtd. ? in] their view may not be directly threatening Egypt. They have made it clear that they would be even more unwilling to commit themselves in advance to allow us to use Egypt as a base for a war in which they were nominally to remain neutral than to commit themselves to war. They would regard any such suggestion as completely and humiliatingly incompatible with their sovereignty and independence, and with their position in the United Nations.

6.   I am not clear whether you consider your new Article 2 would give us a right of re-entry or merely place us in a better position to insist on coming back. It does not appear to us that the words of your re-draft could be interpreted as giving us this right unless there were a private agreement to this effect. We are convinced that the Egyptians would never agree to your Article 2 if they were to understand its purpose was to give us the right of re-entry, and that any attempt to make them do so would confirm their worst suspicions [sic] of our intentions, and seriously increase our difficulties.

7.   We suggest therefore that we should be authorised to press for the acceptance of your new Article 2 on the basis that its intention is as suggested in paragraph 3 above. I would be grateful for your approval for taking this line.

8.   As regards the Evacuation Protocal [sic] we will do our best to get 3 years, but probably our only chance of succeeding would be to agree to the early removal of combatant troops. You will remember from paragraph 4 of my telegram No. 39[2] that Sidki Pasha has reverted to this point.

9.   I must emphasise that there is a danger that if there is further delay in reaching agreement the Egyptians may terminate the negotiations.

---

[2] See 64.

72 FO 371/53308, no 3333   7 Aug 1946[1]
[Anglo–Egyptian treaty negotiations] : outward telegram no 33 from Mr Bevin to Lord Stansgate on the line to be taken with the Egyptians

[The Cabinet met on 7 Aug to discuss the treaty negotiations with Bevin now in attendance. He hoped there would be no further concessions to Egypt and in particular that Britain should not yield on article 2. Bevin believed that Britain had gone to the utmost limit if it was to maintain its Middle Eastern position and rather than yield the Cabinet should face the alternative of having no new treaty. The Cabinet did not formally endorse this view but simply took note of it (CAB 128/6, CM 77(46)1, 7 Aug 1946).]

We have now got to the point where, if conversations in Alexandria with Sidky, foreseen in my telegrams Nos. 30[2] and 31, fail to secure agreement on a treaty, and if the plan for inviting Sidky to negotiate in London is tried and yields no result, we have got to decide whether to content ourselves with an unsatisfactory treaty on basis of the Egyptian draft of Article 2 and even, may be, to reconcile ourselves to some concession over the Sudan, or whether to tell the Egyptians that we prefer to have no new treaty at all.

2.   The King and many other Egyptians are clearly anxious for a Treaty not for love of us but out of fear of Russia. If so the possibility that their present behaviour may lose them the Treaty might make them realise that the time has come to drop their present "take it or leave it" attitude. I am aware that there is a feeling in favour, in the last resort, of concluding a mere "good-will" treaty which would at least provide the machinery of the Joint Defence Board for purposes of consultation, and might prove a starting point from which, given Egyptian good-will, we might in time reach a satisfactory understanding with the Egyptians on matters of defence, in other words fill "the vacuum" gradually.

3.   This course may be a tempting one since it would give us a breathing space in Egypt while our hands are full in Palestine and elsewhere, and I am aware that it is also favoured by the most knowledgeable members of the British community on the grounds that, in the absence of good-will, our economic and cultural interests will suffer damage, if not eclipse, apart from what may happen to our defence interests.

4.   But I am not prepared to accept that view, which seems to me to be the short view. Are we not crediting the Egyptians with a unity and a determination which they are in reality very far from possessing? In your telegram No. 33 you have referred to the possibility of disorders on a scale which would wreck our military objective of a base, place the British civilian community in a grave danger and prejudice our relations with whole Arab world. I am not myself convinced of the inevitableness of disorders when we are manifestly clearing out of the cities. Are we in fact incapable of dealing with such disorders as might follow a suspension of negotiations? Might not such a situation result in the advent to power of an administration more friendly and more representative than the present (whose record e.g. in the matter of the Alexandria disturbances[3] and other outrages will hardly bear examination)? In any case is Egyptian good-will in fact likely to be secured by giving way to Egyptian demands as we have now done uninterruptedly for the past three months? Certainly there is precious little sign of it at the moment, (c.f. the recent insulting references

---

[1] The telegram was despatched at 11.30pm GMT after the Cabinet had met.
[2] See 70.   [3] Demonstrations on 4 Mar in which two British soldiers were killed.

in the Egyptian press to Dunkirk) and if we are not going to get it by signing at Egyptian dictation, we shall be worse off than ever, for the 1936 treaty (on which we can legally take our stand) will then have gone beyond recall. And the more we continue to give way, the less disposed will such as friends as we still possess in Egypt be to declare themselves. Again, in the international field, I do not see that we now stand to lose anything if the Egyptians do appeal to the U.N.O. About what, in fact, can they appeal? Least of all about the Sudan, however juridically interesting the sovereignty question may be. In their latest note they appear in fact to have over-reached themselves and given us a useful weapon against them. In fact it is clear to me that so far as the Sudan is concerned the King and Sidki are trying it on, and I am prepared to accept their challenge.

5. While I see the risks most clearly, I am myself disposed to take the firm line from now onwards.

6. I shall be sending you within 24 hours a reply to your telegram No. 46[4]

---

[4] See 71.

---

73   FO 371/53310, no 3579   8 Aug 1946[1]
[Anglo–Egyptian treaty negotiations] : inward telegram no 48 from Lord Stansgate to Mr Bevin on the mishandling of the negotiations

The purpose of this message is to look forward.

2.   We had at the outset of these negotiations two slender advantages; the first was the ambition of Sidki Pasha, Egypt's most able administrator, to crown his life by securing evacuation and desire of a group of elder statesmen to share in the honour; and the second was general goodwill of the country and a wish to conclude with us a treaty of mutual assistance.

3.   Both of these advantages have been diminished almost to vanishing point by protracted delays and repeated insistence on unacceptable points. Our evacuation promises are not unnaturally beginning to appear bogus and the general wish for a treaty is weakening.

4.   Having thus thrown away our small advantages we have to consider how to obey the Cabinet's decision still to be "firm". There is now only one way to be firm and that is to threaten to break off negotiations. We may indeed be anticipated in this by the Egyptians themselves. Our periods of firmness have given them leisure to prepare memorandum which you have and which no doubt will be the basis of an appeal either to U.N.O. or to the world and the outline of more violent manifestos for local use.

5.   In other telegrams we have tried to express what failing hopes of agreement still exist, but now a rupture is certainly possible if not probable and clearly we must have plans made carefully to meet it.

6.   We must consider our public justification. Firstly we must state why we asked for five years for the evacuation of our troops, nine-tenths of whom are here with no treaty rights at all. Secondly we must explain why we insist that Egypt should agree

---

[1] The telegram was despatched at 1.30am and composed on 7 Aug. It is therefore unlikely that Stansgate saw FO tel 33 (see 72) before sending it.

in advance to our right to return. And thirdly we must justify our refusal to accept Egypt's case in the Sudan. In the eyes of the world the first is our weakest and the third is our strongest card.

7.   We must then consider the local situation. Business of course will be hampered and may in the long run be severely damaged. Moreover, all our schemes for providing economic and social help to the Middle East countries for which we have set up a special office will be prejudiced.

8.   There will certainly be public manifestations and there may be public disorders. The story of 1919 is worth the study even if we do not see a repetition of it on the same scale.

9.   The military on whom the main task will fall will need instructions. Firstly are they to rely on specific treaty rights of 1936? If so a careful examination should be made of that treaty. Are facilities what we require? Are our installations and stores in fact in the prescribed area? Are we entitled to a headquarters for the whole Middle East?

10.   Then as to the right of return where do we stand under Article 7? I notice that the Law Officers in their opinion of jurisdiction of 1946 state that the provisions of Article 7 are likely to be of little value in the event of Egypt not wishing to implement the spirit of the treaty. And when all this is done we shall not have achieved our main objective which is to set up an operable base.

11.   To fall back on our legal rights therefore would seem to be of small use. Furthermore to exercise these rights in an Egypt uncooperative or hostile would require additions to our forces.

12.   The alternative would seem to be a plain military occupation.

13.   In any case unless after breaking the seals of offices[2] we come to agreement on evacuation Egypt may well decide to refer to U.N.O. the question of the continued presence of British troops in her territory. We should presumably be preparing our case against that event.

14.   These practical questions may have to be faced soon, and I think should be examined at once.

15.   It will of course be for you and the Cabinet to decide whether it is wise to add the hostility of the Arabs to the hostility of the Jews.

---

[2] An FO official queried the decoding of the words 'the seals of offices'.

74   FO 371/53309, no 3412   8 Aug 1946

[Anglo–Egyptian treaty negotiations] : outward telegram no 34 from Mr Bevin to Lord Stansgate on article 2 of the proposed treaty

Your telegram No. 46[1]

My Article 2 imposes not merely a moral obligation but a definite commitment upon the Egyptians. I do not wish to burke this. I am not merely trying to make the treaty more defensible here at home. I wish to make it clear beyond doubt what are the obligations of Egypt and ourselves under the Treaty. The whole of Article 2 must moreover be read in conjunction with Article 3.

---

[1] See 71.

2.   Paragraph 1 of my Article 2 is designed to secure that as soon as Egypt or the countries adjacent to Egypt become the object of armed aggression Great Britain will have the right to re-enter Egypt in accordance with plans which will already have been made by the Joint Defence Board. This, is necessary for Egypt's defence and the protection of communications. In plain English that is what it means and I do not desire to hide it. Anything else will be too late and would mean disaster to both countries. As regards paragraph 2, the wording is designed to enable the Egyptians to consult with us in the event of a war which, although outside the adjacent countries, is within neighbouring countries, as defined in paragraph 4 of my telegram No. 30.[2]

3.   Your paragraph 6. You imply that the Egyptians will never agree to joint consultations in order to protect their territory against a likely or impending attack, even though we are apparently to be placed under an obligation to protect it. Nor for that matter would they allow us to re-enter Egyptian territory for the purpose of defending it. If this is really the last word of the Egyptians then I must say that they are asking me to undertake an impossible obligation and that I would prefer to stand on the 1936 Treaty.

4.   Your paragraph 8. I really cannot offer anything better than I have done in my telegram No. 30 on the question of the dtae [sic] for evacuation.

5.   I have noted what you say in your paragraph 9 about the possibility of the Egyptians terminating the negotiations. I am not prepared to swallow everything that the Egyptians say in the course of negotiations. If, however, negotiations are terminated in this way the responsibility will rest with the Egyptians. Should trouble thereafter break out the Egyptians will be held responsible if any bones are broken.

6.   Please now resume negotiations on the lines of the present telegram and my telegram No. 30 and put the redraft of Article 2 in my telegram No. 31 to the Egyptians.

---

[2] See 70.

75   FO 371/53309, no 3477   8 Aug 1946
[Anglo–Egyptian treaty negotiations] : outward telegram no 38 from Mr Bevin to Lord Stansgate reporting a conversation with Amr

At an interview with the Egyptian Ambassador today I explained to him that we had reached the utmost limit of concession and the only alternative would be to go back to the 1936 Treaty if our new Article 2 was unacceptable. I would regard this as a tragedy in view of the distance we have gone. I indicated to him quite firmly that the first paragraph of our new draft presupposes that the Defence Board would have all plans ready. In fact it would be interpreted as being a directive to them so that in the event of any power showing an agressive [sic] attitude to Egypt or to the communications in the Canal zone we should be ready to take action at once. Anything less would be an humiliation for Great Britain and I could not sign any treaty that would bear that interpretation.

2.   Under paragraph 2 of our new Article 2, as I explained to the Ambassador, the High Contracting Parties would consult because it would be quite clear that if countries further away, but still in the Middle East, were in danger of attack the Intelligence Services would know pretty well whether or not there was danger to Egypt. The Joint Defence Board would be in possession of all the facts. I told him that I thought the bargain which Sidki was trying to drive was one that could not be carried in the House of Commons or in the country and therefore I had gone to the limit.

3.   His Excellency then raised the question of the time for evacuation and I repeated to him that my attitude had been that I preferred that no date should be fixed but that there should be agreement with the Joint Defence Board who stage by stage should fix a date but as Egyptians pressed for a date I thought anything earlier than the end of 1950 would be a mistake. I pointed out that if we were handing over to Egypt this time we intended to train the Egyptians to handle this highly technical business properly. Whatever had been done in the past we were acting quite genuinely in this matter and our own experience had shown how long it takes to train effectively the administrative staffs and officers of a modern army, especially on the technical side. I further pointed out that if my new Article 2 was accepted it would state clearly to the world that we were in alliance. It would act as a deterrent. Our people would know their obligations and the Egyptians would know theirs and I thought that the best form of defence.

4.   The Ambassador then asked me whether I could go to Egypt or whether the Egyptians would come here. I said that if our Article 2 is accepted and the period for evacuation is agreed, which were fundamental principles, I thought there need be very little delay, but I could not promise him, whether I would go to Egypt owing to my state of health, or whether the Egyptians would come here.

5.   Amr Pasha said it would be preferable not to present the new draft to Sidky until he had had a chance to talk to the King. In the light of this statement it might be wiser to hold it for a day or two as suggested in my immediately preceding telegram.

6.   If I may express a personal opinion, when you present the draft do it with confidence in it and with an attitude of mind that this is the minimum we can accept. I gather from the Ambassador that there is a very great desire not to have a breakdown.

7.   The Ambassador then asked me if we could secure acceptance of the draft and get it signed quickly. He asked me whether I could make a gesture regarding the Sudan and I said I did not see how I could do this. He then pointed out that they were concerned about the water and I informed him that they need have no fears about that. I told him that I had taken steps to reopen negotiations in regard to Lake Tana itself. I also said that I had been trying to study whether it is not possible to use the Nile in certain parts for electrification in Egypt as this would help to raise the standard of life. I told the Ambassador that I should prefer to say nothing about the Sudan now but that after the Treaty was signed there would no doubt be many exchanges of views on that and other problems and I reiterated that we had reached the limit.

76   FO 371/53309, no 3466   10 Aug 1946

[Anglo–Egyptian treaty negotiations] : inward telegram no 54 from Lord Stansgate to Mr Bevin on article 2 of the proposed treaty

Your telegrams Nos. 34,[1] 37, and 39.
    For Secretary of State for Foreign Affairs from Secretary of State for Air.
    I am anxious to be entirely clear both about exact interpretation of your Article 2 and about manner in which you want it to be presented to Sidki Pasha. This is

---

[1] See 74.

particularly important in view of Amr's return; we must be clear to represent matters in the same light as he does.

2.   Firstly as regards first paragraph of your Article 2, I understand I am to tell Sidki Pasha that "such action as may be recognised as necessary" definitely means that we return to Egypt. I should have thought the words "recognised as necessary" imply that any action taken would have to be so recognised by both parties and that anyhow they gave the Egyptians a loophole to deny that our return was necessary if they felt so inclined. But I suppose if war did reach limitrophe countries our return would obviously be necessary and would have to be recognised as such by the Egyptians. If you are satisfied therefore that this paragraph fully safeguards our right to return in the circumstances referred to I have no more to say.

3.   I am, however, more doubtful in regard to the second paragraph of your Article 2. Do I understand I am to tell Sidki Pasha that this paragraph also gives us the right to return (with or without Egyptian consent and whether or not they themselves declare war) when in our opinion a threat to the security of the neighbouring countries (i.e. the Eastern Mediterranean or Middle East) makes this necessary? Am I further to understand the word "consultation" in this Article is in these circumstances of hardly more than academic interest since it does not imply the necessity of Egyptian agreement to any action we may consider necessary?

4.   This appears to me to be your intention. But even if the Egyptians accept paragraph 2 of your Article 2 as interpreted above it would surely not give us a legal right to return which you say we must secure (paragraph 3 of your telegram No.30[2]) if a future Egyptian Government not wishing us to return chose to take its stand on a strict interpretation of this paragraph, which must surely take "recognised as necessary" as meaning "agreed as necessary by both parties". I am supported in this view of the legal interpretation of the second paragraph of your Article 2 by the Law Officers' opinion on the 1936 Treaty where a somewhat oblique reference to consultation in the agreed minute referring to Article 7 was held to give the Egyptians the right to refuse to recognise the existence of emergency referred to in that Article and hence to refuse to provide us with facilities described therein to enable us to conduct operations of war in Egypt.

5.   You have I am afraid misinterpreted paragraph 6 of my telegram No. 46.[3] I did not say the Egyptians would never agree to consultations about likely or impending attacks on their territory. They have agreed to such consultations in their Article 3. Neither did I say they would not allow us to re-enter Egyptian territory for the purpose of defending it in such circumstances. They might do so when the time came. What they will not agree is to commit themselves now to give us the right to re-enter without their consent and that, apparently, is what the second paragraph of your Article 2 is intended to make them do.

---

[2] See 70.   [3] See 71.

77   FO 371/53309, no 3498   12 Aug 1946
[Anglo–Egyptian treaty negotiations] : inward telegram no 56 from Lord Stansgate to Mr Bevin on the dangers of falling back on the 1936 treaty

When we have seen Amr whose impending visit had been announced in the Press we shall of course press to the utmost with Sidki Pasha same suggestions taking advantage of any new support which Amr may bring. I should warn you that after our four months procrastination Sidki Pasha's influence is on the wane and whatever momentum our mission had has almost gone. So we must be quick. Should we fail then, I think you should immediately invite Sidki Pasha or whoever is Prime Minister and his delegation to come to London. This might gain time though I fear little else.

I do not quite understand your plan for [grp. undec. ? managing] the Government. If you are thinking of some united front with the Wafd the suggestion is difficult. The King will never work with Nahas Pasha. That is the price we pay for the tank incident. Will the Wafd desert Nahas Pasha?

I am more concerned with the next stage. If as is most unlikely the Egyptians agree to let us "fall back on *legal* rights of the 1936 treaty" we have something namely 10,000 men and 400 pilots on the Canal whose *legal* duty is to ensure the "liberty and entire security of navigation of the Canal". They have no legal right to set up Middle East base which is our military necessity, nor could they count on co-operation of Egyptian manpower and industrial resources.

But will the Egyptians accept that position? They might declare unilaterally that they were no longer legally bound by the 1936 Treaty. It is with that in view that situation must be examined.

Will there be disorders, and if so on what scale? Everybody here forecasts trouble but if you wish, for confirmation, it might help you to consult men like Sir Thomas Russell[1] who has just returned to England after being head of Cairo Police for 30 years or Sir K. Cornwallis.

You question unity of Egypt. I think you are wrong. It is certain that no one would be found actively to support us.

You say that we should be moving out of the towns. On the contrary, if we foresee trouble it is our plain duty to stay in Cairo and Alexandria to protect and if need be to evacuate our own people. Commander-in-Chief would ask for reinforcements. Soldiers could tell you how many. Now look at the probability of political consequences. In 1919 Egypt was a Protectorate. We controlled whole administrative machinery and we committed large numbers of troops. There was trouble then. We deported Zaghlul twice and General Bulfin[2] was given subsequently some six divisions to clean up the country which he did very thoroughly with the loss of many Egyptian lives. There never was a better example of firmness. But that was not the end of the matter. Within less than three years the British Government was driven to a policy of scuttle. Protectorate was abandoned and Zaghlul moved from his prison cell to be Prime Minister and Master of Egypt and he gave us plenty of trouble

---

[1] Sir Thomas Russell, commander of Cairo police, 1917–46; director of Egyptian Central Narcotics International Bureau, 1939–1946.
[2] Commander of 60th Division and 21st Army Corps in Palestine, Egypt and Syria during World War I.

thereafter. If that was forced on Lloyd George who had no scruples how would we do better?

But it may be said that when all this is over we are still established with our forces in the country. That is true. And what we have to compare is the relative advantage of sitting tight in a hostile country—if we can find the forces—or accepting a plan of two and a half years evacuation plus what the Egyptians offer in the way of co-operation with Joint Board and the rest. My own estimation is that however thin the treaty might be a friendly Egypt would in time of trouble give us a welcome. If we have to oppress why not postpone application of force until the need arises.

Let me add that I think we ought not to be afraid to do the right thing. We should be able to give a positive justification for what we are doing. In 1915 we abandoned our old time policy of leaning on Turkey and called into being the Arab States. We made an appeal to the spirit of liberty and in consequence among them we enjoy at this moment a high prestige. We are in fact building on the foundations of our own Commonwealth. This is the true bastion against Russian influence. If we apply force and invoke hatred in this country of glaring contrasts between starvation and riches then we are inviting its leaders (not Lufti[3] and Sidki Pasha who are the Redmonds[4] and Dillons)[5] but some new leaders to look elsewhere.

---

[3] Member of the Egyptian delegation and renowned intellectual.

[4] Sir John Redmond, Irish nationalist politician and supporter of Home Rule. He became chairman of the Nationalist Party in 1900 and aimed not at separation but at the attainment of a free Ireland within the Empire.

[5] John Dillon, Irish nationalist who succeeded Redmond in 1918 but whose political career was effectively undermined by the rise of Sinn Fein.

78   FO 371/53309, no 3495   13 Aug 1946
[Anglo–Egyptian treaty negotiations]: inward draft telegram no 490 from Mr Bevin (Paris)[1] to Lord Stansgate on article 2 of the proposed treaty

Your telegram No. 54[2] to Foreign Office.

This bore no urgency prefix and has only just become available to the Foreign Office and me in Paris. I have given it immediate personal attention.

2.   Your paragraph 2. Yes we contemplate that plans involving our re-entry will have been drawn up by the Defence Board and ratified by the two Governments long before any attack on Egypt or adjacent territory; in other words that such prepared plan of action will be kept up to date and will have been "recognised as necessary". Please see the first sentence of paragraph 2 of my telegram No. 34.[3] So long as Article 3 with its provision for a Defence Board is read in conjunction with our Article 2 I do not think there can be cause for misunderstanding. There is apparently no doubt that the Egyptians will be prepared to go to war in the event of an attack on Egypt or the

---

[1] Bevin was in Paris for the Peace Conference to finalise treaties with Germany's allies. The tel became tel 47 from the FO to Alexandria.

[2] See 76.   [3] See 74.

adjacent countries. They will therefore not be able to avoid recognising as necessary such action as we will have to take in such circumstances, i.e. entering Egypt in fulfilment of our side of the Treaty.

3.   Your paragraphs 3 and 4. Under paragraph 2 of our Article 2 there is no legal right to enter Egypt without consultation: nor is there a legal right to enter if after consultation, the Egyptians object to our doing so. But we do not regard such consultation as academic any more than we regard the work of the Defence Board as academic. In the case of a threat to the security of a neighbouring country e.g. Iraq, we should, no doubt, ask for facilities to return. Again this paragraph must be considered in relation to the Defence Board which "shall meet as often as may be necessary . . . to examine the military repercussions . . . of all events which may threaten the security of the Middle East . . ."

4.   I realise that legally the Egyptians might refuse us permission to re-enter under paragraph 2; but as you point out in your paragraph 4 even the 1936 Treaty was imperfect and would have enabled the Egyptians on a purely legalistic interpretation to stultify the purpose of the Treaty. On the other hand I am certain that our paragraph 2 gives us something that we do not get under the Egyptian Draft which you were anxious for us to accept. We gain a chance to consult about what should be done to meet a situation already examined by the Defence Board. I do not call this academic. At the same time it enables action to follow from such consultation which will not of necessity involve the Egyptians in war. Please read my telegrams Nos. 30[4] and 34[5] in the light of the foregoing.

5.   I hope this telegram will have cleared up a misunderstanding between us and that when I give you the signal to re-enter negotiations you will have no doubts about the obligations imposed on both parties.

6.   Of course I must leave it to you how best to present the matter to the Egyptians. But do not please give the impression that we are driving a hard bargain; because I have no sense of this. Do not forget that before the negotiations even began we made the Egyptians a great concession by declaring our willingness to withdraw from Egypt. This was made for no consideration; but in the belief that the friendly nature of our relations would secure such mutual and commonsense arrangements as would make sure that we both could fulfil our obligations under the new Treaty. After all, this is a Treaty of mutual assistance. We will not be able to assist unless we are given the means to do so. All the proposals, it must be remembered, are on terms of equal sovereignty and quite different from the old occupation idea. I think now you have a great chance of success on this basis and I have confidence you will pull it off.

---

[4] See 70.   [5] See 74.

79   FO 371/53310, no 3606   21 Aug 1946

[Anglo–Egyptian treaty negotiations]: inward telegram no 75 from Lord Stansgate to Mr Bevin reporting on meetings with Sidky, Amr and Hassan Youssef

[Attempts to redraft article 2 continued throughout August and the details of every word change are not referred to. The Egyptian delegation discussed it on 14 Aug and all members except Makram Ebeid accepted the British version of paragraph 2. Paragraph 1 of article 2 (cf 70, note 3) was unacceptable to the Egyptians because it omitted the phrase 'in the event of armed aggression against *Great Britain* in the countries adjacent to Egypt' (FO 371/53310, no 3538, Alexandria tel 63, 15 Aug 1946). The point was significant because of the distinction between British and non-British territory. Bevin argued that certain countries which were at present subject to British authority might not be so in the future and therefore it would be dangerous to accept the limitations of the Egyptian draft. Instead the following redraft was proposed: 'in the event of Egypt or countries adjacent to Egypt becoming the object of armed aggression, or in the event of armed aggression against Great Britain in those adjacent countries.' The Egyptians argued this gave the impression that Egypt and the adjacent or limitrophe territories were being regarded as a British sphere of influence (FO 371/53310, no 3549, Paris tels 515 and 516, 16 Aug 1946). Amr believed that the delegation might accept 'in the event of Egypt becoming the object of armed aggression, or in the event of Great Britain being involved in war in the countries adjacent to Egypt' (FO 371/53310, no 3563, Alexandria tel 67, 19 Aug 1946), which the British were also prepared to accept (FO 371/53310, no 3575, Paris tel 1037, 20 Aug 1946). However, even if this had been officially accepted by the Egyptian delegation there was still a problem over the second paragraph of article 2. By 21 Aug the negotiations appeared deadlocked.]

My telegram No. 73.
Following for Secretary of State from Secretary of State for Air.
Sidki Pasha called on us this morning to deliver at the request of the Egyptian Delegation the text of the decision reached at their meeting yesterday (see text included in my telegram No. 74). This done he stated that his Delegation for their part did not desire nor consider the decision to involve a rupture of negotiations adding his own ardent desire for a continuance and his conviction for the necessity for a treaty. Egyptian Government's and he felt sure Egyptian Delegation's sentiments on this point were contained in an oral communication which he made (see text in my immediately following telegram).

2. We said that all we could do was to inform you of his communication since as he knew you considered that in your last proposals you had gone as far as you could go to meet [grp. undec. ?Egyptians] (he evidently was apprehensive that this was a threat of rupture). We asked in what respect he considered our texts had proved unacceptable. He said (1) that we had omitted from Article 2 paragraph 1 any reference to mutuality to which they attached importance (to this you have already consented in your telegram No. 57). (2) That we had continued to insist on inclusion in Article 2 of a paragraph dealing with a threat of war and this moreover outside limitrophe countries. This as he had often explained to us occasioned apprehension and suspicions. He then argued that proper place for dealing with threats of war was Article 3 (which dealt with preparations) and said that he could get the Delegation to agree to add words to paragraph 3 of Article 3 so as to cover the second paragraph of our Article 2. We then asked whether the only difference between us was the position in the treaty of these two articles and he said it was. We pointed out that you attached greatest importance to the position of paragraph 2 of our Article 2 for reasons already given and which we repeated and there the matter was left.

3. Sidki Pasha then turned to question of the Sudan but only to repeat familiar arguments. In reply to our question he said the idea of an exchange of letters on sovereignty question had not commended itself to the Delegation and averred that if he were to give way over sovereignty he would have the whole country against him.

4. [Grp. undec. ?With regard to] evacuation we pointed out that Egyptian draft treaty contained no provision. What were we to understand was position in respect of

your proposal on this point? He said he had informed us of the opinion of Egyptian military experts that evacuation could be carried out in one year but recalled that in conversation he had risen [sic] two and a half years. He said entirely between ourselves he could say that he could get Egyptian side to accept three years if an overall agreement were in prospect.

5. Amr Pasha called with Hassan Youssef this afternoon to assure us that the whole Egyptian Delegation (except Mackram Ebeid) were set on avoiding a rupture and that the King who had been much upset by developments was ardently desirous of a treaty. Close friendship with Great Britain was his long term policy and for this he considered a treaty necessary.

6. Although uncompromising tone of Egyptian note is no doubt partly due to the internal political situation which makes them all afraid of appearing to give way in public, it should not be assumed that Delegation will in the end agree to accept your proposals as they stand especially on Sudan. As for King Farouk Amr Pasha and Hassan Bey stated that he personally would accept your Article 2 and three years for evacuation. Hassan Bey adumbrated real difficulty over Sudan. It would be unsafe to assume that in face of divided opinion over your proposals in Delegation His Majesty will wish to intervene in favour of acceptance. Moreover from what these two said this afternoon it now seems that he had not definitely accepted the idea of getting round the sovereignty question by an exchange of letters or that he has receded from it. Amr expressed optimism on the point but it looks as if he is inclined to over-optimism. Although Amr and Hassan Yousef have informed us that individual members of Delegation were given to understand by them that King Farouk favoured our proposals this has certainly not so far been communicated to the Delegation as a whole. Moreover in view of divisions of opinion in the Delegation His Majesty may well hesitate to declare himself openly in support of one section against another. We hope to see King Farouk very shortly.

7. I fear it appears probable Sidki Pasha is trying to put us in the position of making the break if there is one.

80 FO 141/1082, no 520   30 Aug 1946
[Egyptian political situation]: memorandum by Sir W Smart on the political intrigues in Egypt

The situation which we have come up against in our Treaty negotiations is one of fundamental internal politics and is based on the disequilibrium caused by a minority régime speaking for the community. To this is added the misfortune that the minority régime is led by the most minority and mistrusted politician, with whom many fear to be associated in the signature of an Anglo–Egyptian Treaty.

The present intrigues to get the Treaty signed are merely a reflection of this internal situation. Some are intriguing to bring the Wafd into participation in the negotiations and in the Government, others are intriguing to consolidate the present régime against the Wafd by giving as many plums as possible to the leaders of the régime. Amr's story as regards the Egyptian Delegation appears to be one of an attempt to win over the Independents to acquiesce in the consolidation of the present régime, although the Infant Samuel[1] is so immature that one cannot always be sure whether he knows what he is doing.

Until this internal struggle is settled, the chances of any successful Treaty negotiations are poor.

In former days we would have intervened in this situation to promote the combination which would have given us the best chance of getting a Treaty and of securing Egyptian acquiescence in the Treaty subsequently. Our policy of non-intervention forces us to stand aside and to let the Egyptians go on intriguing and fighting against one another until some combination emerges which will give us our desiderata indicated above. This may take a considerable time. Meanwhile I confess that I personally am beginning to feel that we are in an atmosphere of unreality with all these intrigues and counter-intrigues, which are only incidentally concerned with the Treaty but are more fundamentally concerned with the perhaps decisive battle which is being fought on the internal political stage. It is a pity that we all cannot go off on leave and return after a couple of months when possibly something less unreal may have emerged from the present internal political embroglio.

---

[1] A reference to Ismail Sidky and his relationship with King Farouk. As a child Samuel attended Eli the high priest and later ruler of the Israelites.

81 FO 371/53311, no 3858 11 Sept 1946
[Political situation in Egypt]: inward telegram no 120 from Sir R Campbell to FO on the political conflicts affecting the Egyptian delegation

[A rupture in the negotiations was avoided when King Farouk suggested eliminating the second paragraph of article 2 and using 'neighbouring' in paragraph one (FO 371/53310, no 3639, Alexandria tel 87, 25 Aug 1946). The FO accepted the elimination of paragraph two but insisted on a redraft of paragraph one on the following lines: 'In the event of armed aggression on Egypt, or in the event of Great Britain becoming involved in war in the neighbouring states of Egypt, the High Contracting Parties agree to take in close co-operation such action as may be recognised as necessary until etc' (FO 371/53310, no 3639, FO tel 68, 26 Aug 1946). Bevin, on discovering that this would not be acceptable to the Egyptian delegation (FO 371/53311, no 3752, Alexandria tel 113, 3 Sept 1946), was clearly annoyed, perhaps because of his understanding with Amr. He instructed Stansgate to withdraw the latest British suggestion on article 2 and return to the draft of 4 Aug (cf 70, note 3) with some slight amendment. Thus there were now two paragraphs to article 2 again (FO 371/53311, no 3772, Paris tel 22, 5 Sept 1946). Bevin was determined that there should be no compromise on article 2 or the Sudan (FO 371/53311, no 3838, FO tel 106, 12 Sept 1946) and the British draft was submitted to the Egyptian delegation as a final proposal on 17 Sept. Paragraph one of article 2 now read: 'The High Contracting Parties agree that, in the event of Egypt being the object of armed aggression or in the event of Great Britain being involved in war in the countries adjacent to Egypt, they shall take in close co-operation such action ...' Paragraph two read: In the event of a threat to the security of any of the neighbouring countries of Egypt the High Contracting Parties agree to consult together in order that such action should be taken as may be regarded as necessary until the Security Council has taken the necessary measures for the re-establishment of peace'.]

Your telegram No. 103.

Following is our appreciation of the present situation.

The position of Sidki Pasha in the Egyptian Delegation was becoming difficult owing to growing opposition of the Independents and Liberal Saadists.[1] This attitude of the Delegates was partly due to their annoyance with Sidki Pasha's monopolisation of negotiations and their feeling that they were being left out of the picture. Some Independents were known to be favouring a widening of the Government to include Wafdists under an Independent Prime Minister. These Independents were actuated both by ambitions to secure the Premiership and by reluctance to be associated with Sidki Pasha, who is an unpopular figure and without any appreciable support in the country, in the signature of a treaty involving concessions which the Majority party namely the Wafd would inevitably represent to the people as a betrayal of the Egyptian cause. The matter came to a head when Sidki Pasha with King Farouk's support too openly announced by Sidki Pasha to the Delegation, tried to persuade the Delegates to compromise on the basis of the last treaty proposals officially put up by us. In view of unanimous opposition by the Delegates Sidki Pasha decided to join the band wagon and returned, on behalf of the Egyptian Delegation, the reply maintaining integrally the position taken up by the Egyptian Delegation in its previous note of 1st August.[2]

2.   King Farouk was somewhat compromised by his intervention and criticised by the Delegates and by the Wafd for unconstitutional interference for playing our game. Sidki Pasha's position was shaken by manifest opposition of at least half of the Delegates to him. It was therefore decided by the Palace in consultation with Sidki Pasha to introduce Saadists into the Government in order to secure at least an overwhelming majority in the present régime and in the present parliament in support of the Sidki Pasha Government and of any treaty which might be accepted by the Egyptian side. It was also thought that such a reconstruction of the Government would deprive certain Independent delegates of their hopes of upsetting Sidki Pasha in favour of their own ambitions and dispose them to desist from their manoeuvres in favour of a widened Government including the Wafdists and to be less obstructive within the Treaty Delegation. The Saadists were accordingly approached and apparently agreed to enter the Government. At this juncture the Akhbar el Yom to which Sidki Pasha had previously made improper revelations regarding the Treaty proposals came out with an announcement of this proposed cabinet reconstruction before the Liberal Minister in the Cabinet had heard anything about it. It was generally thought that Sidki Pasha had divulged the news to this newspaper (presumably in order to counter the statements of Wafdists and Independents in favour of Wafdist participation in a Government under an Independent Prime Minister) but he denied having [?grp, omtd.] so. The Liberal Minister of Communication at once tendered his resignation and the Liberal Party after a subsequent meeting announced that in view of the delicate circumstances it was prepared to agree to the proposed reconstruction provided the Liberal Ministers retained the post they held in the present Cabinet. Sidki Pasha had meanwhile announced his intention to include three Liberals and three Saadists as Ministers with Portfolio and one Liberal and one Saadist as Ministers without Portfolio. Apparently this decision was partly due to King Farouk's insistence on the exclusion from any Ministry of the Liberal Minister of Communications

---

[1] The Liberals and the Saadists were two separate parties, both splinters of the Wafd, founded in 1922 and 1938 respectively.
[2] See 68.

because of his hasty resignation and dubious character. Discussions ensued between Sidki Pasha and the Liberals without an agreement being reached and finally it was decided to leave the question for consideration of King Farouk who had chosen this inopportune moment to go off on a cruise in the Eastern Mediterranean from which he has not yet returned. The long absence of His Majesty considerably weakened Sidki Pasha's position and gave time for intrigues not only among disgruntled Liberals but even apparently among Saadists who also are not without hope that their leader may take Sidki Pasha's place. Yesterday Haikal, the Liberal leader got tired of waiting for His Majesty's return and went off in a huff to Port Said. It would seem then that the Liberals are now disgruntled not only with Sidki Pasha but with King Farouk.

3.   The public has been unfavourably impressed by the King's absence from the country in the midst of a Cabinet crisis particularly as all administrative activity comes to a semi stand-still on the eve of a change of Government. The Wafd still entertains hopes of participating in the Government and while attacking Sidki Pasha violently is again piping down as regards us.

4.   It is thought that King Farouk on his return may be able to induce the Liberals to enter Sidki Pasha's Cabinet with which we would then be able to resume negotiations. Owing, however, to mismanagement of the Liberals, divisions have become apparent among them and Sidki Pasha's Cabinet may not be able to count on the whole-hearted support of the Liberal party. Moreover it is not certain that the opposed reconstruction of the Cabinet will have the hoped for effect on the Independents (see paragraph 2 above) and some of them may still continue to work for a wider Government with Wafdist participation and to be obstructive within the delegation. It is possible that a Government formed under such auspices may not be long lived and that sooner or later the need of a Government of national union including the Wafdists will make itself felt more imperatively. Hafez Afifi tells Campbell that in his opinion a Government under Sidki Pasha with the addition of the Liberals will be formed at once on the King's return—Afifi thinks too that it will stick at any rate long enough for the conclusion of a treaty indicating that in his view at any rate the Independents will not be factiously obstructive in the Delegation. Amr believes that the Independents are now "quite vertical". This is not certain.

5.   If we are to adhere strictly to our policy of non-interference in the internal affairs of Egypt our line, it would seem, can only be to present our last treaty proposals to the Government reconstructed on the basis of entry of Saadists into the Cabinet if that is what emerges from the present crisis. It would be useless, indeed harmful to present any treaty proposals to Sidki Pasha before such reconstruction, as until he feels his position more secure, at least temporarily, he will not dare to present them in any favourable light to the Egyptian Delegation. Incidentally all Egyptians are taking it for granted that negotiations cannot be resumed pending reconstruction of the Cabinet. Although we cannot refrain from presenting our proposals to Sidki Pasha once his Government has been thus reconstructed we cannot count on the Independents in the Delegation being much less obstructive in view of the fact that there will be no conviction that this new Government is durable and Independents in the delegation may still be reluctant to sign a treaty with Sidki Pasha and expose themselves to Wafdist obloquy.

6.   As regards Article 2 of the Treaty Amr states that owing to political crisis there

has been no lobbying of Sherif's[3] version; he also now says that anyhow it was dependent in Sherif's mind on a settlement of the Sudan protocol on a basis acceptable to the Egyptians. In any case it never attained a status which would permit us to refer to it with Sidki Pasha or the delegation as a suggestion of theirs failing which we must fall back on our own last version (in this connexion see my telegrams Nos. 94, 101, and 109). It is problematical whether it will ever be endorsed by the Egyptian delegation. We are therefore at present still on our own last version of Article 2 which has been rejected by the Egyptian delegation without any alternative. It seems unlikely that our proposed Sudan protocol will be accepted. We must therefore face the prospect of a break-down of negotiations before they insist on our present terms. Such a breakdown may lead to an appeal by Egypt to U.N.O. and to disorders in the towns. It may also lead to such a weakening of the present régime as to render impossible further exclusion of the Wafd from participation in the Government.

---

[3] Mohamed Sherif Sabry, member of the Egyptian delegation. This was the version of article 2 agreed with Amr.

82   FO 371/53311, no 3652   30 Sept 1946
'Egypt': outward circular despatch no 890 from DO to dominion governments summarising the Egyptian reply to the British treaty proposals

Egyptian reply to our treaty proposals was communicated to United Kingdom Delegation 28th September and published same day.
  Summary Begins.

British draft of article 2
Paragraph 1 re-establishes reciprocity but omits consultation which should precede common action. Paragraph 2 contemplates entirely different situation, namely threat to security of neighbouring countries of Egypt. Since beginning of negotiations Egyptian delegation have made it known that they cannot accept as was done in 1936 treaty, that menace to security may lead to common action involving return of British troops in time of peace to Egyptian soil. Moreover, expression "threat to security" is open to various interpretations. From 1935 to outbreak of last war most of European states rightly regarded themselves as permanently under this menace and today also, public opinion in many countries is convinced that security of their country is threatened. Moreover, British delegation have fully accepted this point of view and various earlier texts present [sic] by them, particularly the three alternative versions presented in July referred only to the event of war. For these reasons Egyptian delegation cannot accept text proposed by British delegation for paragraph 2 Article 2.

Evacuation protocol
Egyptian delegation consider three years excessive, particularly as evacuation should have started immediately after termination of hostilities. They consider, moreover,

that protocol should only lay down broad outlines of evacuation and that details should be settled later.

The Sudan

In course of negotiations it has become clear that object of British delegation is to settle finally regime in Sudan according to 1899 arrangement, as at present applied by British authorities in Sudan. For her share in Sudan campaign British Government claimed right to share in administration (see paragraph 3 of preamble of agreement of January 1899). 1899 Agreement therefore sets up joint Anglo–Egyptian administration but Great Britain's position in Egypt, encroachment of British officials in Sudan and unilateral measures imposed by British Government by force in 1924 have reduced Egyptian share in administration of Sudan provinces to nothing.

First draft protocol proposed by British delegation was merely reproduction of Article II of 1936 Treaty with addition of joint commission charged with task of making recommendations on future of Sudan. Same idea is reproduced in second draft, which departs even further from Egyptian point of view since it makes no provision for subsequent agreement about Sudan.

British protocol lays down that object of high contracting parties is actively to prepare Sudanese for self-government. This is also sincere desire of Egypt. But Egyptian delegation are not prepared to accept this merely as declaration of principle in execution of which Egyptian Government will have no share. On contrary Egyptian Government must take effective part in elaborating democratic regime towards which Sudanese should be moving. 1899 and 1936 agreements give Egyptian Government no means of sharing in this task. In arrangement proposed in British draft protocol it will be Governor General who under instructions from London alone will elaborate new Sudan statute. The only amendments protocol makes to Egyptian Government's objections are that they will be informed from time to time by reports from Governor General of Sudan of progress made by Sudanese towards self-government and to make appropriate recommendations.

Sovereignty

British draft states that protocol does not prejudice claim of King of Egypt to be sovereign of Sudan. Egyptian sovereignty does not need to be claimed. It exists; it has never been possible to contest it. British Government can no longer maintain their refusal to pronounce on this question. Either Great Britain admits right of Egyptian sovereignty, in which case she can have no objection to recognising it, or she contests it, in which case she must state fact in order that Egyptian people may know that Great Britain is denying them only link which still units [sic] them with Sudan at very moment that she is asking them to become ally of Great Britain and to share with her grave responsibilities which derive from alliance.

For all these reasons Egyptian delegation cannot accept draft protocol presented by British delegation. Ends.

83 CAB 131/3, DO(46)124
23 Oct 1946

'Anglo–Egyptian treaty negotiations': memorandum by Mr Bevin for the Cabinet Defence Committee

[When Bevin began the negotiations with Sidky he was convinced that if the Egyptians got satisfaction on the Sudan they would accept a three year evacuation period and the British draft of article 2 as presented on 17 Sept (FO 371/53314, no 4213, conclusions of FO meeting in Paris with embassy officials to discuss the Anglo–Egyptian treaty, 4–5 Oct 1946). Sidky, however was reluctant to agree, under what had again become the second paragraph of article 2 (cf 81, note) to arrangements to reactivate the base on war or the threat of war in neighbouring countries and to any provisions being made for automatic joint action, and insisted that consultation should precede any such commitment in order to determine whether action was necessary (FO 371/53315, no 4384, FO memo on Bevin/Sidky talks, 21 Oct 1946). This was taken into consideration in the draft which was shown the Defence Committee.]

I have now had three meetings with the Egyptian Prime Minister and Minister for Foreign Affairs to discuss the questions outstanding in connection with the revision of the Anglo–Egyptian treaty. These questions were, in ascending order of difficulty:—

    (a) Air transit rights.

    (b) The period of complete military evacuation of Egyptian territory.

    (c) The provisions of the draft treaty defining the obligations of the parties in war or threat of war (Articles 2 and 3 of the last British draft).

    (d) The Sudan.

(a) The Egyptian Ministers have agreed that the question of air transit rights subsequent to our evacuation should be discussed by the proposed Joint Defence Board. I regard this assurance as satisfactory since under our existing draft there was doubt whether this matter was within the Board's competence.

(b) Sidky Pasha has agreed to fix the final date of evacuation at 1st September, 1949. This I regard as acceptable.

(c) As a result of my first two meetings with Sidky Pasha and of a subsequent meeting between the Egyptian Minister of F.A. and officials of the Foreign Office, the texts reproduced as articles 2 and 3 in the attached draft[1] were accepted *ad referendum* to Sidky Pasha and myself. Sidky Pasha has accepted these articles, and I recommend their acceptance by the Defence Committee. I have again received explicit assurances from the Egyptian Ministers that the provision for "consultation" in Article 2 is a pure (but from the Egyptian view point essential) matter of form. It need only amount to an intimation from His Majesty's Government to the Egyptian Government that the plans of the Joint Board for this contingency should be put into effect. The provision for consultation in the case of threat to the security of "neighbouring" countries is now contained in Article 3.

(d) The Egyptian Ministors have again assured me that in asking for recognition of Egyptian "sovereignty" over the Sudan they are not asking for any change in the existing status of the Sudan; and in particular it is not their intention to touch the existing system of administration until the Sudanese people themselves have decided what their ultimate future status is to be; nor the arrangements under which the military defence of the country is at present conducted. All they ask is that Egyptian

---

[1] Not printed, but on this see 85.

Sovereignty, which certainly exists in some measure as witness the fact that the Governor-General is appointed by Egyptian decree, shall receive recognition instead of being passed over in silence. Having regard to the agreement now reached on the defence clauses of the treaty, I have authorised my Department to meet the Egyptian officials in an endeavour to reduce these assurances, and our recognition of the King of Egypt's sovereignty to a mutually acceptable form which shall not prejudice our present position in the territory or the ultimate freedom of the inhabitants. I wish particularly to emphasise that under the proposed arrangements the Sudan will be in the same position from the point of view of imperial defence as it is at present. At the same time, I must add that any reference to the existence of Egyptian sovereignty may create considerable political tension—even if only temporary—in the Sudan, and that the possibility of disorder cannot be excluded. In that event we must be prepared to give full support, military and political, to the Governor General.

84   CAB 131/1, DO 30(46)   24 Oct 1946
'Anglo–Egyptian treaty negotiations': Cabinet Defence Committee
minutes   [Extract]

The Committee had before them a memorandum[1] by the Secretary of State for Foreign Affairs explaining the position now reached after three meetings with the Egyptian Prime Minister, during which he discussed the questions outstanding in connection with the revision of the Anglo–Egyptian Treaty. These questions were, in ascending order of difficulty:—

(a) Air transit rights;
(b) The period of complete military evacuation of Egyptian territory;
(c) The provisions of the draft Treaty defining the obligations of the parties in war or threat of war (Articles 2 and 3 of the last British draft, annexed to the above memorandum);
(d) The Sudan.

The Foreign Secretary said he wished it understood at the outset that the Egyptian Prime Minister had no power to settle an agreement with the British Government in this country. The discussions which had taken place were to prepare the ground for a form of Treaty which might have a chance of acceptance by both the Egyptian and British Governments. The outstanding questions divided themselves generally into two aspects—first of Defence and secondly the Sudan. On the question of air transit rights, the Egyptian Ministers had agreed that these rights, subsequent to our evacuation, should be discussed by the proposed Joint Defence Board. He was satisfied with this assurance since, in the existing British draft Treaty there was no[2] doubt that this matter was within the Board's competence to discuss. On the second outstanding point, the Egyptian Prime Minister had agreed to a final date for the total evacuation of our forces from Egypt as the 1st of September, 1949. When the discussions had first started with the Egyptians, we had originally proposed that the evacuation should take place over a period of five years. In making this proposal,

---

[1] See 83.   [2] Attlee commented in the margin: 'the "no" ought to come out, I think'.

he, the Foreign Secretary, had in mind the necessity to allow time for the British Service authorities to find an alternative base in the Middle East and, secondly, to provide a guarantee that during present international tensions we should not too quickly lose the Egyptian facilities at our disposal. Nevertheless, remembering the progress made in examining the potentialities of East Africa as a base, he regarded the final evacuation date of the 1st of September, 1949, as acceptable, and as allowing sufficient time to determine an alternative base in the Middle East. With regard to the third outstanding problem, he would point out that Article 3 was an innovation and covered the functions of the Joint Defence Board. Originally, the provision for the establishment of this Board had been included in Article 2, but he had thought it correct to make this a separate Article, which in its present wording would make the Board an advisory body holding a continuous function, whose duties were also defined. The present texts of both Articles 2 and 3 were accepted *ad referendum* to Sidky Pasha and himself. The Egyptian Prime Minister had accepted these Articles and he had obtained explicit assurances from the Egyptian Ministers that the provision for consultation in Article 2 was a pure (but from the Egyptian point of view essential) matter of form. It need only amount to an intimation from His Majesty's Government to the Egyptian Government that there was a need for consultation on the Joint Defence Board over any contingencies for this to be put into effect. The provision for consultation in the case of threat to the security of neighbouring countries was now contained in Article 3.

There were two further general points of advantage in negotiating this form of Treaty. From the international point of view, he wished to remove any possibility of interpreting in the Treaty, that our idea was concerned mainly with the defence of the Canal. Our present attitude towards Russian claims on the Dardanelles had been that the defence of these straits was the responsibility of the Riparian states. He did not therefore wish to risk any unfavourable comparison with our attitude over the Dardanelles by reference to any agreements we had reached governing the defence of the Middle East. He also had hopes that, once the Joint Defence Board was established, it would confine itself not so much to covering the problems of defence in Egypt alone, but would ultimately cover the defence of the Middle East as a whole, possibly in co-operation with other Arab States.

The Chief of the Imperial General Staff said the Chiefs of Staff could accept the discussion of air transit rights by the Joint Defence Board. As regards the period of complete military evacuation of British forces from Egyptian territory, they would agree to the final date being settled at the 1st of September, 1949. They would also agree with the present wording of Articles 2 and 3 of the draft Treaty. In this connection, he emphasized that the Treaty was now in such a form that we should depend entirely for any military rights in Egypt on the goodwill of the Egyptians. The present wording of these Articles gave us no specific military rights and we should have to depend on the efficient functioning of the Joint Defence Board, which again would depend on whether or not the Egyptians intended this Board to become an effective organ of co-operation. He stressed also the importance of realising that, as we were to evacuate from Egypt, the question of retaining military rights and facilities in Palestine must assume a growing and vital importance in the defence of the Middle East. Similarly, if the Middle East was to be held and fought for, a Headquarters in this area was necessary and in his opinion if, after the Treaty had been signed and present tensions had relaxed, we were to propose to the Egyptians that a small G.H.Q. consisting of approximately 1, 500 men might be established at (say) Fayid in the Canal Zone, there might be good prospects of the Egyptians accepting this proposal. . . .[3]

---

[3] Attlee sidelined the last lines of this sentence and commented in the margin: 'None whatever!'

85 FO 371/53317, no 4634, appendices   25 Oct 1946
[Anglo–Egyptian treaty negotiations]: draft treaty, taken from the record of the fifth and final meeting between Mr Bevin and Sidky

[This draft treaty, modified to take account of Sidky's points, was the draft accepted by Bevin that was taken back to Egypt for approval. Sargent proposed that in addition to the agreed draft, Britain should get written confirmation of the verbal undertakings given by Sidky on the right of the Sudanese to choose their future status, the transit rights to be accorded to Britain, the right of British troops to be stationed in the Sudan and the assistance to be granted by Egypt during the period of evacuation (FO 371/53317, no 4549, minute by Sargent, 30 Oct 1946). The final agreed version of article 2 should be compared with the original Egyptian draft and the drafts of article 3 in July when article 2 became a key source of disagreement (cf 57 note).]

Appendix 1 to 85

(1) *Draft Anglo–Egyptian treaty*
His Majesty The King of Great Britain, Ireland and the British Dominions beyond the Seas, Emperor of India, and His Majesty the King of Egypt:

Animated by the most sincere desire to consolidate the friendship and good relations which exist between them, and to establish these relations on foundations more suited to the development of this friendship:

Desiring to conclude a treaty of mutual assistance with the object of consolidating the friendly relations which exist between them and of strengthening by mutual co-operation and assistance the contribution which each of them will be able to make to the maintenance of international peace and security in accordance with the provisions and principles of the Charter of the United Nations:

Have accordingly appointed as their plenipotentiaries. . . .

Article 1

The Treaty of Alliance signed in London on 26th August, 1936, together with the agreed minute, notes and the Convention of 26th August, 1936, concerning immunities and privileges which accompanied the said Treaty, shall cease to have effect upon the entry into force of the present Treaty.

Article 2

The High Contracting Parties agree that in the event of Egypt becoming the object of armed aggression or in the event of the United Kingdom becoming involved in war as the result of armed aggression against countries adjacent to Egypt, they shall take, in close co-operation and as a result of consultation, such action as may be recognised as necessary until the Security Council has taken the necessary measures for the re-establishment of peace.

Article 3

In order to ensure the mutual co-operation and assistance of the High Contracting Parties, and in order to permit of the effective co-ordination of the measures to be taken for their mutual defence, the High Contracting Parties agree to establish a joint Board of Defence composed of the competent military authorities of the two Governments, assisted by such other representatives as the two Governments shall appoint.

The Board is an advisory body whose functions are to study, with a view to proposing to the two Governments the measures to be taken, problems concerning the mutual defence of the High Contracting Parties by land, sea and air, including questions of material and personnel connected therewith and, in particular, the technical requirements of their co-operation and the steps to be taken to enable the armed forces of the High Contracting Parties to be in a position effectively to resist aggression.

The Board shall meet as often as may be necessary in order to carry out these functions. If need arises, the Board shall also examine, on the invitation of, and on the information supplied by, the two Governments, the military repercussions of the international situation, and, in particular, of all events which may threaten the security of the Middle East, and shall make in this respect suitable recommendations to the two Governments, who in the case of events threatening the security of any one of the neighbouring countries of Egypt will consult together in order to take in agreement such measures as may be recognised as necessary.

Article 4

The High Contracting Parties undertake not to conclude any alliance and not to take part in any coalition directed against one of them.

Article 5

Nothing in the present Treaty can in any way prejudice the rights and obligations which devolve, or may devolve, upon one or other of the High Contracting Parties under the Charter of the United Nations.

Article 6

The High Contracting Parties agree that any difference on the subject of the application or interpretation of the provisions of the present Treaty, which they are unable to settle by direct negotiation, shall be determined in accordance with the provisions of the Charter of the United Nations, having due regard to the declarations made by both High Contracting Parties under Article 36 (2) of the Statute of the International Court.

Article 7

The present Treaty is subject to ratification. Ratifications shall be exchanged in Cairo as soon as possible. The Treaty shall come into force on the date of the exchange of ratifications. The present Treaty shall remain in force for a period of twenty years from the date of its coming into force and thereafter it shall remain in force until the expiry of one year after a notice of termination has been given by one High Contracting Party to the other through the diplomatic channel.

(2) *Draft Sudan protocol*

The policy which the High Contracting Parties undertake to follow in the Sudan (within the framework of the unity between the Sudan and Egypt under the common Crown of Egypt) will have for its essential objectives to assure the wellbeing of the Sudanese, the development of their interests and their active preparation for self-government and consequently the exercise of the right to choose the future status of the Sudan. Until the High Contracting Parties can in full common agreement realise this latter objective after consultation with the Sudanese, the Agreement of 1899 will continue and Article 11 of the Treaty of 1936, together with its Annexe and paragraphs 14 to 16 of the Agreed Minute annexed to the same Treaty, will remain in force notwithstanding the first Article of the present Treaty.

(3) *Draft evacuation protocol*

The High Contracting Parties agree that the complete evacuation of Egyptian territory (Egypt) by the British Forces shall be completed by the 1st September, 1949.

The towns of Cairo and Alexandria and the Delta shall be evacuated by the 31st March, 1947. The evacuation of the remainder of the country shall proceed continuously during the period ending at the date specified in the first paragraph above.

The provisions of the Convention of the 26th August, 1936, concerning immunities and privileges will continue provisionally to be applied to the British Forces during the period of their withdrawal from Egypt. Such amendment of the agreement as may be necessary in view of the fact that British troops will after the 31st March, 1947, be withdrawn from the Delta and the two cities shall be settled by a subsequent agreement between the two Governments to be negotiated before this date.

Appendix 2 to 85: confidential record of conversation between Sidky Pasha and Mr. Bevin concerning the evacuation protocol

1.   It is understood that the Egyptian Government will lend their co-operation and provide the facilities which the Government of the United Kingdom require in order to enable them to carry out withdrawals of the forces provided for in the Evacuation Protocol.

2.   With reference to Paragraph 2 of the Evacuation Protocol it is understood that the British personnel required to man the wireless stations at Abbassia, Maadi and Heliopolis, may remain at their present stations until a new location is found for these wireless stations. This will be done as soon as possible.

3.   The disposal of the installations, stores of material, equipment and communication facilities made or accumulated by British forces in Egypt, shall be settled by the two Governments on the advice of their respective experts.

4.   It is understood that financial terms on which any installations, stores, equipment and communication facilities which the Egyptian Government may wish to acquire shall be transferred to that Government will be the subject of later discussion between the two Governments.

5.   It is understood that until the completion of the evacuation in accordance with the provisions of the Evacuation Protocol, the British Forces shall continue to

enjoy their present rights of transit and flight over Egypt. It is also understood that the two Governments shall, after the signature of the Treaty of Alliance, discuss with a view to arriving at a mutual agreement the transit rights which shall be enjoyed for their aircraft by the British Forces after the evacuation of Egypt is completed. Reciprocal treatment will also be accorded to Egyptian Air Forces in British territory.

6.   It is understood the abrogation of the Treaty of 1936 does not affect the position of either party with regard to financial rights and liabilities which had accrued under the Treaty of 1936 at the time of the coming into force of the new Treaty of Alliance which abrogates it.

86   CAB 128/6, CM 96(46)3   14 Nov 1946
'Anglo–Egyptian treaty negotiations': Cabinet conclusions on the Sudan protocol and the proposed Anglo–Egyptian treaty

The Prime Minister said that the premature disclosure in Cairo of partial accounts of the Sudan Protocol to the proposed Anglo–Egyptian Treaty had gravely prejudiced the prospects of persuading the Sudanese to accept the protocol. The Governor-General of the Sudan had returned to London to represent to the Government the strength of the feeling which these disclosures had aroused in the Sudan. He believed that, if this formal recognition of Egyptian sovereignty over the Sudan were now given, force would be required to maintain public order and all the confidence engendered by fifty years of co-operation between British and Sudanese would vanish over-night. Many of the Sudanese officials in the administration would resign, and some of the British officials might also resign. At the worst, there might be widespread disorder and bloodshed. The Governor-General had asked that the Cabinet should be made aware, before taking their final decision, of the change in the situation caused by these disclosures in Cairo. In the changed circumstances he could no longer subscribe to the sovereignty clause of the Protocol. If, however, the Cabinet decided to proceed with the Protocol and still wished him to continue as Governor-General, he was ready to do so and would use his personal influence to mitigate the feeling in the Sudan and to reduce the amount of force required to maintain public order. A letter to this effect which the Governor-General had addressed to the Prime Minister was read to the Cabinet.

The Prime Minister said that there was little doubt in law about Egypt's sovereignty over the Sudan, and it was recognised in practice by the facts that the Governor-General was appointed by the King of Egypt, that the Egyptian flag was flown in the Sudan, and that Egyptian troops had been stationed there. For the last twenty years, however, the Sudan Government had allowed the Sudanese to close their eyes to the Egyptian connection to such an extent that the explicit recognition of Egyptian sovereignty in the Protocol would come as a severe shock to Sudanese opinion. The Governor-General's view on this point must be accepted. Even so, however, the Prime Minister felt that it was impossible to withdraw from the understandings about the Protocol which the Foreign Secretary had reached with Sidky Pasha. Such a withdrawal would mean the loss of the Anglo–Egyptian Treaty, with all that this entailed for our future relations with Egypt and our strategic position in the Middle East. Egypt would probably refer the whole issue to the United

Nations and the sovereignty question to the International Court, which was likely to uphold the Egyptian claim. In that event, our position in the Sudan would be worse than it would be under the Protocol; and meanwhile we should have lost our position in Egypt and the Middle East. In these circumstances the Prime Minister recommended that, despite the risk of disorders in the Sudan, we should proceed with our present plans for the Anglo–Egyptian Treaty and the Sudan Protocol. We should, however, endeavour to mitigate feeling in the Sudan by hastening the establishment of Sudanese legislative and executive organs so as to make it clear to the Sudanese that they were being put in a position to control their own affairs with no more interference from the Egyptian Government than in the past.

The Prime Minister said that he had put these considerations to the Foreign Secretary in a telegram (No. 2079 of 11th November); and the Foreign Secretary, in his reply (telegram No. 1613 of 12th November), had endorsed the recommendations which were now being made to the Cabinet.

Discussion showed that it was the view of the Cabinet that, notwithstanding the possible reactions in the Sudan, we should not withdraw from the understanding reached with Sidky Pasha about the Sudan Protocol. There were good prospects that within the next few days the Egyptian Government would accept the latest proposals regarding the Anglo–Egyptian Treaty; and it was most important that nothing should be said or done at this stage to prejudice these prospects. At the same time, we should lose no opportunity of averting serious trouble in the Sudan. Apart from long-term measures for expediting Sudanese progress towards self-government, more immediate action could be taken to reassure the Sudanese. Thus, some of the leaders of political parties in the Sudan might be brought to this country, so that they might satisfy themselves at first-hand of the desire of His Majesty's Government to enable the Sudanese to achieve self-government. Though it would be inexpedient to issue such an invitation before the Egyptian Government had reached their decision on the Treaty, preliminary arrangements could be made at once so that the invitation could be issued as soon as the decision of the Egyptian Government was known. Further, the Prime Minister could send to the Governor-General of the Sudan a letter, which he could show to some of the Sudanese leaders, assuring him that His Majesty's Government had considered his representations and were satisfied that the position of the Sudanese was fully safeguarded. This would be separate from the personal letter which the Prime Minister had already decided to send to the Governor-General inviting him to continue in office despite his apprehensions about the effect of the sovereignty clause in the Sudan Protocol to the Treaty.

The Cabinet:—

(1) Endorsed the Prime Minister's recommendation that, despite the possible reactions in the Sudan, we should not withdraw from our understandings with Sidky Pasha about the text of the Sudan Protocol to the new Anglo–Egyptian Treaty.

(2) Asked the Minister of State to put in hand preliminary arrangements for inviting leaders of political parties in the Sudan to visit this country.

(3) Took note that the Prime Minister would ask the Governor-General of the Sudan to continue in office and that the Foreign Secretary was also sending him a letter which he could show to British Members of the Administration explaining the reasons why His Majesty's Government had recognised the Egyptian claim in

regard to the Sudan and stating that the position and prospects of British officials would not be jeopardised.

(4) Suggested that a further letter should be sent to the Governor-General in suitable terms to be shown to the Sudanese leaders assuring him that His Majesty's Government had considered his representations and were satisfied that Sudanese interests were fully safe-guarded by the proposed Sudan Protocol to the new Anglo–Egyptian Treaty.

87   FO 371/53319, no 4973   26 Nov 1946

[Anglo–Egyptian treaty]: inward telegram no 1756 from R J Bowker to FO summarising the statement by some members of the Egyptian delegation on their opposition to the draft treaty

Following is summary of statement published in press of November 26th over the names of Sherif Sabri, Ali Maher, Abdel Fattah Yehia, Hussein Sirry, Ali Shamsi, Lutfi El Sayed and Makram Ebeid Pasha,[1] who met twice on November 25th.

[Begins]

2.   After meeting of Egyptian delegation to examine the new draft texts brought from London 7 delegates were unable to approve the texts as they were although Sidky Pasha stated that they were not subject to modification. Sidky Pasha's explanatory note is a unilateral document not binding on His Majesty's Government. It is connected with statements in the House of Commons and with the activities of the Governor General of the Sudan which conflict with Sidky Pasha's explanation. When some time elapsed after the delegation's meeting on November 16th without delegation being summoned again delegation charged Hussein Sirry to get in touch with Sidky with a view to resumption of discussion but it was learned that Sidky did not intend to summon delegation before November 26th (date for discussion of Treaty interpellation in Chamber). Above mentioned delegates therefore had no option but to issue statement embodying main reasons for rejecting present Treaty draft.

3.   Draft of Article 2 presented by British side on September 17th was rejected by Egyptian delegation on September 23rd because it meant Egypt might become base for military operation and again liable to British occupation. Moreover the term "threat to security" was elastic and capable of various contradictory interpretations. Although suppressed in the Bevin-Sidky draft of Article 2 it had been reproduced almost textually in draft of Article 3. It was impossible to accept what had been already unaninmously [sic] rejected. Moreover this Article might jeopardise friendly relations between Egypt and other Nations.

4.   Delegation considered period of 3 years for evacuation excessive. Evacuation of forces brought to Egypt for purposes of war should have begun immediately on cessation of hostilities. 1936 Treaty restricted location and numbers of British forces.

5.   Latest version of Sudan Protocol, as drafted in London, destroys essential features of unity of the Nile Valley, maintains the status quo without promising negotiations for its modification, and by giving Sudanese right to choose their future

---

[1] Seven of the Egyptian delegation's members

status, opens the way for the separation of the 2 parts of Nile Valley. Unity of Nile Valley does not carry any implication of expansion or imperialism.

6.   For these reasons signatories refuse Treaty draft in its present form and consider it useful to publish concise statement in order to explain the attitude they have adopted with a view to fulfilling their duties and the mission entrusted to them.

88   FO 371/53319, no 5059   29 Nov 1946
[Anglo–Egyptian treaty]: inward telegram no 1779 from R J Bowker to FO on the problem of exchanging letters on the Sudan protocol

[On 26 Nov the Egyptian delegation was formally dissolved and therefore the fate of the treaty rested with the Egyptian parliament and King Farouk's ability to secure a vote of confidence based on his interpretation of the Sudan protocol. In Cairo the chargé d'affaires, analysing the political groupings, was pessimistic about any outcome on terms acceptable to Britain (FO 371/53319, no 4994, letter from Bowker to Scrivener, 21 Nov 1946). In London there was some surprise at the stance taken over the Sudan issue. Scrivener said Sidky was right to argue that Egypt must have some say in the declaration of Sudanese independence, as opposed to saying the Sudanese should never be independent (FO 371/53319, no 5060, minute by Scrivener, 1 Dec 1946). Stansgate stated that Sidky had never agreed to a free choice of independence for the Sudan and commented that it would be interesting to know when the British government took the decision that Sudan should have the choice of independence. Howe noted that it grew naturally out of the development of Sudanisation. (FO 371/53321, no 5311, minute by Lord Stansgate, 6 Dec 1946, and marginal note by Howe.]

The Prime Minister asked to see me this morning on pretext of giving me an opportunity of delivering to him direct the message from Secretary of State which I delivered yesterday through Minister for Foreign Affairs[1] about Egyptian amendment on subject of the presence of foreign troops in minor States of members of U.N.O. The Minister for Foreign Affairs was present throughout the interview. The Prime Minister said that Egyptian delegate had been instructed yesterday to get into touch with United Kingdom delegate and that the matter had now been satisfactorily settled. The Egyptian delegate had further been instructed to maintain in future close contact with his British colleague. Moreover the Minister for Foreign Affairs had been instructed to keep him informed of political developments.

2.   The Prime Minister then asked me if I had any news about when it would be possible to sign the treaty. I said that I understood this was being discussed between the Egyptian Ambassador and the Foreign Office. The Prime Minister and Minister for Foreign Affairs then emphasised most earnestly the necessity for haste since any delay would be exploited by the Opposition and the whole position might be endangered. The Wafd had to-day announced their intention of carrying out a campaign in the provinces "to spread the good word". The Government were prevented from coming full out in favour of the treaty and so effectively counteracting the Wafd until the treaty was signed.

3.   I said that I knew you appreciated the necessity for speed but that there was first the question of exchange of letters to be settled. This led to an argument which lasted an hour and as usual was quite inconclusive. Sidky Pasha insisted as usual that His Majesty's Government should appreciate his difficulties and now make things

---

[1] Abdel Hadi.

easy for him. The Minister for Foreign Affairs maintained that it had been understood in London that no exchange of letters would be necessary. I said that if this was the case the position since then had been entirely changed by all that had been said and written about the proposals here and it was as a result of this that Mr. Bevin found it necessary now to require that various points should be confirmed in writing. Sidky Pasha argued at length about the impossibility of agreeing in advance to Sudanese independence which he said could only result from discussion between the Sudanese and Egyptian Governments. I pointed out that this point had been made a public issue by the Egyptian and not British side and that since he had found it necessary to publish a precise interpretation of this provision in Sudanese protocol it was now necessary to give Sudanese as well as British Parliament an explanation. I emphasised how patient His Majesty's Government had been in the face of continual publicity and misrepresentation at this end and Mr. Bevin was now appealing to him to appreciate his difficulties.

4.   I fear I made no impression whatever on either the Prime Minister or the Minister for Foreign Affairs and they gave me no reason whatever to think that there was any chance of their agreeing to sign an exchange of letters. I gave them no reason to think this requirement would be waived.

89   FO 371/53320, no 5168   6 Dec 1946
[Anglo–Egyptian exchange of letters]: inward telegram from Mr Bevin[1] (New York) to FO suggesting text of letter to Sidky

My telegram No. 2326.

Following is text of the letter which I would suggest sending to Sidky. He should be asked either to write to me in similar terms or to confirm in writing his agreement to my letter.

[Begins]

At the moment of signing the treaty of to-day's date I am happy to place on record my understanding of our agreement in regard to the meaning of certain parts of the Sudan protocol annexed to the treaty.[2] We are agreed that the provisions of the Sudan protocol involve no change in the present status of the Sudan and that the protocol in fact amounts to an affirmation of the existing status. As to the future, the Sudan protocol provides that the Sudanese people shall when they are ripe for self-government be free to choose the future status of the Sudan. This future status may take several forms: the Sudanese people may choose an association with the crown of Egypt similar to that of the self-governing Dominions with the British crown; they may choose some other form of self-governing association with the crown of Egypt; or they may choose independence. We are agreed that in the Sudan protocol, a completely free choice on the part of the Sudanese people is implied.

We are also agreed that the Sudan protocol in no way affects the right of the United Kingdom to secure the defence of the Sudan with whatever troops and facilities they may require.

---

[1] Bevin was in New York for the Council of Foreign Ministers which met from 4 Nov to 12 Dec.

[2] Upon receipt Attlee inserted 'There will therefore be no changes in the present administration except in so far as this is necessary for the preparation of the Sudanese people for self-government'.

We also agreed that until the completion of the evacuation in accordance with the provisions of the evacuation protocol, the British forces shall continue to enjoy their present rights of transit and flight over Egypt. It is also understood that the two Governments shall, after the signature of the Treaty of Alliance, discuss with a view to arriving at a mutual agreement the transit rights which shall be enjoyed for their aircraft by the British forces after the evacuation of Egypt is completed. Reciprocal treatment will also be accorded to Egyptian air forces in British territory. We finally agreed that the abrogation of the treaty of 1936 does not affect the position of either party with regard to financial rights and liabilities which had accrued under the treaty of 1936 at the time of the coming into force of the new Treaty of Alliance which abrogates it. [Ends]

90   FO 371/62960, no 86   1 Jan 1947

[Failure of the Anglo-Egyptian treaty negotiations]: minute by Sir O Sargent to Mr Bevin on the likely situation in Egypt if the talks break down

The following is an endeavour to describe the situation which will arise in Egypt if the negotiations for a new treaty finally break down.

The dominating factor in the situation at the present moment appears to be not so much the treaty issue as the feud between the King and the Wafd, or, differently expressed, between palace government and party government. The treaty, it is true, has become the immediate bone of contention between the two, but it is *now* more a pretext for quarrelling than a fundamental issue. Last winter and spring there was a fairly unanimous agitation against the 1936 treaty in all its aspects, at any rate amongst the politically minded. This has been allayed by the admission on our part of a large—or at any rate of the more spectacular—parts of the Egyptian thesis, viz. evacuation and the unity of Egypt and the Sudan. The unreality of the present position is shown by the attitudes of some of the independents who admitted that the treaty was a very good one but said that it could not be signed with Sidky—and for practical purposes Sidky and Nokrashi are the same. Moreover the Wafd, if in office, would quite probably have been glad to get such a treaty.

The alignment of forces is now complete viz. Palace, Liberals, Saadists and some independents on one side and the Wafd, Watanists, Kotla, some independents, Moslem Brothers and semi-Fascist bodies such as Young Egypt on the other. By giving full support to the treaty (the particular point of difference at the moment) the King has eliminated, for the moment, the possibility of creating something like a national Government. In fact he seems to have decided to fight. Whether this is the first move in a struggle on the lines of the Civil War in England remains to be seen.

If the treaty negotiations *finally* break down, the Palace régime's difficulties are likely to be greatly increased and its ability to control the turbulent forces of the Opposition greatly decreased. Things having gone as far as they have, it is questionable whether the King could revert to the idea of a coalition and maintain his position. He and his supporters would be more likely to introduce a diversion (however clearly they may recognise its dangers) by appealing against us to the

Security Council and having the whole question of Anglo-Egyptian relations debated there. In spite of Egyptian misgivings regarding the danger of a reference to U.N.O., there would be virtual unanimity on this policy, and by adopting it the King would go far to silence his opponents, at any rate in the foreign field. His enemies would be likely to find, very shortly, some pretext for attack elsewhere.

In these circumstances there is no obvious reason why there should be a serious disturbance of internal order. Demonstrations in Egypt take place against the Government or against the British. There would be no *immediate* grievance against the Government provided they had hauled us before U.N.O., though maybe demonstrations (which the Government would be loth to suppress) would take place in favour of more direct action. And, except on general principles, there would be no overpowering grievance against the British, who would obviously be in process of evacuating, and whose concessions are now well known. Also, (though this is rather flattering the political intelligence of the average student) any disturbance of public order would be calculated to *slow up* evacuation. Thus, even though there might be some sporadic disorder in the towns, it is difficult to see (from here) the likelihood of a nation-wide movement with a real head of steam behind it, as in 1919. It is presumably only such a movement that would require a reinforcement of the present garrison. It should be borne in mind, however, that Egyptian Governments sometimes have encouraged disorderly demonstrations to impress or frighten us, and might do so again, though probably on a moderate scale, to impress U.N.O.

In the Sudan the effects of a rupture on the Sudan issue would be wholly beneficial from the point of view of the Sudan Government. Faith in His Majesty's Government would be fully restored, and the Governor-General could carry on his Sudanisation plans in a much more favourable atmosphere than at present. It is doubtful whether the Ashigga party could make much trouble, though they would certainly try.

If the Egyptian Government decide to take to U.N.O. the situation resulting from a breakdown of the Anglo-Egyptian negotiations, they may be expected to demand, first of all, the evacuation of all British forces and installations on the ground that they are stationed in Egypt, an independent state, without the consent of the Government of that state. They may be expected to invoke clause 8 of the recent resolution of the Assembly on the general regulation and reduction of armaments which reads as follows:— "The General Assembly . . . recommends the members to undertake . . . the withdrawal without delay of armed forces stationed in the territories of members without their consent freely and publicly expressed in treaties or agreements consistent with the Charter and not contradicting international agreements". They might then go on to claim that the Anglo-Egyptian treaty of 1936, on which His Majesty's Government would base their right to maintain troops in the Suez Canal Zone, was no longer valid. In so doing they might argue as follows:—

> "The Treaty of 1936 was bound up with the League and the League Covenant: it is clear that any future relations between the United Kingdom and Egypt must be based on and consistent with the Charter. Amongst other things the Charter says it overrides all other treaties: we, Egypt, say that according to the Charter there is no scope for a Treaty of Alliance on the old lines. We not only say that we think the Charter renders it unnecessary but we also say that it is really contrary to the whole principles of the Charter that there should be a treaty of this kind. The negotiations have broken down and the British

troops are remaining on in Egypt. According to our view and on the basis of the Charter the troops should now go."

As regards the Sudan it must be supposed that the Egyptians would either say nothing about the Sudan at all or claim that the present situation there was not in accordance with Egypt's rights, and would invite U.N.O. to endorse the thesis that politically, racially and historically Egypt and the Sudan are one country and that the question of the secession, or the separation, of the Sudan cannot consequently arise, or at any rate is not one for discussion with any other Power even if that Power possesses a share in the administration.

Our line in reply would no doubt be, in brief, that the 1936 treaty (as the Law Officers have advised) is a perfectly valid instrument and in complete accord with the provisions of the Charter, that we are not in default in its execution, that we agreed to negotiate for its revision before we were under any obligation to do so and that, negotiations under the ten year provisions having failed, the treaty automatically continues.

91 FO 371/62961, no 413   27 Jan 1947
[Intervention in Egyptian politics]: letter from Sir O Sargent to Sir R Campbell on the possibility of bringing the Wafd back to power

[After the fall of Sidky in December 1946 Farouk reappointed Nokrashi as PM. By 14 Jan Nokrashi had made it clear that he could not accept any statement granting the Sudanese the 'freedom to choose their future status' when the time came. The FO therefore told the Egyptians that they had said their last words and expressed relief that the talks had broken down on an issue where Britain had a very good case (FO 371/62940, no 209, minute by Sir R Howe, 14 Jan 1947). As expected Nokrashi made clear his intention to present the whole treaty issue (not just the Sudan) before the Security Council (FO 371/62961, no 405, Cairo tel 243, 25 Jan 1947).]

You will no doubt remember that when the question of treaty revision became acute in 1945 we were strongly recommended in certain quarters not to deal with any but a united Egyptian delegation. Since the Wafd refused to enter such a dele-gation except on conditions, such as the holding of free elections, which would have meant their return to political power, for us to insist on such a delegation would have meant a strong intervention by us in the internal affairs of Egypt. The Secretary of State had however decided that our policy should be to avoid returning to our old habits of Cabinet making. We had moreover been assured that if we would support the King he would see us through the Treaty. Events have falsified these assurances. I think it is a fair assumption that if the Wafd had been in power they would have been agreeably surprised to have been offered a treaty on the lines we agreed with Sidky last October and would have signed it and seen it through the Egyptian Parliament, since the latter would *ex hypothesi* have been a Wafd Parliament.

We are told that the Wafd still commands the support of the majority of the Egyptian people. If His Majesty's Government were again to throw its weight into the scales of internal politics in Egypt, with the result that they came back into office might we not expect that we could negotiate better with them?

The purpose of this letter and the enclosed minute[1] therefore is to ask you to reflect on the above considerations and to advise us whether we should not again take a hand in internal politics with a view to putting an end to the succession of Palace governments which are getting us nowhere. Would our intervention be effective and if so how should it be contrived? Would Abboud be the man to approach? Would an intimation to Nahas that he would have our support for a return to power with a policy of economic and social reform in return for his collaboration and support for a revised treaty be a gambit worth trying? I should like you to explore the whole matter with Smart and let me have your ideas as soon as possible. You would not of course consult anyone else yet.

---

[1] Not printed.

---

92   FO 371/62942, no 723   8 Feb 1947
[Anglo-Egyptian treaty negotiations]: memorandum by Lord Stansgate for Mr Bevin on the reasons for their failure   [Extract][1]

... The negotiations in Egypt for various reasons were greatly protracted. This robbed us of the advantage we had initially gained. Undoubtedly it was a mistake in July, 1945, to take no steps towards evacuation and not to change the Ambassador. The memory of the tanks in 1942 was very much in the minds of the Egyptians. The arrival of the new Ambassador produced a burst of sunshine and had we made then the offer of evacuation which was later agreed on our chances of success would have been brighter. Instead of this, during March, April and May, we thought it wise to present a number of proposals, such as, for a skeleton base, and for a prolonged occupation, which were totally unacceptable to the Egyptians and destroyed what then existed—their desire to agree.

8.   The one success we had at this time was the acceptance of the Joint Defence Board secured by the Foreign Office and the Ambassador. From then onwards we made no progress at all.

9.   In July the Egyptians offered us a draft which, saving the Sudan, was as good as that we ultimately agreed. We should have accepted it for discussion at that time. There followed another two months of effort, all of which proved fruitless.

10.   It appears to me that throughout we have set too much store by the cooperative spirit of the Egyptian Ambassador. He has been a devoted friend of agreement, but the Egyptian Cabinet and Parliament are of much tougher material and I think this was not fully realised in London.

11.   In particular we over-estimated the personal power and willingness of the King. In August a direct effort was made by Amr Pasha to enlist his positive help. It was a failure. The King's position is too insecure to permit him opposing the national will. His presence the other night in the Egyptian Parliament, where he was

---

[1] This memo was enclosed with a letter of the same date from Stansgate to Bevin. The first paragraphs of the memo were an attempt to justify Stansgate's policy of accommodation. The remaining paragraphs, which refer to the Sudan and the difficulty of ensuring that whatever government in Egypt was brought into office would accept British terms over the Sudan, are reproduced in BDEEP series B, vol 5, Douglas H Johnson, *Sudan*, part 1, 129.

acclaimed by the members, is some evidence that he intends to be himself at the head of Egyptian demands. Generally speaking Kings in the Middle East don't count as they once did.

12.   My own view is that we have been too much inclined to think that the Prime Minister of the moment was being obdurate and that a little pressure would bring him to reason. The fact is that both Prime Ministers, and particularly Sidki, have been doing their best to persuade their public opinion to come to agreement. Sidki might have been the more helpful. We made much of his indiscretions and so discredited him and, perhaps, contributed to the King's decision to dismiss him, but in point of fact the first indiscretion, that is to say, the first declaration, in recent time, of independence for the Sudan was made by the Governor-General in his speech to the Advisory Council in April, where being a servant of both parties he declared his policy without consulting Egypt, thus going, as the Egyptians say, outside his proper function. His speech, of course, angered them and was the subject of complaint to me by the King. Sidki, who, by his indiscretions, was striving to defeat his opponents and come to an agreement with us, was destroyed and Nokrashi took his place. The whole episode, for which Sidki was only partly to blame, was disastrous.

13.   Nokrashi is a totally different man, stubborn and straightforward, and his method was to rally behind him, not only the two parties supporting the Government, but all the other members of Parliament.

14.   This he has effectively done and for the moment may be regarded as the real spokesman of a unanimous Egypt. The lull, therefore, so far from being reassuring is ominous for we are not dealing with a Sidki, trying to find a way round the difficulties, but with a tough representative who will bring all difficulties into the open. . . .

93   CAB 131/4, DO(47)23   7 Mar 1947
'The defence of the Commonwealth': memorandum by the COS for the Cabinet Defence Committee on the general requirements for survival in a future war

[On 13 Jan Attlee finally gave way (cf 32, note) and accepted that the defence of the Middle East would form a central part of British defence strategy (DEFE 4/1, COS 9(47)2). The rejection of the idea of a Lagos-Mombasa line as a replacement for a Middle Eastern defence line and the restatement of the Middle East's vital role in Commonwealth defence had formalised British strategic priorities. This ended the great debate which had been underway since the autumn of 1945 and had implications for the future of the base in Egypt. In the FO, one official commenting on the confirmation of the Middle East's vital importance to the empire claimed that 'our position in Egypt is the keystone to our position in the whole area and there can be no doubt that the recent developments in Egypt, coupled with our difficulties in Palestine have seriously affected our prestige right throughout the Arab world'. Therefore a treaty with Egypt 'at any price' would have a further harmful effect on Britain's Middle East position (FO 371/62968, no 1405, minute by I P Garran, 1 Apr 1947). Egypt's importance had to be conceived in this way as there were still no specific plans for defending the Middle East if the Soviets were to attack in the immediate future. The memorandum reproduced below was not brought before the Defence Committee for discussion.]

The series of developments during the past nine months have each, when considered singly, had far-reaching effects on our strategic situation. But, when viewed collectively, it is clear that our essential strategic requirements as a whole, and indeed the security, not only of the Commonwealth but of the United Kingdom itself, are gravely threatened. We therefore feel it our duty to His Majesty's Government, who we realise are facing immense political problems in all parts of the world, to re-affirm and confirm our views and advice as to what, in our opinion, are the essential and fundamental strategic requirements which it is necessary for our political action to ensure if the security of Britain and the Commonwealth is to be maintained.

2.   We have agreed that our strategy demands:—

(a) The ability to defend the resources on which the Commonwealth must draw to prosecute a major war, until, with our Allies, we can develop an all-out offensive.
(b) The holding of bases from which this offensive can be launched at the earliest possible moment.

3.   It was further agreed that the fulfilment of these basic objectives rendered the following absolutely essential:—

(a) The defence and safety of the United Kingdom.
(b) The maintenance of our sea communications.
(c) A firm hold in the Middle East area.

4.   The above fundamental principles were endorsed by the Prime Minister, Foreign Secretary and Minister of Defence on 13th January, 1947.

5.   In the last six months:—

(a) The Egyptian negotiations have failed.
(b) The future of Palestine is to be referred to U.N.O.
(c) British material support to Greece, upon which her independence depends, will not continue after June 1947. Unless ample American assistance is forthcoming, Greece is likely to become a satellite of Russia to the detriment of our strategic position in the Mediterranean and to the position of Turkey.
(d) Nothing has been achieved to ensure our position in Cyrenaica.
(e) His Majesty's Government have decided to hand over power in India by June 1948.

On each of the individual points (a) to (d) above, the Chiefs of Staff have taken a stand on strategic grounds. In the case of (e) the Chiefs of Staff were not consulted before the Cabinet decision was taken.

6.   Taken separately, each of the above events is extremely serious, but viewed as a whole they mean that:—

(a) We would not have the ability to fight in, and to hold, the Middle East in war. Without rights in Egypt and Palestine, the time factor at the outbreak of war would be very heavily weighted against us. With the loss of the Middle East we lose the air bases vital for the action which alone can decrease the weight of attack on the United Kingdom, and we lose the bases necessary for the security of our communications through the Mediterranean.
(b) The vast man-power and resources and the vital air bases of India may not be available to the Commonwealth. This, in addition to denying us India's immense potential, would remove a most important link in our communications to

Australia and the Far East, and in the maintenance of the security of those communications.

7.   There are no proper alternatives to the above essential areas. The abandonment of our positions in them means that we risk starting a war from the "outer ring" of the North American Continent, South Africa, Australia and New Zealand and, except for the United Kingdom, with no air bases available from which to operate. Such a withdrawal to the "outer ring" would entail long, arduous and costly operations before we could even start hitting back at the enemy; in fact, the United Kingdom would begin the war by fighting in the last ditch, and it is open to serious doubt whether she could survive so long.

8.   If the present trend of events continues, it must eventually lead the Commonwealth to disaster. His Majesty's Government must be left in no doubt of the seriousness with which the Chiefs of Staff view the position.

9.   It is our national policy to prevent war, and we should therefore do everything we can to improve our relations with Russia. But, both to enable us to deter aggression and also to ensure our survival if war should be forced upon us, in our opinion it is of supreme importance that His Majesty's Government should:—

Employ every means within their power to incorporate our minimum strategic requirements in the final settlements of the international problems in paragraph 5 above.

10.   To this end, the following principles stand out clearly:—

(a) We should have the closest possible tie-up with the United States and the Dominions.

(b) We should retain our essential strategic requirements in Palestine.

(c) We should negotiate a treaty with Egypt which will:—
(i)   Safeguard our right of re-entry into that country in the threat of war;
(ii) Ensure the maintenance in peace of the minimum base facilities which we shall require on the outbreak of war.

(d) In the event of failure to negotiate such a treaty, we must have military rights in Cyrenaica. But the necessity to return to Egypt in the event of war, despite the lack of a treaty, would remain.

(e) Nothing should be allowed to interfere with the improvement of our relations with the Arab States.

(f) We should not relinquish our sovereignty over Cyprus.

(g) We should ensure that an arrangement is concluded with India which allows us all essential military facilities.

11.   We recognise that His Majesty's Government are committed to certain policies which may profoundly affect our Commonwealth strategic position, *e.g.*, the reference of the Palestine question to U.N.O. Nevertheless, we feel strongly that the measures outlined in paragraph 10 above should be the aim of our policy and that we should strive with all the means at our disposal, in consultation as appropriate, with the Dominions and the United States, for its achievement.

94   FO 371/62967, no 1178   12 Mar 1947

[Policy towards Egypt]: inward telegram no 636 from Sir R Campbell to FO suggesting a tougher policy

[On 3 Mar Nokrashi announced at a press conference that because there had been no immediate British evacuation of Egypt and because Egypt's administrative rights in the Sudan had not been restored, British troops must leave the Sudan to enable the Sudanese to determine their own future. He claimed, along with the unity of Egypt and the Sudan, that the Egyptians were best placed to prepare the Sudanese for self-government (FO 371/62966, no 1019, Cairo tel 557, 3 Mar 1946). On 27 Jan Bevin had assured parliament that the 1936 treaty would be adhered to (*H of C Debs*, vol 432, cols 616–620), and he informed parliament on 11 Mar that Britain had fallen back on its rights and while evacuating from Cairo would be going to the Canal Zone (*H of C Debs*, vol 434, col 1134).]

Nokrashi's statement makes it most undesirable if not futile for us to pursue any longer the task of getting the Egyptians to reopen treaty negotiations. Efforts by His Majesty's Government to this end would only be regarded as indicating a degree of weakness on our part which must encourage those Egyptians who are so minded to go further and further towards destruction of our positions not only in Egypt but also in the Middle East. I think therefore that the time has come to stiffen our whole attitude to Egypt as long as the present situation continues.

2.   A small reactionary group in Egypt is deliberately and strongly promoting anti-British feeling in Egypt and is trying to do the same thing in Arab countries perhaps as a long term policy likewise for the purposes of its policy in connexion with Treaty revision. This move is making considerable progress largely owing to the bewilderment of Egyptians who think that our failure to react against this obvious anti-British drive is due to Great Britain's weakness. If this goes on much longer friendly Egyptians (whatever exhortations we may make in appropriate quarters) will little by little fight shy of us and we shall find with difficulty Egyptians ready to collaborate with us. One by one our different institutions will be attacked as has already been the case with Marconis and the Anglo–Egyptian Union.[1] There will be no halting the Egyptians on this road as long as they think we are powerless to hold our friends here and make things unpleasant for our enemies. Sources of this move are both Nokrashi himself and the Palace. Nokrashi is taking this line because when aggrieved he can become "awkward". The Palace is encouraging it partly because of an innate anti-British tendency which is one facet of King Farouk's character dating from his very accession, partly because of royal pique over reference to a minority Government, partly because His Majesty desires to reinsure with the public after failure of the treaty policy. Both Nokrashi and the Palace are actuated partly by the need of a minority régime to compete with the majority in anti-British extremism. The majority meanwhile likewise indulges in extremism in order not to be outdone by the Palace and in order to make it difficult for the present régime to accept any settlement by forcing them yet higher in the ascending spiral.

3.   There is every indication that King Farouk and Azzam are endeavouring to undermine friendly Hashemite rulers in Iraq and Trans-Jordan; thus the Egyptian influence is being used to alienate Arab states generally from Great Britain. Causes of this are (a) fear of a Hashemite Greater Syria which would compete for leadership of

---

[1] The Anglo-Egyptian Union was a wartime association inspired by Amin Uthman and encouraged by the British for propaganda purposes. It was opposed by the opponents of the Wafd.

the Arab countries with Egypt, (b) belief that we are backing Greater Syria and resultant fear that Saudi Arabia is most likely to desire to back us at U.N.O.

4.   It seems to me that an essential condition of maintaining our positions in the Middle East is that we should show firmness by which both friends and enemies will realise that we are not going to allow ourselves to be driven out of the Middle East by Egypt and that our patience and conciliatory attitude during negotiations does not mean we can be driven to any position the Egyptians choose.

5.   I think the line we now should take is that the Egyptian Government have by this statement of Nokrashi grossly misrepresented causes of the breakdown of negotiations and been guilty of bad faith, that we will always be prepared to negotiate revision of the 1936 Treaty with any Egyptian government, prepared and able to study our common problems on their merits and that meanwhile we will stand on the 1936 Treaty particularly on Article 8 which makes Egypt a strategical area as being an essential means of communication between different parts of the British Empire and also a universal means of communication. As regards temporary presence in Egypt of military elements in excess of those stipulated in the 1936 Treaty we would [grp. undec.] troops came here to save the world and Egypt from Nazi and Fascist domination during the World War. They had incidently saved Egypt from complete material destruction. They were being removed as quickly as circumstances would permit. It would in my opinion be well for us to get this line taken in general terms in the press as soon as possible (tone should be good tempered) and we should prepare a closely argued and detailed case on this basis for use at U.N.O. We should seek America's support at U.N.O. for this attitude.

6.   As regards the Sudan we would stand on the principle of self determination while we would be prepared to consider any reasonable extension of claim as regards their participation in the preparation of the Sudanese for self Government, this would be impossible as long as the Egyptians maintain their present unreasonable attitude and continue to mis-represent British past and present policy.

7.   I submit that we are forced to take up an attitude on these lines unless we are prepared to be driven from pillar to post until we are driven out of the Middle East.

95   FO 371/62967, no 1254   15 Mar 1947
[Intervention in Egyptian politics]: outward telegram no 97 from Sir O Sargent to Mr Bevin (Moscow)[1] on the possibility of replacing the existing government.

If there is a progressive or accelerated deterioration in our relations with Egypt, we may have to consider whether we should not go further than the line advocated by Sir R. Campbell and see whether there are any means open to us of replacing the present minority régime by a more representative form of government. You will remember recent correspondence on the subject of the Wafd's return to power and in this connexion I am repeating to you Cairo telegram No. 535 [of March 1st] from which you will observe that the Ambassador sees no worth while results likely from

---

[1] Bevin was in Moscow for the Council of Foreign Ministers which was convened on 10 Mar to consider the German peace treaty and which ended in failure on 25 Apr.

an approach to the Wafd. It may be of interest in this connexion that Abboud Pasha has telegraphed to the Minister of State expressing hope of arriving here shortly and of seeing Minister of State. This indicates that Abboud may raise question of our support for a return of the Wafd and in this event you may wish to consider whether Minister of State or some official should not receive him, listen to what he has to say, and endeavour to find out, without commitment on our part, what, if anything, the Wafd would require from us in the way of support.

96 FO 371/62943, no 1409   28 Mar 1947

[Policy towards Egypt and the Sudan]: outward telegram no 425 from Sir O Sargent to Mr Bevin (Moscow) on the inadvisibility of concessions[1]   [Extract]

> [Bevin replied objecting to the idea that British policy had been based on concessions. He suggested that the defence aspects of the proposed treaty had been satisfactory and suited to the empire's needs in the post-war world. The talks, Bevin claimed, had broken down on the Sudan not only because satisfying Egyptian claims would have prejudiced the rights of the Sudanese but because Britain's imperial defence was at stake (FO 371/62943, no 1553, Moscow tel 524, 1 Apr 1947).]

Your telegram No. 353 [of 25th March].

I do not think I have misunderstood the way your mind is working and I agree that a better atmosphere over the Sudan is a necessary preliminary to the resumption of negotiations. But I should not have said that a talk between the Ambassador and the King as suggested in Foreign Office telegram under reference need necessarily be excluded on this account. It would at any rate enable us to judge what prospects there are of an early change of Government and outlook as regards which we are at present very much in the dark.

2.   But what I am sure we must avoid is to say or do anything at this stage which will give the impression that His Majesty's Government are still making concessions because they are frightened of Egyptian displeasure or because they are doubtful of the strength of their case before United Nations Organisation. (As regards this latter point, I shall send you a further telegram on the legal issue). I do not believe that any Egyptian sincerely thinks that Egyptian interests are endangered by the present British administration or policy in the Sudan. On the contrary, every thinking Egyptian knows that his own Government has neither the authority nor the men necessary to rule and hold the Sudan. But we have, I fear, reached a point where it has become for the time being the object of every ambitious politician in Egypt to claim popular credit by representing each British concession as an Egyptian victory over British weakness. Any change of policy therefore in regard to the administration of the Sudan must I suggest be put through very gradually and cautiously. Any sudden introduction of Egyptians into the administrative machine in the place of British or Sudanese, or even an announcement that this was going to be the policy of His Majesty's Government in the future, would, I am sure, be treated by Egyptian politicians as yet another concession exacted by them from a weak and frightened Great Britain. If so, far from lessening the present anti-British trend such a reform

---

[1] Repeated to Cairo no 686 (personal for the ambassador)

would I fear increase it, for experience shows that anti-British feeling inevitably grows each time the Egyptians feel that they have achieved yet another victory.

3.   A year ago we had a large fund of goodwill in Egypt and if this has been now more or less dissipated and replaced by growing hostility, I cannot help feeling that this is largely due to the long series of concessions which we have made to Egypt over the last twelve months without exacting any immediate return. First of all we agreed to revise the Treaty. We then agreed to complete evacuation—both of these were concessions due in Egyptian eyes to clamour and agitation. Later on we waived our right to maintain the military facilities we enjoyed under the 1936 Treaty; then we waived our rights to intervene in the event of menace of war, substituting for these rights a mere consultative body. Lastly we admitted the unity of the Nile Valley under a common Crown, and now even the departure of Sir H. Huddleston[2] is being represented as an attempt to placate Egyptian public opinion (see Cairo telegram No. 747 paragraph 12).

4.   My conviction is that this series of concessions, however justifiable at the time, has been interpreted as a sign of the growing weakness of Great Britain, the proof of which is seen daily in Arab eyes in our inability to put down terrorism in Palestine and the humiliations imposed by Jewish gunmen on our soldiers there. By contrast any sign of our growing strength would produce I should hope a pro-British feeling and greatly encourage our friends who at present remain silent and perplexed. I would submit that in the present circumstances we cannot in dealing with the Egyptians afford to play from anything else but strength, and this means showing ourselves hard bargainers at every stage.

5.   I therefore feel that at any rate as long as Nokrashi remains in power we should be very careful not to take any action which in Egyptian eyes would appear as a concession to the present Government; and for this same reason it seems to me that we must feel our way very cautiously before announcing changes in our Sudan policy. . . .

---

[2] Gov-Gen of the Sudan, replaced in March 1947 by Sir R Howe.

97   FO 141/1187, no 28A   2 Apr 1947
[Policy towards Egypt]: memorandum by Sir W Smart on the need to frighten the Egyptians

The gravity of the situation in Egypt is evident to everyone and it seems clear that this situation must get worse and worse unless we find any way of re-acting and frightening the Egyptians. Nothing but fear will prevent the development of the present terrorist and semi-terrorist campaign which is being carried out in Egypt with the encouragement of the present Palace régime which thereby hopes to win nationalist sympathies as against the Wafd which has the majority of the people with it.

The terrorism that is going on now consists mainly in frightening the Egyptians of having anything to do with us and in attacking British Institutions. These attacks on British Institutions are bound to spread and after that British shops and British business houses will likewise be affected. For instance, campaigns will be made to frighten the Egyptians from working in British Institutions. British schools likewise will be affected. This movement, however, is not only anti-British but also anti-Christian and xenophobic. King Farouk is of course playing with fire and is so irresponsible that he does not see where he is going. It is more than likely that in the near future foreign nationals will be beaten up on odd occasions or things made unpleasant for them. Already on Evacuation Day a Greek shopkeeper, according to a report of Major Sansom, was badly handled by the crowd.

Respect for us is disappearing in view of the growing belief that we are really impotent. In considering, therefore, the Egyptian situation, it is quite useless to think of what concessions may bring the Egyptians round. What we have to consider is can we or can we not take any effective action against the Egyptians to stop this deliberate campaign which, if not checked, will end in anti-British and anti-foreign violences on an increasing scale.

98   FO 371/62969, no 1653   3 Apr 1947
[Policy towards Egypt and Sudan]: minute by Sir O Sargent to Mr Attlee on the debate over concessions to Egypt

> [The draft telegram attached to this minute which Attlee approved for despatch to Bevin, apologised for Sargent's previous recital of British concessions (see 96). It argued that the Egyptians, owing to their oriental mentality, had taken unfair advantage of Britain's efforts to secure a freely negotiated treaty. Sargent also referred to his suspicions of King Farouk whom he regarded as no friend of Britain's.]

Prime Minister
You have already seen Cairo telegram No. 636[1] of March 12th, but I attach a copy of it at Flag A for ease of reference.

2.   In commenting on this telegram to the Secretary of State in Moscow, we agreed with Sir R. Campbell's view that it would be futile to try to get the Egyptians to re-open negotiations, but thought that we should do nothing to discourage mediation by the other Arab States. As regards the line proposed by Sir R. Campbell in paragraph 5 of his telegram, we noted that your own statement in the House on March 11th was almost identical, except for the point on extension of Egyptian participation in the preparation of the Sudanese for self-Government.

3.   In a subsequent telegram we suggested that, should relations with Egypt continue to deteriorate, it might be wise to examine the means of replacing the present minority régime in Egypt by a more representative form of Government.

4.   The Secretary of State agreed with our comments as in paragraph 2 above, but did not approve the idea of under-mining Nokrashi's position until we had had the chance to see whether Sir R. Howe's appointment would have any affect on the situation in Egypt. The Secretary of State suggested that Sir R. Howe might talk to King Farouk on the lines of paragraph 6 of Cairo telegram No. 636. If, thereafter, relations continued to deteriorate, we might attempt to change the political set-up in Cairo and the Secretary of State asked that we should make concrete proposals with this end in view.

---

[1] See 94.

5.   In reply we advised that the removal of Nokrashi might be accomplished by
(a) an approach to King Farouk or (b) an approach to the Wafd in the first instance.
On the whole we preferred course (a). We also suggested that Sir R. Campbell
should be authorised, when he judged it opportune, to give the King a message
from the Foreign Secretary to the effect that while not wishing to interfere in
Egyptian internal affairs, he felt that our special relations with Egypt entitled him
to give a word of advice; that with the present régime Mr. Bevin saw no chance of
establishing Anglo–Egyptian relations on a basis which the King himself had
frequently assured us was his aim, and that he regarded the present internal
situation as very threatening and its continuation as likely to have serious
consequences not only on Anglo–Egyptian relations, but on the King's own
position.

6.   At this point in the correspondence the Secretary of State expressed some
doubt as to whether we had understood his intentions. (Moscow Delegation telegram
No. 353, at Flag B). The first step to his mind should be an attempt to create a better
atmosphere over the Sudan. He did not feel that the policy we had followed in 1924
and again in 1942 would do us credit, if the dispute came before the United Nations.
The question arose whether an improvement in the atmosphere could be achieved by
negotiation with the Egyptians or by taking administrative measures in the Sudan.
The Secretary of State suggested that Sir R. Howe (whose early departure for
Khartoum he advocated) should see King Farouk in Cairo and acquaint him with the
policy he had been instructed to carry out in the Sudan. This policy would broadly be
the association of the Egyptians with ourselves in the administration of the
condominium without compromising the right of the Sudanese to self-
determination. Such an approach to the King might give the Egyptian Government a
chance of changing their attitude and so make possible a resumption of talks. If this
approach failed, the Secretary of State thought it useless to seek to change the
Government through the King's instrumentality and favoured an attempt to put the
Wafd back into power. In a subsequent telegram (Moscow Delegation No. 448, at Flag
C), the Secretary of State indicated the lines on which Sir R. Howe should speak to
King Farouk.

7.   In the meantime I had replied to the Secretary of State suggesting that we
should avoid giving the appearance of making any further concessions. I attach a
copy of this telegram (Foreign Office telegram No. 425,[2] at Flag D) together with a
copy of the reply that it has provoked (Moscow Delegation telegram No. 524 at
Flag E).

8.   I apologise for having to burden you with this long story, but I feel that the
discussion has reached a stage where I can go no further without your express
approval. I therefore attach a draft telegram (Flag F)[3] for your consideration and, if
you concur in it, would like to add in a final sentence that you have been
acquainted with the tenor of this correspondence and have approved the present
reply.

---

[2] See 96.   [3] Not printed.

99   FO 371/62970, no 2064   24 Apr 1947

[Enforcement of British rights in Egypt]: minute by J P E C
Henniker[1] to Mr Bevin on the difficulties of enforcing British rights
under the 1936 treaty

Both the Chiefs of Staff and the Cabinet have considered your suggestion that we
should take firm measures to put a stop to the Egyptian attempts to break the 1936
Treaty.

The conclusion of the Chiefs of Staff as regards the possibility of using force to
ensure that we get our Treaty rights is apparently to the effect that the troops now
available in the Middle East could enforce the two specific rights which have been
challenged. If, however, serious disturbances follow our troops would not be
sufficient to protect British lives and property as well as to retain the initiative in
Palestine. I think that if we are to take forcible action we must reckon with the
possibility of widespread disturbance. The Chiefs of Staff have also apparently pointed
out that the First Armoured Division is shortly to be transferred from Italy to
Palestine to replace the Third Armoured Division. We shall be in a strong position in
the Middle East while this change-over is taking place and both the divisions are
there.

The conclusion to be drawn seems to be that we cannot enforce our Treaty rights
by the use of force at the present moment but we might be in a position to do so
fairly shortly.

Chiefs of Staff also decided that the two rights i.e. freedom to move our vehicles in
the Delta and freedom for our troops from the Sudan to pass through the Delta, were
very important from a military point of view, the latter particularly if we had to send
troops quickly to reinforce either Cyrenaica or the Sudan.

It seems to me that it is going to be extremely difficult to make the moment when
we want to stand on our rights to co-incide with the when [sic] we are strong enough
to do so. We seem, moreover, at present to be rather pulling in two directions. We are
urging the speedy run-down of our forces in the Canal Zone while if we are to take
forcible action it will be essential to build them up. If, therefore, it is decided that a
policy of force may be essential we must stop the evacuation of our troops. This
would weaken our case for the time when it comes before the United Nations. My
own feeling is, I am afraid, that we shall find it extremely difficult to use force unless
we have a really good case. Neither of the two cases at the moment in question are
really strong enough to allow us to risk a conflagration in Egypt in order to enforce
our rights. The only circumstances under which I feel that the use of force would
really be justified in world opinion and our own public opinion would be if the
Egyptians made the mistake of injuring or killing British soldiers. Even if they were
to arrest them we should have a strong case. If such a case does arise I think we must
use force.

On the two cases in point we are at present taking a very firm line with Nokrashi. It
looks as if it may be succeeding. If it does not I am afraid we shall probably have to
reach some accommodation with Nokrashi on them. In the event of our requiring
urgent reinforcements either in Cyrenaica or the Sudan we would just have to push

---

[1] J P E C Henniker, Bevin's assistant private secretary.

the troops through Egypt under heavy armed escort but until such a case arises I do not think the game is really worth the candle. Our present attitude as regards our Treaty rights on these two points should, however, be maintained for as long as possible. It may be that in doing so we shall find that the Egyptians provide us with an incident which will really justify us in the eyes of our own public in intervening forcibly.

In the meantime I think we should consider urgently what steps we can take to get rid of Nokrashi.[2]

---

[2] It was noted by one official at the end of the document that Sir R Campbell regarded the FO feeling that Farouk would dismiss Nokrashi as wishful thinking.

100   FO 141/1173, no 24   5 May 1947
'The possibility and desirability of un-seating Nokrashi': minute by Sir O Sargent to Mr Bevin

[This minute was sent to the embassy in Cairo for consideration and the reply came in a letter from Sir R Campbell to Sir O Sargent on 19 May (FO 371/62973, no 2423) stating that Britain did not have the means to bring about a change of government. The ambassador advised leaving things as they were in the hope of some favourable development even though he regarded such a development as unlikely.]

In regard to this question, which formed the subject of telegraphic exchanges with you while you were still in Moscow, there have been two new developments:—

(1) Dr. Rifa'i Bey, a Wafdist politician who may have been used by Nahhas as an emissary, has made to us certain suggestions for encompassing the fall of Nokrashi and the emergence of a more representative Egyptian Government including, of course, the Wafd.

(2) The Treasury have been urging that Egyptian representatives should be invited to come to London at once for discussions in connexion with the Egyptian sterling balances. The Foreign Office view is that, provided that we can do so without falling foul of the Americans, we should use the timing of this invitation as a card in the political game, since the Egyptians are most anxious to resume the financial discussions, and this anxiety provides us with a certain amount of political leverage.

A third development may be said to be the more reasonable and forthcoming line which Nokrashi has taken in response to Sir R. Campbell's representations of April 24th about the various incidents in connexion with British troops.

For the reasons developed below, the recommendations submitted by the Egyptian Department are as follows:—

(a) That in view of Nokrashi's present more reasonable line, and of the fact that he is not yet absolutely certain to decide upon an appeal to the United Nations, we should take no immediate step with a view to dislodging him;

(b) That if and when Nokrashi does address an appeal to the United Nations, we should for our part publish the texts comprising the Bevin-Sidky Agreement;

(c) That before publishing we should warn King Farouk that we are going to do so, adding that if the United Nations advise the two parties to try again to break the present deadlock and reach a settlement, the only hope in our view of our being able to achieve agreement will be if in the meantime free elections have taken place and a fresh Parliament is sitting in Egypt.

It is submitted that Sir R. Campbell's views should first be sought on the foregoing programme of action.

Foreign Office telegram No. 827 of the 19th April to the Secretary of State in Moscow raised the question of attempting to unseat the Egyptian Prime Minister, Nokrashi Pasha, by political means. There were some slight indications (not amounting to definite evidence) that the Palace was getting tired of him and was sufficiently doubtful of the success of an Egyptian appeal to the United Nations to be toying with the idea of dismissing him in order to facilitate a resumption of treaty negotiations. The Foreign Office telegram emphasised, however, that such an attempt *might* have the opposite effect of strengthening Nokrashi's position.

2.   Sir R. Campbell's comments on this suggestion (Cairo telegram No. 964 of April 24th) were not encouraging. The Ambassador agreed that the attempt to unseat Nokrashi might have the opposite effect, and he doubted whether King Farouk was contemplating the Prime Minister's dismissal. Both the King and Nokrashi himself would, of course, prefer a one-hundred per cent. acceptance of their demands to the risks of an appeal to the United Nations, but it was doubtful whether the former wished to appoint another Prime Minister able to conclude a treaty on our terms.

3.   The possibility of securing Nokrashi's dismissal had been considered at an earlier stage—in January last. Sir R. Campbell was then asked for his views on the question whether, since we were getting nowhere with the last of a series of unrepresentative Palace governments, the time had not come to revert to a policy of intervention in Egyptian internal affairs in order to secure the return of the Wafd to power. At that time it was thought here that the Wafd might well be prepared to let us have a treaty on, roughly, the basis of the Bevin-Sidky texts, but dressed up to appear difference [sic] and better from the Egyptian point of view. Sir R. Campbell was, however, very doubtful about this, feeling that although the Wafd might have accepted a treaty based on the Bevin-Sidky texts at the outset of negotiations, the subsequent crystallisation of the Sudan issue had altered the picture to our disadvantage. He also felt that, as "strong hand" methods on the 1942 model were no longer possible, the necessary pressure could not in fact be brought to bear upon the King—whom he evidently regarded as the only possible instrument that we could employ for installing the Wafd. (In point of fact we here had been thinking on the lines of an approach to the Wafd itself rather than to the King.) At Flag "L" is an extract from Cairo telegram No. 535 of March 1st, giving the form of approach to the King which Sir R. Campbell favoured at that time. Nothing positive came of this exchange of views with Cairo at the time. The Secretary of State, in his telegram No. 167 of the 18th March from Moscow to the Foreign Office, ruled that we should make no attempt to secure Nokrashi's removal until we had had time to see whether Sir R. Howe's appointment had a favourable effect on the situation.

4.   Sir R. Howe's appointment certainly did not have the desired effect of lessening Angle-Egyptian tension; and the renewed proposal, mentioned in para. 1 above, to attempt to unseat Nokrashi was prompted by the series of obstructive

measures taken by him in the matter of troop leave, transit through the Delta, the registration of military vehicles, etc. We not unnaturally regarded these cases of obstruction as deliberate pinpricks. Nevertheless Sir R. Campbell's most recent representations to Nokrashi (on April 24th) have apparently produced at least a temporary *détente*: the Egyptian Prime Minister has gone a little way towards meeting us (though only, it is true, on an interim basis and pending further consideration of the legal position as set forth by the Ambassador); and Sir R. Campbell has derived the impression that Nokrashi's attitude has been at least partly dictated by a genuine fear of complications resulting from popular demonstrations against our troops in the Delta. If this impression is correct, it is arguable that, in respect of our day-to-day relations with the Egyptians, we might fare worse if we succeeded in securing a change of government. On the other hand, in respect of the wider problem of Anglo–Egyptian relations, it is evident that a deadlock will continue so long as the Nokrashi Government remains in power. Nokrashi is more irrevocably committed than any other Egyptian to the continuance of this deadlock or, alternatively, to breaking it by an appeal to the United Nations—a solution which we of course do not want; and whoever else on the Egyptian side could afford to resume treaty negotiations, he certainly cannot. For this reason there is still a good *prima facie* case for attempting to unseat him. But it must be added that, at the stage now reached, it is extremely doubtful whether any other Egyptian who might conceivably replace him would in fact be able to agree to a resumption of treaty negotiations on anything approaching the basis of the Bevin-Sidky texts. The fact is that Nokrashi has fouled the course not only for himself but also for everybody else.

5.   A new factor which has now been introduced into this question is the approach recently made by Rifa'i Bey, a Wafdist politician, to Mr. Nevile Butler[1] please see record at Flag "G" attached). The gist of Rifa'i Bey's suggestion is as follows:–

> In response to an inspired Parliamentary Question as to how H.M.G's offer, embodied in the abortive negotiations with Sidky, now stood, the Secretary of State would intimate that we did not intend to repeat our previous action in negotiating with a government that was not based on free elections nor widely representative of Egypt, but that our generous offer still stood if a properly representative Egyptian Government were formed. Thereafter Sir R. Campbell would invite Prince Mohanned [sic] Ali[2] and other respected Egyptian figures to the Embassy and repeat to them the substance of the Secretary of State's reply in Parliament. It would then be for his guests to make it clear to Egyptian public opinion that the King's adherence to a minority government was hindering the conclusion of a satisfactory treaty with the United Kingdom.

Rifa'i Bey of course suggested that our new treaty offer should be "more generous", but he could suggest no practical means of making it so beyond expressing the hope that the forthcoming negotiations over the sterling balances might provide the necessary appearance of increased concessions on the British side.

6.   In connexion with Rifa'i Bey's mention of the sterling balance negotiations,

---

[1] (Sir) Nevile Butler, deputy under-secretary in the FO, 1944–1947.

[2] Mohammed Ali, one of the royal regents before Farouk came of age.

it is relevant to point out that there has been an inconclusive exchange of views between Sir Orme Sargent and Sir W. Eady of the Treasury concerning the possibility of using these financial negotiations as a lever for use in the political game. The Treasury, of course, are opposed to this, and would like to keep the financial negotiations entirely separate. They consider, moreover, that any prolonged stonewalling by us in connexion with the financial negotiations (we here had contemplated using these negotiations, or a refusal to initiate them for the present, to quell Egyptian obstructiveness rather than, as suggested by Rifa'i Bey, to sweeten a future Egyptian government) would be likely to get us into trouble with the Americans, who are keenly interested in the ability of the Egyptians to make dollar purchases in the U.S.A. The Treasury may well be right about this; and it is fair to add that, according to Sir W. Eady, they anyhow intended to be pretty tough with the Egyptian negotiators when the latter came to London). The Minister of State, however, in commenting on the exchange of view with Sir W. Eady, has minuted:—

> "I am hoping the Secretary of State will review our whole attitude to Nokrashi. We ought therefore to tell Sir W. Eady this, while agreeing to the telegram [authorising Sir R. Campbell, subject to his seeing no objection, to invite the Egyptian financial negotiators to London]."

> * Note: On Sir Orme Sargent's instructions the telegram is being held up pending discussion with Sir W. Eady.

7.   The Minister of State's minute on the record of the conversation between Mr. Nevile Butler and Rifa'i Bey is attached at Flag I. It will be seen that he suggests the possibility, in view of the difficulty of taking a really firm stand on any of the incidents which have so far occurred, of presenting Nokrashi, via King Farouk, with a sort of ultimatum. This would consist of an intimation to the King that H.M.G. would soon be pressed by Parliament on the question of the Treaty, and that in reply they would have to point out the futility of further negotiation with Nokrashi's minority government and the consequent necessity for standing on the 1936 Treaty as long as that government remained in power.

8.   Egyptian Department cannot help doubting whether a hint to this effect made to King Farouk would achieve any positive result. It will be remembered that the Secretary of State's reference in the House of Commons on January 27th to the minority status of the Nokrashi government, though doubtless necessary and desirable from the point of view of British public opinion, had no effect in *Egypt* save that of further antagonising both King Farouk and Nokrashi himself. It would perhaps be more accurate to say that the first effect in Egypt of the Secretary of State's remarks was considerable, since it was generally assumed that they were the prelude to some sort of positive action; but that when nothing further happened the final effect was the negative one mentioned above. It is true, too, that the Secretary of State on that occasion did not say (as is now proposed) that because Egypt had a minority government we should have to continue to take our stand on the 1936 Treaty. There was not, in fact, the same clear hint that an alternative government would be able to come to satisfactory terms with us. It must however be emphasised that, at any rate once the treaty negotiations broke down, there has not been the slightest sign of willingness on the part of the Wafd to resume them with us should

they come to power. On the contrary, the general line of Wafdist propaganda has been even more hostile to the Bevin-Sidky agreement than that of the Egyptian Government itself, and has in addition implied that it was the Wafd that prevented that government from concluding a treaty which would have betrayed Egyptian interests. It seems fairly clear, therefore, that public references in this country to the unrepresentative quality of the Nokrashi régime are hardly likely to get us any further, and might well merely increase the determination of the Palace and the Government to exploit the various weaknesses and difficulties of our treaty position in regard to such matters as troop leave and transit between the Canal Zone and the Sudan. Naturally such public criticisms by us are always welcome to the Wafd, who stand to lose nothing by them and to gain a certain amount of international support. But something much more positive would almost certainly be required to throw the present government out and get the Wafd in.

9.   It is difficult to see what this "something" can be. Our old technique of political interference in Egypt was based on our known ability to use physical force if need be. Quite apart from the extreme inadvisability, in present international conditions, of a recourse to the methods that were still practicable in 1924 and 1942, we cannot in fact have recourse now to precisely the same methods, but would have to adopt still more flamboyant ones, i.e., to bring troops *back* to Cairo from the Canal Zone as a preliminary move to using them for political intimidation. We have reason to know (from most secret sources) that this is precisely what King Farouk fears we may do, and there is thus some chance of bluffing him into submission (i.e. into dismissal of Nokrashi and acceptance of Nahhas, whom he intensely dislikes); but if he decided to call the bluff we should either forfeit our prestige in Egypt completely by doing nothing, or have to go ahead at the risk of serious international complications including an Egyptian appeal to the United Nations on a very good wicket. It would, be worth while to ask Sir, R. Campbell for his views on the scheme propounded by Rifa'i Bey (see para. 5 above); but that the Ambassador will probably reply in the sense that an Embassy flirtation with Egyptian Elder Statesmen and/or the Wafd, coupled with threats of more public criticism here on the subject of the unrepresentative quality of the Nokrashi regime, would *not* gain the trick in the absence of the joker we used to hold. The fact is that, because the average Egyptian no longer believes (though the King may) in our readiness to use force, the chances of our having actually to use it on a considerable scale, as distinct from merely making a demonstration indicative of our readiness to do so, are greatly increased.

10.   Sir R. Campbell is also likely to maintain a view which he has expressed in the past, that any attempt to un-seat Nokrashi must take the form of an approach to the King in the first place, since a direct approach to the Wafd would immediately become known to H.M. before we could "get going" with them, and might well drive him and Nokrashi into extreme courses. In this connexion it is well to remember that although the Wafd can count on a large measure of popular support, the King, who has recently been posing with some success as a heroic figure and liberator, can probably count for his part on the loyalty of the Egyptian Army and Police—except of course in the event of our actually using force, when they would fold up at once. It is likely therefore that the Wafd would *not* attempt a coup on the strength of mere blandishments by the Embassy and encouraging "noises off"; and that if they did attempt one, they would fail. Either way we should merely have made our relations

with the present Egyptian Government, which are none too good as it is, entirely impossible—though the resultant suppression of popular liberties would no doubt provide us with plenty of additional grounds for public criticism of the Nokrashi régime.

11.   In connexion with the foregoing, the question has once more been raised of our making public the Bevin-Sidky texts. When this question has been mooted in the past, two objections have been raised to our doing so: (1) that it would be better publicity timing to await the moment when the Egyptian appeal to the United Nations became really imminent and world opinion was correspondingly interested; and (2) that if and when we do publish the Bevin-Sidky texts, the Egyptians for their part may retaliate by publishing (a) related documents which might be construed to imply that our plans for joint defence envisaged the Soviet Union as the aggressor. The documents in question are the F.O. aide-mémoire explaining the British views as to the objects of the proposed new Treaty of Alliance, and Sidky Pasha's Note commenting thereon—please see pages 24, 25 and 26 of Mr. Scrivener's memorandum, copy attached. It is true that it is the second of these documents (i.e. the Egyptian one) rather than the first which permits of this construction being placed upon them as a whole; but the most natural interpretation of the Egyptian Note would be that it referred, not only to the official British aide-mémoire, but also to oral explanations which had accompanied it. Sidky says, for instance, "it is now apparently a question of a danger from the East. . . . But may we remark that these perils are often presented in a light in which a sometimes deliberate pessimism plays a leading part. Russian policy is certainly disturbing; but it is more suspicious than dangerous. . . ." etc. The Egyptians might also publish (b) our attempt, when the negotiations broke down, to secure by an exchange of letters transit rights for our aircraft across Egyptian territory and payment by the Egyptians for our installations. (The Egyptians could make play with (b) as disproving our contention that the negotiations broke down on the question of ultimate self-determination for the Sudanese). As regards (2), it seems almost inevitable that we should have to publish the Bevin-Sidky texts, and hence take this risk, in the event of the Egyptians actually appealing to the United Nations; and consequently the only reason for not taking the risk now is that increasingly faint hope that the Egyptians will not appeal. As regards (1), this seems to the Egyptian Department to be still a valid reason for waiting; the publicity experts with whom we have recently been discussing the dissemination of guidance and background material are unaninous [sic] that a full propaganda blast by us at the present stage would be premature, i.e., would be half-forgotten by the time the Egyptians had got in with theirs.

101   FO 371/62971, no 2102   6 May 1947

[Policy towards Egypt]: FO note of an inter-departmental meeting with the Treasury on unseating Nokrashi and negotiations on the Egyptian sterling balances

Sir O Sargent said that the main question was whether or not an attempt should be made to unseat Nokrashi.

The S/S thought it would be a mistake to try to do so. If we did and it proved a flop we should be in a very bad situation. If we pressed for free elections etc he would find himself in the same position as in e.g. Poland. He had followed the Americans and their policy had led to no useful result at all.

Sir O Sargent said that all that was suggested was a warning to the King. Maybe the Security Council would tell us and the Egyptians to go away and negotiate. The suggestion was that in that event the King should be warned privately that we saw no point in negotiating with an unrepresentative Government.

The S/S said that the King would immediately come back with an enquiry whether he, the S of S, had changed his policy of non-interference. He thought that nothing should be done until the Egyptians actually made their appeal to the Security Council. Then he would make his decisions after considering the matter again. In the meanwhile Sir R. Campbell could be consulted but he must not be given the idea that the S/S intended to do anything. He should be told that the Secretary of State had considered proposals for such intervention and that if the Egyptians did go to the Security Council it might be a possibility. At that time he would also consider the publication of the Bevin-Sidky texts. We had kept cool so far and there had been no serious incidents; the same tactics should be continued until the Egyptians appealed to the United Nations.

The S/S said that the suggestion that there should be a united front on both sides for negotiations i.e. on the British as well as the Egyptian side, was impracticable.

For some time to come he had to bluff his way through in foreign policy, given the financial weakness of this country.

Sterling balance negotiations

Sir W Eady said that he had the impression that the Egyptians were scared about our intentions on this issue. At the talks in Cairo they had been very cock-a-hoop until we refused their suggestion that they should have our Suez Canal shares in part payment. All the Treasury wished to do now was to take the next normal and essential step in the negotiations i.e. to ask the Egyptians to come to this country. There was no intention of being particularly civil to them and they were very anxious to come.

The S/S said that he thought it best to go ahead. The people whom they would be likely to meet should be well briefed. He agreed that in the negotiations we should be cold and business-like.

Sir W. Eady explained that the Egyptians could make it difficult for us in the event of a failure to agree by (a) refusing to accept sterling for our troops' expenditure and insisting on payment in gold and (b) by evading the blocking of their balances in this country. But on the other hand under similar conditions they would initially be in a mess, they were very frightened, and they wanted a commercial agreement.

102   DEFE 5/4, COS(47)112   29 May 1947

'Anglo–Egyptian treaty negotiations: meeting of the Security Council':
letter from Sir O Sargent to Lt-Gen Sir L Hollis on the reduction of
British troops to the numbers permitted by the 1936 treaty

[The 1936 treaty stipulated 10,000 troops could be maintained in the Canal Zone within clearly defined areas. Many of the facilities necessary for the maintenance of the base were outside the designated areas including key installations and depots. As the COS pointed out, withdrawal to comply with the treaty posed greater problems than complete withdrawal leaving the bulk of stores in place under the aegis of the joint defence board proposed in 1946 (DEFE 5/5, COS(47)143, 10 July 1947). Although stores were being transferred to Kenya the decision to dump the Palestine problem in the lap of the UN meant stores were now arriving from Palestine. The COS concluded that it would not be possible to evacuate the base by Sept 1949 unless some £300,000,000 of stores were abandoned (DEFE 5/5, COS(47)149, 17 July 1947). The other problem to which Bevin referred was the embarrassment of 90,000 troops in Egypt. At a COS Committee meeting Attlee insisted that as such large numbers were the consequence of the HQ of Middle East forces being in Egypt, immediate attention should be given to its re-location (DEFE 4/5, COS 90(47)2, 21 July 1947). The most suitable alternative, given the Palestine situation, was Cyrenaica. Unfortunately the Council of Foreign Ministers, having fruitlessly argued over the fate of the Italian colonies since July 1945, agreed at the Paris Council, which ended on 12 July 1946, to give the foreign ministers' deputies twelve months to find a solution. Their report would then have to be considered by the council and if there was still no agreement the matter would have to be placed in the hands of the UN. Consequently the British could not readily establish a new base for Middle Eastern HQ or provide permanent accommodation for British forces while the fate of Cyrenaica was still undecided. The option of temporarily removing troops from the Middle East was ruled out because Cunningham believed that 10,000 troops in Egypt were insufficient for him to command Middle Eastern forces in general and the troops in Palestine in particular (DEFE 4/5, COS 92(47)11, 23 July 1947). In reply to Attlee's demand for the removal of Middle East HQ from Egypt the COS argued that no decision could be taken on this until there had been an examination of the forces required in peacetime now that the commitment to Middle Eastern defence had been finally accepted by the prime minister. The COS also informed the FO that the assumptions about requirements in Egypt on which the Bevin-Sidky draft agreement had been based no longer held good (DEFE 4/6, COS 97(47)6, 30 July 1947, Annex II).]

In the course of the preparation of our reply to the Egyptian case before the Security Council (the presentation of which can hardly be much further delayed), we have come across one serious gap in our line of argument which we feel it is essential to fill if we are to hope to secure the sympathy of the Council for our case as a whole.

2.   You will know that the Evacuation Protocol which formed part of the text agreed between the Foreign Secretary and Sidky Pasha in London last October provided for the total evacuation of Egypt by the British Forces to be completed by the 1st September, 1949. The text of this Protocol has been published in the press in Egypt; and though it has not been released to the press in this country, there is no doubt that the texts of all the documents forming the Bevin-Sidky Agreements will have to be laid beofre [sic] the Security Council when the case comes before it, even if we do not decide to issue them as a White Paper beforehand. Moreover the Prime Minister, in his reply to Mr. Eden in the House of Commons on the 11th March last, stated that the British Government had agreed "to complete evacuation of British troops in Egypt by 1949". We must, therefore, take it as certain that the date of the 1st September, 1949 for *total* evacuation will be known to the Security Council.

3.   We shall maintain in our reply to the Egyptian case that the sole reason why the Anglo–Egyptian Treaty negotiations broke down was the Egyptian insistance [sic]

on an erroneous and unacceptable interpretation of one phrase in the Sudan Protocol. It is a necessary corollary of this (and indeed essential to our case) to maintain that we are still prepared to agree to the military clauses of the revised draft treaty and the Evacuation Protocol as a whole. We may be exposed to a charge that we have failed to carry out the 1936 Treaty in that our troops are not reduced to the numbers specified in paragraph 1 of the annexe to Article 8 of the Treaty. Our reply must be that the situation envisaged in Article 7 of the Treaty did in fact last a considerable time and necessitated the building up of enormous forces and installations on Egyptian territory, but that we are reducing these as fast as physically possible. We should then have to add that we had agreed to arrange for the total withdrawal of our Forces by the 1st September, 1949.

4.　It is here that the lacuna in our case occurs. If we were physically able to arrange for the total evacuation to be completed by the 1st September, 1949, we must have also been able to arrange for a reduction to Treaty numbers before that date. We are now taking our stand on our military rights under the 1936 Treaty, which only entitle us to maintain certain stated numbers of troops in Egypt and we shall certainly be pressed by the Egyptians and their friends to name the exact date by which the reduction to Treaty numbers will have been accomplished. Indeed so inevitable is this, and so disastrous would be any hesitation or ambiguity in our reply, that it would certainly be preferable for us to take the initiative and announce spontaneously the date by which we shall have reduced to Treaty numbers.

5.　We should be grateful, therefore, if the Chiefs of Staff would go into this question and give the Foreign Secretary a firm date as soon as possible. I should add that it is naturally preferable that this date should be sooner rather than later; and also that it will of course be necessary that when our Forces have been reduced to the Treaty figures, they should also be quartered in the areas defined in paragraph 2 of the Annex to Article 8, as interpreted in respect of the GENEIFA[1] area by sub-paragraph 5 (v) of the Agreed Minute.

---

[1] An area south of the Sweet Water Canal and east of Little Bitter Lake.

103　DEFE 6/3, JP(47)105　　　　　　　　　　　　6 Aug 1947
'Middle East defence–military requirements in Egypt': report by the
JPS to the COS. *Annex* 1　　　　　　　　　　　　　　　　[Extract]

[Four days later Attlee commented to Bevin: 'I cannot see how the fact of our needing a Commonwealth base in the Middle East gives us any ground for demanding that the base should be in Egypt, a sovereign state. We have no case to retain more troops than we are allowed under the Treaty. Our only defence is the difficulty of removal in the time at our disposal. COS must press on with alternative arrangements' (PREM 8/837, minute by Attlee, 10 Aug 1947).]

We were instructed to examine our peacetime strategic requirements in the Middle East and to draft a reply to a Foreign Office letter asking for the views of the Chiefs of Staff on certain proposals for the co-ordination of Middle East Defence and contributions to be made by the Arab countries concerned.

2.　In the course of our examination it has become clear that the crux of the whole problem of Middle East Defence lies in our ability rapidly to establish ourselves in and operate effectively from Egypt on the threat of war, and that the chances of our being able to do so under the terms of the Bevin-Sidky draft now seem much less than at the time when this draft was drawn up. We have therefore deferred for the present the detailed examination of our strategic requirements in the Middle East in peace as they affect Arab States other than Egypt, until we can establish the assumption we ought to take about Egypt.

The Bevin-Sidky draft

3.   It will be recalled that when the suggestion was first mooted in April 1946, the Chiefs of Staff stated that agreement to withdraw all British armed forces from Egyptian soil would mean the forfeiture of the minimum military requirements necessary for our retention of a firm hold on the Middle East. They hoped, however, that this line would result in friendly co-operation by Egypt which might give us the right of re-entry in war and the maintenance in Egypt in peace of a shadow headquarters and certain other installations. As the alternative then appeared to be the permanent ruining of our relations with Egypt, the need to send considerable reinforcements to restore and maintain order in the country, and the reference of the case to U.N.O., the Chiefs of Staff very reluctantly agreed to the line of negotiations which led to the Bevin-Sidky draft.

The conditions obtaining when this reluctant acquiescence was given have now changed. The hope of effective Egyptian co-operation has faded and our case has been taken to U.N.O. The chances of our 1936 Treaty rights being upheld are reasonable. Even so, it is probable that U.N.O. would invite us to resume negotiations with the Egyptians for the revision of that Treaty.

There is also the possibility that the Egyptians may try to come to agreement with us before the case before U.N.O. has been finished.

If negotiations were reopened, under existing Government policy the Foreign Office would be entitled to reach an agreement on the lines of the Bevin-Sidky draft.

4.   In the changed circumstances we believe that the Bevin-Sidky draft is even less likely to meet our requirement to be able to establish ourselves in and operate effectively from Egypt on the outbreak of war than in April 1946. We are convinced, in fact, that only the presence of our forces on Egyptian soil can really guarantee this requirement being met, since events have shown that the value of any written agreement with the Egyptians without the presence of our forces will always be illusory and of little practical value.

Minimum military requirements

5.   We have accordingly set out at Annex I what we consider to be our minimum military requirements in Egypt in peace to assure retention of a firm hold on the Middle East in war. The failure to obtain these rights will seriously weaken our ability to hold the Middle East in war. We fully realise, however, that for political reasons it may prove impossible for H.M.G. to secure all the rights we require. Nevertheless, even if we do not get our full requirements it is essential that we should strive to maintain our position in the Middle East in peace and do our utmost to defend it in war. Failure to secure all these rights must not, therefore, be used as a reason for abandoning our position in the Middle East. It may be that if the retention of forces in Egypt is judged to be politically unobtainable, we should have to concentrate upon obtaining an agreement which will give us the best possible case in the eyes of the

world for re-entry into Egypt on threat of war. An essential corollary to this line, however, must be the retention in the Middle East of the force necessary rapidly to re-establish our position in Egypt.

Suggested action by the Chiefs of Staff

6.   We suggest that as the whole question is likely to be reopened between the Egyptians and ourselves at any moment now, the Chiefs of Staff will wish to make their views quite clear to the Foreign Office, and to find out what is the present Foreign Office view of our chances of obtaining our full requirements and thus to establish the assumptions on which we can proceed to assess our strategic requirements in the other Arab States.

Annex 1 to 103

The following are our essential minimum requirements in Egypt in peace if we are to maintain a firm hold on the Middle East in war.

Base organisation

2.   We must maintain in Egypt in peace the nucleus organisation for an operational and administrative base which is capable of rapid expansion at the commencement of a war. Only Egypt possesses the communications, facilities and reserve of skilled and unskilled man-power which are essential to the operation of such a base in war. Therefore, there is no alternative location in the Middle East area which would be suitable for development as a base.

Right of re-entry

3.   We must have the certainty of rapid re-entry into Egypt at the outset of a war or on imminent threat of war. We can only be assured of this right of immediate re-entry in war if we maintain small forces in the country in peace. Any delay while negotiations take place about the re-entry of British troops into Egypt would endanger our whole position in the Middle East.

Air defence and airfield requirements

4.   We must be able to operate offensive and defensive air forces from Egypt at the very outset of a war. Airfield facilities in the Canal Zone are insufficient to meet our requirements in full, and we shall therefore require further airfields in other parts of Egypt, and an air defence system for the protection of the base. In order to maintain these facilities in a state of operational efficiency the Egyptians will require assistance from the Royal Air Force.

Naval operational requirements

5.   We must have the right to operate our naval forces from the outset of a war from Egyptian ports, and we require that the port facilities, installations and local defence arrangements which will be required in the event of war are adequately developed and maintained.

Imperial communications

6.   The maintenance of facilities, including transit rights for military aircraft,

necessary for our Imperial communications to India, Australasia and the Far East and the right to use then.

Headquarters Middle East
7.   We must have established at the outset of a war a headquarters capable of controlling and co-ordinating all our resources for the defence of the Middle East. This control and co-ordination can only be exercised from Egypt which is the political and communication centre of the Middle East. The work of the headquarters would be at very great intensity just before the outbreak of a war. It is most important, therefore, that it should be established in its war location in peace. . . .

104   FO 371/62987, no 4912   11 Oct 1947

'Egypt–future policy': FO memorandum opposing any moves to break the deadlock between Britain and Egypt

We have examined the possibility of making some gesture or other move to break the present deadlock between ourselves and Egypt.

Various proposals have been made, centring round telegrams sent by Sir A. Cadogan and Mr. Bowker at the time of the hearing of the case at the Security Council.

Sir Alexander Cadogan's suggestion was that, primarily in order to relieve pro-Egyptian feeling in New York and to make it more difficult for Egypt to raise the question in the Assembly, we should formally renew the offer made last year to settle with the Egyptians all outstanding matters except the Sudan.

Since this proposal was made matters at the Security Council have reached an impasse and it is too late for the Egyptians, even if they wish to raise the question at the Assembly. The Americans also have agreed, if rather reluctantly, that it is best to leave things as they are at the Security Council; and for some time no further move has come from that quarter.

Mr. Bowker's suggestion is that we should inform the Egyptians that, while maintaining the validity of the treaty, we have decided no longer to avail ourselves of the facilities afforded under Article 8 and that we are withdrawing our troops from Egypt. His argument is that, although the Egyptians have adopted the attitude that they would accept no offer to reopen negotiations except on the basis of unconditional evacuation, there is considerable nervousness in Egypt about the situation and a genuine desire to reach a settlement. And he suggests that, if we took the step proposed, the Egyptians would be faced with the alternative either of negotiating a revised treaty or of leaving us with the 1936 treaty less Article 8, which in some respects gives us more than the Bevin-Sidky draft.

It is felt to be more than doubtful whether such action would have any effect on the Egyptians in present circumstances except to make them open their mouths still wider. They would accept the proposal for evacuation and then proceed to insist that this evacuation must be immediate. They would reject the explanation that evacuation would take a considerable time and would then proceed to stir up even more feeling against us by maintaining that our offer to evacuate was specious and insincere. They would not be moved by fear that the Treaty less Article 8 would give them disadvantages over the present situation, since they would argue that we had practically admitted their thesis that the treaty was no longer applicable and would proceed so far as possible to ignore its existence and infringe its stipulations.

From our point of view, waiving our rights under Article 8 would mean that we would be left with the obligation to defend Egypt while renouncing the means by which alone we could carry this obligation into effect. Although Article 8 is technically facultative, the treaty is a balanced whole, our duty to defend Egypt depending on our ability to maintain a base there in time of peace. We would not want to be put in the position of continuing an empty guarantee which we could not implement,—the position we got ourselves into over Poland before the war.

Again, a gesture at the present moment would enhance the reputation of Nokrashi, who is now being attacked in Egypt for his failure to win complete acceptance of the Egyptian case at New York. If we refuse to make advances to him there is at least a chance that he might be replaced. There are signs that the King and responsible Egyptians were anxious about the situation.

The effect on the Arab countries of our Egyptian policy should also be considered. We are about to open negotiations for a revised treaty with Iraq. At present the signs were favourable; but the Iraquis [sic] might well try to slip out of the military obligations which we hope to secure from them if we give any further impression of weakening as to our rights in Egypt.

If we wished to turn the tables on the Egyptians, the only effective course would be to denounce the Treaty, withdraw our troops, and say that in the circumstances created by the Egyptian Government we did not intend to have any treaty with them, thus facing them with a situation where, if there was trouble in the Middle East, they would be without any guarantee of British assistance. There is of course the point that our title to the Sudan under the agreement of 1899 is not so strong as that under the Treaty of 1936. But it is felt that this in itself was not an insuperable objection, since our moral position in the Sudan is so strong now that the Egyptians would hardly dare to call it in question merely because we had denounced the 1936 Treaty.

In any case an overriding reason for delay is the situation in Palestine. We must see further how the situation there develops before deciding on any new departure in Egypt.

Finally we do not wish to anticipate or prejudice in any way the outcome of the discussions with the Americans on the Middle East generally.

There have been telegrams recently from the Embassy in Cairo and from the Commanders-in-Chief, Middle East, describing the possibilities of Egypt attacking our economic and military interests; and we have considered whether they disclose a situation serious enough to compel us to make some political gesture. It is admitted that the Egyptians have it in their power to cause serious trouble on these lines. Not only might they make things difficult for British business and private interests, but they might ask for dollar payments for our military expenditure (amounting at present to £12,000,000 a year) and they might refuse to supply food, labour or other necessaries to the army. Their present policy seems to be one of making our position difficult rather than of resorting to violence as we at one time feared. But it is felt that the Egyptians might well be frightened of extreme measures against the army, knowing that, if they made the position of the army impossible, we had various means of making ourselves unpleasant in retaliation. In any case there is no certainty that any political gesture to which we could consent would prevent the Egyptians from resorting to such tactics. On the contrary, they might well work up an even stronger feeling against us if our gesture failed, as it was bound to do, to meet their extreme demands over the date of evacuation.

To sum up. It is agreed that it would be unwise to take any further step for the following reasons:—

(1) It is unwise to give away any cards pending the discussions in Washington and a knowledge of the degree to which we can rely on American support. If the Americans were to support us effectively in Egypt and in the Middle East generally the whole situation in Egypt might change for the better.

(2) The only offer we could make, namely evacuation spread over a period, would not content the Egyptians, who would still demand immediate evacuation and would stir up further trouble when we made it clear that this was a concession we would not make.

(3) A gesture now would strengthen the position of Nokrashi, with whom it was fairly obvious we could not do business. He would interpret it as a sign of weakness, and proceed to open his mouth still wider. If we hold firm, there is at least a possibility that a new Government might come into power.

(4) In any case it would be wise first to secure the revision of the treaty with Iraq.

This paper has been shown in draft to Sir Ronald Campbell, who agrees with its conclusions.

105   DEFE 6/4, JP(47)137   4 Nov 1947
'Redeployment of Middle East forces': report by the JPS for the COS Committee   [Extract]

[The problems of evacuating Egypt to comply with the 1936 treaty increased with the decision to leave Palestine by May 1948, as it appeared the Palestine garrison would have to go to Egypt. More difficulties appeared in the way of reconciling the requirements of what appeared to be the key element of a military strategy with the political and economic realities. The military strategy was not however geared to meeting an immediate military threat from the Soviet Union. Not only was there still no emergency plan but a strategic summary considered by the COS on 31 Oct concluded that Russia was not yet ready to undertake an offensive war. Britain's military strategy was defined as preventing the spread of hostile influences in peacetime because any such spread would make future operations in wartime more difficult. In order to carry out such a task it was deemed vital that Britain's prestige throughout the world should be maintained especially in the Middle East (DEFE 4/8, COS 134(47)3, 31 Oct 1947, JP(47)139, 31 Oct 1947, Annex II). The redeployment of British forces from Palestine and Britain's relations with the Arab states were considered by the Defence Committee in that light and in the knowledge that the departure from Palestine would make it difficult to comply with Britain's treaty obligations in Egypt by the date they had offered to evacuate by in 1946. On 7 Nov it was pointed out in the Defence Committee that Egypt would have to be used as a transit area for the Palestine evacuation (CAB 131/5, DO 23(47)1). The Egyptian problem was now being discussed with the Americans as part of a broader attempt to co-ordinate the various strands of Anglo–American policy in the Middle East and the eastern Mediterranean. The informal talks at the Pentagon on political and strategic matters began on 16 Oct and lasted until 7 Nov, and the Americans agreed that facilities in Egypt manned by British personnel were needed. In these circumstances it appeared sensible to aim for some agreement with Egypt rather than to stand on the 1936 treaty and Bevin was encouraged to do so by reports from Cairo. The foreign secretary suggested abandoning the idea of stationing operational units of the armed forces in the Canal Zone in peacetime and requested a new military appreciation of Britain's strategic requirements in Egypt on the assumption that Cyrenaica would be available and that it might be possible to lease a base in Sinai (DEFE 4/8, COS 141(47)2, 14 Nov 1947).]

As instructed we have examined the main factors and tasks involved in the reorganisation of our Middle East forces and their deployment in their permanent peacetime locations. We have taken into account a note by the Chief of the Imperial General Staff which deals with certain Army aspects of the problem. We have consulted the Joint Administrative Planning Staff.

2.   Since the issue of our terms of reference the Prime Minister has set up a special Palestine Committee to study the implications of withdrawal from Palestine. This Committee is about to produce a report for consideration by the Defence Committee on Friday next, 7th November. The object of the report will be to show the nature of the problems which will arise if a definite date for withdrawal is announced.

We suggest, therefore, that the Chiefs of Staff should use the conclusions and arguments in this paper as a brief from which to argue the problems of withdrawal at the Defence Committee on Friday when the Palestine Committee's report is considered.

Our strategic position in the Middle East

3.   Recent and continuing political changes in Egypt and Palestine have made it clear that:—

(a) We can no longer hope to obtain our long term strategic requirements in Palestine.

(b) In Egypt the most we can hope for is some form of Joint Defence Board and possibly an agreement with the Egyptians that the assistance of British technicians will maintain the nucleus of a base organisation which will be available to us in the event of war.

4.   The only method by which we can now hope to retain a hold in the Middle East is by:—

(a) Obtaining our long term strategic requirements in Cyrenaica.
(b) Retaining temporary control of Tripolitania.
(c) Ensuring continued freedom of action in the Sudan.
(d) Retaining permanently the sovereignty of Cyprus.

Our strategic position in the Middle East, with which our redeployment plan is bound up, is dependent upon the satisfaction of the above requirements. Since, however, the report of the Deputies to the Foreign Ministers on the future of the Italian Colonies is unlikely to be considered by the Council of Foreign Ministers much before September 1948, it is clear that no decision can be taken now by H.M.G. which will safeguard our long term strategic requirements in Libya. Nevertheless, in order to complete our redeployment we must start development in Cyrenaica which includes construction of accommodation and the development of a port, airfields, administrative installations and facilities, amenities and public utilities. Any delay in giving authority to start new construction in Cyrenaica would retard our evacuation of Egypt and Tripolitania and mean the housing of forces in the Middle East in entirely inadequate accommodation under quite unacceptable living conditions; alternatively, we should be unable to maintain in the Middle East at least for a period until construction can be completed, sufficient forces to maintain a firm hold in the area.

Our examination is based on the assumption that the requirements outlined in (a) to (d) above are satisfied. It is in any case essential that H.M.G. should give immediate approval for the development of Cyrenaica as outlined above on the assumption that ultimately we shall obtain control of that territory.

Redeployment of our forces in the Middle East

5.   The proposed peacetime size of our forces in the Middle East on which we have based our examination is the best estimate that can be made at the present time in advance of a final decision on the future shape and size of the armed forces and the effect that such decision may have on the strength of our forces in the Middle East, but bearing in mind the overall strength of the three Services and the tasks which have to be performed in maintaining our world strategic position.

6.   The proposed location of these forces is as follows:—

(a) The Royal Navy will continue to be based on Malta.

(b) Armed forces comprising one division, one brigade and administrative troops will be located mainly in Cyrenaica with garrisons in Cyprus and the Sudan.

(c) The Royal Air Force will be deployed largely in Cyrenaica with units in Iraq, Aden, Cyprus, Sudan, Malta and possibly a small detachment in Transjordan.

Even if the size of the forces on which we have based our examination were the subject of moderate changes the problems of redeployment would differ only in degree from those we have discussed.

Conclusions

7.   The conclusions of our examination at Annex[1] are:—

(a) The main problems of implementing our redeployment are connected with:—
   (i)   the evacuation of Palestine,
   (ii)   the evacuation of Egypt,
   (iii) the provision of accommodation in Libya.

(b) The evacuation of all stores from Palestine will take 18 months.

(c) The evacuation of Palestine will result in our being unable to evacuate Egypt before the middle of 1950.

(d) To ensure the most economical implementation of the proposed redeployment, approval should be given to begin work sufficiently early to permit of temporary accommodation in Cyrenaica being ready to receive the appropriate forces on their withdrawal from Palestine and Egypt. This work would take 20 months to complete from the date of final financial approval.

(e) If for any reason it is impossible to retain our forces in Palestine until they can be moved direct to their proposed redeployment areas, alternative arrangements can be made. By using Tripolitania as a temporary location and by undertaking repairs on existing accommodation both there and in Cyrenaica, it will be possible some eight months after repair work is started to accommodate in Cyrenaica and Tripolitania the whole of the operational forces destined ultimately for Cyrenaica, with the exception of one brigade. One brigade will in any event be located in the

---

[1] Not printed.

Canal Zone until the final evacuation from Egypt in order to safeguard the withdrawal of stores.

This solution would therefore be acceptable provided that the work of providing full temporary accommodation in Cyrenaica is completed before the final evacuation of Egypt takes place. . . .

106 DEFE 5/6, COS(47)236   18 Nov 1947
'Egypt-military requirements': letter from the FO to Lieutenant-General Sir L Hollis, 14 Nov 1947. *Annex*   [Extract]

As I explained when you were so good as to attend our meeting yesterday, the Foreign Secretary has been turning over in his mind the possibilities of making a fresh start in negotiations with the Egyptians on some basis other than that of the Bevin-Sidky agreement. From a talk which he had with the Egyptian Ambassador on November 12th, and from the recent audience which Campbell has had with King Farouk (Cairo telegram No. 159 Saving of November 10th, of which a copy has been sent to you separately), he feels that the Egyptians may now be beginning to come round to a rather more amenable frame of mind; and of course a new and very important factor is the extent to which the Americans now seem likely to agree to exert pressure on the Egyptian Government in our interest.

2.   The Secretary of State was particularly struck by the views of the American Service and State Department representatives as recorded in Washington telegram No. 5965 of October 26th (copy attached for convenience of reference). As you know, there is unfortunately no possibility of obtaining Egyptian agreement (which ultimately we shall need in practice, if not in theory) to the embodiment in a new treaty of the arrangements provided in the 1936 Treaty for a garrison in the Canal Zone. There may, however, be some chance of obtaining their agreement to our maintenance in some part of Egypt of our minimum requirements in the way of physical installations including airfields or air facilities and stores, together with the minimum personnel to guard and maintain these, provided that it is not a question of formed units; and the chance would clearly be increased if such installations could be located well outside the inhabited areas. For this reason the Secretary of State has been turning over in his mind the possibility of location in Sinai on the basis of a lease of the whole or some part of the Sinai Peninsula from the Egyptian Government.

3.   The question of a base in Sinai has, I believe, been considered in the past by the Chiefs of Staff with negative results. There are, however, certain new factors apart from those which I have mentioned above, e.g. the recent developments in regard to Palestine and the decision that, in view of these developments and of the evident impossibility of reaching any wholly satisfactory agreement with Egypt, a base in Cyrenaica is essential and must be planned now despite the continuing political uncertainty as to the disposal of the ex-Italian colonies.

4.   We should like, therefore, to have as soon as possible, the views of the Service authorities concerned on the general feasibility of abandoning the Canal Zone in favour of a new base (bracketed with the one which we must ensure our ability to establish in Cyrenaica) somewhere East of the Canal; and of maintaining such a

base—if it is to be located in Egyptian territory—with other than formed units, preferably in civilian clothes and with the assistance for guard duties of Egyptian army personnel.

5.   In considering this, we must I think rule out a mere transfer to the Eastern bank of the Canal. From the psychological point of view such a short move would not be at all likely to appeal to the Egyptians—we should still be almost as much "in evidence" as before. We should not, however, rule out the possibility of a base outside Egypt, Aqaba in Transjordania; or alternatively of linked bases at Aqaba and in North Eastern Sinai (though this last would certainly raise awkward problems of communication across the international frontier). Needless to say, the acquisition of a base wholly in Transjordania would present a far less difficult political problem, and would thus be greatly preferable from our point of view provided that it met our minimum strategic requirements.

6.   As you will remember, the American Service representatives laid great stress on the necessity of our having the right of rapid re-entry into Egypt in time of war. Clearly we do need to secure this right if we are to withdraw our forces from Egypt; indeed, we need something still more difficult to get, namely the right of re-entry when *we* judge the threat of war sufficiently imminent to necessitate it. I think that, for the purposes of the problem which I have outlined above, we must assume that we shall enjoy this right.

7.   In estimating our chances of inducing the Egyptians to lease us a base in Sinai, much will of course depend on the size of the base which we should require, on the number of British personnel needed to maintain it and on the extent to which it can be confined to areas at present wholly uninhabited. It is on these points, in particular, that we should be grateful for the views of the Service authorities concerned. Naturally too, we should have to have an approximate idea of the cost which such a transfer would involve; and of the proportion of this cost which would be offset by the corresponding reduction in the size of the Cyrenaican base. (We realise, of course, that to get an answer on this last point will take a considerable time, and we do not suggest that your answer on other points should be held up until you are able to deal with this one).

8.   For political reasons, there could I think be no question of including G.H.Q. in the Sinai base or elsewhere in Egypt. . . .

Annex to 106: copy of telegram no 5965 from Washington to FO, 26 Oct 1947

Following for Sir O. Sargent from Mr. Wright.

Following is point we have now reached in discussion with State Department and American Service representatives about Egypt.

2.   American Service representatives put forward with great emphasis the view that the maintenance of His Majesty's Government's position in the Middle East, which they considered to be essential to the security of the United States and to world peace, postulated the maintenance of minimum strategic facilities in the canal area in peace time, coupled with the right of rapid re-entry in time of war.

3.   They pointed out that the importance of facilities in Cyrenaica increased as the prospects of adequate facilities in the canal area diminished, but could never afford a fully satisfactory substitute.

4.   State Department representatives agreed, but appreciated our political difficulties in obtaining what we require in Egypt. Both American [? grp. omtd.] and State Department representatives recognised that of course the lower we scale down our requirements in Egypt, the more chance we have of obtaining them. American Service representatives considered that physical installations, e.g. airfield installations, radar equipment and general stores or supplies were the most important element, with the minimum of personnel, whether in uniform or dressed as civilians, to guard and maintain them. Figure of 3,700 or less was discussed and possibilities of some mixed Anglo–Egyptian body for this purpose was touched upon. Americans recognise difficulties of obtaining Egyptian consent to the maintenance on Egyptian territory in peace time of any formed units, and doubted whether this was essential.

5.   Americans expressed their agreement to following general principles which have not (repeat not) so far been put into any agreed form of words:—

(a) United States Government recognises that it is desirable that His Majesty's Government should retain minimum strategic facilities in the canal area in peace time, with the right of re-entry in war time.

(b) United States Government is prepared to give His Majesty's Government such diplomatic support as His Majesty's Government may desire, and as both Governments may, at any given moment, agree to be helpful in order to assist His Majesty's Government to obtain the required facilities.

(c) United States Government considers that it is desirable for any revised treaty with Egypt to be negotiated with a majority or a national government.

6.   State Department representatives believed that any future American approach to the Egyptian Government would be more likely to carry weight if it were based on general need of countries of Middle East of strategic help, and protection by His Majesty's Government with American support, than any other argument.

7.   Both American Service and State Department representatives welcomed and approved our idea of common defence arrangements between Middle East countries and His Majesty's Government. They considered this would be the best solution if it could be achieved, and that the United States Government ought to give us any support with Middle East countries which we might desire to help us in obtaining it. They were glad to learn that Iraqi Government favoured the idea and thought that Ibn Saud would do so also, and that United States Government might be able to help with him. Failing common defence arrangements, bilateral arrangements were desirable.

8.   In the case of Egypt, American representatives were inclined to think, subject to our views, that any approach from the United States Government would be most likely to achieve its object if made personally to the King. It is for this reason that they already suggested that it might be helpful if, at some moment to be agreed upon with us, they were to invite the King of Egypt to the United States and, during his visit, impress strongly their views upon him. We thanked them for the suggestion and said we would think it over.

9.   I have at two meetings explained to the American representatives our dilemma over resumption of negotiations with a Palace Government. State Department representatives are inclined to agree that a treaty with a Palace Government would have no (repeat no) value since it would inevitably be opposed, and probably in due course repudiated, by the Wafd, and that it is therefore desirable that any revised

treaty should be concluded with a majority or with a national government, but they think that we should weigh carefully whether a categoric intimation that we should not negotiate with any other Government would be tactically wise, and if we judge that it would be wise, how we should make it.

10.   The American representatives mentioned the requests which the United States Government had received from Egypt for a military mission for help with training and equipment. I said that the Egyptians were playing the game of trying to put an end to all British facilities in Egypt, and at the same time turning to the Americans for assistance. The American Service representatives interjected that these were the familiar tactics of trying to play off the British and Americans against one another. After discussion, the American representatives agreed that they would refuse all such requests from the Egyptians until the question of British strategic requirements in Egypt was settled. They would consider informing the Egyptians of their decision and of the reasons for it.

11.   I informed American representatives that we were bound to consider the situation which would arise if riots took place in Egypt which threatened the lives of British or other foreign residents. In that event, reference would no doubt be made at once to United Nations, but meanwhile we should have to consider whether to send armed convoys to rescue, protect and evacuate British or other foreign residents. . . .

107   FO 371/62989, no 5901   20 Nov 1947
[Policy towards Egypt]: minute by M R Wright on the new factors affecting a possible Anglo–Egyptian agreement

I attach copies of Cairo telegrams nos. 159 saving, 2179 and 2191, Foreign Office telegram no. 2093 to Cairo and Washington telegram no. 5965 about Egypt.[1]

2.   *New factors*
We are now reviewing the whole position in the light of the new factors which have emerged. The most important of these new factors are the prospects of American support coupled with the importance the Americans attach to the right of re-entry in addition to minimum facilities in peacetime, a fresh examination by the Chiefs of Staff of our minimum requirements in peacetime and of the possibility of using Sinai, and the overtures from the King of Egypt over the head of and presumably without the knowledge of his government.

3.   *Minimum requirements in peacetime and possible use of Sinai*
The following are the views of the Chiefs of Staff. The Services do not require the retention in Egypt in peacetime of any units in uniform, or of any men in uniform except possibly about 150 R.A.F. personnel for a transit airfield. The use in peacetime of any airfields in Egypt is not essential (although desirable) with the exception of one airfield for transit use which might be in Sinai. But in wartime there is no practical alternative to the use of Egypt because neither ports, railway facilities,

---

[1] See 106.

roads, oil pipelines or labour are available in Cyrenaica, Sinai or Transjordan. In order to make sure that these facilities are available for rapid use in the event of war or threat of war, it is necessary to provide for their maintenance by Egyptians in a sufficient state of readiness and for certain construction and operational stores to be kept in Egypt and guarded by Egyptians with the assistance of some British personnel. The minimum total of such personnel from the three Services combined would be about a thousand, all of whom could wear civilian clothes with the possible exception of the 150 R.A.F. personnel for the transit airfield. If this field were in Egypt proper and not in Sinai, in other words was guarded by Egyptians, even these 150 men might be in civilian clothes.

4. *Sinai*

Since the requirements of the Services are now so low and are confined to the maintenance of physical installations which cannot be elsewhere than in Egypt, the lease of the whole or a part of Sinai would not be necessary unless the Egyptians prefer the transit airfield to be in Sinai rather than in Egypt. In that case it would have to be in the north of Sinai and probably at Rafa on the Palestine border. Anything else in Sinai would be in addition to and not in substitution for the maintenance of minimum physicial [sic] installations in Egypt.

5. *Minimum requirements for a treaty*

The above clarifies and simplifies the position about our minimum requirements in peacetime. But there remain three other major difficulties, namely the right of re-entry, the Sudan, and the awkward but inescapable fact that if a treaty is not to be disowned it ought to bear the signature of all the principle [sic] parties including the Wafd.

The questions of the right of re-entry and of the Sudan are under fresh study by the department concerned. But it looks as though on neither point can we now regard the Sidky proposals as any longer meeting our requirements.

6. *Prospects for renewed negotiations*

It is difficult to see our way clearly at least until decisions have been taken on the Washington talks and we know more definitely what are the prospects of American support over Egypt and Cyrenaica; until the Assembly has reached a decision on Palestine; and until we know the result of the Iraqi negotiations. Meanwhile the 1936 Treaty remains in force with such bargaining advantages as that carries with it. If we were to embark now on renewed negotiations we should be hard pressed at once over evacuation and it would be more difficult for us during such negotiations to pursue the almost inevitable staging through Egypt of some of the troops to be withdrawn from Palestine. Finally the King of Egypt is acting in an irregular and perhaps even unconstitutional manner in suggesting what are virtually negotiations with us over the head of and perhaps behind the back of his government and we may get ourselves into an awkward position with the Egyptian Parliament and parties if we go far down this road. All these considerations point to the desirability of feeling our way cautiously. By repeating our general willingness to resume negotiations but waiting for an actual approach from the Egyptian side we have already elicited feelers, although not of the most desirable kind. On balance it looks as though we may improve our position still more by continuing to take the same line. In undertaking to resume negotiations we have always had in mind open negotiations with the government of Egypt whichever it may be and not secret negotiations with the King acting independently.

7.   Overall defence arrangements in the Middle East

There is the further consideration that our desire is for common defence arrangements with all the Middle East countries, and that we want an arrangement with Egypt which will fit into this pattern. Here again the pattern may well become clearer as the weeks go by and in particular as the Palestine situation develops and the revision of the Iraqi Treaty takes shape.

8.   Conclusions

For these reasons it would be difficult and perhaps dangerous to make any definite and precise reply at this moment to the overture from the King, and a non-committal attitude seems to be wiser. We might however consider whether anything would be gained by following up the King's suggestion that Sir R. Campbell might come back to London for further discussion following the talks he has already had with the King. This might serve to keep the ball in play, and it would be desirable to discuss the various new developments with Sir R. Campbell personally. On the other hand it is doubtful whether the Secretary of State could see him until the Council of Foreign Ministers is over. Both on this ground and because the position about the Washington talks, Iraq and Palestine may be clearer by then, a visit soon after Christmas might be more fruitful. We might perhaps put the point to Sir R. Campbell and ask for his views.

I submit a possible draft telegram to Sir R. Campbell covering the above briefly and answering some of the questions he has put to us.

108   DEFE 4/8, COS 144(47)1   21 Nov 1947
'Middle East policy': COS Committee minutes on the Washington talks with the Americans

The Staff Conference considered a minute (P.M./47/169) from the Foreign Secretary to the Prime Minister covering a record of the Washington talks about the Middle East.

The Foreign Secretary said that when the Egyptians referred the revision of the Anglo–Egyptian Treaty to the United Nations there were inconsistencies in the views held by different United States Government Departments and expressed by the United States Delegates in the United Nations. The United States had attempted to exert pressure on H.M.G. to accept their proposals for the future policy to be adopted in Greece and on their proposed solution of the Palestine problem. The British Delegation had often been faced with statements by the U.S. Delegation, which differed from agreements reached even shortly before the statements were made.

In spite of the political risks, he had felt it essential to discuss, secretly and confidentially with the American Government, the situation in the Middle East so as to avoid the risk of the Americans and ourselves pursuing opposed policies. He had made it clear before the start of the talks that he would be opposed to the adoption of a combined Anglo–American policy for the Middle East, as this area was primarily of strategic and economic interest to the United Kingdom. The Delegation was, therefore, briefed to seek the United States views on the Middle East and to ascertain to what extent they would be prepared to support us in maintaining our position in that area.

The records now before the Staff Conference described the results achieved at the talks. He thought great credit was due to the British Delegation in having reached so large a measure of agreement with the Americans. Annexures B and C[1] to Mr. Wright's memoranda set out the respective views of officials of the United States Government and H.M.G.. It now remained for both Governments to consider the identic record. If the record was approved then each Government could inform the other that they intended to be guided by the general principles described. He did not know if the U.S. Secretary of State, Mr. Marshall, had yet obtained the views of the United States National Security Council, but he hoped that it would be possible to discuss the record with Mr. Marshall when he arrived in this country. He, therefore, hoped that the general principles might be approved so that he could assure Mr. Marshall that they represented the guiding principles to be adopted by His Majesty's Government in the Middle East.

He stressed that the record set out no more than general principles on which the policy of both Governments should be guided. There would be no necessity, indeed it would be undesirable, for there to be any Treaty between the two Governments, secret or otherwise, and it represented, therefore, only an exchange of agreement on fundamental principles, covering economic, cultural as well as strategic policy.

The Minister of Defence said he shared with the Foreign Secretary his pleasure at the valuable results achieved at the confidential discussions. He felt also that the Foreign Secretary had contributed greatly to their success by his decision to initiate the discussions.

The exchange of telegrams on the talks had led him to believe that the Americans had agreed to include in paragraph 2 a definition, agreed by both sides, of the word "vital". This definition was not contained in paragraph 2 of the identic record and he enquired the reason for its omission.

The last half of Mr. Wright's memoranda led him to think that as the fundamental decision to maintain our economic, strategic and political position lay with H.M.G., it would now be necessary for us to give the Americans an assurance of what we were prepared to do to implement our policy. Before any detailed planning could proceed, however, it would be essential to obtain from the United States an estimate of the time that would elapse between the outbreak of hostilities in the Middle East and the time at which we could expect to receive effective American assistance. The length of this hiatus during which we would stand alone would determine the military and economic expenditure required from us.

Apart from these observations, he recommended that the Staff Conference should endorse the recommendations in the Foreign Secretary's minute to the Prime Minister.

Mr. Wright said the omission of the definition of the word "vital" in the identic record had been made at the request of the United States Delegation, who felt that its

---

[1] Wright's memo and its annexures are not printed.

inclusion might lead to some difficulty in obtaining the approval of the United States National Security Council. The meaning of the word "vital" was, however, apparent from the text in which it was used and the definition was, therefore, inferred, although not directly stated.

In reply to a question from the Chancellor of the Exchequer, he said that if the United States Government approved the identic record it was expected that the United States diplomatic posts in the Middle East would be verbally informed of the approved fundamental principles and instructed to act accordingly. He suggested that His Majesty's Government, if they approved the principles, might wish to do likewise.

The Chancellor of the Exchequer said he thought the results of the discussions were most valuable. Approval of the record would not commit either Government in any way on the implementation of the agreed policy. In view of our economic and manpower difficulties, freedom of action must remain with H.M.G. On the other hand, H.M.G. could not easily expect the United States to agree to carry out such a policy unless H.M.G. indicated to them determination to maintain our strong strategic, political and economic position in the Middle East and Eastern Mediterranean within the limits of her resources. This understanding was recognised and it should be possible for the two Governments to adopt the similar objectives described.

He drew attention to the success of the economic negotiations set out at Annex A, with which he was in agreement. He stressed that, similarly to other issues discussed, the economic discussions had been limited to a frank exchange of views on general principles, and that His Majesty's Government was in no way committed to its detailed implementation.

The Chiefs of Staff said that the agreements on strategic issues reached between the two Delegations were entirely consistent with the previous recommendations of the Chiefs of Staff and with the present policy, in so far as it affected strategic intentions and military dispositions in the Middle East.

The Foreign Secretary emphasized that unless His Majesty's Government was prepared to assure the Americans that we intended to maintain our economic, political and strategic position in the Middle East and the Eastern Mediterranean, it was certain that the United States would feel compelled to disinterest herself in that area. The U.S. Government wished to be assured that we regarded the Middle East as an area vital to the defence of the British Commonwealth; that we should continue to do so; and that we should take the necessary steps to this end. If he was in a position to give these assurances to Mr. Marshall, it might well be that the present American plan for assistance to Europe would be extended to the Eastern Mediterranean and the Middle East countries. This, if it could be achieved, would be of incalculable benefit to the countries concerned and directly to the defence of the British Commonwealth.

After the fundamental principles had been approved by Governments, it would require close and continuous collaboration between them to implement the agreed policy. He did not think that the Americans thought that in peacetime this would occasion the stationing of large numbers of U.S. or British troops in that region. He believed that the Americans felt that we were placing too great a value on the physical presence of troops there in peacetime and were not relying sufficiently on obtaining guarantees of adequate facilities to be available in the event or imminent threat of war. Detailed planning in the event of the policy being approved would naturally have to await the solution of the Palestine problem, but he foresaw close collaboration with the Americans through the medium of the British Middle East Office. He would have no objection to the continuation of combined military discussions, provided they were conducted under conditions of strict secrecy.

The presence of Field Marshal Smuts[2] and Mr. Mackenzie King[3] in the United Kingdom would provide a good opportunity for them to be informed of the present negotiations. He suggested that he could conveniently discuss the matter with them privately and separately.

The Prime Minister said he agreed with the action proposed by the Foreign Secretary and that the agreed general principles and objectives contained in the identic record should guide and direct the policy of H.M. Government in the Middle East. Military discussions with the Americans must be continued only under conditions of strict secrecy. He agreed that the Foreign Secretary should inform Field Marshal Smuts and Mr. Mackenzie King, privately, of the progress of the negotiations with the United States Government.

The Conference:—

(a) Approved the identic record of the Washington talks.

(b) Approved the general principles and objectives described in the memoranda submitted by the Foreign Secretary, as forming the foundation and guide for the policy of H.M. Government towards the Middle East.

(c) Authorised the Foreign Secretary to inform the U.S. Secretary of State of the decision in (a) and (b) above and to seek, through discussions with him, adoption by the U.S. Government of the same general principles and objectives in their policy towards the Middle East.

(d) Agreed that complete freedom must be retained by H.M. Government in the executive implementation of this policy, but that the planning necessary to fulfil this policy could proceed.

(e) Authorised the Foreign Secretary to inform Field Marshal Smuts and Mr. Mackenzie King privately of the outlines of the agreements achieved with the Americans.

(f) Recorded their appreciation of the success achieved in the Washington discussions and of the work of the British Delegation.

---

[2] Field Marshal Jan Smuts, South African prime minister, 1919–1924 and 1939–1948; Field Marshal of the British army 1941.
[3] William Lyon Mackenzie King, Canadian prime minister, 1921–1930 and 1935–1948 and leader of the Liberal Party, 1919–1948.

109   FO 371/69192, no 598   15 Dec 1947

'Egypt': draft minute by Mr Bevin to Mr Attlee on how best to approach the Egyptians

[Attlee agreed with the proposed line of approach with the proviso that the proposals would have to be acceptable to both parties to be of any value (FO 371/69192, no 63, Attlee to Bevin, 16 Dec 1947).]

Prime Minister

I. *The problem*

We have been considering afresh how best to break the deadlock in our relations with Egypt. A few weeks ago certain very tentative approaches by King Farouk and his entourage to our Ambassador, and by the Egyptian Ambassador to myself, seemed to indicate the possibility of resuming negotiations for a general settlement. The King, whose position is none too secure, would certainly like to see the deadlock broken and negotiations resumed; but from Sir R. Campbell's most recent telegrams it is clear that no adequate basis for resumption exists. The Egyptians are still demanding as much as ever, and this is a great deal more than we could profitably concede. They want, that is, an impossibly early date for the complete evacuation of our troops from Egypt; and they also want us to acknowledge explicitly King Farouk's status as Sovereign of the Sudan and to open the higher grades of the Sudan Administration to Egyptians. These, in Sir R. Campbell's opinion, are likely to be their minimum terms.

2.   We therefore must, for the present at any rate, give up hope of reaching a general settlement and try instead to tackle our immediate problems from another angle. Our position so far has been that we stand on the 1936 Treaty, under which we have the right (but not the obligation) to keep troops in the Canal Zone. But in practice it would almost certainly be impossible to keep troops there indefinitely against the Egyptian people's will. There are many ways in which the Egyptian Government could make the position of our forces extremely difficult, e.g. by withholding labour and supplies. Moreover, we were under strong pressure from many quarters, during the hearing of the Egyptian Appeal at Lake Success, to withdraw our troops from Egypt as a gesture which would be compatible with our stand on the Treaty.

3.   In any negotiations with Egypt for a general settlement there are four main problems:—

(a) Our peace-time requirements for the maintenance of Egypt in a state of readiness to serve as an essential strategic base for Middle Eastern defence, i.e. the maintenance of the necessary physical installations and the guarding of our stores. This would involve leaving in Egypt about 1,000 men, all, or almost all, of whom could be in civilian clothes;
(b) Facilities for re-entry in an apprehended emergency;
(c) The Sudan;
(d) The desirability of any revised treaty being signed by representatives of all Egyptian parties.

4.   Sir R. Campbell considers that we are unlikely to get anything better on (b) than Article 3 of the Sidky protocol,[1] which provided for an Anglo–Egyptian Joint Defence Board, and that the Egyptians would probably press for something even less specific. This would not meet our requirements.

5.   As regards (c) (the Sudan) my view is that we cannot now go as far as we were prepared to do at the time of the Sidky negotiations since the text which we were then prepared to adopt has been exploited and misinterpreted. Moreover, to admit

---

[1-] See 85.

Egyptians to the higher grades of the Administration would certainly retard, and probably wreck, our programme of "Sudanisation" and self government. We are therefore faced with a deadlock.

6.　As regards (d), Sir R. Campbell considers that the prospects of a government of National Union remain extremely remote.

7.　On points (b), (c) and (d) above, therefore, the prospects of agreement are slight; and even as regards (a) the Egyptian insistance [sic] on a very early date for the completion of evacuation is likely to prove a complicating factor.

II.　*Recommendations*

8.　I should like therefore to try the following new line of approach. At the appropriate moment we would say to the Egyptians that although we and they desire an agreement which would place our relations on a new footing, the obstacles to the conclusion of a new treaty acceptable to both sides seem difficult to surmount at the moment. We are therefore prepared to go beyond the reduction of our forces to the Treaty level, and to offer the withdrawal of all formed units from Egypt altogether by a date X, provided that the Egyptian Government will agree on their side to cooperate in the maintenance of physical installations in a state of readiness and to guard our stores, allowing us to keep about 1,000 men (all, or almost all, of whom would be in civilian clothes) for these purposes only. As I have indicated above, the tempo of withdrawal and the final date by which it will be completed are the crucial factors in the eyes of the Egyptians. The Chiefs of Staff, in their latest paper, agreed that the stores could be guarded by Egyptians provided we leave behind the 1,000 men. We should therefore have to press the Chiefs of Staff to agree on this basis to earlier evacuation than they have so far been prepared to accept. Their calculations, ever since the Sidky Protocol was rejected, have been based on the need for withdrawing a vast accumulation of stores and for retaining troops to perform this work. If arrangements can be made for leaving the stores in Egypt, it should be possible to evacuate the men much faster, though the difficulty created by the shortage of shipping will remain. If we could get the date fixed sufficiently early, we should have offered to meet the main Egyptian preoccupation.

9.　By making this offer, even if the Egyptians refused to accept it, we should have largely cut the ground from under the feet of our critics, whether at U.N.O. or elsewhere, the main burden of whose accusation centres round continued British occupation of Egypt.

10.　We might make our offer in the form of an undertaking not to avail ourselves (short of an apprehended international emergency) of the facilities accorded to us under the 1936 Treaty for the maintenance of troops in Egypt. For the rest the Treaty would remain in force until 1956 (in particular Article 7 providing for re-entry). This would mean that the Egyptian Government and H.M.G. would have to agree *not* to continue negotiations for the revision of the Treaty which we and they decided on in 1946 in virtue of the last sentence of Article 16 (which provides that with the consent of both parties negotiations for revision *may* be entered into any time after the expiration of a period of ten years from the date on which the Treaty comes into force). This would further mean that for the life of the Treaty, i.e. at least until 1956 (and perhaps longer in virtue of Article 16), we should retain the right of re-entry which we need.

11.　At the same time we might make it clear that it is our intention that our treaty arrangements with Egypt *should* eventually fall into the framework of those common defence arrangements which we hope will in due course be made for the Middle East as a whole.

12.　　If we could reach an agreement with Egypt on the above lines we should keep our present re-entry facilities, and avoid the dilemma about negotiating a new treaty with a government other than a government of National Union. The question of the Sudan would remain for separate treatment. We should therefore avoid the greater part of the difficulties now facing us over points (b), (c) and (d) in para 3 above.

110　FO 371/69192, no 255　　　　　　　　　　10 Jan 1948
'Egypt and Sudan': note of an FO meeting with Mr Bevin　[Extract]

[On 3 Jan the FO wrote to the COS outlining the new line of approach to Egypt proposed by Bevin (FO 371/69192, no 63, Sargent to Hollis). They replied that they wished to reserve judgment. A successful outcome to the Anglo–Iraqi treaty negotiations might help to secure more favourable terms from the Egyptians. The COS feared that if requirements were set too low the pursuit of Egyptian goodwill might lead to a further whittling away of British needs. Therefore any new approach should be on a take it or leave it basis (DEFE 4/10, COS 3(48)4 Annex II, 7 Jan 1948).]

The *S. of State* had before him the paper on the Sudan constitutional reform question and the draft reply to Amr Pasha. He said he did not disagree with the course of action suggested, but he was anxious to get ahead with the general negotiations with Egypt. If we failed to bring off a settlement before next March he felt that we should probably never bring one off at all. The political situation was boiling up in Palestine, Greece and Germany. The Egyptians were showing increased willingness to reach a settlement, and anxiety over the international situation played a part in this.

Sir O. Sargent pointed out that it was a question of what we could get in the way of a settlement and how much we should have to pay for it. These things might be clearer once the Palestine problem was out of the way and we were safely installed in Cyrenaica.

The *S. of State* did not agree that we should wait. We might not get Cyrenaica, and might lose Egypt also through waiting. He would like to have the bird in the hand *and* the bird in the bush.

Sir O. Sargent observed that the Egyptians wanted a settlement even more than we did, and had been brought to this state largely by our policy of sitting tight.

The *S. of State* repeated that the time to settle was now. Soviet policy might before long become less intolerable to the world in general, and if that happened people would begin once more to run after them. He had discussed the Egyptian problem with the Prime Minister, who agreed with him. As for the price of a settlement, there was no reason to pay anything.

As regards the Sudan, he considered that the line of approach suggested was the right one. We should confine our negotiations in regard to the Egyptian side of the problem to the question of withdrawal of troops. We could not go back to the Bevin-Sidky agreement, and in particular we could not go back to the sovereignty formula in that agreement. . . .[1]

---

[1] The remaining section of the text discussing the Sudan is not printed.

Egyptian aspect of negotiations

The *S. of State* said that he wanted to get away from the question of the withdrawal of troops and onto new ground. On the assumption that the Iraqi treaty went through, it would surely have a great effect on the Egyptians, and we should try to take it as a model. Why should he not say to the Egyptians that the defence of Egypt should be on a new basis? In the past we had treated them unfairly by failing to train their armed forces adequately or take them seriously. This had given them an inferiority complex. He did not, indeed, consider that there was any real need to keep 10,000 men in Egypt, nor was the expense involved possible to justify. The Cabinet wanted to announce that we were pulling out of Egypt. But the difficulty was to give a date. The evacuation of our stores was a vast job, and at present it was being still further complicated and retarded by the withdrawal from India and Palestine. In these circumstances, evacuation from Egypt by September 1949 would be the earliest that we could manage.

Sir R. Campbell thought that the Egyptians, while they could not pretend to doubt that we were faced with grave evacuation difficulties in other parts of the world, would say that they did not see why *they* should be made to suffer from these difficulties by being given the lowest priority.

The *S. of State* said he had been wondering whether, instead of a new treaty, we could not simply lease from the Egyptian Government the necessary areas in which to leave our stores and installations. This was after all quite an established practice as between independent States: there was the precedent of the American leased bases. He did not like the idea of getting the Egyptians to guard our stores for us—they would probably appropriate them. It would not be a question of a long lease such as the Americans had in the West Indies: four years would be enough.

Sir R. Campbell said he doubted whether the Egyptians would steal our stores; after all, they would regard their preservation as necessary for their own defence in the event of war. As regards the question of leasing the necessary areas, he had understood King Farouk to say, when a similar suggestion had been tentatively put to him not long ago, that he was precluded by the terms of his coronation oath from allowing this.

Mr Wright pointed out that if we failed to get a satisfactory right of re-entry in any new agreement with Egypt this would probably have serious repercussions in all other Middle Eastern countries where we had got, or were hoping to get, this right. They would object strongly to being committed to a greater extent than Egypt was, and would tend to back out. The plan which we had envisaged would at least preserve our existing right of re-entry, since the 1936 Treaty would remain in force.

Sir R. Campbell thought that, by continuing to take our stand on the 1936 Treaty and to rely on the right of re-entry which the treaty gave us, we might be filling the defence vacuum on paper, but not in practice. Willing Egyptian cooperation was in practice essential.

The *S. of State* said that we should re-examine the question of the right of re-entry in the light of the new Iraqi treaty.[2] He did not like our present ideas for approaching the problem. We could not give a date for the completion of withdrawal—Amr Pasha's suggestion that we should announce a date with no intention of keeping to it was of course ridiculous – and he did not like the idea of keeping 1,000 men in Egypt

---

[2] See 119, note 1.

in civilian clothes. He wished he knew what our stores really consisted of: the figures which he had been given from time to time for the total value of these stores had varied enormously, and we had never yet been given a clear picture by the Chiefs of Staff.

Sir R. Campbell said that according to what he had gathered from the British military authorities in Egypt it was an exceedingly difficult matter to estimate the value of the stores. Some of them were modern and of great value, and these would anyhow have to be removed. There was also a lot of less modern but still valuable equipment which was regarded as a useful reserve, especially during the present phase when we were producing so little. And finally there was a good deal that was of little or no value. The problem had been eased by the Palestine evacuation, since hitherto the Canal Zone had served as a dump from which to feed and equip our forces in Palestine.

The *S. of State* repeated that we must now get a clear idea of the nature and value of the stores. Some while ago the Cabinet had actually ruled that an independent mission should be sent out to Egypt to investigate this question, but apparently nothing had been done about this. He instructed Mr Roberts to find out from the Ministry of Defence how this matter stood and to keep the Prime Minister informed. Before the decision to evacuate Palestine he had repeatedly been given alarming figures of the value of the stores there which we should have to abandon, but when it came to the point a large proportion of these stores had turned out to consist of bricks and other building material which could perfectly well be sold to the Jews.

If the Egyptians pressed us about the date of our withdrawal we should reply "what about a treaty? If you will agree to buy a proportion of our stores, withdrawal can be accelerated."

Sir O. Sargent said that it would all depend on how much we were in fact prepared to sell to the Egyptians; and for this we must have a proper inventory.

The *S. of State* said that Sir R. Campbell, when speaking to the Egyptians, should emphasise that the question of the date of withdrawal depended on physical factors and not on good will. The Ambassador should go on to remind them that they professed to want efficient defence arrangements, and that we must therefore get down to practical business: how much of our stores did they want to buy?

Sir R. Campbell thought that the efficacy of an approach on these lines would depend on two things: how much of value we could offer the Egyptians, and how much their purchase of it would affect the tempo of evacuation.

The *Secretary of State* said that, if the tempo were *not* materially affected, this would mean that the excuse invariably given by our military authorities in the past for the slowness of the run-down would have been shown up as false. The Cabinet's view was that what we really needed was air facilities, not infantry. Our stores could be kept in Aden and British Somaliland, but the trouble was that British officers didn't like being stationed there and did like the Canal Zone. The C.I.G.S. now wanted the Combined Headquarters to be in the Canal Zone, but this was out of the question.

Sir R. Howe observed that the Sudan Government had expressed their readiness to accommodate all non-military stores in the Sudan.

Sir R. Campbell though there might be some possibility of camouflaging the Combined Headquarters in Egypt provided that we got an agreement. The Joint Defence Board would, he thought, provide the necessary camouflage. The prerequisite for a new agreement was that the Egyptians should be certain that we were really evacuating and should have definite evidence of this.

The *S. of State* said he could not accept the view that the Canal Zone was the only possible main base for operations. It was no doubt the best one, but it was not essential. The Jews had always laughed at him when he had told them that we might clear out of Palestine, and had maintained that we never could do so since Palestine was strategically essential to us. We must get it out of the heads of the Egyptians that the Canal Zone was essential to us, and that we are consequently dependent on them in all circumstances. After that, we must try to get a worth-while treaty, and if we can't get it we must get out without one, telling them that we can and will make other arrangements.

Sir Orme Sargent said that Cyrenaica was undoubtedly the best "aircraft carrier" in Africa—though admittedly the territory lacked the necessary manpower and other resources.

The *S. of State* spoke of the value to us of Egyptian manpower during the last war, especially as ground personnel for our airfields. He would far rather have properly and technically trained Egyptians at our disposal in the event of war than 10,000 British troops occupying an unwilling country. In the past we had made the mistake of neglecting the potentialities of the Middle East reserve of military manpower. The Russians treated all the different races of the Soviet Union, from the Pacific to the Baltic, on exactly the same footing in this respect, and the result was that they had at their disposal one vast and homogeneous force. We should do the same. We must exploit the manpower resources of the Middle East by means of joint defence boards set up under treaties between H.M.G. and each of the States concerned and reporting direct to the two governments—i.e., in our case, to the Defence Committee of the Cabinet, not to the Chiefs of Staff. Thus we should have one great Middle Eastern Army. This was the more necessary now that we could no longer count on India as a manpower reserve.

Sir O. Sargent observed that this had a bearing on the Foreign Office proposals for the expansion of the Sudan Defence Force, which the C.I.G.S. had disparaged.

The *S. of State* agreed, and was not prepared to take the Field Marshal's disparagement too seriously.

Sir R. Campbell saw great advantage in drawing the Sudan into the common defence arrangements for Egypt.

Sir O. Sargent enquired whether the Egyptians would be ready to pay, under such arrangements, for the expansion of the Sudan Defence Force.

Sir R. Campbell thought that they might even be *too* willing to pay, i.e. too proprietary about it.

Mr Wright suggested that we should pursue all these ideas further in the light of the Iraqi treaty and while Sir R. Campbell was still here.

The *S. of State* agreed: he had not yet, he said, made up his mind definitely about the best method of approaching the Egyptians except that he felt sure that now was the time to do so. He would consider further the line of approach already proposed to the Prime Minister. Meanwhile we must get the facts about the nature and value of the stores in Egypt.

111 FO 371/69192, no 554 20 Jan 1948
'Egypt': note of an FO meeting with Mr Bevin on future talks with the Egyptians [Extract]

The Secretary of State held a meeting on the 20th January to discuss the lines of our next conversations with the Egyptians. Sir Orme Sargent and Sir Ronald Campbell attended from 5 p.m. and at 5.30 p.m. Mr. Wright, Mr. Lascelles, Mr. McDermott[1] and Mr. Johnston[2] joined the meeting. This record refers only to the latter part of the meeting.

The Secretary of State emphasized the importance of getting a Treaty with Egypt between now and say next May. He believed that the Soviet Government would for tactical reasons reverse their present policy of hostility to non-satellites as soon as it was clear that the Marshall Plan was to be put into effect. The Egyptians would not realise that this was merely a tactical manoeuvre and would think that the danger had passed.

Sir Ronald Campbell agreed both that this was the moment to talk to the Egyptians and that we should try to get a real Treaty.

The Secretary of State said that the question was how? He suggested that we should try the method of cutting out all reference to the Sidky-Bevin Agreements and attempt to shelve the Sudan question. He would like to get our own and the Egyptian technical military experts together to discuss the practical questions affecting the withdrawal of our troops from Egypt (We should have to use forceful methods to get our own military authorities moving on this). Many of his colleagues in the Cabinet wanted us to leave the Middle East altogether: he had stood out against this because he was convinced that the Middle East was essential for the defence of the United Kingdom. If we were to propose unconditional withdrawal from Egypt we should lose the goodwill of the other Middle Eastern countries and our position as regards even Afghanistan and Pakistan would be adversely affected. (Pakistan had already declined an offer from the Soviet Government of a Treaty of Friendship). If we were in difficulties in our relations with Egypt the Soviet Government might try to step in. He thought that Sir Ronald Campbell should say to King Farouk that he must know that our intentions were good and should suggest that technical experts of the two countries should get together to advise on a practical date for withdrawal. The Secretary of State had emphasized to the Regent of Iraq that the cost of research and production of modern weapons and appliances, such as jet-planes and radar, was so great that, on the one hand, small countries simply could not afford them although they were essential in modern warfare, while on the other hand we could not afford to give them to countries with whom we had not a treaty. The Secretary of State would like to bring the Egyptian experts to the United Kingdom and show them just what is involved in the defensive measures demanded in modern warfare. They should be shown the R.A.F. in particular. In our own interest we would do well to equip the Egyptians with the most efficient armaments. Our position was such that we could not provide much at the moment

---

[1] G L McDermott, on temporary assignment to the FO. Until December 1947, acting first secretary at the Cairo embassy.
[2] W J Johnston, financial counsellor at the Cairo embassy.

but if we got relations on a proper basis we could treat them as well as we were treating the Iraqis. In the past we had tended to ridicule the Egyptian army rather than to train it efficiently. This must be remedied. In the recent war the Egyptians had trained into good technicians and without them we might not have been able to keep for instance our air effort in the Middle East operating.

Sir Ronald Campbell confirmed that any concrete evidence of help that we would give to the Egyptian army would have a good effect.

The Secretary of State said that he had told the Iraqis that when trouble came we all wanted to be able to spring to arms immediately, our allies such as the Iraqis on a basis of equality with ourselves. There was a large manpower potential in Egypt backed up by further good manpower resources in the Sudan. We must create confidence in Egypt by wiping out the past and giving a new basis of quality. The Egyptians were not in fact such bad soldiers as had been made out; and with properly organized conscription, better health services in Egypt would follow. The Secretary of State felt that discussions must be with the Palace because there was no-one else worth talking to in Egypt. He would try to get a directive from the Cabinet the same evening to the effect that a detailed break-down of British military sources in Egypt must be provided by the British military authorities.

Sir Orme Sargent said that it would also be useful to have the British military authorities' considered view on what was the real value of the Egyptian base, in view of the facilities that were being provided at various places around Egypt.

The Secretary of State said that we should talk to the Egyptians on the basis that we should be prepared to withdraw if they would give us the necessary help over our installations, etc.

Sir Orme Sargent added that they must also give us re-entry rights similar to those in the Treaty with Iraq.

The Secretary of State said that re-entry rights were no good unless they became effective in time for the outbreak of war, which in modern conditions would be very sudden. He had no desire to use British labour in Egypt, nor to keep 10,000 men in the Canal zone. Conditions were very difference [sic] from what they were in 1936 when the Treaty was made. The next war would start with violent air attacks. As regards re-entry into Egypt we would effect this by force if necessary, treaty or no treaty.

Mr. Lascelles pointed out that a treaty giving re-entry rights would enable us to take action on a basis of legality and thus to avoid being branded as aggressors.

The Secretary of State agreed that this was a good point.

Sir Orme Sargent emphasised that the important point was to be able to put in our Air Forces immediately. We could not ask less from Egypt than from Iraq or Iraq would protest.

Sir Ronald Campbell said that some Egyptians would no doubt claim that Egyptian forces could defend Egypt alone if we trained them. In any case visits by British military technical experts to Egypt would be valuable.

The Secretary of State felt that if we began discussing political formulas and so on with the Egyptians we should get bogged. Let us put to them a date for the withdrawal of our troops from Egypt and get their experts in collaboration with ours to investigate the matter and to work out what was necessary for the defence of Egypt. Sir Ronald Campbell should be given the record of the Secretary of State's talks with the Regent of Iraq about the great cost of essential modern armaments and he could then explain to the Egyptians that they must possess these if their defence was to be effective but could not afford them themselves and must therefore obtain them by way of an agreement with His Majesty's Government. The Secretary of State did not consider that Marshal of the Royal Air Force Sir Sholto Douglas, who was shortly to visit Egypt, would be a suitable spokesman on these matters. He would prefer to send some high-ranking R.A.F. technical expert to Egypt for this purpose, and afterwards to invite Egyptian experts to come to the United Kingdom and see for themselves. He thought King Farouk would be helpful. He would like to bring King Farouk here himself but there were grave objections.

Sir Orme Sargent said that we must not put all our money on King Farouk.

Sir Ronald Campbell thought it might be helpful if King Farouk could be made honorary commodore of an Air Squadron or Colonel of a Regiment or something of the kind.

Mr. Lascelles mentioned that General Allfrey (until recently G.O.C. British Troops in Egypt) had said that a high decoration might influence King Farouk.

Mr. Wright wondered whether we could make him a present of a jet-plane.

The Secretary of State said that he would very much like the Chief of the Air Staff, Lord Tedder, to pay a visit to Egypt. . . .

112 FO 141/1285, no 6 7 Feb 1948
[Regional defence arrangements for the Middle East]: note by E A Chapman Andrews of a conversation with Azzam on a regional agreement with the Arab states

I had half an hour's talk with Azzam Pasha at the Mohamed Ali Club a couple of days back. He said he had had a long talk with Mr. Bevin last September and had afterwards written him a letter (of which he would show me a copy some time) advising him to seize the opportunity of coming to a regional agreement through the intermediary of the Arab League with all the Arab nations as an essential first step to the setting up of a regional defensive scheme. He much preferred this way of tackling the problem to that which we had in fact adopted of trying to get individual treaties with the Arab nations. He would like to have another talk with Mr. Bevin now because although we had followed the wrong policy the denunciation of the Iraqi Treaty presented us with the opportunity of reconsidering the whole matter. If we let slip this opportunity another might not recur for some time. Goodwill towards us throughout the Arab world was still deep and widespread but we should have to cash in on it soon if we were not to lose it altogether as a result of misunderstanding. I here interposed that the Arab nations seemed to [sic] preoccupied with British evacuation. They seemed to have British troops on the brain. To this he replied that we seemed to have treaties on the brain. Treaties were not worth anything unless rooted in the goodwill of the people bound together by them. For example, he said, we had a treaty with Russia but we had none with the United States. The *sine qua non* is goodwill and we should be very unwise to risk losing this further by insisting in individual treaties on terms unacceptable to the Arab nations as a whole. The approach was all wrong. What was needed was a new approach. I asked him what he envisaged as a workable arrangement for a regional understanding. He said nothing very much was required. We still had a treaty of alliance containing military clauses with Transjordan. The Arab world understood that, because Transjordan had as yet hardly emerged from the mandatory stage. Let that treaty stand with its military clauses. It was sufficient to link us with the Arab world. If Transjordan were a party to an Arab regional defensive alliance and if one of the participating Arab states were involved in war which in its turn involved the other participating states including Transjordan, Britain would automatically through her link with Transjordan be at war too. I said this was all very well. The object of our policy was not to go to war and less still to be involved in a war as a result of a guarantee which we had no proper means of rendering effective. What we wanted, and the rocks on which our previous treaty-making efforts seemed to have foundered on, were minimum strategic facilities in peacetime which would render effective rapid action in war. Azzam Pasha replied that if only we would concentrate for the time being on getting goodwill these things might be added to it. I asked him how long he thought it would take if we were in fact to change our approach (I expressed doubts on our ability to do this especially in the case of evacuation from Egypt at an early date) for us to find ourselves in a position where we had a military alliance with all the states of the Arab world which would enable us to honour our side of the bargain and render both rapid and effective aid in the event of war. He said he thought that if the thing were properly handled it would not take more than six months.

It might be worth sending a copy of this minute to Mr. Wright.

113   FO 141/1292, no 13   14 Feb 1948
[Regional defence arrangements for the Middle East]: outward telegram no 255 from Mr Bevin to Sir R Campbell giving instructions on how to respond to King Farouk

Addressed to Cairo telegram No. 255 of February 14th for information to Amman, Bagdad, Jedda, Beirut and Damascus.

Your telegrams Nos. 182, 190, 20 Saving and 24 Saving.

You will now have seen my telegram No. 141 which explains generally our point of view on the question raised by King Farouk. I will deal more fully later with your telegram No. 20 Saving. Meanwhile, a reply to King should not be outstanding.

2.   First of all I may again make it clear in the light of a number of statements that it is not His Majesty's Government who are trying to persuade the Middle East countries to undertake new Treaty commitments with His Majesty's Government. We already have treaties with Egypt, Iraq and Transjordan which give us the facilities we require. It is these countries who are asking us to revise their treaties before their date of expiration. We have responded by saying we are prepared to consider treaty revision in the sense they desire provided the new treaties give us minimum facilities which our common security requires. In the case of Saudi Arabia we have told the King that we are willing to conclude a treaty with him if he desires, in order to remove any feeling in his mind that we desire treaties with Hashemites and not with him. In the case of the Lebanon and Syria, we have a more open mind but if they desire to participate we would certainly consider this and it might be desirable to round the arrangement off by including them.

3.   Our object is that we should have strategic facilities in the Middle East which will enable us both to defend it effectively in time of war and to show clearly to any would-be aggressor that we are able and ready to do this. Some of these facilities will be required in peace, some on menace of war and some in time of actual war. We realise that in order to make full use of these facilities we must also have the goodwill of the inhabitants. As our requirements differ in each country we must have separate agreements with each country. If as appears to be the case we can only retain the goodwill of the inhabitants by a further general agreement, either between various states or between various states collectively and us, then we would be ready to consider such an agreement in addition to individual agreements.

4.   But it is clear that general agreement could not be a substitute for individual agreements and there appears to be no difference of opinion on this point between us and King Farouk. In case of further discussion of principle, the argument is that a general agreement would tend to limit facilities to a general minimum while imposing on us the maximum obligation to guarantee the security of the whole group of states. Furthermore, the differences between various Middle East countries themselves make it most improbable that it would in fact be easy to reach any general agreement which would be of more than an extremely vague kind.

5.   King Farouk suggests that if we make a general agreement first, individual agreements will easily follow from it. In view of his efforts to prevent conclusion of individual revised treaties we cannot help feeling that his motives in arguing thus are somewhat suspect and that he may in fact be hoping to be able to use the policy of general agreement as a ruse, refusing us meanwhile some or all the facilities we want in Egypt.

6.   The above does not, repeat not, imply that we desire bilateral agreements to be unnecessarily piecemeal or that we wish to ignore the natural ties between the various Middle East countries or to decline to consider an overall arrangement at all. We are quite ready to see bilateral agreements co-ordinated and linked up so as to form a comprehensive security system. Indeed we should welcome such a co-ordination since we have no wish to accentuate the regrettable divisions in the Arab world. Equally, we do not want either individual defence arrangements or partial collective defence arrangements which would exclude Hashemite countries or if necessary vice versa.

7.   To sum up therefore you should make it plain to King Farouk that while we are not averse to suggestion of an overall arrangement in some form we cannot contemplate it either as a substitute for, or as a preliminary, of bilateral agreements with the countries to whose assistance we should be expected to come in time of war. If we got into a discussion with Arab countries as suggested any one of them might canalise a settlement or want to water it down to such a point that it would be useless. Alternatively, if we have to accept the principle of coming in only by invitation it might be made a condition of agreement in the case of entry into any one country that all Arab countries must agree. The result would be to bog us down completely. We cannot and will not undertake obligations that we are hindered from fulfilling especially having regard to information we got from secret German documents of the last war. We feel we must have a clear basis well understood by all concerned.

114   FO 371/69174, no 1803   11 Mar 1948
[Military requirements in the Middle East]: letter from Lieutenant-General Sir L Hollis to Sir O Sargent on military requirements in the countries adjacent to Egypt

I am replying to your letter dated 2nd February in which you conveyed to me the Foreign Secretary's request to obtain the views of the Chiefs of Staff on the development of facilities in an outer ring[1] of Middle East countries around Egypt, especially those which are British possessions or in which we have a special position. In particular, he wanted to know what would be required on two different assumptions:—

(a) That we obtain our minimum peacetime requirements in Egypt;
(b) That we get none of our requirements in Egypt.

2.   The Chiefs of Staff have considered these points and on the first assumption, though they have recently made a number of studies bearing on the problem, it might be convenient to you if they are summarised below.

3.   Although the Foreign Secretary's question refers to the facilities in an outer ring it cannot be emphasised too strongly that the countries of the outer ring can only be considered in their relationship to Egypt. Egypt, with its ports, communications, manpower and industrial potential is the key to the defence of the Middle East and the Middle East cannot be defended without it. Therefore all our studies of strategic requirements in other countries in the Middle East deal with what we need in those countries either to enable us to move into Egypt at the beginning of another war or alternatively to help us in a defence of the Middle East conducted from Egypt as its main base area.

4.   Thus the development required in Aden, Somaliland, Kenya and the Sudan is not very great. Each of these places has its limited use both for peace and war, and each will be developed to the extent required by its uses. These uses may be summarised as follows:—

(a) Aden is a fuelling and replenishment base for the Navy and R.A.F. and its retention is essential for the control of sea and air communications in the Red Sea and Persian Gulf;
(b) British Somaliland occupies a strategic position for the control of sea and air communications at the mouth of the Red Sea;
(c) Kenya offers facilities for the control of sea communications in the Indian Ocean and is also being developed as a storeholding area in peacetime;
(d) The Sudan is an important link in our Imperial air, sea and potential land communications.

5.   Libya, however, is a different matter. Quite apart from the fact that it is an area from which offensive air operations can be developed and our sea

---

[1] An outer ring of countries adjacent to Egypt was distinct from the Outer Ring which was a defence line running through Turkey and the Zagros mountains down to Iran and the Persian Gulf.

communications in the Eastern Mediterranean protected, it is also virtually the only area from which land forces could enter Egypt immediately on the threat of war. It is chiefly for this reason that the Chiefs of Staff have pressed so strongly that we should obtain control of this territory by means of an agreement. They have recently stated their requirements in this territory as follows:—

(a) the right to develop the country as a Naval, Military and Air base from which we could:—
    (i) start strategic air action at the outset of a war;
    (ii) rapidly deploy forces for the establishment and defence of the main base in Egypt, which is vital to the conduct of a war in the Middle East.
(b) The right to locate in the country in peacetime both armed forces and stores depots.

6.   Your letter mentions all the territory noted above but it does not mention either Malta or Cyprus. These two islands are of course of immense importance to the outer ring of the Middle East defences. The strategic value of Malta speaks for itself; but considerable developments of such facilities as underground storage and power stations will be necessary if Malta is again to withstand heavy attack with modern weapons.

7.   Cyprus might be said to occupy a strategic position which, in its relation to an attack by Russia from the north, is not unlike Malta's position on the flank of the German attack in the late war. But much development of port facilities, communications and indeed of every nature would be necessary before Cyprus could be used as an offensive base.

8.   This completes the list of countries around Egypt which are British possessions or in which we have a special position. We therefore come to the second part of your questions which assume that we get none of our requirements in Egypt, not even the right to re-entry in war.

9.   But Egypt—as we have already seen—is essential to the defence of the Middle East; and if we are to defend the Middle East at all we should have to go into Egypt, with or without Egyptian consent, immediately on or before the outbreak of war, so as to allow early development of a base of the required size in that country. This fact cannot be over-emphasised.

10.   This does not mean that our needs in countries of the outer ring are any less important. On the contrary, it makes it even more vitally important that we should retain full strategic rights in Libya. It would only be by using troops stationed in Libya in peacetime that we should be able to secure a base in Egypt immediately on the outbreak of a war and thus be able to take the necessary measures in its defence. If the rights that we required in Libya were not obtained, thus preventing us from entering Egypt on the outbreak of a war, then our ability to maintain a firm hold in the Middle East would be destroyed.

11.   The Minister of Defence has seen and agreed this reply.

115   FO 371/69193, no 1872   12 Mar 1948

[Policy towards the Sudan and Egypt]: FO note of a meeting with Mr Bevin and E A Chapman Andrews on the Sudan ordinance and military questions   [Extract]

[There was a growing disagreement between the FO and the Cairo embassy over the line of approach to Egypt and the demands that Britain should make on the Egyptians. The ambassador believed that all that mattered was the Egyptians' willingness to permit re-entry. If they granted re-entry rights then Britain did not need a treaty. If they were unwilling to do so then any treaty provisions would have little value. Consequently the embassy was more inclined to favour a general agreement rather than the securing of specific rights (FO 371/69174, no 1685, minute by M R Wright, 27 Feb 1948). In March, the new minister at the embassy was recalled to London to discuss these questions.]

... *Mr. Chapman Andrews* said in reply[1] to a question that the Embassy had been making good progress with the Egyptians on military questions until difficulties became acute over the Sudan ordinance. It had been proposed that the Egyptian Minister of Defence who had himself been a soldier should come to the U.K. rather as suggested in the instructions to Sir R. Campbell. Now everything was held up on account of the difficulty with the ordinance. If the new proposal succeeded we might also put across our ideas on military questions. King Farouk thought that there would be war this year. Mr. Chapman Andrews therefore considered that the Egyptian authorities were in a mood to talk about strategic requirements now. But he wondered whether the instructions given to Sir R. Campbell now represented the best method. King Farouk had put forward his scheme on a regional basis. Mr. Chapman Andrews would suggest that while standing firmly on our existing treaties with the Middle Eastern countries we might send someone like Lord Wavell or Lord Tedder around the Arab capitols [sic] to talk to their governments about the defence of the Middle East. If these talks went well we might then persuade Azzam Pasha, who he thought was well disposed to us, to organise the Arab League in favour of our ideas.

The Secretary of State pointed out that this was a difficult moment for such action because we might appear to be interfering indirectly with the question of the partition of Palestine. Supposing, for instance, that the United Nations were to propose sanctions against the Arab States for their opposition to the partition at a moment when we were negotiating with those States, we should be in a very awkward position.

Mr. Chapman Andrews thought there was a chance that the Arab States would accept a Jewish State sooner or later. They would fight against partition unless there were a strong armed force to defend it. The Arab States feared that the Russians would come through Azerbaijan to Iraq.

The Secretary of State said that he had little faith in Azzam Pasha and in a fact thought that he hated us.

Mr. Chapman Andrews said that he could not agree. He thought that Azzam respected us and the Secretary of State personally.

Mr. Roberts agreed that Azzam did not hate us but thought that he was not very effective in practice.

---

[1] The first part of the talks dealt with the Sudan.

Mr. Chapman Andrews admitted that the method he had suggested would entail delicate handling, but pointed out that a considerable body of opinion including Brigadier Clayton[2] was in favour of an approach on these lines.

The Secretary of State said that he had hoped to approach the question in another way. He had shown his willingness to revise the Egyptian and Iraqi Treaties and he had made the 1946 Transjordan Treaty. Thus there would have been a firm basis of three Treaties with Middle East States of a similar type perhaps with more to come. On this basis we could withdraw our forces but keep the necessary facilities and work through Joint Defence Boards. He still thought that this was the best approach. Otherwise there was the danger that the Arab League would immediately demand a revision of all existing treaties with the implication that the facilities now available would be withdrawn from us. Iraq might again want to sign a new treaty after the elections which were due in some three months. He was afraid that, if we adopted the approach suggested by Mr. Chapman Andrews, Egypt would induce the other States to insist on weakening the position we held under our existing treaties.

Mr. Chapman Andrews thought that the other States would not agree to any such suggestion by Egypt because they would want us to be in a position to organise effectively the defence of the Middle East.

The Secretary of State said that he would like an alliance with the Middle East States on the lines of the Western Union which would have the U.S. behind it. This could be called the Middle East Union. Such a union would not, of course, affect existing treaties.

Mr. Roberts pointed out that the trouble was the question of our reentry facilities. Since the Middle East Governments were so much less relaible [sic] than the Western Governments, and also so much less well organised from the military point of view, we had to insist on explicit arrangements.

The Secretary of State agreed. The Middle East States did not possess highly developed defensive systems like the Western States, so that we had to insist on such facilities. We must be able to leave stores in the Middle Eastern States because the Mediterranean might be closed at the very start of the next war.

Sir R. Howe said that the necessary facilities could be offered in the Sudan.

The Secretary of State said that the Western Union meant that five States worked together, instead of two as in the case of ordinary alliance. They worked together not only for defence purposes but economically and he would like to do the same with Egypt and the Middle East Governments. But he did not wish to propose this to the Egyptian Government because they must not be allowed to think that H.M.G. were running after them. He had told the Egyptian Ambassador that the time had come to clear up one way or another the question whether the Egyptian Government wanted a friendly agreement with H.M.G. or not.

---

[2] Brigadier Iltyd Nicholl Clayton, minister at the Cairo embassy, 1947-Feb 1948, and head of the British Middle East Office until 1948.

116 FO 371/69193, no 2130   23 Mar 1948

'Egypt-defence arrangements': minute by D W Lascelles on the defence proposals and the attitudes of the Egyptian government

The problem

It will be recalled that when Sir R. Campbell returned to Egypt with fresh instructions a few weeks ago and proposed to the Egyptians that our common defence problems and evacuation difficulties should be studied by Egyptian Service personnel, King Farouk seemed disposed to favour the idea. It was only later, when the same suggestions were made to Nokrashi, that there was a definitely unfavourable reaction. The question therefore arises whether it is possible and desirable for us to continue to press our suggestion upon the Egyptian authorities at the stage now reached.

2. Although in Sir R. Campbell's conversation with Nokrashi the latter did not specifically link his negative attitude towards our defence proposals with the question of the Sudan ordinance on constitutional reform, it is evident that the two questions were in fact linked together in his mind. Even the more favourably-disposed Egyptians, such as the Minister for Foreign Affairs[1] and Hassan Youssef, had shown considerable nervousness of anything becoming known about the proposed talks and visits of Egyptian Service authorities; and it may be assumed that in the state of increased tension brought about by the controversy over the Sudan ordinance they would now be more nervous still. Any renewed proposals which we now make to the Egyptians in regard to defence and evacuation will have to be made to the King rather than to Nokrashi. But Mr. Chapman Andrews when he was here agreed that so long as Nokrashi remained in office we were most unlikely to make any progress with the Egyptian Government. He went back to Egypt with authority for Sir R. Campbell to make one further attempt to induce the Egyptians to accept the Sudan ordinance. That attempt, it was recognised here, stood no chance of success unless it could be combined with Nokrashi's dismissal. Sir R. Campbell was therefore given three weeks, from the date of Mr Chapman Andrews' return, to try his luck on these lines.

3. Mr Chapman Andrews took back with him his own draft,[2] of which a copy is attached, of the sort of lines on which King Farouk might be tackled about our defence problem. We discussed the draft with him here, and I think that there is much to be said for a harangue on the lines proposed at some stage, though not immediately. No action will of course be taken till we telegraph the recommendations.

4. It is recommended that no further attempt should be made to secure Egyptian acceptance of our defence proposals (i.e. inter-Service talks about defence and evacuation) until we see the result of Sir R. Campbell's final bid to secure acceptance of the Sudan ordinance and incidentally to unseat Nokrashi. Thereafter the matter can be considered further, but our decision will then naturally depend largely on the extent to which we may have decided to ignore Egyptian reactions in regard to the Sudan ordinance. Only if we were to adopt some comparatively mild course, such for example as a proposal for official talks under a neutral arbitrator, would there be any chance of our making any immediate progress on the defence side of the problem.

---

[1] Khashaba Pasha.   [2] See 117.

117   FO 371/69193, no 1872   Mar 1948

'Egypt and defence: suggested manner of approach to King Farouk': draft memorandum by E A Chapman Andrews

[The memorandum was drafted following the meeting Chapman Andrews had in London on 12 March and was taken back to Egypt by him.]

To speak in this wise:-

As your Majesty is aware, the total number of British military personnel in Egypt, including British troops of all arms and German prisoners of war, amounts to very nearly ten times the Treaty figure of 10,000. This high figure is not surprising in the light of the fact that we had approximately ten times the present figure in or based on Egypt at the end of the war. Since then we have reduced numbers everywhere as rapidly as possible and the process would have been more rapid in respect of Egypt but for our withdrawals from India and Palestine.

2.   His Majesty's Government wish to give your Majesty an assurance that every effort is being made to get down to the Treaty figure in Egypt in the shortest possible time, if only for reasons of economy of manpower and overseas expenditure. That process is estimated to take at least eighteen months from the present date.

3.   Reduction to the Treaty figure can, however, be hastened, if Your Majesty will agree to accept the suggestion made by Sir Ronald Campbell that a joint Anglo–Egyptian committee or commission of technical military experts be appointed to study the detailed technical aspects of the problems. This is necessary mainly because of the problem of stores, of which our military hold something like 1,000,000 tons in Egypt.

4.   The committee would, as proposed by Sir Ronald Campbell, also consider together general problems of Egyptian and Middle East defence. In this respect they would make recommendations to their two Governments, though these need not be *agreed* recommendations, for the committee would be one of fact-finding and enquiry and in no sense of negotiation. Any negotiations for the settlement of the defence problem would be for the two Governments later.

5.   Once we have reached the Treaty figure, further reductions will depend entirely on any progress the two Governments may have made, in the light of the recommendations of the joint technical committee, towards agreement. His Majesty's Government want to reach agreement with Egypt over this problem because, for one thing, it will save us manpower and money, and, for another, it will mean more effective and wholehearted co-operation. The Middle East is a vital strategic region for us, however, and we are not prepared to sacrifice our existing Treaties with countries in that region merely in exchange for general agreements that do not give us the strategic facilities we need. This is solely because of the distance of the Middle East region from the United Kingdom. In the case of Western European nations their proximity to our island renders it unnecessary for us to seek from them strategic facilities in peace-time. Moreover the technical and scientific standards of achievement and the modern military equipment, organisation and experience of those nations enables them, with a minimum of advice and assistance from us, to maintain stores, equipment, technical installations, fuel reserves, air-fields and accommodation for troops in a state of complete readiness for war. Under our existing Treaties we guarantee the defence of certain Middle East countries. We

are willing and prepared to continue to guarantee them and possibly others in the Middle East region. This is a heavy obligation on our part and we must look to the nations concerned to appreciate our difficulties and the threatening nature of the general world situation and to support our unremitting efforts to safeguard peace by agreeing to our minimum strategic requirements on a basis of mutual aid. We have no wish to interfere in the internal affairs of the Middle East States. All we intend to do is to ensure their security and independence, because, by so doing, we ensure our own. If there were a future war, the period of the out-break of hostilities would be a vital one. We must be able to hit so hard from the air during that period that we can prevent or hamper the enemy from mustering and deploying his own assault forces, whether land or air. Swift and effective action by our air forces will be Egypt's first line of defence. Hence our insistence on certain minimum peace-time facilities in the Middle East which we do not require in Western Europe. Finally there is the point that, though it is known that Your Majesty's own ideas on the subject are in agreement with those of His Majesty's Government, there are certain Egyptian politicians who affect to believe that once British troops are out of the way, it will be possible for Egypt to follow a course of neutrality in a future world war. This is of course not only a false and unfounded hope but might, if unchecked, become a fatal weakness to our alliance. His Majesty's Government therefore ask Your Majesty to leave the politicians in no doubt about your intention at once to declare war in the event of a future war between His Majesty's Government and another European Power.

6.   If Your Majesty is in agreement with the above we shall on reaching the Treaty figure be prepared further to reduce our forces in the Canal Zone to as few as 1,000 men. We should naturally, however, not be precluded from reinforcing these men in an apprehanded [sic] international emergency. We shall be prepared to do this by a date which can only be fixed in the light of the report of the joint technical committee referred to above, because it will depend entirely upon the disposal of the 1,000,000 tons of military stores. If Egypt will agree to cooperate with us in the disposal of part and the guarding on the spot of the remainder of these stores, the date can be advanced substantially beyond that which will be necessary if we have to remove the greater part. We must assume that, at the beginning of the next war, the Mediterranean will be closed. It will therefore be best for us to leave and maintain in good order the greater part of our stores now in Egypt. This, however, we can only do in agreement with the Egyptian Government and the cooperation of the Egyptian Army. In addition we should require cooperation of the Egyptian forces in the maintenance of a transit airfield which could be used by the Royal Air Force. These arrangements could be covered by an exchange of notes.

7.   As for the prospects of agreement with the Egyptian Government, His Majesty's Government confess that their experience of the past two or three years has made them unhopeful. It has been suggested that the Egyptian Government, knowing full well that practical difficulties alone make the early military evacuation of Egypt impossible, have felt it quite safe from the international security point of view, to pursue a positively obstructive and unfriendly line towards us in order to enhance their reputation in the country for 'patriotism'. We know that Your Majesty, however, on the contrary, has done your best to smooth the path to agreement. Your Majesty's suggestion about a new approach to the whole problem of British strategic requirements in the Middle East was studied with great interest by His Majesty's

Government. They do not exclude the possibility of the success of such an approach, but feel that the most important first step is the settlement in a friendly manner of our relations with Egypt and a return to that sort of mutual aid that characterised our association during the war. His Majesty's Government urge Your Majesty, therefore, to take strong measures with the Egyptian Government to secure their cooperation with us, without further loss of time, on the lines suggested above. Great Britain is the only European state on which Egypt can safely rely. His Majesty's Government appeal to Your Majesty to bring the Egyptian Government into line, without further obstruction and delay, with British efforts to preserve freedom in Europe, without which there can be no freedom in Egypt.

8.   Your Majesty will appreciate that His Majesty's Government for their part are satisfied with the existing Treaty, on which they intend to rely. This does not mean, however, that they will not be prepared, should the situation warrant it in the light of the success of the plan outlined above, to include any new agreement of a military nature affecting our alliance in a new treaty which, while providing for our minimum needs as set forth above, would be valid for a much longer period, say 20 years, or even 50 years, like the Western Union, and therefore be a much more stable element in the security system of the Middle East and therefore in the peace of the world.

9.   Finally, His Majesty's Government would welcome a general regional alliance with the States of the Middle East, or a group of them, of a general political, financial, economic and military nature similar to that which His Majesty's Government has just concluded with certain Western European nations, commonly called the Western Union. His Majesty's Government would welcome the establishment of a Middle Eastern Union which, as in the case of the Western Union, would not affect any Treaties already in force with the separate States of the union. The pursuance of this object could, therefore, quite conveniently be in parallel with that by which we now suggest that Anglo–Egyptian relations and mutual security be put upon a satisfactory footing.

118 FO 141/1292, no 32   25 Mar–1 Apr 1948
[Evacuation from Egypt]: minutes by E A Chapman Andrews and Sir R Campbell

As recorded elsewhere I was told to make it clear on my return to Cairo that there could be no question now of H.M.G. agreeing to withdraw from Egypt or evacuate Egypt. The diminution of our forces in Egypt below the Treaty level which cannot in any case occur much before 18 months' time can only occur then as a result of a reasonable agreement with Egypt giving us our minimum strategic requirements. I was told in the Foreign Office that evacuation or withdrawal were terms that did not accord with the realities of the present international situation.

E.A.C.A.
25.3.48

But readiness to reduce our troops to 1,000 men, probably in civilian clothes, is equivalent to evacuation as we have hither to discussed it with the Egyptians. It has always been, in effect, conditional on our getting the facilities we require. The difference now, I take it, is that we must have a right of re-entry in writing and are not ready to give the appearance of 'Evacuating' independently of agreement on 'facilities', or of agreeing to evacuate prior to securing written agreement on facilities. The nature of 'evacuation' (or non-evacuation) remains, as far as I can see, unchanged.

R.C.

1.4.48

119   FO 141/1285, no 20   21 Apr 1948

[Nationalist agitation in the Middle East]: inward despatch no 31 from J M Troutbeck (BMEO) to Mr Bevin. *Enclosure*: note from a British subject resident in the Middle East, nd

I have the honour to acknowledge the receipt of your despatch No. 44 of the 7th of April in which you invited my observations on a memorandum concerning the reaction in Iraq to the Treaty of Portsmouth[1] and the general subject of nationalist agitation in Middle East countries.

2.   The memorandum appears to me, if I may say so, to cover the ground with such clarity and common sense that few comments are required. I venture, however, to offer a few observations on one or two points.

3.   In paragraph 2(f) of the memorandum the question is raised whether we should not in future give more weight to the advantage of early public discussion of treaty negotiations. Here we seem to be between the devil and the deep sea. One of the reasons for the rejection of the Treaty of Portsmouth is said to be the secrecy in which the preliminary talks were conducted. On the other hand, public discussion of our relations with Egypt seems to have no other effect than to render a solution more and more difficult. Perhaps the answer is that it matters less how the negotiations are conducted than whom we conduct them with. Our difficulty both in Iraq and Egypt is that public opinion has not been behind the governments with which we have negotiated. Whether we negotiate in secrecy or otherwise, we shall always be incurring a risk if we negotiate with a weak and unpopular government. On

---

[1] On 15 January 1948 representatives of Britain and Iraq signed the Treaty of Portsmouth which was to replace the treaty of 1930 and under which Britain guaranteed to come to the aid of Iraq if the latter were attacked. The treaty was never ratified owing to the opposition and violent protests it produced in Iraq. These centered on the annexure to the treaty which laid down the conditions under which the RAF would continue to use bases at Habbaniya and Shaiba. In the event of 'a menace of hostilities' or if Britain or Iraq were involved in hostilities, the King of Iraq undertook to invite Britain to bring all necessary forces to Iraq and to furnish all the aid and assistance in his power. This was to include the use of railways, rivers, ports, aerodromes and lines of communications on the same financial terms as Iraqi forces. Britain would provide the technical staff at Habbaniya and Shaiba that were deemed necessary for the operational efficiency of the bases. In addition, until the peace treaties with all ex-enemy countries entered into force (meaning when all allied forces were withdrawn), the King of Iraq agreed to grant the RAF free access to, and use of, Habbaniya and Shaiba including their use by aircraft in transit. After the treaties entered into force the King of Iraq would invite the RAF to use the bases on the advice of the Anglo–Iraqi Joint Defence Board which would be established under the terms of the treaty.

the other hand if there is a strong and popular government to negotiate with the actual method of negotiation will be a matter of secondary importance.

4.   This leads to two other points brought out in the memorandum, viz: the Arab capacity for hero-worship and the dangerous influence of the extreme right in Arab countries. There is always the possibility, is [sic] not the likelihood, that the "heroes" will be found among the ranks of the extreme right and therefore that governments based upon it may be the only ones with whom it is worth while negotiating. This may place us in a certain dilemma, as the "heroes" may be persons who sided openly against us in the last war, or who at any rate hold and preach views indistinguishable from Fascist. Each case would presumably have to be decided on its merits, but I suggest that we should be guided more by the effects on our relations with the Arab States than by ideological prejudices. It seems clear from the memorandum on Stalinsim enclosed in your circular despatch No. 046 of the 31st March that the Soviet Government would have no compunction, if it suited its purpose, in supporting a national movement led by an ex-Fascist. Similarly experience shows that Fascists are always prepared to compromise with Communism if they think it expedient, and I doubt if we should be wise to rely on an Arab extremist being an exception despite the religious obstacle. If so, the possibility of a deal between communists and extreme right in the Arab world cannot safely be excluded. This seems a further reason why it would be a mistake to give the impression to the extreme right, whatever the past history of some of its members, that we would never in any circumstance have dealings with it.

5.   In paragraph 13 of the paper attention is drawn to the innate Arab admiration for ruthlessness and violence. This has particular relevance to our own propaganda, one of the main planks of which is to protest that we ourselves are no longer ruthless and violent. I suggest that in addition to persuading the Arabs that we have changed our spots, we need to show them that we still have strength behind us.

6.   Paragraph 15 of the memorandum draws attention to our main difficulty in all the countries of the Middle East, namely that we have always been forced into the position of appearing to back the forces of reaction since we cannot risk a violent upheaval. This paragraph might perhaps be read in connection with the suggestion referred to in the last paragraph of the paper in which the importance is stressed of increasing social contacts between the effendis[1] and the British official and unofficial residents.

7.   Mention of the effendis raises a further point to which attention might perhaps be drawn. A large proportion of the Arabs who receive a western education receive it in French institutions. It is difficult to believe that many kind words are heard about the United Kingdom in a French school or university in the Middle East. The staff are probably for the most part bitterly anti-British. The result must be that many educated Arabs start their adult life with a prejudice against ourselves taught to them from their earliest years in French institutions. I read in the press not long ago that we have recently concluded a cultural agreement with France and, though I am unable to refer to its text as no copy appears to exist in Cairo, it occurs to me that advantage might be taken of the agreement to discuss the whole question of education in the Middle East from this point of view.

---

[1] The professional classes of Egypt.

8.   I should like, if I may, to endorse the suggestion made at the beginning of paragraph 16 that we should not modify our policy of advocating social progress and economic development. At the same time it would be difficult to over-emphasise the unlikelihood of quick results in these respects. This follows not merely from the reasons given in paragraph 14 of the memorandum. There are others of equal validity. Before economic development can make much progress in the Arab states, the whole mentality of the Moslem Arabs will have to be transformed. They will have to learn to do patient, honest, plodding work instead of looking only for quick profits and results. I was much struck by a conversation I recently had with the manager of a foreign bank in Bagdad. He told me that the only Moslems that his branch had been able to employ were porters and such like. No Moslem was capable of or inclined to undertake ordinary, honest work on an office stool and such jobs had to be given to Jews and Christians. A further impediment to economic development is the financial straits into which the Arab countries are drifting. Not only is foreign exchange likely to become more and more of a problem, but the governments are having difficulties in finding even the local currency they require. Finally, economic development demands a modicum of political stability. Things are not going well in that direction. It is only necessary to point to the sanguinary riots that took place in Alexandria this month, to the recent telegrams from Bagdad on the situation in Iraq, and to the appeals lately made to us by the Lebanese government to save their country from a situation in which it would be likely to break up.

9.   I venture to suggest that the words "and at home" might usefully be added at the end of paragraph 16(c) of the memorandum. Rash and frequently smug remarks made at home are reported out there and cause great irritation.

10.   I have some doubts whether we should be wise to rely too much on the effectiveness of Ibn Saud or Abdulla as our allies in the Middle East, as suggested in paragraph 16(e) of the memorandum, even though their loyalty may be unquestioned. Moreover if it became apparent that we are placing our chief confidence in the most reactionary rulers, our sincerity in preaching democracy and social reform elsewhere is bound to be called in question.

11.   With regard to paragraph 16(e) (3), it is worth mentioning that in fact many present members of government in the Arab countries started as members of the effendi class and have risen to their present position.

12.   While I entirely agree with paragraph 16(e) (4) I suggest that we should avoid making invidious comparisons and should always bear in mind the yardstick we are using, which would not be that of the home civil service. Condemnation should, that is to say, be absolute and not comparative.

13.   Finally I have the honour to enclose a copy of a note embodying some ideas which were put to me in a conversation I recently had with a British subject who has lived many years in the Middle East. It seems to me that these ideas are worthy of consideration, particularly the suggestion of endeavouring to associate the non-official British community still more closely with our national effort and projection in the Middle East. I think too that the patient approach which he advocates is more likely to produce results than any dramatic appeal to the imagination of the effendis, even if any appropriate appeal could be devised.

14.   I am sending a copy of this despatch to His Majesty's Representatives at Washington, Cairo, Bagdad, Jedda, Amman, Beirut, Damascus and Teheran, and to the Political Resident in the Persian Gulf.

Enclosure to 119

1.   British representatives and their staffs should be encouraged to give their social patronage to those people who are sincerely trying to do something constructive in their own countries. They should also be encouraged gradually to avoid the blandishments and parties of the ultra-rich and social climbers, and quietly to indicate their disapproval of the matter's [sic] mode of living. This attitude should gradually be inculcated in all British working throughout the Middle East, through bank managers, oil companies, British Council, Arab Centre of Studies and so forth.

2.   Accombined [sic] Anglo–American campaign through educational and missionary establishments with the co-operation of big business, oil, etc. to inculcate by instruction and example the principles of social responsibility. It is very important to get the material *young*—witness the success and influence of Victoria College and the English School.

3.   Organize an approach to the semi-educated intelligentsia, to win them from politics and to give their energies to constructive social work in these countries. I believe something *can* be done on these lines with the co-operation of certain English and local pesonalities [sic].

4.   Avoid giving the impression, which some facets of our present policy do, that we are interfering in these countries' local affairs and are weaving over-all schemes, political, strategic and economic, etc. etc. for *our* own benefit.

5.   When occasion demands, go in for devastatingly plain speaking in public and private, a facing of realities and a truce to wishful thinkings.

6.   I firmly believe that with the guidance and influence of the Foreign Service and the help of a number of obscurer but most admirable people, who still carry the torch quietly but most effectively, we *can*, given a few years, steady public opinion in these countries.

120   DEFE 5/11, COS(48)111   13 May 1948
'Staff study "Intermezzo"': report by the Commanders-in-Chief, Middle East to the COS   [Extract]

[On Apr 14 the Committee on Service Stores in Egypt produced a skeleton interim report on the factors involved in a move from Egypt. The speed of evacuation depended on the completion of the transfer of stores and the preparation of alternative accommodation for Middle East HQ and the troops then in Egypt. The report concluded that the transfer of stores should be completed by Mar 1950. Therefore the limiting factor on a speedy evacuation was more the provision of new accommodation than, as had been claimed, the removal of stores. Given that the only suitable site for HQ was deemed to be Cyrenaica, preparations could not begin until it was decided that Britain would remain in Cyrenaica permanently or some other site was chosen. Unlike the departure from India which coincided with a rapid run down of the services, and unlike the evacuation of Palestine when troops could be fitted into existing accommodation, there were no alternative areas for troops from Egypt in which new construction and additional expenditure would not be involved (FO 371/69174, no 2712, report on stores in Egypt and evacuation, 14 Apr 1948). Unfortunately the future of Cyrenaica had still not been determined and the commission of the Council of Foreign Ministers' Deputies had only visited Libya in Mar. British policy remained the securing of the trusteeship of Tripolitania and Cyrenaica or the creation of an independent Libya which was expected to grant Britain the desired facilities (CAB 129/24, CP(48)43, 4 Feb 1948). The 'Intermezzo' study was therefore undertaken when pressure was mounting to abort the planned Egyptian evacuation. It was based on estimates of forces available in 1957–1958 which current military thinking assumed was the earliest possible date the Soviets would be likely to start a major war.]

1.   In the summer of 1947 it was decided by the Commander-in-Chief *Melf* that the time had come to start a Study of *Middle East* strategy in the event of a war with *Russia*. At the same time a paper arrived from the Commander-in-Chief *East Indies* Station, which brought to the notice of Commanders-in-Chief, *Middle East* an appreciation on the tactical aspects of the *Persian Gulf*.

2.   In October, 1947 Commanders-in-Chief *Middle East* decided that this paper pointed the way to the setting of the Study they wished to make, because it had been thought by some that our *Middle East strategy laid too much emphasis on the importance of the Eastern Mediterranean* area and that perhaps the strategical centre of gravity had now shifted further East. They accordingly agreed to hold an interservice study in the spring of 1948.

3.   Before a start could be made, certain information and estimates only available in *London* had to be obtained. These were received in January, 1948 and included:—

(a) An estimate of the forces that might be available to us and to the Russians in the *Middle East* ten years hence. It should be noted that the air forces allotted by the Air Ministry were for study purposes only.

(b) A Foreign Office forecast of the political situation in the *Middle East* in 1958.

(c) An appreciation of the importance of *Middle East* oil. This stated that should the Allies be denied the *Bahrein/Saudi Arabian* oil for more than twelve months, their war effort would be severely restricted.

The above information was used to draw up the opening narrative for the Study.

4.   Because of the effort and time that it would take to re-capture the *Bahrein/Saudi Arabian* oilfields, should they be lost, together with the fact that physical re-occupation would not necessarily make available immediate supplies of oil, and because the restriction mentioned in 3(c) above was considered so crippling, the aim of the Study was taken to be:—

> "To study strategy in the *Middle East*, with the direct view to ensuring the supply of oil from the *Persian Gulf* area in the event of a war against *Russia*".

5.   JIC(ME) and JPS(ME) then appreciated the situation from the Russian and Allied points of view.

6.   During the conduct of the Study the above papers were elaborated in a series of presentations and discussions, and in addition consideration was given to the administrative problems involved. The administrative development required is summarised at Annex.[1]

7.   It was not practicable in this Study to evaluate the effects on *Russia* of an Allied strategic air offensive, applying the full Allied resources in absolute weapons. Weight must, however, be given to the view that these agents might not be immediately decisive, might be successfully countered, or considerations of policy might forbid their use.

8.   With this in mind, and taking into account the Allied forces given in the setting, we appreciated that it was within the capacity of the *Russians* to overrun

---

[1] Not printed.

Persia, *Iraq* and the *Saudi Arabian* oilfields and to be ready to carry out an offensive against *Egypt* in the first few months of a war. We further appreciated that the Russians, realising the importance of the *Eastern Mediterranean countries* to us, would deploy the greater part of their effort against this area.

Thus, in fact, one of the Pillars of our Imperial strategy would be imperilled.

9.   It emerged that there was only one method of slowing down the *Russian* advance both *Southwards* to the *Persian Gulf* and Westward to the *Mediterranean* to a degree sufficiently great to enable our small Army to hold them before reaching areas vital to us and that was by an all out policy of air interdiction on their limited lines of communication.

10.   To make this possible we concluded that whether the conduct of the next war is absolute or conventional the following are our fundamental minimum requirements:-

(a) A powerful air force operating from a belt of modern and secure airfields in *Egypt*, *Cyprus* and along the north coast of *Africa*, with the task of strategic bombing, interdiction on the enemy's Lines of Communication, and defence of our vulnerable areas.

(b) Security of sea communications in the *Mediterranean* for maintaining the airfields of North *Africa* and the base in *Egypt*. This demands continuous fighter and anti-submarine cover for shipping in the *Mediterranean*, for which the functioning of *Malta* as a base for Naval and Air Forces is vital. *Alexandria* will also be required as a forward Fleet base.

(c) The deployment in *Transjordan* of an Allied army, fully supported by air forces, with the task of preventing the Russians from establishing themselves on the Eastern Bank of the *Jordan*, and of eventually eliminating the Russian threat to *Egypt*. To do this, it will be necessary to enter *Palestine* quickly and establish advanced air bases there, as those in *Transjordan* will be insufficient.

(d) The existence in *Egypt* at the outbreak of war of a base capable of supporting the forces in (a) (b) and (c) above. The capacity of *Cyrenaica* is too small to meet these requirements.

11.   The above fundamental requirements will be greatly assisted by:—

(a) In peace, the coordination of *Middle East* defence by means of Missions and Joint Defence Boards, and by increasing the efficiency of indigenous forces.

(b) The existence of an efficient *Iraqi* army which will assist in delaying the Russian advance, supported by Allied Air Forces operating for as long as possible from forward bases in *Iraq*.

(c) Attacks by Allied Air Forces on the Russian flank from bases in *Turkey*. On account of its position, this country is particularly suitable for such action.

(d) The preparation of *Cyprus* as a fully stocked fortress for operations by fighter and bomber aircraft.

(e) The introduction into *Persia* and *Iraq* of agents to inspire and organize guerilla activity.

12.   The successful defence of the *Persian Gulf* is not in itself vital to the defence of the *Middle East*. But since it is not possible to state at this stage whether the next war will be long or short, and since the loss of the oil from the *Saudi Arabian* oilfields for a period longer than twelve months would be crippling, we must plan to secure at least these oilfields by the following measures—these measures must be without

prejudice to the forces deployed and the essential development in the Eastern *Mediterranean*.

(a) The deployment of Allied sea, land and air forces in the *Persian Gulf*, before the outbreak of war, with the task of ensuring the continued use of the oil from the *Bahrein/Saudi Arabian* oilfields. Once these oilfields are lost, their recapture would be a long and costly operation.

(b) The establishment of an advanced base at *Karachi* to hold reserves for, and to support operations in, the *Persian Gulf*.

(c) The existence in East *Africa*, at the outbreak of war, of an army base for the forces in the *Persian Gulf* area.

13.   Though as mentioned in paragraph two there has been some thought here that too much emphasis was being laid on the more Western part of the *Middle East*, this Study has made clear to us that:—

(a) Our *Middle East* strategy cannot lay too much emphasis on the importance of *Egypt* being available to the Allies at the outbreak of war as a base. *Egypt* is still the corner stone of our defence plans for the *Middle East*. We must, therefore, have a treaty with *Egypt* which enables us to have ready and use that country as a willing base against Russian aggression from the outset. This point must be fully appreciated in future treaty negotiations with the Egyptians . . . .

121   DEFE 4/14, COS 98(48)9   12 July 1948
'Middle East defence policy – potentialities and scale and direction of attack—1950': report by the JIC to the COS, 7 June 1948, (JIC (48) 12/1). *Annexes*

At the request of the Joint Planning Staff, we prepared for use in their discussions with the Americans a report on potentialities and scale and direction of attack on the Middle East in 1950. This report was prepared at short notice, and the Joint Intelligence Committee had not intended to finalise it. However, the Joint Planning Staff have informed us that the report (with the general terms of which the Americans were in agreement), would be useful as providing the necessary intelligence background on which to base the directive which they are drawing up for the Commanders-in-Chief, Middle East for the preparation of outline plans to meet an attack by enemy forces in the period up to July 1949.

2.   In view of the time factor involved, we accordingly recommend that the Chiefs of Staff approve the report for the purposes of this directive to Commanders-in-Chief, Middle East. We are, however, basing future assessments of enemy intentions on a new and, we hope, more realistic approach to the problem, and in particular we are reassessing enemy intentions in the Middle East. We suggest, therefore, that the Chiefs of Staff approval to the present report should be without prejudice to our subsequent appreciation (re Nature and scale of enemy attack in the Middle East).

3.   In the present report we have estimated at Annexes A, B and C respectively:-[1]

---

[1] Annex A and the appendix to Annex C are not printed.

(a) The individual and collective potentialities both in armed forces and material of the Middle East countries.

(b) The place in Russian strategy which an attack on the Middle East is likely to take.

(c) The probable scale and directions of attacks against the Middle East countries by the Soviet Union between now and 1950.

We have consulted the Joint Administrative Planning Staff and their logistic assessments are attached as an Appendix to Annex C.

4.   Our assumptions are as follows:—

(a) War with the Soviet Union will start between now and 1950.

(b) The frontiers of the Soviet Union are the same as in 1948.

(c) The present Satellite States are under complete Russian domination.

(d) We retain the sovereignty of Cyprus.

(e) Greece, Turkey and Persia remain outside the sphere of Soviet influence and opposed to it.

(f) (i) We have control of the sea communications throughout the Mediterranean.

(ii) The Russians have a general knowledge of the strength and dispositions of the Anglo–Saxon forces in the Middle East.

(g) We are either still in the Canal Zone or have the right to re-enter Egypt on the threat of war; the base facilities we shall require there are maintained in peace.

(h) We have strategic rights in Libya.

Annex B to 121: the place in Russian strategy which an attack on the Middle East is likely to take

Significance to the Soviet Union of the Middle East countries
The advantages which the Soviet Union would derive from the military occupation of the Middle East countries are considered under two headings, Economic and Military.

Principal resources
2.   The principal resources of the countries under review are discussed below. The strategic importance of Middle East oil resources is discussed separately at Appendix.

3.   *Persia*
Mainly oil. (See Appendix).

4.   *Turkey*
Turkey's production of chrome ore is estimated at about 1/5 or 1/6 of the world's production. There are also deposits of other non-ferrous metals.

5.   *Iraq*
Mainly oil. (See Appendix).
   Iraq annually has an annual exportable surplus of about 225,000 tons of barley.

6. *Kuwait and Saudi Arabia*
Only oil. (See Appendix).

7. *Palestine, Syria and Lebanon, Transjordan*
This area in itself is economically not a rich one, but the pipelines from the Iraq oilfields run through it, and Haifa and Tripoli with their refineries at the terminals are the only outlets for the removal of Iraq oil. (See Appendix) Production of potash in Palestine (a source of fertilisers and bromine, explosives, drugs and dyes) averaged 70,000 tons a year before the war when it was the third largest production in the world. Its relative importance has, however, declined since then and will probably continue to do so. In Transjordan there are large deposits of phospates [sic] but exploitation is difficult and output is at present negligible.

8. *Egypt*
Oil resources (see Appendix).

Egypt produces about 5% of the *world's cotton* and normally has about 400,000 tons for export a year. She has an important exportable surplus of common salt and phosphate of lime.

9. *Greece*
Greece is a source of non-ferrous metals but the deposits are not suitable for large-scale exploitation. Production of bauxite in 1938 was 180,000 tons, amounting to 10% of European and 4% of World output.

Economic advantages to the Soviet Union of occupation of the Middle East countries
   10.   The economic advantages to the Russians of occupation of Middle East countries are of two kinds; those to be derived from the positive value of the resources of these countries and those resulting from denial of these resources to the Western Powers. The advantages of denial would in fact far outweigh the positive benefits to be gained by the Russians.

(a) *Importance to the Russians of denial to the Western powers*
By depriving the Western Powers of the Middle East oilfields the Russians would deny them rather over 10% of their present available supplies rising to about 20% by 1950. This would leave the Western Powers almost entirely dependent on sources of supply in the American Hemisphere (see Appendix). The Russians will probably consider that the Western Powers will be unable to wage a Middle East campaign without the benefit of Middle East oil, and that they will be seriously handicapped in the conduct of their overall war effort. (The factual justice of this appreciation, particularly as it affects the British war effort, is now under investigation by another body).

   The denial to the Western Powers of the other economic resources of the Middle East countries, such as chrome, potash and bauxite would represent an inconvenience but not a serious loss.

(b) *Positive advantages to be gained by the Russians*
Apart from the immediate operational advantages to be gained by seizure of stocks of refined oil and oil products, food and transport facilities of all kinds, particularly

motor transport, the economic advantages to the Russians would be entirely of a long-term nature and would in fact provide no commodities of which the Soviet Union is likely to be critically short.

Military advantages to the Soviet Union of occupation of the Middle East countries

11.   Occupation of the Middle East countries would have the following general military significance:—

(a) It would give the Soviet Union control over the Eastern Mediterranean and the Suez Canal and, in consequence, sever the most direct sea lines of communication between Europe and the Far East.

(b) It would give the Soviet Union an outlet on the Persian Gulf and access to the Indian Ocean.

(c) It would give the Soviet Union control of land routes and it would enable her to sever direct air routes to Pakistan.

(d) It would increase the protection from air attack of the industrial centres of South European Russia:—

   (i) by extending the distance between these areas and any air bases from which they might be attacked by the strategic air forces of the U.S.A. and the U.K.

   (ii) by providing the Soviet Union with fighter bases beyond her frontiers for the interception of any such strategic air attacks.

(e) It would provide the Soviet Union with a foothold in Africa for further exploitation along the Mediterranean coast and towards East Africa.

12.   The economic and military advantages of the occupation of the whole of the Middle East are so great that the Soviet Union would be unlikely to be content with anything less. On the other hand the logistical problems are such that the advance of the Soviet Forces might be slow and might be carried out by stages. Even in the early stages however, the Soviet Union would achieve a number of strategic advantages; thus by the occupation of Persia, Iraq, Turkey and Greece, the Soviet Union would be able:—

(a) To deny the Iraq and Persian oilfields to the Anglo–Saxon powers.

(b) To control the Dardanelles, the Aegean and the sea communications along the Turkish coast.

(c) To improve the air defence of the Soviet Union and to build up in these countries land and air bases for further advance.

Annex C to 121: scale and direction of attack

The Joint Administrative Planning Staff have examined the logistical considerations of a Russian attack on the Middle East other than Greece. Their examination is attached at Appendix.

Capabilities of the Russian air force in 1950

2.   Although some modern jet fighters might be available the Soviet Air Force would be largely equipped with aircraft similar to those in use in the late war. These aircraft would be incapable of providing adequate air cover for operations in the Baghdad-Mosul or Tehran areas until they were deployed South of the present Russian frontier. Although a considerable number of aircraft similar to the B.29 type are likely to be available for a general strategic offensive, any Russian strategic air effort in the Middle East is likely to be of a limited nature.

3.   We consider that these factors will affect the logistic estimates in the following ways:—

(a) *Air interdiction*

Air interdiction by Allied Air Forces cannot be excluded and in fact excellent opportunities are offered at a very difficult stage in the Russian advance, namely as they emerge southwards from the Lake Urmia-Tehran bottleneck. The effect of allied air interdiction can only be assessed when it is known what allied air forces will be available.

(b) *Airborne and air-transported operations*

In order to use the available transport aircraft for airborne operations in the Baghdad-Mosul area it will be necessary to delay such operations until such time as the support aircraft can be deployed South of the present Russian frontier, or to undertake these operations without air cover. This would also apply to air transport operations in the Tehran area. The advantages to the Soviet Union of employing airborne forces to seize the Iraq oilfields intact and to obtain surprise are so great that they might be prepared to take the risk of interference from British fighter aircraft. Such interference would not prevent this Soviet airborne attack from achieving a measure of success even though heavy losses in both aircraft and personnel were inflicted.

Turkish resistance

4.   We consider that the Joint Administrative Planning Staff may have overestimated the delay factor which can be imposed by the Turkish armed forces on a major Russian threat, unless direct aid is provided by British and American forces. We therefore consider that a Russian force of two divisions may well arrive in Northern Syria in 2 to 3 months and not 3 to 4 months.

Administrative considerations

5.   We believe the administrative efficiency of the Russian armed forces to be lower than our own but, by comparison, the Russians can accept lower standards and are adept at emergency improvisation, with the result that mistakes in administration are likely to have less serious consequences.

6.   We have considered how these factors might apply in the Middle East to see if it is necessary to adjust the estimates made by the Joint Administrative Planning Staff which are based on British standards. Our evidence indicates that the Russians have carried out very careful administrative planning before large offensives and it is inconceivable that they have not already studied the administrative aspect of a campaign in the Middle East. Moreover they have available in Turkistan an area where topographical conditions are similar to these of the Middle East and, during the war they gained detailed local knowledge of Persia. An example of their administrative efficiency is the recent withdrawal of five divisions from Bulgaria which was carried out with great speed and efficiency. We do not, therefore, consider that any adjustment, on the grounds of inefficiency, is necessary to the estimates of the Joint Administrative Planning Staff.

Timing of the campaign

7.   If it is assumed that war between now and 1950 would break out by accident, some time may be expected to elapse between the outbreak of war and the start of a

campaign in the Middle East. If the Russians should have failed to concentrate the necessary air transport and airborne forces prior to D day, and if they should then decide to wait until these are in position, it is unlikely that they could start a campaign until D + 1 month. Should they decide, however, to move before airborne troops are in position, again assuming that this has not been done prior to D day, they could cross the frontier with light forces within some 2 weeks of the outbreak of war, though the total force envisaged on the line Mosul-Basra would not be in a sound administrative position until D + 3 months. Meanwhile our estimates are based on the day when leading Russian forces cross the frontier. We refer to this day as "F day".

8.   Our estimates are based on the campaign taking place at the most favourable time of year from the Russian point of view. As a result of preliminary examination we do not consider that there is any time of the year when the Russians would be prevented from undertaking a campaign in the Middle East, but their advance would probably be subject to some delay during the months of March to May in Turkey and March to June in Iraq, when climatic conditions are at their worst. We are undertaking a more detailed examination of this point.

Conclusions

9.   We conclude that, without making allowance for allied air interdiction (See paragraph 3 (a) above), Russian forces would be capable of advancing as follows, until making contact with Allied ground forces:—

(a) Tehran Area.	Leading elements by F + 5.
(b) Baghdad–Mosul Area.	Leading elements of ground forces by F + 6.

If surprise can be ensured, one airborne division could be used on F-Day or shortly afterwards.

(c) The oilfields area of S.W. Persia and Kuwait.	Leading elements by F + 14 increasing to two divisions by F + 25. Airborne forces could not be employed in this area.
(d) Bahrein Area.	Leading elements by about F + 30 with a limitation of one regimental group.
(e) Bandar Abbas.	Leading elements by F + 23 increasing to 1½ divisions by F + 45.
(f) Mediterranean Coast.	Leading elements of three divisions by F + 31 or of a force of nine divisions by about F + 82.

We consider that the attacks in (a) to (f) above could be supported by some 500 support aircraft of equivalent performance to those in use in the late war.

(g) *Northern Syria via Turkey*

If the Turkish Army were defeated in less than three months it would then be possible for Soviet Forces of strength up to two divisions, supported by about 250 aircraft, to operate against Northern Syria via Turkey not earlier than F + 2 months.

10.   We consider that some 1,500 transport aircraft might be available in support

of operations throughout the Middle East. Although a considerable number of aircraft similar to the B 29 type are likely to be available for a general strategic offensive, we consider that any Russian strategic air effort is likely to be of a limited nature.

122   DEFE 4/15, COS 118(48)6   25 Aug 1948
'Egypt-short term requirements': COS Committee minutes on the need to postpone the rundown of forces in Egypt

[In May 1948 the British finally withdrew from Palestine and the CIGS instructed the JPS to prepare another paper restating the minimum requirements in Egypt in the light of that withdrawal (DEFE 4/13, COS 75(48)4, 1 June 1948). Also in May the first global emergency war plan, codenamed 'Doublequick', was drawn up after consultation with the Americans.[1] Consequently for the first time actual plans had to be prepared for the defence of the Middle East within the framework provided by 'Doublequick' (DEFE 4/14, COS 90(48)2, 30 June 1948). In order to do this the C's-in-C Middle East had to be informed of what forces would be deployed in the region to meet a surprise attack, and therefore the number of troops available in Egypt assumed significance and would require a formal decision to be taken in London. In view of the consideration recently given to the moving of Middle East HQ out of Egypt and the evacuation of all but one thousand non-combatant personnel, the COS were increasingly concerned that such ideas, which neither they nor the Defence Committee had endorsed, might gain acceptance because of the political requirements of the Egyptian situation. And as a result the new military determination to avoid evacuation of the base would be ignored. The crucial fact was that the terms of the Bevin-Sidky agreement and the idea of leaving only one thousand administrative personnel would not permit the immediate re-activation of the base. The JPS were now adamant that it was essential to have a main base in working order in the Canal Zone at the outbreak of war. Indeed the services had begun to plan for the extension of the HQ in the Canal Zone and were arguing that there should be no further reduction of British forces for the next eight months (FO 371/69175, no 4289, minute by G L McDermott, 23 June 1948). The COS wanted the Defence Committee to approve a directive to the C's-in-C stating that British forces would remain in the Canal Zone in accordance with the 1936 treaty, that a main base in Egypt was essential, that Middle East HQ would remain in the Canal Zone and that the army would be run down to the numbers permitted by the treaty as soon as possible (DEFE 4/14, COS 94(48)3, 1 July 1948, JP(48)72). When asked to reconsider the COS remained adamant that they should direct the C's-in-C to reduce the troop levels to the treaty numbers but no lower (DEFE 4/14, COS 110(48)1, 6 Aug 1948). As the views of the COS hardened in August, as seen

---

[1] The full version of 'Doublequick' (DEFE 5/11, COS(48)110, 18 May 1948) was finally released in 1995. The plan was drawn up in the wake of discussions by British, Canadian and American planners in the spring of 1948. It was the equivalent of the US global war emergency plan codenamed 'Halfmoon'. There were a number of important differences between 'Halfmoon' and 'Doublequick', notably the references to the evacuation of Europe which were removed before the final version of 'Doublequick' was produced in June 1948. 'Doublequick' embodied the British abandonment of plans to deliver a strategic air offensive into the Soviet Union and envisaged five US bomber groups being deployed from bases in the UK (2), Japan (2) and the Cairo-Suez area (1) at D+1 month. Subsequently emergency global war plans were produced on an Anglo–American–Canadian basis after the production of national plans. Joint planning was never fully implemented in the period covered in these volumes because the Americans always refused to supply the vital information on the exact role of the Strategic Air Command which was responsible for the US strategic nuclear arsenal. The British therefore were never sure what was targeted for nuclear destruction. In the Middle East 'Doublequick' envisaged Soviet forces of eleven divisions being deployed against Palestine and Syria by D+3½ months and, if unopposed, threatening the Canal Zone by D+6 months. These estimates were reduced by the JIC in Dec 1948 to the extent that the committee believed the Soviets could threaten Syria with six divisions at D+80 days and the Canal Zone with eleven divisions at D+180 days (DEFE 5/9, COS(48)210, 16 Dec 1948).

below, the door was left open to argue that it was impossible to reduce the numbers of British troops by an early date. The most effective argument was not now the problem of stores or the construction of accommodation but the deteriorating international situation. The Czech coup in February 1948 and the Berlin blockade in June led the military, who still did not believe the Soviet Union would deliberately start a war, to suggest that it was now much more likely that war would break out by accident. The key fact was that any preparations to mount a defence against Soviet attack were not reconcilable with the evacuation of Egypt.]

The Committee considered a Note by the Chief of the Imperial General Staff on the facilities which must be retained in Egypt in order to allow us in a short term emergency to fight to maintain our position in the Middle East.

Lord Montgomery said that a directive approved by Ministers had recently been sent to the Commanders-in-Chief, Middle East, on the future deployment of our forces in the Middle East. This directive had been based on reducing the British forces in Egypt to the 1936 Anglo/Egyptian Treaty figure of 10,000 as urgently as possible and was a long term peace-time arrangement. The present world situation was such that peace-time arrangements were incompatible with the arrangements that must necessarily be made to meet the possibility of a sudden emergency in the near future.

The Commanders-in-Chief, Middle East, had already been instructed to prepare plans to meet such an emergency under the code name "Plan SANDOWN", which was based on emergency "Plan DOUBLEQUICK".

If an emergency occurred in the near future, it was essential that we should have certain facilities in Egypt, otherwise we could not hope to defend our position in the Middle East. These facilities were mainly an Army requirement though the R.A.F. was directly affected as the Army was responsible for providing a wide variety of equipment and stores to the R.A.F. in the Middle East. It was necessary, therefore, that the rundown of our forces in Egypt should be postponed until the threat of war receded.

Sir James Robb said he agreed in general with the Note by the Chief of the Imperial General Staff. The R.A.F. were dependent on the Army for the provision of a wide variety of equipment and stores in the Middle East and would be gravely affected if they had to meet a sudden emergency unless the present rundown in Egypt was stopped. The terms of the 1936 Anglo/Egyptian Treaty were incompatible with the strategic needs of a modern war.

In discussion general agreement was expressed with the Note by the Chief of the Imperial General Staff and with the recommendation that it should be submitted to the Minister of Defence as an expression of their views, with the request that early Ministerial decision be given on the points at issue.

The Committee:—

(a) Endorsed the Note by the Chief of the Imperial General Staff and instructed the Secretary to submit it to the Minister of Defence.

(b) Instructed the Joint Planning Staff to complete as a matter of urgency the report called for on 4th August.

123   FO 371/69176, no 6110   10 Sept 1948

[Finance for military requirements in Egypt]: letter from M R Wright
to E A Chapman Andrews on construction work and the currency
needs of the military authorities   [Extract]

Thank you for your letter No. 500/29/480 of the 1st of September about the alleged
Foreign Office ban on construction work outside the permitted areas of the Canal
Zone.

2.   There is obviously a misunderstanding here, whether wilful or not I am not
prepared to say. The position is as follows. For the past year we have been exerting
pressure on the Services departments to reduce their forces in the Canal Zone to
Treaty level, and to confine themselves to the areas permitted under that Treaty. The
political reasons for this are obvious and are still valid. Although the Egyptians may
not be raising any objections to the fact that we are at present far above Treaty
strength, there is nothing to say that their attitude might not change at very short
notice, and if, for instance, we were taken again to the Security Council, the fact that
we had seven times the permitted number of troops in the Canal Zone would
seriously embarrass us in maintaining that the 1936 Treaty was still valid and that we
had a perfect right to remain in Egypt. I doubt if, in fact, we shall be able to force the
military authorities to reduce the number of troops to Treaty level by September,
1949, the target date, but we may get them down to reasonable limits. Moreover, as
regards retirement into the permitted areas, we have raised no objection to the Army
retaining Geneifa and the R.A.F. Abu Sultan, nor to the Navy having a depot at Lake
Timsah.

3.   In the meantime, a very serious development has occurred in that there is
every reason to believe that owing to the unsatisfactory manner in which the
Anglo–Egyptian financial agreement has worked out, the Egyptians will ask for
dollars or gold in exchange for local currency required by the military authorities
in Egypt. The hard fact is that we have not this gold or dollars, and in default we
could only obtain the Egyptian currency at the expense of our cotton imports
which are absolutely vital to our textile industry. In these circumstances, the
Chancellor of the Exchequer has told the Minister of Defence that he must reduce
our forces in the Canal Zone to Treaty level as soon as possible. At first he asked
that this should be done by the end of 1948. His argument is that all round
economy in our expenditure in Egypt is necessary in itself and that if we can
reduce to Treaty level we may be able to claim that the spirit of the Treaty entitles
us to ask the Egyptians to provide the local currency we require even though there
is nothing to justify this claim in the letter of the Treaty. I imagine that the ban on
even temporary construction outside the permitted areas is the consequence of the
Chancellor's stern warning to the Service Chiefs. At any rate it is not a Foreign
Office ban. . . .

124 FO 371/69176, no 6290   13 Sept 1948
[Military requirements in Egypt]: letter from Mr Bevin to Mr Alexander on the views of the COS

[In the light of the conflict between military and financial requirements, the COS discussed the Egyptian dilemma again on 9 Sept. It was pointed out that while it would be possible to remove all essential stores and equipment within twenty-one months, there was a contradiction between the preparation of an emergency plan to defend the Middle East and the requirement to run down forces in Egypt and reduce installations there (DEFE 4/16, COS 125(48)2, 9 Sept 1948). When these points were put to the minister of defence a letter was sent to Bevin to which this letter was a response. The subsequent discussion with Cripps and the COS on 17 Sept proved inconclusive except in as much as it was agreed that in the short term the HQ should remain in the Canal Zone contrary to the earlier instructions of the PM (DEFE 4/16, COS 130(48)1, 17 Sept 1948). This was to a large extent determined by an investigation into the cost of moving to Cyrenaica which was estimated at £7 million. At no point were the issues of cost, in terms of potential dollar losses or the construction of accommodation outside Egypt and their possible conflict with military requirements, discussed by the Cabinet. The only traceable involvement of the Defence Committee was to agree that the COS should discuss their strategic requirements with the ambassador in Cairo (CAB 131/5, DO 18(48)6, 13 Sept 1948), who pointed out that the Egyptians would never agree to the presence of 20,000 troops in peacetime (FO 371/69176, no 6558, minute by Sir R Campbell, 16 Oct 1948). Following an approach by the Egyptian foreign minister for talks on Anglo–Egyptian relations, the problem did however produce yet another request from Bevin to the COS for an examination of the prospects of getting out of Egypt and using other Middle Eastern territories. The idea of technical discussions by the military that had been shelved because of Nokrashi's attitude to them was then revived (DEFE 5/12, COS (48)224, annex, 30 Sept 1948). The COS believed that if agreement was wanted all but 3–4,000 combat troops could be pulled out of Egypt but the total figure for British forces could still not be reduced below 20,000. To mollify the Egyptians it was suggested that installations in the Canal Zone could become joint ones and that Britain should supply Egypt with military equipment (DEFE 4/16, COS 140(48)1, annex, 1 Oct 1948).]

Thank you for your letter of the 9th September enclosing the papers about our strategic requirements in Egypt. Roughly speaking, what the Chiefs of Staff now want is authority to plan in the Middle East on the basis that they may maintain 20,000 troops in Egypt and continue to use the base establishment at Tel el Kebir, outside the permitted areas.

While it is true that at present we have many more than 20,000 troops in the Canal Zone besides depots and establishments outside the permitted areas and that the Egyptians are not objecting, I do not think that at the moment there is the remotest hope of the Egyptians agreeing to admit that they do not object. Indeed, if we were to approach them and ask them to agree to the comparatively limited increase in the facilities available to us under the 1936 Treaty suggested by the C.I.G.S., I am certain the reply would be that they did not even regard the 1936 Treaty as valid and that we have no right to any troops at all in Egypt.

It seems to me that the future of Egypt as our main base in the Middle East is nearly as problematical as the future of Cyrenaica. At any moment the present accommodating attitude of the Egyptians may change and if we were taken again before the Security Council, we might well be ordered to reduce our forces to Treaty strength within a period that gave us no time to make other arrangements, even if the Council did not rule that in view our [sic] our continued abuse of our rights under the Treaty, the Treaty itself had now become invalid.

Are we therefore being wise in basing no large a part of our future strategic plans on Egypt? Even though it may not be as good a location as Egypt, would it not be more prudent to plan to locate Regional Headquarters in Cyrenaica? Cyrenaica, if we get it, will be in the sterling area and this will have the advantage of relieving the strain on our Egyptian currency resources. Moreover, as the proposed Regional Headquarters will have an establishment of some four thousand odd persons, we would, by locating it in Cyrenaica, avoid making so large a hole in the permitted number of 10,000 troops in Egypt.

All these are questions which I agree could be most usefully discussed between the Chiefs of Staff, Sir Stafford Cripps and Sir Ronald Campbell. I have called him back from leave and he will be in London on Friday, 17th September. He will be available for a meeting any time after 11.30 a.m.

I am sending a copy of this letter to Sir Stafford Cripps.

125   DEFE 4/16, COS 145(48)2, annexes   11 Oct 1948
[Emergency planning for the defence of the Middle East]: report by the JPS to the COS, 7 Oct 1948 (JP(48)106)

Annex I: Summary of plan 'Sandown'
Plan '*Sandown*' has been prepared by the Commanders-in-Chief Committee, Middle East, as the result of a Directive by the Chiefs of Staff. The Directive gave the necessary assumptions on which the plan is based, the probable Russian aims and the minimum Allied Military aims which last are:—

(a) to provide secure bases for strategic air forces.
(b) to defend the Egyptian base.
(c) to retain control of our Mediterranean and Red Sea communications.

2.   The Commanders-in-Chief call attention to the most serious weaknesses of the plan, namely the vulnerability of Egypt to air attack and the inadequacy of fighter and ground attack aircraft. They point out that much of the Plan depends upon a 28-day precautionary period, which would enable them to effect considerable re-deployment of the present Middle East forces before D Day.

Allied strategy

3.   Because of the need to concentrate all available land and air forces to meet the main land threat to Egypt, the Allies cannot undertake any major subsidiary operations. Certain areas will therefore be left without Allied forces or with inadequate support. These are set out below:-

(a) *Turkey*
The Allies will not have sufficient forces in the early stages to render direct assistance except by naval and air attack on the Russian L. of C. Should the Russian attack on Turkey be delayed and the Turks remain neutral, for political reasons the Allies will not be able to pass ships or submarines through the Darndanelles and Bosporus for operations in the Black Sea.

(b) *Greece*
British land forces, if still in Greece, must be withdrawn as soon as possible after the outbreak of war. Allied Missions will, however, remain to stimulate Greek resistance but may subsequently be withdrawn if circumstances permit.

(c) *Cyprus*

The Allies cannot undertake the defence of the Island against even small scale airborne attack but will continue to use it as an advance air base for refuelling for as long as circumstances permit. According to the air situation it may prove possible to deploy fighter aircraft after the strength of the Allied air forces has built up. One Infantry Battalion will remain for internal security duties.

(d) *Persian Gulf*

The Allies cannot undertake the defence of this area, and will have to withdraw their forces at the outbreak of war.

(e) *Crete*

Allied land and air forces cannot be spared for the defence of Crete but the Greeks must be persuaded to defend the Island in conjunction with such Allied naval forces and Allied logistic support as can be afforded.

The plan

4.   The Plan covers three periods:—

(a) A precautionary period (D – 28 to D. Day)
(b) A period of initial concentration after the outbreak of war (D. Day to D + 15).
(c) The move into the Levant and subsequent operations.

Precautionary period

5.   The Commanders-in-Chief have assumed that there will be a precautionary period of about a month during which they intend to make unobtrusive preparations confined to measures which are unlikely to embarrass His Majesty's Government. They list the principal measures which consist in the main of establishing various war organisations and re-deploying the forces already in the Middle East: they include the setting up of Regional Headquarters at Fayid and of Army Headquarters and R.A.F. Tactical Group H.Q. in the Ismailia area.

Air forces will be concentrated in Egypt and Transjordan with two ground attack fighter squadrons deployed in Iraq.

Initial concentration

6.   *Navy.* Immediately war breaks out convoys will be instituted in the Mediterranean and Allied shipping will be withdrawn from the Persian Gulf. Concurrently, offensive operations will begin with submarine attacks in the Black Sea and air mining and bombing of the ports in the Black Sea and the Caspian. Offensive operations in the Black Sea pre-suppose that Turkey is already in the war.

7.   *Air Force.* Simultaneously, Tempest aircraft from Habbaniya and Mosul will begin bombing attacks against potential Russian Communications. Aircraft of the two squadrons concerned will also be responsible for the air defence of these stations. The R.A.F. Regiment and the Iraq Levies will be responsible for the defence of Habbaniya against the airborne threat.

8.   Plans for the destruction of oil installations and for demolitions on the Trans Persian Railway will be put into effect. These plans have still to be formultated [sic] and are not discussed further in '*Sandown*'. Security plans for combatting 5th column activities in areas under British control will also be implemented.

Move into the Levant

9.   During the third period starting at D + 15 days the Allied land forces have to gain time for the Allied air forces, including naval aircraft, to be reinforced, to achieve air superiority and to disrupt the enemy's advance. The object of the land operations will therefore be to impose the maximum delay on the enemy as far from the Egypt base as administrative resources will allow. The operations will consist of a series of delaying and harassing actions by mobile forces in Transjordan and later in Palestine.

10.   A prepared defensive position will be constructed on the general line Jericho-Ramallah-North of Tel Aviv. The Allied land forces will not withdraw into it unless forced to: there they will fight it out and from this position there will be no withdrawal.

Subsequent operations

11.   Subsequent operations are dealt with in five phases:—

$$D + 15 \quad \text{to } D + 30$$
$$D + 30 \quad \text{to } D + 60$$
$$D + 60 \quad \text{to } D + 90$$
$$D + 90 \quad \text{to } D + 120$$
$$D + 120 \text{ to } D + 180$$

12.   *Phase I-D + 15 to D + 30 days*

This period covers the rapid deployment of a mobile force of 1 Brigade group and 2 armoured regiments, to delay the enemy forward of the main defensive position. This force will establish itself in the Mafraq area and will carry out bold offensive operations with the object of delaying and harassing the enemy. It will be supported by the Arab Legion. The R.A.F. will withdraw from Iraq (if this has not already been done) and will operate from Mafraq with 3 ground attack squadrons and 1 fighter reconnaissance squadron, a maximum of 56 aircraft, until an airfield in Palestine is ready for them. 1 group of 30 U.S. strategic bombers will arrive in Egypt.

13.   *Phase II-D + 30 to D + 60 days*

During this period the Allied ground forces will be built up to 2 British divisions, 1 U.S. infantry division and 1 U.S. airborne regiment. The plan assumes that the American troops will operate in the Tiberias area and the British in the general area Jericho-Ramallah-Jerusalem.

The initial task of these Allied formations will be to reach forward in such strength as administrative resources will allow in support of the mobile force, while preparing defensive positions in their respective areas. They will also have to be responsible for the security of the L of C, in particular the railways, against sabotage.

During this and subsequent phases the three primary roles of the R.A.F. will be:—

(a) to delay the enemy advance and build up.
(b) to secure air superiority and protection.
(c) to afford close support to our land forces.

The medium bomber force will be built up to 96 Lincolns which will operate by night from the Canal zone against vulnerable points on the numerous L of C in the

Caucasus area and in Central Persia. The 24 tactical light bombers will operate from airfields in Palestine against enemy movements and supplies.

14.   *Phase III–D + 60 to D + 90 days*

Towards the end of this phase the army in the Levant will be reinforced by a further British infantry division and an infantry brigade. During this phase it is probable that the Allied forces will be heavily engaged with the enemy and adjustments to our deployment may have to take place. The preparation of the Ramallah position should by now be well advanced.

Air force operations will continue as before. A further 8 tactical light bombers will be moved to Palestine from Aden as soon as American forces are established in Aden.

The Navy must be prepared to give direct support to the army by air action or bombardment on the left flank.

15.   *Phase IV–D + 90 to D + 120 days*

During this stage the need for air support will be at its greatest as the build up of Russian land forces will probably outstrip that of the Allies. Greater numbers of aircraft, possibly up to a total of about 400 fighter and ground attack aircraft, operating from airfields in Palestine, may be required.

During this phase air reinforcements arrive in the theatre in significant quantities. The most important of these are 4 groups of day fighters, 1 group of tactical reconnaissance aircraft and 1 group of all-weather fighters, all of which are U.S.A.F.; and 2 R.A.F. night fighter squadrons. Depending on the scale of Russian air attack on the Egypt base, a proportion of the day fighters will have to be deployed in Egypt together with the night fighters for the air defence of the base. The plan is for the remainder to go to the Levant area. In addition there will be reinforcements of light bombers from the Dominions which will also go to Palestine. When the air reinforcements are deployed the security of the main bases will be greatly improved and the tactical air forces, together with naval aircraft, should have a numerical superiority over the Russians. It is at this stage that an all-out offensive will be carried out against the Russian air force with the aim of obtaining air superiority over the area of land operations and disrupting the Russian L of C to the battle area. By now we can expect to have sufficient air fields south of the Ramallah position to operate all available tactical aircraft.

If the land battle becomes critical it may be necessary to request assistance from the U.S. strategic air force operating in a tactical role.

16.   *Phase V–D + 120 to D + 180 days*

The progress of operations after the fourth month of the war is impossible to forecast, but by this time it is possible that the land forces may have been forced to withdraw to the Ramallah position. In that event the Commanders-in-Chief intend to group the allied forces with the British formations on the right and the American on the left.

Towards the end of this phase a second U.S. infantry division and a further British infantry division and an armoured brigade will be deployed in Palestine.

Communications

17.   The Commanders-in-Chief call attention to the need for introducing an Anglo/U.S. inter service radio and cyphering organisation. They state that U.S.

methods and books will in general be employed. Joint "Y" and D/F organisation on land, and joint convoy and fleet radio organisation will be required.

Annex II: points for discussion with the Americans
In addition to obtaining the general agreement of the Americans to Plan "*Sandown*", it will be necessary to discuss with them certain particular points in the Plan. In this Annex we give our views on the outstanding points which require discussion.

Strategy

Greece and Crete
2.   It is proposed to leave the British Service Missions in Greece to encourage and organise Greek forces of resistance. We hope that the Greeks may be persuaded to attempt to hold Crete but no British assistance can be provided.
3.   We intend to ask the Americans:–

(a) Whether they intend to leave their Missions in Greece and to continue to supply Greek forces.
(b) Whether they propose to use Crete and whether they will supply logistic backing for Greek forces defending the island.

Trieste
4.   This will be discussed separately and we will use as a brief our report on the withdrawal of Allied forces from Austria and Trieste which has received the general approval of the Chiefs of Staff.

Persian Gulf
5.   We are most reluctant to leave, completely unprotected, the whole of the Persian Gulf area, thus abandoning all the Middle East oil and presenting the enemy with a large area from which he can develop threats to our sea and air routes along the Red Sea and Southern Arabia and organise activities which may threaten our main Middle East positions. The loss of our air bases in the Persian Gulf will, moreover, make any possible return to this area an operation of considerable difficulty. With the resources available to us no other course is possible.
We propose to ask the Americans what has become of their previous proposal to move a force of Marines to the Persian Gulf from the Marianas.

Turkey
6. Under Plan "Sandown" no British assistance is given to Turkey. We propose to ask the Americans what their intentions are regarding Turkey.

The plan

Security of the base
7.   *Air defence*. With the total forces available at the outbreak of hostilities, namely 2 day fighter squadrons, 1 AA AGRA of 2 weak regiments and no night fighters at all for 3 months, the air defence of the Middle East base is extremely thin. We propose to ask the Americans if they can expedite the arrival of one U.S. Fighter Group, at the same time mentioning that the U.K. Chiefs of Staff are finding out whether any Commonwealth reinforcements can be made available earlier.

8. *Internal security*

We feel that we must point out to the Americans that we do not propose to retain any regular forces in Tripolia, the Sudan and Aden to back the local forces in the maintenance of internal security when once American forces are deployed in these areas.

Main defensive line

9.   The Chiefs of Staff are not convinced that we can accept a main defence line so far to the south as that selected by the Commanders-in-Chief, Middle East. If the Americans make the same criticism we will reply in the light of the examination now being undertaken by the War Office.

Availability of airfields

10.   The question of improving airfields so that they will be available for U.S. air forces is being considered at a high level, the chief point being that we will want very great American help in doing this. We propose to tell the Americans that pending formal Anglo/U.S. agreement the Chiefs of Staff are, as a start, pressing for an extension of Abu Sueir from British resources.

Air forces

11.   The whole plan ignores the effect of strategic bombing of the Russian bases facing the Middle East. The J.I.C. are examining what would be the likely effect of atomic attack on towns such as Baku, Tiflis and Batum. We hope to get this information in time to discuss the matter with the Americans.

Warning period

12.   If the Americans raise the question of the warning period, we will say that the Chiefs of Staff have asked the Commanders-in-Chief, Middle East, what affect it would have on the Plan if the 28 days warning was not forthcoming.

Demolitions—Oilfields and Trans-Persian Railway

13.   We know that the Americans are particularly interested in the demolition of:–

(a) the oilfields
(b) The Trans-Persian Railway.

As regards (a) we will inform them that we have had discussions with the Oil Companies and that a reconnaissance on the ground is now in hand. The aim is to destroy stocks of refined oil and refining plant as we consider that Russian transportation problems will prevent them making use of crude oil.

As regards (b) the Chiefs of Staff consider that the beat means apart from bombing, would be to enlist the help of the Persians.

We will ask the Americans whether they have received any views from their Mission in Persia on this subject.

Administration

14.   Considerable co-ordination will be required with the Americans over administrative planning for operation "Sandown." In the main our requirements are

for more detailed information from the Americans. Attached at Appendix[1] is a list of the points which the representative of the Joint Administrative Planning Staff, who will accompany us to Washington, proposes to raise.

---

[1] Not printed.

---

126   FO 141/1292, no 73   19 Nov 1948

[Military talks and the removal of Nokrashi]: minute by E A Chapman Andrews to Sir R Campbell on the attitude of King Farouk to military talks and a new Egyptian government

The points Amr made to me in his hour's talk on the morning of the 18th coincide with those he made later in the day to H.E. I gather that the meeting with the King referred to took place most secretly at Maadi in the middle of the night and was attended by a good deal of emotional display. Amr had to swear on his life that if the King went through with all this "the British would not let King Farouk down".[1] Amr must realise that his life was at stake. He would be hanged like a dog if after King Farouk had trusted us we let him down.

I was rather worried about all this because I did not quite see where it was all leading. The picture seemed to me for a moment to become a little clearer when Amr went on to say that in reply to questions from Abdel Hadi the King asserted that if Nokrashy or Parliament opposed his will he would sweep them away. If necessary he would call in the Army. He would have a purely military form of government.[2] King Farouk had said that they had all learned many lessons as a result of the Palestine episode. The King was not at all sorry that he had embarked on that warlike adventure. Today not a single Egyptian Army officer could hold up his head and say that the Egyptian Army was sufficient unto itself and the needs of the country and that there was no need of a military understanding with Great Britain.

It is therefore in the back of my mind that having, let us say, pushed through successfully military talks on the technical level with us the King may then suspend the constitution and try and rule through a military dictatorship something like Franco,[3] making to us the excuse that this was the only way in which he could safeguard our joint security which depended upon the military agreement. If this were to cause something like revolution here and Britain had once again to step in to safeguard foreign lives and property the King would expect us to do so (as we did under the Khedive Tewfik[4] in 1882) to re-established [sic] the royal authority. If at such a time having stepped in we were to facilitate the advent to power, on the

---

[1] At this point Sir R Campbell noted in the margin that: 'This anxiety may relate – at least partly – to a fear that after getting rid of Nokrashi HM would be faced by a further demand from us i.e. for a government of national unity'.
[2] At this point Sir R Campbell noted in the margin that: 'This is much in my mind. I have put in some further warning words – this time to Amr'.
[3] General Franco, fascist ruler of Spain, 1939–1975.
[4] Khedive Tewfik, ruler of Egypt 1879–1892 who, in Feb 1882, in the face of army pressure, appointed Urabi as PM to deal with the grievances of Egyptian officers against their Turkish counterparts. In July 1882 the British occupation brought the army back under foreign control.

grounds of expediency, of people like Nahas, this would be "letting the King down" and would lead to the unfortunate death of poor little Amr.

Another point was that the King is impatient to get results. Abdel Hadi's attitude was that the whole question of any arrangement with England was a political one. There could be no technical arrangement affecting the presence of British troops in Egypt that did not so impinge upon wider political considerations as to make it necessary for the politicians to be kept closely informed and finally to approve or reject the suggested arrangements. King Farouk came down heavily upon this and made the remark mentioned above about ruling through the military. It seems pretty clear to me that whatever may be King Farouk's ideas of how the situation might forward any personal aspirations of his own towards a more autocratic form of government, His Majesty is scared stiff about the security of Egypt. Quite apart from the imminence or otherwise of a world war, I think His Majesty now really believes that unless he has a clear military understanding with us and if the situation in Palestine is allowed to drift as it has been drifting in recent years and months, the Zionists will rapidly become so strong that it will be not only possible but easy for them to invade Egypt.

127   FO 371/69195, no 8150   7 Dec 1948
'Egypt': memorandum by G L Clutton on the instigation of military technical talks

After his consultations with King Farouk, Amr Pasha has now returned to Paris and is shortly expected in London when he will pursue further with the Secretary of State and the Department the question of instituting military technical discussions on defence in the Middle East. In anticipation of Amr Pasha's call, His Majesty's Ambassador at Cairo has sent us a despatch (J 7714, flag A) giving us an idea of some of the points which may be raised. This has been supplemented by three private letters which will be found in J 7784/G, J 7745/G and J 7732/G (flags B, C and D).

The correspondence is somewhat lengthy and not very clear, but there are four main points which emerge for consideration:—

(1) King Farouk is continually asking for an assurance that if he pursues the idea of military conversations we shall not let him down. What exactly he means is open to doubt. Amr Pasha has denied that it means that we should support a military dictatorship which would crush any opposition to the King's policy with regard to us or with regard to any other point. What the King wants to be assured of is that if for the purposes of reaching agreement with us he appoints a man like Khashaba Pasha as Prime Minister, we will not suddenly say that we want a Government of national unity, the formation of which has proved impossible. All this may be partly true. On the other hand, there seems no doubt that one of the reasons why the King wants agreement with us is because of his precarious position in a steadily worsening domestic political situation. Any Anglo–Egyptian agreement, therefore, will be used for bolstering up a corrupt régime which will probably more and more rely on the Army as it did in the recent police strike. It is difficult to believe that the King cannot appreciate this. Another very possible motive behind the King's request is his fear that in the worsening internal position

we may start flirting with the Wafd who apart from the mob are the real danger to his position. Crudely put, part of the King's idea may be that in return for an agreement we shall agree to renounce any idea of supporting a return of the Wafd to power and back him exclusively. If this analysis is correct, then the situation is tricky.

(2) On our side we have also been impressing on Amr, and through him on the King, that we want to be assured that if an agreement is reached it will be honoured. This has raised the question of whether it is possible to do business with Nokrashy. We have been given more than a hint that if we say the word the King will get rid of him, and the Ambassador in his letter to Sir Orme Sargent in J 7084/G at flag B, strongly recommends that we should get rid of him. Here again we are getting into very deep waters indeed. If Nokrashy is dismissed at our request, we shall commit ourselves very largely to supporting his successor who will be even more of a Palace nominee than Norkashy is himself. We shall therefore be placing all our cards on the King, an action which, as indicated in the preceding paragraph, is far from being without its dangers. Nokrashy is a man of some personality and in certain matters not without judgment. He has a certain amount of political backing. If, for instance, Khashaba Pasha was appointed in his place, we would find ourselves dealing with a weak, if well disposed man, and a man without political connections at all. Nokrashy would be in the wilderness, a martyr, etc. It is true that it is practically impossible to conduct any business whatsoever with Nokrashy but to get rid of him on so delicate a subject as our military requirements in Egypt seems most unwise, especially as if, in fact, he did carry out the King's policy, the fact that it was he who did so would have some weight. If he is to be got rid of, he should be got rid of on the general grounds that he is the obstacle to the conduct of business of any sort between any power and Egypt independently of the present proposed conversations.

(3) If the military conversations succeed, and agreement is reached giving us what we require in Egypt, the question arises whether there should be a second stage where these purely technical arrangements are given permanence in a political agreement. It should be remembered in this connexion that the whole object of the talks is to discuss the defence of Egypt as a joint Anglo–Egyptian problem, leaving aside the whole question of the revision of the treaty itself. It could, however, be argued that the conversations themselves are part of the mutual consultation provided for by the Treaty and that any agreement on defence matters is, in fact, the revision before 1956 of Article 8 of the Treaty (the Article which gives us the right to base our troops in Egypt) provided for in the last paragraph of Article 16. There are obvious objections to treating the results of the military conversations in this manner. Another idea is that the results of the conversations should be incorporated in an entirely new political agreement which would be accompanied by a renunciation on our part of our rights in Egypt as the successor of the Ottoman Empire, these rights being in fact the basis of the rights accorded us in the 1936 Treaty. Any such suggestion would have to be considered very carefully by our legal experts because such a renunciation would create an entirely new basis for our being in Egypt at all. Any power can at Egypt's invitation station troops in Egypt in time of peace but under the Suez Canal Convention only the Ottoman Empire, and now ourselves, can do so in time of war.

(4) In the annexe to Sir Ronald Campbell's despatch at flag F may be found the sort

of Agenda King Farouk has in mind for the military talks. This Agenda seems sensible, especially as in addition the King contemplates the institution of a joint headquarters. Considerable work will, however, have to be done on the Agenda by the Chiefs of Staff. It is also suggested that Lord Tedder, accompanied by Lord Douglas[1] who is a personal friend of King Farouk's, should visit Egypt in connexion with the Agenda. The only possible objection to such a course is that the visit might be regarded as a sign that the military power of Great Britain was behind the King.

Conclusions

If Amr raises these points, it is recommended that the following line be taken:-

(1) We should be very wary about giving the King assurances that we will not let him down. We can, however, be quite explicit that if an agreement is reached, we shall honour our side of it. We must not, however, put all our cards on the King.

(2) Until Nokrashy has shown that he will not carry out the King's policy regarding the proposed conversations, we should not attempt to get rid of him. The sooner, however, our talks with the Egyptians are transferred to normal channels and we know whether or not Nokrashy will play, the better. If he will not play then we can think again.

(3) The question of whether the results of the military talks should be incorporated in a political agreement should be left over for the time being. The very basis of the proposed talks is to shelve politics for the time being.

(4) As regards the Agenda for the military talks, Amr Pasha can be told that the F.O. are in general agreement with his rough draft which, however, we would like to be elaborated and considered by our technical military experts.

---

[1] Lord Douglas, assistant chief of the air staff, 1938–1940 and C-in-C Middle East Air Forces, 1943–1944.

128   DEFE 5/9, COS(48)210, annex   16 Dec 1948

'Digest of plan "Speedway"':[1] COS Committee memorandum on the global war emergency plan for the period to July 1950

[By the summer of 1948 the first emergency plan for the defence of the Middle East had been drawn up. Plan 'Sandown' confirmed the importance of the use of nuclear weapons by American strategic bombers if the Middle East, and indeed anywhere else, was to have any chance of repulsing a Soviet offensive (see 125). The British expected that the US would not only use airfields in the Middle East but contribute the bulk of the forces in all three services that would be deployed in the region within the first year of conflict (DEFE 5/9, COS(48)209, 16 Dec 1948). Unfortunately there were few if any Middle Eastern airfields large enough to take American strategic bombers. Cyprus would take too long to develop and Abu Sueir, the most suitable airfield in Egypt, had runways which were too short and which could not be extended within the likely period of warning prior to a major conflict (FO 371/69286A, no 6615, Alexander to Cripps, 5 Oct 1948). Work therefore had to begin at once, preferably financed by the Americans (DEFE 4/16, COS 138(48)2, 27 Sept 1948). However by April 1949 it became clear that the US was unwilling to pay, and the Defence Committee reluctantly authorised the work on Abu Sueir, which was eventually paid for on a joint basis, but not on the other airfields that would now by required under plan 'Sandown' (FO 371/73552, no 3630, minute by M N F Stewart, 19 May 1949). The

---

[1] The successor to 'Doublequick'.

revision of 'Doublequick' provided for by 'Speedway' contained a number of significant changes embodying the information on the role of the SAC disclosed by the Americans in the October 1948 planning discussions. New long range heavy bombers, the B 36s, would be introduced by D+6 months and staged in Britain, Egypt and Okinawa. (The US would not agree to store atomic bombs under the control of a foreign government.) A bomber group formerly assigned to the Cairo-Suez area would now operate from Britain. This no doubt reflected the lack of suitable airfields in Egypt but it also indicated growing US doubts about the value of operating strategic bombers from the Middle East. SAC strategy was to attack specific targets relating, for example, to oil and submarine production with conventional bombs, and launch the atomic offensive against the main Soviet industrial centres (DEFE 6/7, JP(48)131, 18 Nov 1948). Discussions with the Americans were also held on long-term strategic plans for global war which, as with emergency plans, were accompanied by British attempts to draw up long-term plans for Middle East defence. The first such British plan for the Middle East was geared to 1957 and the defence of the outer ring, which was the only way the oilfields could be protected. The Tel Aviv-Ramallah line was deemed to be too close to the Nile delta and was not considered. The Russians were assumed to have sixteen divisions and 600 aircraft that would attack in four separate sectors. Without allied action, Force P would seize the Erbil-Kirkuk-Mosul area by D+40 days and capture Tripoli and Beirut by D+60. Force Q would secure Baghdad by D+45 and capture Amman and Damascus by D+80. Force R, with landings near Pahlevi-Resht, Nau Shah and Bandar Abbas, would seize the Straits of Hormuz at D+5, Tehran between D+10 and D+15 and Basra at D+45. Force S would land at Bandar Shah and move behind force R to secure Qom by D+20. A separate force would attack Turkey with the result that Iskenderun (Alexandretta) would fall at D+80. Between D+80 and D+130 force P and Q would attack positions in the Palestine and Jordan valleys with a combined strength of nine divisions and reach the Suez Canal by D+140 capturing Cairo and Alexandria before D+6 months. To prevent this the British planners believed it would be necessary to retard the Russian advance in its early stages with 665 strategic bombers. Hitting key targets only would require 260 long range strategic bombers and thirty two light bombers with the latter based in Iraq along with 112 fighters and reconnaissance aircraft. If this were done the attack on the most northerly of the passes into Iraq would be reduced, it was claimed, to two divisions at D+30. If it were not done the outer ring could not be defended. The strategic bombers could not be provided by Britain alone, and with only ninety-six Lincoln bombers planned for deployment in 1957, 163 SAC bombers would be required. In addition one brigade would need to be in the Mosul area on D Day and one division by D+5 days with the SAS undertaking road demolition in Persia. Another division would have to be in place in Iraq at D+14–20 having arrived by road. By D+45 one other infantry division and one armoured division would be required. In the Turkish sector one armoured division and one other division would be needed between D+70 and D+90 along with 112 aircraft. If the outer ring was not held, by D+120 defences would be built up on the Palestine-Lebanon line, which ran north-south along the Lebanon and anti-Lebanon mountain ranges, with a force of ten divisions (DEFE 6/6, JP(48)61, 12 Oct 1948).]

The attached Annex gives a digest of the plan which has been agreed with the Americans for use should war break out before July 1950.

2.   The forces available, in particular their rate of build-up in the Middle East, and the availability of A.A. artillery will require material reduction after the Defence Votes for 1949/50 have been determined. The figures given in the plan are therefore optimistic in these respects.

3.   The outstanding feature of this plan is that the only means we have of striking direct at the heart of the enemy is the American strategic bomber force using atomic weapons. We are at a disadvantage in that, apart from the fact that the U.S.A.F. can put 400 strategic bombers in the field, we do not know the details of the number of atomic weapons to be used and so cannot assess with any accuracy the results which may be achieved.

4.   There are certain weaknesses in this plan as it stands:—

(a) Our inability to withstand a Russian advance in Western Europe, even with the full defence co-operation of the Western Powers.

(b) The Anglo–American air striking force is not big enough to carry out the strategic attack on Russia and at the same time make any significant direct contribution to the defence of Western Europe, the Middle East or the United Kingdom. This, together with our shortage of fighter aircraft, radar and A.A. artillery for the defence of the United Kingdom, will make the situation critical about D + 6 months unless the strategic air offensive has by then achieved material results.

(c) The Allied shortage of minesweepers, which will be serious if the assessed scale of enemy mine-laying attack develops.

(d) The critical shortages of vehicles and equipment, particularly in the Army. The forces which we shall deploy for the defence of the Middle East will only be partially equipped and the administrative resources available will at the best be barely adequate.

(e) The Allied shortage of escorts. The escorts available are only sufficient to give all convoys an average of two-thirds of the desirable strength.

5.   It will be noted that the plan takes account of possible Commonwealth assistance in the Middle East, South-East Asia and in the Atlantic. With the exception of the Canadian contribution, these forces are only assumed to be available, as no military conversations with the Commonwealth countries on emergency plans have yet been authorised.

Annex to 128

Speedway is the British version of the combined American-British-Canadian plan, recently revised in Washington, to cover the possibility of war breaking out between now and 1950.

The plan is confined to the opening months of the war.

Assumptions

2. (a) War may break out without warning.

(b) The United States and United Kingdom Governments authorise the use of atomic bombs. The U.S.S.R. will have none.

(c) Egypt and Palestine will be re-occupied immediately, without active opposition, by our forces in the Canal area.

Military aims

3. The Soviet are expected to launch two major offensives:—

(a) to seize the Middle East and its oil resources;

(b) to destroy all the forces of the Allies on the mainlands of Europe.

In conjunction with the above, other early objectives of the Soviet will be to:—

(c) seize or neutralise those areas from which the Allies are delivering an air offensive; this will include the United Kingdom:

(d) expand and consolidate their positions in China, Manchuria and Korea:

(e) disrupt the Allied war-making capacity by sabotage and subversive action:

(f) disrupt essential Allied sea communications by submarine warfare, mining and air operations.

4.   The only offensive action which the Allies can take strategically in the early stages of the war is from the air. With the exception of some strategic missions to be undertaken by British aircraft based on the Middle East, these operations will become the responsibility of the American Air Force, since they only possess the equipment required for this task. These vital interests must be the defence of bases for the air offensive, of main support areas, and of their sea communications.

Our forces will be too small to plan on being able to defend the countries in Western Europe or to hold the Middle East oil.

5.   During 1949/50 the initial Allied military aims are, therefore:—

(a) to attack the Soviet Union with strategic bomber forces based on the U.K., the Egypt-Aden area and Okinawa; this can at present only be undertaken by the U.S. Air Forces:

(b) to defend the U.K. and to fight the enemy as far to the east in Europe as possible:

(c) to defend Egypt by fighting the enemy as far to the north and east as possible:

(d) to control essential sea and air communications:

(e) to hold Japan and the essential Western Pacific Islands:

(f) to defend the American continent, Africa, Austria [sic] and New Zealand.

Strategic air offensive

6.   Plan *Speedway* depends on the success of the strategic air offensive, using atomic weapons, during the first six months. The strategic air offensive will be undertaken by some 400 U.S. bombers operating from the U.K., the Egypt-Aden area and Okinawa. The British bomber force (160) will have too short a range to deliver an effective offensive into Russia. Its primary task will be to assist in the defence of the Middle East and the U.K., but it is at present quite inadequate in size to be really effective in preventing the enemy build-up in Western Europe and at the same time slowing the Russian advance into the Middle East.

7.   The plan for the air offensive will be made by the U.S. Chiefs of Staff, who alone know what atom bombs are available. We have insufficient information properly to assess the effect of this plan.

The plan depends for its full effectiveness on our completing as quickly as possible in peacetime certain work on airfields in the Middle East.

Western Europe

8.   The Allies intend to fight on the line of the Rhine as long as possible. The forces available, i.e. British and U.S. garrisons in Germany and those of the Western European countries, cannot exceed some 11 divisions and 500 aircraft in all. Some of the British and U.S. garrisons in Austria, which total 1 division in all, may also join them.

The assessed scale of enemy attack is some 50 divisions and 5,000 – 6,000 aircraft. Therefore, if the enemy presses his attack we cannot hold Western Europe.

United Kingdom

9.   The defence of the U.K. will be a British responsibility, except for some help from U.S. fighters attached to their strategic air forces.

10.   The plan assumes that the forces available during the first six months will be

200–300 fighter and 80 bomber aircraft, 88 heavy A.A. regiments, 42 escorts, 233 minesweepers and 6–7 territorial divisions (90% last war reservists and on a low scale of equipment).

11.   Air attack, which may start at once, is unlikely to become really serious until the enemy can support it by short range air forces operating from Western Europe. The Russian forces then available might amount to 800 long range bombers, 700 tactical bombers and 1,000–2,000 fighters.

Enemy submarines will probably attack shipping, particularly in the approaches to the U.K. Further, a serious mine-laying threat by aircraft and submarines is likely to develop.

12.   A threat of air or seaborn invasion will not become serious until the enemy has consolidated his position in Western Europe and attained air superiority. This will be about D + 6 months, unless our air offensive has achieved substantial results.

Middle East

13.   Our minimum aim in the Middle East is to defend Egypt by holding the enemy at all costs on the line Ramallah-Tel Aviv. Russian communications are, however, extremely vulnerable and the Middle East Commanders will be instructed to exploit to the full any delays which can be imposed.

14.   The Allied forces assumed to be available are of the order of 3 scratch divisions and 300 combat aircraft by D + 1 months, including 80 heavy bombers from the United Kingdom; rising by D + 6 months to 4⅔ British and 3⅓ U.S. divisions, and 250 British, 150 Commonwealth and 350 U.S. aircraft.

This build up is dependent on keeping open the Mediterranean.

15.   The assessed maximum enemy threat in this area by about D + 3 – 4 months is of the order of 11 divisions supported by 400 aircraft and in addition some 700 aircraft operating from airfields in Turkey. This makes no allowance for opposition to and attrition of the enemy forces. Owing to the length and vulnerability of his communications the enemy's build up is likely to be appreciably less. The Allies should thus have a reasonable chance of at least defending Egypt.

Control of sea communications

16. The plan for the control of sea communications allows for provision of naval forces as follows:—

(a) Atlantic   Half British and half U.S. with a small Canadian contribution.
(b) European Waters   – British assisted by Western Union navies.
(c) Mediterranean   – ⅔ US, ⅓ British.
(d) Indian Ocean   – British.
(e) Australia,   – Australia and New Zealand
New Zealand & South
East Asia
(f) Pacific   – US.

17.   The main threat will be from air, submarine and mine-laying attack, mainly in Atlantic and European waters, the Mediterranean and Western Pacific.

The initial submarine threat is assessed at 160 Soviet ocean-going submarines. Their operational efficiency is likely to be low.

Air attack in the early stages will not constitute a powerful threat. As the Soviet land forces advance in Western Europe, however, tactical air forces will join the Soviet naval-air forces to constitute a serious threat to the approaches to the UK and in the Mediterranean.

18.   The naval forces are adequate except for Escorts and Minesweepers. The Allied totals for the world's oceans are:-

	British	U.S.	Common-wealth	Western Union	Total
Escorts (including Fleet Destroyers)	208	208	46	55	517
Minesweepers	282	25	49	96	452

19.   It will be necessary to operate a large force of US aircraft carriers in the Mediterranean to help in curtailing the enemy's build up of air strength in areas from which our Mediterranean communications can be threatened.

The Escorts available should be sufficient to give all convoys an average of two-thirds the desirable strength.

If and when Scandinavia and Western Europe are overrun, the threat to sea communications will be greatly increased.

Japan and the West Pacific Islands

20.   The US should be able to maintain a strategic defence in the Far East with the small forces available.

Redeployment of allied forces in Europe

21.   *Greece.* British forces in Greece will be withdrawn. The British and US Military Missions will remain as long as the Greek forces are fighting.

22.   *Austria and Trieste.* Action by Allied forces in Austria and Trieste is still under examination. As at present planned, if Italy remains neutral, Allied forces in Austria will attempt to withdraw to the Rhine. If Italy fights, these forces, in conjunction with those in Trieste, will withdraw to Italy and fight as long as is practicable.

If Italy remains neutral, Trieste forces will try to withdraw by sea for deployment in the Middle East.

Review by D + 3 Months

23.   The plan allows for a major review at about D + 3 months, when the initial atomic campaign should be substantially completed. By this time a considerable proportion of forces being mobilised will not have definitely been committed.

24.   The situation which may have to be faced by about D + 3 months will lie between the two extremes of such complete success of the atomic offensive that even with the forces available some exploitation will be possible, or failure of the offensive to prevent a critical air situation developing in the U.K., with or without a critical situation in the Middle East.

25.   In the first case, the problem will be whether to exploit from the U.K. or Middle East.

To meet the second situation, two major changes in policy, or a combination of the two, may be needed:-

(a) to shift some of the strategic air effort in order to prevent the Russian build up in Western Europe or the Middle East;

(b) to shift the emphasis of the Allied effort to the U.K. at the expense of the Middle East, by diverting forces, especially fighters, from the Middle East.

129   FO 141/1292, no 89   21 Dec 1948

'Treaty': minute by Sir R Campbell on technical talks and the timing of Nokrashi's removal

I only had quarter-of-an-hour with Kerim Tabet[1] this afternoon because Prince Mohamed Aly arrived unannounced, twenty minutes before Kerim Bey was due, to stay his usual hour, and Kerim Bey had an appointment he had to keep.

He told me he thought there must be some slight delay in prosecuting the programme for the technical talks, though he thought the delay should not go beyond the second half of January. While confirming the fact that on a word from Mr. Bevin, Nokrashy would be dismissed, Kerim Bey said it was felt that the present was not the moment for doing so. First of all there was the blow at the Ikhwan el Muslimeen, which (a) had slightly raised Nokrashy's prestige, and (b) made it desirable that he should be left where he was a little longer in order (i) to press the suppression of the Ikhwan further, and (ii) to avoid any appearance that there was a change of policy in respect of the Ikhwan or any letting up on the action against them. A change of Government at this moment might be so interpreted. (He asserted strongly that the action was being successful).

A further consideration was the fuss about the Sudan, which should be given a little further time to die down. I said that it appeared to be continuing at full blast, and that it showed little signs of dying down, and urged that something should be done about this. He said that it would yield to some other matter of interest whenever that occurred. I said that the Ikhwan matter was surely such a subject, but that the campaign still went on. Kerim Bey said that unfortunately it was not possible yet to give enough sensational details about the Ikhwan to deflect public interest from the Sudan. This, however, would be done when the enquiry into the whole matter started. Further, a change of Government, when it came, would deflect attention from the Sudan. Everybody would be talking about the new Ministers, etc. etc.

In the circumstances, Amr would very shortly ask to see Mr. Bevin, but to begin with would go gently. He would work up to giving Mr. Bevin an opening for saying that technical discussions with, or under a Government headed by, Nokrashy would be impossible, and the King would then immediately take the action already decided upon. Kerim Bey here rehearsed the sort of thing that Mr. Bevin might say, which was almost exactly the language suggested in paragraph 4 of my telegram No. 1757. But as he had said, he thought that this action would not be opportune until two or three weeks had passed. I said that from what he had told me this period seemed

---

[1] Kerim Tabet, a Lebanese adviser and press counsellor to King Farouk who was working for the return of Nahas and the Wafd.

rather short for reaching the conditions where a change of Government could take place, but he said he thought it was enough. I said that that seemed a good thing, since as the whole idea of technical discussions was based on the demands of the international situation, and since the international situation was what it was, I did not think that we had time to lose. He did not contest this.

Kerim Bey said that while King Farouk did not think it well to dismiss Nokrashy at once, at the same time, as the almost certainty of his dismissal existed, he did not like to be on very cordial terms with him, and Kerim Bey thought that Nokrashy sensed this. I do not quite know what was the point of this remark. Kerim did not seem himself to think that Nokrashy would necessarily be too bad a man with whom to negotiate, but he realised that Mr. Bevin probably thought differently, and that if that proved so, the only thing was for him to go. He admitted that as far as the record went, negotiations or discussions with Nokrashy seemed unlikely to succeed. He said "Nokrashy says this must happen and that must happen, and no "No". He is like that – and yet he is not like that, that is the curious thing". From further remarks I think he was trying to express the idea which Amr had once or twice expressed to me, i.e. that, Nokrashy being very positive and definite, if he was convinced of the necessity of something he would agree to it definitely.

With regard to a new Government in succession to Nokrashy's, Kerim Bey said that he was putting into King Farouk's mind the advantage of a more broadly based one, and he thought the King was biting. He had to get round the attitude of the King that a coalition Government would lead people to think that this was a preparation for the Wafd, and that waverers would therefore get on to the Wafd band-waggon. It was too early to get this preoccupation out of the King's mind. He was therefore suggesting that the new Government should be a variation of the present, (i.e. the present members of the Cabinet should not all be changed) with the addition of other elements, e.g. independent people. He saw no reason why independents should not be brought in to some of the technical Ministries. There would be others without portfolio. The King had seemed to think this all right. Kerim Bey hoped to be able, after he had put this over, to suggest approaching certain members of the Wafd. He did not know whether they would accept, but he thought it important that the King should make the gesture so as to avoid the accusation that he was intransigent and an obstacle to the adhesion of Wafdists. There was a pretty wide demand for them. Kerim Bey did not even despair that, if the gesture was made by the King and turned down because of Nahas Pasha's refusal to budge from his principle of not entering a coalition Government, some of the members of the Wafd would begin to feel that but for this refusal they could have been Ministers, and that a process might be started by which members of the Wafd would no longer abide by Nahas's ukase against entering non-Wafd government.

I have arranged with Kerim Bey to see him again tomorrow morning at 12, when I will go into these matters a bit further.

130   FO 371/73494, no 407   7 Jan 1949

[Effect of the Palestine issue on the possibility of obtaining an agreement with Egypt]: letter from E A Chapman Andrews to G L Clutton

Your letter J 7929/24/G of the 17th December, about the effect of the Palestine issue on the possibility of obtaining a new Anglo–Egyptian agreement.

I hope that I did not give, in my letter 1/137/48G of 29th November, the impression that we do not consider the Palestine and Egyptian problems closely inter-related. No-one, I think, would for one moment deny the interaction of the two, and the events of the past few weeks have made the relationship between them still closer. We still do not, however, appreciate the force of your contention that "unless the situation in Palestine stabilises it is difficult to see how conversations of any value can take place".

We agree, of course, that an unprovoked renewal of the fight in Palestine by Egypt (a most unlikely contingency in the event of a compromise settlement on something like fair lines) would make conversations politically impossible (penultimate sentence of your second paragraph); but if unchecked and unpunished Jewish aggression and cynical contempt for the Security Council's resolutions should finally succeed in "stabilising" the Palestine situation by a Jewish imposed peace, I think we may be pretty sure that no military conversations could possibly be of any value unless they were aimed at collaboration not only against a looming Russian danger but *also* (eventually, at any rate) against Israel; avowedly or unavowedly, liquidation of Israel would indeed be War Aim No. 1 in order of importance.

If, however, on the other hand, the basis of a *reasonable* settlement in Palestine were reached as a result of British military aid (e.g. arms and a British insistence on Jewish withdrawal to the October 14th position) military conversations could develop out of this collaboration and we ought to be able to exercise restraint and to influence the military advice given by the Egyptian general staff to the Egyptian Government.

In general, it seems to us here that, by a policy of hanging back, we have brought the Egyptians to approach us. This object having been achieved, we should surely wish to clinch it—rather than to continue to hold back—and seize, if warily, the Egyptian hand.

131   WO 216/304,   Jan 1949

'Long term policy in Egypt': note for the Cabinet Defence Committee by Mr Shinwell

[In the autumn of 1948 the Council of Foreign Ministers failed to reach agreement on the future of Cyrenaica and the question was passed to the UN with no decision possible before April 1949 (CAB 129/30, CP(48)261, 9 Nov 1948). This had implications for the accommodation of British troops in Egypt following the withdrawal from Palestine. The note prepared for the Defence Committee followed the JPS's redefinition of Britain's minimum requirements in Egypt. The paper reaffirmed the need for 20,000 troops with between 5–10,000 of them as combat troops. In addition Britain would need the use of areas outside the treaty area, the right to station naval personnel and the presence of more than 400 pilots; none of these were provided for under the 1936 treaty (DEFE 4/19, COS 19(49)2, 7 Feb 1949, JP(48)126, 1 Feb 1949). The note's history provides a good illustration of the problem of getting decisions on practical issues made by high policy makers and the even bigger problem of getting them implemented. Without alteration the note became DO(49)23 of 23 Mar, but did not come before the Defence Committee because of the discussions that began with the Egyptians (see 133). The paper eventually had to be revised as DO(49)86 and was not considered by the Defence Committee until Dec 1949 (see 155).]

It is necessary to review the existing policy on the location of administrative installations and of reserves of Army equipment and stores in the Middle East.

2. In June, 1947, the Defence Committee agreed (14th Meeting 1947) that a Store Holding Area should be constructed in East Africa to hold the equipment less vehicles that would be required in war by a force of two corps each of two divisions, together with a comparable holding of Engineer project stores. These stores were to come from India and Egypt. Later stores from Palestine were also sent to East Africa. This decision was made at a time when it seemed that, whether we liked it or not, we should certainly have to contract into the 1936 Treaty Area and would eventually have to evacuate Egypt altogether.

3. Since June, 1947, the situation has changed very materially. The importance of the Middle East, both in peace and war, has been more generally accepted. The development of plans for the defence of the Middle East and an examination of the relative rates of build up of our own and Russian forces in the area have made it more and more apparent that we must, at the outbreak of war, have an established base in Egypt. A base for a large force can only be established where there is a good deep water port, some internal communications and a reasonable supply of local skilled and unskilled labour. These conditions exist only in Egypt.

4. Even when these conditions are present, much expenditure of time, money and labour is necessary before a base can be fully established. In Egypt in the early days of the last war, it was necessary to construct in the desert camps for personnel and depots to hold vast tonnages of stores and equipment, covered work-shops and hospitals. To all these places it was necessary to lay on water and electric power. It was essential to improve communications, both by road and rail, and this entailed the building of many bridges. It was necessary to develop the ports and to establish signal communications. It is estimated that what was required in the last war took three years to construct and cost no less than £200,000,000. At their peak, local labour forces amounted to 250,000 men. If we were to evacuate the whole of Egypt now, nearly all these wartime developments would be lost. All buildings would be torn down by the local Arab in search of corrugated iron. The expensive water-pumping machinery would be removed and only the roads, and perhaps some of the buried pipelines and railways would remain. In war we could again only establish ourselves in Egypt at the expense of time and money, and time, at any rate, is very unlikely to be available.

5. It was these considerations which led to my colleagues agreeing to a short term policy by which we should retain in working order our existing installations in Egypt including those outside the Treaty Area. This was given to Commanders-in-Chief, Middle East, in COS(ME)293 of 2nd November. The need for these installations is however, not a short term one, and what is required is the recognition that we must retain in Egypt as a long term policy the administrative facilities necessary for our strategy. Without such recognition by my colleagues I cannot provide the facilities and accommodation which the Army in Egypt must have.

6.   The policy for retention of base installations in Egypt also requires a revision of the previous proposals for the construction of personnel accommodation for the troops required to man and guard these installations. At the moment, authority has only been given for development of existing accommodation in the Treaty Area on the minimum scale necessary for a short tenure of two or three years. Even so, it has been obvious for some months that living conditions in Egypt and in fact throughout the Middle East are far below the standard which should be provided for the Army in peacetime. If, therefore, we are to accept a long term commitment for the retention of troops in Egypt we must plan immediately for the early construction of more permanent accommodation for them. Any delay in reaching a decision on this point will react unfavourably on the troops and will prolong the discomforts which are already affecting their morale and efficiency.

7.   Under the instructions of the Chiefs of Staff, a more precise statement of our long term military requirements in Egypt has been prepared by the Joint Planning Staff in consultation with the Foreign Office. This report is intended for use in any negotiations which may take place with the Egyptians. Our exact detailed requirements can only be determined by the Commanders-in-Chief, Middle East. It is, however, apparent that these requirements cannot be met within the limits of the present Army Treaty Area. At the moment, of course, our troops are occupying areas which are outside the Army Treaty Zone.

8.   Illogical as it may seem, there are in Egypt two Treaty Areas; the Army Treaty Area, which consists of two small areas on the Canal, quite inadequate in size for the formation of a base and containing few of the installations erected at such expense during the war; and the Royal Air Force Treaty Area which embraces the greater part of the Canal Zone but does not include those Army installations located in the neighbourhood of Tel el Kebir. It does however contain the considerable storage depots at Geneifa and in the Suez Area and the ammunition depot at Abu Sultan.

9.   The storage and workshop installations in the Tel el Kebir area are essential to us. Their replacement within the Army Treaty Areas would be impossible for lack of space, and elsewhere in the Canal Zone would cost a very large sum – roughly estimated at £4,000,000 to £5,000,000. Moreover, the skilled and unskilled Egyptian labour essential to the operation of these installations is readily available in the Tel el Kebir area but is not available elsewhere in the Canal Zone.

10.   In their present mood I believe that the Egyptians would not raise any objection to work carried out in these areas already occupied by our troops or in fact in any of the sparsely populated desert areas between the Canal and the Delta. The majority of the areas in which work should be done, with the exception of Tel el Kebir, fall within the Royal Air Force Treaty area and this should help to obviate Egyptian objections.

11.   I therefore consider that authority should be given now to go ahead with permanent and semi-permanent construction essential to the efficiency and welfare of our intended permanent Garrison in the areas already occupied by our troops, that is to say within the present Army Treaty area, at Geneifa, at Fayid, in the Suez Area, Abu Sultan, Kantara, El Ballah, in the Port Said Area and within the Tel el Kebir appendage.

The numbers for which accommodation will be required are about 20,000, of which only approximately 4,000 will be teeth [sic] Arm troops. The remainder being the personnel of the nucleus Base, the Regional Headquarters, and for the Anti-Aircraft defence of Egypt.

12.   As a natural corollary to our new policy in Egypt it is necessary to revise the project for building a store holding Area in East Africa. This has been examined in the War Office and it is recommended that:-

(a) No additional storage shall be constructed in East Africa beyond that already completed or so advanced that its completion is economically desirable. This decision involves the completion of 36 sheds (out of an original total of 70) and a REME Workshop. All of this accommodation will eventually be required for stores which are, in any case, to be held in East Africa.

(b) The storage part of this reduced project to be completed by March, 1950, the necessary ancillaries (barrack accommodation, offices etc.) in 1951.

The reduced project will allow the holding in East Africa of about half the stores which it was originally proposed to send there. The remainder should be held in Egypt.

13.   I recommend therefore that my colleagues should agree:-

(a) To confirm that our future administrative policy in the Middle East shall be based on our retention in Egypt of the facilities and installations essential to our strategy.

(b) To go ahead with permanent and semi-permanent construction of installations and accommodation in areas already occupied by our troops.

(c) To a curtailment of the project for the construction of a Store Holding Area in East Africa. Details to be on the lines in the attached Memorandum.[1]

---

[1] Not printed.

132   CAB 131/7, DO(49)26   21 Mar 1949
'Egyptian defence talks': memorandum by Mr Bevin for the Cabinet Defence Committee on technical defence talks

In the course of conversation with His Majesty's Ambassador at Cairo on 26th February King Farouk said that he was now prepared to proceed with the suggestion made last autumn that there should be defence talks between the Egyptians and ourselves on a technical basis.

2.   The object of these talks would be to try and break the deadlock between the Egyptians and ourselves on defence matters. The Egyptians, of course, hope that if we could make satisfactory arrangements on a basis other than that of the Treaty we should at some stage be prepared to scrap the Treaty. We have never committed ourselves to saying that we would dispense with the 1936 Treaty, and must be extremely careful what we say about it. But we have made it clear that what we are concerned with is the reality of defence arrangements which meet our requirements as well as those of the Egyptians, and that if these were secured the Treaty might lose its importance.

3.   We must, of course, remember that in Egypt policy and governments may change overnight, and that a new government may disown agreements concluded by

a previous government. The largest party in Egypt, the Wafd, has for many years been out of power, but if the elections due to take place this summer are free, would certainly come into power. We must bear in mind the obvious risks of relying on arrangements which are revocable while a Treaty strictly speaking is not.

4.   None the less with these reserves I consider that we should actively follow up the suggestions for technical defence talks now made by the King, the Prime Minister and the Foreign Minister.

Visit of the C.I.G.S. to Cairo

5.   In the course of his recent visit to the Middle East the Chief of the Imperial General Staff has had talks with the King, the Prime Minister and the Minister for War. His Majesty's Ambassador, of course, took part.

6.   Cairo telegrams Nos. 412[1] and 413 reporting the result of these conversations which were generally encouraging, have already been circulated.

7.   The proposal now made by the Prime Minister—see paragraph 1 of telegram No. 413—is that we should provide him with a statement listing our military requirements, and also with an indication of our general defence plans for the Middle East. His Majesty's Ambassador and the Chief of the Imperial General Staff concur.

8.   The Chiefs of Staff recently reviewed our military requirements in Egypt—see C.O.S. (49) 48 of 8th February. A paper is now being prepared at Fayid, presumably on the basis of that review, which if approved will be ready for presentation to the Egyptians in ten days' time.

9.   The Defence Committee are asked to decide whether we approve this procedure—see paragraph 4 of Cairo telegram No. 426 (already circulated).

10.   Our original views had been that it might be wiser to conduct the talks by stages, beginning with subjects such as joint training and joint use of airfields on which agreement might be easiest, and having thus created an atmosphere of confidence and success to proceed to the more difficult questions such as maintenance of a base in Egypt and right of re-entry in case of apprehended emergency. His Majesty's Ambassador and the Chief of the Imperial General Staff, however, both recommend that we should fall in with the Egyptian suggestion of giving them an outline of our full requirements at once. In view of the attitude of the King and his Ministers as reported to us, and of the atmosphere created by the publication of the terms of the Atlantic Pact, there is much to be said for striking while the iron is hot and taking this risk.

11.   On balance, therefore, I recommend that we should approve the procedure advocated by His Majesty's Ambassador and the Chief of the Imperial General Staff.

Arms

12.   One of the most important factors in any defence agreement or arrangement with Egypt and with other Middle East countries will be our ability to provide them with at least the minimum of the arms they require to equip their forces to take a share in at least local defence. To meet these requirements it may be necessary:-

(a) To lay down what degree of high priority the requirements of Middle East countries up to a minimum scale should have as compared with Western Union requirements.

---

[1] See 133.

(b) That our own production of arms should be stepped up to make delivery possible. In considering the economic effects it should be remembered that the countries concerned will pay for the arms. In any case the delivery of arms to Egypt is probably a condition of the successful outcome of the talks.

United States government

13. We should, of course, keep the United States Government fully informed. The United States Government are most anxious that we should maintain military facilities in Egypt and have expressed willingness in principle to help us to do so. We are already keeping the United States Government generally informed.

Recommendations

14. It is recommended that:-

(a) As proposed by His Majesty's Ambassador at Cairo and the Chief of the Imperial General Staff, a statement of our military requirements in Egypt and an indication of our general defence plans for the Middle East should be given to the Egyptian Prime Minister.
(b) All possible steps should be taken to enable us to meet essential arms requirements of Egypt and other Middle East countries.
(c) We should continue to keep the United States Government informed of the progress of Anglo–Egyptian Defence talks.

133 CAB 131/7, DO 8(49)2 22 Mar 1949

'Egyptian defence talks': Cabinet Defence Committee minutes. *Annex I*: copy of Cairo telegram no 412 on talks between Field Marshal Sir W Slim and King Farouk, 17 Mar 1949

The Committee had before them the following documents:-

(i) Cairo to Foreign Office telegrams No. 412,[1] 413, 418 and 426 of 17th, 18th, 19th and 20th March respectively, reporting the results of interviews which His Majesty's Ambassador and the Chief of the Imperial General Staff had had with King Farouk and the Egyptian Prime Minister, and seeking approval to the further procedure that had been agreed with the Egyptian Prime Minister.
(ii) A memorandum (D.O. (49) 26)[2] in which the Secretary of State for Foreign Affairs put forward his views on further procedure.

The Foreign Secretary said that his original idea had been to start the proposed defence discussions on the purely technical level in the hope that it would there be possible to avoid the more difficult and controversial questions, at least until an atmosphere of confidence had been created. The Egyptian Prime Minister had, however, insisted that the discussions should start by our presenting him with an outline of our full requirements, and the main question before the Committee was whether they should agree with His Majesty's Ambassador and the Chief of the Imperial General Staff that this was now the right course to take. There were obvious risks in taking it. The

---

[1] Only tel 412 is reproduced here.   [2] See 132.

Egyptians might at once raise the question of the 1936 Treaty, or embarrass us by pressing us to disclose the nature of our plans for the defence of the Middle East; and there were risks in embarking on discussions on the political level with a régime which was so unstable. But on the whole his own view was that all these risks should be accepted. With the signing of the Atlantic Pact he felt that there was a general stirring of interest in defence which provided the exact physchological [sic] moment in which to make a fresh start with the Egyptians. If the Committee agreed with this view he thought the next step would be for His Majesty's Ambassador to present the Egyptian Prime Minister with the outline of our full requirements which was now being prepared by the Commanders-in-Chief, Middle East; after which it was to be hoped that it would be possible to transfer the discussions to the military plane.

The Chief of the Imperial General Staff did not think that there would be any need to discuss with the Egyptian Prime Minister our plans for the defence of the Middle East to the security of which, therefore, very little risk would attach. The Commanders-in-Chief in the Middle East were fully alive to the security question and, if pressed, intended to take the line described in paragraph 5 of Cairo telegram No. 413, i.e., they would explain that the general plan was to defend Egypt as far forward as possible and lay stress on the fact that defence would depend on the efficiency of the Egyptian base and the speed with which it can receive and forward reinforcements. No particular lines of defence would be stated, but a description of possible lines of advance which the Russians might alternatively take could be described without danger.

The main points in the discussion which followed were:-

(a) There was general agreement with the views of the Foreign Secretary that as a first step a statement of our requirements in Egypt should be handed to the Egyptian Prime Minister, and that the risks inherent in this procedure should be accepted.

(b) Throughout the discussions the aim should be to get away from the conception of a *British* base in Egypt and get the Egyptians to regard the base as a *joint* base which we would both share. There was no reason, for instance, why Egyptian units should not share areas and installations occupied by British units and indeed a great deal to be said for encouraging them to do so.

(c) The Sinai Peninsula could not be regarded as Egyptian territory proper and from the political point of view less difficulty with the Egyptians might be encountered over our requirements if we were able to suggest in the discussions that some of them might be met in this area. The Chiefs of Staff undertook to look into this suggestion with the Foreign Office, to which the Foreign Secretary attached considerable importance.

(d) In a short discussion on the question of the provision of arms and equipment to Egypt in particular and the Middle East countries in general, the *Chief of the Imperial General Staff* suggested that it would pay us to make an outright gift of a couple of thousand repairable lorries from the reserve stocks in Egypt.

Sir Edward Bridges reminded the Committee that we owed Egypt some £300 million, and said that the Chancellor of the Exchequer hoped that any supplies and services, which we might render under any new defence arrangements with the Egyptians, would be paid for; and the *Minister of Defence* said that, as the Foreign Secretary recognised in his paper, the requirements of Egypt and the Middle East could not be considered in isolation. Before any decisions could be taken on the scale of supply to any particular country or on the extent to which our own production might be stepped up to make delivery possible, it was first essential to assess the total foreign demand. He was glad to say that a working party was assembling all the likely demands and would shortly be putting up a report in which the whole problem could be seen in perspective.

(e) At present it was vitally necessary to ensure the secrecy of any further discussions with the Egyptians on defence matters. Commonwealth Governments should not, therefore, at present be informed of the talks and in American circles it was most undesirable that any information concerning them should go beyond Admiral Conolly[3] who had already been told the position by the Chief of the Imperial General Staff.

The Committee:—

(1) Endorsed the procedure advocated by His Majesty's Ambassador at Cairo and the Chief of the Imperial General Staff, and invited the Secretary of State for Foreign Affairs to proceed accordingly.

(2) Agreed that all possible steps should be taken to enable us to meet the essential arms requirements of Egypt and other Middle East countries, and took note that the Minister of Defence would shortly be submitting to the Committee a comprehensive appreciation of the supply of arms to foreign countries.

(3) Invited the Chiefs of Staff to consider the point at (c) above.

Annex I to 133

Following from C.I.G.S. for Defence Committee:—

I was received by King Farouk with the Ambassador this afternoon. The King was cordial and forthcoming, and expressed special pleasure at the opportunity of meeting me as I was no doubt constantly studying strategic matters.

2. I mentioned the good relations between British and Egyptian troops. His Majesty said he was well aware of this and glad of it, and he hoped that it would be expanded. I seized the opportunity of this to suggest closer and more practical contacts, but he sheered off at this point and said he much regretted that Great Britain had missed a very great opportunity while the Egyptian forces were fighting the Jews. He said that we should remember that a friend in need is a friend indeed. He realised that this had nothing to do with the British army; still he feared that it would be remembered that we had missed this opportunity. He also doubted whether so good an opportunity would recur.

3. We then raised the question of Russia's intentions. He showed himself as entirely agreed as ever that it was necessary to prepare for aggression in the Middle East and agreed that we had interests in common here. On that point I told him that I thought that Russia, dangerous as she was, was not so formidable at this moment as Hitler's Germany in 1939. The only hope of preventing an attack was for the democratic nations to keep together. I did not mean that if an attack occurred Russia would not endeavour to push us back in Europe, but we would certainly win in the end. His Majesty said that he was glad to hear what I said, but he felt sure himself that it would be from the Channel coast that we should have to push Russia back, adding that he

---

[3] US naval commander in Mediterranean (NATO c-in-c South, under SACEUR).

did not know about the Pyrenees because he knew that the Americans were fortifying them. But it was not only Europe that Russia would attack. She would also attack the Middle East and he was convinced that before final victory the Middle East as well as Europe would have gone through a very nasty time. I here said that Egypt would be the main target because of her geographical position and her wealth. He entirely agreed with this. I then said that this being so everything, and both our interests coinciding, we should surely get together. I would like to see our staffs discussing measures together. He said that the Ambassador knew his opinion on this point and that the Egyptian Ambassador had received instructions. He hoped that the Egyptian Prime Minister would be speaking to me on this subject later in the evening. The Prime Minister knew his mind from the time he had been head of the Royal Cabinet, and His Majesty was confident I would be approached by him and discuss ways and means. I pressed him on the point whether he himself approved of such staff contacts, saying that I would appoint the Commanders-in-Chief in the Canal Zone to get in touch with whomever he would appoint. He said he did approve of it, and he would appoint his best man (not that he had many of these) for the purpose. He said that I now had it from the horse's mouth. I said what then would be the next step, and he said that the Prime Minister would be talking to me on this point to-night. His Majesty hinted at a knowledge of American preparations in this part of the world mentioning specificially [sic] underground airfields in Saudi Arabia. He did not, however, pursue this nor mention the question of Anglo–American planning.

4.   Talking of the threat of the Jews, His Majesty expressed pleasure at the presence of our troops at Akaba, and clear statement by His Majesty's Government of their position, which he said was about the one good thing we had done in the Palestine affair. Speaking of the narrow apex of the triangular cone of Akaba, he said he had given instructions for an Egyptian force to move to the Palestine frontier in that area with a view to preventing Jewish troops patrolling over Egyptian frontier which there was nothing otherwise to prevent them doing.

5.   In the course of conversation, His Majesty said that his intelligence had given him the line dividing the point up to which the Russian *saboteurs* were to destroy communications in the Middle East from that behind which they were to preserve them. I pressed His Majesty to give me what his line was, but he said that he was confident that it coincided with the line which I had received from my own intelligence. His Majesty also said that through counter-espionage organisations he had received complete information as to what our requirements were for bases and installations in Egypt in the event of war. He said that the British officer through whom this leakage had occurred had been punished. He further said that with this knowledge, and in order to avoid clashes on arrival of British reinforcements he had instructed the Commanding Officers of the areas concerned to be prepared to evacuate them. I used this as a peg to impress on him further necessity of co-operation between our staffs even if only to avoid such clashes and that I should be glad for them to make such arrangements together before the necessity for them arose. He agreed and said that it was for this purpose that he mentioned the matter. He reiterated that we had a friend in him, and one that we did not deserve (reference 4th February, 1942, on which he expanded at some length) and that he said this both from his heart and because of the interests of his country. In closing the audience he asked me to express his good wishes to the British troops.

6.   I will report further result of talk with the Prime Minister at dinner to-night.

134   DEFE 5/13, COS(49)100, annex   23 Mar 1949
'Middle East defence agreements': note for COS by Brigadier C Price[1]
circulating a minute by Mr Bevin and an FO paper

The Foreign Secretary has sent the Minister of Defence the attached paper under
cover of the following Minute:-

> "I enclose for your consideration a paper on Middle East defence agreements
> which I think ought to be reviewed in a general way in relation to various new
> factors which have recently appeared and which I do not think have yet been
> properly co-ordinated.
>
>   2. I shall be very glad if you can let me have your views on this whole
> problem fairly shortly. We can then perhaps decide whether we ought to
> circulate the paper to the Defence Committee or take the matter further in
> any other way.
>
>   3. I appreciate of course, that some of the questions raised in paragraph 4
> of the enclosed paper are largely political in character, but they all have
> military implications and it would be most valuable to have the views of the
> Chiefs of Staff on them from this point of view".

    2.   In anticipation of your instructions, the Joint Planning Staff have been asked
to examine and prepare a draft report on the Foreign Secretary's paper.

Annex to 134

The last general paper on this subject appears to be that sent to the Foreign Office in
Group-Captain Stapleton's letter of 16th January, 1948. Since the date of that paper
various new aspects of the matter have come to notice and the time seems to have
come for a general review on which future policy may be based. This paper sets out a
list of the more important factors which it seems necessary to take into consideration
and attempts to put some of the main questions which require to be answered.

    2.   Discussions are already proceeding about the particular case of Egypt and it
has seemed most convenient in this paper not to try to include questions relating to
these discussions but to proceed on the assumption, which has always been held by
the Service Departments, that some arrangement with Egypt is the absolutely
essential part of our strategic requirements in the Middle East and that sooner or
later and somehow or other we shall get an arrangement which will meet some or all
of our requirements for a main base there. If we failed to do this the whole picture
would be different and we should have to start again from the beginning. On this
assumption, therefore, the remaining points for consideration and the questions on
which the views of the Service Departments are required, are set out below.

    3.   The points for consideration seem to be:—

(1) Closer American interest in the Middle East defence planning as exemplified
by the appointment of Admiral Connolly.
(2) The probable continuance of the temporary United States-Saudi Arabian
agreement for the use of Dhahran by American military and civil aircraft but

---

[1] Secretary to COS Committee.

without any undertaking on the part of the United States Government with regard to the defence of Saudi Arabia and without any general grant of facilities by Saudi Arabia. There are indications that a somewhat similar pattern of local arrangements might be contemplated between the United States Government and the Lebanon and possibly Syria.

(3) The possibility of a statement on Persia being made at the time of signature of the Atlantic Pact. This would, if made, probably be to the effect that in the event of a threat to the integrity of Persia the signatories (or some of them) would urgently consult together.

(4) The question how far north we could in the event of war attempt to defend the Middle East. This is particularly relevant to defence arrangements with Iraq and Syria.

(5) The difficulty of supplying war material from the United Kingdom to Middle Eastern States even after the raising of the Palestine arms embargo.

(6) The establishment of the State of Israel. Some of the considerations relevant to this factor are set out in C.O.S. (49) 64 of 17th February, 1949.

(7) The probable establishment of Greater Transjordan (though we cannot yet tell whether this would include territory in the Negeb allowing of a common frontier with Egypt).

(8) A new approach which has been made to us by the Syrian Government with a view to technical advice being given to Syria by British Service representatives on defence measures which might be taken in Syria, leading possibly to an agreement somewhat on the lines of our arrangements with Turkey.

(9) French attempts to improve relations with Syria and the Lebanon, notably by the supply of war material for internal security purposes.

(10) The refusal by the Saudi Arabian Government to allow a British reconnaissance party to examine sites for airfields, etc. in Saudi Arabia accompanied, however, by a proposal for a tripartite Anglo–American–Saudi agreement.

(11) The possibility of supply of British war material to Persia in addition to that supplied by the United States Government.

(12) The existing Anglo–Iraqi Treaty of 1930 is due to remain in force until January, 1956, though it has a provision for the conclusion of a new treaty at the request of either party at any time after January, 1951. A new treaty can of course be substituted for it at any time with the consent of both parties. This date may be rather inconvenient in relation to the most likely period of emergency as this has appeared from the planning discussions.

4. The main questions on which the views of the Service Departments are required appear to be as follows:—

(a) Should we seek to retain in all cases the essential structure of defence agreements as we have at present got them with Iraq and Transjordan, i.e. a firm undertaking on our part to come to the assistance of the other state in return for the grant of definite facilities in the other state for our military requirements? Can we conscientiously retain this structure in relation to Iraq if there is in fact very little chance of our defending that country in practice?

(b) To what extent would our requirements be met by arrangements, in some countries at least, more on the American model as described in paragraph 3(2) above, i.e. British financial and technical contribution to the preparation of say an airfield or port in return for permission to use the airfield or port but without any general commitments on either side?

(c) In view of the great anxiety shown by all Middle East states to acquire war material, what attitude can we adopt in defence discussions on this subject in the light of our own supply position and the requirements of Western Union?

(d) What response are we to make to the Syrian proposal mentioned in paragraph 3 (8) above and further explained in Foreign Office telegram to Damascus No. 120 (copy attached)? The Syrian Government will expect a reply fairly soon and it is hoped that this question may perhaps be dealt with in advance of more general consideration. The first question to be decided is whether we should agree to send a small party of British Service representatives into Syria for reconnaissance purposes to be followed by technical talks with Syrian representatives. The decision on this question will have to take account of French susceptibilities but it would be useful to have advice from the Service point of view in the very near future. Service comments on a previous Syrian approach were given in Colonel Waterfield's letter to the Foreign Office C.O.S. 1553/11/9/8 of 11th September, 1948.

(e) If the Auja-Beersheba-Hebron road is not in Egyptian or Transjordan control as a result of the final settlement of Palestine should we develop or contribute to the development of the Suez-Aqaba-Amman track as an all-weather road capable of carrying heavy transport? The expense in Transjordan territory would almost certainly fall entirely on His Majesty's Government. Are there in any case military reasons for building up port facilities at Aqaba? Should any British forces be retained there after the Palestine settlement?

(f) What are the possibilities of developing alternative road and/or rail communications between Beirut and the Red Sea south of Aqaba and again from this point to Basra?

(g) Assuming that the Egyptians retain the Gaza-Rafah strip of Palestine territory, should we ask for any military facilities there?

(h) Is there any military advantage in any closer grouping of Middle East States among themselves? The future of the Arab League is uncertain. There has been some talk of reviving instead the idea of a federation between Iraq, Syria, Transjordan and possibly the Lebanon. There are some signs of renewed Turkish interest in closer relations with the Arab States.

(i) Assuming that no such closer grouping of Middle East states would of itself have much effect on the military situation, should we try to link these states with the United Kingdom or the United States or both in some similar manner to that to be adopted in the Atlantic Pact or should we continue to rely on individual arrangements between His Majesty's Government and Middle East Governments on the assumption that United States would in fact come to our assistance in carrying out our obligations under such arrangements? The Arab States cannot be directly attacked by Russia without first passing through Turkey or Persia. The American attitude would no doubt in any case already have been decided as a result of Russian attack on one of these two countries.

(j) It is too early politically for any step to be taken towards a defence arrangement of any kind with Israel and it must be doubtful whether any such step may be possible for a considerable time. Meanwhile is there any indirect method by which the ground could be prepared for some such possibility, e.g. by contact between British and Israeli Services? Should it be our policy to supply limited and specialised types of war material to the Israeli forces after a final settlement has been reached in Palestine or would this be too dangerous in regard to our relations with armed forces of Arab States?

135   FO 371/73464, no 2414   26 Mar 1949
[Dictatorship in Egypt]: minute by D J D Maitland on the future nature of the Egyptian regime

Last summer King Farouk presumably had in mind the establishment of a military state on present Spanish lines. The defeat of the Egyptian army in Palestine, the consequent collapse of morale and the shortage of military equipment have ruled out this possibility for some time to come. But a dictatorship need not be a military one and so long as martial law continues there will be a Palace dictatorship in Egypt. If, during that time, the King can secure an arrangement perpetuating British occupation of a part of Egypt he will be able to substitute the measures which we will be bound to take to counter any threat to our base e.g. disorders in Egypt, for martial law and continue his more or less benevolent dictatorship.

136   FO 141/1347, no 33   30 Mar 1949
[Middle Eastern defence]: inward telegram no 479 from Sir R Campbell to FO on the talks with General H Pyman[1] and Abdel Hadi

> [The murder of Nokrashi in Dec 1948 had produced martial law in Egypt and a new government under the Saadist Abdel Hadi. The British were considering whether these developments would provide the opportunity for a new agreement or whether a government of national unity including the Wafd would be more advantageous. In the event the Wafd refused to participate in a Hadi led government and the British were left to try and convince the new prime minister of the value of defence co-operation pending the promised elections. It was not until July 1949 that Abdel Hadi was replaced by a 'national' government under Hussein Sirry which included the Wafd.]

General Pyman and I presented to the P.M. this morning the paper promised him by the C.I.G.S. After reading it through, he said that it did not supply the answer to his question whether Egypt was in the first line, and what was the rôle of Turkey. Was Egypt in the statement of our requirements considered in isolation, or in the setting of a wide strategic plan for the Middle East? Presumably it was the latter, and he wished very much to know what were our plans in respect of other M.E. countries. We said that, as the paper stated, there were a number of possible alternative lines of Russian attack, that one could not say before-hand which would be chosen or, therefore, how the situation would be met. As he would see, the paper contemplated keeping the attack as far away as possible from the Egyptian base. Where this would be must depend on the circumstances, and the means available at the moment. P.M. replied that we had arrangements with Turkey and Iraq. Surely in the case of land

---

[1] Chief of staff, Middle East Land Forces.

attack, which must come through those countries or Persia, we would wish to have some forward bases for their defence on such strategic lines as existed. What facilities and help were these countries going to provide? Surely we had arranged this. We said that we had alliances with Turkey and Iraq. We knew of no arrangements of the kind referred to but we personally assumed that the alliances would be honoured. But we repeated that how and where operations should be carried out seemed impossible to tell beforehand. To fix on a prearranged line in defence had been shown to be dangerous in, e.g., France at the beginning of the war. We were convinced that Egypt was the only possible main base from which whatever operations were decided on at the time must start and be controlled, and this was the basis of the paper. P.M. said he well understood that no General could or should fix his line arbitrarily before-hand, but we must have formed ideas on where it should be in the various alternative possibilities. As we knew, Egypt had decided that she must be with us in a future war, and work hand in hand. That was a definite decision, but he begged to be given the information he asked for. Though it would not affect the decision (which he repeated again with emphasis) it would be "very very useful" that he should be told.

2. He said he wished to study the paper before discussing it with us further, adding twice that he would not waste any time. We knew that he was anxious to go ahead.

3. P.M. made no comment on the statement of our requirements. He gave no sign of being shocked during his single reading, but I would not like to conclude that he will prove ready to accept it whole. We got the impression that in his reading of it today, he was chiefly concerned to seek an answer to the question mentioned above, and we are impressed by his keenness on getting one. We do not know whether it may be possible, without giving him more than we and/or the Americans hold desirable, to meet his request in a less general way than attempted in the paper. I will telegraph further after Gen Pyman has reported to the C's-in-C and ascertained their views.

4. Text of paper follows immediately by bag.

137   FO 141/1347, no 38   1 Apr 1949
[Middle East defence arrangements]: record by Air Marshal Sir W Dickson of a meeting between Sir R Campbell and Abdel Hadi

The meeting took place at the Prime Minister's house. No one else was present. After an exchange of courtesies, I opened the talk by saying that we understood from the Ambassador that he (the Prime Minister) was anxious to have answers to certain questions which might assist as a background for the proposed discussions. I explained that it was not possible for the three of us to be in Cairo on this particular day but that he could take it that I spoke for the three Commanders-in-Chief. I also mentioned that since I would be speaking from a strictly military point of view I hoped he would regard anything I said as being in strict confidence to himself and off the record.

The Prime Minister then said that he had been very glad to get our paper which would be of much help to him, but frankly it was not quite what he had been expecting. What he had expected was a more specific list of our requirements. What barracks we wanted, what airfields, where we wanted to put our forces, and so on. He had also wanted to have a clearer picture as to our general Middle East defence arrangements, and he went on to expound the identical points and questions he put to the Ambassador and General Pyman on the 30th March.[1]

To this I said that the truth of it was that we had had some difficulty in drafting the paper we had sent him, because we were not quite sure how much detail he wanted at this stage. To set out all the various points big and small which would be important in working out a joint defence plan involved a lengthy document, and also we did not think that this could be done without both our staffs working together. So as a first step we had set out what we thought were the basic requirements and we were expecting to be able to develop these in detail at the next stage of the discussions. I hoped he would believe that this was the only reason why our paper was written in rather general terms.

As to his particular questions about defence arrangements with other countries in relation to Middle East Defence, I said I felt sure I could explain the position if he would allow me to speak at some length.

I then said that it was only in the comparatively recent past that we had been working on the assumption that there was no immediate danger of war and that we had perhaps five years or more before that danger became imminent. Under such an assumption we were working on longer term plans of development and no question arose of discussing plans with anyone in the Middle East to meet an immediate threat.

It was true that American and British aid had been given and was being given to Greece and Turkey. But the reason for this was clear. Greece was immediately threatened by the cold war and the Communist technique. If Greece succumbed it would be a serious blow to Middle East security and particularly to the security of Egypt. Turkey had also been under great pressure and it was vital to support Turkish resistance. In fact both Greece and Turkey were at present fighting in the front line of the cold war. But, I could assure him, in the strictest confidence, that this help had not extended to the discussion of plans of defence in the event of war.

The situation to-day was different. Tension had increased and there was now a serious risk that some accident might precipitate war even if war was contrary to the general policy of the potential enemy. We were thus faced with the immediate necessity of preparing for such an eventuality which might come without warning.

In this situation we had to put first things first, and there was no question that the primary need was an understanding about the defence of Egypt. That was why we now came to them first and why, I imagine, His Majesty the King and he himself had also seen the need for these discussions. The reason why Egypt was all important we had explained in our paper and I expanded on this to rub the point in. I also said that it was not until we could jointly agree on arrangements for the mutual defence of Egypt and its development as a base that we could properly consider detailed plans for the outer defence.

The Prime Minister here interjected that he was quite convinced as to the essential importance of the Egypt base but he still did not quite understand why it was not important to consider first the use of Turkey and, say, Iraq as front line bases

---

[1] See 136.

complementary to Egypt where our forces might meet the impact of attack. Why had they got to be in Egypt to start with?

To this I said that whatever forward positions we might try and hold and whatever forward bases we might use, it was not practicable to consider, say, Turkey as an alternative base to Egypt. The enemy might by-pass Turkey and Turkey at any rate to start with might remain neutral. Because of such a possibility it was obviously impractical to consider Turkey as a base. Similarly Iraq would not be suitable as an alternative to Egypt in view of its exposed position and the difficulty of the communications leading to it.

I said he must not take this to mean that we had not thought a good deal about the outer defence of the area. It was misleading to think in terms of fixed lines of defence. To take, for example, an enemy advance on Egypt through Persia and Iraq. Our intention would be as he had heard to fight and hold the enemy as far away from Egypt as possible. The problem was, however, one of time and space. In fact it was a race with the time. If we had forces ready to operate, and if, together, we had done the right amount of development to receive reinforcements in Egypt and deploy them quickly then we might have good prospects of meeting and holding the enemy a long distance from Egypt. But, if on the other hand we had nothing in Egypt ready to operate and had to start planning and development when the war started vital delays would occur and we might not be able to meet and hold the enemy until he was very close to Egypt. This might be fatal bearing in mind that it would bring his short range aircraft within range of Egypt.

It could be said therefore that the distance of the outer line of defence from Egypt was in direct relation to the preparations and plans which together we could make in Egypt and to the readiness of our land and air forces to operate from Egypt at the outset. This would explain why it was so necessary for Egyptian/British defence talks to precede anything else.

I turned then to the air threat pointing out that that was not a matter of lines. Egypt could not escape the danger of air attack from the start. The scale of attack might not be heavy to begin but neither of us could afford not to meet such an attack at once. The weaker the defence the heavier the attack would be. He must agree that there was virtually no effective defence system at present. It was essential to be ready. Remembering the possibility of no warning period and the suddeness with which air attack could come from distant bases, it would be suicidal to leave preparations and plans until the emergency arises and not to have a joint Egyptian/British force of fighters and guns ready to meet the initial attacks and trained to work within the same air defence system.

The system must cover the whole of the Delta area. Our arrangements in the Canal Zone would not protect Egypt. Plans were needed for the proper selection of airfields, guns and radar sites, construction of operations rooms and for a telephone network and so on.

I then put in the thought that it must be our object to prevent war, and that to the extent that the possible enemy could see that we were prepared and strong the risk of war diminished. But if on the other hand we were obviously unprepared, and if, for example, there were no British forces on the spot to assist in the defence of Egypt, then the enemy to that extent might be tempted. Our joint defence arrangements were thus a deterrent to war.

I asked the Prime Minister if my general explanation had answered his questions. He nodded and appeared to be quite satisfied.

He then started on a new line. He fully saw the importance of developing the Egypt base and having it brought up to a state of readiness to receive immediate reinforcements. There was no argument coming from him about this. But we had to remember his problem and the importance of obtaining the right attitude of mind in the Egyptian people. Neither of us could hope for much success if the Egyptian people were to be brought into the war with a sense of grievance against us. But if, on the other hand, they could be made to feel that the defence of Egypt, at least in the initial stages, rests primarily on themselves, then it would be quite different; one did not fight properly or meet the sacrifices necessary for defence unless one's heart was in it. Was there no possibility that our defence discussions might not lead to an arrangement whereby all the development of installations could be put in hand on a modern basis and all the plans completed for the working of our forces together in Egypt in war without the necessity of maintaining British troops actually in Egypt. By this he did not mean that we need be far away. He realised that if it were a question of being weeks away it would be fatal. He, however, was thinking of us being only a few hours away. Did I think that some such solution might not come out of the talks because if that was so his problem and our problem would be easy.

To this I replied that he would not expect me to be able to speak about the political problem but speaking from the military aspect I said that I fully sympathised with his problem and that indeed we agreed that without the goodwill of the Egyptian people the problem of the defence of Egypt would be serious indeed. At the same time I frankly did not see how it would be possible to defend Egypt, and indeed the Middle East, against the emergency which threatened us in the present situation unless the advanced element of British forces, which we had indicated in our paper, were actually present in the Canal Zone and assisting in the development of the defence arrangements which nowadays was an intricate and elaborate matter. I could not speak about the future when the present threat might disappear. Then perhaps some other defence arrangements might be possible. The issues both for Egypt and the future of the world were, however, too great at the moment to take any risks. He must realize that neither the Egyptian army nor the Egyptian Air Force would for some long time be able to provide an adequate defence against such a strong enemy even in the initial stages.

I asked if there was not some way by which the Egyptian people could be made to feel the extent of the threat and to look upon the presence of the relatively small British force in the Canal Zone as a partner in the defence of Egypt against this serious threat. He said that this might be possible and indeed was what they would have to try and do but it would be difficult and it was important for us to make his task easier.

The Prime Minister dropped this point and said he would like our assurance that we really were genuine in our desire to see the Egyptian Army and Air Force made strong and effective. He hoped that this would not be pushed on one side in the discussions. He did not want the Egyptian forces relegated to a minor role. Egypt must feel that she had the means to contribute to her own defence. This did not mean only internal security. He wanted to fight to keep the enemy outside the frontiers of Egypt. He had rather expected that our paper would have stated more precisely what size the Egyptian forces would be and what would be the requirements to make them effective.

I said, at once, that we were sincere when we said that it was an important part of our joint defence policy that there should be strong, well trained and well equipped Egyptian armed forces. We had, indeed, made special mention of this in our paper. We had thought of setting out in more detail what we thought Egyptian requirements might be but we soon found that we could not do this without first discussing the problem with the Egyptian staffs. After all, it was not for us to stipulate the size and composition of the Egyptian armed forces. We did not know, for instance, how much the Egyptian Government could afford to spend on defence. We were, however, only too ready to give any advice that might be required. As to the question of the Egyptian forces taking their share of the field force role, we were only too anxious that this should happen. We had, however, felt diffident in pressing this suggestion in our paper in case it might not have been in accord with his views.

The Prime Minister then questioned me about the kind of requirements we had in mind in the way of airfields and installations in the Delta. I said that this was a matter of detail and that whereas we had certain general ideas, we were anxious to consult with the Egyptian staffs and to reach an agreed conclusion. The immediate requirements in peacetime were not likely to be considerable. There was no question of our asking that British units should move into locations in the Delta area in peacetime unless, of course, it turned out later that it was the Egyptians wish that we should do so. The important thing now was to get together and to arrive at agreed plans. This was particularly necessary in the case of air defence. Airfields must be selected, some improvements made, telephones laid out, places earmarked for occupation in war etc. Ports would want some development, dredging etc. The work was not very considerable and much of it might be made to assist Egyptian economy. It would take time and there might not be much time to lose. All these plans were matters of detail but it must be thought out and agreed. I spoke for a bit on this line with the object of making the task ahead seem as profitable as possible and in the Egyptian interests.

The Prime Minister took this all very well and showed a good deal of interest. I then asked him whether he had thought about what might be the procedure for the next stage of the discussions. I said that we were quite prepared to meet him or anyone he deputed to have a preliminary talk as to how these discussions might be split up, that is, to arrange a plan of work. Or we were ready to nominate senior experts to meet their Egyptian appropriate numbers. He said that he was anxious to begin but that there were one or two difficulties he had to overcome and that he wanted to discuss these first with the Minister of National Defence. As soon as he had made up his mind he would let us know through the Ambassador.

I ended up by assuring him that we were anxious to help in any way possible and to give our full attention to the problem so as to ensure the success of the discussions. We would wait until we heard further from him and would like him to know that we would remain ready at Fayid at his disposal and willing to fit into any arrangements that were suitable to him. He was extremely cordial throughout and gave me the impression that he had not weakened in any way in wanting to get something moving.

138   FO 141/1347, no 43   15 Apr 1949

[Negotiations for an Anglo–Egyptian settlement]: inward telegram no 561 from Sir R Campbell to FO on the timing of discussions with the Egyptians

I hope that the following review may be useful in any contacts at Lake Success or in London with Egyptian representatives.

2.   Until recently the Palace and the present Prime Minister were concentrating on the idea of technical military discussions in order to meet the security requirements of the prevailing international situation, while at the same time avoiding the political snags which any attempt at negotiation for a revision of the 1936 Treaty would present. About a month ago there began to be indications that Khashaba Pasha, for his part, looked to the possibility of achieving an early full settlement with His Majesty's Government, both in respect of the alliance and of the Sudan. This line of thought was based both on Khashaba's definite policy of conciliation all round, and particularly with regard to Great Britain, and also on the improvement in sentiment towards Great Britain. The tendency seemed to spread from Khashaba Pasha to the Prime Minister, and it seemed that these two Ministers, at any rate, were now aiming at reaching full settlement with H.M.G. within the next few months, that is, before the elections, which it is the present intention to hold in November. In this context, they were looking to a successful outcome of technical military talks as a means (amongst others) of preparing the way for such settlement. Later indications, supported by public statements, have been that both the Prime Minister and the Minister for Foreign Affairs have realised that since negotiations cannot be undertaken if there is any risk of failure, and since the ground must therefore be fully prepared and the chances of success be almost certain before they can be undertaken, it may not be possible to tackle a full settlement before the elections.

3.   However, it is clear to me that Abdel Hadi and Khashaba desire a settlement at the earliest possible moment, and that they might think the moment had come before the elections. For I suppose that at no time in the last few years has the general sentiment in Egypt been so favourable to an Anglo–Egyptian settlement. The Government would like to take advantage of this sentiment—which may not last— both on grounds of the general interest of the country and of party interest. It is doing its best to clear the air and the ground for this. But what may be thought now to be the party interest may turn out to be incompatible with both the general and the party interest—see below.

4.   It is tempting for us on our side also to seek to take advantage of the present phase of sentiment, more especially as moods change quickly in Egypt. Moreover, I have advised in the past that if our chief concern was to secure our new military requirements to meet an immediate situation, then we should regard any military arrangement resulting from technical discussions, and any instrument which might eventually enshrine the military arrangement, as a short term affair, and take the risk of its not long outlasting the present Government and Parliament.

5.   Meanwhile time has been passing and the situation is not a simple one; and it is well to bear the following considerations in mind. In the first place, it will not be easy to reconcile Egyptian aspirations, such as they still remain, in respect of the

presence of British troops and perhaps more particularly of the Sudan, with our requirements and views. These aspirations may have become slightly modified, and the approach to their achievement is probably more flexible than during Nokrashy Pasha's term of office. But is the Government yet a free agent? There are, first, Watanist Ministers who may be troublesome. Next, and more important, the Wafd has so far refused to join the Government, and seems likely to maintain its refusal. The prospects of the formation of a neutral Government to hold the elections are at the moment dim. Hence the Wafd must be expected to fight the elections, and the present signs are that it will fight them hard. This means almost inevitably that it will also oppose the Government's foreign policy, more especially as far as the "Egyptian question" is concerned, and the Press will be whooped up both against negotiations and against any successful outcome they might have, if entered upon.

6.   It is not inconceivable that the Government may hope to settle the question of the maintenance of British troops in Egypt by a severing of "the link" (see my unnumbered despatch of November 27th, 1948, paras. 4, 10 and 11) consequent upon a military arrangement resulting from technical military talks. It may consider that if by doing so it can claim that H.M.G. have agreed to substitute a military arrangement for Article 8 of the 1936 Treaty, it can spike the opposition guns. In respect of the Sudan, it may hope for a compromise based partly on the Sidky-Bevin protocol and partly on the abortive agreement with Khashaba Pasha of last summer, and hope by this again to assuage the opposition's maw. But supposing it succeeds, however good (especially in the light of the present international situation) the settlement might be, and however much general sentiment might really welcome it, the Wafd would almost certainly condemn it, and probably manage to whip up sufficient agitation against it for it to fall to the ground. Thus a calculation by the Government that it would be in its party interest to secure a settlement before the elections might be wrong, and even if the opposition failed to prevent negotiations or the signature of a settlement, the Government's party interest might be incompatible with the general interest.

7.   The Government, moreover, is faced with this dilemma:– To cope with the Moslem Brethren, and perhaps with communism, the continuance of Martial Law appears necessary: and Martial Law doubtless can be useful in the eyes of the Government for keeping the opposition in its place, for evading awkward opposition questions, and perhaps for ensuring satisfactory elections. But the maintenance of Martial Law, since it will anger and frustrate the Wafdists on the ground that it consigns them to silence, is sure to sharpen their general resentment and may encourage acute and factious opposition by the only course left open—that of violent agitation, at any rate at election time.

8.   Again the Government may calculate that it may not after all be able to conclude a settlement before the elections, and that this may have to be left to the Government resulting from them. If the elections have not been free and the Wafd is largely excluded, the result will be the same as in the case of a settlement made before the elections. The elections may, however, produce a Wafd Government, a National Government, or a Government of the present régime with a well-balanced Parliamentary situation resulting from strong opposition representation. This would not necessarily make things easier for us, but whatever was agreed with us in such circumstances (and it might be less satisfactory than what we might get with the present régime) would go through.

9.   I am inclined to think that, until they can see things more clearly, His Majesty's Government should deliberate carefully before letting themselves be drawn on by Khashaba and Abdel Hadi into negotiations for a settlement. Desiring both to secure their immediate strategic requirements and to improve relations with Egypt, but refusing to have a further failure, H.M.G., like the Egyptian Government, decided on technical discussions for a military arrangement, intending thus to avoid the political snags, and hoping an arrangement of the kind might be the first step towards an eventual settlement. Even in the case of technical discussions, H.M.G., as I understand it, do not wish to risk a failure, and might sheer off rather than fail, if prospects don't seem good. The *settlement* that the Egyptian Government wants is still one on pretty well its own conditions.

10.   It may be, therefore, that H.M.G. should go slowly, risk a change of general mood, and spin things out until, after the elections, they can judge of the possibility of a settlement on sound foundations. I do not want to make too much of all this but, as suggested above, think it should be present in our minds.

11.   I would see no harm in use being made of the contents of this telegram for soundings with Khashaba Pasha and Amr Pasha. But I recommend, if I may, that any use of them should take the form of innocent and interested enquiries in a tour of the horizon when discussing prospects in a general way. It is important also that no impression should be given (on the contrary) that there is any diminution in our keenness for very early technical military discussions, which, as stated above, I am satisfied the Egyptian Government desires, as distinct from, but also as a step towards, an eventual full settlement.

12.   If the Egyptian Government become insistent in expressing a wish for a settlement before the elections, it may be necessary for us, as a condition of proceeding, to consider insisting on something which will furnish us with a definite assurance that the settlement would not be rejected. But we cannot be sure at this stage what would be required in the way of such an assurance, and even if we should decide later that one is necessary, the time for insisting on it, or emphasising it, has not yet arrived.

139   DEFE 4/22, COS 90(49)2   17 June 1949
'Anglo–Egyptian defence talks and arms for the Egyptians': COS Committee minutes on Egyptian equipment requirements   [Extract]

The Committee had before them:—

(a) A telegram from the Commanders-in-Chief Middle East stating that the satisfactory outcome of the defence discussions would depend largely on our ability to meet the Egyptian equipment requirements; and requesting authority to inform the Egyptians that we agreed in principle to meeting their demands to the best of our ability as soon as possible.

(b) A Minute by the Secretary stating that an interim reply had been sent to the Commanders-in-Chief Middle East drawing their attention to certain previous telegrams on this subject.

The Committee first discussed whether it was possible to give the Commanders-in-

Chief Middle East any additional guidance on the equipment aspect of the defence discussions to that contained in two previous telegrams.

The Committee were informed that the War Office had informed Commanders-in-Chief M.E.L.F. on 3rd June of the various items of equipment that could be provided for the Egyptians immediately. This should enable the British Delegation to make a favourable impression during the opening stages of the Discussions. The defence talks had started on the 3rd June but very little ground had been covered at the first meeting. A further meeting had been held on the 15th June, but no report had yet been received of what had transpired.

It was pointed out (*by Sir William Elliot*)[1] that the Commanders-in-Chief Middle East did not appear to realise fully how important it was that we should have firm orders from the Egyptians for all major items of equipment before new production could be planned. The defence talks had clearly not yet reached the stage when the Egyptians could put in a schedule of their complete requirements. It was possible, however, that there was already sufficient common ground for the Egyptians to give us a fair indication of what they needed. For example although we hoped to dissuade the Egyptians from having the large army which they had in mind we did agree that they would need land forces of the order of one Division and one Armoured Brigade. It would seem therefore that a firm bid could now be made for the equipment required for these formations. On the air side it was most important that the Air Ministry should know as soon as possible what aircraft the Egyptians would require.

It was therefore agreed that it would be of value to send a further telegram to the Commanders-in-Chief Middle East explaining these points and asking them to obtain an indication of the Egyptian equipment requirements as soon as possible.

The Committee were informed that the defence discussions were being conducted under conditions of the strictest secrecy. Very few Egyptians knew that the discussions were taking place. This was known only to the King and one or two highly placed Egyptian Officials, in addition to the Egyptian Officers taking part— who were of comparatively junior rank. There would be extremely undesirable political repercussions in Egypt if the fact became known that the defence talks were going on. It was therefore most important that no unguarded reference should be made on this subject in London.

The Committee then referred to the question of the arms embargo on the supply of equipment to the Arab States.

Sir Gerald Templer said that it had been reported in a recent telegram that the Foreign Secretary had discussed with Mr. Acheson at Paris the effect of the arms embargo on our relations with the Egyptians. He had pointed out that it was quite impossible for H.M.G. to make any progress if they were not in a position to supply Egypt with arms of any kind. He was hoping that he would be able to hold the position for another 2 months. In the meanwhile Egypt and other Arab countries would be given such small arms and equipment which might be regarded as necessary for internal security. No heavy guns and fighter aircraft would, however, be supplied for 2 months. He (Sir Gerald Templer) considered that it would greatly ease the present negotiations with the Egyptians if the British Delegation could inform them that it had definitely been decided to lift the arms embargo in 2 months time if this was the case. He suggested that the Chiefs of Staff should represent this to Ministers. . . .

---

[1] Chief staff officer to Ministry of Defence and deputy secretary (military) to Cabinet, 1949–1951.

140   FO 371/73464, no 5644   24 June 1949
'Egypt': minute by G L Clutton on the value of bringing the Wafd into the Egyptian government

The Egyptian elections, which at the latest will take place some time between November and January next, will to some extent be a turning point in Egyptian affairs, and we should consequently consider carefully what, from the point of view of British interests, we would like the result of these elections to be, and whether we would take any action to secure the result we desire.

The defects from the point of view of British interests of the present régime are too obvious to require enumeration. There seems no doubt that a Wafdist majority in the Egyptian Parliament would serve British interests better than anything else. The Wafd party are probably still supported by an absolute majority of all politically minded Egyptians. Both with regard to the Treaty issue and the Sudan, the Wafd alone is in a position, by reason of the support it enjoys in the country, to honour any agreement that may be reached with H.M.G. on the subject. The Wafd again, having played no part in the direction of Egyptian affairs since the war, is in a position to disown and amend Egyptian policy with regard to Palestine and the tiresome restrictions imposed by martial law. The Wafd, representing all classes in Egypt, is probably the only party capable of instituting and carrying out the internal social and economic reforms so badly needed by the country. Lastly, the Wafd would probably put a stop to plans for the expansion of the Egyptian Army which will have so fatal an effect on plans for social reform and by which it appears the King wishes to prepare the way for the entry into the Egyptian scene of a new political force (incidentally, these Egyptian plans are opposed by our military authorities who wish Egypt's contribution to Middle East strategy to be the provision of air defence and not the formation of large land forces as at present proposed). At the same time, it would be unwise to believe that the return of the Wafd would solve the issues in dispute between H.M.G. and Egypt. It seems to the Department doubtful whether any Egyptian Government could conclude a formal Treaty giving us the strategic facilities we require in Egypt. As regards the Sudan, the day for any formal agreement disappeared forever when the Egyptian Government declined to participate in the constitutional machinery established under the Sudan Constitutional Ordinance. The problem of the Sudan can only be solved by the process of time. Nevertheless, agreement on working arrangements on both these subjects would be much easier if H.M.G. had to deal with a Wafdist Government.

As a footnote, it should be here remarked that a coalition Government of all parties, including the Wafd, would not be a satisfactory solution. Rivalries in Egypt are such that sooner or later on some such issue as the presence of British troops in Egypt, or the Sudan, one of the component parties would break away and for its own political purposes upset any agreement reached between the Government and H.M.G.

If, therefore, it is in the interests of H.M.G. that the Egyptian elections should result in a Wafdist victory, we next have to consider whether we have means at our disposal to influence the elections, and if so, whether we should use them. At present, as will be seen from Sir R. Campbell's two letters (see J 4495, flag A) and his letter of the 7th June (flag B), he is discreetly working for the formation of a coalition

Government before the elections. Such a Government would ensure that there was Wafdist participation in the voting and that as a result there was at least a Wafdist opposition in the Parliament elected. On the other hand, it does not ensure that the elections will be free, and consequently result in a Wafdist majority. Should we, therefore, go further and ensure that the elections are free? As will be seen from the records of the two conversations which Mr. Maitland recently had with Makram Ebeid and a prominent Wafdist, (see J 4276 and J 4279/1105/16 at flags C and D) intervention on our part would not be unwelcome, and at some suitable date Sir R. Campbell could inform King Farouk frankly that while we are anxious to settle outstanding differences with Egypt, we would only be prepared to do so if the Wafd were returned to power. Such a declaration would amount to an ultimatum, but short of armed intervention it is as far as we could go.

Whether such intervention would be successful seems to the Department to be open to doubt. It is quite possible that the King might reject our ultimatum, go to the country with an anti-British platform, and with the help of his Minister for the Interior, return a satisfactory majority for his own purposes. He would then as likely as not proceed with his suspected plans for some form of military dictatorship. In the meantime, of course, the present comparatively favourable atmosphere in Egypt which has enabled us to avoid friction over the presence of British troops in the Canal Zone and to a certain extent over the Sudan, and which has also enabled us to make progress on the Nile Waters issue, would be destroyed and a period of great uneasiness in Anglo–Egyptian relations would result. Internationally, moreover, we would have laid ourselves open to criticism both in the Arab states and in the Asiatic states. Moreover, even if our intervention were successful, the Wafd at any rate for the beginning of its period of power would be obliged to adopt a strongly anti-British line, even if eventually it were possible for H.M.G. to work better with them than with the present Government. In the interval, all progress in connexion with the Nile Waters schemes would probably beheld up.

Recommendation

The Department feel that in the light of the foregoing, drastic intervention is not to be recommended. There is no chance of a final settlement of either the Treaty or the Sudan issue, even if the Wafd were returned to power. As things are at present, neither issue is causing us immediate anxiety and we do not wish to cloud the present atmosphere which is enabling us to proceed with the important Nile Waters schemes. On the other hand, there is much to be said for doing everything in our power to secure Wafd participation in the elections. If they do participate, the possibility at any rate is not excluded that they will gain a majority. Even if they only return as an opposition party we shall reap considerable advantage. Their presence in Parliament will keep in check, especially if supported by public opinion outside, the King's plans for military expansion. There is also the possibility (pointed out by Makram Ebeid) that in the course of the life of the Parliament they will over-throw the Government and assume power by constitutional means. If such a Parliament were to result from the elections, it would also be open to H.M.G. if it came to concluding an agreement on the Treaty or Sudan issues to insist that the Egyptian Delegation included Wafd representatives.

In short, the aim of any intervention on H.M.G.'s part should be not the return of a

Wafd majority but Wafd participation in the elections. The concrete action for this purpose should be on the following lines:—

(1) Continuation by Sir R. Campbell of his advocacy of a coalition Government, including the Wafd, before the elections.

(2) Discreet encouragement of the Wafd leaders to take part in the elections (the danger of the King building up an Army to establish a military dictatorship if unchecked might be pointed out to them as the most urgent reason for their participation).

(3) Evasion of any attempt by the present Egyptian Government to come to an agreement with us either over the Treaty issue or over the Sudan until after the elections.

141 DEFE 4/22, COS 97(49)3, annex   6 July 1949
'Overall strategic concept for war in 1957':[1] report by the JPS to the COS, 20 July 1949 (JP(48)59)[2]   [Extract]

. . .

Allied strategic aims

24.   Our strategy must therefore aim:—

(a) To defeat the Russian onslaught by land, sea and air against areas and communications vital to the Allies.

(b) To achieve a negotiated peace; this involves:-
    (i) the adoption of an air strategy aimed primarily at breaking the Communist control of the Russian people.
    (ii) the adoption of a political strategy aimed primarily at breaking the faith of the Russian people in their rulers.

(c) to wean the Satellites away from Russia.

Part II
Military measures to implement our strategy

25.   The military measures to implement our strategic aims are:—

(a) to launch an air offensive against Russia and the satellites.

(b) to hold securely the air bases and sea areas essential for launching this air offensive.

(c) to defend the Allied main support areas, and in addition, certain other areas whose retention is essential to our strategy.

(d) to control the sea communications essential for the security of the above bases and areas.

(e) to be prepared to establish control of Russia and her occupied territories and to enforce surrender terms.

---

[1] 1957 was the earliest date it was thought the Soviet Union would deliberately start a major war.
[2] JP(49)59 went through a number of drafts. The extract is taken from the final draft amended in the light of the COS discussion on 6 July.

The basic assumptions upon which our strategy is based, are attached at Appendix.[3]

The strategic air offensive

26.   The character of this offensive will follow from the aims given in Part I of the paper, i.e., it should be directed at the centres of control. *Since these centres of control are in the large towns, attacks upon them will at the same time reduce the war making capacity of the USSR by physical destruction.*

The only strategic offensive which the Allies can adopt at the outbreak of war is in the air. The fact that the attack on strategic targets in Russia may not immediately affect the enemy offensives makes it the more necessary that the air offensive should be mounted at maximum intensity from the outbreak of war. At the same time this requirement will have to be reconciled with the requirements of other air operations aimed directly at Soviet offensives on land and sea.

In discussing the effectiveness of the air offensive against *Soviet* centres of control it is essential to decide the weapons which are to be employed.

Weapons of mass destruction

27.   A basic assumption for war in 1957 is that both sides will be capable of using Weapons of Mass Destruction. It is probable that Russia will use these weapons at any time she considers that it will be substantially to her advantage to do so. Should she initiate their use the allies must retaliate.

28.   It is possible, however, that Russia might consider that her war aim, at any rate for Western Europe and the Middle East, could be achieved without the use of W.M.D. and might appreciate that the Allies would hesitate to initiate this form of warfare. She might therefore think that it would be to her advantage to reserve the use of these weapons until she had reduced the danger of retaliation by occupying the allied air bases in these two areas. She might even decide that the Allies could not defeat her without employing weapons of mass destruction and might therefore declare publicly that she did not propose to initiate the use of such weapons.

29.   The decision whether or not to initiate the use of W.M.D. may well therefore rest with the Allied Governments. We therefore consider the advantages and disadvantages to the Allies of initiating their use from the outset of war.

30.   *Advantages*

(a) We are advised that an air offensive by conventional weapons would not achieve decisive results against Russia. It would appear therefore that W.M.D. provide the only means whereby the Allies can achieve their strategic aims.

(b) If Weapons of Mass Destruction are not used at the outset Russian advances on land are likely to bring about conditions more favourable to the Russian strategic air offensive than to our own.

(c) In 1957 the Allies will certainly possess a marked numerical and technical lead over Russia in atomic weapons but we cannot forecast the relative position in other forms of weapons of mass destruction.

(d) The use of W.M.D. will produce an effect *much* more rapidly than conventional weapons.

---

[3] Emphasis throughout in original. The Appendix is not printed.

31. *Disadvantages*

These, although stated with particular reference to the United Kingdom, apply to a greater or lesser degree to all the Allies and must be considered in relation to the Allied war effort as a whole. They are as follows:—

(a) A fairly small number of Weapons of Mass Destruction could cause such damage against a highly concentrated target such as the United Kingdom that the areas might become useless as an offensive air base and the country might never recover.

(b) By 1957 it is unlikely that active defence measures will have progressed so far as to prevent the arrival of at least some of the W.M.D. directed against Allied countries. Similarly civil defence measures may well be far short of the standard necessary to provide *reasonable* protection against atomic bombs.

(c) As public opinion amongst the Allies may well be against initiating atomic attack, the use of such weapons may adversely affect the war effort.

32. From the point of view of the Allies as a whole we consider that there is an unanswerable military case for the use of Weapons of Mass Destruction against Russia from the outset in order to achieve our strategic aims. It must be appreciated however that the use of weapons of mass destruction will entail the risk of the United Kingdom and other Western European countries suffering fatal damage.

Bases and sea areas essential for the strategic air offensive

33. We must select our air bases so that all the important towns are within range. In order to achieve the maximum intensity of attack, the bases should be as near as possible to the targets. At the same time, they must be secure from any enemy ground threat and capable of adequate defence against air attack.

In addition to the main bases, advanced air bases and possibly aircraft carriers *will be used*.

34. Bearing in mind the great distances to be covered over enemy territory, the aircraft employed in the atomic offensive must be of sufficiently high performance to ensure an acceptable casuality rate. This applies particularly to attacks on targets west of the Urals, which area includes the majority of large Russian towns and will probably be covered by a highly organized defence system.

It is estimated that the *high performance jet* bombers in service in 1957 will be able to bomb effectively *up to a radius of action of from 1,500 to 2,000 nautical miles*.

35. With this radius of action, *most of* the major towns *in Soviet territory* could be reached from bases in Western Europe, the Middle East, Pakistan and the *Japanese Islands*. No other shore bases, from which aircraft with the above radius of action could adequately cover the same area, are likely to be available to the Allies.

36. Some important towns in the Karaganda, Kuzbas and Lake Baikal areas would, however, be out of range from Western Europe, the Middle East *and the Japanese Islands*. These towns could be covered from bases in Pakistan, by increasing the range of shore-based bombers or possibly by aircraft operating from carriers in the Barents Sea.

142   DEFE 4/23, COS 102(49)4, annex   15 July 1949
'Middle East strategy and defence policy': report by the JPS to the
COS, 11 July 1949 (JP(49)59). *Appendix "A"*   [Extract]

The object of this paper is to define British strategy in the Middle East and relate it to allied world wide strategy.

For convenience of military command, the area of responsibility of the British Defence Co-ordination Committee, Middle East, which is illustrated on the map at Appendix "B",[1] covers a very much wider area than is normally associated with the expression 'Middle East'. This paper only deals with those countries within this area which have an important bearing on allied Middle East strategy. We set out at Appendix "A" the peace time defence policy which we consider should be followed in these countries.

The threat to world security

2.   We appreciate that the only two Powers who are singly capable at the present time of menacing our strategic security are the United States and the U.S.S.R. It is unthinkable, in view of the close political and other ties and the considerable community of interest between ourselves and the Americans, that we should ever engage in hostilities against the United States or against a combination of Powers which includes the United States.

3.   On the other hand, the Soviet policy and aims, which we discuss below, make it abundantly clear that the U.S.S.R. must be regarded as a potentially hostile power.

Fundamental aim of the Soviet Union

4.   The fundamental aim of the Soviet leaders is to impose Soviet Communism in all parts of the world. They foresee this happening in the course of a revolutionary struggle carried out primarily by every method short of war and lasting possibly for many years; but, on the other hand, they may consider it desirable to assist this process by war should favourable conditions arise.

5.   The Soviet leaders are convinced that our system of political democracy contains the seeds of its own decay. Therefore, although they may fear that the Allies may ultimately have to resort to war to avert the collapse of their political system, the Soviet [sic] are unlikely themselves to precipitate a war until they are ready.

Capabilities of the Soviet Union

6.   It is not considered likely that before the end of the second post-war 5 year Plan the Soviet Union will be capable of supporting her armed forces in a major war entirely from the natural resources and industrial potential now under her control. Nevertheless, if Russia wished to go to war, economic considerations alone would not be enough to prevent her from doing so if she felt confident of attaining her primary aims rapidly.

7.   The Soviet armed forces, despite certain deficiencies, could embark on a land war at any time and would, at least in the early stages, have the advantage of numbers against any likely combination of opposing forces. In any major war,

---

[1] Only Appendix "A" is reproduced here.

however, that started before 1956/60 at any rate, this initial advantage would be increasingly counter-balanced, as hostilities continued, by the incompletion of Russia's industrial plan. Moreover the strategic air situation is, at least at present, unfavourable to the Soviet Union; her air striking force and air defences are still comparatively backward despite the efforts she is making. She can thus not yet adequately protect those centres of population and industry which are within range of air attack. Her future readiness to embark upon a major war is likely, therefore, to be conditioned by the relative efficacy of her air strength.

8.   We consider it improbable that the Soviet Union will have sufficient atomic bombs for some years to offset the allied preponderance in that weapon, though as time passes, she may have all stock capable of neutralising small areas such as the United Kingdom. It is a reasonable deduction that a realisation of her relative backwardness in atomic development may cause, or has already caused, the Soviet Union to hasten her preparedness to wage biological warfare. Although there are no raw material difficulties comparable to those for atomic development, Biological warfare presents many technical problems.

9.   Failing the early development of biological or other weapons of mass ˙ destruction to a point which she believed would ensure her rapid victory, the Soviet Union's economic situation is likely to militate strongly against her provoking a major war until, at any rate, the aims of the second post-war 5 year Plan have been achieved.

Resultant policy

10.   We believe that the present Soviet policy has the following aims:—

(a) First the consolidation of her strategic security by the establishment of a belt of subservient states around her frontiers.

(b) Second, the restoration of Russian economy and its development to a point where it will rival and eventually outstrip that of the United States.

(c) Third, the avoidance of a major war unless she considers a Soviet vital interest is menaced or conditions are judged to be sufficiently favourable to the Soviet Union.

(d) Fourth, the continued aggressive promotion of communism by all means short of war throughout the non-communist world.

(e) Fifth, an endeavour to weaken and disintegrate the non-communist world both by political infiltration, leading to unrest and economic distress, and by the fostering of nationalist movements and thus unrest in colonial territories or those under Trusteeship.

11.   The emergence of the United States as the Soviet Union's main rival in world affairs, and the recognition of United States superiority in war potential, particularly as regards the atom bomb, are factors of decisive importance to the Soviet Union.

12.   The close co-operation between the British Commonwealth and the U.S.A. together with the development of the North Atlantic Treaty, the Western Union, the European Recovery Programme and the Council of Europe are most disquieting to the Soviet leaders. Given the present balance of strength, the Soviet Union will pursue a policy of communist penetration aided by economic distress rather than of open war.

It is clear, however, that there is a risk that the aggressive policy of the U.S.S.R.

might cause an accidental war owing to a miscalculation on the part of the Soviet of the extent to which she could pursue a policy of ideological and territorial expansion without becoming involved in war with the non-communist Powers.

Allied defence policy

The prevention of war

13.   It should, therefore, be the aim of all the non-communist countries of the world to adopt a common policy to meet the communist threat. The primary aim of this policy must be to prevent war, always provided that our vital interests are not prejudiced. The United Nations Organisation has shown itself unable to give us the necessary security and we must, therefore, plan accordingly.

14.   We should plan to prevent war in two ways:—

(a) by showing that the Commonwealth and its Allies possess forces and resources on a scale adequate to convince the Soviet Union that war is unprofitable and further that the Allies are fully prepared to act offensively from the outset.
(b) by taking all possible means, short of war, not only to resist the further spread of communism, but also to weaken the Russian hold over countries she now dominates.

15.   None of the non-communist countries of the world, except possibly the US, have the resources to fight alone against Russia. If we are to fight successfully we must, therefore, have a common policy and co-ordinated plans.

16.   Towards this end the United Kingdom, apart from defence arrangements within the Commonwealth, is participating in the following measures:-

(a) Collaborating with the US on defence matters.
(b) Working to create an effective defence organisation for the Western Union, comprising the UK, France and the Benelux countries.
(c) Working for the full development of the potentialities of the North Atlantic Treaty.
(d) Giving assistance in individual defence arrangements to countries subject to communist pressure, e.g., Greece, Turkey, Burma and Persia; and to certain countries which occupy an important strategic position, e.g. Egypt and the Arab States.

17.   Similarly, within the Commonwealth discussions are taking place with South Africa, Australia and New Zealand to agree a common defence strategy and to determine their contribution to it.

Discussions with India and Pakistan may follow later.

British strategy in war

18.   The three pillars of British strategy are:—

(a) the defence of the United Kingdom and its development as an offensive base;
(b) the control of essential sea communications;
(c) a firm hold on the Middle East and its development as an offensive base.

Short and long term plans

19.   Our preparations for war are considered in two distinct categories, short term and long term. Short term preparations are confined to plans for the use of

existing armed forces in the event of an unforeseen emergency, and are kept up-to-date cover [sic] a period of about 12 months ahead. Long term plans include the intention to re-equip the armed forces with modern weapons by 1957.

In both the above sets of plans, the military measures required to implement our strategic aims are:-

(a) To launch an air offensive against Russia and the satellites.

(b) To hold securely the air bases and sea areas essential for launching this air offensive.

(c) To defend the Allied main support areas, and in addition, certain other areas whose retention is essential to our strategy.

(d) To control the sea communications essential for the security and development of the above bases and areas.

The place of the Middle East in world strategy

20.   The Middle East is important because:—

(a) it is an offensive air base;
(b) it is a source of oil;
(c) it is a centre of communications;
(d) it gives depth to the defence of Africa.

These points are elaborated below.

21.   *Offensive air base.* The Allies' plan is to launch a strategic air offensive at the outbreak of war. In order to reach all the targets with bombers likely to be developed in the foreseeable future it will be necessary to have bases in Western Europe, the Western Pacific, and the Middle East. A base in Pakistan would be a desirable addition. Present plans rely on using the Middle East as a base.

22.   *Sources of oil.* Subject to final confirmation by the Official Oil Committee, it seems clear that the Middle East oilfields, including those of Iraq, South Persia and Saudi Arabia, will be essential to the Allied war effort in 1957. The defence of the Middle East must therefore be included as a basic requirement in our long-term strategy.

23.   *Centre of communications.* The main importance of the Middle East is as an essential link in the air routes. It also commands the shortest sea route from Europe to the M.E. and the land route between Europe and Africa.

24.   *Depth to the defence of Africa.* One of the main support areas needed for the Allied war economy would be southern Africa, of which the keystone would be the Union of South Africa. The easiest way in which Russia, primarily a land power, could hope to establish herself in Africa would be through Egypt. The retention of that country in Allied hands is, therefore, essential in order to block the only practicable land approach by large forces into the African continent.

Allied strategy in the Middle East

25. The map at Appendix "C" shows the main geographical features referred to below.

Enemy threat

26.   We appreciate that the Russians will launch, simultaneously with campaigns in Europe, a campaign to seize control of the Middle East, including Greece and

Turkey and the Suez Canal area. The advance on Egypt is expected to be carried out by two main forces, which, starting from the Caucasus area and advancing on the respective axes Mosul-Aleppo, Baghdad-Damascus, could, if not seriously opposed each arrive in the Beirut area some 80 days after the outbreak of war. Further forces advancing south from the Caspian Sea would have Basra and Bandar Abbas as their objectives. Simultaneously, Turkey would be invaded and could be overrun in 80–120 days, thus eventually furnishing the enemy with an extra line of communications for the attack on Egypt. At the same time Greece could be overrun in 75 days. These timings take no account of Allied reactions to Soviet moves, and are only an estimate of the maximum Russian rate of advance.

Allied defensive strategy

27.   The Allies will be numerically inferior and must therefore plan to hold the Russian advance on a natural defensive line as far north as possible. There are three natural defence areas:—

(a) The line along the mountain passes leading into southern Turkey and western and southern Persia as far as Bandar Abbas. This is referred to as the "Outer Ring."
(b) The parallel mountain ranges of the Lebanon and Anti-Lebanon running north and south on each side of the Jordan and Baalbek valleys. The system of defence based on this natural barrier is referred to as the Palestine–Lebanon Line.
(c) The line Jericho–Ramallah–Tel Aviv. Referred to as the Ramallah line.

28.   *The Outer Ring.* The strategic advantages of holding this line are very great; it is, in fact, the only way of securing the Middle East oil. Provided the necessary air and land forces and their administrative installations could be deployed in time, no larger forces would be needed than for the shorter but less defensible Palestine-Lebanon line.

Conditions are not favourable to this plan in the short term, but we are examining the ways and means of adopting it by 1957.

29.   *Palestine–Lebanon and Ramallah Lines.* Until we are in a position to hold the "Outer Ring", the only possible plan is to hold the Palestine–Lebanon or Ramallah lines. The latter suffers from a grave disadvantage in being so close to the Delta, but could be held by smaller forces with considerably less administrative backing.

The holding of either of these lines entails the abandonment of most of the Middle East oilfields, and it would be necessary to deny by demolitions, their use to the enemy for as long as possible. It should, however, be feasible to defend the Dahran/Bahrein oilfields against a light scale of attack should this be considered sufficiently important.

Allied offensive strategy

30.   It is planned to start delivering a strategic air offensive from Middle East bases immediately on the outbreak of war. Air bases in the short term plans would be located in Egypt, but it is probable that they will be supplemented by bases in Cyrenaica, Aden and possibly the Sudan in the long term.

Main base

31.   The vital strategic area of the Middle East is Egypt since it alone possesses

the essential air bases, ports, internal communications, water supplies, industrial potential and manpower necessary for the maintenance of a main base of the size required for the defence of the Middle East.

Conditions necessary for allied strategy

32.   Our ability to carry out these plans depends upon certain conditions, many of which can only obtain as a result of political negotiation. These are listed below:-

(a) the basic requirements are:—
(i)   right of entry of armed forces into Egypt, Syria, the Lebanon, Israel, Transjordan, Iraq;
(ii) the right to maintain forces in Egypt and Cyrenaica in peace;
(iii) availability of a main base in Egypt, the nucleus of which must be maintained in peace;
(iv) availability of airfields for strategic bombers, for the defence of Egypt, for the defence of sea communications and for the support of land forces.
(b) Our ability to hold the Outer Ring will depend on certain additional factors which have not yet been fully assessed.

Allied planning in the Middle East

United States

33.   United States authorities agree with us on the importance of the Middle East, and the prospects of U.S. co-operation in all main theatres, including the Middle East are good.

34.   *Other Commonwealth countries.* We have already sent a planning team to South Africa, with a view to persuading the Union authorities to participate in the defence of the Middle East.

Planning discussions have also been arranged with Australia and New Zealand, to take place in Melbourne and Wellington during August, in the course of which we shall attempt to secure their agreement to dispatch forces to the Middle East in war.

35.   *Western Union countries.* The other Western Union countries, particularly France, are so preoccupied with their own defence that they tend to depreciate the importance of holding the Middle East. Consequently they hold the view that we should give priority to the allocation of forces for the defence of Western Europe.

Defence policy in Middle East countries

36.   Although our ultimate object will be to combine all the Middle East countries into one comprehensive security arrangement, the time is not yet opportune. As is the case with other regional defence pacts, such as Western Union and the North Atlantic Treaty, it would be essential for any grouping of Middle East countries to be backed by both the United States and Great Britain. The increasing interest of the United States in the Middle East, with particular reference to the security of the Middle East oil supplies, is a political factor of major importance. Every effort should be made to foster this interest and to secure the increasing participation of the United States in the defence and economic development of the Middle East on the basis of a common policy.

Until a Middle East pact is possible, however, the United Kingdom must continue to obtain her essential military requirements by bilateral agreements with individual countries concerned, or by joint agreements which include the United States.

Appendix "A" to 142: peacetime defence requirements in individual Middle East countries

In this Appendix we deal, in the following order, with those countries within the area which have an important bearing on Allied Middle East defence strategy.

Cyprus
Egypt
India and Pakistan
Iraq
Israel
Libya
Persia
Saudi Arabia
Sudan
Syria and the Lebanon
Transjordan
Turkey

Cyprus

2.   *General considerations.* The strategic importance of Cyprus lies chiefly in the use that could be made of it as an air base in the early days of the war. The establishment of an advanced base for strategic bombers there would enable us, from the very outset of war, to penetrate further into Russia than is possible from any other likely base in the Middle East. Tactical air forces could also operate from bases in the Island in support of land forces defending Turkey, and of an Allied campaign in North Syria. The use of Cyprus as an air base could be denied to us once Turkey was overrun.

3.   *Strategic requirements.* The only Allied strategic requirement in Cyprus is to station there such forces as are needed in peace and war, and to develop in peace such airfields and other military facilities as would be necessary in war. Important factors are the very limited port facilities and the lack of adequate fuel storage.

Egypt

4.   *General considerations.* In peace Egypt, with the Suez Canal, is a focal point on our trade routes, and is a most important centre of air communications. In war the retention of Egypt will be vital to the defence of the African continent. It is the only country in the Middle East where the resources in manpower, both skilled and unskilled, industries, communications, water supplies, port facilities and airfields are adequate for an Anglo–American main base. The minimum requirement is therefore that the security of Egypt from the outbreak of war must be ensured.

Egypt is the most suitable location for air bases in the Middle East, not only on account of her manpower and facilities but also because she is comparatively close to targets in Russia and is defensible against a ground threat.

5.   *Strategic requirements.* Allied forces in the Middle East will initially be dependent upon those British facilities which it has been possible to prepare and maintain in peace time. In order to maintain adequate facilities the British must continue to occupy at least those areas which they hold at present, and which are much in excess of those permitted by the 1936 Treaty. The British must also retain in Egypt considerably more personnel than authorised by the treaty, to man and protect

the British base installations and headquarters, and provide the covering forces to protect the initial concentration of our forces at the beginning of an emergency.

In war, the Allies will require freedom of entry and movement for all reinforcements and the use of airfields, ports, and communications, not only in the Canal Zone, but throughout Egypt. Air attacks on Egypt can be expected from the outbreak of war and the organisation of an efficient air defence system in peace, including the construction of airfields and the installation of radar cover for the projected main base area is therefore necessary.

It is thus essential to the success of the Allied plans that the British should come to a working agreement with the Egyptians on these matters. Where possible the Egyptians themselves should undertake as great a share in their own defence as their resources and technical ability permit.

6. *Defence co-operation*. The Allies would like the Egyptians to be able to contribute to their own defence, particularly against air attack. We are therefore trying to dissuade them from creating a large field army and to induce them to develop air defences. Since the Egyptians look to Great Britain for supply of arms, and for advanced technical training of selected personnel for their armed forces, we are able to exercise some influence in defence matters.

7. *Rectification of the western frontier*. From the military point of view, so long as the goodwill of the Arab States is retained it is immaterial whether the disputed areas on Egypt's frontier are allocated to Egypt or to Cyrenaica.

India and Pakistan

8. Although India and Pakistan are not normally considered as part of the Middle East they are within the sphere of the responsibility of the British Defence Co-ordination Committee Middle East and have been included here because of their importance in relation to Allied strategy in the Middle East.

9. *Political considerations*. The clear cut alignment in peace of India and Pakistan with the Western Powers would greatly assist in resisting the spread of Communism. Pakistan, particularly, being the largest Moslem state, could exercise a favourable political influence in the Middle East. Neither country has yet entered into any defence agreement with the United Kingdom.

10. *General considerations*. The role that we shall wish India and Pakistan to play in our general strategy has not yet been decided. On the one hand, these countries have large manpower resources and they could form an important minor support area, assist in the control of sea communications and provide air transit facilities. Pakistan, in particular, could provide air bases for the strategic bombing of Russia.

On the other hand, their active assistance in war would require of the Allies arms, equipment and air defence which they could ill-afford; it is unlikely, moreover, that either country would agree to provide manpower in other war theatres until mutual confidence had been established between them and they were convinced of their own safety from invasion.

It seems possible, therefore, that we may decide that their benevolent neutrality at the beginning of war would be preferable to their active intervention, but that their assistance at a later stage will be desirable.

11. *Strategic requirements*. The Allied strategic requirements in India and Pakistan which, if fulfilled, would directly affect the Middle East are:-

(a) the early despatch of forces for the defence of the Middle East;

(b) the development of required base facilities;

(c) the use of air staging posts.

Iraq

12.   *General considerations*. To secure the oilfield area, the defence of the Middle East would have to be conducted on the Outer Ring. This would necessitate the deployment of tactical air forces on forward Iraqi airfields. In addition, ground forces must take up positions in mountain passes leading from Persia to Iraq in sufficient strength and in time to forestall the enemy.

The port of Basra, the land communications northward from Basra and the Haifa – Baghdad road would be strategically important, for the transit of supplies and reinforcements, if the allies were holding the Outer Ring.

13.   *Strategic requirements*. Considerations of time and space make it essential that, at least in the long term, the British should obtain from Iraq the right to maintain military installations and army troops in that country in peacetime. In addition to the right, under the existing Treaty, to station air forces on Iraqi airfields it is also desirable to have the right to move these air forces to forward airfields should war appear imminent.

Israel

14.   *General considerations*. In any war with Russia, Palestine will either be a battle ground or an area through which our vital communications will pass to a front further north. We appreciate, that at present, whatever government is in power, some resistance will be offered to an armed advance through Israel. If an extremist government is in power the resistance will be strong, although it is still too early to assess its probable effectiveness. We must, therefore, take in peace every possible step which will facilitate on the outbreak of war both the speedy movement of our troops through Palestine and the setting up in that country of the necessary administrative organisation.

15.   *Strategic requirements*. We consider that the allies should aim at obtaining the following strategic requirements:—

(a) that the ports (particularly Haifa), communications and airfields should be maintained in peace so that we can make use of them immediately on the outbreak of war;

(b) that Russian influence should be excluded from Palestine;

(c) that the entry of Allied forces into Palestine at the outbreak of war should not be delayed, and to this end the United Kingdom or the United States should conclude a military agreement with Israel which would afford the Allies:—

    (i)   the maximum facilities in peace;

    (ii)   the right of entry on the threat of war;

    (iii) facilities to set up the necessary administrative organisation;

    (iv)   if possible, the actual assistance of the armed forces of Israel.

(d) that the production of the oil installations, particularly the Haifa refineries, should be available to the Allies in peace and if possible in war.

Libya

16. *Cyrenaica*. Cyrenaica is strategically of great value as an area from which our sea communications in the Eastern Mediterranean can be protected, as a potential

strategic air base, and as an important link in our air reinforcement route. It is also the most convenient area from which land forces could reinforce Egypt on threat of war.

17. *Tripolitania*. Despite the fact that Tripolitania is a better developed country and possesses the useful port of Tripoli, it is not so well placed strategically.

18. *Strategic requirements*. Allied long term requirements in Libya, particularly Cyrenaica, are therefore:—

(a) the right to develop the ports, airfields, communications and public utilities;
(b) the right to locate armed forces in the country in peace time.

Persia

19. *General considerations*. Persia's armed forces are incapable of defending her frontiers if attacked by Russia, and owing to her geographical position it would be impossible for Allied forces to give her effective assistance unless they were already in position in Persia before the outbreak of war. This, we understand, is not politically possible as it would give the Russians a pretext under the terms of the 1921 Treaty for occupying northern Persia.

The only Allied requirement, therefore, is that a stable and friendly government should be maintained in Persia willing to withstand Russian diplomatic pressure and capable of preventing civil disorders, particularly in the oilfield area.

The Allies require no military facilities in peace, but it would be necessary to send forces into Persia on the outbreak of war to demolish communications and, in the short term, the oil installations. In the long term the Allies would wish to introduce forces to defend the Persian passes.

It is desirable that the Allies should supply any arms that can be spared to Persia with the object both of raising her morale and of enabling her to maintain internal security.

From the military point of view, we consider there is little to be gained by including Persia in any Middle East pact.

20. *Strategic requirements*. The Allies have no strategic requirements from Persia, but it may be politically necessary to include her in any Middle East Defence Pact, though militarily undesirable.

Saudi Arabia

21. *General considerations*. The chief importance of Saudi Arabia at present is the fact that it includes the increasingly important oil field area around Dahran. In the Allied short term plan, it is intended to defend these oilfields against a surprise attack by flying in a special force, which will also ensure the neutralisation of the oilfield installations if they have to be abandoned. In our long term plan, the oilfield area should be adequately safeguarded by the defence of the Outer Ring.

22. *Treaty proposals*. Early this year Saudi Arabia proposed an Anglo–American Saudi-Arabian Treaty. It was unacceptable to the Chiefs of Staff because they considered that such a Treaty would lead to Anglo–American clashes and would make complications when we came to weld Treaties into our pact with the Arab States.

It was further agreed that a defence agreement with Saudi Arabia, whose military contribution to the defence of the Middle East was nil, was undesirable at a time when we were having difficulty in providing war material for other more deserving countries and when we were likely to have over-riding commitments in connection with the North Atlantic Treaty and when the Pakistan situation was still fluid.

We have since agreed to send a small reconnaissance party to Saudi Arabia to study the location of possible airfields; no funds are, however, likely to be available for their development.

23. *Strategic requirements.* Allied strategic requirements are broadly as follows:—

(a) arrangements to allow for the entry of Commonwealth forces on threat of war, and the discretion to decide when such a threat exists;

(b) the right to develop and maintain:-

(i)   the necessary airfields and communication facilities;

(ii) strategic road and, if possible, rail communications along the west coast of the Persian Gulf;

(iii) port facilities and administrative installations, including the development of adequate water supplies;

(c) freedom of action in obtaining oil supplies, and the right to construct oil pipelines through any part of the Arabian Peninsula, should this prove necessary.

Except for (c) above, these strategic requirements are at present of relatively minor importance.

Sudan

24.   Whilst it is appreciated that the political future of the Sudan is uncertain, her geographical position makes the territory important as a link in British imperial communications and as a possible base for strategic bombers. The Allied requirement, therefore, is to retain all the present British facilities.

Syria and Lebanon

25.   *General considerations.* Although the Allies at present cannot station any forces in the Levant in peacetime, they will need to operate through the Lebanon and Syria, certainly in a long term war and probably in any war in the near future. Whether these countries form part of the Allied final defended area or not, it would be greatly to the Allied advantage if certain facilities, particularly airfields and an air warning system, were maintained in peace and were immediately available to the Allies in war.

It is appreciated, however, that it would be impolitic to try to reach an agreement with Syria and the Lebanon without consultation with the French. On the other hand it will be in our interest to ensure the security of the proposed oil pipe line from the Persian Gulf to the Mediterranean, with its refinery in Syria. We understand that Colonel Zaim[2] also realises the security implications of this project, and would welcome some gesture on the part of His Majesty's Government. Whilst desiring certain facilities in Syria in wartime, or on the

---

[2] Colonel Husni Zaim, Syrian president, prime minister, minister of foreign affairs and minister of the interior who seized power on 30 Mar 1949 from Qwaitli only to become a victim of a coup in Aug 1949.

threat of outbreak of war, we do not at present feel able to enter into new engagements to secure them. We should, however, be very glad to arrange for a party of technical experts to visit Syria, if necessary incognito, to study where any facilities that are needed should be located.

26.   *Strategic requirements*. Allied strategic requirements are:—

(a) arrangements to allow for the entry of Allied forces on the threat of war and the discretion to decide when that threat exists;

(b) the maintenance and development by the Levant States, in consultation with H.M. Government, of:—

(i) the operational airfields and other military installations which the Allies will require in war, including arrangements for the possible storage of fuel and munitions;

(ii) the existing rail and road communications and port facilities.

Transjordan (including Arab Palestine)

27.   *General considerations*. Transjordan possesses, in the Arab Legion, the only Arab force which is properly trained and equipped for modern war. The Southern area of the existing pipeline from Kirkuk and several projected pipelines pass through Transjordan territory. In the event of a campaign being fought in the Palestine Lebanon area, an important, though at present ill-developed, line of communications would run through the port of Aqaba. In the short term Transjordan would afford us advance airfields from which to delay the enemy and would be an area in which we would engage him with mobile land forces. In the long term, Transjordan would be an area in which we might wish to station forces for deployment on the "Outer Ring".

British defence policy in Transjordan is, on account of our Treaty obligations, particularly affected by the outcome of the Arab/Israeli conflict. In the event of Arab Palestine being incorporated in Transjordan and H.M.G. recognising this fact, the existing Anglo/Transjordan Treaty would automatically cover Greater Transjordan. Should Israel attack Transjordan it would be impractical to confine our intervention to the defence of Transjordan territory and the only way of giving effective assistance would be by engaging in general hostilities against Israel.

28.   *Strategic requirements*. The strategic requirements of the Allies are satisfactorily covered by the rights afforded to the United Kingdom by the existing Treaty with Transjordan. These requirements may be summarised as:—

(a) arrangements to allow for the entry of Commonwealth forces in peace and war;

(b) full transit rights for personnel and stores;

(c) training facilities for land and air forces;

(d) the safeguarding, maintenance and development by Transjordan, in consultation with the United Kingdom of:—

(i)   strategic road communications;

(ii)   oil pipelines and installations;

(iii) airfields;

(iv) the port of Aqaba;

(v)   telecommunications.

Turkey

29.   *General considerations*. A strong Turkey capable, with Allied air and technical help, of offering substantial resistance to a Russian attack would be of great assistance to any defence of the Middle East. In the short term it would delay the advance of the Russian forces in the critical first weeks of the war; in the long term it would contribute to the defence of the Outer Ring. With this in view, the United States are at present providing Turkey with considerable material aid.

The importance of her position in the Middle East, political and military as well as geographical, clearly makes it desirable that Turkey should be associated with any Middle East pact. The implications of her joining such a pact would need detailed examination.

30.   *Strategic requirements*. Allied strategic requirements are considered to be:-

(a) in both the short and long term, the use of Turkish airfields;
(b) in both the short and long term, free passage through the Dardanelles as long as Turkey in Europe is held;
(c) in the long term, the use of the communications in the South and the lateral railway from Aleppo to Mosul, which for a portion of its length passes through Turkish territory;
(d) in peace, certain photographic intelligence, mainly of ports, airfields, communications, and of certain portions of coastline.

143   DEFE 5/15/1, COS(49)245, annex   21 July 1949
'Arms and equipment for the Egyptians': note by the War Office for the COS on the military talks and Egyptian requirements

1.   In February 1949, the Chiefs of Staff recorded their opinion that the Anglo/Egyptian Treaty of 1936 did not make provision for our present Military requirements in Egypt in peace. They, therefore, recommended to the Defence Committee that we should negotiate a mutual defence agreement which, whilst providing for our requirements would in exchange offer to integrate our defensive, training and administrative arrangements with the Egyptians, and provide them with equipment for their forces. The Defence Committee considered the problem on 22nd March, 1949, and:—

(a) authorised the Secretary of State for Foreign Affairs to proceed to negotiate with the Egyptians
(b) agreed that all possible steps should be taken to enable us to meet the essential arms requirements of Egypt.[1]

2.   At a meeting held in Cairo on 18th March, 1949, at which H.M. Ambassador and the Chief of the Imperial General Staff were present with the Egyptian Prime Minister, the Minister of War, and the Acting Head of the Royal Cabinet it was agreed that we should follow the procedure of first presenting the Egyptian Prime Minister with a statement of our requirements and then proceed with technical detailed discussions with their Military representatives. This statement of our requirements

---

[1] See 133.

was presented to the Egyptians at the end of March and the discussions with the Military representatives began on 3rd June, 1949.

3.   Important factors to bear in mind, at this stage, are that, at a subsequent audience, King Farouk personally stated to H.M. Ambassador and to the Chief of the Imperial General Staff, that he desired inter-staff discussions between the Egyptian and the British troops; and also that the Egyptian elections, by the rules of the Constitution, are due to be held before 4th November, 1949. We are therefore assured of an element of continuity in our negotiations, but on the other hand, it would probably save us having to start all over again with a new government, if we can reach an agreement on the principles of the supply of arms and equipment in the next month.

Staff talks

4.   The talks with the Military representatives have proceeded in an atmosphere of cordiality. The Egyptian team do not accept, presumably for political reasons, the premise of an immediate threat, although this has been accepted by King Farouk. They have agreed, but are not authorised to sign, a summary on which the plan for the defence of Egypt must be based and both sides have listed their requirements.

5.   The Egyptian representatives on the talks were comparatively junior officers of the three services, acting under the instructions of King Farouk, through the Prime Minister, and it is not clear to what extent their Service Chiefs have been kept informed. Their statement of the overall Egyptian requirements is not therefore suitable for detailed consideration except from the view-point of the principles at issue.

Egyptian requirements

6.   The Egyptian requirements are based, as regards the composition of their forces, on their experience in their recent war in Palestine, and as regards scales of equipment, and ammunition on British practice. They desire to expand, re-organise and re-equip their forces on the following programme:—

   (a) *Phase I – To be completed by March 1950*
       One infantry division
       One armoured regiment
   (b) *Phase II – To be completed in subsequent years*
       One additional infantry division
       Balance of units to complete one armoured division
       Fourteen anti-aircraft regiments
   (c) *Comparison between the Egyptian requirements and the Chiefs of Staff's assessment of their needs.*

Total Egyptian requirements *(Phase I plus Phase II)*	*Chiefs of Staff's assessment of Egyptian needs*
Two infantry divisions	One infantry division
	Two infantry brigades
One armoured division	One light armoured brigade
Fourteen A.A. regiments	Twelve AA regiments
	Four light searchlight regiments
	Two coast artillery regiments.

7.   Based on the above, the Egyptian delegation have now given details of the ammunition and equipment required to implement Phase I of the programme under the headings:-

(a) Urgent equipment and ammunition demands i.e. of highest priority.
(b) Deferred equipment and ammunition demands i.e. required by March, 1950.
(c) Spare parts required to enable training to proceed.

They have not yet submitted equipment and ammunition demands for Phase II.

The whole re-equipment programme for Phases I and II has been very roughly estimated by the Egyptians to cost a sum of the order of £50 million, of which the Egyptian Delegation maintains that £10 to £15 million, to cover items under (a) and (b) could be met within the sum voted for the year ending March 1950.

8.   They expect the equipment for their re-organisation programme to be new ex factory, but will accept, as an interim measure reconditioned tanks and limited quantities of other equipment required to allow training to proceed.

Order of battle for the new Egyptian army

9.   The order of battle proposed by the Egyptian Delegation exceeds the Chiefs of Staff assessment of their needs. It is, however, considered probable that when the Egyptian Service and Finance Ministries have examined more closely the manpower, training and financial aspects involved, they will reconsider both their total requirement and the scales of unit equipment; particularly of those units which are not likely to move far from their own home country. We will therefore obtain no better approximation of their requirements till the appropriate Egyptian authorities have confirmed the plan so far agreed in the technical talks and have begun to make a detailed examination of their requirements. Before they can be expected to do this, or say how much reconditioned equipment they will accept, they must be assured that we will supply them with the equipment they need and be given some information as to when supplies will begin and an indication of the rate of supply thereafter.

10.   It is clear that we will have to accept a considerable increase in our plans for new production if we are to meet these demands. The Defence Committee, however, agreed that steps should be taken to meet the essential Egyptian needs. We have not obtained agreement with the Egyptian Government as to what is essential, but we can agree that they will need, over a period of years, at least the equipment for the size of Army given in the Chiefs of Staff's assessment. We can consider any increase on this later, after further discussions with the Egyptians.

Action now required

11.   To sum up, the stage has been reached in the negotiations in Egypt when it has become essential to give the Egyptians some clear indication of our intentions with regard to the supply of equipment. There are still many unknowns with regard to the exact quantities of equipment likely to be demanded by the Egyptians, and as to the period, during which, the Egyptians will be prepared to accept delivery.

12.   We consider, however, that the Commanders-in-Chief, Middle East, must be given some authority to make a concrete offer, and we therefore suggest that we should ask Ministers to give:—

(a) Their agreement that we will supply the Egyptians with arms, ammunition and equipment of British origin, to enable them to reorganise and re-equip their Army and maintain the necessary reserve holdings on a programme to be agreed with them. The ways and means of meeting this requirement from reconditioned equipment or new production, together with the timing and rate of supply, will be left to be worked out between the Ministry of Supply and the Egyptian authorities, in consultation with the War Office and the Air Ministry.

(b) Their agreement that, for the present, the order of battle which we consider essential for Egyptians' needs, and for which we will supply equipment, will be limited to that recommended by the Chiefs of Staff (see paragraph 6(c) above). Any additional expansion beyond this will be considered when the Egyptian Government has presented their detailed proposals for their overall requirement.

13.   We would emphasise that the agreement to the above imposes a definite limitation on the quantity of equipment which we could offer to provide, and leaves considerable latitude for negotiations with regard to:—

(a) the exact order of battle of the Egyptian Forces
(b) the period of provision
(c) the conditions of sale.

It would also permit us, when it suited, to meet Egyptian demands from available reconditioned equipment and replenish our stocks with new equipment from new production.

14.   The War Office has prepared a detailed analysis of the items of equipment and ammunition likely to be required. It is recommended that this should be examined by the J.W.P.S. together with any likely demands by the Egyptian Air Force if these are known.

Recommendation
15.   The War office recommends:—

(a) This paper should be used as a basis for a Note by the Chiefs of Staff to the Defence Committee.
(b) Chiefs of Staff should invite the J.W.P.S. to examine the likely Egyptian demands and that Service Ministries be asked to provide the necessary information.

144   DEFE 4/23, COS 113(49)3   3 Aug 1949
'Short term strategy and plans': COS Committee minutes recording a conversation between the COS and the United States JCS on the new American strategic concept

Lord Tedder asked the United States Chiefs of Staff to give their views on the broad strategic concept to be followed in framing regional defence plans.

At the request of the United States Chiefs of Staff, *Major General Gruenther*[1]

---

[1] Major General Alfred M Gruenther, deputy chief of staff, 1949; chief of staff to General Eisenhower, 1950 and, in May 1953, supreme allied commander, Europe.

explained the difficulties with which they were faced on account of severe cuts in the United States Defence Budget which must inevitably result in severe reduction in the size of the United States Defence Forces and in their effectiveness. It had therefore been necessary to review the whole concept for war in the event of an early emergency. As a result of this examination the United States Chiefs of Staff had drawn up a new strategic concept in which there were three main elements:-

(i)   The basic defensive tasks on which both the United States and the United Kingdom were agree[d].

(ii)   The waging of a strategic air offensive with the object of inflicting the maximum damage on the Soviet war making capacity and on the rate of advance of their invading forces.

(iii) A strategic offensive in Western Eurasia combined with a strategic defensive in the Far East.

Major General Gruenther then explained in some detail the United States strategic concept for Western Eurasia. This was conditional not only by the reduction in American Armed Forces consequent upon the smaller Defence Budget but also by the necessity for supporting the Western European countries now that the United States was a signatory to the North Atlantic Treaty. In the opinion of the United States Chiefs of Staff the left flank of the front in Western Eurasia should rest upon the United Kingdom which must be firmly held so as to ensure its use as a base for offensive action. The right flank should rest on the Cairo-Suez area. The centre should be held as far to the East as possible but until such time as there was a reasonable possibility of holding the line the main object should be to retain a substantial bridgehead on the mainland of Western Europe so that the offensive could be assumed on land at a later date when the necessary forces were available.

In pursuance of this concept the United States Chiefs of Staff believed that the allocation of forces and the conduct of operations should be governed by an order of priority as follows: first, the defence of the United Kingdom; second, the security of the Western Mediterranean area as far east as Tunisia; third, the defence of the Cairo-Suez area.

An analysis of the United States Forces likely to be available in the early days of a war showed that there were insufficient resources to satisfy these three priority requirements; there were not even enough to satisfy the first two; in the near future we were unlikely to be able to provide sufficient forces to hold the enemy on the line of the Rhine. In the early stages of a war the United States would only be able to open one line of logistic support; and in the view of the United States Chiefs of Staff it would be militarily unsound to develop this line through to the Cairo-Suez area, since the enemy could and quite probably would disrupt it by invading Spain. It would also be politically unacceptable to put the main American effort into the Middle East when the North Atlantic Treaty required the United States to assist in the defence of Western Europe. The United States Chiefs of Staff therefore proposed to operate along the axis; Morocco–Spain–France, deploying in such positions along this axis as proved militarily feasible at the time. For instance, if the forces of Western Europe were holding on the Rhine, then the United States forces could be deployed to assist them. On the other hand, if the enemy were over-running France, it might still be possible to deploy so as to hold the line of the Pyrenees. In any case it was essential to hold a foothold in Europe, even if this was only the southern part of

Spain covering the Straits of Gibraltar, because once we withdrew altogether we should be unlikely to be in a position to return in under two years.

The United States Chiefs of Staff therefore proposed to assemble their forces first in Morocco, and then deploy them as the situation might require. It might be that, in the event, they would be deployed in the Middle East, though this must have a lower priority than the other two bases of their strategy. This meant that no United States land forces could be allocated for the Middle East initially, but some United States naval forces, especially carriers, could be made available and there could be some part of the United States strategic air force deployed in the Cairo-Suez area provided suitable airfields were available. It was considered that this should not change the British allocation of forces to the defence of the Middle East, but this was clearly a subject for mutual discussion and examination between the two Planning Staffs: it had been suggested in some quarters that it would be militarily more sound to concentrate both the British and American forces in the centre.

Lord Tedder said that he did not agree with the relatively low priority accorded to the security of the Middle East which the British Chiefs of Staff regarded as vital to our strategy. They rated its defence as second only to the security of the United Kingdom base. They regarded the use of bases in the Middle East as essential to the successful conduct of the air offensive which in itself would be an essential part of the defence of the United Kingdom base. The area was essential to us for other reasons too: the oil resources of this area, important as they were in the near future, would probably become of vital importance in eight or ten years' time; and the loss of the Cairo-Suez Canal gateway would open up the whole of Africa to Soviet penetration. Admittedly, the loss of a foothold in Western Europe would be a disaster, but the loss of the Middle East would entail a major campaign to restore the position there.

He thought that in this approach to the problem the risks of the Mediterranean being closed by the loss of Gibraltar had been over estimated in the same way as had been done during the planning of Operation "Torch". The Germans had not pushed South through Spain and it seemed unlikely that the Russians would be able to do so, at any rate during the early stages of a war. There was a limit to the range at which Armies and Air Forces could operate effectively from their main sources of supply. It was a long way from Soviet Russia to the Straits of Gibraltar. Over insurance as regards Gibraltar had seriously delayed the development of the North Africa Campaign, and he felt we should avoid repeating a mistake which in the new circumstance would jeopardise the security of the vital Cairo-Suez area.

General Bradley[2] said that because the Germans had made the mistake of leaving Spain alone, it would be rash to assume that the Russians would do likewise. He felt there was a real danger that they might appreciate that the best way of neutralizing any threat from the Middle East would be to close the Straits of Gibraltar. There was, however, another aspect of this question. The United States would lack the essential services and material resources to open up and maintain more than one base area and line of communication during the early stages of another war. Every effort must be made to preserve some foothold in Western Europe. We could not afford the delay involved in staging another operation "Overlord". If Western Europe were left under

---

[2] General Omar N Bradley, first chairman of the US JCOS, 1948–1953.

the Communist carpet too long all would be lost. Even if United States forces could not arrive in time to assist in the defence of the Rhine, the plan for their deployment must give the option of using them in Western Europe as far forward as circumstances might permit. It was doubtful how much oil we should actually be able to get from the Middle East oilfields in war unless we could spare the necessary forces to hold the Persian Gulf. In any case there was probably enough oil available from other sources to meet war requirements over the period of the next five years. He agreed that there was an effective limit to the range at which land and air forces could operate; the Russians would be near this limit by the time they reached the Pyrenees which was an added reason for striking at them then. Finally, it was a choice between supporting the two flanks (Britain and the Middle East) and leaving the centre unsupported or concentrating on the support of the United Kingdom and Western Europe. The former line of action would be indefensible politically under the terms of the Atlantic Pact.

Lord Fraser said that he did not agree that the Germans had made a mistake in leaving Spain alone. One should visit the country and see its rugged nature, and one should read the histories of military campaigns in Spain: the Germans had been right not to get bogged down in a campaign in Spain. It seemed to him all wrong to deploy forces in the Western Mediterranean area to meet a threat which might never mature instead of engaging them to meet a certain Russian advance into France or the Middle East: it seemed to him so much better to use our forces to hold an essential position, rather than hold them back and be forced to use them later to re-take what had been lost. As far as he could see we should have the ludicrous position of the French withdrawing their forces as rapidly as possible from North Africa for the Battle of the Rhine at the same time that the Americans were moving their forces into North Africa.

General Vandenberg[3] said that if the Middle East air base could be held during the early months of a war it would have served its offensive purpose. He regarded the Middle East area as a pocket from which no real overland threat could be developed into Soviet territory. It would be possible, with the aircraft coming into service, to use North Africa as a complementary air base to the United Kingdom.

General Bradley said that one of the reasons that the Germans did not attack Spain was the fact that she [sic] was threatened on two fronts. The Russians would not be exposed to such a threat in the early days of a war. The United States must retain an option on the deployment of their forces in Western Europe during the early stages of a war. It was impossible to forecast how the Russian campaign would develop and the extent to which their forces could be delayed or held up on the Rhine. If things went well and the threat to the Western Mediterranean did not develop then it would be easy to reinforce the Middle East. With the limited resources now likely to be at their disposal, the United States Chiefs of Staff could not undertake the early reinforcements of British land forces in the Middle East. The first United States division, which would be air-transported, could not arrive in Europe until D + one month, and would not be ready for combat until about D + three months. The second and third divisions could not arrive in Europe until D + three months and would not be ready for combat for some time after their arrival.

---

[3] General Hoyt Sanford Vandenberg, chief of US air staff.

Lord Tedder said that this new United States strategic concept presented the British Chiefs of Staff with a very difficult problem. The United Kingdom and the Commonwealth could not hope to hold the Middle East unaided by United States forces and at the same time re-inforce Western Europe. The French had demanded to know what contribution the United Kingdom was prepared to make to the defence of the Rhine in addition to forces already committed in Germany, and the British Chiefs of Staff had expressed their inability to answer this question until more was known about the deployment of United States forces. The French would raise this question again at the next meeting of the Western Union Defence Ministers in October and would expect some answer. It was important there should be agreement on the line the British and United States should take with the Western European countries on this vital question.

Sir William Slim emphasised the importance of what Lord Tedder had said. There had been a marked improvement recently in Western European morale which had been buoyed up by the ratification of the North Atlantic Treaty, but continental morale was still very brittle. The French were thinking in terms of pulling divisions out of North Africa to re-inforce the forces on the Rhine. Any indication that the United States were thinking of putting forces into this Western Mediterrenean area in anticipation of a French collapse would precipitate a crisis. He was not in favour of promising re-inforcements to Western Europe until the French themselves could put adequate forces into the field, but the time would come before very long when they might expect to do this.

General Vandenberg said that much would depend upon the vote on the Military Aid Programme now before Congress. The amount of money voted under this programme would govern the rate at which French forces would be equipped: at present it would not provide equipment for more than five French divisions. This in turn would determine the date by which allied prospects of holding the Rhine could be regarded as reasonable.

General Bradley, in reply to Lord Tedder, said that he did not foresee that we should be much stronger in 1957 than we were now. He also agreed that no resources were likely to be available in the foreseeable future to help the Italians in the defence of Northern Italy. The United States Occupation Forces in Austria, while they remained there, and the Anglo–American forces in Trieste, might be able to help the Italians to impose some delay on any Russian advance into Southern Italy.

After some further discussion it was agreed that it would not be politically possible to make any approach to Spain under present circumstances in spite of the importance of Spain in the "centre" strategy which the United States Chiefs of Staff had outlined. It was also agreed that no answer could be given to the French until the Military Aid Programme had been passed by Congress: after that, there would have to be a carefully co-ordinated Anglo–American approach to the French with the object of conducting a frank discussion with them on this problem. Our policy, when making this approach, should be to withhold the promise of re-inforcements until the stage had been reached when the total forces available for the defence of the Rhine would have a reasonable chance of holding that line.

In the meantime the British and United States Planning Staffs should meet and examine the implications and consequences of the United States strategic concept, and to draw up, if possible, a mutually agreed plan for war should it occur during the next Fiscal Year.

145   DEFE 4/23, COS 115(49)1   5 Aug 1949
'Anglo–Egyptian defence talks': COS Committee minutes on the
supply of equipment to Egypt and the nature of future discussions
[Extract]

The Committee had before them the following papers:—

(a) A Minute by the Secretary covering a draft telegram to the Commanders-in-Chief, Middle East, informing them of the decisions taken by the Defence Committee on the equipment aspect of the Anglo/Egyptian Defence Talks.

(b) A Minute by the Secretary containing certain amendments to the above telegram proposed by the War Office and the Foreign Office on the subject of the arms embargo.

(c) A telegram from the Acting Ambassador in Egypt to the Foreign Office reporting an interview which he had had with the Prime Minister of Egypt about the Anglo/Egyptian Defence Talks. The Acting Ambassador expressed the view that it would be inadvisable to press the Egyptian Prime Minister to sign the agreed Military Appreciation; and that in the meanwhile it was in our interest to continue the technical military talks and make such progress as was possible in the field of joint training and re-equipment of the Egyptian Armed Forces.

(d) A personal telegram from the Commander-in-Chief, Middle East Land Forces to the Vice Chief of the Imperial General Staff giving his views on the present state of the negotiations. General Crocker expressed the view that while it was clearly in the interests of the Egyptians to continue the talks on the present basis the time would soon arrive when it would be militarily imprudent for us to proceed unless the way was opened for discussions on a higher level to resolve the wider issues. He emphasised the danger of offering equipment and military aid to the Egyptians without achieving our main aim of securing our strategic requirements in Egypt.

Mr. Wright said that the Government which had recently taken office in Egypt was a "caretaker" Government of a Nationalist character who would remain in power until the elections, which were due to take place in September or October, had been held. He agreed with the Acting Ambassador that it was pointless to press the present Egyptian Prime Minister to commit himself on the Defence Discussions. Our aim should, he felt, be to keep the technical discussions going until after the elections had been held. The Commander-in-Chief, Middle East Land Forces seemed to imply that our policy should be to use the promise of equipment as a bargaining counter to obtain base facilities in Egypt. He considered, however, that the equipment question must be considered in the broader setting of our general relations with the Egyptian Government – i.e., in the political sphere as well as in the defence field. There were other outstanding issues with the Egyptians to be taken into account such as the question of Lake Tana and the Nile waters and the removal of restrictions on shipping in the Suez Canal. He felt, therefore, that there were arguments against using the supply of arms as a bargaining counter for base facilities alone. He stressed that he had not yet had an opportunity of consulting the Foreign Secretary on this question. He (Mr. Wright) was inclined to the view that in the long term the best approach was to try to improve our relations with Egypt step by step on a gradual basis. He would, however, like to discuss the matter further with the Ambassador, who was now in the

United Kingdom, and would then inform the Chiefs of Staff of the views of the Foreign Office on the broad policy which should be pursued for the conduct of the talks.

In the course of the discussion which followed the following points were made:—

(a) The draft telegram to the Commanders-in-Chief, Middle East reflected closely the decisions which had been taken by Ministers on the equipment aspect of the Defence Discussions. The instructions to the Commanders-in-Chief, Middle East were on very broad lines and this guidance was being given because it had been understood that unless some offer of equipment could be made to the Egyptians, the Defence Talks would break down. Since the original request had been received from the Commanders-in-Chief, Middle East it appeared that their views on the broad policy for the conduct of the talks had changed, as Commander-in-Chief, Middle East Land Forces now considered that in certain circumstances it would be imprudent to pursue the discussions. The talks were now not to be resumed until about the 15th August. There would, therefore, be sufficient time to give the Commanders-in-Chief, Middle East, further broad policy guidance after the Foreign Office had consulted Sir Ronald Campbell. The Commanders-in-Chief, Middle East, should, however, be informed as soon as possible of the rulings which had already been given by the Defence Committee.

(b) A debate on the arms embargo was now proceeding in the Security Council. No decisions had yet been reached, but it was possible that a favourable decision would be taken in the course of the following week. It was considered advisable to include a word of warning in the telegram to the Commanders-in-Chief that delivery of equipment was dependent on a decision on the arms embargo.

(c) It was pointed out that so far only the views of the Commander-in-Chief, Middle East Land Forces on the future policy for the conduct of the talks had been obtained. It appeared that his views differed in certain respects from the advice tendered by the Acting Ambassador to the Foreign Office. It was considered that the Commanders-in-Chief, Middle East, should be invited to discuss the matter with the Acting Ambassador and inform the Chiefs of Staff officially of their views on this question. *Major-General Redman* undertook to ask General Crocker to arrange for this to be done.

(d) It was suggested that one way of keeping the talks going would be to offer the Egyptians certain equipment to meet their training requirements. The wider question of the equipment needed for Egyptian Operational Units could be dealt with on a longer term basis. It was agreed that this question should be further explored and *Major-General Redman* undertook to arrange this.

(e) *The Committee* were informed that the Chief of the Imperial General Staff would be visiting Fayid on his way to the Far East in October and also on his return on about 4th November. *Mr. Wright* said that he thought that there would be every advantage if the Chief of the Imperial General Staff could visit in November King Farouk and also the new Prime Minister of Egypt who would by then have assumed office, as the elections would have been held.

The Committee agreed that the draft telegram to the Commanders-in-Chief, Middle East, should be amended to include a reference to the arms embargo and also to the fact that further policy guidance would be given at a later date. It was also agreed that when the Foreign Office had discussed the problem with the Ambassador, the Chiefs of Staff would give further consideration to the whole question.

The Committee:—

(1) Approved the draft telegram to the Commanders-in-Chief, Middle East as amended in discussion and instructed the Secretary to despatch it.

(2) Took note that Mr. Wright would inform the Chiefs of Staff by 10th August, of the views of the Foreign Office on the policy for the conduct of the Defence Discussions. . . .

146 FO 371/73496, no 6509   5 Aug 1949

[Anglo–Egyptian technical military talks]: letter from E A Chapman Andrews to M R Wright on talks with Hussein Sirry and Hassan Youssef

Please refer to my telegram No. 65 of the 29th July, reporting my conversation with Sirry Pasha concerning Anglo–Egyptian technical military talks.

In this same conversation, Sirry also argued that there was no reason why we should not safely withdraw from Egypt though "not immediately". Technical personnel in sufficient numbers "in civilian clothes" could be left behind to look after technical equipment and to see that all was kept in proper order at the ports, airfields and other installations. There would be no difficulty in the way of agreeing to the immediate inflow of British aircraft and troops on the outbreak of war. Sirry alleged that the delay in arranging such inflow would be infinitesmal because British aircraft and forces could be stationed nearby in Cyrenaica, the Sudan "and at Gaza".

Sirry was, of course, seeking to bolster up his contention that "no Egyptian political leader could accept any military agreement with Great Britain that did not provide in some way or another for evacuation"—(see paragraph 2 of my telegram under reference). The argument that our joint military needs could be covered by British technical staff disguised as civilians, is a familiar one and had to be dealt with firmly when both Abdel Hadi and Khashaba raised it shortly after Field Marshal Slim's visit. I shall, of course, do my best to disillusion Sirry Pasha.

As regards Sirry's reference to Gaza, this too is a point which has cropped up before. Both Hassan Youssef and Hassouna Pasha tried out on me last May the idea that if the Jews could be got out of the Southern Negeb, Egypt should allow us to have all the military facilities we wanted there, thus making it militarily possible for us to evacuate Egypt itself. Hassan Youssef told me at the time that the King was much attracted by this idea. He also later mentioned the same scheme to the Ambassador, though (perhaps more realistically!) substituting the Gaza Strip for the Southern Negeb. We warned the Commanders-in-Chief that this suggestion might be put forward by the Egyptian representatives at the technical talks. This has not in fact happened so far but the idea is still evidently in the air here.

Incidentally, I had an hour's talk with Hassan Youssef Pasha the other day about the situation in regard to these technical talks. He had not previously seen the full Appreciation which I therefore went through with him word for word. It had a marked effect for he grasped at once the points about the immediacy of the threat, its scope and nature and the resultant necessity for our forces to be in position in Egypt on D Day; also the need for immediate preparatory work for the organisation of civil defence, etc. He said that he believed that Abdel Hadi Pasha had kept the King in the dark about all this for His Majesty had been at a disadvantage in this connexion when he received the Ambassador for his farewell audience; and this was one of the reasons why His Majesty had decided to get rid of Abdel Hadi now. Hassan Youssef went on to say that we should undoubtedly find Sirry Pasha easier to get on with for he would accept the immediate threat and would leave the three Egyptian Service representatives on the Technical Talks Committee in no doubt about his wholehearted endorsement of the Appreciation. When I pointed out that the Prime Minister was nevertheless chary of putting his name to the Appreciation Hassan Youssef said that there really never had been any question of the Prime Minister or anyone else signing anything of this nature. The technical talks were intended to clear the way to a political agreement. This alone would be signed. Prime Ministers came and went but records remained and no Egyptian Prime Minister could afford to leave behind him a record proving beyond dispute that he had agreed with and put his name to a military agreement with Great Britain that implied the necessity for British troops to remain in Egypt and did not, at the same time, safeguard the age-long Egyptian national aspiration concerning evacuation. Nevertheless we need have no qualms concerning both the King's and Sirry Pasha's endorsement of the Appreciation and approval of the work of further planning now required to be done.

I then raised the point about the need for further planning to be carried out by a wider circle of British and Egyptian officers. Hassan Youssef Pasha at once said that there was of course no objection to a wider circle of British officers being let in on the plan if we thought this advisable; but so far as Egyptian officers were concerned knowledge of the actual Appreciation and of the plan should be confined strictly to those who already possess it, i.e., on the Egyptian service side, the three officers and Haidar Pasha (Minister for War and Marine). This would in no way delay the progress of further planning. Indeed the work of the various sub-committees ought to proceed simultaneously. Haidar Pasha and his three experts would see to it that the right Egyptian officers were given the right instructions regarding the work of the various committees but these officers would not (repeat not) be told anything about the background. They would simply obey orders to collaborate with our people in carrying out various tasks and though they might draw their own conclusions they would be given severe warnings about the secrecy of what they were doing and, in any case, the master plan would be safe. Hassan Youssef Pasha said that one of the most encouraging features of these technical talks was the complete secrecy with which they had been conducted. It was essential that this secrecy should be maintained. He ended by reassuring me most solemnly that we could trust them.

I am sending five copies of this letter to Wall (B.M.E.O.) for Commanders-in-Chief.

147 DEFE 4/23, COS 118(49)2 12 Aug 1949
'Anglo–Egyptian defence talks': COS Committee minutes on the supply of equipment to Egypt

The Committee had before them the following papers:—

(a) A minute by the Secretary covering a letter from the Foreign Office on the attitude which should be adopted by the British Delegation on the delivery of arms and equipment to the Egyptians.

(b) A telegram from the Commanders-in-Chief, Middle East suggesting how the basis of the Anglo–Egyptian defence talks might be broadened.

(c) A telegram from the Commanders-in-Chief, Middle East giving their views on the broad policy for the future conduct of the defence discussions.

Mr. Wright said that since the last meeting with the Chiefs of Staff he had had an opportunity of discussing with Sir William Strang and Sir Ronald Campbell the whole question of the defence discussions. The Foreign Office view remained broadly as stated at the meeting the previous week.[1] The Foreign Office were of the opinion that the supply of equipment must be considered not only in relation to the Defence Talks but also in regard to various outstanding political problems, such as the restrictions on shipping in the Suez Canal, the Nile Waters and the Sudan. It must be borne in mind that the Egyptians were obliged by the 1936 Treaty to take equipment from us unless we were unable to provide it—in which event they could look elsewhere. The Foreign Office, therefore, did not entirely subscribe to the views of the Commanders-in-Chief, Middle East, which appeared to be that we should use the supply of equipment as a bargaining counter to get the base facilities which we required. It would be a grave mistake, just after the lifting of the arms embargo, to make the supply of equipment to Egypt conditional on an Egyptian undertaking in writing to grant us base facilities. There was no prospect of opening political negotiations with the Egyptians until after the elections had been held in the autumn. A certain amount of equipment had been promised to Egypt for a long time and had been awaiting the raising of the arms embargo. He considered that this equipment should be issued immediately; and should be followed by an instalment of such equipment as could be made available for training purposes. This was a matter on which the Commanders-in-Chief, Middle East could be given considerable latitude during the negotiations. He had heard that the Commanders-in-Chief, Middle East had not yet had an opportunity of discussing the question with the acting Ambassador in Egypt before the telegram had been dispatched. His views were therefore to some extent conditional on what Mr. Chapman Andrews might have to say. Although Sir Ronald Campbell had approved the views he (Mr. Wright) had expressed, Sir Ronald Campbell had pointed out that it was possible that there might have been developments during his absence in the United Kingdom which would make him modify his views.

In the discussion that followed there was general agreement that the broad policy for the supply of equipment should be on the lines indicated by Mr. Wright. The equipment already promised to Egypt against routine demands should be released as soon as possible. In addition a certain amount of equipment should be offered to the Egyptians for training purposes. In the case of the Army it would be possible to make quite an impressive offer of training equipment. Such quantities of aircraft as could be made available should also be offered to the Egyptians. Our strongest bargaining counter was our ability to offer to equip the operational units of the Egyptian Forces. This was our trump card which should not be played until the later stage of the negotiations.

Sir Gerald Templer then circulated a draft telegram to the Commanders-in-Chief, Middle East, outlining the policy on the equipment aspect of the discussions. The

---

[1] See 145.

Committee went through this telegram paragraph by paragraph and agreed a number of amendments. It was agreed that the telegram would give the Commanders-in-Chief sufficient guidance on the broad policy. It was important that Service Ministries should inform the Commanders-in-Chief, Middle East as soon as possible of the availabilities of equipment. *Mr. Wright* asked that the telegram should be cleared with Sir William Strang before despatch.

The Committee:—

(1) Instructed the Secretary to clear the telegram to the Commanders in Chief, Middle East, as amended, with the Foreign Office before despatch.

(2) Invited the War Office and the Air Ministry to inform the Commanders-in-Chief, Middle East, as a matter of urgency, of the equipment that could be made available to the Egyptians.

148   FO 371/73496, no 6509   17–24 Aug 1949

[Securing a secret agreement with Egypt]: minutes by D J D Maitland on the means of obtaining the desired agreement

I mentioned the Egyptian Prime Minister's counter proposal to Lieut.-Colonel Calvert (War Office) yesterday. He agreed that it would be useful for the Foreign Office and Mr. Chapman-Andrews to know to what extent Hussein Sirry's proposal falls short of our requirements.

I think we can only put such ideas as this out of the Egyptians' heads if we tell them that there can be no question of a new or revised Treaty being negotiated. King Farouk, Sirry Pasha, all the Egyptian party leaders, and Amr Pasha and his staff are all obsessed with the idea of negotiating a Treaty. As Sirry Pasha says, no Egyptian political leader can accept any military arrangement that does not provide in some way or another for evacuation. The Egyptians' idea is that a new Treaty would provide for:—

(a) evacuation of the Canal Zone by British Forces;

(b) the granting to us of facilities which they, the Egyptians, think will be adequate for our purpose without allowing us actually to station troops in uniform in Egypt proper;

(c) some accommodation over the Sudan.

We have recently seen in our discussions with Sir R., Campbell and Sir R. Howe that (c) is possible. We have been advised so far that (a) and (b) are impossible and therefore a Treaty is out of the question; and perhaps the idea of a Treaty is out of date.

Until the Egyptians are convinced of this and are prepared to agree to a secret arrangement (on the lines of the agreement between ourselves and the U.S. Government which provides for the stationing of U.S. Forces in peacetime in the U.K.) whereby we shall be allowed to establish a base in Egypt, I cannot see that the technical talks will make any progress at all. Nor, I am afraid, can I see even a national or majority government in Egypt readily agreeing to such a secret arrangement. The Egyptian Government which made such an arrangement, whatever its character, would still be under pressure, inspired by Communists or malcontents, to secure the evacuation and unification of the Nile Valley, and our relations with Egypt would continue in the same uneasy way so long as we did not take account of Egypt's so-called "national aspirations". The separate components of a national government are each to be possessed of a piece of information (the fact that such a secret agreement had been concluded) which they are ingenious enough to use to the detriment of the other components of the national government.

I think that it would be useful for our strategists to examine Hussein Sirry's counter proposals even though they do so only as a military exercise starting out from the assumption that facilities on the lines he has mentioned are all that we are going to get.

D.J.D.M.
17.8.49

Mr. Stewart has asked me to expand my minute above.
The important points to my mind are that:—

(a) the 1936 Treaty does not give us the facilities we require;
(b) a new or revised Treaty is out of the question;
(c) we cannot in present circumstances rely on a Wafdist or a Coalition Government being able to carry out their part of a secret arrangement (on the lines of the unwritten arrangement between ourselves and the Americans).

By some means we must therefore alter the present circumstances so that a Wafdist or Coalition Government will be able to carry out a secret, and perhaps unwritten, military agreement.

The means available to us are few. We can threaten to withhold the arms which the Egyptians want for internal security, for defence against Israel or for the sake of becoming a force to be reckoned with in the Mediterranean. If we carried out this threat, the Egyptians might be able to get arms from elsewhere. If they could not, they could make things difficult for us in other ways, e.g. in the Sudan, in the Suez Canal Zone, in the Canal itself, over Nile Waters or British interests in Egypt. We are of course infinitely more vulnerable in this way than they are.

While the threat to withhold arms is a good weapon, I do not think it is good enough by itself when we are dealing with a person as astute as King Farouk. I think that we should do all in our power to get King Farouk resolutely on our side. In the last resort, he is the one person who can make a secret arrangement acceptable to an Egyptian Government and, should it ever become public, acceptable to the Egyptian people. We can either frighten him or woo him into doing so, or both. We might invite him to this country, show him round Harwell, let him see the latest weapons of war and allow him to read some of the Chiefs of Staff's appreciations. The wooing might be done by a member of the staff of the Embassy at Cairo whose principal task would be to become King Farouk's friend and incidentally his confidential adviser.

D.J.D.M.
24.8.49

149   FO 371/73504, no 6968   5–7 Sept 1949
[Anglo–Egyptian treaty negotiations]: minutes by D J D Maitland and G L Clutton on a response to an Egyptian request for talks   [Extract]

The purport of this important despatch[1] is that in the near future the Egyptian Government are going to ask us formally to open negotiations for the revision of the 1936 Treaty. The Egyptians, of course, want the negotiations to take place on the understanding that we shall evacuate the Canal Zone and shall agree to some accommodation over the Sudan.

This is not an unexpected development but it means that the crisis in Anglo–Egyptian relations which we have successfully avoided since the Bevin/Sidky Talks of 1946 is about to arise. The only unexpected thing is that in spite of what has happened in the past two years, the Egyptians are remarkably incapable of facing facts.

For the reasons set out in the minutes on J 6509/1053/16G,[2] which is submitted simultaneously, a new or revised treaty with Egypt is out of the question. It was agreed at the meeting on the 9th August that an accommodation over the Sudan is possible, but agreement about strategic questions is impossible. The arguments in the previous minutes were based on the assumption that it is our intention to defend the Middle East in time of war, and that we can only do so if we have certain facilities in the Canal Zone of Egypt. There is perhaps a remote chance that such facilities as the Egyptians are prepared to offer us will be sufficient for our needs. This has never been studied in detail and I think that we must first of all ask the Chiefs of Staff to study Hussein Sirry's proposals[3] (see J 6509) even if they do so as a military exercise.

On the assumption that the Chiefs of Staff tell us that facilities outside the Canal Zone are useless, there are two courses of action open to us. First, we can endeavour to prevent the Egyptians from requesting the opening of negotiations. Secondly, we can tell them when they do make such a request that it is pointless. To follow the first course of action we should have to show good reason for dissuading the Egyptians from negotiating. Any arguments that we put forward would, I think, be less convincing than the Egyptian argument that they have now fulfilled one of the conditions that we have laid down hitherto, namely that there should be a majority or national government in Egypt. If the Egyptians want to begin negotiations they could make it very difficult for us to refuse to comply. The second course of action is, therefore, the only possible one. This means taking advantage of the fact that King Farouk has already recognised in the context of the current defence talks that an immediate threat to the safety of Egypt exists. It may be that he has recognised this threat merely to manouevre us into the position (in which we now are) of talking defence matters on a technical level behind the backs of the kind of government with which we have said we will be prepared to negotiate. The solution appears to be to convince King Farouk once and for all of the terrifying danger which threatens Egypt. I think we can only do this by bringing him to this country and showing him how, where and with what weapons a future war will be fought. During such a visit we could kill two other birds. We could let him know our views about the economic

---

[1] From Chapman Andrews, dated 29 Aug.   [2] See 148.   [3] See 146.

situation of Egypt and about the folly and iniquity of the past few years' discriminatory legislation in Egypt.

D.J.D.M.
5.9.49

The Treaty issue is an insoluble problem and we have for long recognised it as such. Although we were prepared to evacuate Egypt two years ago, this is now, because of the change in the international situation, out of the question. At the same time, we realise that the 1936 Treaty does not give us the minimum facilities we require. On the other hand, we recognise the impossibility of any Egyptian Government agreeing to a Treaty which did not provide for the complete evacuation of British troops from Egypt.

The whole basis of the present talks is that we are dealing with an [sic] problem to which there is no solution. The object of the talks is to short-circuit the problem and come to practical arrangements to meet the realities of the situation to the mutual benefit of both Egypt and the United Kingdom. Such arrangements might or might not be incorporated in an inter-governmental agreement. In addition, as the Secretary of State pointed out repeatedly to Khashaba Pasha and to Amr Pasha, Treaties are out of date conceptions as far as military strategy is concerned.

The present despatch on the face of it seems to show that the Egyptians have forgotten all this. What was the motive of the three prominent Egyptian public figures in making their views known to Mr. Chapman-Andrews I do not know, and in view of the complexity of the Egyptian mind, I do not think it is much worth while wracking our brains too much . . . .

G.L.C.
7.9.49

150   DEFE 4/24, COS 131(49)8   8 Sept 1949
'Examination of United States strategic concept for war in 1950/51': report by the JPS to the COS, 5 Sept 1945 (JP(49)85)

[The British military was seeking alternatives to the new American strategic concept that was developed after the creation of NATO. A bridgehead in Brittany was suggested but it was later pointed out that there would not be enough forces to hold one there (DEFE 4/24, COS 131(49)8, 8 Sept 1949; DEFE 4/24, COS 139(49)5, 21 Sept 1949). The future position improved slightly in October when the Americans agreed to put forces to defend the Rhine as part of a medium term plan for 1954 (DEFE 4/25, COS 151(49)1, 10 Oct 1949; DEFE 4/26, COS 175(49)4, 23 Nov). In the short term the NATO powers, let alone the British, lacked the forces to defend western Europe while Britain was clearly unable to defend the Middle East without US support.]

As instructed[1] we have examined the new United States strategic concept for war in the fiscal year 1951. We attach at Annex[2] an examination of this. It will be seen that among our conclusions are:—

(a) The American strategic concept is not sound militarily since land forces, and in part their air forces, are unlikely to be effectively engaged during the first vital

---

[1] See 144.   [2] Not printed.

six months. Thus, it does not deploy forces to the best advantage to achieve our political object of preventing Western Europe being overrun.

(b) Under the American strategic concept the British Empire and Commonwealth will be unable to attain the three objects of the British defence policy (defence of the United Kingdom, control of essential sea communications and a firm hold of the Middle East) unless part of the United States strategic air force is employed tactically in defending the Middle East and unless part of the United States naval air force is employed to keep control of the Middle East communications. Even with this United States air support our hold on the Middle East will be precarious.

(c) No United Kingdom or United States forces other than the land force garrison of Germany can be made available for the defence of Western Europe; thus we have simultaneously jeopardised our hold on the Middle East and invited serious political repercussions in Western Europe.

2.   The American strategic concept has been approved by their Chiefs of Staff and their Secretary of Defense, after more than nine months of discussion: it will, therefore, be difficult at this stage to get American agreement to a change in their strategic concept. We consider, however, that we should use all the arguments at our disposal to discredit this concept. Although we may well fail to get the Americans to change their concept during the meeting, yet we shall have sown the seeds which may bear fruit in a new strategic concept next year.

Recommendations

3.   We recommend, however, that in order to have some agreed emergency plan and to keep in being the direct Anglo/American planning machinery, we have the authority of the Chiefs of Staff to agree as a last resort to an emergency plan for the year 1950/51 on the following lines. We would of course make it clear that it would be impossible to agree to this strategic concept for long term planning.

(a) The British Empire and Commonwealth to be responsible for the defence of the United Kingdom and the Middle East.

(b) The United States to be responsible for the defence of the Western European Continent.

(c) The United Kingdom to be responsible for providing three-quarters of the naval forces required for control of sea communications in the North Atlantic and for the naval forces required for close escort of British Mediterranean convoys, and for supporting the Army's flank in the Middle East.

(d) The United States to be responsible for providing the naval forces required for:—

    (i)   The Central/South Atlantic.

    (ii)   The Pacific.

    (iii) The Mediterranean other than a close escort of British convoys and the flank force in the Middle East.

    (iv) One-quarter of the forces required in the North Atlantic.

(e) The United States to employ three-quarters of their strategic air effort on strategic targets in Russia and one-quarter to assist the defence of Western Europe and the Middle East (at least 15% of the United States strategic air force to be employed in the defence of the Middle East).

(f) The tasks of the Royal Air Force to be the security of the United Kingdom and the Middle East.

(g) The United Kingdom and United States forces of occupation at present in Germany to be allocated to the Western European theatre.

(h) Australia and New Zealand to be responsible for the defence of South-East Asia and the Indian Ocean except that the United Kingdom will provide one Gurkha division.

(i) Canadian forces to be deployed in the United Kingdom and in the control of North Atlantic sea communications.

(j) At least one American regimental combat team to be deployed in Israel so as to encourage the co-operation of that country with the forces defending the Middle East.

(k) The American and Canadian forces as they become fit for combat after D + 6 months to be regarded as a strategic reserve disposable by the Combined Chiefs of Staff as the situation at that time may require.

4.   We recommend the Chiefs of Staff approve the paper at Annex as a brief for our discussions with the American and Canadian Joint Planners and authorise us, in the last resort, to agree to an emergency plan on the basis given in paragraph 3 above.

Appendix to Part I

Extract from the treaty of alliance between His Majesty, in respect of the United Kingdom, and His Majesty the King of Egypt, London, 26 August 1936 Cmd 5360, 1936

ARTICLE 1

The military occupation of Egypt by the forces of His Majesty The King and Emperor is terminated.

ARTICLE 2

His Majesty The King and Emperor will henceforth be represented at the Court of His Majesty the King of Egypt and His Majesty the King of Egypt will be represented at the Court of St. James's by Ambassadors duly accredited.

ARTICLE 3

Egypt intends to apply for membership to the League of Nations. His Majesty's Government in the United Kingdom, recognising Egypt as a sovereign independent State, will support any request for admission which the Egyptian Government may present in the conditions prescribed by Article 1 of the Covenant.

ARTICLE 4

An alliance is established between the High Contracting Parties with a view to consolidating their friendship, their cordial understanding and their good relations.

ARTICLE 5

Each of the High Contracting Parties undertakes not to adopt in relation to foreign countries an attitude which is inconsistent with the alliance, nor to conclude political treaties inconsistent with the provisions of the present treaty.

ARTICLE 6

Should any dispute with a third State produce a situation which involves a risk of a rupture with that State, the High Contracting Parties will consult each other with a view to the settlement of the said dispute by peaceful means, in accordance with the provisions of the Covenant of the League of Nations and of any other international obligations which may be applicable to the case.

ARTICLE 7

Should, notwithstanding the provisions of Article 6 above, either of the High Contracting Parties become engaged in war, the other High Contracting Party will, subject always to the provisions of Article 10 below, immediately come to his aid in the capacity of an ally.

The aid of His Majesty the King of Egypt in the event of war, imminent menace of war or apprehended international emergency will consist in furnishing to His Majesty The King and Emperor on Egyptian territory, in accordance with the Egyptian system of administration and legislation, all the facilities and assistance in his power, including the use of his ports, aerodromes and means of communication. It will accordingly be for the Egyptian Government to take all the administrative and legislative measures, including the establishment of martial law and an effective censorship, necessary to render these facilities and assistance effective.

ARTICLE 8

In view of the fact that the Suez Canal, whilst being an integral part of Egypt, is a universal means of communication as also an essential means of communication between the different parts of the British Empire, His Majesty the King of Egypt, until such time as the High Contracting Parties agree that the Egyptian Army is in a position to ensure by its own resources the liberty and entire security of navigation of the Canal, authorises His Majesty The King and Emperor to station forces in Egyptian territory in the vicinity of the Canal, in the zone specified in the Annex to this Article, with a view to ensuring in co-operation with the Egyptian forces the defence of the Canal. The detailed arrangements for the carrying into effect of this Article are contained in the Annex hereto. The presence of these forces shall not constitute in any manner an occupation and will in no way prejudice the sovereign rights of Egypt.

It is understood that at the end of the period of twenty years specified in Article 16 the question whether the presence of British forces is no longer necessary owing to the fact that the Egyptian Army is in a position to ensure by its own resources the liberty and entire security of navigation of the Canal may, if the High Contracting Parties do not agree thereon, be submitted to the Council of the League of Nations for decision in accordance with the provisions of the Covenant in force at the time of signature of the present treaty or to such other person or body of persons for decision in accordance with such other procedure as the High Contracting Parties may agree.

Annex to Article 8

1. Without prejudice to the provisions of Article 7, the numbers of the forces of His Majesty The King and Emperor to be maintained in the vicinity of the Canal shall not exceed, of the land forces, 10,000, and of the air forces, 400 pilots, together with the necessary ancillary personnel for administrative and technical duties. These numbers do not include civilian personnel, *e.g.*, clerks, artisans and labourers.

2. The British forces to be maintained in the vicinity of the Canal will be distributed (a) as regards the land forces, in Moascar and the Geneifa area on the south-west side of the Great Bitter Lake, and (b) as regards the air forces, within 5 miles of the Port Said-Suez railway from Kantara in the north, to the junction of the railway Suez-Cairo and Suez-Ismailia in the south, together with an extension along the Ismailia-Cairo railway to include the Royal Air Force Station at Abu Sueir and its satellite landing grounds; together with areas suitable for air firing and bombing ranges, which may have to be placed east of the Canal.

3. In the localities specified above there shall be provided for the British land and air forces of the numbers specified in paragraph 1 above, including 4,000 civilian personnel (but less 2,000 of the land forces, 700 of the air forces and 450 civilian personnel for whom accommodation already exists), the necessary lands and durable barrack and technical accommodation, including an emergency water supply. The lands, accommodation and water supply shall be suitable according to modern standards. In addition, amenities such as are reasonable, having regard to the character of these localities, will be provided by the

planting of trees and the provision of gardens, playing fields, &c., for the troops, and a site for the erection of a convalescent camp on the Mediterranean coast.

4.   The Egyptian Government will make available the lands and construct the accommodation, water supplies, amenities and convalescent camp, referred to in the preceding paragraph as being necessary over and above the accommodation already existing in these localities, at its own expense, but His Majesty's Government in the United Kingdom will contribute (1) the actual sum spent by the Egyptian Government before 1914 on the construction of new barracks as alternative accommodation to the Kasr-el-Nil Barracks in Cairo, and (2) the cost of one-fourth of the barrack and technical accommodation for the land forces. The first of these sums shall be paid at the time specified in paragraph 8 below for the withdrawal of the British forces from Cairo and the second at the time for the withdrawal of the British forces from Alexandria under paragraph 18 below. The Egyptian Government may charge a fair rental for the residential accommodation provided for the civilian personnel. The amount of the rent will be agreed between His Majesty's Government in the United Kingdom and the Egyptian Government.

5.   The two Governments will each appoint, immediately the present treaty comes into force, two or more persons who shall together form a committee to whom all questions relating to the execution of these works from the time of their commencement to the time of their completion shall be entrusted. Proposals for, or outlines of, plans and specifications put forward by the representatives of His Majesty's Government in the United Kingdom will be accepted, provided they are reasonable and do not fall outside the scope of the obligations of the Egyptian Government under paragraph 4. The plans and specifications of each of the works to be undertaken by the Egyptian Government shall be approved by the representatives of both Governments on this committee before the work is begun. Any member of this committee, as well as the Commanders of the British forces or their representatives, shall have the right to examine the works at all stages of their construction, and the United Kingdom members of the committee may make suggestions as regards the manner in which the work is carried out. The United Kingdom members shall also have the right to make at any time, while the work is in progress, proposals for modifications or alterations in the plans and specifications. Effect shall be given to suggestions and proposals by the United Kingdom members, subject to the condition that they are reasonable and do not fall outside the scope of the obligations of the Egyptian Government under paragraph 4. In the case of machinery and other stores, where standardization of type is important, it is agreed that stores of the standard type in general use by the British forces will be obtained and installed. It is, of course, understood that His Majesty's Government in the United Kingdom may, when the barracks and accommodation are being used by the British forces, make at their own expense improvements or alterations thereto and construct new buildings in the areas specified in paragraph 2 above.

6.   In pursuance of their programme for the development of road and railway communications in Egypt, and in order to bring the means of communications in Egypt up to modern strategic requirements, the Egyptian Government will construct and maintain the following roads, bridges and railways . . . .

ARTICLE 9

The immunities and privileges in jurisdictional and fiscal matters to be enjoyed by the forces of His Majesty The King and Emperor who are in Egypt in accordance with the provisions of the present treaty will be determined in a separate convention to be concluded between the Egyptian Government and His Majesty's Government in the United Kingdom.

ARTICLE 10

Nothing in the present treaty is intended to or shall in any way prejudice the rights and obligations which devolve, or may devolve, upon either of the High Contracting Parties under the Covenant of the League of Nations or the Treaty for the Renunciation of War signed at Paris on the 27th August, 1928.

ARTICLE 11

1.   While reserving liberty to conclude new conventions in future, modifying the agreements of the 19th January and the 10th July, 1899, the High Contracting

Parties agree that the administration of the Sudan shall continue to be that resulting from the said agreements. The Governor-General shall continue to exercise on the joint behalf of the High Contracting Parties the powers conferred upon him by the said agreements.

The High Contracting Parties agree that the primary aim of their administration in the Sudan must be the welfare of the Sudanese.

Nothing in this article prejudices the question of sovereignty over the Sudan.

2.   Appointments and promotions of officials in the Sudan will in consequence remain vested in the Governor-General, who, in making new appointments to posts for which qualified Sudanese are not available, will select suitable candidates of British and Egyptian nationality.

3.   In addition to Sudanese troops, both British and Egyptian troops shall be placed at the disposal of the Governor-General for the defence of the Sudan.

4.   Egyptian immigration into the Sudan shall be unrestricted except for reasons of public order and health.

5.   There shall be no discrimination in the Sudan between British subjects and Egyptian nationals in matters of commerce, immigration or the possession of property.

6.   The High Contracting Parties are agreed on the provisions set out in the Annex to this Article as regards the method by which international conventions are to be made applicable to the Sudan.

Annex to Article 11

1.   Unless and until the High Contracting Parties agree to the contrary in application of paragraph 1 of this Article, the general principle for the future shall be that international conventions shall only become applicable to the Sudan by the joint action of the Governments of the United Kingdom and of Egypt, and that such joint action shall similarly also be required if it is desired to terminate the participation of the Sudan in an international convention which already applies to this territory.

2.   Conventions to which it will be desired that the Sudan should be a party will generally be conventions of a technical or humanitarian character. Such conventions almost invariably contain a provision for subsequent accession, and in such cases this method of making the convention applicable to the Sudan will be adopted. Accession will be effected by a joint instrument, signed on behalf of Egypt and the United Kingdom respectively by two persons duly authorised for the purpose. The method of depositing the instruments of accession will be the subject of agreement in each case between the two Governments. In the event of its being desired to apply to the Sudan a convention which does not contain an accession clause, the method by which this should be effected will be the subject of consultation and agreement between the two Governments.

3.   If the Sudan is already a party to a convention, and it is desired to terminate the participation of the Sudan therein, the necessary notice of termination will be given jointly by the United Kingdom and by Egypt.

4.   It is understood that the participation of the Sudan in a convention and the termination of such participation can only be effected by joint action specifically taken in respect of the Sudan, and does not follow merely from the fact that the United Kingdom and Egypt are both parties to a convention or have both denounced a convention.

5.   At international conferences where such conventions are negotiated, the Egyptian and the United Kingdom delegates would naturally keep in touch with a view to any action which they may agree to be desirable in the interests of the Sudan.

ARTICLE 12

His Majesty The King and Emperor recognises that the responsibility for the lives and property of foreigners in Egypt devolves exclusively upon the Egyptian Government, who will ensure the fulfilment of their obligations in this respect.

ARTICLE 13

His Majesty The King and Emperor recognises that the capitulatory régime now existing in Egypt is no longer in accordance with the spirit of the times and with the present state of Egypt.

His Majesty the King of Egypt desires the abolition of this régime without delay.

Both High Contracting Parties are agreed upon the arrangements with regard to this matter as set forth in the Annex to this Article . . . .

ARTICLE 14

The present treaty abrogates any existing agreements or other instruments whose continued existence is inconsistent with its provisions. Should either High Contracting Party so request, a list of the agreements and instruments thus abrogated shall be drawn up in agreement between them within six months of the coming into force of the present treaty.

ARTICLE 15

The High Contracting Parties agree that any difference on the subject of the application or interpretation of the provisions of the present treaty which they are unable to settle by direct negotiation shall be dealt with in accordance with the provisions of the Covenant of the League of Nations.

ARTICLE 16

At any time after the expiration of a period of twenty years from the coming into force of the treaty, the High Contracting Parties will, at the request of either of them, enter into negotiations with a view to such revision of its terms by agreement between them as may be appropriate in the circumstances as they then exist. In case of the High Contracting Parties being unable to agree upon the terms of the revised treaty, the difference will be submitted to the Council of the League of Nations for decision in accordance with the provisions of the Covenant in force at the time of signature of the present treaty or to such other person or body of persons for decision in accordance with such procedure as the High Contracting Parties may agree. It is agreed that any revision of this treaty will provide for the continuation of the Alliance between the High Contracting Parties in accordance with the principles contained in Articles 4, 5, 6 and 7. Nevertheless, with the consent of both High Contracting Parties, negotiations may be entered into at any time after the expiration of a period of ten years after the coming into force of the treaty, with a view to such revision as aforesaid.

ARTICLE 17

The present treaty is subject to ratification. Ratifications shall be exchanged in Cairo as soon as possible. The treaty shall come into force on the date of the exchange of ratifications, and shall thereupon be registered with the Secretary-General of the League of Nations.

In witness whereof the above-named plenipotentiaries have signed the present treaty and affixed thereto their seals.

Done at London in duplicate this 26th day of August, 1936.

Index of Main Subjects and Persons

This is a consolidated index of the three parts of the volume. It is not a comprehensive index but a simplified and straightforward index to document numbers, with page references to the introduction in part I, the latter being given at the beginning of the entry in lower case roman numerals. The index is designed to be used in conjunction with the summary lists of the preliminary pages to all three parts of the volume. A preceding asterisk indicates inclusion in the Biographical Notes at the end of part III. Where necessary, particularly in long documents, and when possible, paragraph or section numbers are given in round brackets. The important articles of the 1936 Anglo–Egyptian treaty are reproduced as an appendix in each of the three volume parts. Arabic names are indexed in the form in which they appear in the Biographical Notes, not as they generally appear in the introduction and documents. The Foreign Office is not indexed but its individual departments are. The rank of military officers is given as the one held at the end of their service.

The following abbreviations are used:

A	– Annex	
App	– Appendix	
E	– Enclosure	
N	– editor's link note (before main text of document)	
n	– footnote	

Documents are divided between the three parts of the volume as follows:

nos	1–150	Part I
nos	151–368	Part II
nos	369–646	Part III

Abadan 11 (22), 177 (26, 29), 182, 204 n, 245, 271, 288 N, 317, 348, 369 N, 377, 395, 446 N, 448, 450, 643 A
  evacuation of British personnel from 225, 349, 358
* Abboud 91, 95, 155–156, 166, 172, 313
Abdullah, King of Jordan 11 (14), 119, 177 (16, 34, 64), 191 (12), 211 n, 611
Abu Sueir xliii, lv–lvi, 125 A, 128 N, 159 N, 165 (33), 177 (20), 181, 187, 376, 387, 424–426, 444, 488–489, 496, 511, 515, 518, 521, 523, 528 App, 532, 541
Abu Sultan 123, 131, 181, 554 A
Acheson, D (US) lxiv, lxviii, 292, 336
Adabiya 181, 385, 554 A
Addison, Lord 35, 53
Aden lv, 41, 56 A, 105, 110, 114, 125, 128 A, 191

(29), 216, 316, 409, 447, 475 App, 600, 610, 627, 635, 640, 643, 645
Afghanistan 111, 588
Africa xxxvii, lxxviii, lxxxvi, xciv, 120, 159, 180 A, 213, 258, 356, 430, 458, 469, 490, 527, 563, 566, 575, 604, 643
  bases in north west of 33 (11), 144, 159 N, 447
Africa Department (FO) 204, 395, 521, 605
Agrud 554 A
air interdiction 120, 257 App, 580 A
Air Ministry 522
Akrotiri 642, 646
Ala, Husain (Ala Hussein) 204 n
Ala, M 595 A, 595 n
* Alanbrooke, Field Marshal Lord 35, 39, 44, 53, 55
Albania 257 App

Aldrich, W (US)   446

Aleppo   142 (26), 257 App, 323, 337, 580

Alexander, A V   liii, 1–2, 108, 114, 193 N

* Alexander, Field Marshal Lord   lxvi, lxviii, 293,
    297, 303–304, 307, 333 N, 336, 393, 420, 434,
    443–444, 466, 484, 504, 523, 525, 530

Alexandretta   (see Iskanderun)

Alexandria   11 (17, 19), 13, 23 App, 30, 32 (14,
    20), 44, 56 A, 56 App, 120, 128 N, 170, 193, 236,
    245, 247, 252, 262, 288–289, 302, 339, 359, 393,
    416, 475, 557
  evacuation of 40, 57–58, 68, 220, 385
  riots in 119

Ali, Muhammad   100 n

* Allen, R   xxxvi, lxiv, lxvii, 161–163, 166, 196 N,
    203–204, 208, 249, 251, 278, 302, 306, 310,
    329–330, 332, 353, 359–360, 371, 381, 383–384,
    394, 408, 497

Allfrey, Lieutenant-General (Sir) C   48, 111

Al Misri   156, 206, 397

Al Nida   207

Alpha, plan   lxxxv, lxxxviii, xc, xcii, 589 N, 590,
    601 n, 602, 610, 614, 634, 640 N

* Altrincham, Lord   xlv, 8 N, 11, 15

Amery, J   lxxviii, 377 n, 408

Amery, L S   lxxiv

Amman   128 N, 157, 257 App, 337 A, 643, 646

* Amr, Abd al-Fattah   liv, 4, 6, 60–61, 75, 79, 81,
    92, 110, 126–127, 129, 148, 156, 169,
    300–302

Amr, Hakim   386 n, 441, 556–557

Amr, Sirri   313

Anderson, R B (US)   xcii

Andimeshk   580

* Andraos, E   224 n, 260, 302, 313

Anglo–American relations   xliii, lxii–lxiii, lxxxv,
    lxxxix, 460

Anglo–American–Turkish defence talks   (1955)
    577, 580, 587 (1), 621 A

Anglo–Egyptian agreement   (1954) 531, 541,
    548–549, 554, 563, 566–568, 571, 576, 583, 594,
    618, 625, 638–639
  difficulties with heads of 544

Anglo–Egyptian Control Board   200 A

Anglo–Egyptian Council   54–55

Anglo–Egyptian Joint Defence Board   xlviii, 44,
    52–55, 57, 59, 61, 64–66, 68, 70, 72, 74–75,
    77–78, 83–85, 92, 105, 109–110, 115, 157

Anglo–Egyptian negotiations on Suez Canal base
    (see also Anglo–Egyptian treaty, negotiations
    for revision of)
  (1946)   xlvi–xlix, 23, 26, 30, 32 (2), 34, 37–39,
    41, 47, 51–52, 87
  (1948)   lii
  (1949)   lvi, 132, 139, 145, 147
  (1950)   lviii, lx–lxi, 172, 174 E, 176
  (1951)   lxiii, 200, 203, 209–210, 347

  (1952)   268, 284 A, 285, 291–292, 300–302,
    309, 328–329
  (1953)   lxxv–lxxviii, 354–355, 366, 384, 388,
    392–393, 412, 416, 419, 425, 430–442,
    444–446, 464–467, 472
  (1954)   lxxxiii, xciii, 468–470, 474, 476,
    480–481, 484, 486–487, 489, 492, 503–504,
    511, 513, 518–520, 523, 526, 529–530,
    532–536, 539–541, 543–544, 547, 550, 557
  American support in   347, 384
  Cases A, B and C
    (1952)   339–340, 344, 346–347, 349, 351 N
    (1953)   lxxii–lxxiv, lxvi–lxxvii, 354–355, 364
      N, 374–376, 379–380, 382, 387, 391,
      394–396, 398, 401, 402 N, 406, 408, 411,
      413–415, 424, 426, 443
    (1954)   519
  Case D
    (1952)   340, 344, 347, 349
    (1953)   lxxii–lxxiii, 382
  Egyptian views on (1946)   45, 68
  military technical discussions about (1949)
    124, 126, 132, 138, 143, 145–146, 151, 157,
    384
  on Article 2 (Article 5 of British draft) of
    proposed treaty (1946)   xlviii, xlix, 47 N,
    53–55, 59–62, 64, 66–67, 69, 70 N, 70 n, 71,
    74–76, 79, 81–85, 87

Anglo–Egyptian Oilfields Ltd   248

Anglo–Egyptian treaty (1936)   intro l, liii, lx, lxiii,
    lxxx, lxxxii, 1, 7, 9, 12–13, 19, 22, 26, 28, 30, 32
    (1), 45, 48, 52–55, 65, 68, 73–75, 77, 82, 90, 94,
    99, 104–105, 122, 127, 132, 138, 148–149, 151,
    157–158, 167–168, 180, 186–187, 191 (5), 198,
    200, 222, 251, 272, 294–295, 318, 435, 457, 472,
    478 N, 479–480, 484, 488–489, 492, 497, 499,
    502, 505, 535, 539, 541, 547
  abrogation of   lxiii, 186, 211, 217, 220, 225,
    243, 247, 250, 252 A, 253, 267, 283, 314,
    317, 358, 361, 377, 416, 428, 488, 493, 594
  negotiations for revision of
    (1945)   19, 22
    (1946)   26–27, 36, 39, 42–45, 50, 52, 58–60,
      63–67, 69–77, 79–80, 83, 85, 88
    (1947)   90, 93, 100, 102
    (1949)   151
    (1950)   157, 187
    (1951)   196–198, 202

Anglo–Egyptian Union   94 n

Anglo–Iranian Oil Company   lxii, lxxvi, 204 n,
    206, 208, 242, 314, 372, 377

Anglo–Iraqi Joint Defence Board   119 n, 577

Anglo–Iraqi treaty (1930)   lxxxi, 21, 110, 134 A,
    157, 462–463, 472, 478, 542 N, 548–549,
    561–562, 573, 577, 583
  (1948 unratified) 157, 177 (27), 191 (10)

Anglo–Jordanian defence board   598

Anglo–Transjordanian treaty (1946) 157; (1948) 157, 496, 642–643, 646, 648
Ansar (Sudanese sect) 556 n, 594
anti-imperialism 262, 265
ANZUS, pact 525
Aqaba 106, 133 A, 142 A, 269, 277, 467, 643, 646
  gulf of 605
  line of communication with Amman 168
Arabian American Oil Company (ARAMCO) 607 A
Arab–Israeli conflict lxxxv–lxxxviii, xcii, 159, 286, 556, 560, 563, 565–566, 603–604, 614, 620, 627, 642
  armistice in 189
  settlement of xci, 180, 194, 573, 578, 587 (4, 37), 589 N, 594, 614–615
Arab League lxxxv–lxxxvi, xcii, 11 (32, 36), 15 (6, 8, 12, 30), 21, 26 A, 28, 52 A, 112, 115, 134 A, 159, 177 (11), 229, 527, 561–562, 568, 571–573, 582, 585, 626
Arab League Collective Security Pact 250, 350–351, 369–370, 386, 394, 411, 432, 441, 444–445, 476, 542 N, 549, 556, 567, 574 N, 579, 623, 626, 632
Arab Legion 177 (33, 56, 63), 409, 519, 581, 598, 600, 633, 643
Arab prime ministers' conference (1955) 571 N, 574
Ardahan 177 (11)
Armistice and Post-War Planning Committee 3 n
Army, British 308 (120–129), 334 A
* Arthur, G G 494, 590, 601
Ashigga (Sudanese political party) 90
Assheton, (Sir) R 1
Astara 337 A
Aswan dam xc, xcii, 313, 579, 602–603, 608–610, 612, 619, 629, 632, 635
Ataqa 181, 385
atomic demolitions 177 App, 182
atomic disarmament 165 (16), 308 (41)
atomic warfare 308 (107), 562
atomic weapons (see nuclear weapons; also nuclear deterrent)
* Attlee, C R xliv, xlvi, xlviii–l, liii, xciii–xciv, 1–2, 8 N, 32 N, 35, 44, 46, 49, 58, 66 N, 67, 84 n, 86, 88, 89 n, 93 N, 98 N, 102 N, 103, 108–109, 133 A, 154, 210, 227, 634
Auriol, President V 358
Australia 3, 33 (11, 23), 93, 142 (34), 153, 165 (36, 56, 60), 177 (60), 183, 201, 216, 308 (62–63, 76), 328, 342, 369, 377, 423, 453, 472, 563–564, 566
Austria 128 A, 308 (77)
al-Azhari, Ismail (Azari, I) 556 n
Azerbaijan 115, 184, 191 (3, 14), 257 App
* Azzam Pasha 94, 112, 115, 188

B 26 bomber 600
B 29 bomber lv
Badawi (Bedawi) 4, 6–7, 22
Baghdad 128 N, 142 (26), 142 A, 257 App, 323, 337 A, 566, 577, 580
Baghdad–Mosul area 121 A
Baghdad Pact (1955) xxxvi, lxxvii, lxxxvii–lxxxviii, xc-xci, xciii–xciv, 587 N, 598, 604, 606, 611, 614–615, 618, 620–626, 628, 631–636, 640–648
  expansion of 614–615
Bahrain 56 A, 120, 121 A, 142 (29), 177 (27), 199, 257, 309, 451, 551, 640
Bahrain–Ras–Tanura defence line 177 (54)
Bahri, Yunis (Younis Bahri) 623
Baikal, Lake 141
Baker, Air Marshal (Sir) J 170, 188, 347
Baku 125 A
Balfour, Colonel R 259 n
Bancroft, I P 412 n, 425
Bandar Abbas 121 A, 128 N, 142 (26–27), 177 (41, 54), 182, 257 App, 577, 580
Bandar Shah 128 N
Bandung conference (1955) 592 n, 600
Barents Sea 141
Barnes, A 189 n
Basra lxxxv, 142 (26), 142 A, 257 App, 276, 323, 329, 337 A, 369, 551, 566, 577
Bat Galim 556 n
Batum 125 A, 311
Beaumont, R A 583
Beckett, W E 48 n
Bedell-Smith, W (US) 380 n, 396, 428 n, 502
Beersheba 562, 612
Beirut 128 N, 177 App, 323, 337–338, 455, 508
* Bendall, D V 204, 233, 249, 280, 288 N, 299
Benghazi 56 App, 154, 519
Ben Gurion, D lxxxviii
Benina 56 App
* Bennett, Sir J Sterndale 468–469, 490, 493
Benson, Major-General E 541 n, 556
Berlin, blockade of (1948) 122, 165 (11)
Bermuda conference (1953) 395, 399–400, 402–404, 407, 454, 459 N, 460
Bevan, A 470 n
* Bevin, E xlv, xlviii–lii, lix–lxi, xciii, 12 N, 16 n, 26, 30–31, 32 N, 36, 38 N, 44–45, 49, 52–53, 55, 58, 60–62, 66, 69, 72, 74, 78–79, 81 N, 83–85, 88, 89 n, 94 N, 96 N, 98, 101, 108–111, 113, 115, 124 N, 129, 132–134, 154, 179, 186–190, 193 n, 197
Bevin-Sidky agreement 103, 151, 167, 196, 225
Bidault, G 407 n
Binnacle, plan (1950) lxii, 159 N, 257
Birch, N 538 n
Bison bomber (see Ilyushin IL28)
Bitlis 580
Black, E (US) 609

Black Sea   125
Board of Trade   607 A
bomber command   165 (55), 308 (93), 334, 447
Bonn Convention   387 n
* Boothby, E B   481, 496, 499
* Bowker, (Sir) J   28–29, 87–88, 104, 203, 208,
    220, 227, 251, 262, 275, 320, 335, 340, 347,
    358 n, 359, 383, 394, 402 N, 506
Boyle, H   327 n
Bradley, General O (US)   144 n
Brenchley, T F   535 n
* Brewis, J F   561, 590
Bridges, Sir E   8 N, 133, 517 n
Britain, defence of (see United Kingdom, defence
    of)
British Broadcasting Corporation   607 A
British Council   607 A, 645
British Defence Co-ordination Committee, Middle
    East   xlii, lxxi, lxxv, lxxxiv, 142 (1), 159, 254,
    323, 344–346, 369, 428, 493, 511–513, 642
British empire
    perceptions of   xxxvi–xxxvii
British Middle East Office   244
British Somaliland   216
broken backed warfare   474 n
* Bromley, T E   521 N, 546, 561, 590, 605
Brook, (Sir) N   641 N
Brownjohn, General (Sir) N   lix, lxxxiv, 324, 559 n
Brussels treaty   157, 165 (28), 177 (35)
    Military Committee of 308
al-Bughdadi, Wing Commander A (el-Boghdadi)
    541 n, 557
Bulfin, General Sir E   77 n
Bulganin, Marshal N   602, 634
Bulgaria   257 App
Buraimi oasis   xliii, xc, 450, 581 N, 600, 612–614,
    640 N
Burma   165 (38), 308 (59)
* Burroughs, R A   292, 312
Butler, (Sir) N   100 n
Butler R A B   270, 293, 334 N, 352, 418, 434,
    453, 466, 473, 525, 608–609
Byroade, H A (US)   xc, 312 n, 351 N, 382, 582 N,
    601

Cabinet minutes and memoranda   xliii, xlv, xlvii,
    xlviii, xlix, lx–lxii, lxvi, lxvii–lxxi, lxxx–lxxxiv,
    26, 33, 34 n, 45 N, 46, 50, 53, 55, 67, 86,
    186–187, 189–190, 196–198, 200, 202, 209–210,
    235, 248, 252, 264, 267, 270, 272–274, 281,
    284–285, 291, 293–294, 296, 303–304, 314, 331,
    333, 342, 352, 355, 361, 364, 374, 388, 393, 411,
    415, 418, 420–423, 426, 428, 431–434, 439,
    443–444, 452, 459, 466, 472, 475, 479–480, 482,
    484–486, 488–489, 491, 496, 503–505, 514–515,
    523, 525, 530, 539, 584, 603, 607–609, 629, 631,
    633, 635

* Caccia, (Sir) H   599–600
Cadogan, Sir A   10 N, 104
* Caffery, J (US)   lxx, 229, 312, 320–321, 351 N,
    378, 383, 405, 413, 417 N, 446, 454, 458, 470,
    483, 582 N
Cairo   128 N, 220, 231, 236, 247, 252, 262, 271,
    289, 302, 359, 393, 395–396, 416, 469, 471, 488
    evacuation of   11 (19), 15 (10), 29–30, 40, 44,
        53–55, 57–58, 68, 385
    riots and demonstrations in (1952)   lxvi, 217,
        277, 288, 594
Campbell, Lieutenant-Colonel (Sir) C   244 n, 279
* Campbell, Sir R   liii, 6, 27, 31, 32 N, 36, 51, 52
    A, 81, 94, 100, 109–111, 118, 129, 136–138,
    147, 156–157, 167 n
Campbell, P   298 n, 316
Campbell, Admiral (Sir) I   170 n
Canberra bomber   308 (134), 596, 644 A, 648
Carney, Admiral R (US)   lxvi, 201 n, 264 N, 303,
    326, 338
Caucasus   308 (58), 311, 570 A, 580
Celery, plan (1949)   lix, xlii, 257
Central Intelligence Agency (CIA)   lxx
Centurion tank   187–189, 331, 600, 602, 605
Ceylon   153, 423
* Chapman-Andrews, (Sir) E   112, 115–118, 126,
    130, 146, 167, 448, 626
Chauvel, J   586 n
Cherine, Ismael (see Shirin, Ismail)
Chiefs of Staff Committee minutes and
    memoranda   xli, xlvi–xlvii, xlviii, lii–lv,
    lviii–lix, lxi, lxviii–lxix, lxxi–lxxiii, lxxvii, lxxxi,
    lxxxiii–lxxxiv, lxxxvii, 20, 24, 38–39, 43, 47, 49,
    54, 56, 65, 93, 99, 108, 110, 122, 128 N, 139,
    144–145, 147, 153, 158–159, 161–162, 164, 174,
    176–177, 195, 216, 227, 236, 245, 257–258, 308
    318, 325, 329, 334–335, 338, 340, 347, 353, 365,
    387, 404, 451, 467, 474, 488, 496, 513–514, 564,
    566, 577, 580, 587, 595 A, 598, 604, 620,
    624–625, 628, 636, 643
Chilton, Major-General (Sir) M   329
China   165 (37, 39–40), 298, 308 (2, 4, 19, 23, 30,
    43, 60, 71), 459, 461, 563, 566
* Churchill, (Sir) W   xxxvii, lxvi–lxviii, lxx,
    lxxvi–lxxvii, lxxx–lxxxi, lxxxiii, xciv, 10, 178,
    235, 270–271, 273–274, 282, 286 N, 288,
    293–295, 296 N, 300, 308 (2), 317, 325,
    333–334, 342, 352, 356, 364, 368, 373–374, 388,
    390, 393, 396, 399, 411 n, 416, 426, 432, 434,
    439, 444, 452, 456, 459, 461, 464, 466, 477, 478
    n, 480, 481 n, 484, 486, 489, 504–505, 513, 525,
    530, 537
Cicilian Gates   177 (42), 257 App, 337 A
Cinderella, plan (1951)   lxv, 257 App
civil defence measures   141
Clayton, Brigadier (Sir) I   115 n
* Clutton, G L   xxxvi, lvii, 127, 140, 149, 157

cold war   li, lxix, lxxvi, lxxxi, lxxxv, cx, 159, 165
(5–6, 8, 13, 26, 29–30, 34, 37, 44, 47–49), 177
(2, 11, 23, 66), 180 A, 256, 308 (15, 20–22,
43–68, 71, 74, 76, 81, 92, 111, 123–124, 127,
129, 139), 325, 334, 341, 345–346, 348, 357,
365, 369, 377, 430, 447, 472, 491 N, 559, 563,
566, 570 A, 574 N, 596 N, 598, 607 A, 608, 610,
620, 621 A, 625, 642–644, 648
meaning of   xxxvi, lvii
need for a more offensive strategy in   165
(11–12, 49–50), 308 (64–68)
phases in   165 (13)
Coleraine, Lord (*see* Law, R)
Colonial Office   15 (24, 36), 49, 630
Commanders-in-Chief, Middle East   xlviii, lii,
lvii–lviii, lx, lxiv, lxxii, lxxiv, lxxxiii, 22–23, 29,
32, 41, 59, 104, 120, 125, 133, 139, 147, 158,
162, 174, 180 A, 231, 234, 239, 252, 326, 347,
469, 488 App
Commonwealth, British (*see also* Middle East,
Commonwealth contribution to defence of)
15 (2), 32 (1), 77, 93, 165 (39), 446 N, 450, 473
consultation with members of   421
defence of   xxxviii, xlvi–xlvii, liii, lxix, xciii, 26
A, 33, 56, 108, 159, 262, 308 (75), 377
communism   lxxv–lxxvi, lxxviii, 15 (21), 40, 119,
142 (2), 158, 160, 165 (2, 4, 37, 49), 168, 177
(14, 32), 186, 191 (1), 207, 256, 258, 287, 301,
305 A, 306, 308 (2, 5, 22, 54, 64, 67, 74, 79, 86),
341, 377, 383, 447, 450, 472–473, 556, 562–563,
566, 574 N, 595 A, 598, 604, 612, 614, 621 A,
641, 647–648
Conolly, Admiral R (US)   133, 159
Conservative Party   lxii, lxvii, lxxiii, 282, 368, 371
N, 446 N, 459, 525
Cornwallis, Sir K   11 (6, 22) n, 15 (23, 33, 36), 77
Council of Europe   142 (12)
Council of Foreign Ministers
London 1945   xliv
Moscow 1945   25, 27 n
Moscow 1947   95 n
New York 1946   89 n
Paris 1946   46, 102 N
Council of the Revolutionary Command (*see*
Revolutionary Command Council)
Coutts, W F   630 n
* Coverley-Price, A V   10 E
Cranborne, Lord (Lord Salisbury from 1947) (*see*
Salisbury, Lord)
* Creswell, M J   240, 243, 246, 264, 276 n, 279,
301 n, 305, 307, 312–313, 315–316, 319 n,
350 n, 378, 383–384, 386, 390, 470
Crete   125, 159
Cripps, Sir S   liii, 108
Crocker, General (Sir) J   145
Crombie, (Sir) J   268 n, 349, 522, 553
Cromer, Lord   15 (19) n, (31), 51, 178, 242

Crookshank, Lord H   433–434
* Cumberbatch, A N   310
Cunningham, Admiral of the Fleet Lord   18, 20,
102 N
Cyprus   lxxv, lxxxiv–lxxxv, lxxxvii, lxxxix 11 (5,
16–17), 15 (24), 30, 56 A, 93, 105, 114, 120,
125, 128 N, 142 A, 159–160, 168–169, 175, 177
(9–10), 180 A, 184, 191 (23, 29), 216, 223, 252
A, 269, 286 N, 298, 308 (80), 333, 336, 342, 346,
350–351, 357, 365, 377, 394, 447, 453, 455–457,
475 App, 484, 488 App, 494, 504, 513, 519, 525,
567, 587 (46), 597, 608, 624, 627, 641–646
Cyprus National Party   160
Cyrenaica   xlvii–xlviii, li–lii, 1, 11 (26), 23 A, 23
App, 25, 29, 32 (4, 7), 41, 49, 56, 63, 93, 102 N,
105–107, 110, 120 N, 124, 131 N, 142 App, 146,
153–154, 168–170, 175, 180 A, 191 (15, 23, 29),
199, 216, 308 (80), 377
Czechoslovakia, coup in (1948)   122

Dakar   165 (31)
Dalton, H J N   49
Damascus   128 N, 142 (26), 177 App, 508, 580
Dardanelles, Straits of   xliv, 84, 121 A, 125, 257
App, 308 (54, 82), 323, 620
Dawson, Air Commodore W   18, 20
Dayan, General M   lxxxviii
Dean, P H   559 n, 627
Defence Committee minutes and memoranda
xlvii, liii, lv, lvii, lxi, lxvii, lxxi, lxxiii, 32 N, 35,
44, 49, 84, 105 N, 132–133, 143, 154, 158, 165
defence cuts, British   xlii, lxix–lxxii, lxxv, lxxx,
lxxxiv, lxxxix, 308 (72), 334, 453
defence research, British   165 (14)
De Lisle and Dudley, Lord   426, 444, 530
Denmark   165 (26)
Deversoir   511
Dharhan   134 A, 142 (29), 159 N, 177 (27), 309,
369 N
Diameter, plan   385
Dickson, Marshal of the RAF Sir W   lxxxiv, 24,
137, 365, 387, 404, 474, 513, 564
Diocletian, Emperor   327 n
* Dixon, (Sir) P   lxv, 214, 220, 263
Djulfa   337 A
Dodecanese, islands   30, 49
Dominions Office   82
Doublequick, plan (1948)   liii–lv, 122, 128, 369 N
Douglas of Kirtleside, Marshal of the RAF Lord
111 n, 128 n
Dove, P A   61 n
* Duff, A A   292
* Duke, C B   321, 327, 350
Dulles, A (US)   516
* Dulles, J F (US)   lxxvi–lxxvii, cx, 382, 393–394,
396, 398, 401–403, 411, 417 N, 418–419, 445 N,
458, 459 N, 480, 505 N, 582 N, 602–603, 614

Dumbarton Oaks conference 7 n,
Duncanson, Sir J 557

Eady, Sir W 15 (27) n, 100–101
East Africa 63
  British base in 11 (26), 27, 30, 32 N, 34–35,
    41, 49, 56, 84, 120, 131, 154, 175, 180 A,
    181, 377, 457
Eban, A 602 n
Economic and Reconstruction Department (FO)
  3 n
* Eden, A lxvi–lxviii, lxx, lxxiii–lxxiv, lxxx–lxxxiii,
    xc, 1, 3, 12, 235, 238, 243, 248, 251 n, 252, 255,
    259–261, 264, 267, 270, 273–275, 281, 283–284,
    289–291, 293–294, 296, 301, 303, 331, 333, 336,
    342, 354–355, 360 N, 361–362, 367, 372, 380,
    386 N, 396 N, 442 N, 444, 445 N, 449, 452, 454,
    457–458, 459 N, 463, 465–466, 472, 475 N,
    478–480, 481 n, 484, 493 n, 497, 501, 503–505,
    509, 524–526, 529–530, 539, 545 n, 546, 560,
    578, 582 n, 584, 589, 601, 608–609, 614 N, 631,
    633, 635, 640 N, 640 n
Edmonds, R H G 171
Egypt (see also Middle East, British vital interests
  in; Suez Canal Zone, British military presence
  in)
  armed forces of 35, 43, 45, 100, 140, 143, 157,
    166–167, 179, 207, 229, 231, 252 A, 264,
    274, 281–282, 305 A, 319, 321, 384–385,
    415, 469, 507
  arms supplies for (see also Soviet arms supplies
    to Egypt) 106, 132, 139, 143, 145, 147,
    159, 163, 174, 176–177 (33, 35), 186, 188,
    200 A, 202, 207–208, 300 N, 306–307,
    320–321, 333, 354, 360, 476 N, 556, 560 N,
    603, 605, 610
  British community in 178
  cotton production and trade in 248, 252, 290,
    359, 429
  defence of xxxvii, lv, lvii, lix, lxi, lxx, 26 A, 56,
    74, 111, 116–117, 128 A, 137, 159, 161, 165
    (33, 44), 167–170, 172–175, 182, 186
  dictatorship in 135
  economic conditions in 15 (17), 51, 172, 177
    (18), 186, 208, 287, 305 A
  elections in (1950) 138, 140
  evacuation of (see also Anglo–Egyptian
    negotiations) li–lii, lvii, lx–lxi, lxvi–lxviii,
    lxxii, lxxx–lxxxi, lxxxvi, xciii, 7 N, 34, 36–43,
    46, 47 N, 48, 51, 52 A, 56, 58–59, 61–65, 67,
    70–71, 73, 75, 82–85, 89, 96, 102, 104–105,
    109, 111, 118, 120, 122 N, 124, 146,
    148–149, 157–158, 162, 166, 168, 173, 174
    E, 176, 177 (17), 179–180, 186, 187 A, 189,
    191 (34), 195, 200, 202, 209, 222–223, 225,
    249–251, 253, 255, 267, 274, 279–281, 284
    A, 288 N, 292–293, 296, 298, 317–318, 321,

    335, 339, 346, 351, 354–355, 357, 360–363,
    365, 367–368, 371 N, 374, 377, 384, 386,
    389, 394, 407, 411 A, 413, 416, 426, 447,
    453, 467–468, 472–474, 479, 482, 488–489,
    493, 497, 500–501, 521–523, 525, 528, 531,
    538, 541, 561–562, 592, 597, 625
  expenditure by Britain in 123
  land reform in 320, 429
  martial law in 138
  measures to maintain British position in 227,
    229–231, 234–235, 252, 254, 261, 428, 450,
    471
  propaganda in 172, 490
  re-entry rights for Britain in 106–107, 111,
    114–115, 142, 157, 168, 180 A, 197, 200 A,
    398, 472, 480, 513, 519, 529
  sanctions against lxiv, 231, 237–238, 245,
    248, 252, 261, 264, 286, 385
  social and economic reform in 243–244, 246
  social conditions in 11 (18), 15 (20–22), 16,
    51, 208, 242 N, 248, 277, 319, 508
  Soviet threat to 23 A
  sterling balances of xxxix, 53, 100–101, 157,
    186 N, 193, 231, 248, 262, 352, 356, 466,
    525, 565, 603, 635
  terrorism in 97, 515, 520
Egypt Committee 262 N
Egyptian arms purchase (1955) lxxxix
Egyptian delegation for 1936 treaty revision (1946)
  members of 87
Egyptian Department (FO) 32 N, 100
Egyptian/Israeli Mixed Armistice Commission
  186
Egyptians
  British views on racial characteristics of 28,
    178, 185, 188, 192, 535, 594
Egyptian–Saudi–Syrian defence arrangement
  581–582, 585–586, 592, 604, 610
Egyptian–Saudi–Yemeni pact (1955) 640
* Eisenhower, President D (US) lxvi, lxxvi xcii,
    165 n, 308 (18), 342, 382, 396, 398, 402, 414,
    420 N, 460
El Abassa 385
El Adem 56 App
El Agrud 181
El Arish 385
Elath 472
El Ballah 131
Elburz mountains xc, 182, 620, 622
El Ferdan (see also Ferdan bridges) 203, 385
El Hemra 181
Elliot, Air Chief Marshal Sir W 139 n
Erbil 128 N
* Erskine, Lieutenant-General G 226, 229–230,
    250, 377
Erzerum-Masla-Bitis, defence line 570 A, 580
Euphrates, river 257 App

European Defence Community 308 (45), 365, 453, 472

European Recovery Programme 142 (12)

* Evans, T E 319, 321, 327

Faisal, King of Iraq 495 N

* Falla, P S 463, 548–549

Fanara 181, 385, 496, 518, 554 A

Faraj, Ibrahim (Farag, I) 217 n

* Faruq, King of Egypt (Farouk) xliv, xlix, intro l, liv, lvi–lvii, lxiv, lxx, 4, 6, 8–9, 12, 22, 27 N, 28, 36, 40, 42–43, 47, 52 A, 66, 79, 81, 88 N, 90–92, 94, 97–98, 101, 107, 109, 111, 113, 115–116, 126–127, 129, 132–133, 140, 143, 146, 148–149, 152, 155, 156 N, 166, 170, 172, 174 E, 177 (16), 186–187, 208–209, 211, 225, 249–250, 252, 260, 262, 278–279, 281, 288, 302, 306 N, 320, 594
    overthrow of lxx, 315

* Fawzi, M 435, 441, 449–450, 470, 541, 557, 562, 578, 613

Fayid 84, 125, 131, 145, 168, 316, 385, 496, 511, 554 A

Fechteler, Admiral A (US) lxvi, 303

Federation of Rhodesia and Nyasaland 566, 596

Ferdan bridges 358, 498

fertile crescent scheme 593

Festing, Field Marshal (Sir) F 307n , 316, 385 n

Fighter Command 334 A

Fikri Abaza 63 n

Fitzmaurice, (Sir) G 487 n

Fleetwood, plan (1948) lvi

Flett, M T 266 n, 349, 363

Four power proposals (Middle East Command) 223, 232, 250, 252 A, 254–255, 260, 262, 264, 267, 272–273, 283, 290, 293, 312, 384

France 144, 308 (70), 358
    and supply of arms to Israel 602
    and the Baghdad Pact 615
    and the Turco–Iraqi pact 575–576, 584–585
    role of in Middle East 5, 11 (31–36), 18, 174, 262, 403

Franks, (Sir) O 212

Fraser of North Cape, Admiral of the Fleet Lord 144, 176, 245

free officers 594

* Fry, L A C 590

Fuad, King of Egypt 28

Fuchs, K 308 (94 n)

Furlonge, G W 175

Gaitskell, H T N 198, 202, 634 n

Gallman, V J (US) 647 n

Galloper, plan (1950) lix, lxii, lxv, 159 N, 164, 177 (55)

* Garvey, T W 593

Gaza lx, lxviii, 146, 170–171, 174, 180 A, 199, 252, 259, 270, 276, 282, 286 N, 308 (80), 377, 385, 448, 457, 472, 562
    Israeli raid on (1955) lxxxviii

Gazarene, Group Captain 169, 298 n

Geneifa 102, 123, 131, 181

Geneva summit (1955) 599, 602–603

Germany 165 (23–25), 297, 308 (40, 48–53, 71), 453, 472, 579
    rearmament of 334 N

Ghalib, Major-General Abd al-Hamid (Ghaleb) 626 n

al-Ghazali 240 n, 243

Gibbon, E 327

Gibraltar 144, 377

global strategy, British xxxviii, li, lv–lvi, lix, lxviii–lxxi, lxxxi, 32 N, 159 N, 164–165, 177 (3), 184, 323, 325, 328–329, 334, 365, 563, 566, 598, 620

Glubb, General (Sir) J xci, 562, 623, 632 N, 633, 640, 643 A

Goulburn, Brigadier C 316 n

Grady, H F (US) 378 n

Graham, W M (US) 267 N

Grantham, Admiral (Sir) G 329

great power status lxxi, 35, 597 N

greater Syria 94

Greece 93, 121, 125, 128 A, 137, 177 (7–8), 180, 183–184, 186–187, 269, 308 (40), 311, 328, 341, 597, 642, 643 A
    and the Baghdad Pact 615

Greenhill, D A 215

* Grigg, Sir E (see Altrincham, Lord)

Gruenther, Major-General A (US) 144 n

Habbanyia lxxxi, 11 (22), 119, 125, 157, 199, 257 App, 316, 350, 447, 475 App, 478, 514, 519, 577, 584, 643, 648

* Abd al-Hadi, I (Abdel Hadi) lvi, 126, 133, 136 N, 137–138, 146, 157, 267 N

* Hadow, R M 600, 611

* Hafez Afifi 64, 81, 225, 262, 301, 313, 319

Haidar, General M 146, 186, 205 n, 240, 313

Haifa 142, 198, 203, 205, 229, 233, 235, 276, 338, 455, 519

Halfmoon, plan 122

Hall, Lord 32 N, 49 n

* Hamilton, J de C 178, 192, 262, 269, 327

Hankey, Lord 358 n, 516

* Hankey, R M A lxxvii–lxxviii, 395–396, 405–406, 408, 413, 429–430, 435–436, 438, 440–442, 445–446, 450

* Harding, Field Marshal (Sir) J lxxx, 338, 340, 347, 353, 355, 365, 404, 439, 451, 455, 474, 480, 489, 497, 513, 579

Hare, R (US) 383 n, 602

Harvey, Sir O 241 n

Hasanain (Hassanein)   4 n, 6, 146
Hassuna (Hassouna)   296 N
Head, A   lxxxiv, 540–541
Helm, (Sir) K   194 n
Henderson, A   154
Henderson, L (US)   383 n
Henniker, J P E C   99 n
Higher Military Committee (Egypt)   320
* Hilali, A   lxvii–lxviii, lxx, 251, 279 N, 281, 288
   N, 290, 292, 296, 300–301, 313, 319
Hitler, A   179
* Hollis, General (Sir) L   114
Homs   257 App, 580
Hong Kong   334, 416
Hood, Lord   404
* Hooper, R W J   495, 567, 569
Hoover, H jnr (US)   615 n
Hormuz, Straits of   128 N, 177 App, 182, 257 App,
   551, 580
hot war   165 (9, 18, 22, 47), 357, 430, 506, 570 A,
   587 (5)
* Howe, (Sir) R   xlviii, 16 N, 34, 62, 91 N, 98,
   100, 110, 115
Huddleston, Sir H   86, 96 n
Humphreys-Davies, G P   268, 362, 517, 522
Husain, A (Hussein)   246 n, 313, 327 n,
Husain, (Hussein) King of Jordan   lxxxix, xcii,
   614 N, 617, 623, 632 N, 633
hydrogen bomb   lxxxix, xci, 513, 525, 529, 563

Iceland   159 N
Idris, King of Libya   xcii, 153 n
Ilyushin IL28 bomber   lviii
imperialism   373, 567, 592
Implacable, plan   385
Independents (Egyptian political grouping)   lvii,
   6, 81, 90
India   33 (6, 13, 22), 53, 56 A, 142 App, 153, 177
   (63), 191 (4), 341–342, 423, 434, 447, 547, 631,
   646
   air bases in north west of   33 (6, 22–23), 93,
      248, 257 App
Indo-China   165 (38–40), 308 (8, 19, 24, 59, 71,
   86), 371 N, 377, 460, 509, 524
inner ring defence line   lix, lxii, lxv, lxix, lxxi,
   lxxxi, lxxxvii, 177 (41, 46–49, 51–53, 59, 62,
   64–66), 182, 191 (4), 257 n, 276, 309, 311 N,
   323, 326, 337, 357, 474
Intermezzo, exercise   liii, 120
International Bank   608–609, 612
Invoke, plan (1954)   511
Iran (Persia)   xlix, lxxvii, lxxxi, 25, 40, 43, 46, 49,
   56, 69, 120–121, 134 A, 142, 160, 165 n, 172,
   177 (7–8, 26–27, 29), 180 A, 184, 199, 204,
   206–208, 225, 237, 245, 247, 257 App, 262, 268,
   298, 305 A, 308 (58), 311, 323, 332, 337 A, 339,
   342–343, 350, 354, 357, 369 N, 383, 409, 412,

431–432, 444, 454, 460, 474, 476, 483, 487, 489,
   491, 495, 503–504, 521, 529–531, 533, 535–536,
   541, 558, 561, 567, 570 A, 577, 579–580,
   583–584, 588, 590, 595, 598, 602, 607 A, 608,
   620, 621 A, 622, 626, 643 A, 644 A, 648
   and Baghdad Pact   608, 615
   armed forces of   587 (4), 595 A
   nuclear bombing of   621 A
   passes in   338
Iraq   xlix, lx, lxxi–lxxii, lxxxi–lxxxvi, lxxxix, xcii 11
   (29), 15 (20), 30, 33 (26), 34, 49, 56, 61, 63, 67,
   69, 104, 113, 115, 120, 121 A, 125, 128 N, 134
   A, 142 A, 157, 159–160, 177 (5, 12–13, 16, 26,
   45, 47), 180, 184, 199, 228, 276, 286, 298, 308
   (58, 80, 82), 309, 311, 323, 325–326, 334,
   342–343, 346, 350, 354, 357, 365, 369, 386, 399,
   403–404, 409, 434, 447–448, 453–454, 462, 464,
   468, 472–473, 475, 491, 494–495, 506, 508, 514,
   521, 524, 527, 548, 551, 558, 561–562, 566–569,
   570 A, 571 N, 574, 577, 579, 581–584, 587 (4,
   26), 590, 592, 595, 597–600, 602–604, 607 A,
   610, 615, 619–620, 626, 628, 631, 633, 635, 641,
   643, 644 A, 646–648
   military facilities in   549, 558, 581 N, 584, 588
   passes in north east of   lxxxii–lxxxiv, lxxxix,
      xci, 177 App, 191 (3, 10, 14, 23), 214, 257
      App, 258, 323, 337, 339, 343, 472, 514, 564
      N, 587 (32), 598
Iraqi–Levant forward defence strategy   xlix,
   lxxi–lxxii, lxxv, lxxxii–lxxxiii, lxxxvii, 311,
   337–338, 340, 343–345, 514
Iskanderun   257 App, 276, 323, 329, 337 A, 338,
   340, 369, 394, 455, 475, 580, 583
Ismailia   125, 188, 217, 226, 240, 243, 245, 252 A,
   261–262, 264, 358, 385, 468–469, 496, 505,
   552–553
   massacre at   xlvi, 317
Ismay, General H   43 n
Israel   lvii, lxi, lxxxviii, 130, 142, 158–159, 168,
   170–171, 175, 177 (12, 16, 21–22, 26, 47, 51,
   56, 62, 64), 181–182, 186, 188, 191 (6–11,
   23–24, 29), 194, 196–197, 201–203, 216, 245,
   257 App, 259, 275, 308 (82), 309, 314, 327, 332,
   337, 341, 345, 350, 369–370, 377, 385, 390, 403,
   407, 447, 453, 457, 460, 463, 473, 475, 487, 491,
   493, 495, 527, 541, 548–549, 556, 562–563, 574,
   576, 579–580, 584–586, 587 (37), 593, 598–600,
   602, 604–605, 608, 610, 614, 616, 632, 634–635,
   643 A, 645–648
   British military mission to (1952)   422 A, 472
   contraband for   314
Italian colonies
   future of   xliv, 32 n, 49, 105
Italy   128 A, 165 (26)
   and Baghdad Pact   615

Jabr, S   583

Jacob, Major-General I   xlvii, 40 n, 43–44
al-Jamali, M   463 n, 495 N, 508, 567
Japan   165 (41), 308 (62), 602
Japanese islands   141
Jernegan, J D (US)   593
Jessup, P (US)   213 n
Johnston, plan   602 n, 611
Johnston, W J   111 n
Joint Chiefs of Staff (US)   144, 165 (35), 182, 184, 325, 570 A, 580
Joint Intelligence Committee   xxxix, lxxxv, 121, 159 N, 160, 165 n, 570 A
Joint Intelligence Committee (Middle East)   397
Joint planners (US)   182
Joint Planning Staff memoranda   intro l, liii, lvi, lxxi–lxxii, lxxxii, lxxxv, lxxxviii, xc, 17, 19, 22–23, 57, 103, 105, 125, 141–142, 150, 168, 181, 191, 311, 326, 328, 337, 339, 341, 357, 447, 473, 551, 563, 596–597, 615, 621–622, 646, 648
Jones, L (US)   212 n, 215, 405, 575
Jordan   lxxi–lxxii, lxxxvii, lxxxix, xci, 157, 168, 177 (5, 11, 14, 29, 47, 56), 191 (10, 12, 23), 194, 199, 228, 270, 282, 308 (80), 323, 325, 337, 342–343, 346, 350, 354, 357, 365, 369, 377, 386, 399, 404, 409, 447–448, 453, 457, 472–473, 475, 493–494, 504, 519, 521, 527, 556, 562–563, 566, 571 N, 579–582, 584–585, 589, 592–593, 597–598, 600, 604, 607, 610, 614, 623, 628, 633–635, 641, 643, 645–646, 648
and Baghdad Pact   615, 617, 640 n

Kabrit   511
Kantara   131, 276, 385
Karachi   120, 369, 647–648
Kars   177 (11)
Kashmir   201, 216, 341, 491 N, 506
Kazvin   337 A
Keightley, General Sir C   513 n
Kemal, Mustafa   249, 327 n
Kenya (see also East Africa)   114, 409, 624, 627, 630, 643
Keown-Boyd, Sir A   31 n
Kermanshah   337 A, 369 N
Khanaquin, pass (see Paitak, pass)
Khartoum   lxxx, 456–457, 504
Khashaba, A   116 n, 127, 138, 146, 157, 163, 225
Khatmiya (Katmia) (Sudanese sect)   556 n, 594
Khrushchev, N   634 n
Khurramabad, pass   177 App, 337 A, 577, 580, 595 A, 622
* Killearn, Lord   xlv–xlvi, 4, 9–10, 14, 16 N, 23, 25, 27 N, 28
* Kirkbride, (Sir) A   236, 410, 527
* Kirkpatrick, (Sir) I   xc, 481, 560, 576, 586, 610, 614
Kirkuk   128 N, 142 App, 177 App, 182, 323, 337 A, 580

Kléber, General J-B   327 n
Korea   170, 308 (8, 19, 59, 88–89, 126), 373, 416, 425, 453, 459, 487, 602
war in   lix, lxxv, 165 n, 327, 377
Kubrib   385
Kuwait   56, 121 A, 177 (27), 199, 466, 551, 607 A

Lagos-Mombasa defence line   93 N
Lakeland, W (US)   378 n
* Lascelles, D W   111, 116
Lathbury, General (Sir) G   630 n
Law, R   1
Leathers, Lord   1, 420 n, 433
Lebanon   11 (22, 36), 15 (9), 18, 31, 43, 113, 121 A, 134 A, 142 App, 160, 177 (13–14, 16, 47), 191 (13), 354, 473, 527, 562, 571 N, 574, 580–582, 584–585, 589, 592–593, 598, 600, 604, 610, 614, 634
and the Baghdad Pact   615, 617
Lebanon-Jordan defence line   lix, lxv, 177 (41, 50–53, 59), 182, 191 (4), 194 N, 257, 337 A
Lee, Air Chief Marshal D   644 n
Lennox-Boyd, A   432 n, 433, 505, 525, 530
Levant Department (FO)   590, 600
Liberals (Egyptian political party)   6, 81, 90, 301
Liberation squads (Egypt)   240, 428
Libya   lxxxvii, 32 (4), 105, 114, 142 App, 153, 180, 186, 191 (15), 199, 223, 268, 342, 346, 350–351, 357, 447, 453, 456–457, 472–473, 475, 484, 504, 518–519, 521, 524, 527, 566, 576, 587 (18), 597–598, 600, 604, 618, 621 A, 624, 635, 639, 641, 643, 645
and the Baghdad Pact   617
Lincoln bomber   xlviii, 125
Lisbon force goals   lxxi, 308 N (7), 325 n, 334 A
Lloyd, Selwyn J   lxxxiii, 389, 395, 418, 482, 484, 486, 489, 491–492, 514–515, 520, 619, 629, 631–632, 635
Locket, plan (1954)   494
Lucky Break   xci, 640 N

MacArthur, D (US)   602
McCarthy, J (US)   459 n
McDermott, G L   111 n, 122 N
McGhee, G C (US)   lxii, lxvi, 215
McGrigor, Admiral of the Fleet Sir R   24, 39, 338, 340, 347, 474, 564
Mackenzie King, W L   108 n
McLean, D   151 n
McClintock, R (US)   351, 378
Macmillan, M H   602–603, 607–608, 614 N, 641 N
* McNeil, H   155
McNeill, Major-General J   570 n
* Mackworth-Young, R C   249, 427
Madfai, J   583
Mafraq   125, 519, 580, 643, 646
al-Mahdi (El Mahdi)   243 n

Mahir, Ahmad (Ahmed Maher)   4, 6, 28, 327 n
* Mahir, Ali (Ali Maher)   lxvi–lxvii, lxx, 28 n, 243, 260, 264 n, 265, 278–279 N, 281, 315, 319–320, 557
Mahmud, Muhammad (Mohamed Mahmoud)   28 n, 42
main support areas   xlvi, 33 (3, 13, 16, 24, 27), 56, 141, 570 A
* Maitland, D J D   135, 148–149
Makins, (Sir) R   417, 491, 502, 569, 602
Makram Ebeid (see Ubaid, Makram)
Makramites   16
Majlis (Iranian parliament)   204 n
Malatya   177 (41–42), 257 App
Malaya   165 (38–40, 47, 56), 308 (8, 19, 24, 59, 86, 90, 126, 139), 325, 334, 416, 453
Malta   105, 114, 120, 159, 165 (26), 168, 170, 180 A, 191 (29), 216, 223, 268, 308 (80), 316, 365, 393, 620, 643, 645
   Anglo–American Conference at (1951)   201 N
Mardin   472, 474–475, 478, 519
Marshall Plan   111
Masirah Island   624
Mason, P   407 n
Massigli, R   228, 586 n
Mau Mau   450, 630, 643
Mauritian guards   170, 174, 181, 186, 188, 229, 519
Mediterranean   165 (32)
   British position in   xlvi, 35, 46
   command arrangements in   lxii, lxv–lxvi, lxxiv–lxxv, 201 N, 303–304
   sea communications through   lv–lvi, 33 (7, 26–27), 56, 114, 120, 128 A, 257 App, 338, 369, 475
Menderes, A   571, 578–579, 583
Meteor fighter   lxx, 193, 331, 354 N, 635
MI6   xci–xcii
Middle East
   air barrier in   624, 627, 643
   American commitment to defence of   liv–lvi, 142 (36), 144, 153, 159, 165 (35), 177 (62), 201 N, 422
   American interest in   li, lix, 106 A, 107–108, 134 A, 142 (33), 202, 204, 258, 427, 525, 570 A
   American reinforcements for   35
   Anglo–American association in   525
   British garrison in   447, 604
   British reinforcement plans for   559, 596, 598, 621 A
   British retreat from   xl
   Commonwealth contribution to defence of   liv–lv, lviii, lxii, lxv, lxxv, lxxxvii, 56, 153–154, 159, 165 (53–55), 177 (60), 180 A, 182, 308 (63, 76, 85, 139), 563, 564 N, 566, 570 A, 587 (47), 596, 620

   deception plans for   621
   defence needs   xlvi–xlvii, li–lvi, lviii–lx, lxv, lxvii, lxxx, lxxxiv, cx, 11 (1–2, 11–13, 20), 12, 23 A, 23 App, 32 (6), 35–36, 49, 56, 84, 93, 103, 105, 114, 117, 120, 125, 128 A, 134, 142 (31), 153, 157–159, 165 (29–31), 168, 174, 177 (58, 60–64), 180, 184, 187 A, 198–199, 200 A, 213, 256, 257 App, 267 A, 305 A, 328–329, 338, 354, 357, 409, 447, 450, 455, 563, 597
   defence of without a base in Egypt   337 A
   definition of   258
   difference between US and British strategy for defence of   182
   economic aspects of British policy towards   15 (7, 14–18), 56 A, 177 (31)
   façade of defence of   lxxv, lxxvii, 180, 350, 369, 644
   forward defence strategy for (see Iraqi–Levant forward strategy)
   idea of regional defence grouping in   xlvi, lii–liii, lx, lxxxvi, 15 (12), 21, 25, 32 (2), 34–35, 36 N, 39, 44, 53, 112, 117, 161, 177 (24), 204, 206–207, 250, 294, 308 (71, 81), 327, 360, 411, 561, 564, 567–568, 574, 587 (36), 597–598, 601, 604, 615
   nuclear targets in   622
   policy of scuttle in   453, 465
   political aspects of British policy towards   15 (8), 159, 361, 494
   propaganda in   177 (37), 305
   redeployment of British forces in   105, 182, 191 (20–21), 195, 376, 413, 426, 453–454, 467, 472–473, 484, 488–489, 494, 503–505, 511, 519, 526, 528 App, 532, 537–539, 563, 596, 643
   regional headquarters in   56 App, 124, 191 (26–30), 525, 597
   social aspects of British policy towards   15 (19–23)
   Soviet threat to   liv, lvii, lix, lxv, lxix, lxxi, lxxv, lxxxiv, lxxxvii, 13, 33 (9–10, 25), 56, 63, 105, 120, 122 n, 125, 128 N, 142 (26), 159, 165 (31, 53), 172, 177 (26, 39, 42, 54), 182, 186, 191 (2–3), 257–258, 350, 369, 398, 404, 551, 563, 566, 570 A, 577, 580, 615, 620, 621 A, 642
   vital British interests in   3, 11 (3), 33 (1, 20–21), 54, 93, 108, 177 (1–4), 191 (1), 216, 308 (78), 309, 450, 506, 603, 607
Middle East Arms Co-ordinating Committee   603
Middle East Command   lxii–lxviii, 201, 204, 209–210, 212–214, 216, 218, 222, 228, 233, 236–238, 240–241, 248, 251, 255, 264 N, 267, 272–274, 278, 281, 283, 292 A, 293, 301, 308 (55), 309, 311–312

Middle East Confederacy   17–18, 21, 23, 26 A, 29, 32 (3)
Middle East Defence Committee   15 (34)
Middle East Defence Organisation   lxvi, lxix–lxx, lxxii–lxxiii, 223, 281, 300 N, 308 (55), 309, 318, 321, 324–325, 330–331, 333–335, 338, 341, 345–348, 350, 354 E, 360–361, 364 N, 365, 369, 377, 379, 381, 384, 391, 394, 401, 403–404, 408, 419, 450, 473, 487, 506, 556, 570 A, 584
Middle East Office   15 (30, 32, 34–35), 51, 108
Middle East Oil Committee   607
Middle East Redeployment Committee   518, 532
Middle East Supply Centre   15 (3, 16)
Middle East Union   liii, 115, 117
Military Assistance Advisory Group   615
MIG 15 fighter   lviii, 257 App, 308 (38)
Military Committee (Egypt)   378
* Millard, G E   518, 543–544, 561, 565
Ministry of Defence   521, 628
Ministry of Fuel and Power   56 App
Ministry of Transport and Civil Aviation   591
Moascar   181, 488–489, 512, 544, 550, 552–553
mobile strike force   170, 180 A, 357, 365
Mohammed Ali   405 n, 549
Molotov, V   32 n, 602 n
Mombasa (see East Africa British base; Lagos-Mombasa defence line)
Monckton, Sir W   641 N
Monroe doctrine
  British form of   12
* Montgomery, Field Marshal Lord   li, 84, 110, 122, 336
Montreux Convention   xliv, 1–2
Morocco   144, 262, 308 (54), 516
* Morrison, H S   lxii, 196–198, 200, 202, 209–210, 220, 223, 634
Mosul   lxxxvi, 125, 128 N, 142 (26), 177 App, 182, 323, 337, 343, 369 N, 566, 577, 580
Mossadeq, M   204 n, 207, 237, 332, 342, 405 n, 427 n
Muhy ad-Din, General K (Mohieddin)   606 n
* Murray F R H   555, 557, 562, 565
Musa Shabandar   567
Muslim Brotherhood   liv, lxxxii, 4, 40, 90, 129, 138, 177 (14), 186, 207, 240, 262, 279, 321, 327, 393, 395, 406, 429, 507, 555 N, 557, 562, 594, 606
Mussolini, B   28, 53, 180 A
Mystère, fighter   604, 635

* al-Nahas, M   lx, 4, 12–13, 16, 22, 47, 77, 100, 129, 155–156, 185, 188, 209, 211, 225, 250, 282, 288, 313–314, 606
* Najib, General M (Neguib)   lxx, lxxii, lxxxii, 313, 315, 317, 319–320, 327, 331–332, 334–335, 351, 358, 360, 372, 377, 384–385, 390, 395–397, 400, 408, 411, 413, 417 N, 418, 429, 450, 458, 465, 490, 504, 505 N, 555, 557, 562, 594

* al-Nasr, Colonel J (Nasser)   lxx, lxxxi–lxxxiii, lxxxv–lxxxvi, lxxxviii–xc, xcii–xciv, 360 N, 385, 413, 429, 435–436, 441, 449–450, 483, 502, 536, 541, 552, 555–557, 561–562, 571, 574, 578–579, 581–582, 585, 588–590, 592, 599–600, 602–603, 605–606, 608, 610, 612–614, 617, 623, 632, 634–635, 637–640, 648
National Bank of Egypt   248
National Front (Egypt)   265
National Security Council (US)   108
nationalism, Arab, Egyptian and Middle Eastern   11 (19), 12, 15 (6), 23 A, 249, 262, 267, 272, 277, 288 N, 308 (25), 325, 350, 361, 399, 413, 563, 566, 590, 594, 607 A, 627, 643
nationalist movements   11 (6), 321
Nau Shah   128 N
Near East Arms Co-ordinating Committee   354 N, 604, 608
Nefisha   554 A
Negev   146, 199, 377, 472, 556, 562
Nehru, J   405 n, 413, 600, 602
neutralism   600, 605
New Zealand   3, 93, 142 (34), 153, 159, 165 (36, 56), 177 (60), 183, 201, 216, 308 (62–63, 76), 311, 328, 342, 377, 423, 453, 472–473, 521, 563–564, 566
North Atlantic Treaty Organisation (NATO)   xxxvi, lvi, lx, lxii, lxvi, lxxi, 142 (12), 144, 150, 157, 165 (28, 45), 179, 183, 187, 211, 222, 303–304, 308 (6, 14, 46, 69, 74–75, 77, 82, 92, 133), 325–326, 328, 334, 341, 351, 354 A, 405, 447, 450, 453, 472, 504, 514, 525 N, 556, 580, 587 (43), 616, 643 A, 648
  command arrangements   lxvi, lxxv, 201
northern tier   lxxvi, lxxxi, lxxxiii–lxxxviii, xc–xci, xciv, 491 N, 506, 514, 525 N, 548–549, 561, 568, 570 A, 573–574, 582, 588, 590, 592, 596 N, 599, 601–603, 608, 610, 615, 617, 621
Norway   165 (26)
nuclear deterrent   xlix, 165 (13, 17), 308 (17, 26, 36–41, 71, 74, 96), 646
nuclear weapons   lxix, lxxxiii–lxxxv, lxxxvii, xc, 13, 32 N, 128 N, 141, 165 (6, 13, 15, 18), 308 (6), 520, 539, 563, 566, 580, 587 (6, 38–39), 596, 620, 621 A
  defence against   308 (12, 71)
  pre-stocking in Middle East   596
  tactical use of   35, 308 (11, 71), 563, 570 A, 577, 580, 596 N, 597, 644 A
  US provision for Britain   308 (94)
* Nuqrashi, M F (Nokrashi)   xlvi, intro l, liii–liv, 4, 6, 9–10, 14, 22, 27 N, 90, 91 N, 92, 94, 99–101, 104, 116, 126–127, 327
  proposed British removal of   98, 100, 129, 136 N, 186

* Nuri Said   lxxxv–lxxxvi, xcii, 188, 191 (14), 346,
     369–370, 431, 462, 495 N, 506, 542 N, 548–549,
     556, 558, 561, 567, 571–572, 574, 583–585, 592,
     599, 623, 626
* Nutting, H A   395, 431, 535, 550, 552, 556–557,
     565
Nye, Lieutenant-General (Sir) A   18, 20

oil
     British imports of 607
     defence of in Middle East   xlviii, lix, lxv, xcii,
        46, 49, 55–56, 63, 120, 128, 142 (28), 159,
        182–183, 191 (4), 258, 309, 337 A, 473, 598,
        608, 641, 644 A, 646, 648
     installations destruction of 125, 142 App, 257
     reserves of in Middle East 56 App, 566, 595 A
Okinawa   lv–lvi, 128 N, 128 A, 159 N
Omega, plan   xcii, 637 N, 639 N, 640 N
outer ring defence line   lviii, lxii, lxxxvii, xc, 114,
     128 N, 142 (27), 177 (41, 43–45, 59), App, 182,
     184, 191 (4), 257, 276, 369, 472, 474–475, 564
     N, 614

* Page, C H   185
* Paget, General Sir B   17, 21–22, 36, 55
Pahlevi-Resht   128 N
Paitak, pass   177 App, 337, 577, 595 A, 622
Pakistan   lxxxi, lxxxiii, 111, 121 A, 141, 142 A,
     153, 177 (63), 191 (4), 201, 216, 257 App, 308
     (54), 341–342, 403, 423, 434, 447, 467, 474,
     491, 506, 525 N, 530, 542 N, 548, 558, 561–562,
     564, 566–567, 569–570, 579–580, 583–584, 587
     (4, 26), 588–590, 595–596, 598, 615, 617, 620,
     628, 631, 645
Palestine   xlvii–xlviii, li, liv, 11 (5, 14, 20, 38), 13, 15
     (8, 18, 24), 18, 20–21, 23, 25, 29, 32 (5), 34, 39,
     41, 49, 56 A, 56 App, 69, 72, 84, 102 N, 104–106,
     110, 115, 120 N, 121 A, 122 n, 125, 130, 157, 186,
     199, 257 App, 377, 450, 547, 584, 607 A, 614
     Anglo–American commission on   49, 50
     Anglo–Jewish conference on   xlix
     refugees from   177 (12, 31), 236
Palestine-Lebanon defence line   128 N, 142 (27, 29)
Palmer II, J (US)   383 n
Panama Canal   1–3, 169, 237, 314, 450
Paris Peace Conference   66 n, 77 n
* Pelham, G C   448
Penjwin, pass   337 A, 577, 580, 595 A, 622
Pentagon talks on Middle East (1947)   li, 105 N, 108
Persia (see Iran)
Persian Gulf   liii, lxxx, xci, xciv, 11 (29), 56 A,
     120, 125, 142 App, 144, 175, 177 (27, 41, 54, 59,
     63), 182, 199, 257 App, 308 (54, 58, 82, 85),
     309, 314, 323, 325, 349, 369, 377, 450–451,
     453–455, 457, 467, 473, 524, 551, 563, 566, 570
     A, 580, 584, 587 (24), 595 A, 610, 622, 627, 631,
     633, 635, 641–43, 648

Point Four aid   182, 206 n, 242, 244, 380, 406,
     566
Port Emergency Planning Committee   308 (108)
Portal of Hungerford, Marshal of the RAF Lord
     18, 20
Port Said   23 App, 32 (14, 20), 131, 180 A, 181,
     243, 259, 262, 339, 354, 358, 385, 450, 455, 469,
     472, 475, 488–489, 496–498, 505, 554 A
Portsmouth, treaty of   119
Post-Hostilities Planning Committee   3 n
Post-Hostilities Planning Staff   3 n, 5 n, 56 App
Potsdam conference   xliv, 32 n
Powell, (Sir) R   387, 518
* Powell-Jones, J E   558, 589 N
prestige, British (see also great power status)   xli,
     xlii, lxv, lxviii–lxiv, lxxv, lxxviii, lxxx, lxxxiv,
     lxxxvi, lxxxix, xci–xciv, 93 N, 100, 105 N, 168,
     178, 192, 203, 254, 267, 283, 308 (57), 321, 334,
     350, 357–358, 368, 377, 387, 398, 408, 446 N,
     447–448, 451, 453, 472, 474, 482, 499–500, 504,
     511, 515, 525 N, 526, 528 App, 532, 538–539,
     597, 626
Price, Brigadier C   134 n, 164
propaganda, Egyptian   547, 579, 630, 632, 640,
     643 A
Pyman, General H   136 n
Pyrenees defence line   144

Qom 128 N

Radical review of British defence policy   357, 409
Ramallah (see Tel Aviv-Ramallah defence line)
* Rapp, (Sir) T   237, 239, 286, 343, 346, 350
* Ravensdale, T C   151
Reform Party of the Working People   160
Revolutionary Command Council   lxxix,
     lxxxi–lxxxii, 384 E, 389, 397, 417 N, 429, 441,
     450, 458, 483, 490, 507, 557, 594, 606
Reza Khan   327 n
Rhodesia   11 (26)
Riad es Solh (see al-Sulh, Riyad)
Riches, D M H   627
Rifa'i Bey   100
Robb, Air Chief Marshal (Sir) J   122
* Roberts, (Sir) F   115
Roberts, Lieutenant-General (Sir) O   49 n, 338,
     474, 519 n
* Robertson, General (Sir) B   lxi, lxxv, lxxix, 170,
     174, 180, 188, 202, 229, 262, 346, 379, 387, 393,
     398, 401, 411, 415 N, 429 N, 432–434, 441, 449,
     487
     visit to Israel of   194 N
Rodeo, operation   264, 279, 302, 328, 331, 333,
     385, 467, 469, 473, 475, 511
     Rodeo Bernard   264 n, 385
     Rodeo Flail   264 n, 385
Roosevelt, President F (US)   11 (39)

Roosevelt, Kermit (US)   502 n
* Rose, E M   572, 576, 584
* Ross, A D M   332, 370
Rowan, Sir L   268 n
Royal Air Force (RAF)   lxx, lxxxi, lxxxvii, 298, 308 (130–138), 334 A, 595, 644 A
Royal Navy   308 (110–119), 334 A, 351, 621 A, 635
Russell, F (US)   560 N, 599 n, 601–602
Russell, Sir T   77 n
Russia (see Soviet Union)
Ruwandiz, pass   177 App, 337, 577, 580, 595 A, 622
Ryukyus, islands   165 (41)

Saadists   6, 16, 81, 90, 301
Sabri, Ali (Sabry)   606 n
Sabri, Sharif (Sherif Sabry)   81 n
Sadat, A   lxx
* Salah al-Din, M (Saleh el Din)   lviii, lx, 166, 169, 172–173, 179, 190, 193, 200, 205, 210, 217, 224–225, 242, 250, 301
Salim, Jamal (Salem, Gamal)   606
Salim, Kamal (Kamel Selim)   51 n
Salim, Major Salah (Salem, Saleh)   367 n, 441, 541–542, 549, 555–557, 562, 593, 606, 623
Salisbury, Lord (Lord Cranborne before 1947)   lxxvii, 1, 261 n, 411, 415, 419–422, 424–426, 434, 439
Samsun   580
Sanders, Air Chief Marshal (Sir) A   245, 346 n, 387
Sandown, plan (1948)   liii–liv, lxii, 122, 125, 128 N, 159
San Francisco conference   7 n, 11 (39), 12, 15 (9), 22, 32 n, 45
* Sargent, (Sir) O   xlv, intro l, 66, 70 N, 85, 91, 95–96, 98, 100–102, 110–111
Saud, Abd al-Aziz, King of Saudia Arabia   11 (24), 52 A, 106 A, 119, 177 (16), 342, 398
Saud, ibn Abd al-Aziz, King of Saudi Arabia   xcii, 634 n, 637
Saudi Arabia   lxxvii, 11 (21, 24, 39), 113, 120, 121 A, 134 A, 142 App, 177 (11, 13–14), 258, 309, 342, 383, 399, 447–448, 453, 492, 527, 548–549, 551, 574, 581–582, 584, 590, 592, 602, 610, 612, 614, 627, 635, 640–641, 643 A, 647
   arms supplies to 603
al-Sayyid, Ahmad Lufti (Lufti al-Saiyid)   52 A
Scandinavia   33 (18)
Schuman, R   218
* Scrivener, P S   4 E, 9 n, 10 E, 12, 27, 32 N, 88
Searight, R G   242 N, 244
Senna, pass   177 App
Senussi   153
* Serag al-Din (Serag ed Din)   156, 167, 169, 172, 301, 313, 358, 606

Serpell, D R   349, 553
Shaiba   lxxxi, 11 (22), 119 n, 157, 350, 478, 514, 577, 584
Shallufa   511
Sharett, M   614 n
Sharjah   199, 457, 635
Shinwell, E   131, 154, 198, 202, 208, 223
Shirin, Ismail (Cherine Ismael)   313
al-Shishakli, Colonel A   346 n, 581 N
* Shuckburgh, C A E   lxxxvi, 336, 535, 560 N, 562, 564, 568, 573, 576 n, 582 N, 586, 599, 601–602, 614, 627, 634
Siam (see Thailand)
* Sidqi, I (Sidky)   xlvii, xlix, intro l, 27 N, 28, 31, 36, 40, 42, 45, 48, 51–53, 61, 62, 64, 66, 73, 75, 77, 79, 80 n, 81, 83, 85, 87–88, 90, 92
Sidqi, M K   319, 320 n
Silifka-Ulukiala-Malatya-Razaieh defence line   182
Simonds, Lord   486, 488–489
Simpson, General (Sir) F   24, 49
Sinai   106–107, 170, 199, 498
Singapore   627
* Sirri, H (Sirry)   lvi, lxx, 22, 136 N, 146, 148, 156, 312, 557
Slessor, Marshal of the RAF Sir J   227, 264 N, 318, 329, 336, 340
* Slim, Field Marshal (Sir) W   lviii, lxvii, 132–133, 144, 162–163, 166–168, 186, 236, 245, 264, 286 N, 288 N, 292 N, 318, 329, 333, 374–375
* Smart, Sir W   13, 42, 47, 63, 80, 97, 327
Smuts, Field Marshal J   108 n
Somaliland, British   110, 114, 409, 643, 645
South Africa   93, 142 (24), 153, 177 (60), 182, 201, 216, 342, 369, 377, 453, 472, 521, 563–564, 570, 596, 598, 604, 620
   and the Baghdad Pact 615
South-East Asia   33 (23), 165 (36, 40, 56) n, 308 (2, 6, 59, 89), 325
South-East Asia Treaty Organisation (SEATO)   xxxvi
southern Africa   33 (11, 13), 56 A, 142 (24)
Soviet Union (see also Middle East and Tripolitania)
   arms supplies to Egypt   599 N, 600, 602, 604, 606, 607 A
   atomic offensive against   308 (9, 29, 34, 38), 559
   attitudes to west   165 (11, 24)
   capabilities of armed forces of   142 (6–8), 165 (31), 308 (27, 39)
   claim to a position in the Mediterranean   19, 23
   role in Middle East   5, 11 (37), 35, 40, 43 n, 45, 119–120, 121 A, 153, 182, 286, 323, 602
   vulnerability to conventional bombers   165 (13)

Spain   lvi, 144, 165 (26), 201 N
Special Air Service   551, 595 A
Speedway, plan (1948)   lv–lvi, 128, 159 N
Stalin, J   xliv, lv, 27
Stanley, Col O   1
* Stansgate, Lord   xlvii–xlix, xciii, 38, 40 n, 51,
   53, 55, 57–59, 61, 64, 71, 73, 76, 79, 88, 92,
   288 N
State Department (US)   lxxxvi, 204, 207, 212, 215,
   233, 249, 383, 491, 502, 504 N, 568–569, 601
* Steel, C E 204, 382
* Stevenson, (Sir) R   lviii–lx, lxiv, lxviii, lxxxiv,
   167 n, 169–170, 172–173, 176, 180, 193–194,
   207, 211, 217, 219, 221–222, 224–225, 230, 232,
   242, 246 n, 247, 250, 253, 261–262, 265, 269 n,
   276–277, 287, 288 N, 290, 292 N, 300, 301 n,
   306 N, 316, 322, 346, 348, 360, 366, 381, 383,
   391, 469–471, 477, 483, 507, 510, 527, 534, 536,
   541, 542 N, 546, 571, 574, 579, 581–582, 585,
   588, 592, 594, 600
* Stewart, D L   350
* Stewart, M N F   152
Stokes, R R   202 n
Strachey, E J St Loe   49 n, 168
* Strang, (Sir) W   228, 371, 383
Strategic Air Command (US)   xliii, lvi, lxxxix, 125,
   128, 159 N, 308 (9), 551
strategic air offensive   120, 125, 128, 141, 142
   (21), 144, 165 (18), 182, 184, 308 (54, 92, 139),
   311, 559, 563, 566, 570 A, 577, 580, 587 (11),
   596–598, 621 A, 622
strategic reserve, British   lxxx, lxxxv, 5, 32 (10),
   416
* Street, J E D   500
Sudan   xlviii–xlix, lxi, xliii, 25–26, 64, 66, 68, 72,
   75, 79, 82–84, 86, 89–90, 94, 96, 98, 100,
   104–105, 109, 114, 142 App, 146, 148–149, 151,
   157, 174, 180 A, 187 A, 196, 198, 200, 202, 209
   App, 210, 216, 224, 235, 243, 248, 250 N, 251, 252
   A, 255 n, 262, 267, 272–273, 278, 288 N, 290, 292
   A, 296, 301, 312, 342, 353, 354 N, 372, 409,
   449–450, 456, 480, 493, 503–504, 525, 527, 547,
   556, 579, 594, 602, 604–605, 609–610, 635, 643 A
   and the Baghdad Pact 617
   Anglo–Egyptian agreement on (1953) 366 n,
   503–504
Sudan ordinance   lii, 115–116, 140, 186
Sudan protocol   59, 85–87, 88 N, 89, 102
Suez, port of   231, 261, 339, 354, 385, 450, 455,
   468–469, 472, 475, 484, 488, 554 A
Suez Canal
   defence of   xliv, lxx, lxxxi, 1, 3, 5, 12, 23 App,
      168, 191 (21), 282, 294, 415, 472, 493
   freedom of navigation in   186, 189, 196, 292 A,
      314, 361, 372, 395, 407, 415, 421, 432–434, 442
      n, 450, 452, 455, 468, 472, 479, 485, 488, 498,
      503, 522, 525, 530–531, 539, 556, 591, 598

importance of   169, 430
main user countries of   314, 423
passage through   lxii–lxiii, lxxiii, lxxviii–lxxix,
   xcii, 1 248, 504
tonnage of users' ships   358
Suez Canal Committee   1, 3, 5, 591
Suez Canal Company   xcii, 1–2, 5, 248, 252, 306,
   314, 358, 371–372, 377, 385, 407, 429, 450, 591
Suez Canal Convention (1888)   lxxviii, 127, 157,
   186, 314, 358, 371, 377, 423, 442 n, 476, 531,
   554, 556 n
   signatory powers of   314
Suez Canal Zone (see also Anglo–Egyptian
   negotiations on Suez Canal base;
   Anglo–Egyptian treaty, negotiations for revision
   of; Egypt, evacuation of)   xxxvii, xlii, lxxi–lxxii,
   lxxv, lxxvii–lxviii, lxxx
   British military presence in   xxxv, xliv, xlvii,
      xlix, lxxii–lxxiii, lxxxv, xci, 23 A, 23 App,
      31–32 (6–42), 34, 36, 38, 41, 43, 47, 49,
      53–54, 68, 85, 99, 102–103, 105 N, 106–107,
      109, 112, 117, 122–124, 131, 133, 137, 140,
      149, 151, 153–154, 157, 161, 165 (33), 166,
      168–171, 174, 177 (20), 179, 180 A, 181,
      186–189, 191 (24, 27, 32), 195–196, 198,
      208, 220, 222, 238, 248, 266–267, 270, 273,
      279, 290, 292, 297, 299, 305 A, 307, 314,
      316, 339–340, 342, 344, 348, 354, 359,
      361–362, 371, 374–375, 377, 379, 384 E,
      385, 387–388, 392–393, 395, 398, 411, 415,
      418, 425, 428, 443, 456, 467, 469, 472, 479,
      484, 489, 496, 498–499, 503–504, 509, 512,
      520, 526, 529, 547
   civilian contract labour for   lxxxiii, 23 App,
      504, 509–510, 515, 517–523, 528–529, 554
      A, 556
   contraction of base in   505 N
   courses A, B and C in   473, 482, 497, 499–501
   Egyptian actions against British presence in
      231, 233, 237, 248, 252 A, 449
   invasion of   xcii–xciii
   nucleus base in   518, 521
   possible numbers of technicians in   398, 408,
      418, 426, 429 N, 431–432, 434–437, 444, 449
   problems of military government of   252, 469,
      471, 498
   reactivation of base in (see also Egypt, re-entry
      rights for Britain in)   417, 424, 426, 442
      App, 447, 449, 483, 487, 503, 523, 563, 566,
      598, 604, 620
   reason for base in   455
   uselessness of base in   643
Suez group   lxxviii
al-Sulh, Riyad (Riad es Solh)   211 n
Supreme Headquarters Allied Powers Europe
   304, 308 (18, 58, 81, 84–85, 126), 311, 369
Suwaidi, M   495

Sweden 165 (26)

Swinton, Lord 4 n, 434

Syria liv, lxxxvi–lxxxvii, 11 (21–23, 36) 15 (6, 9),
18, 31, 43, 56 A, 67, 113, 121 A, 122 n, 134 A,
142 App, 160, 177 (13–14, 36, 47), 191 (13),
199, 257 App, 258, 298, 309, 327, 346, 354, 357,
369, 403, 527, 548, 558, 562, 567, 571 N, 574,
576, 581–586, 589–590, 592–593, 599, 602, 604,
610, 625, 635, 643 A, 646, 648
and Baghdad Pact 615
arms supplies to 603

Tabat, Karim (Kerim Tabet) 129 n, 186, 313

Tabriz gap 337 A

Tacitus 327 n

Taurus mountains 177 App, 257 App, 258, 309

Tawfik, Khedive of Egypt (Tewfik) 126 n

* Tedder, Marshal of the RAF Lord 35, 39, 127,
144

Tehran 121 A, 369 N

Tel Aviv-Ramallah defence line liv–lv, lviii–lix,
lxv, xciii, 125, 128 N, 128 A, 142 (27), 175, 177,
(41, 55–57, 59–61), 182, 257, 369 N

Tel el Kebir 124, 131, 181, 186, 190, 328, 333,
385, 488–489, 496, 519, 521–523, 528 App, 532,
554 A

Templer, Field Marshal Sir G 139, 147, 614 N,
627

Thailand 165 (38), 308 (59)

thermo-nuclear weapons (see hydrogen bomb)

Third Force li, liii

Thompson, Brigadier G 20

Thorneycroft, P 609 n

Tiberias, Lake 125, 177 App

Tiflis (Tblisi) 125 A, 580 A

Tigris, river 257 App

Timsah, Lake 123

Tobruk 56 App, 154, 199, 484, 519

Transjordan (see also Jordan) 11 (5–6, 21–22) 15
(9, 18, 20, 24), 30, 63, 105, 107, 112–113, 121 A,
125, 134 A, 142 App
treaty with (1946) 115

Transport Command 216, 256, 308 (139), 316,
323

Treasury xlix, lxxi–lxxiii, lxxxii–lxxxiv, 1–2, 15
(15, 25), 100, 412, 425, 498, 522, 565

* Trevelyan, (Sir) H 600, 606, 612–613, 617,
623, 637–638, 640

Tripartite declaration (1950) 187 A, 354 N, 369,
447, 598, 602, 608, 634

Tripoli (Lebanon) 11 (23), 128 N, 323

Tripoli (Libya) 180 A, 252 A, 519

Tripolitania 30, 105, 142 App, 153–154, 180 A,
191 (15, 23), 216
Soviet Union desires for trusteeship of 23 A,
32 (4)

* Troutbeck, (Sir) J 119, 462, 478 n

Trucial Sheikdoms 342, 409, 581 N, 598,
603–604, 607 A, 645

Truman, President H (US) 206 n, 308 (63)

T.U.2. bomber 257 App

T.U.4. bomber 257 App

Tunis 262

Tudeh Party 177 (26), 204 n, 342, 595 A

Turco–Iraqi pact (1955) lxxxvi–lxxxviii, 495, 562,
572–579, 581–586, 588–590, 592–593, 595,
600–602, 612, 617

Turco–Pakistani pact (1954) lxxxi, 495, 506, 508,
514, 533, 548, 556, 562–563, 566, 568–569,
570 A

Turkey lix–lx, lxv–lxvi, lxxvii–lxviii, lxxxi–lxxxiii,
11 (23), 121, 125, 137, 142, 159, 165 (34), 177
(5, 8–11, 47, 52–53, 62), 179, 180 A, 182–184,
186–187, 191 (4, 17–19, 23), 214, 216, 218,
257–258, 262, 264 N, 269, 286, 308 (27, 54, 58,
79, 82, 139), 309, 311, 323, 326, 328–331, 333,
336–337, 340, 342, 346, 350, 354, 365, 369, 373,
386, 403–404, 412, 431–433, 444, 447, 453, 455,
472–474, 476, 483, 487, 489, 491–492, 494–495,
502, 504–506, 515, 521, 529–531, 533, 536, 541,
542 N, 548–549, 554–559, 561–563, 566–567,
571, 574, 577, 580–581, 584, 587 (31), 595 A,
598–599, 608, 610, 620, 622, 626, 628, 642–643

Turton, R 611 n

Ubaid, Makram (Makram Ebeid) 4 n, 12 n, 38,
79, 140

al-Umari, A 583

Umma (Sudanese political party) 556

United Front (Egypt) 13, 28

United Kingdom
defence of 56, 93, 128, 142 (18–19), 144, 150,
165 (19, 43–44, 52), 308 (96–109)

United Nations 142 (13), 153, 186, 203, 262, 265,
425, 431–433, 469, 487, 489, 504, 567, 602
responsibility for Middle East security 5

United Nations Relief and Works Agency 177
(31), 385

United Nations Security Council 13, 18–19, 21,
26–27, 52–53, 61, 104, 157, 314, 479, 547,
556 n
Egyptian appeal to intro l, 43–44, 86, 90, 91
N, 101, 196, 488

United States (see also Middle East) 469
aid for the Middle East 287, 349, 354, 413,
429, 449 N, 459, 461, 508, 514, 521, 645
and Baghdad Pact 604–605, 610, 615, 647
anti-imperialism 215
attempts to reach agreement with Britain and
Egypt lxxii–lxxiv, lxxvii, 186–187, 213, 327,
364, 374, 380, 384 E, 387, 408, 411, 418,
432, 481, 520, 522, 524–525, 529
bomber groups 122 n, 128
British views on 410

United States (*continued*)
  forces in Britain   157, 213
  interest in British position in Egypt   132, 200,
    202, 204, 210, 213, 215, 244, 383–384, 419
  military aid programme   14
  role in Middle East   5, 11 (38–39), 165 (30),
    174, 177 (7, 34), 182, 258, 262, 308 (57,
    139), 321, 369, 406, 450
  strategic concept for global war (1949)   144,
    150, 308 (109)
  supplanting of Britain in Middle East   359, 491
Urmia, Lake   121 A, 337 A
Uthman, Amin (Amin Osman)   22 n

Van, Lake   177 (41)
Vandenberg, General H (US)   144
Voice of the Arabs   640
Vyshinsky, A   243n

Wafd   intro l, lvi, lviii, lxiii–lxiv, lxvii, lxx, lxxv, 4,
  6, 10 N, 12–13, 16, 26 N, 27 N, 28, 36, 40, 43,
  47, 77, 80, 88, 91, 95, 100, 129, 132, 136 N, 138,
  140, 156–157, 167, 170, 174, 177 (17, 20), 188,
  196, 206–207, 210, 225, 229–231, 233, 236, 243,
  247, 261–262, 265, 272, 277, 279, 281–283, 288,
  290, 300–302, 306, 313–314, 320, 327, 384 E,
  386, 429, 438, 594
Wafd Kotla   12 n, 90
* Wall, J W   206, 244, 262, 292, 301, 310, 312
War Cabinet minutes and memoranda   2
* Ward, J G   lxxxvi, 545, 573
* Wardle-Smith, J H   172, 205, 246, 262, 292
War Office   522, 528, 618
Washington talks (1954)   524–525
Watanists   6, 90, 138, 327

Waterhouse, Captain C   526 n
* Watson, J H A   627, 630, 639
weapons of mass destruction (*see* nuclear
  weapons)
Wells H G   15 (38)
western bloc   5 N
western Eurasia   144
western Europe   33 (18)
  defence of   lii, lv, lxxi, 128, 144, 150, 159 N,
    164, 165 (21–28, 35, 39, 52), 177 (61), 308
    (18, 47, 77, 96)
Western Union   liii, lv, 115, 117, 142 (12), 144,
  165 (24–25)
Wilkins, F (US)   602
Wilson, E (US)   568 n
* Wilton, A J   610, 616
* Wright, (Sir) M   lxxxvi, 106 A, 107–108,
  110–111, 115 n, 123, 145, 163, 182, 647
Wyman, General W (US)   369 n

Yemen   627
Young Officers movement   lxx
* Yusuf, Hasan (Hassan Youssef)   52 A, 61, 79,
  116, 146, 225

Zafrullah Khan, M   506 n
Zaghlul, Saad (Saad Zaghloul)   12 n, 15 (10), 16,
  77
Zagros mountains   lxxxiv, lxxxvii, cx, 177 App,
  182, 257 App, 337 A, 339, 563, 564 N, 570, 577,
  580, 587 (3), 588, 590, 595–596, 615, 620, 622,
  627, 636
Zaim, Colonel H   142 App
Zanzibar   630
Zionism   11 (22), 327